Macroeconomics and Business

Macroeconomics and Business

An Interactive Approach

Nadia Tempini Macdonald

INTERNATIONAL THOMSON BUSINESS PRESS
I(T)P An International Thomson Publishing Company

London • Bonn • Johannesburg • Madrid • Melbourne • Mexico City • New York • Paris
Singapore • Tokyo • Toronto • Albany, NY • Belmont, CA • Cincinnati, OH • Detroit, MI

Macroeconomics and Business: An interactive approach

Copyright © 1999 International Thomson Publishing

 I(T)P A division of International Thomson Publishing
The ITP logo is a trademark under licence

British Library Cataloguing-in-Publication Data
A catalogue record for this book is available from the British Library

---

First published 1999 by International Thomson Business Press

Typeset by Saxon Graphics Ltd, Derby
Printed in Great Britain by T.J. International, Padstow, Cornwall

---

ISBN 1-86152-450-1

International Thomson Business Press
Berkshire House
168–173 High Holborn
London WC1V 7AA
UK

http://www.itbp.com

to Alan and Camilla

Contents

PART II   THE INTERNATIONAL SCENARIO   323

List of figures

List of tables

Preface

This book has been written with the non-specialist student in mind. It particularly addresses the needs of students studying by themselves, at their own pace. The topics have been clearly organized and dealt with in a very concise way to provide students of economics and business with a practical and engaging, yet rigorous alternative to more traditional all-embracing texts. The experience gained through teaching macroeconomic foundation courses over many years seems in fact to suggest that the richer and the more comprehensive the book, the more difficult it is for students to isolate what really matters for the understanding of a specific topic, and to see clearly the bones of the model under the larger amount of flesh. A deliberate effort has therefore been made to keep matters as simple as possible, so that macroeconomic models and concepts stand out quite clearly. For its distilled, theoretical simplicity this textbook fulfils a useful function and occupies its own distinct place in the literature on the subject.

The focus of the book is not, however, exclusively on theoretical models. While Part I, Chapters 1–10, aims at formalizing the economic relationships within the domestic economy and between the domestic economy and the rest of the world, Part II, Chapters 11–13, looks at the international institutions which frame business operations and constrain governments' policies, discusses the European Union (EU) and introduces global issues of income distribution and development.

ACTIVITIES AND CONTENT ORGANIZATION

Each chapter is organized in the same way, starting with a list of **learning objectives**. Readers are urged to try the suggested activities in the order in which they appear in the text, without reading the answers provided.

Topical activities are generously interspersed in the text. The activities form an integral part of the didactic approach of the book, which intends to be interactive. The readers are never 'left alone', but constantly challenged to test their own understanding of a topic. The use of economic jargon has also been kept to a bare minimum and everyday language is used as much as possible. Each chapter ends with a **case study** – intended to provide a real-life application of the concepts introduced.

STATISTICS

The use made in the book of graphs and statistics is radical and new. While in most cases such material is used 'passively', simply to support a theory or a main point explained in the text, here graphs and statistics have been incorporated into the core part of the text and used as a main vehicle for teaching and learning. Each is presented to the reader as an **activity**: material to work through, before moving on to read the 'correct' interpretation, which is also always given in the text. This approach fulfils two main objectives:

- It teaches students, particularly business students, how to read graphs and use statistical information. This is a skill essential in its own right, particularly for anyone dealing with business and the economy. For anyone who works through the book, and the word 'works' is chosen with care, graphs and statistics are in the end so familiar as to be no longer feared or shied away from, but instead positively needed. After you have read this book, a theory or a point will no longer seem 'complete' without some supportive statistics.
- Statistics help to bring real life into abstract theory, which would otherwise seem totally irrelevant and unrelated to the crucial, contemporary issues it sets out to explain. In so doing it helps readers to see not only how models and theories relate to real life and are supported by evidence, but also how they have developed from a study of real life situations, in an effort to explain their complexities.

Part I

Macroeconomics and business

1 Macroeconomics and business

Objectives

After studying this chapter, you will be able to understand:

- what characterizes the macroeconomic environment of business and the difference between microeconomics and macroeconomics;
- how business investment decisions are affected by interest rates;
- how business is affected by inflation;
- how exchange rate changes affect the profitability of the export sector;
- how businesses are affected by labour market conditions;
- how macroeconomic conditions affect business expectations;
- what characterizes business cycles;
- how government policies can reduce business cycles;
- the main macroeconomic objectives of governments;
- the conflicts between governments' macroeconomic objectives.

MICROECONOMICS AND MACROECONOMICS

Economics is conventionally divided into two distinct branches: microeconomics and macroeconomics. As suggested by the Greek prefix 'micro', which means 'small', microeconomics takes as the subject of its study the individual – the individual household and the individual consumer, the individual firm and the individual market. Microeconomics helps observers and businesses in particular to analyse the effect of changes in the demand or the supply of a product; it explains how government taxation, European Union (EU) regulations, the imposition of a tariff, a quota restriction, a legally enforced price ceiling might affect the market for a specific product; how the existence of competition or rather the lack of it will affect firms' pricing and output decisions.

Macroeconomics, in contrast, studies the economy as a whole; the use of the Greek prefix 'macro', which means 'large', helps to convey this meaning. The focus of macroeconomic analysis is broad. Macroeconomics does not aim to explain what affects the demand for an individual good, but rather what affects the demand for all goods produced in the economy. It does not concern itself with the price of individual products, but rather with the general price level. It studies what influences the aggregate supply of the economy, its total output, rather than the output of an industry or of an individual firm.

The main difference between microeconomics and macroeconomics is not, however, merely one of size, but rather one of approach. The 'whole economy' that macroeconomics looks at and investigates is not just 'the sum of its parts'. It is like going to watch a race: what do you do, use a pair of binoculars or your naked eye? Microeconomics is rather like watching a race through a pair of binoculars; it is great for details, but you miss the big picture and you cannot predict who is going to win. Macroeconomics is more like watching the race with a naked eye. You cannot see the tensing of the muscles on the athletes' faces but you can enjoy the unfolding of the race itself. You have a broader picture. In the same way, macroeconomics achieves a broad picture of the whole economy, 'standing back' from it, so to speak, through the use of models.

What we wish to gain, however, at this early stage, is an appreciation of how the 'whole economy' affects individuals and businesses, but businesses in particular. To achieve that we need to explain what characterizes the 'macroeconomic environment of business'.

MACROECONOMICS AND BUSINESS

Interest rates, exchange rates, the level of inflation, unemployment, government spending and taxation, international trade policies and monetary policies all affect businesses and all affect one another in the macroeconomy. Let's begin to introduce here some of the links between these macro-variables and business decisions. It will be the task of the rest of this book to explain how these macro-variables are in turn all linked to one another and how together they contribute to determine the final outcome: the economy in which we live and in which businesses operate.

'Industry needs succour' is the title of a recent newspaper article, which goes on to argue that 'the Bank of England was wrong to raise interest rates by another 0.25 per cent to 7.5 per cent. This is the sixth interest rate rise since Labour came to power and the fifth since the Bank of England was granted independence. The Bank's monetary policy committee knows that by raising rates yet again it will make sterling stronger just when it was starting to show signs of subsiding from the crazy heights of the past year, which have plunged manufacturing industry towards a premature and unnecessary recession' (*Guardian*, 5 June 1998).

Why should industry worry? In what way do interest rates affect business decisions and, more specifically, what is the link between interest rates and the export sector, by which we mean UK firms selling abroad?

To a firm borrowing money from a bank, the **interest rate** represents the cost of money, the 'price' of the loan. The higher the interest rate, the more costly the loan. Firms that were thinking of borrowing to finance their expansion or to start up something new will think twice. Firms who are already indebted to banks will see their costs rise and their profits being squeezed. Some may even go bankrupt. But to an individual or an institution saving money by either placing it in a bank account or buying a financial asset, the interest rate determines the return from those savings or financial investments: hence, the higher the interest rate, the larger the financial reward. Even relatively small changes, like a quarter of a point, can make a huge difference in returns when the sums of money 'invested' are very large. To give you an idea of the sums often involved, just the UK occupational pension fund industry is worth £650bn, two-thirds of which is controlled by only five fund management companies (Mercury Asset Management, Schroder, Morgan Grenfell Asset Management, now part of Deutsche Bank, PDMF and Gartmore, owned by NatWest Bank). Multinationals, government and pension funds, unit trusts and commercial banks, that control and manage huge funds, tend to place their money worldwide, in those countries where the interest rates, and therefore the returns on financial assets, are higher, for the same degree of risk. A quarter-point increase in UK interest rates is enough to attract huge sums of this speculative capital into Britain.

This inflow of foreign money in turn has an effect on the value of our currency vis-à-vis foreign currencies, known as the **exchange rate**, causing its appreciation. If £1 used to cost a German fund manager DM2.50, as the pound appreciates it will cost more, say DM3. This adversely affects UK firms producing for foreign markets, as the stronger sterling will make their products more expensive and consequently less competitive and harder to sell on foreign markets. An increase in interest rates then hits industry in many ways: it prejudices domestic investment, it reduces businesses' profitability and, via its effect on exchange rates, reduces the competitiveness of export-oriented firms.

'French companies braced for extra tax. Profitable corporate sector asked to stump up in an attempt to narrow budget deficit closer to 3 per cent' (*Financial Times*, 18 July 1997). This is another example of how macroeconomic variables, such as **taxation** and the size of the government **budget deficit**, have an impact upon business. A deficit within 3 per cent of gross domestic product (GDP) is the level required for EU countries to join the European single currency. France's government deficit in 1997 seemed to be likely to exceed 3.5 per cent of GDP, hence it needed to be reduced. The French government did so by a one-off increase in corporation tax which was levied at 36.6 per cent in 1997.

Why, one may ask, does France want to join the **single currency**? What will a single currency mean for business? We have just stated how important are interest rates and the value of the exchange rate for business. With the single currency, decisions about the level of interest rates will not be taken at national government level any more. Interest rates will have to be uniform throughout the single currency area. Decisions about their value will be taken by all EU countries, at least in theory.

Why, in order to have a single currency, do governments need to reduce the size of their deficits? Why do governments run deficits in the first place? One reason, it could be argued, is to sustain **demand** and reduce **unemployment**. Government spending adds to the demand for firms' products, giving them a greater incentive to expand their output and take on more people. For the same reason, a reduction in government spending is likely to result in higher unemployment.

In what way does high unemployment impact on business? For a start, people who lose their jobs and become unemployed suffer a cut in their incomes and have to cut their spending. This, in turn, will reduce the demand for firms' output, causing firms to cut down on employment even further, in a vicious circle of deepening contractions. Furthermore, high unemployment creates insecurity and resistance to organizational and technical change. The rise in youth unemployment means that many young people are not gaining skills and are losing employability; the businesses of the future will have a deskilled labour force as a result (OECD 1994). Unemployment increases governments' **social welfare costs**, which are likely to lead to higher taxation. Unemployment, however, also reduces wage demands, hence costs for firms.

To complicate matters further, economies to not grow smoothly, at a steady pace. Instead, they go through what are known as **business cycles**, periods of contractions – when the economy's output and employment fall and many businesses have to close down – followed by period of expansions – when everything is on the up, demand, output, employment, but also often prices and balance of trade deficits. What determines these business cycles? Can they be avoided? One of the main causes of business cycles seems to be the volatility of investment spending by businesses, which tends to overexpand during boom periods, only to fall equally dramatically during recessions. Government, particularly in the first thirty years after World War II, have tried to use the macroeconomic policies at their disposal to try and eliminate, or at least reduce, the size and duration of the business cycles.

Once more, the effects on business decisions of these important macro-variables – the phase of the business cycle, the strength of the economy's demand, the level of unemployment and taxation, the introduction of a single currency, the size of the government deficit, the value of the interest rate and the exchange rate can only be really understood when the whole map of the economy, with its complex interconnections, is finally drawn.

MACROECONOMIC MODELS

Macroeconomics achieves a broad picture of the whole economy through the use of models. A model is a deliberate simplification of a situation that helps us to see more clearly its fundamental features. What we call 'economy' is ultimately the result of the interactions of millions and millions of decisions made by individuals. These are decisions about what to buy and how much;

decisions about how much to invest and in what, how many people to employ; whether to buy a cottage, a car or some government bonds; whether to spend the holidays abroad or at home. If you are the government, decisions have to be made about whether to expand the National Health Service and tax corporate profits more; whether to cut down spending on education and reduce the rate of income tax. These decisions, although apparantly independent, are mostly interdependent.

To keep the analysis of this variety of decisions manageable and to simplify the complexity of the real world, macroeconomics models divide the economy into various sectors of decision-making. Each sector is then examined separately, in order to understand what forces operate in each sector, before looking at the interdependence between them and explaining the final, overall result.

Macroeconomic models provide us with a logical framework for the analysis of economic phenomena. The framework consists of hypothesis about how people, or better still **economic agents**, behave in different situations and how their behaviours are linked or affected by one another.

The macroeconomic model that dominated western economic thinking for about 30 years, after World War II, was developed by John Maynard Keynes in his seminal book *The General Theory of Employment, Interest and Money*, published in 1936. The main focus of Keynes's work was the problem of unemployment; his ambition was to put forward a consistent and perfectly general solution capable of curing it. Increasing dissatisfaction with this model, due to its inability to explain the persistence of both high unemployment and high inflation, which plagued most western economies in the 1970s, led in the mid-1970s and 1980s to a radical swing towards a different 'model' or explanation of how the economic system works.

This alternative model centred around the work done by a group of Chicago economists led by Milton Friedman and is often referred to as the 'monetarist' model. The monetarist model represents in a sense a return to the 'classical' economic theory that had preceded Keynes. The core of the classical model is the belief that markets find their equilibrium and clear reasonably fast. From this it follows that the economy should be allowed to regulate itself, that unemployment can only be temporary or voluntary and that government intervention to regulate aggregate demand is not necessary. The main preoccupation of the monetarists is the control of inflation. Governments should make the fight against inflation their main policy objective and should achieve its reduction through a tight control of the money supply.

The unemployment ridden 1990s have failed to bring about a full swing back of the theoretical pendulum towards Keynesianism. The approach to macroeconomic modelling nowadays is somewhat more eclectic.

MAIN MACROECONOMIC ISSUES

What then are the main issues that affect the economy as a whole, and which are at the heart of macroeconomic theory? Macroeconomics tries to provide an answer to the major questions that concern most people, ordinary individuals, business people, government officials, politicians and bankers; the same questions that fill the front pages of the newspapers every day of the year.

✍ Activity 1.1

Make your own list of the major questions macroeconomic theory should provide an answer to.

✓ Answer 1.1

Among the main questions that macroeconomics aims to answer we can list the following:

■ What makes people and countries rich?
■ Why are some countries wealthier than others?
■ Why are some economies growing faster than others?
■ Why is unemployment so high in most industrial countries? Are wages too high? What can be done to reduce unemployment?
■ What causes inflation? Does inflation cause unemployment? Is inflation such a bad thing? Should people mind about inflation?
■ Why, when trading with each other, do some countries run into difficulties and experience balance of trade or balance of payments deficits, while others experience surpluses?
■ Should governments intervene in the economy? Should they use their control over the money supply and interest rates, over spending and taxation to try and steer the level of economic activity? Should governments fight inflation or unemployment? Why can't they fight both?

AIMS OF GOVERNMENT POLICY

Right across the political spectrum, there is a general consensus about the broad aims of government economic policy.

✍ Activity 1.2

Before you read on, make your own list of what you think the aims of government policy should be.

✓ Answer 1.2

Government aims are:

■ full employment;
■ price stability;
■ balance of payments equilibrium;
■ positive rate of economic growth;
■ some degree of redistribution of income and wealth.

Full employment

The maintenance of a fully employed labour force was certainly accepted by most post-war governments as the main objective of their economic policy. However, since the 1970s, western governments have abandoned their pledge to full employment and have increasingly focused on the fight to control inflation.

Unemployment is measured in the UK as the number of adult people capable and willing to work, who are registered at a job centre as looking for a job and are in receipt of job seeking allowance. The total of those working and in employment and those looking for a job constitutes what economists call the **labour force**. The **unemployment rate** is the percentage of those willing to work but currently without a job relative to the labour force as a whole.

✍ Activity 1.3

Study Figure 1.1 and Table 1.1 and describe the unemployment trend in Britain, comparing it with the average unemployment rate of the main western economies.

Table 1.1 Unemployment rates in major OECD economies, 1996–8

	1996 %	1997 %	1998 %
Japan	3.3	3.2	3.1
Germany	10.3	11.1	10.2
USA	5.4	5.0	5.1
Britain	7.4	6.1	5.6
Canada	9.7	9.4	9.1
France	12.4	12.6	12.2
Italy	12.1	12.1	11.9
Average	8.8	8.9	8.7

Note: Average includes: Japan, Germany, USA, Canada, France, Italy
Source: OECD statistics

Figure 1.1 Unemployment trend in Britain, 1979–98

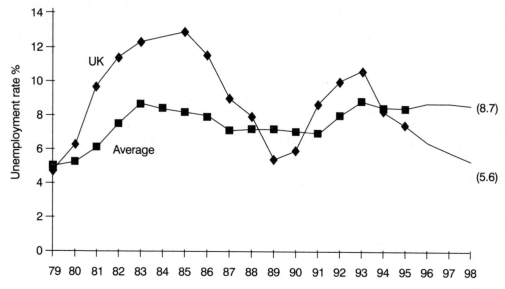

Source: ONS 1998. Note: Average includes: Japan, Germany, USA, Canada, France, Italy. You will note some discrepancies between national and international statistics. These are caused by different ways of calculating unemployment.

✓ Answer 1.3

The increase in unemployment in the UK since the late 1970s has been quite dramatic, from around 5 per cent of the labour force in 1979 to 13 per cent in the mid-1980s. By 1985, over 3 million people in the UK were unemployed. Figure 1.1 also shows that there was a substantial fall in UK unemployment rates in the second half of the 1980s, to an unemployment rate of 5 per cent. However, this downward trend was reversed in 1989, when the rate of unemployment started to rise again relentlessly, reaching double figures once more with over 10 per cent of the labour force being unemployed in 1993. Since 1993, the unemployment rate has been slowly but steadily coming down. It fell more rapidly from 7.4 per cent in 1996 to 5.6 per cent in 1998, the lowest recorded value since 1990.

Over the same period, most of the large industrialized economies of the west have suffered equally from high levels of unemployment, although never quite as high as in the UK. The average figures, which include figures for the USA, Canada and Japan, as well as Germany (although figures for Western Germany only are taken into account up to 1993), France and Italy, show a steadier, slightly upward trend with an unemployment rate of around 8 per cent for most of the last decade. However, the average rate rose to 8.8 per cent in 1996, its highest level since 1979, to stabilize around a similar value, 8.7 per cent, in 1998.

While, at the beginning of 1996, UK unemployment rates (7.4 per cent) were fairly close to the average rate (8.8 per cent), they differed by 3.1 percentage points by 1998, with Britain continuing to improve its unemployment record with respect to the average. However, one must not forget that the average includes countries with a very low rate of unemployment, like Japan (3.1 per cent) or the USA (5.1 per cent), as well as countries with a very high rate of unemployment like Italy (11.9 per cent) and France (12.2 per cent). During this period Britain also changed the official definition of unemployment, on the basis of which unemployment statistics are collected. This may account for the relatively more favourable record shown by Britain, with respect to other economies.

The persistence of these high rates of unemployment throughout the industrialized world is particularly worrying. What complicates matters further is the fact that market economies tend to fluctuate. We learn about booms and recessions even from reading the daily press. Economies have bad years and good years and the bad tend to follow the good in a kind of regular cycle which takes up to ten years overall. These, as we mentioned before, are what economists call business cycles.

The bad years of a business cycle are called recessions or slumps if the contraction is very pronounced; the good years of expansion are called recoveries or booms if very buoyant. In bad years, unemployment tends to rise and the output of the economy to fall as less of everything is produced. In good years, the opposite tends to happen; unemployment falls, output increases and the economy expands. Now, what the unemployment figures of Figure 1.1 show us is that each cycle of good years (second half of the 1980s; to the mid-1990s) has failed to reduce unemployment to its previous level. Average unemployment has been climbing up with each cycle, causing a 'ratchet' effect. It still remains to be seen if the UK improved record of unemployment in 1998 will be maintained in the years to come.

We must also remember that unemployment is often a regional or localized phenomenon. A 5.6 per cent unemployment rate represents an average for the whole country; this could mean, however, as much as 30 per cent unemployment in some regions and full employment in others. Unemployment is also a social-, colour- and gender-related phenomenon. A 10 per cent average unemployment rate for the country might nonetheless mean a 30 per cent unemployment rate among women or 35 per cent for Pakistani men. But as one British Labour Prime Minister once remarked: 'For the man who is unemployed, unemployment is 100 per cent.'

🖎 Activity 1.4

Look at the UK unemployment rates shown in Table 1.2 and comment on the distribution of regional unemployment in Britain in 1996.

✓ Answer 1.4

The average unemployment rate for the UK in 1996 was 7.5 per cent. The region with the highest unemployment rate was Merseyside, with 13.0 per cent, while the region with the lowest unemployment rate was the Eastern region with 6.1 per cent.

However, it remains true that the importance attached to full employment as a policy objective has declined dramatically since the 1970s. In the 1950s and 1960s, full employment was regarded by governments in western Europe as the most important macroeconomic objective. This was partly due to the experience of many western economies, including the USA, during the inter-war period, when high and persistent levels of unemployment caused social unrest and misery for millions.

The emphasis on the control of unemployment also resulted from Keynes's *General Theory*. Keynes was mostly concerned with trying to explain the persistence of high rates of unemployment. In the early 1930s, more than one-quarter of the labour force was unemployed in the UK and unemployment had reached unprecedented levels throughout the western world. According to the classical economists that had preceded Keynes, free market forces would always automatically bring about full employment. Classical economic theory could not therefore explain the persistence of high levels of unemployment. Keynes's theory could; what is more, it also seemed able to provide a 'cure for it'.

According to Keynes, unemployment was caused by a lack of demand in the economy and could be reduced by increasing government spending. In the post-war period, it became generally accepted that governments could and should regulate their own expenditure in order to maintain a level of effective demand in the economy sufficient to preserve full employment. And that is what most western governments did with considerable success; although one could also argue that after World War II the main problem experienced by most of the industrialized economies was one of excess demand rather then lack of it. However, governments did their best actively to sustain and stabilize demand. Unemployment was virtually defeated in the 1950s and 1960s, when it averaged less than 2 per cent.

In the mid-1970s, as shown in Tables 1.3 and 1.4, the emergence and persistence of stagflation, a combination of high inflation and high unemployment, seemed to defeat Keynesian policy prescriptions.

Governments began to perceive inflation as an even greater threat to economic and social stability and gradually moved away from Keynes, in favour of a new economic theory: **monetarism**. Milton Friedman's monetarism in many ways represents a return to the classical economic thinking that had preceded Keynes.

🖎 Activity 1.5

Look at the figures in Table 1.5 and comment on the unemployment trends for the economies in question. What do you think might have caused them?

✓ Answer 1.5

All the eastern European countries considered here show a sudden and severe increase in the rate of unemployment in 1991 together with an upward trend, which levels off and in some cases is slightly reversed in 1995. These figures can be explained with the move of these economies away from socialist regimes of state control, where work was seen not only as a duty but also as a right. The state had an obligation to guarantee people jobs and job security. With the move of these economies towards a free market system, their

Table 1.2 UK unemployment rates by region, 1993–7 (seasonally adjusted)

	UK	North East	North West (GOR)	Mersey-side	Yorkshire and the Humber	East Midlands	West Midlands	Eastern	London	South East (GOR)	South West	Wales	Scotland	Northern Ireland
1993	10.3	12.9	9.5	15.1	10.2	9.5	10.8	9.4	11.6	8.7	9.5	10.3	9.7	13.7
1994	9.3	12.4	8.7	14.8	9.6	8.7	9.9	8.1	10.7	8.1	8.1	9.3	9.3	12.6
1995	8.2	11.5	7.6	13.7	8.7	7.6	8.3	6.9	9.7	7.0	7.0	8.7	8.1	11.4
1996	7.5	10.6	6.9	13.0	8.0	6.8	7.4	6.1	8.0	6.2	6.2	8.2	7.9	10.9
1997														
Jan	6.5	9.1	5.9	11.8	7.0	5.8	6.3	5.1	7.7	4.4	5.3	7.2	7.1	9.2
Feb	6.2	8.8	5.7	11.5	6.8	5.5	6.1	4.8	7.5	4.2	5.0	7.0	6.9	8.9
Mar	6.1	8.7	5.5	11.4	6.6	5.4	6.0	4.7	7.3	4.1	4.9	6.8	6.9	8.7
Apr	5.9	8.5	5.4	11.1	6.4	5.3	5.8	4.5	7.0	3.9	4.7	6.6	6.6	8.4
May	5.8	8.5	5.3	10.9	6.4	5.2	5.7	4.4	6.9	3.8	4.6	6.6	6.6	8.4

Source: Adapted from ONS, Economic Trends, July 1997

Table 1.3   Unemployment rates, selected countries, 1977–98

	1993 Unemployment (thousands)	1977	1978	1979	1980	1981	1982	1983	1984	1985	1986
USA	8927	7.0	6.1	5.8	7.2	7.6	9.7	9.6	7.5	7.2	7.0
Japan	1666	2.0	2.2	2.1	2.0	2.2	2.3	2.7	2.7	2.6	2.8
Germany	3419	3.8	3.7	3.2	3.2	4.5	6.4	7.9	7.9	8.0	7.7
France	2946	4.9	5.2	5.9	6.2	7.4	8.0	8.3	9.7	10.2	10.4
Italy	2335	7.2	7.3	7.8	5.6	6.3	6.9	7.7	8.5	8.6	9.9
UK	2884	5.2	4.9	4.5	5.3	8.3	9.7	10.5	10.7	11.0	11.0
Canada	1649	8.1	8.3	7.4	7.5	7.6	11.0	11.9	11.3	10.5	9.6
Total of above countries	23 826	5.3	5.0	4.9	5.3	6.1	7.6	7.9	7.3	7.2	7.2

	1987	1988	1989	1990	1991	1992	1993	1994	1995	1996	1997	1998
USA	6.2	5.5	5.3	5.6	6.8	7.5	6.9	6.1	5.6	5.4	5.0	5.1
Japan	2.8	2.5	2.3	2.1	2.1	2.1	2.5	2.9	3.1	3.3	3.2	3.1
Germany	7.6	7.6	6.9	6.2	6.7	7.7	8.9	9.6	9.4	10.3	11.1	10.9
France	10.5	10.0	9.3	8.9	9.4	10.4	11.7	12.2	11.5	12.4	12.6	12.2
Italy	10.2	10.5	10.2	9.1	8.6	8.8	10.2	11.3	12.0	12.1	12.1	11.9
UK	9.8	7.8	6.0	5.8	8.2	9.9	10.2	9.2	8.1	7.4	6.1	5.6
Canada	8.8	7.8	7.5	8.1	10.4	11.3	11.2	10.4	9.5	9.7	9.4	9.1
Total of above countries	6.8	6.2	5.7	5.6	6.5	7.1	7.3	7.1	6.8	6.9	6.7	6.6

Source: OECD, *Economic Outlook*, 1998

Table 1.4   Inflation rates, selected countries, 1974–96

	Average 1970–73	1974	1975	1976	1977	1978	1979	1980	1981	1982	1983	1984
USA	4.6	11.1	9.1	5.7	6.5	7.6	11.3	13.5	10.3	6.1	3.2	4.3
Japan	7.6	23.1	11.8	9.4	8.2	4.2	3.7	7.8	4.9	2.7	1.9	2.2
Germany	5.9	7.0	5.9	4.6	3.7	2.7	4.1	5.5	6.3	5.3	3.3	2.4
France	6.3	13.7	11.8	9.6	9.4	9.1	10.8	13.6	13.4	11.8	9.6	7.4
Italy	7.0	19.4	17.2	16.5	18.1	12.4	15.7	21.1	18.7	16.3	15.0	10.6
UK	8.6	16.0	24.2	16.5	15.8	8.3	13.4	18.0	11.9	8.6	4.6	5.0
Canada	5.1	10.9	10.7	7.5	8.0	8.9	9.1	10.2	12.4	10.8	5.8	4.3
Total of above countries	5.8	13.5	11.3	8.2	8.4	7.3	9.8	12.7	10.2	7.2	4.7	4.7

	1985	1986	1987	1988	1989	1990	1991	1992	1993	1994	1995	1996
USA	3.5	1.9	3.7	4.1	4.8	5.4	4.2	3.0	3.0	2.6	2.8	2.9
Japan	2.0	0.6	0.1	0.7	2.3	3.1	3.3	1.7	1.2	0.7	–0.1	0.1
Germany	2.2	–0.1	0.2	1.3	2.8	2.7	3.5	4.0	4.5	2.7	1.8	1.5
France	5.8	2.7	3.1	2.7	3.6	3.4	3.2	2.4	2.1	1.7	1.7	2.0
Italy	8.6	6.1	4.6	5.0	6.6	6.1	6.5	5.3	4.2	3.9	5.4	3.8
UK	6.1	3.4	4.1	4.9	7.8	9.5	5.9	3.7	1.6	2.5	3.4	2.4
Canada	4.0	4.2	4.4	4.0	5.0	4.8	5.6	1.5	1.8	0.2	2.2	1.6
Total of above countries	4.0	2.1	2.9	3.4	4.5	5.0	4.3	3.0	2.7	2.2	2.4	2.2

Source: OECD, *Economic Outlook*, 1997

Table 1.5 Unemployment in eastern Europe, 1990–95

| | Percentage of civilian labour force, end of period: unemployed | | | | | |
	1990	1991	1992	1993	1994	1995
Bulgaria	1.6	11.7	15.6	17	17	16
CSFR	1.0	6.8	5.1	—	—	—
Czech Republic	—	—	2.6	4	8	8
Slovak Republic	—	—	10.4	15	18	18
Hungary	1.6	7.5	12.3	13	13	12
Poland	6.1	11.5	15.0	14	14.4	14
Romania	—	2.7	6.2	9	15	15

Sources: National sources; OECD estimates

labour markets too fell under the law of supply and demand and international competition. This situation is further illustrated by Figure 1.2, which shows the rate of unemployment in Poland from 1988 to 1998.

Price stability

Inflation is a generalized and persistent rise in the price level. The annual **inflation rate** is the percent-age increase per annum in the average price of goods and services. The **retail price index** (RPI), a weighted average of the prices which households pay for goods and services, is used in the UK to measure inflation. What we normally refer to as the 'inflation rate' is the percentage annual growth in RPI.

Fluctuations in the general level of prices can cause harmful distortions in the economy. They particularly affect the level of production, the distribution of real

Figure 1.2 Unemployment rates in Poland, 1988–98

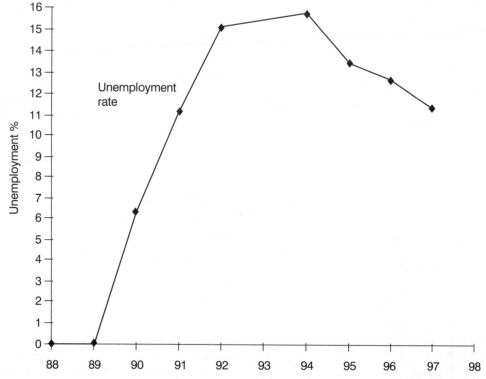

Source: Adapted from OECD statistics

income and balance of payments situation. A rapid increase in prices reduces:

1 the real income of those on fixed money incomes, relative to those whose incomes are rapidly adjusted to the changing price level;
2 the purchasing power of savings;
3 the real burden of debt, so that debtors repay less in real terms than they borrow.

Inflation increases the prices of exports and makes them less attractive to foreigners, so that balance of trade deficits will emerge if the currency exchange rate is fixed. Alternatively, if the exchange rate is flexible, domestic inflation will cause a depreciation of the exchange rate, which in turn may be inflationary. All governments are therefore concerned to hold prices steady and to eliminate or reduce such harmful developments (see Table 1.6).

In many ways, the decreasing importance attached to the control of unemployment has been mirrored by an increasing concern with controlling the rate of price inflation. In the 1950s and 1960s, moderate levels of inflation, between 2–4 per cent per annum, were the norm in most western countries. This was known as 'creeping inflation'. But in the 1970s, inflation rates in a number of western countries increased dramatically and for brief periods, in particular after the oil price shocks of 1973 and 1979, when inflation exceeded 20 per cent in some cases. Governments throughout the west, but particularly in the USA and UK, began to attach the greatest importance to controlling the rate of inflation. President Reagan described inflation as 'public enemy number one', while in the UK, Prime Minister Margaret Thatcher saw the control of inflation as a prerequisite for any sort of economic success.

Table 1.6   Inflation rates, selected countries, 1994–6

	Average last 15 years	1994	1995	1996
Japan	2.6	0.7	−0.1	0.1
WG	3.3	+2.7	+1.8	1.5
USA	5.6	+2.6	2.8	2.9
France	6.8	+1.7	1.7	2.0
Canada	7.2	+0.2	2.2	1.6
Britain	7.9	+2.5	3.1	2.4
Italy	10.7	+3.1	5.4	3.8

Source: Derived from OECD statistics
Note: Average includes: Japan, WG, USA, France, Canada, Italy

✍ Activity 1.6

Study Figure 1.3 and describe the inflation trends in Britain compared with the average trend of the six major industrial economies over the same period.

✓ Answer 1.6

Inflation in the UK reached its peak in 1980 when it stood at about 18 per cent. The contractionary monetary policies introduced by Margaret Thatcher in the early 1980s brought inflation under control. By 1985, inflation was down to 6 per cent, it fell again to just over 3 per cent in 1986 only to restart its ascent in the second half of the 1980s as government policies had become less restrictive. In 1990 the spectre of inflation, by then disappointingly high (9.5 per cent), was back at the top of the political agenda and the fight against it was resumed with renewed vigour. The first part of the 1990s saw inflation brought under control once more, down to 2.4 per cent by 1996. The same pattern, although less jagged, has been followed by the other major industrialized countries; among them Japan and Germany are the least inflationary countries. In Japan in 1995 the rate of inflation was negative, which means that the average price level actually fell. Germany recorded a low 1.5 per cent in 1996, followed in Europe by France with 2.0 per cent. If we compare the recent rates of inflation with individual countries' averages over the last 15 years, we see that for all of them the trend is distinctly downwards. By the mid-1990s in western Europe, the rates of inflation had been reduced to rather modest levels, typically less than 5 per cent per annum. In central and eastern Europe, however, the newly 'marketized' economies such as those of the former Soviet Union experienced high rates of inflation. Moreover, as we have just seen, these high rates of inflation were coupled with high levels of unemployment as the forces of a market system began to bite.

✍ Activity 1.7

Study Figure 1.4 and describe the inflation trends in Poland.

✓ Answer 1.7

As Figure 1.4 shows, inflation in Poland reached 'explosive levels', almost 600 per cent, after liberalization, in 1990. Remember, 100 per cent inflation means that prices have doubled over the period. A 600 per cent annual rate of inflation indicates that prices have increased sixfold in a year. Since 1990, inflation has been brought under control, gradually coming down to a 'more acceptable' 15 per cent in 1997.

Figure 1.3 UK inflation rates, 1979–96

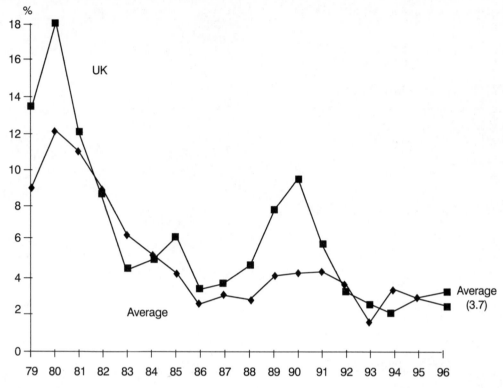

Source: OECD

Emerging markets too, as Table 1.9 shows, are not immune from inflationary pressures.

Economic growth

Despite the importance attached to the control of unemployment and inflation by many politicians, the most important of the economic objectives remains economic growth. Economic growth – measured as the average annual rate of growth of real gross domestic product (GDP) – is an indication that the economy produces a greater volume of goods and services. Real GDP divided by total population – per capita GDP – is the economic indicator most commonly used to measure the standard of living in an economy. Changes in per capita GDP indicate whether people's standards of living have improved or deteriorated. Note that we are talking here about the rate of growth of GDP measured in real terms, that is, once the figures have been adjusted for the effect of inflation. GDP comparisons over time give an indication of how much better off we have become.

✍ Activity 1.8

Look at Table 1.7 and comment on what it shows.

✓ Answer 1.8

Real growth rates of the main industrialized countries fell from an average of 3.6 per cent per year in the 1970s, to an average of 2.8 per cent in the 1980s and 2 per cent a year on average from 1990 to 1998.

✍ Activity 1.9

Look at Figure 1.5 and Table 1.8 and comment on what they show.

✓ Answer 1.9

As Figure 1.5 shows, the major industrial economies have grown at a modest average rate of about 2.5 per cent per annum in real terms over the period, though overlaid on this long-term trend there are substantial fluctuations in economic activity. For example, in some years the economies will be growing at 4 per cent and in

Table 1.7 Real GDP percentage changes from previous period, 1980–98

	Average 1970–79	1980	1981	1982	1983	1984	1985	1986	1987	1988	1989	1990	1991	1992	1993	1994	1995	1996	1997	1998
USA	3.5	-0.3	2.5	-2.1	4.0	6.8	3.7	3.0	2.9	3.8	3.4	1.3	-1.0	2.7	2.3	3.5	2.0	2.4	3.6	2.0
Japan	4.6	2.8	3.2	3.1	2.3	3.9	4.4	2.9	4.2	6.2	4.8	5.1	3.8	1.0	0.3	0.6	1.4	3.6	2.3	2.9
Germany	2.9	1.0	0.1	-0.9	1.8	2.8	2.0	2.3	1.5	3.7	3.6	5.7	5.0	2.2	-1.1	2.9	1.9	1.4	2.2	2.8
France	3.5	1.6	1.2	2.5	0.7	1.3	1.9	2.5	2.3	4.5	4.3	2.5	0.8	1.2	-1.3	2.8	2.1	1.5	2.5	2.8
Italy	3.6	3.5	0.5	0.5	1.2	2.6	2.8	2.8	3.1	3.9	2.9	2.2	1.1	0.6	-1.2	2.2	2.9	0.7	1.0	1.8
UK	2.4	-2.2	-1.3	1.7	3.7	2.4	3.5	4.4	4.8	5.0	2.2	0.4	-2.0	-0.5	2.1	3.8	2.5	2.1	3.0	2.7
Canada	4.9	1.5	3.7	-3.2	3.2	6.3	4.8	3.3	4.2	5.0	2.4	-0.2	-1.8	0.8	2.2	4.1	2.3	1.5	3.5	3.3
Total of above countries	3.6	0.8	1.9	-0.3	3.0	4.8	3.5	3.0	3.1	4.4	3.6	2.5	0.7	1.8	1.0	2.8	2.0	2.3	2.9	2.4
Australia	3.5	2.3	3.6	-0.6	1.0	7.5	4.4	2.1	4.8	4.1	4.1	1.2	-1.4	2.6	3.9	5.3	3.7	4.0	3.5	3.5
Austria	3.7	2.9	-0.3	1.1	2.0	1.4	2.5	1.2	1.7	4.1	3.8	4.2	2.8	2.0	0.4	3.0	1.8	1.1	1.5	2.4
Belgium	3.2	4.4	-2.3	1.5	0.2	2.3	0.9	1.9	2.0	4.9	3.4	3.7	1.6	1.7	-1.4	2.3	1.9	1.4	2.2	2.6
Czech Republic	—	—	—	—	—	—	—	—	—	—	—	—	—	—	—	2.6	4.8	4.4	2.6	2.0
Denmark	2.5	-0.4	-0.9	3.0	2.5	4.4	4.3	3.6	0.3	1.2	0.6	1.4	1.3	0.2	1.5	4.2	2.7	2.5	2.5	2.9
Finland	3.3	5.3	1.6	3.6	3.0	3.0	3.3	2.4	4.1	4.9	5.7	0.0	-7.1	-3.6	-1.2	4.5	4.5	3.3	4.6	3.6
Greece	5.0	1.8	0.1	0.4	0.4	2.8	3.1	1.6	-0.5	4.5	3.8	0.0	3.1	0.4	-1.0	1.5	2.0	2.6	3.0	3.1
Hungary	—	—	—	—	—	—	—	—	—	—	—	—	—	—	—	2.9	1.5	0.8	2.4	3.5
Iceland	6.4	5.7	4.3	2.2	-2.2	4.1	3.3	6.3	8.5	-0.1	0.3	1.2	1.3	-3.3	0.9	3.5	1.2	5.7	4.5	3.3
Ireland	4.9	3.1	3.3	2.3	-0.2	4.4	3.1	-0.4	4.7	4.4	7.0	8.4	2.1	4.0	3.1	6.5	10.3	7.3	6.7	7.0
Korea	8.8	-2.7	6.2	7.6	11.5	8.7	6.5	11.6	11.5	11.3	6.4	9.5	9.1	5.1	5.8	8.6	8.9	7.1	5.3	6.5
Luxembourg	2.8	0.8	-0.6	1.1	3.0	6.2	2.9	7.8	2.3	10.4	9.8	2.2	6.1	4.5	8.7	4.2	3.2	3.9	4.1	4.0
Mexico	6.4	8.3	8.8	-0.7	-4.3	3.6	2.8	-3.8	1.9	1.2	4.2	5.1	4.2	3.6	2.0	4.4	-6.2	5.1	5.4	4.7
Netherlands	3.1	1.2	-0.5	-1.2	1.7	3.3	3.1	2.8	1.4	2.6	4.7	4.1	2.3	2.0	0.8	3.4	2.1	2.7	3.0	3.2
New Zealand	1.7	0.4	4.7	3.3	2.5	8.5	1.6	0.6	0.7	2.3	-0.6	0.3	-2.3	0.6	5.1	5.5	2.7	2.1	2.8	3.2
Norway	4.8	4.2	0.9	0.3	4.6	5.7	5.3	4.2	2.0	-0.5	0.9	1.9	3.1	3.3	2.8	5.0	3.3	4.8	3.8	3.4
Poland	—	—	—	—	—	—	—	—	—	—	—	—	—	—	—	5.2	7.0	6.0	5.0	4.9
Portugal	4.8	4.6	1.6	2.1	-0.2	-1.9	2.8	4.1	6.4	4.9	4.9	4.6	2.5	1.8	0.3	3.5	1.9	3.0	3.3	3.4
Spain	3.8	1.3	-0.2	1.6	2.2	1.5	2.6	3.2	5.6	5.2	4.7	3.7	2.3	0.7	-1.2	2.1	2.8	2.2	2.8	3.0
Sweden	2.0	1.7	0.0	1.0	1.8	4.0	1.9	2.3	3.1	2.3	2.4	1.4	-1.1	-1.4	-2.2	3.3	3.6	1.1	2.0	2.3
Switzerland	1.1	4.4	1.4	-0.9	1.0	1.8	3.7	2.9	2.0	2.9	3.9	2.3	0.0	-0.3	-0.8	1.0	0.1	-0.7	0.8	1.8
Turkey	4.8	-2.4	4.9	3.6	5.0	6.7	4.2	7.0	9.5	2.1	0.3	9.3	0.9	6.0	8.0	-5.5	7.0	7.2	5.2	4.7
Total of smaller countries	4.6	2.2	2.8	1.6	2.2	4.2	3.5	3.1	4.6	4.2	3.9	4.5	2.4	2.3	1.8	3.3	2.8	3.8	3.7	3.8
Total OECD	3.8	1.1	2.1	0.1	2.8	4.7	3.5	3.0	3.4	4.4	3.6	2.9	1.0	1.9	1.2	2.9	2.2	2.6	3.0	2.7
Memorandum item																				
European Union	3.2	1.4	0.1	0.9	1.7	2.3	2.5	2.9	2.9	4.2	3.5	3.0	1.5	1.0	-0.5	2.9	2.4	1.6	2.3	2.7

Source: OECD, *Economic Outlook*, 1998

Figure 1.4   Inflation in Poland, 1988–97

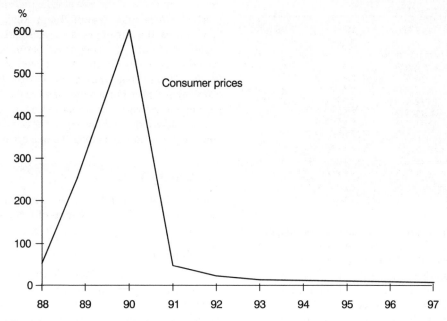

Source: Adapted from OECD, *Economic Outlook*, several issues

Figure 1.5   Real GDP growth trend in Britain, 1979–98

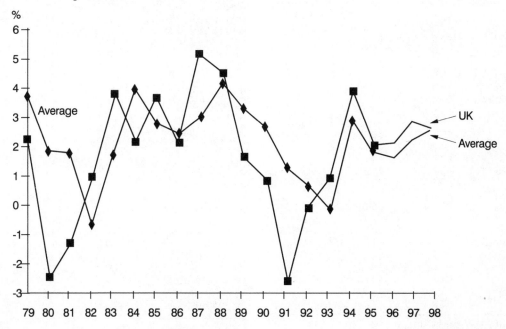

Source: OECD

Table 1.8   Real GDP percentage changes at annual rate: selected countries, 1996–8

	1996 %	1997 %	1998 %
Japan	3.6	2.3	2.9
Germany	1.4	2.2	2.8
USA	2.4	3.6	2.0
Britain	2.1	3.0	2.7
Canada	1.5	3.5	3.3
France	1.5	2.5	2.8
Italy	0.7	1.0	1.8
Average	1.85	2.5	2.6

Note: Average includes: USA, Canada, Germany, France, Italy, Japan
Source: OECD, *Economic Outlook*, 1998

others the rate of growth will actually be negative. A positive though modest rate of economic growth ensures, however, that on average people become 'better off' through time. In broad terms, living standards double each generation – today's children can expect a material standard of living twice as high as that of their parents. However, this is a broad approximation that applies to the economies of western Europe and North America. In some of the newly industrializing countries (NICs) of Asia, like Taiwan, Hong Kong, Singapore, South Korea, the rate of growth is substantially faster, as Table 1.9 shows. The staggering performance of the Japanese economy in the 1960s and 1970s is well known. At one stage during the 1970s, the Japanese economy was growing at a rate of more than 10 per cent per annum. However, as we have seen, Japan's growth rate has slowed down dramatically in recent years and is now one of the lowest among the western economies.

✍ Activity 1.10

Using the figures in Table 1.10–1.12, comment on the rates of growth of the economies of central Europe.

✓ Answer 1.10

As we can see from Table 1.10, the transitional economies of central Europe have all experienced very substantial negative rates of growth in the immediate years following the changeover to a market system.

Table 1.9   Emerging markets indicators

	GDP	% change on year earlier Industrial production	Consumer prices
China	+9.4	+12.1	+2.8
Hong Kong	+5.5	−3.0	+5.8
India	+7.0	+2.9	+9.2
Indonesia	+7.8	+7.1	+5.0
Malaysia	+8.2	+11.4	+2.2
Philippines	+5.0	+9.3	−4.8
Singapore	+3.8	−1.6	+1.6
South Korea	+5.4	+6.1	+4.0
Taiwan	+6.8	+7.3	+1.8
Thailand	+6.7	+2.4	+4.4
Argentina	+8.1	+5.2	+0.9
Brazil	+4.2	+2.5	+7.0
Chile	+3.8	+4.2	+5.3
Colombia	+2.4	−11.7	−18.7
Mexico	+5.1	+15.0	+20.4
Venezuela	−1.6	n a	+43.5
Greece	+2.0	+3.8	+5.5
Israel	+2.5	+2.0	+8.4
Portugal	+3.6	+4.7	+1.8
South Africa	+2.3	+7.7	+9.5
Turkey	+6.7	+11.2	+78.0
Czech Republic	+1.5	−0.7	+6.8
Hungary	+1.2	+1.7	+18.7
Poland	+7.3	+19.9	+15.3
Russia	−0.6	+0.5	+14.6

Source: World Development Report, 1997

Table 1.10   Countries in transition, real GDP, 1991–3

	Annual % change		
	1991	1992	1993
Central Europe	−27.7	−7.8	3.5
Albania	−11.7	−5.6	−2.0
Bulgaria	−15.9	−8.6	—
Former Czechoslovakia	—	—	1.0
Czech Republic	—	—	−9.3
Slovak Republic	−11.9	−4.4	—
Hungary	−7.6	1.0	4.0
Poland	−15.1	−15.4	−2.5
Romania			
Former USSR	−11.8	−40.0	—
Armenia	−0.7	−26.3	−10.0
Azerbaijan	−1.9	−10.0	−14.4
Belarus	−11.9	−23.3	−2.3
Estonia	−20.6	−45.6	−5.0
Georgia	−13.0	−14.0	−7.5
Kazakhstan	−5.0	−26.0	−11.8
Kirghizia	−8.3	−32.9	−10.0
Latvia	−13.4	−35.0	−9.4
Lithuania	−18.0	−21.3	−15.0
Moldova	−12.9	−18.5	−14.9
Russian Federation	—	—	—
Tadjikistan	−4.7	−5.3	3.9
Turkmenistan	−13.4	−14.0	−18.0
Ukraine	−0.9	−9.5	−5.3
Uzbekistan			
Other	−9.9	−7.6	−1.3
Mongolia			

Source: OECD statistics

Table 1.11 Central and eastern European countries and the Russian Federation: key economic indicators[a], 1994–7

	1994	1995	1996	1997
Bulgaria				
Output	1.4	2.5	2.5	3.0
Inflation	125.0	38.0	30.0	30.0
Unemployment	12.8	10.8	12.0	12.0
Fiscal balance[b]	−5.5	−6.5	−6.0	−5.5
Current account balance	0.2	0.3	0.3	0.3
Czech Republic				
Output	2.6	4.0	5.0	6.0
Inflation	10.0	9.0	8.0	8.0
Unemployment	3.2	3.2	4.5	4.5
Fiscal balance	0.6	0.0	0.0	0.0
Current account balance	0.0	−1.9	−2.4	−2.9
Hungary				
Output	2.5	1.0	3.0	4.0
Inflation	19.0	29.0	20.0	18.0
Unemployment	10.4	10.0	9.0	9.0
Fiscal balance[c]	−8.0	−6.0	−4.0	−3.0
Current account balance	−3.9	−2.8	−2.2	−2.0
Poland				
Output	5.2	6.5	5.5	5.0
Inflation	29.0	23.0	20.0	15.0
Unemployment	16.0	14.8	14.2	13.5
Fiscal balance[b,d]	−2.5	−3.0	−2.8	−2.5
Current account balance	−0.9	−1.4	−2.5	−3.3
Romania				
Output	3.4	3.0	4.0	4.0
Inflation	137.0	45.0	35.0	30.0
Unemployment	10.9	12.0	12.5	12.5
Fiscal balance	−4.0	−2.5	−2.5	−2.5
Current account balance	−0.4	−0.6	−0.6	−0.7
Russian Federation				
Output	−15	−4	2	4
Inflation	226	140	60	40
Unemployment	6.0	8.0	9.0	10.0
Fiscal balance	−10.1	−4.0	−4.0	−3.5
Current account balance	0.0	2.5	2.5	−0.6
Slovak Republic				
Output	4.8	6.0	5.0	5.0
Inflation	13.0	10.0	8.0	8.0
Unemployment	14.8	14.0	13.0	13.0
Fiscal balance	−4.0	−3.0	−3.0	−2.0
Current account balance	0.7	0.3	0.0	0.0
Slovenia				
Output	5.5	4.5	5.0	5.0
Inflation	20.0	14.0	10.0	10.0
Unemployment	14.2	13.5	13.0	12.0
Fiscal balance	−0.2	−0.9	−0.5	−0.5
Current account balance	0.5	0.0	0.3	0.1

Source: OECD statistics

[a] The figures given for output (real GDP) and prices (CPI) are average annual percentage changes, with the exception of consumer prices in Bulgaria, Poland and Russia, which are expressed in end-of-year terms. Unemployment is registered unemployment as a percentage of the labour force, end year. Fiscal balances are expressed in per cent of GDP. Current account balances are in US$ billion.
[b] Cash basis; excludes accrued interest on foreign debt.
[c] Excluding privatization.
[d] State budget excluding local authorities but including extra-budgetary funds.

Table 1.12   Central and eastern Europe trade flows, 1993–7

	1993	1994	1995	1996	1997
Central and eastern Europe and the FSU[a]					
Goods export volumes (% change)	10.0	8.6	14.5	10.6	7.5
Goods import volumes (% change)	11.0	6.9	11.8	12.3	9.6
Exports ($ billion)	123.5	136.9	163.9	183.5	200.4
Imports ($ billion)	123.7	135.4	159.9	181.6	202.6
Six central and eastern European countries[b]:					
Goods export volumes (% change)	4.4	11.0	23.4	9.3	7.2
Goods import volumes (% change)	10.6	4.5	20.4	10.4	7.2
Exports ($ billion)	48.7	55.7	71.4	79.0	86.0
Imports ($ billion)	57.5	61.1	78.1	87.2	95.2
Current balance ($ billion)	−8.5	−4.4	−6.2	−7.4	−8.6

Sources: OECD statistics
[a] Former Soviet Union, excludes intra–FSU trade
[b] Poland, Hungary, Czech Republic, Slovak Republic, Romania and Bulgaria

The output of these economies has been contracting rather than expanding. In much of central Europe, however, the liberalization of trade and prices, progress toward enterprise reform and sound macroeconomic policies are beginning to succeed, as Tables 1.11 and 1.12 show.

✍ Activity 1.11

Study Figure 1.6 and comment on the rate of growth of the Polish economy.

✓ Answer 1.11

As we can see from Figure 1.6, in Poland output took a dramatic dip after 1988 from a positive rate of growth of plus 4 per cent per annum in 1988 to a dramatic minus 12 per cent in 1990. Economic performance has, however, improved since then and the annual rate of growth of real GDP has once more reached pre-1988 levels, at 4 per cent in 1993 and 5.2 per cent annual rate of growth in 1994, 6.5 per cent in 1995, only to slow down to 5 per cent in 1997.

Figure 1.6   Polish GDP growth trend, 1988–97

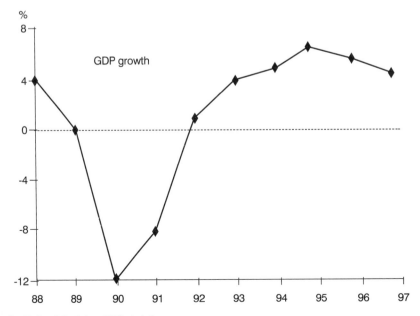

Sources: IMF, Office for National Statistics, OECD statistics

✍ Activity 1.12

Look at Table 1.13 and comment on the performance of China and the dynamic Asian Economies.

✓ Answer 1.12

In China policies aimed at controlling inflation, which was brought down from 21.7 per cent to 15.5 per cent in 1995, have slowed down the rate of growth of real GDP from 11.8 to below 10 per cent.

The deceleration of the domestic economy in 1995 coincided with a rise in exports with the USA and other Asian economies.

Led by strong exports, growing domestic demand and using foreign direct investment, particularly from Japan, economic activity in the DAEs (dynamic Asian economies) has continued to be strong in 1995. Rapid

Table 1.13 China and dynamic Asian economies: key economic indicators[a], 1994–7

	1994	1995	1996	1997
China				
GNP	11.8	9.5	10.0	10.5
Retail prices	21.7	15.5	13.0	13.5
Current account balance	7.3	7.8	6.3	5.4
DAEs total				
GDP/GNP	7.6	7.8	7.0	6.4
Consumer prices	5.4	5.0	5.3	4.9
Trade balance	−4.9	−10.2	−9.9	−9.2
Current account balance	3.2	−7.4	−7.4	−5.8
Korea				
GDP	8.4	9.0	7.5	7.0
Consumer prices	6.2	5.0	6.0	5.5
Trade balance	−3.1	−7.0	−6.0	−4.8
Current account balance	−4.5	−8.5	−9.0	−7.5
Chinese Taipei				
GDP/GNP	6.1	6.3	6.0	5.5
Consumer prices	4.1	3.8	3.8	3.5
Trade balance	11.9	10.5	8.3	7.0
Current account balance	5.9	5.0	6.0	6.5
Hong Kong				
GDP/GNP	5.5	5.0	4.8	4.5
Consumer prices	8.1	9.0	8.8	8.0
Trade balance	−10.9	−11.7	−11.3	−11.0
Current account balance	2.8	2.3	1.2	1.5
Singapore				
GDP/GNP	10.1	8.2	7.5	7.0
Consumer prices	3.5	2.3	2.5	2.5
Trade balance	−0.2	2.0	2.0	2.1
Current account balance	11.9	10.6	10.0	9.5
Thailand				
GDP/GNP	8.5	8.7	8.2	7.2
Consumer prices	5.1	5.5	5.3	4.8
Trade balance	−4.0	−4.5	−4.4	−4.0
Current account balance	−8.5	−9.6	−9.6	−9.3
Malaysia				
GDP/GNP	8.7	9.6	8.5	7.5
Consumer prices	3.7	3.6	3.5	3.5
Trade balance	1.4	0.5	1.5	1.5
Current account balance	−4.4	−7.2	−7.0	−6.5

Sources: IMF, International Financial Statistics, Chinese Taipei sources, Hong Kong Census and Statistics Department, Monthly Digest of Statistics, OECD estimates and projections

[a] The figures given for GDP/GNP and consumer prices are percentage changes from previous period. Trade and current account balances are in $ billion. Current account estimates for Hong Kong correspond to net exports of goods and services on a national account basis and therefore exclude investment income and transfers. The trade balance corresponds to net exports of goods on a national account

growth has exacerbated problems of infrastructure bottlenecks and labour shortages. This has resulted in increased cost pressures and increased demand for imported capital equipment, needed to support high investment requirements.

There were, however, some signs of a deceleration during the second half of 1995, particularly in Thailand and Malaysia. Hong Kong and Chinese Taipei have been particularly affected by the moderate slowing down of growth in China and by the negative consequences of falling property and assets prices. Growth rates, however, are still high, around 8–9 per cent per annum. Inflation and current account deficits remain key policy concerns for 1996.

Summing up, the statistics analysed above show that economic growth has been the norm rather than the exception this century. Despite the disruption caused by two world wars, substantial increases in gross national product per person have been recorded. Growth was exceptionally high in the industrialized economies in the 1950s and 1960s, often referred to as the economic miracle years. The miracle ended in the 1970s and 1980s when much lower rates of growth were recorded.

If one looks at the whole post-war period, from 1950 to 1990, national output per capita grew by an annual average of 1.9 per cent in the USA, 6 per cent in Japan, 2.4 per cent in the UK, 3.7 per cent in Germany, 3.1 per cent in France. These rates do not seem particularly impressive, but if sustained over an extended period of time they can make a big difference in a country's standards of living; a 3 per cent annual growth rate will double living standards in 33 years, the time span of a generation. Today's children in Germany, France and Italy enjoy a standard of living twice as high as that of their parents. We can now sum up the growth statistics as follows:

■ Economic growth has been the norm rather than the exception since World War II.
■ Countries which were relatively well off in the 1950s and 1960s have continued to enjoy high standards of living, although growth rates have considerably slowed down in the 1980s and 1990s.
■ Dramatic changes have occurred in the economic development of some developing countries since the 1960s, notably the rapid growth of the Japanese economy in the 1960s, followed by Korea, Taiwan, Singapore and Hong Kong in the 1970s, and by China, Indonesia, Malaysia and Thailand, among others, in the 1980s and 1990s.
■ Resource-rich countries did not fare equally well. Oil-producing countries benefited from the large increases in oil prices of the 1970s, but were sub-

sequently unable to sustain the cartelized prices. The price of oil fell in real terms to pre-1973 levels in the 1990s. Many other primary product exporting countries have suffered a deterioration in their terms of trade; in other words they have seen the price of their exports fall in relation to the price of their imports. This has contributed to their poor growth records.
■ From 1989 to 1994, the economies in transition of the former Soviet Union have suffered a cumulative fall in their real output, recording negative rates of growth. Most of them seem, however, to be now firmly on the road to economic recovery.

Balance of payments

International trade in goods and services and factors of production can greatly increase an economy's wealth, output and employment. International trade requires, however, the operation of an efficient mechanism for international payments.

A country's transactions with the rest of the world over a year are recorded in its balance of payments. These transactions are divided into two main groups: the current account, which shows cross-border transactions in 'visible' goods and 'invisible' services, such as tourism, banking services or factor incomes. The balance of trade refers only to the trade of goods. It is in surplus when exports are greater than imports and in deficit when imports are greater than exports. Common expressions like 'the UK deficit' or 'the Japanese surplus' are often used as an abbreviation for the balance of payments on the current account. A country with a deficit is therefore buying more than it is selling and will need to obtain more foreign currency than it is earning from its foreign transactions. A country with a surplus is in exactly the opposite situation, as it is selling more than it is buying.

Current account transactions constitute only a small proportion of the total value of international transactions. With the growing size of capital movements and investments on a global scale, the importance of the capital account of the balance of payments has greatly increased in recent years. The capital account of the balance of payments records UK direct investment and portfolio investment flows abroad and overseas investment and portfolio investment inflows into the UK. A capital account deficit indicates that the UK direct investment abroad and outflow of capital is greater than overseas direct investment and inflow of capital into the UK.

For reasons that will become clear later on in the book, it is quite obvious that a disequilibrium in the balance of trade or in the capital accounts cannot be sustained forever. External equilibrium is therefore a policy objective that governments actively pursue. However, if balance of payments difficulties occur, governments often have to impose remedies which are likely to have negative effects on other domestic policy objectives. Thus a country with a large balance of payments deficit may be forced to raise interest rates as a short-term measure and this may adversely affect domestic investment, employment and growth. In short, the objective of achieving external balance may conflict with the achievement of internal balance and vice versa.

✍ Activity 1.13

Study Table 1.14 and Figure 1.7 and comment on the UK current account position.

✓ Answer 1.13

The current account as a whole from a deficit of £11 billion in 1993 to a surplus of £4 billion in 1997. Figure 1.7 shows however that the UK current account is expected to turn negative again in 1998 and to continue to run a modest deficit in 1999 and 2000.

Table 1.14 UK current account, 1993–7 (figures rounded up to nearest integer)

			£ billion			
	Manufacturers	Oil	Other	Total visibles	Invisibles	Current balance
1993	–8	2	–8	–13	2	–11
1994	–7	4	–7	–11	10	–1
1995	–9	4	–7	–11	5	–6
1996	–9	5	–6	–10	5	–5
1997	–9	5	–6	–9	5	4

Source: HMT, *Financial Statement Budget Report*, 1998

Figure 1.7 UK current account, 1976–2000

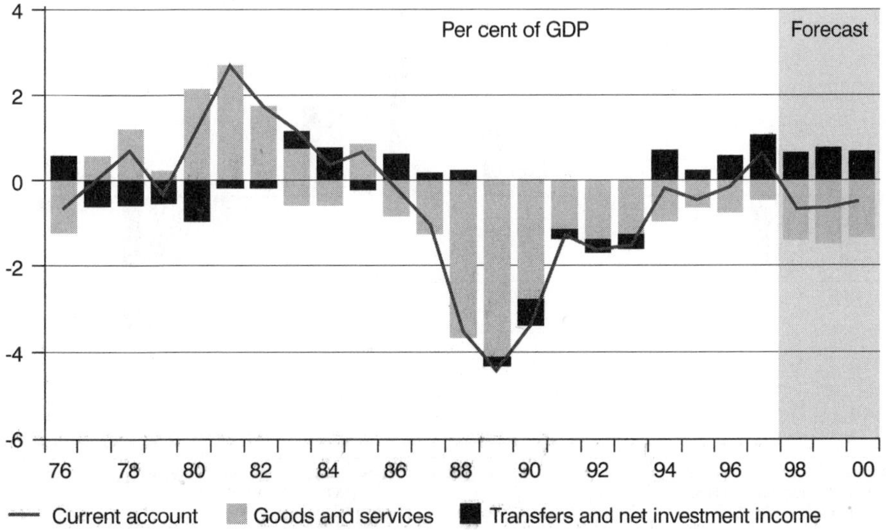

Source: Her Majesty's Treasury, *Financial Statement Budget Report*, 1998

Other macroeconomic objectives

In addition to the four main objectives we have already discussed, policymakers wish to influence a number of other variables in the economy. They may be concerned, among other things, about regional imbalances within a country. In the UK, for example, the south-east is comparatively affluent with low levels of unemployment, whereas the north is characterized by higher levels of unemployment and lower wages. In Italy, the reverse is true: the predominantly agricultural south is poorer than the more affluent industrialized north. Thus, a government may be concerned not just with the macroeconomic impact of its policies but also with the different ways in which they affect various regions or sectors of the economy.

A government may also be concerned with the distribution of income between individuals or households in the economy. Policies which raise taxes – on goods and services or on incomes – have an impact on the distribution of real incomes and the government may wish to take this into account in assessing the desirability of some of its policies. Most people would agree that large inequalities in income and wealth are socially divisive and undesirable, but the disagreement may lie in how we define 'large inequalities'. In the UK over the last 15 years, the distribution of income has become more unequal as a result of various government policies on taxation and public spending.

A government may also be concerned to some extent with the impact of its policies on the environment. For example, in considering ways in which taxation can be raised to finance expenditure, a government may deem it legitimate and indeed desirable to impose high taxes on polluting activities; for example, high taxes might be levied on petrol to discourage people from using their cars. The government may also consider it sensible to impose high taxes on tobacco, the consumption of which affects the health of individuals.

✍ Activity 1.14

Study the Figure 1.8 and Table 1.15 and comment on regional composition of output and distribution of income in the UK in 1995.

✓ Answer 1.14

In 1995 total UK gross domestic product (GDP) was £633 billion, an increase of about 30 per cent in real terms from 1990. Within the UK total, over a third of

Figure 1.8   UK GDP per head

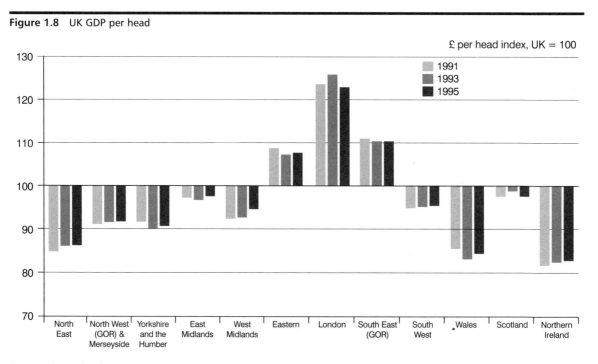

Source: ONS, Regional Accounts, 1997

Table 1.15 Regional personal income, 1985–95

	1985	1990	1991	1992	1993	1994	1995
Personal income							
£ million							
United Kingdom	307 081	485 175	516 732	547 929	572 125	596 929	633 237
North East	12 518	18 569	20 299	21 607	22 390	22 818	23 914
North West (GOR) & Merseyside	35 316	53 978	57 174	60 177	62 419	64 823	68 271
Yorkshire and the Humber	24 922	38 544	41 183	43 592	45 423	47 441	49 891
East Midlands	20 597	32 307	34 227	35 731	37 720	39 617	42 377
West Midlands	25 848	41 508	44 509	47 235	48 779	50 962	54 363
Eastern	27 789	44 778	47 189	49 685	51 126	53 861	57 081
London	44 041	71 133	75 851	79 758	85 067	88 134	94 676
South East (GOR)	44 724	72 572	76 273	80 959	85 344	90 744	97 072
South West	24 370	38 113	40 803	43 819	45 284	46 792	49 640
England	260 125	411 501	437 509	462 564	483 552	505 191	537 286
Wales	13 053	20 795	22 333	23 587	24 212	25 493	26 463
Scotland	26 879	41 914	44 800	48 735	50 502	51 564	53 922
Northern Ireland	7024	10 965	12 088	13 042	13 859	14 680	15 566
£ per head							
United Kingdom	5417	8429	8939	9446	9832	10 222	10 805
North East	4801	7148	7800	8283	8572	8744	9180
North West (GOR) & Merseyside	5146	7861	8304	8734	9043	9392	9894
Yorkshire and the Humber	5078	7767	8265	8714	9059	9441	9920
East Midlands	5286	8049	8482	8797	9239	9658	10 276
West Midlands	4976	7907	8453	8950	9222	9625	10 245
Eastern	5587	8758	9163	9600	9845	10 312	10 857
London	6486	10 380	11 009	11 552	12 270	12 649	13 512
South East (GOR)	6017	9497	9933	10 498	11 031	11 657	12 370
South West	5399	8120	8649	9232	9498	9751	10 284
England	5513	8574	9075	9561	9963	10 372	10 987
Wales	4645	7226	7724	8138	8330	8751	9073
Scotland	5233	8214	8772	9535	9863	10 047	10 498
Northern Ireland	4509	6899	7548	8059	8493	8942	9440
£ per head, UK = 100							
United Kingdom	100.0	100.0	100.0	100.0	100.0	100.0	100.0
North East	89.8	87.0	89.3	89.5	88.9	87.1	86.6
North West (GOR) & Merseyside	95.5	94.8	94.1	93.9	93.2	93.0	93.0
Yorkshire and the Humber	94.9	94.2	94.2	93.5	93.4	93.7	93.1
East Midlands	96.8	96.3	95.4	93.4	94.5	94.8	95.7
West Midlands	92.7	95.0	95.6	95.7	94.6	95.0	95.8
Eastern	99.8	100.4	99.3	98.3	97.2	98.3	97.7
London	120.9	119.6	119.6	118.9	122.2	121.3	122.6
South East (GOR)	109.0	109.9	108.2	108.7	109.7	111.6	111.9
South West	100.4	96.7	97.2	98.4	97.0	95.6	95.6
England	101.7	101.2	100.9	100.6	100.8	101.0	101.2
Wales	87.0	88.0	89.9	89.2	87.0	88.2	86.3
Scotland	96.2	99.4	100.2	103.2	101.9	99.5	98.2
Northern Ireland	85.9	87.8	90.9	91.2	92.5	93.8	93.6

Source: ONS, *Regional Trends*, 1997

GDP is still accounted for by the South East, as Table 1.15 and Figure 1.8 show.

There are wide variations in output (GDP) per head between the regions, with London and the South East having the highest level and Wales and Northern Ireland the lowest (see Table 1.15).

Many of the differences in the levels of regional GDP per head are long standing and there are relatively small year to year changes. Between 1994 and 1995 regional growth in GDP per head was strongest in Wales, while the North West, Scotland and Ireland also performed better than the UK average. There have been significant variations in the economic performance of the regions. Figure 1.8 shows regional GDP per head, indexed to UK=100, from 1991–5.

Part of the explanation for the wide variation in regional GDP per head lies in the marked differences in the industrial structures of the regions. Very significant but short-term factors, such as changes in the sterling price of oil, may affect industries and therefore regions.

CONFLICT BETWEEN POLICY OBJECTIVES

What emerges from the study of macroeconomics is the existence of conflicts between policy objectives. Although all governments would like to bring about rapid rates of growth, full employment, price stability and external payments balance, a fundamental conflict between the policy objectives makes their simultaneous achievements very difficult. As you will able to appreciate after you have read this book, policies aimed at reducing inflation might cause interest rates to rise; high interest rates adversely affect investment and consumption and therefore ultimately increase unemployment. Higher interest rates may in some cases make the currency stronger, which in turn adversely affects exports. Rapid rates of growth might cause a balance of payments problem; policies aimed at reducing unemployment lead to an increase in inflation.

✍ Activity 1.15

Study Figures 1.1 and 1.3 together. What can you infer by comparing the data for UK unemployment and inflation?

✓ Answer 1.15

As you can see from the two sets of figures, inflation and unemployment seem to move in opposite directions. When inflation is brought under control, as in the early 1980s, unemployment rates rise. When the rate of unemployment falls, as in the second part of the 1980s, the rate of inflation rises. The same pattern is displayed by the 1990s.

Targets and instruments

The reason for the existence of conflicts among governments' policy objectives can be expressed more clearly if we introduce the concepts of economic targets and instruments. Price stability, fast growth and full employment, all represent their aims or ultimate **policy goals**. To achieve those long-term goals, governments set themselves some quantifiable, short-term **policy targets**, such as to bring the inflation rate down from 3 per cent to 2 per cent in the next year, to ensure a rate of growth of 2 per cent or an unemployment rate of 4 per cent. To achieve the set policy targets, governments can choose from a series of **policy instruments**, for instance, setting certain values for interest rates, for direct and indirect taxation and government spending.

The difficulty experienced by governments in achieving policy targets stems from the fact that they do not have specific policy instruments for every policy target: there is a shortage of tools. For example, interest rates are a tool which works and can be used to achieve price stability and full employment, but it works in opposite directions. Interest rates need to be lowered to increase employment and raised to reduce inflation. Thus, the use of the same tools to achieve different policy targets creates conflict with regard to government policy objectives.

JOHN MAYNARD KEYNES: PERSONAL PROFILE

John Maynard Keynes (1883–1946), educated at Eton and Cambridge, studied economics under Marshall and Pigou before being offered a lectureship in economics at King's College, Cambridge. During World War I he held a post at the Treasury, from which he resigned because of disagreements over Germany's war reparation payments, considered by Keynes to have been set too high. He explained this in his book, *The Economic Consequences of the Peace*, published in 1919. In his subsequent book, *The Economic Consequences of Mr Churchill*, he was also severely critical of the decision taken by the government in 1925 to return to the gold standard, and at its pre-war parity. In 1930 he published

A Treaty on Money and was subsequently appointed a member of the Macmillan Committee on Finance and Industry. His most famous book, *The General Theory of Employment, Interest and Money*, was published in 1936. Written after the experience of the Great Depression of 1929–33 and the high rates of unemployment and business failures that had persisted throughout the 1930s, the *General Theory* rejected the classical view of the economy as inherently stable and well functioning. Instead Keynes developed an explanation of the workings of the macroeconomy which allows for the possibility of persistent disequilibrium, where mass unemployment can develop and set in, and from which economies can only be rescued by government intervention aimed at stimulating aggregate demand through fiscal and monetary policy. The book seemed to stand classical economic theory on its head. It rejected the theoretical foundations on which the laissez-faire policies of right-wing marketers had rested and caused a revolution of economic thinking. This came to be known as the **Keynesian revolution**. It was not, however, a political revolution. Despite being a strong advo-

cate of government intervention, Keynes was not a socialist engaged in the overthrow of the capitalist system. First tested in America by President Roosevelt during the New Deal, Keynes's policies of aggregate demand management to fight unemployment seemed to work. Most western European governments endorsed them in the 1950s and 1960s and consistently engaged in demand management to stabilize and stimulate their economies. Keynes gave a further important contribution to the post-World War II monetary and economic order by taking part as the British negotiator at the Bretton Woods Conference in New Hampshire in 1944. The world monetary system that emerged from that conference, known as the Bretton Woods system, was to regulate international monetary relationships until the early 1970s. Keynesian demand management policies started to fall into disrepute during the recessionary 1970s, when a combination of high inflation, high unemployment and lack of growth or stagnation, **stagflation**, seemed to defeat any explanation by the traditional Keynesian model. The tide of monetarism was rising.

☆ **For revision of this chapter, see the Chapter Summaries at the end of the book, starting on page 411.**

2 Measurement and structure of the national economy

Objectives

After studying this chapter, you will be able to understand:

- the circular flow of income, output and expenditure;
- the purpose of the National Accounts;
- the conceptual and practical issues involved in measuring economic activity;
- the difference between gross domestic product (GDP) and gross national product (GNP);
- the difference between gross national product (GNP) and net national product (NNP);
- the difference between nominal GDP and real GDP;
- the meaning of disposable income;
- the meaning of per capita Income;
- the limits of GNP as a measure of living standards;
- the function of the Measure of Economic Welfare (MEW) and Human Development Index (HDI).

DATA AND MACROECONOMIC MODELS

The state of the British economy outlined in Chapter 1 highlights the importance of understanding what affects the main macroeconomic variables. Inflation in Britain has been brought under control in recent years, but output growth, although improving, remains unimpressive as well as unbalanced; the unemployment rate is high and the trade balance is in deficit. What is more, this situation has developed within the context of protracted government policy aimed at reducing government spending and reinstating the 'free' forces of the market.

Britain's economy is not behaving very differently from other developed countries' economies. As we have seen, most industrialized economies have suffered from the same macroeconomic problems, although sometimes not as severely as the UK. The members of the EU, the USA and Japan all started the 1990s with a recession – that is a decline in the rate of growth of aggregate output. Most, with the exception of Japan, are now experiencing an expansion, with output growth rates at or above their historical average (over the past 35 years). This growth has also been accompanied by low inflation, again lower than the average over the last 35 years. By 1997, their relative performance varied, however, as shown in Table 2.1.

European unemployment rates, which were very low in the 1960s, are now nearly twice as high as the US rate. In most rich countries, in sharp contrast to the developing countries, output growth appears to be lower than it was before the mid-1970s. Governments' attitudes around the world, in the last twenty years, have also been largely in favour of a gradual disengagement from the management of the economy.

This is as far as one can go without a theory. You can describe how things are, but you cannot explain why they are what they are. We begin to appreciate therefore how important it is to be able to explain what determines these macroeconomic variables and how

Table 2.1 Main macroeconomic indicators, 1996–8

	1996	1997	1998
Real total domestic demand			
USA	2.5	3.9	2.1
Japan	4.5	1.4	2.4
Germany	0.8	1.3	2.5
European Union	1.3	1.9	2.6
Total OECD	2.8	2.9	2.7
Real GDP			
USA	2.4	3.6	2.0
Japan	3.6	2.3	2.9
Germany	1.4	2.2	2.8
UK	2.1	3.0	2.7
European Union	1.6	2.3	2.7
Total OECD	2.6	3.0	2.7
Inflation			
USA	2.0	2.0	2.2
Japan	0.0	0.9	0.8
Germany	1.0	1.2	1.1
UK	3.1	2.3	2.2
Total OECD *less* high inflation countries	1.8	1.8	1.9
European Union	2.4	1.8	1.9
Total OECD	4.2	3.7	3.4
Unemployment			
USA	5.4	5.0	5.1
Japan	3.3	3.2	3.1
Germany	10.3	11.1	10.9
UK	7.4	6.1	5.6
European Union	11.3	11.2	10.8
Total OECD	7.5	7.3	7.1
Current balances			
USA	−2.2	−2.3	−2.4
Japan	1.4	1.9	2.3
Germany	−0.6	0.1	0.3
UK	−0.4	3.0	3.0
European Union	1.0	1.4	1.6
Total OECD	−0.2	−0.1	−0.1
Short-term interest rates			
USA	5.0	5.4	5.7
Japan	0.6	0.7	1.2
Germany	3.3	3.1	3.2
UK	6.0	6.3	6.5
Major four European countries	5.7	5.0	4.8
World trade	6.2	8.1	8.0

Source: OECD, *Economic Outlook*, 1997, estimated values for 1998
Notes:
Growth rate: annual rate of real GDP growth.
Unemployment rate: average over the year.
Inflation rate: annual rate of change of GDP deflator.

need a model. Just like a model of a car engine shows us how its many different parts – pistons, spark plugs, valves, camshaft – are connected to one another and work together to make the car go, in the same way, economic models suggest ways in which the various parts of the economy fit together to produce:

- growth or contraction of aggregate output;
- full employment or unemployment;
- price stability or inflation;
- balance of trade surpluses or deficits;
- currency appreciations or depreciations.

Unfortunately for the students of economics, as well as for politicians, who are often confused by conflicting professional advice, there is more than one way – or one model – of explaining how the macroeconomy works. As we have already mentioned, economists disagree among themselves and tend to divide into two opposing schools of thought: the Keynesians, who agree with Keynes's model of how the economy works, and the monetarists, who favour Friedman's explanation. These two main schools of thought have in turn subdivided into more subtle strands, nowadays represented respectively by the new (or neo-) Keynesians and the new (or neo-) monetarists.

On many issues, however, the disagreement is less dramatic than it is often made out to be. Sometimes it relates to the weight the two schools assign to different objectives: whether unemployment, inflation or income inequalities should be regarded as the worst social evil. Sometimes the disagreement relates to the interpretation of statistical data. Macroeconomics, as a social science, is the result of a continuous process of interaction between models and data, theory and practice, ideas and events, where the models that do not fit the data, the ideas that fail to explain reality are gradually discarded. But unlike a physicist who can conduct a controlled experiment to measure, say, the boiling point for a specific liquid substance by varying only the temperature applied to the liquid, while everything else stays the same, the economist cannot make the world stop in order to conduct its own test. Typically, the data collected will be the result of many influences, all susceptible to change at the same time. Hence the disagreement over the interpretation of the data. This is why different economists looking at the same data can reach different conclusions.

Before we can even begin to understand what the controversy between Keynesians and monetarists is all about, we need to do two things:

- First, we need to organize our thoughts about the macroeconomy. We do this with the help of a much easier model, the **circular flow model**. This model

they are affected by governments' economic policies: we need to understand how the macroeconomy works.

To understand 'what causes what' and how the various parts of the economy fit together as a whole, we is simple and makes such powerful assumptions that it can be regarded as axiomatic, that is, something which is true by definition. In its simplicity, however, this model helps us to understand some fundamental relationships within the economic system which provide the basis for any subsequent, more sophisticated modelling.

■ Second, we need some data to work on. Before we try to explain why the economy works the way it does, we need to be able to describe it. We do so by collecting and examining macroeconomic data. So our preliminary step must be to understand which data to look at and how to collect them. In fact the simple circular flow model also helps us to understand some important characteristics of the macroeconomic data we collect to measure the level of economic activity.

✍ Activity 2.1

Now think about the economy. Think about the many goods produced, the services provided, the contracts and agreements entered into. If you were asked to provide a model of the economy as a whole, a model based on common sense and no specific knowledge, a model of what makes the economy function, a very simple model, what would you say? Try and think about it in terms of relationships and motives and then see if your ideas match those of the circular flow model described below.

CIRCULAR FLOW MODEL

Let's forget about the complications of everyday economic transactions and try to capture instead the very basic features of any macroeconomic system. We can begin by making a list of some simple, indisputable facts:

■ We all need goods and services to survive.
■ Economies are systems for the production and distribution of the goods and services that we all need and want.
■ In the economy, some people produce things for other people's consumption.
■ People have to pay money to obtain the goods and services they want.
■ People earn money by selling or renting out what they have, which in most cases is just their ability to work for others.
■ Those who produce the goods need to use productive resources, including other people's labour, in order to produce goods and services.

These are basically the facts. Is there any way in which we can or should order them? The answer is no, as the order in which we look at them is immaterial. It's like trying to decide where the head of table at a dinner party should sit, when looking at a round table. These facts can be better described as a circular flow rather than as one-directional processes. There are two functionally different types of economic agents: one that we call 'the firm' and the other that we call the 'household'. Firms produce goods and services for households' consumption. What firms produce, and we refer here to all the firms in the economy, represents the **total output** of the economy, what the whole economy has produced over a time period, say in a year. This output 'flows', as it changes hands and goes round in the economy. It is produced by firms for household consumption and is sold to them. Households spend all their money to buy all the goods and services which the firms have produced. As they spend their money to buy the goods and services, households generate a flow of **expenditure**. It is self-evident that if all goods and services produced are also sold, the value of the expenditure generated by their purchase is equal to the value of the goods, which is to say that the value of the economy's **total expenditure** is the same as the value of the economy's **total output**.

So what we have established so far is that the value of total output, which we call Y, is equal to the value of total expenditure, which we call E, generated in order to purchase it:

$$Y = E.$$

✍ Activity 2.2

Where do households get the money they need to buy the firms' output, the total output of the economy?

✓ Answer 2.2

People get their money from the firms themselves, to whom they sell what they have, in terms of productive resources. Households may therefore derive their **income** from:

■ Selling their labour services (i.e. working for someone) or being self-employed. This source of income is what we call **wages** and **salaries**. Individuals who run their own business are self-employed. In this case the household and the firm are the same person, but the economic functions and transactions remain distinct. Self-employed persons pay themselves a salary from the business proceeds. Proceeds in excess of costs – the profits – will also be part of the self-employed income, in addition to salary, but will represent income in return for the capital invested in the business and not for the work done on a daily basis.

■ Letting to firms any land, buildings or households they own. This income is called **rent**.

■ Households may earn income from savings deposited in banks or building societies, pension funds, etc., which in turn can be used by financial institutions to make loans to borrowers. This income is called **interest**.

■ Households may earn an income from any company shares they might have. Companies use shareholders' money to run the business. In return shareholders are entitled to a share of the company's profits in relation to the number of shares held, i.e. in relation to the amount of money they have made available to the company. This source of income is what we call business **profits**.

Summing up, to produce goods and services for household consumption, firms employ people and use up resources. Firms have to pay for such resources as their use is not free. Households ultimately receive their income from firms.

✍ Activity 2.3

Where do firms get the money to pay for households' services and the resources they need to produce the goods?

✓ Answer 2.3

They get it from the households that have paid the firms money for the goods and services purchased. The money spent by the households to buy the goods, the total expenditure of the economy, becomes the firms' revenue, which is then used to pay for the productive resources (labour, land and capital) needed to produce the goods. So firms provide households with their income, which households then spend to buy the firms' output.

So it must be that if all the goods and services produced in the economy by firms are sold to households, and all the factors of production are fully rewarded, the money value of the economy's **total output**, Y, is equal to the value of the economy's **total expenditure**, E, which in turn is equal to the economy's **total income**, Y. So:

total output = total expenditure = total income

or:

$$E = Y$$

where Y is used to denote both income and output.

This is the situation shown by the circular flow diagram in Figure 2.1.

✍ Activity 2.4

Just to reinforce the concepts introduced here, describe in your own words what the inner loop and the outer loop of this circular flow model show.

✓ Answer 2.4

The inner loop shows the transfer of real resources between the two sectors. Households exchange labour services and command over whatever productive resources they own, whether labour, capital or land, in exchange for goods and services produced by firms. The households become the firms' employees, shareholders, owners and landlords. The outer loop shows the corresponding flow of money. Households allow firms the use of their productive resources (land, labour and capital) in exchange for money, their income. Firms pay households wages and salaries in exchange for labour, rent for the use of land or buildings, interest and dividends for the money which households put into businesses either directly in the form of share capital or indirectly through financial

---

Figure 2.1 Circular flow model

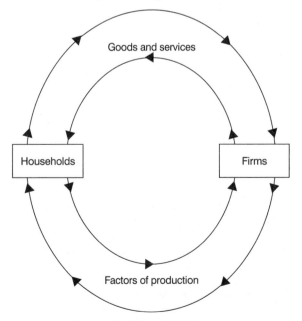

Total expenditure on goods and services

Goods and services

Households

Firms

Factors of production

Rewards to factors: factors' income

intermediaries. The incomes earned by households from firms are then spent by households to buy goods and services produced by firms. The incomes received become a flow of expenditure that flows back to the firms from which they had initially originated, as rewards to factors of production.

It is important to recognize that this circular flow model describes the situation of an economy where:

■ The owners of all factors of production (households) are fully rewarded. It follows from this that the aggregate value of gross factor incomes must be equal to the aggregate value of final output produced in the economy. By **factor incomes** economists mean the payment that accrues to each factor of production for the services rendered. Land, labour and capital are the factors of production needed in the production of any good or service. Payment for those factors will make up the total costs that firms need to meet. Broadly speaking, these payments are rent for land, wages for labour, interest for financial capital and profit for risk capital and enterprise. All these costs make up the price of the finished product. In this sense, the value of national output is equal to the value of national income.
■ All income received by households is in turn spent purchasing the goods and services produced by firms in the domestic economy.
■ All goods are sold; all services provided are demanded. Nothing is left unsold at the end of the period. If this is the case, it must also be true that:

total income = total expenditure = total output

or

$$Y = E$$

where Y stands for total income but also total output of the economy and E stands for total expenditure.

The circular flow model helps us to understand an important aspect of the national accounts.

If we want to measure the level of economic activity in our economy (Figure 2.2), we could do so by measuring the value of the goods and services produced, the value of the total output of the economy at A, when it reaches the households. We could equally do so by measuring the value of total expenditure at B, as all the goods and services produced are purchased by the households. Or we could measure it at C, adding together all factor incomes generated in the economy. We have reached an important point. This circular flow model helps us to see that there are three ways of measuring the level of economic activity in an economy. We could measure:

Figure 2.2   Measuring the flow of economic activity

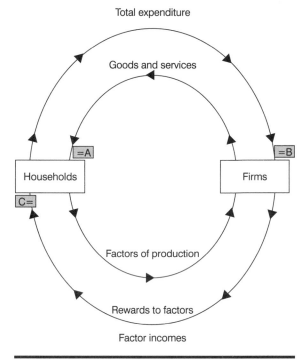

■ the value of goods and services produced, **total output, Y.**
■ the value of total spending on goods and services, **total expenditure, E.**
■ the value of factor services supplied, **total income, Y.**

What is more, the model shows us that if all factors are fully rewarded, all income is spent and all the goods are sold, then the three measures lead, in theory at least, to the same value for the level of economic activity.

The existence in real life of indirect taxes and subsidies may distort this relationship between national output, income and expenditure. Indirect taxes, like VAT, placed on goods and services, are paid at the time of the purchase. They raise the market price of goods or services above the price necessary to cover all the costs or rewards to the factors of production. The money collected by firms as VAT is paid to the government; it does not represent money which firms can share out as income to the factors of production. Subsidies, on the other hand, are payments by the government to firms, which are used to make payments to factors. We must therefore subtract indirect taxes from the value of the output and add on subsidies if we are to arrive at the same figure for the value of the economy's output.

What if a firm cannot sell some of the goods it has produced? Won't the product and expenditure measures then differ? From a national accounting point of view 'unsold goods' are treated as investment expenditure by the firm itself. When a firm cannot sell all its products it stocks up its unsold goods. Accumulation of unsold goods in inventories is treated in the national accounts as part of investment expenditure by firms. This is what economists call **investment** in **working capital** – which includes raw materials, partly finished goods and finished goods – as opposed to investment in **fixed capital** – which refers to firms' expenditure on machinery and buildings. Thus the equivalence between the expenditure and output measures of the level of economic activity is guaranteed, even if some goods remain unsold.

Before we can try to explain how the economy works and how the parts fit together, we need to know something about the state of the economy, that is, we need to be able to describe it. We need to have some measure of the level of the economic activity in the economy. We need some data. This is precisely what the national income accounts give us.

NATIONAL ACCOUNTS: METHODS AND MEASURES

The national income accounts give us an idea of what is going on in the economy and how the economy is doing. Before we examine in some details how the national accounts are compiled and what their data tell us, let's be clear about their purpose.

🖎 Activity 2.5

What is the purpose of the national accounts? Are they important?

✓ Answer 2.5

The purpose of the national accounts is to measure the total value of the output of the economy. The data collected by the national accounts also convey other important information:

■ where the output originates by sector (agriculture, manufacturing, services, etc.) or by region, how much of it is produced by the private sector as opposed to government sector, and so on. This

information allows us to assess the relative importance of the different sectors of the economy, expressed as a percentage of total GDP, and how this has changed over the years.
■ how the output is allocated (between household and government, residents and foreigners).

A system of national income accounting is therefore important for the following reasons:

1 It allows us to measure the level of production in the economy over a given period of time, and to explain the immediate causes of that level of performance.
2 By comparing the national income accounts over a period of time, the long run course which the economy has been following can be detected.
3 The national income accounts will show growth or stagnation in the economy, alerting economic policymakers to the sort of action which ought to be taken. Since national income accounts break the performance of the economy down into its component parts, they provide policymakers with specific information needed for the formulation and application of economic policy.

The most commonly used measure of economic activity used for the purpose of national accounting is the **gross domestic product (GDP)**. Gross domestic product is the value of output produced within the country over a twelve month period, regardless of who owns the factors of production.

The circular flow of output, income and expenditure, which we have just described, shows us quite clearly that there are three methods of calculating GDP.

🖎 Activity 2.6

In the light of what you have learnt about the circular flow, explain what those methods might be and why they should all give the same figure for GDP.

✓ Answer 2.6

The first method of measuring GDP is the **output** or **product method**. This consists of adding up the value of all the goods and services produced in the economy. We simply add up the production of all firms, industry by industry (so many cars, refrigerators, concerts, etc.), sector by sector (manufacturing sector, agricultural sector, etc.). The second method of measuring GDP is called the **expenditure method**. This consists of looking at the money actually spent to purchase the economy's output, adding up the various categories of expenditure. The third method of measuring GDP is the **income method**. This consists of adding up all the households' incomes generated by the production of goods and services. The value of all the wages and salaries earned in the economy are added up together with the value of profits, rents and interests earned. In the simplified model presented so far, where whatever is produced is sold, the value of what is sold must be equal to the value of what is produced. If what is sold generates the incomes in the economy, then it must be true that:

value of total product = value of total
expenditure = value of total income.

REAL-WORLD COMPLICATIONS

Although the circular flow model is very useful in explaining the important notion of circularity and fundamental identity of output, income and expenditure, the real world is slightly more complicated than the one described by it.

First of all, in the real world not all firms produce goods for consumption by households. Some firms produce for other firms:

■ **intermediate goods**, such as raw materials or partly finished goods, are then used by other firms as inputs for the production of final consumption goods;
■ **capital goods**, like tools and machinery, which are called **final goods**, because they are used by other firms producing **consumption goods** (although they are not 'used up' in the sense that they are not, like a raw material, an input of the finished product).

When firms buy from other firms, they engage in what economists call an act of **investment**. Consumption goods also belong to the category of final goods, as they are destined for individuals' consumption and are not an input to the production of anything else.

Secondly, in the real world there are governments. There are several ways in which the government affects the circular flow of income:

■ The government reduces some people's incomes by taxing part of it away (through what are called **direct taxes**, like income tax) and increases some people's incomes by paying them **benefits**, such as social security, child benefit, income supplement payments.
■ The government increases the market price of goods and services by imposing taxes on goods and services sold. These are called **indirect taxes**, like VAT or excise duties, because they are levied as

people buy goods, often as a percentage of the value of the good or service bought.
■ The government also adds to the economy's expenditure, buying part of the goods and services produced by private firms. This is called **government expenditure**, G. As well as a consumer, the government is also a producer of goods and services (through nationalized industries) and a major employer.

Thirdly, in the real world countries trade with one another. The products of the country may be sold abroad: these represent the country's **exports**. The country may be buying goods and services from other foreign countries: these represent the country's **imports**. So incomes earned in one country may be spent on purchasing the products of another country.

How can we accommodate these complexities and still maintain the identity of the three measures stated above? To be able to do so we need to refine somewhat and adjust our methods of national income accounting.

Revised product method: the value added approach

As we said before, the product method of measuring GDP consists of adding up the value of the products of each firm and government department in the economy, industry by industry, sector by sector. The most likely problem to be encountered when using this method in the real world, however, is one of double counting. Double counting originates from the fact that a particular firm's product may not be a **final product**, in the sense that it is intended for household consumption and is sold to households, but rather an intermediate product. Some firms produce for other firms what we have already defined as **intermediate products**, which then become inputs into some other firm's output. Some firms, for instance, are engaged in steel production. Steel is an intermediate product used in the production of many things, like cars and heavy machinery. The value of the final product, the price at which the final product is sold (think of the price of a car, for instance), incorporates the value of its inputs, which are costs to the producer of the final product. If in the calculation of the economy's GDP we were to add up the value of all intermediate products produced, as well as the value of the final products, we would be **double counting** the value of the intermediate products.

So if we were to add the total value of steel produced in the economy to the total value of vehicles and heavy machinery produced, we would be double counting, as the value of the steel used up in the production of cars and heavy machinery is already reflected in their final value, their price.

In order to avoid this, when using the product method to calculate GDP, economists use the **value-added** method. Value added means the value a firm creates as a result of the processing, which is equal to the difference between the price of the final good and the cost of its bought in inputs. A bakery buys flour and turns it into bread; the bread has more value, as a product, than the flour needed for its production. The price of the bread, as a final product, is higher than the price of the flour used to make it. The difference between the value of the flour bought by the baker to make the bread and the bread sold is the firm's value added. Adding the value added by all firms in the economy gives the real value created by the economy as a whole, its GDP, without any double counting.

The value-added method consists therefore in adding up the value added by each firm to the value of the product at each stage of production. Finally to clarify this point, let's look at another example. Consider a suit which can be bought in the shops for £160. For simplicity's sake, let's assume that there are five stages of production involved in making and distributing a suit. These stages are shown in Table 2.2.

As Table 2.2 shows, Firm A, the sheep farmer provides £40 worth of wool to Firm B, the wool processor. Firm A pays out the £40 it receives in wages, rents, interest and profit. Firm B processes the wool and sells it to Firm C, a suit manufacturer, for £65. Of the £65 Firm B receives from Firm C, £40 goes to Firm A to pay for the wool and the remaining £25 is used by B to pay wages, rents, interest and profits for the resources needed in processing the wool. The manufacturer then sells the suit to Firm D, the wholesaler, for £85. From this £85, £65 goes to Firm B to pay for the wool, the remaining £20 becomes the income of the people whose resources have been needed to actually produce the suit. And so on: the wholesaler sells the suit to Firm E, the retailer, for £110, which then, at last, sells it to you, the consumer and final user of the product, for £160.

At each stage, the difference between what a firm has paid for the intermediate product used and what it receives for its sale is paid out as wages, rent, interest and profits for the resources used specifically by that firm in the process of producing and distributing the suit.

✍ Activity 2.7

Look again at Table 2.2. How much should be included in the GDP accounts for the production of this suit?

✓ Answer 2.7

The answer is £160, because this figure includes only the value added to the final product by each firm at the various stages of production. If we were to sum all the intermediate sales figures and the final sale value of the product and add £460 to GDP, we would be grossly exaggerating the value of the economy's output. The real output, the real value generated, is a suit worth £160, not £460. To add £460 in the GDP accounts would be double counting, in other words, counting both the value of the final product as well as the value of the sale and resale of its various parts in the multistage productive process.

The value-added example we used in Table 2.2 is particularly useful as it also shows us the equivalence between the product method (value-added method) and the income method. Since the **source** of value added is the **work** performed on the intermediate product by factors of production, a firm's value added corresponds to what it pays its factors of production. If we add the values of the incomes generated at each

Table 2.2 The value-added method				
Firms	Stages of production	Sales value of materials or product £	Value added £	Income £
Firm A	Sheep farmer	40	40	40
Firm B	Wool processor	65	25	25
Firm C	Suit manufacturer	85	20	20
Firm D	Clothes wholesaler	110	25	25
Firm E	Clothes retailer	160	50	50
Total		£460	£160	£160

stage of the production and distribution of the suit, we see that the resulting figure is identical to the one obtained for the total value of the product, using the value-added method. The value-added approach is equivalent to the income approach.

The value-added method allows us to calculate value added by industry.

An analysis of 11 broad industrial sectors shows that in 1995 the financial intermediation sector provided the largest contribution to value added or GDP at current factor cost, at £156.16 billion out of £608.1 billion. Manufacturing contributed £131.7 billion. Wholesaling and retailing trades with £87.63 billion also featured strongly. More details on the composition of GDP for periods up to 1996 is provided in Table 2.3.

🐾 Activity 2.8

Study Tables 2. 3 and 2.4 and explain what they show.

✓ Answer 2.8

Tables 2.3 and 2.4 show the value of GDP calculated using the output (value-added) method. They show the economy's output by sector over a period of years. This allows us to calculate the change in the output of various sectors of the economy. We can see, for example, that from 1990 to 1995 the output of the agricultural sector has decreased by 3 per cent, the output of mining and quarrying sector has increased by 38.7 per cent. This increase, however, is due to the extraction of mineral oil and natural gas (+ 70 per cent), while the mining of coal and nuclear fuel has in fact fallen by 50 per cent over the same period. Manufacturing production has increased by a meagre 2.5 per cent in five years, electricity, water and gas supply have increased by 16.3 per cent. From 1990 to 1995, total production has increased by 6.7 per cent, construction on the other hand has fallen by 10 per cent, while the output of the service industries has increased by 8.9 per cent.

Revised expenditure method: final goods expenditure

The expenditure method of calculating GDP consists of adding up all the categories of expenditure in the economy. The main categories of expenditure are:

- **consumption expenditure, C:** expenditure done by households buying the goods and services they need.
- **investment expenditure, I:** expenditure done by firms buying capital equipment and production-related items needed to maintain or expand their

business capacity. It also includes the value of the firm's stocks and work in progress. Stocks are a firm's holdings of raw materials and finished products, while work in progress are partly finished products. The value of stocks and work in progress needs to be included in the GDP accounts because it represents some production which will not be included anywhere else.

- **government expenditure, G:** expenditure done by the government and government departments (building and maintaining roads, schools, hospitals, but also the pens and paperclips, the lightbulbs and wastepaper baskets used by government employees in government departments).
- **net export** or **export minus import, X–M:** this represents the value of expenditure by foreigners purchasing British-made goods, or **exports (X)**, net of the expenditure on foreign goods by British residents, or **imports (M)**.

When using the expenditure method, a series of accounting difficulties emerges which requires some careful consideration.

Double counting

When using the expenditure method, care must be taken again to avoid double counting. Here too we need to distinguish between expenditure on 'final goods', by which we mean purchases of goods and services for final use and not for resale or further processing or manufacturing, and expenditure on 'intermediate goods', goods and services purchased for further processing.

🐾 Activity 2.9

Explain as fully as you can why, in the calculation of GDP, expenditure on final goods should be included, while the expenditure on intermediate goods should be excluded.

✓ Answer 2.9

In the computation of GDP, expenditure on final goods is included, while the expenditure on intermediate goods is excluded because the price paid for final goods already includes the value of all the intermediate transactions involved in their production. The inclusion of intermediate transactions in the calculation of GDP by the expenditure method would involve double counting and produce an exaggerated estimate of GDP.

Non-productive transactions

The purpose of compiling national accounts, through whatever method, is to be able to measure the **annual**

Table 2.3   GDP at current factor cost by category of output, 1986–96 (£ million)

	1986	1987	1988	1989	1990	1991	1992	1993	1994	1995	1996
Agriculture, hunting, forestry and fishing Total (net)	6680	7120	7153	8324	8943	8964	9738	10 092	10 231	11 544	11 790
Mining and quarrying including oil and gas extraction Total (net)	13 533	14 128	11 488	11 260	11 318	11 203	11 674	12 261	13 591	14 986	18 068
Manufacturing Total (net)	81 252	88 623	98 784	107 166	111 315	106 896	109 811	115 719	123 941	131 701	137 006
Electricity, gas and water supply Total (net)	9407	9918	10 263	10 583	10 583	13 388	13 558	14 902	14 815	14 092	13 606
Construction Total (net)	19 916	23 158	28 121	32 911	34 568	31 506	29 797	29 030	30 902	32 241	33 746
Wholesale and retail trade, repairs, hotels and restaurants Total (net)	45 617	49 451	56 050	62 343	68 271	71 755	74 742	78 860	83 212	87 633	93 091
Transport, storage and communication Total (net)	27 247	30 037	34 238	37 356	40 523	42 191	43 782	46 327	49 042	50 837	54 056
Financial intermediation, real estate, renting and business activities Total (net)	71 330	79 499	89 939	102 549	114 506	118 813	129 179	138 481	152 350	156 164	164 282
Public administration, national defence and compulsory social security Total	22 604	24 368	26 000	28 028	31 676	34 257	36 774	37 925	37 273	37 123	38 244
Education, health and social work Total	31 645	34 731	39 674	46 633	51 744	58 371	62 998	66 601	72 082	77 199	81 876
Other services including sewage and refuse disposal Total	13 326	14 482	16 198	16 077	17 928	18 387	19 221	20 482	21 969	23 379	24 713

Source: Adapted from ONS, Blue Book, 1997

Table 2.4   GDP at constant 1990 factor cost by category of output, 1986–96

1990=100

	1986	1987	1988	1989	1990	1991	1992	1993	1994	1995	1996
Agriculture, hunting, forestry and fishing	95.5	93.5	92.1	96.7	100.0	103.8	107.7	99.1	98.5	97.1	95.4
Production											
Mining and quarrying											
Mining of coal and nuclear fuel	122.9	117.2	114.4	109.9	100.0	101.5	91.4	71.5	47.5	50.4	49.5
Extraction of mineral oil and natural gas	136.0	136.9	121.7	102.4	100.0	106.7	114.3	129.6	160.7	170.0	178.3
Other mining and quarrying	95.5	100.9	103.7	110.3	100.0	96.1	92.1	94.1	93.8	89.7	79.9
Total mining and quarrying	129.2	129.3	118.4	104.6	100.0	104.6	107.6	114.8	132.1	138.7	143.3
Manufacturing											
Food and beverages	93.9	96.3	98.2	98.5	100.0	99.6	101.1	101.9	104.2	106.2	107.3
Tobacco products	87.4	95.9	98.8	96.2	100.0	101.6	107.3	100.4	107.5	102.8	106.9
Textiles and leather products	101.1	104.9	104.6	101.4	100.0	89.8	90.2	90.2	91.9	90.1	89.2
Wood and wood products	83.3	91.6	102.9	103.2	100.0	89.0	88.0	90.0	97.0	91.2	89.4
Pulp, paper products, printing	78.1	85.5	93.3	97.7	100.0	95.4	96.5	99.7	102.2	102.5	101.1
Solid and nuclear fuels, oil refining	114.2	100.0	99.6	104.8	100.0	108.0	114.3	114.8	115.9	131.2	117.0
Chemicals and manmade fibres	84.0	91.0	95.7	100.2	100.0	102.8	106.0	108.4	114.0	116.9	119.3
Rubber and plastic products	75.5	84.5	92.9	97.3	100.0	94.3	96.5	100.8	111.1	114.5	113.3
Other non-metallic mineral products	91.0	96.3	105.5	106.6	100.0	90.5	86.5	90.6	93.9	92.3	88.7
Basic metals and metal products	84.1	89.0	97.8	100.8	100.0	90.8	86.3	85.4	87.5	89.0	88.9
Machinery and equipment	88.4	88.7	96.7	99.6	100.0	89.4	85.7	85.6	90.4	90.9	89.4
Electrical and optical equipment	78.6	82.8	92.3	99.1	100.0	96.0	97.6	103.0	115.5	121.6	124.8
Transport equipment	79.6	82.7	91.1	102.2	100.0	93.6	91.7	90.1	92.5	92.0	95.5
Other manufacturing	85.0	90.0	99.6	98.7	100.0	87.5	87.1	88.3	91.0	89.6	91.1
Total manufacturing (revised definition)	85.7	89.7	96.3	100.1	100.0	95.0	94.9	96.3	100.8	102.5	102.8
Electricity, gas and water supply	95.1	97.6	97.3	97.4	100.0	105.7	107.4	111.9	113.0	116.3	123.6
Total production	90.1	93.7	98.2	100.3	100.0	96.6	97.0	99.1	104.4	106.7	107.9
Construction	76.0	84.9	92.3	97.6	100.0	92.0	87.9	87.2	90.6	90.0	91.1
Service industries											
Wholesale and retail trade, repairs	85.3	91.9	98.1	101.7	100.0	96.6	96.5	101.8	106.2	108.5	111.9
Hotels and restaurants	85.9	91.3	96.1	99.1	100.0	93.5	89.3	91.7	94.0	93.9	97.5
Transport and storage	85.6	92.6	96.7	100.8	100.0	96.0	99.1	101.6	109.6	115.6	115.9
Post and telecommunication	81.1	85.2	90.9	96.3	100.0	99.4	98.9	104.5	113.2	122.9	135.9
Financial intermediation	75.9	84.8	91.4	95.6	100.0	100.2	94.9	97.7	99.2	104.0	109.7
Real estate, renting and business activities	84.3	88.4	96.3	97.9	100.0	97.3	95.1	98.0	108.2	116.0	125.4
Ownerships and dwellings	98.1	98.1	98.4	98.7	100.0	101.6	102.1	103.4	104.8	106.1	107.2
Public administration, national defence, social security	100.2	98.8	98.3	98.5	100.0	101.3	100.4	98.7	97.0	94.5	
Education	96.0	98.7	101.3	101.3	100.0	100.5	100.3	97.4	100.3	101.8	
Health and social work	90.6	94.1	97.0	98.7	100.0	102.1	103.6	106.5	107.3	110.8	
Other services	85.3	93.8	99.3	99.6	100.0	99.4	100.8	110.4	117.8	125.0	
Adjustment for financial services	78.1	87.3	93.0	96.9	100.0	98.5	94.3	95.9	100.3	108.2	
Total services	88.6	92.7	97.2	99.2	100.0	98.9	98.4	101.2	105.6	108.9	112.6
Gross domestic product	88.6	92.7	97.3	99.4	100.0	97.9	97.4	99.6	104.0	106.9	109.5

Source: Adapted from ONS, Blue Book, 1997

production of the economy, its GDP. When using the expenditure method to calculate GDP, it is therefore also important not to include **non-productive transactions**. There are two major types of non-productive transactions:

- **purely financial transactions**. They include public and private transfer payments and trade in securities. Transfer payments – the payments by the government such as social security, child benefits, pensions, income support supplement – do not require production of any good or service from the recipients, as in the case of a wage payment, but simply the transfer of funds from the government to individuals in the economy. Equally, stock market transactions involve the swapping of claims to real assets and do not involve current production.
- **secondhand sales**. Secondhand sales reflect no current production, if the goods have been produced in previous years, or they involve double counting, if the production of the particular good being resold has taken place during the current year and its value (the first sale) has already been included in the current GDP.

Bearing in mind the points just mentioned, when we use the expenditure approach to calculate GDP, we obtain E by adding up all the categories of expenditure:

$$E = C + I + G + (X–M)$$

where E is expenditure, C is consumption expenditure, I is investment expenditure, G is government expenditure, X is export expenditure and M is import expenditure.

✍ Activity 2.10

Look at Table 2.5 and Figure 2.3 below and explain what they show.

✓ Answer 2.10

Table 2.5 shows how GDP can be calculated using the expenditure method. All the category of expenditure are added together $(C+I+G+X–M)$ to obtain the value of GDP at market prices.

Figure 2.3 shows the composition of final expenditure in 1995. In that year, just under half of total expenditure was household consumption expenditure. The next highest proportion of total expenditure, 22 per cent, was represented by exports (expenditure by foreigners purchasing British made goods), 16.4 per cent was government expenditure, both national and local, the remainder 12.5 per cent was capital expenditure by various industry sectors.

Figure 2.3   Composition of final expenditure, UK 1995

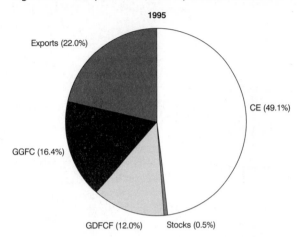

1995

Exports (22.0%)
CE (49.1%)
GGFC (16.4%)
GDFCF (12.0%)   Stocks (0.5%)

CE = Consumers'expenditure, CGFC = general government final consumption, GDFCF = gross domestic fixed capital formation

Source: ONS, *Blue Book*, 1997

Revised income method

When we calculate GDP using the **income method** we measure the value of the incomes generated in the economy by the production of goods and services, using the following formula:

$$Y = W + R + Int + P$$

where Y is output, W is wages, R is rent, Int is interest, P is profit. When using this method, the following points must be remembered:

- **gross income**: Part of people's gross income is taxed away. But gross income is on the other hand the true reflection of the productive contribution of factors to the economy's output. Gross incomes therefore need to be added, when using this method of calculation of GDP.
- **transfer payments**: for the same reason, because GDP only includes the incomes that originate from the production of goods and services, transfer payments must not be included, when using the income method to calculate GDP. Transfer payments include social services payments, pensions, child benefits, etc.
- **profits from stock appreciation**: gains in profits from stock appreciation must be deducted when using this method as they do not originate from an increase in real output.

✍ Activity 2.11

Study Table 2.6 and explain what it shows.

Table 2.5   GDP by category of expenditure at 1990 prices (£ million at 1990 prices), 1975–96

	1975	1976	1977	1978	1979	1980	1981	1982	1983	1984	1985
At 1990 market prices											
Consumers' expenditure	224 580	225 666	224 892	236 909	247 212	247 185	247 402	249 852	261 200	266 486	276 742
General government final consumption	95 748	96 997	95 357	97 443	99 277	101 005	101 260	102 146	104 296	105 177	105 097
Central government	59 156	60 458	59 752	60 437	61 243	63 207	63 725	64 260	65 604	66 146	66 241
Local authorities	36 552	36 549	35 645	36 988	38 008	37 791	37 535	37 886	38 692	39 030	38 856
Gross domestic fixed capital formation	71 170	72 921	71 618	73 777	75 840	71 764	64 888	68 404	71 845	78 270	81 575
Value of physical increase in stocks and work in progress	−4103	1955	4119	3458	4013	−4064	−3859	−1545	1637	1307	990
Total domestic expenditure	386 710	397 225	396 143	411 909	426 915	414 792	408 223	417 916	438 768	450 949	464 316
Export of goods and services	77 179	84 206	90 000	91 683	95 130	94 918	94 211	94 996	96 689	103 019	109 163
Goods	52 293	57 584	62 281	63 849	66 694	67 475	66 838	68 724	70 324	76 028	80 250
Services	25 891	27 590	28 580	28 617	29 134	27 917	27 877	26 441	26 463	26 925	28 883
Total final expenditure	461 473	479 851	485 669	502 752	521 191	509 274	502 120	512 372	534 409	553 528	573 567
Less imports of goods and services	−73 752	−77 308	−78 509	−81 840	−89 714	−86 469	−84 050	−88 146	−93 954	−103 282	−105 957
Goods	−56 643	−60 313	−61 598	−64 409	−70 641	−66 827	−64 170	−67 771	−73 826	−82 221	−84 825
Services	−17 420	−17 240	−17 129	−17 641	−19 301	−20 055	−20 402	−20 849	−20 388	−21 187	−21 189
Statistical discrepancy (expenditure adjustment)	4001	−7818	−3125	−2685	−514	−1420	−2394	−840	−1075	677	—
Gross domestic product	386 867	397 610	407 002	421 073	432 849	423 490	418 026	425 252	440 888	451 131	468 071
At 1990 factor cost											
Gross domestic product at market prices	386 867	397 610	407 002	421 073	432 849	423 490	418 026	425 252	440 888	451 131	468 071
Less factor cost adjustment	−48 158	−50 026	−50 181	−55 223	−56 943	−55 347	−54 054	−54 846	−56 631	−59 064	−60 310
Gross domestic product at factor cost	338 138	347 129	356 100	365 920	375 974	368 216	364 055	370 493	384 351	392 067	407 844

Source: ONS, *Blue Book*, 1997

Table 2.5 continued

	1986	1987	1988	1989	1990	1991	1992	1993	1994	1995	1996
At 1990 market prices											
Consumers' expenditure	295 622	311 234	334 591	345 406	347 527	340 037	339 652	348 164	357 845	364 046	376 648
General government final consumption	106 824	107 858	108 612	110 139	112 934	115 845	115 732	115 521	118 080	119 578	122 418
Central government	67 277	67 122	67 588	68 836	70 108	71 811	72 093	73 942	75 506	76 114	78 752
Local authorities	39 547	40 736	41 024	41 303	42 826	44 034	43 693	41 579	42 574	43 464	43 666
Gross domestic fixed capital formation	83 685	92 339	105 164	111 470	107 577	97 403	95 973	96 586	100 778	102 249	104 090
Value of physical increase in stocks and work in progress	1199	1652	5094	2704	–1800	–4631	–1699	312	2890	4119	2635
Total domestic expenditure	487 330	513 083	553 461	569 719	566 238	548 654	549 658	560 583	579 593	589 992	605 791
Export of goods and services	114 047	120 607	121 197	126 836	133 165	132 252	138 045	142 847	156 089	168 202	179 805
Goods	83 644	88 611	90 508	95 786	101 718	102 898	105 457	109 240	120 481	129 942	138 681
Services	30 403	31 996	30 689	31 050	31 447	29 345	32 588	33 607	35 608	38 260	41 124
Total final expenditure	601 377	633 690	647 658	696 555	699 403	680 906	687 703	703 403	735 682	758 194	785 596
Less imports of goods and services	–113 255	–122 075	–137 443	–147 615	–148 285	–140 598	–150 255	–154 808	–163 381	–107 282	–184 671
Goods	–91 072	–98 128	–111 360	–120 441	–120 527	–114 101	–121 629	–126 286	–131 841	–137 792	–149 550
Services	–22 183	–23 947	–26 083	–27 174	–27 758	–26 497	–28 626	–28 522	–31 540	–32 490	–35 121
Statistical discrepancy (expenditure adjustment)	—	—	—	—	—	—	—	—	—	—	795
Gross domestic product	488 122	511 615	537 215	548 940	551 118	540 308	537 448	548 622	572 301	587 912	601 720
At 1990 factor cost											
Gross domestic product at market prices	488 122	511 615	537 215	548 940	551 118	540 308	537 448	548 622	572 301	587 912	601 720
Less factor cost adjustment	–63 908	–67 798	–71 469	–72 712	–72 232	–71 395	–70 992	–71 822	–74 070	–75 977	–77 172
Gross domestic product at factor cost	424 214	443 817	465 746	476 228	478 886	468 913	466 456	476 800	498 231	511 935	524 548

Source: ONS, Blue Book, 1997

Table 2.6   GDP at current factor cost by type of income, 1986–96 (£ million)

	1986	1987	1988	1989	1990	1991	1992	1993	1994	1995	1996
Income from employment	212 380	230 208	256 537	284 878	315 471	331 967	342 608	351 561	365 035	381 208	400 354
Income from self-employment	35 104	39 361	45 829	51 440	56 727	54 735	55 862	60 110	65 296	68 915	69 898
Gross trading profits of companies	47 339	59 453	64 377	67 880	66 103	60 191	63 168	75 908	88 398	92 530	101 409
Gross trading surplus of public corporations	8213	6993	7554	5951	3426	1410	1669	2438	2698	4230	3959
Gross trading surplus of general government enterprises	155	–75	–32	199	12	–36	206	193	495	623	681
Rent	23 848	26 155	29 904	34 467	38 888	45 632	52 160	56 092	58 466	61 230	63 850
Imputed charge for consumption of non-trading capital	3068	3307	3634	4005	4391	4363	4207	3918	3890	4115	4333
Less stock appreciation	–1835	–4728	–6375	–7061	–6131	–2009	–1778	–2350	–4143	–4761	–973
Statistical discrepancy (income adjustment)	—	—	—	—	—	—	—	—	—	—	–595
Gross domestic product	328 272	360 675	401 428	441 759	478 886	496 253	518 132	547 870	580 135	608 090	642 916

Source: ONS, *Blue Book*, 1997

✓ Answer 2.11

Table 2.6 shows how to calculate GDP using the income method, which consist in adding up the incomes earned in the economy by type of income: income from employment, self-employment, profits, rent and interest.

Summary

There are three methods of calculating GDP: the product method, the expenditure method and the income method. The circular flow model of output, income and expenditure helps us to understand why the final figure for GDP is the same, in theory at least, irrespective of which method we use. In practice, because of the complexity of the calculations involved, there are often substantial statistical discrepancies between the figures obtained using these three different methods.

✍ Activity 2.12

To make sure that you understand the computational equivalence of the three methods, work through the following numerical example. Calculate the total value of the economic activity generated by two hypothetical businesses described below, using the output method, the income method and the expenditure method. If your calculations are correct, you should obtain the same numerical answer.

Imagine a simple economy with only two businesses: a wine producer called Barbera Ltd and a mulled wine producer, called Marchand & Son Ltd. Barbera Ltd owns and operates its own vineyard, selling some of the wine it produces directly to the people of the local village. It sells the rest of its wine to Marchand & Son Ltd, which uses it to produce its own brand of highly spiced mulled wine. In this simple economy there is only a corporate tax on profit: no income tax to be paid on wages, nor indirect tax (like VAT) on purchases. The two companies' financial position and total transactions at the end of the year are shown in the table below:

Barbera Ltd	£ (000)	
Wages	−15	
Taxes	−5	
Revenue from wine sales	35	
directly to public		10
to Marchand & Son		25
After-tax profit	15	

Marchand & Son Ltd	£(000)
Wages	−10
Taxes	−2
Wine purchase from Barbera Ltd	−25
Sales revenue	40
After-tax profit	3

Barbera Ltd pays £15,000 a year in wages to workers to pick the grapes and sells £35,000 worth of wine, part directly to the public, £10,000, and part to Marchand & Son, £25,000. Barbera's profit before tax is £35,000 − £15,000 = £20,000.

Marchand & Son Ltd buys £25,000 of wine from Barbera Ltd, pays £10,000 in wages to employees; it sells £40,000 worth of mulled wine, so that its profit before tax is £40,000 − £25,000 − £10,000 = £5,000.

✓ Answer 2.12

Following the **output method**, economic activity is calculated by adding the market value of goods and services produced, excluding goods and services used up in intermediate stages of production. In this case Barbera Ltd produces an output worth £35,000, while Marchand & Son produces an output worth £40,000. However, if we were simply to add the two, we would be double counting the £25,000 worth of wine that Marchand & Son buys from Barbera Ltd. To avoid double counting we add up the value added by Marchand & Son which is £15,000 (£40,000 − £25,000), rather than the total value of the output, which is £40,000. Barbera Ltd instead produces its own wine and does not buy in any other input, so its value added is equal to the value of its product, which is also the value of its revenue, £35,000. So, the GDP of our simple economy, calculated using the output method, is equal to £35,000 + £15,000 = **£50,000**.

If we follow the **income method** of calculating the value of economic activity, we add together the gross incomes (before tax is paid) received by factors of production in the economy, which includes wages and salaries, profits, interests and rents. In our example, the incomes to be added up are the wages paid by the two businesses to their workers (£15,000 + £10,000) and the before-tax profits of the two producers (£20,000 + £5,000). The value of GDP, calculated using the income method, is equal to £25,000 + £25,000 = **£50,000**.

Following the **expenditure method**, the value of economic activity is calculated by adding up the amount of **final expenditure** spent by the final users of the products of the economy. In our example the final users are those buying wine directly from Barbera Ltd and those buying mulled wine from Marchand & Son. It is true that

Marchand & Son buy wine fron Barbera Ltd, but that wine is not destined for their personal consumption. Rather it is the main ingredient of the mulled wine of their production, so it represents an intermediate expenditure. Hence the expenditure on final goods in our example is: £10,000 of wine sold directly to the public by Barbera Ltd and £40,000 of mulled wine sold to the public by Marchand & Son. The total value of GDP calculated using the expenditure method is therefore equal to £10,000 + £40,000 = **£50,000**. All three methods give us the same numerical result.

OTHER MEASURES

Gross domestic product (GDP) and gross national product (GNP)

There are several important alternative measures of income and output that can be derived from gross domestic product (GDP): gross national product (GNP) is one of them. To understand what this measure really means, we must understand the difference between **domestic** product and **national** product. GDP measures the value of all the goods and services produced in Britain in a year, regardless of who owns the factors of production, provided that production has taken place in Britain.

This is precisely what the word **domestic** means. However, not all the goods and services produced in Britain and British made are also British owned. Some firms operating in Britain and factories producing in Britain are owned by foreigners, who have invested their capital. The Japanese car manufacturer, Nissan, has set up production plants in Britain. The cars are produced in Britain and the value of this car production, if we are using the product method, is included in the calculation of GDP. But would we get the same figure for GDP if we used the income method? Are all the incomes generated by these car production plants British incomes? The answer is no. Part of the income generated, namely some of the profits, will accrue to the Japanese shareholders. Similarly, foreign owners of UK properties, shareholders in UK companies, or foreign workers working in Britain but supporting relatives back home will all want to send home some of their incomes. In other words, some of the incomes generated and earned in Britain from property rents, company dividends or wages will not remain in Britain, and will not accrue to British households.

At the same time, however, some British households will be earning income from properties and shares they have abroad. So there is a two-way flow of what the economists call property income, since it originates mostly from interest, dividends, profits and rents, rather than wages, between countries in the world. Because of this, the product and expenditure measure of GDP is no longer equal to the factor incomes earned by UK citizens. To take account of this fact, economists use a different measure, the gross national product (GNP) which is gross domestic product (GDP) adjusted for net property income from abroad. Net property income from abroad is the difference between the inflow into Britain of property income from abroad and the outflow of property income from Britain. Net property income will show as a positive value when the inflow of property income into Britain exceeds the outflow of property income and vice versa.

So, while we had defined GDP as a measure of the output produced by the domestic economy, regardless of who owns the factors of production, we now define:

GNP = GDP + net property income from abroad.

GNP measures total income earned by British citizens, regardless of the country in which their factor services were supplied.

✍ Activity 2.13

If Britain has an inflow of property income of £2 billion and an outflow of £1 billion of property income going to foreigners, which measure will be greater, GDP or GNP?

✓ Answer 2.13

UK GNP, which measures income earned by British citizens, will exceed UK GDP, which measures the value of the goods produced in the UK, by £1 billion.

Net domestic product (NDP) and net national product (NNP)

Net domestic product (NDP) and **net national product** (NNP) are two further useful measures of the level of economic activity. The need for such measures originates from another real-life complication, and more precisely from the fact that capital stock depreciates because of wear and tear and technical obsolescence. Any measure of the value of the output produced by an economy must, therefore, take into account this fact: capital **depreciation**.

Depreciation or **capital consumption** measures the rate at which the value of the existing capital stock of the economy declines per period (say a year) because of wear and tear or obsolescence. Depreciation is a flow concept, measuring the rate of wearing out of the existing capital stock. It is the opposite of investment, which is also a flow concept and represents the addition of capital equipment to the stock of capital.

The GDP and GNP introduced earlier, as measures of the domestic and national product, ignore depreciation completely. In fact, we should not ignore capital depreciation when trying to assess the net output of the economy, since it needs to be taken into account. The fact that some of the capital stocks wear out means that some of the output of investment goods (capital equipment, etc.) or, some of the investment expenditure does not represent a net addition to the capital stock of the country, but merely a replacement for existing capital stock which has reached the end of its economic life and needs replacing. The concept of capital depreciation leads to the distinction between gross investment and net investment.

Gross investment is the amount spent on capital goods. By simply looking at the figure for gross investment, we cannot really say whether there has been a net addition to the capital stock of the country. Some of the new capital goods produced will simply replace fully depreciated capital and are needed just to maintain the capital stock constant. **Net investment** is therefore the difference between gross investment and capital depreciation and measures the net addition to capital stock.

So NDP takes into account net investment rather than gross investment and is equal to GDP minus capital depreciation, while NNP for the same reasons is calculated as GNP minus capital depreciation.

✍ Activity 2.14

Explain the difference between gross investment and net investment. Give reasons why net investment is used, rather than gross investment, in calculating net national product (NNP).

✓ Answer 2.14

We have defined investment as an increase in the economy's productive capacity, an addition to the economy's stock of capital, for example, machines and factories, etc. During the course of a year, the period over which GDP is calculated, the economy will produce new machines, etc. and will be adding to the stock of capital goods. This is gross investment, which we have already defined as the total amount of newly produced goods. However, during that year a certain amount of capital goods already in use will become obsolete. A certain part of gross investment will therefore be used to replace this depreciated capital. That part of gross investment that replaces old, worn out

capital goods is defined as depreciation and is called a capital consumption allowance in the national income accounts. It does not add to the capital stock, but rather replaces worn out capital goods. For example, if gross investment is £10 billion a year and depreciation is £5 billion, the real addition to capital is only £5 billion and not the reported £10 billion. Net investment (gross investment minus depreciation) is therefore used in calculating net national product.

Market prices or factor cost

Another important distinction that takes care of a further real-life complication is that between GDP at market prices and GDP at factor cost. The need for this distinction arises from the fact that indirect taxes imposed by the government on goods and services increase their prices and therefore affect the value of GDP when calculated at market prices. That part of the price paid by the purchaser which represents the tax, however, goes to the government and not to the factors of production which have produced the good, as a reward for their services. So GDP at **factor cost** will measure the value of the output in terms of what it really cost to produce (resources used up or incomes earned, which is the same); it represents the payments made to factors of production. Adjustments also have to be made for government subsidies to firms that top up the market prices which producers receive from purchasers. The subsidies are used by firms to pay for factors of production and the price plus subsidy represents the true income to factors of production. We can therefore choose to value domestic or national output either at market prices not adjusted for indirect taxes on goods and services and subsidies, or at the prices received by the producers after indirect taxes and subsidies have been taken into account:

GDP at factor cost = GDP at market prices
– indirect taxes + subsidies.

This distinction also applies to GNP. So we can equally distinguish between GNP at market prices and GNP at factor cost.

✍ Activity 2.15

What do GDP at market prices and GDP at factor cost measure respectively?

✓ Answer 2.15

GDP at market prices measures domestic output inclusive of indirect taxes on goods and services and not adjusted for government subsidies to firms. GDP at factor cost measures domestic output exclusive of indirect taxes on goods and services and inclusive of subsidies. Thus GDP at market prices exceeds GDP at factor cost by the amount of revenue raised in indirect taxes net of any subsidies on goods and services.

✍ Activity 2.16

Study Table 2.7 and explain what it shows.

✓ Answer 2.16

Table 2.7 shows how GNP and NNP at factor cost are calculated.

Nominal and real GDP

Another complication, when using GDP figures, is caused by inflation. Inflation, as mentioned before, is a situation of persistent and generalized price rises. One of the main purposes of the national income accounts is to have an idea of the state of health of the economy, how much the economy is really growing, with respect to the previous year or years, for example, or with respect to other economies.

The economic output is measured at current prices: x amount of cars at whatever market price they sell. If prices rise rapidly from year to year, this year's output might appear much greater than last year's simply because **prices** have risen and not because more has been produced. In which case, GDP at current prices becomes useless as an indicator of the real performance of the economy.

Simplifying, the output of the economy, Y, is the volume of goods produced (Q) multiplied by their price (P).

$$Y = P.Q.$$

If the value of Y in 1997 (Q_2) is greater than in 1996 (Q_1), this could be for two reasons: first, that Q has grown ($Q_2 > Q_1$), which would mean that the economy has actually produced more goods and services: secondly, that P has increased ($P_2 > P_1$), i.e. the economy has experienced inflation:

$$Y_{1996} = P_1 \times Q_1$$
$$Y_{1997} = P_2 \times Q_2$$

To have an idea of the performance of the British economy in 1997, we would want to compare its output in 1997 with its output in 1996. But this comparison, undertaken in order to know whether there has been any real growth of the economy in a year, will be meaningless if the output in 1997 appears to be greater than in 1996 because prices have risen and not output. If in 1997 the economy has produced the same physical quantity of output (Q) but all prices are 10 per cent higher than in 1996, nominal GDP (GDP measured at current prices) will be 10 per cent higher than in 1996. This 10 per cent increase in the UK GDP in 1997 does not represent real growth, i.e. a greater quantity of goods and services produced; it merely reflects the increase in their prices.

It can be therefore very misleading to judge the economy's performance by looking at nominal GDP. For this reason, we need to find a way of measuring GDP using constant prices. If we did that, then we would know that any change in the value of GDP would reflect a change in the volume of goods produced. This is precisely what GDP at constant prices or real GDP does. It adjusts for inflation by measuring GDP in different years using the same set of prices prevailing at some particular year, known as the **base year**.

When we use this measure, known as real GDP or GDP at constant prices, i.e. GDP calculated at base year prices, the only way GDP can increase from one year to the other is if the volume of goods produced has increased. To understand how this is achieved it is useful to look at the UK GDP figures provided by Table 2.8.

✍ Activity 2.17

State clearly what is measured by nominal GDP and real GDP respectively.

✓ Answer 2.17

Nominal GDP measures the value of the output in **current** prices, i.e. in the prices that prevailed in that particular year. **Real GDP** measures the value of output in constant (base year) prices, i.e. using the set of prices that prevailed in one specific year or **base year**, chosen as a fixed term of reference. When looking at changes in the value of nominal GDP from one year to the other, we do not know whether those changes reflect changes in the volume of goods or merely changes in prices. Changes in the value of real GDP, on the other hand, measure changes in the volume of output since prices are constant at base year.

The concept of real GDP seems simple enough. But how do we do this in practice? We do this by using so-called **GDP deflators**. To convert nominal GDP to real GDP, we need to use an index that reflects what is happening to the price of all goods. This index is called the GDP deflator. How is the GDP deflator calculated? The GDP deflator is the ratio of nominal GDP to real GDP, expressed as an index. In other words, it is equal to nominal GDP divided by real GDP, multiplied by 100:

$$\text{GDP deflator} = \frac{\text{nominal GDP}}{\text{real GDP}} \times 100.$$

Table 2.7 UK GDP, GNP and NNP at factor cost (£ million), 1975–96

	1975	1976	1977	1978	1979	1980	1981	1982	1983	1984	1985
Gross domestic product	105 852	125 247	145 983	168 526	198 221	231 772	254 927	279 041	304 456	325 852	357 344
Net property income from abroad	891	1560	265	806	1205	−182	1251	1460	2830	4344	2296
Gross national product	106 743	126 807	146 248	169 332	199 426	231 590	256 178	280 501	307 286	330 196	359 640
Factor cost adjustment											
Taxes on expenditure	14 036	16 284	19 834	22 756	29 670	36 474	42 465	46 467	49 500	52 736	56 667
Subsidies	3771	3572	3386	3775	4643	5719	6369	5811	6269	7537	7225
Factor cost adjustment (taxes less subsidies)	10 265	12 712	16 448	18 981	25 027	30 755	36 096	40 656	43 231	45 199	49 442
Gross domestic product	95 587	112 535	129 535	149 545	173 194	201 017	218 831	238 385	261 225	280 653	307 902
Net property income from abroad	891	1560	265	806	1205	−182	1251	1460	2830	4344	2296
Gross national product	96 478	114 095	129 800	150 351	174 399	200 835	220 082	239 845	264 055	284 997	310 198
less capital consumption	−11 621	−13 976	−16 501	−19 378	−22 827	−27 952	−31 641	−33 653	−36 150	−38 758	−41 883
Net national product a factor cost ('national income')	84 857	100 312	113 595	131 285	151 958	172 883	188 382	206 209	228 066	246 239	268 315

	1986	1987	1988	1989	1990	1991	1992	1993	1994	1995	1996
At current market prices											
Consumers' expenditure	241 554	265 290	299 449	327 363	347 527	365 469	383 490	406 569	427 394	446 169	473 509
General government final consumption	80 911	87 045	93 641	101 796	112 934	124 105	131 875	137 756	144 068	149 208	155 732
Central government	50 331	53 736	57 522	63 294	70 108	76 985	82 259	89 074	93 190	96 027	101 140
Local authorities	30 580	33 309	36 119	38 502	42 826	47 120	49 616	48 682	50 878	53 181	54 592
Gross domestic fixed capital formation	65 032	75 158	91 530	105 443	107 577	97 747	93 642	94 293	100 252	108 736	114 623
Value of physical increase in stocks and work in progress	682	1228	4333	2677	−1800	−4927	−1937	329	3708	4748	2917
Total domestic expenditure	388 179	428 721	488 953	537 279	566 238	582 394	607 070	638 947	675 422	708 861	746 781
Exports of goods and services	97 885	106 397	107 273	121 486	133 165	134 289	142 497	160 464	176 602	199 675	217 147
Goods	72 627	79 153	80 346	92 154	101 718	103 413	107 343	121 398	134 664	153 077	166 340
Services	25 258	27 244	26 927	29 332	31 447	30 876	35 154	39 066	41 938	46 598	50 807
Total final expenditure	486 064	535 118	596 226	658 765	699 403	716 683	749 567	799 411	852 024	908 536	963 928
Less imports of goods and services	−101 221	−111 737	−124 796	−142 808	−148 285	−141 009	−150 651	−168 408	−182 955	−204 380	−222 603
Goods	−82 186	−90 735	−101 826	−116 837	−120 527	−113 697	−120 447	−134 858	−145 793	−164 659	−178 938
Services	−19 035	−21 002	−22 970	−25 971	−27 758	−27 312	−30 204	−33 550	−37 162	−39 721	−43 665
Statistical discrepancy (expenditure adjustment)											975
Gross domestic product	384 843	423 381	471 430	515 957	551 118	575 674	598 916	631 003	669 069	704 156	742 300
Net property income from abroad	4629	3927	4566	3502	1269	150	3124	2595	9667	7920	9652
Gross national product	389 472	427 308	475 996	519 459	552 387	575 824	602 040	633 598	678 736	712 076	751 952
Factor cost adjustment											
Taxes on expenditure	62 872	68 971	76 039	79 980	78 298	85 416	87 521	90 336	96 418	103 697	108 484
Subsidies	6301	6265	6037	5782	6066	5995	6737	7203	7484	7631	9100
Factor cost adjustment (taxes less subsidies)	56 571	62 706	70 002	74 198	72 232	79 421	80 784	83 133	88 934	96 066	99 384
Gross domestic product	328 272	360 675	401 428	441 759	478 886	496 253	518 132	547 870	580 135	608 090	642 916
Net property income from abroad	4269	3927	4566	3502	1269	150	3124	2595	9667	7920	9652
Gross national product	332 901	364 602	405 994	445 261	480 155	496 403	521 256	550 465	589 802	616 010	652 568
less capital consumption	−45 085	−48 164	−52 636	−56 716	−61 261	−63 356	−62 485	−65 353	−68 298	−73 014	−77 372
Net national product at factor cost ('national income')	287 816	316 438	353 358	388 545	418 894	433 047	458 771	485 112	521 504	542 996	575 196

Source: ONS, *Blue Book*, 1997

The Central Statistical Office which collects the economy's statistics publishes every year the values of nominal GDP, real GDP and GDP deflators.

✍ Activity 2.18

At the top of the national account statistics tables, you see in some cases the heading 'Gross national product at current prices' or the heading 'Gross national product at 1990 prices'. How do these statistics differ?

✓ Answer 2.18

The value of GDP at current prices has been measured using prices prevailing each year. GDP at 1990 prices means that the prices prevailing in 1990 have been used to calculate the value of GDP in subsequent years. In the first case, we are looking at nominal GDP, in the other case at real GDP.

Let's look at Table 2.8 which shows figures published in 1998 by the Office for National Statistics for the UK economy.

✍ Activity 2.19

Study Table 2.8 very carefully and calculate the rate of change of nominal GDP and real GDP from 1996 to 1997. How do you interpret your results?

✓ Answer 2.19

Nominal rate of growth: $\dfrac{\text{Change in nominal GDP}}{\text{Nominal GDP in 1996}} \times 100$

Nominal rate of growth: $\dfrac{46}{742} \times 100 = 6.2\%$

Real rate of growth: $\dfrac{21}{602} \times 100 = 3.5\%$.

Nominal GDP would suggest a yearly rate of growth of output in Britain of 6.2 per cent. The real growth over the same period was only 3.5 per cent (still respectable). The use of nominal GDP figures grossly exaggerates the growth rate of the economy.

GDP deflators, arrived at by the method we have just described, can be used to calculate the rate of inflation. The most common measure of inflation is the rate of change of the retail price index (RPI). However, the RPI only takes into account changes in the prices of consumer goods and services and leaves out altogether the prices of investment goods. A more comprehensive measure of inflation is therefore provided by changes of the GDP deflators, which are calculated using the prices of all goods and services of the economy, including production goods. Calculating the percentage change in the GDP deflator between any two years will give the rate of inflation between those two years.

✍ Activity 2.20

Using the GDP deflators provided in Table 2.8, calculate the annual rate of inflation in 1997. What was the rate of inflation in 1992?

✓ Answer 2.20

The rate of inflation in 1997 was 2.7 per cent, calculated as follows:

$$\frac{1997\ GDP\ deflator - 1996\ GDP\ deflator}{1996\ GDP\ deflator} \times 100$$

$$\frac{3.3}{123.3} \times 100 = 2.7\%.$$

The rate of inflation is 1992 was: $\dfrac{4.6}{106.4} \times 100 = 4.3\%$

Table 2.8 Nominal GDP, real GDP and the GDP deflator, 1990–97

Year	Nominal GDP (billions of pounds) at market prices	Real GDP (billions of pounds) at market prices	GDP deflator 1990 = 100
1990	551	551	100.0
1991	575	540	106.4
1992	597	537	111.0
1993	630	549	114.7
1994	669	572	117.0
1995	704	588	119.8
1996	742	602	123.3
1997	788	623	126.6

Source: ONS, *Economic Trends*, 1998

GDP deflators, when known, can also be used to deflate nominal GDP figures into real figures. Given that GDP deflators are obtained by the following formula:

$$\text{GDP deflator} = \frac{\text{GDP at current prices (NOMINAL GDP)}}{\text{GDP at base year prices (REAL GDP)}} \times 100$$

If you know the GDP deflator for a given year and the GDP at current prices, you can calculate real GDP as follows:

$$\text{Real GDP} = \frac{\text{GDP at current prices (NOMINAL GDP)}}{\text{GDP deflator}} \times 100.$$

Activity 2.21

Using the above formula and the data in Table 2.9, calculate real GDP for 1996 and 1997.

✓ Answer 2.21

You should have obtained the same real GDP figures as those of Table 2.8.

Disposable income and per capita income

The last two concepts that we need to introduce here are **disposable income** and **per capita income**.

Disposable income

Disposable income measures people's personal income after direct taxes (income taxes) paid to the government have been deducted and benefits received from the government added. It is an important measure which shows how much households have available for spending and saving.

$$Y_D = Y + B - T_d$$

where Y_D is disposable income, Y is income, B is benefits and T_d is direct taxes. This measure is useful for analysing consumer behaviour, as it is income 'disposable' for consumption that affects spending decisions.

Table 2.9 Real GDP, UK, 1992–7

Year	Nominal GDP	GDP deflator
1992	597	111.0
1993	630	114.7
1994	669	117.0
1995	704	119.8
1996	742	123.3
1997	788	126.6

Source: ONS, Economic Trends, 1998

Per capita income

Per capita income measures the quantity of goods and services available on average for each individual. GNP figures relate to the product or income of the whole economy. They are adequate measures for comparing the size of one economy with another, but they are not adequate for comparing living standards.

If we want to know how well off the average British person is in comparison with the average Italian, we need to know the size of the respective populations and not just the size of the GNP of the two countries. Two cakes might be the same size, but how many people have been invited to the party will make all the difference when it comes to deciding how big each slice should be.

If we are interested in comparing living standards between two countries or over time in the same country, we must look at national income per head of population. This is what the Latin expression per capita means. To calculate per capita income is fairly straight forward: we divide national income by the size of the population. In this way, we can find out how much, on average, each person gets of the total output produced.

To be able to compare two countries' per capita income, we must use the same unit of currency. We must therefore convert the per capita figure expressed in the domestic currency of one country into a figure expressed in the currency of the other country. Alternatively, we can use a common currency, usually dollars, in which to convert the values to the domestic currencies. We do the conversions by using market rates of exchange between currencies. However, we could argue that the use of the purchasing power of currencies (PPC) rate of exchange between two countries' currencies, rather than the official exchange rates, would be more appropriate. We look at this again later.

Activity 2.22

Using the figures provided in Table 2.10, calculate per capita income for the UK, Italy, Ireland, Portugal, Switzerland and Turkey. What can you say about the standard of living in these countries?

✓ Answer 2.22

The highest per capita income is enjoyed by people living in Switzerland, followed by Italy, the UK, Ireland and Turkey, as shown in Table 2.11.

Activity 2.23

Study Figure 2.4 and explain what it shows.

Table 2.10   Population and per capita income, selected countries, 1994

Reference period 1994	UK	Ireland	Italy	Portugal	Switzerland	Turkey
Population (000)	58375	3571	57190	9900	6994	60580
GDP US$ bn (using current prices and current exchange rates)	1015.7	51.9	1025.4	87.1	259.7	125.8

Source: OECD, *Economic Outlook*, 1995

Table 2.11   Population and per capita income, selected countries, 1994

Reference period 1994	UK	Ireland	Italy	Portugal	Switzerland	Turkey
Population (000)	58375	3571	57190	9900	6994	60580
GDP US$ bn (using current prices and current exchange rates)	1015.7	51.9	1025.4	87.1	259.7	125.8
Per capita income US$ (000)	17399	14533	17929	8797	37131	2076

Source: OECD, *Economic Outlook*, 1995

✔ Answer 2.23

Figure 2.4 traces the gradual impoverishment of the UK, measured by the decline of UK income per head, from 1870 to 1995, as a percentage of income per head in the USA, Germany, France and Italy respectively. While in 1870 the UK income per head was twice as high as in Germany, France and Italy and 20 per cent higher than in the USA, by 1995 it was merely 71 per cent of the income per head of the USA and 94 per cent of the income per head of Germany, France and Italy. In other words, by 1995 the average British person had become worse off than the average American or German.

Standard of living

We began this chapter talking about the importance of the national income and expenditure accounts as an indication of the economy's performance and general state of health. We conclude, however, by discussing the limitations of the national account figures, particularly as a measure of national well-being.

✍ Activity 2.24

Think of possible reasons why even real, per capita GNP figures might be a poor indicator of a country's well-being and standard of living.

✔ Answer 2.24

The inadequacy of national income figures for international or intertemporal comparison of standards of living remains even when real, per capita GNP figures are used. The main reasons for this are as follows:

1 GNP measures only marketed production; it does not measure all production. For this reason, GNP understates the economy's real output. Non-marketed production concerns:

■ *Non-marketed items:* do-it-yourself activities, produce from the backyard vegetable garden, intangibles such as leisure time, quality of relationships, all of which elude GNP computations. If you decorate your own house rather than paying an interior decorator to do it, if you clean your house rather than paying a cleaner, if you grow your own vegetables rather than buying them from the greengrocer, you are actually producing goods and services worth just as much as the ones you would have to pay for. However, for the GNP accounts it is as if you had produced nothing, as nothing really becomes the object of a recorded

Figure 2.4   UK income per head, 1870–1995

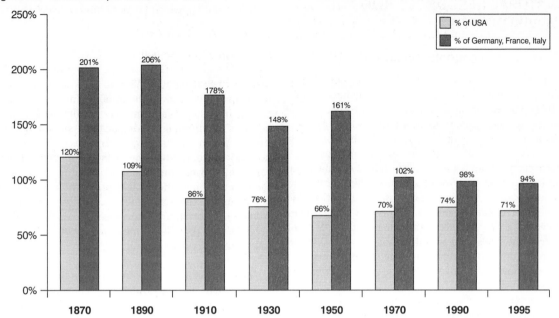

Source: Lloyds Bank Economic Bulletin, July 1997

market transaction. The money you pay the interior decorator, the cleaner or the greengrocer would add to GNP; the money you 'do not pay yourself' does not.

■ *Underground economy or black economy:* there are goods and services which are transacted, i.e. exchanged and paid for, but the transaction goes unrecorded, often because it is criminal or illegal, like drug smuggling or prostitution: the greater the size of the underground economy, the greater the understatement of the real output of the economy by GNP figures.

2   GNP is an indicator of a country's production, and production is in itself a poor indicator of the well-being of society:

■ The production may be of items or activities that may not really add to human well-being. If the rate of criminality is higher in more affluent economies, forcing people to take expensive protective measures like burglar alarms and so on, the money spent on them adds to GNP. But are the people living in such economies really better off, despite their larger GNP? In particular are they better off than people living in economies which record smaller GNPs, but where life is simpler, less threatening and not requiring sophisticated gadgetry? Equally, the GNP figure might be

very high because of an unusually high amount of armaments produced in that economy or because of expensive space exploration projects. However, people's well-being will not necessarily be greater than that enjoyed by others living in more peace-orientated societies. The composition of output, what kind of goods are available to people, is what matters for the well-being of the people, not so much the output value. Production does not equal consumption.

■ GNP figures ignore negative production or consumption externalities. Negative externalities are hidden costs like air or water pollution, or street rubbish in cities, which often go hand in hand with even greater production. These costs are not taken into account by the individual producer or consumer actually causing them, but are nonetheless a social cost that detract from people's well-being.

■ GNP figures do not take into account the distribution of income. An unequal distribution may reduce well-being in society. The suffering endured by a majority of poor people is not compensated by the increased satisfaction of few.

■ GNP figures also ignore the human costs of production. The quality of the working environment may be poor or hazardous and working hours long, despite a high GNP.

NATURAL RESOURCES AND THE ENVIRONMENT

Measures of economic welfare (MEW)

Because of the limitations of GNP as a measure of well-being, economists William Nordhaus and James Tobin (1972), introduced an alternative measure of economic well-being, the measure of economic welfare (MEW), which takes into account all the points raised before: it adds to GNP an estimated value for non-marketed and black economy activities; it also adds a certain value for leisure time and social amenities like parks and communication systems, and private amenities like housing or clothing qualities. It consequently reduces the value of GNP by subtracting the negative effects of growth, the 'bads' like pollution, noise and stress, and the regrettables or disadvantages like time spent sitting in traffic jams, protective expenditures, defence expenditure, etc.

However, MEW has not succeeded in replacing GDP as a standard measure. The main problem with using MEW is the difficulty in finding suitable criteria to calculate the values of the 'goods' and 'bads' that need to be added to or subtracted from GDP figures. The following examples, related to natural resource depletion and pollution control, illustrate this point.

✍ Activity 2.25

When BP pumps oil from an underground field, the value of the oil produced is counted as part of the country's GDP. There is no offsetting deduction to account for the fact that non-renewable resources are being depleted. Can you suggest a way of overcoming this computational problem?

✔ Answer 2.25

In theory, pumping oil out of the oilfield could be treated as negative inventory investment, because it reduces the stock of oil. If this negative inventory investment were to be included in the national income accounts it would substantially reduce the value of the GDP.

✍ Activity 2.26

Suppose that the turnover (value of output) of a firm producing chemicals is £100 million a year. This firm's production process pollutes the local river by dumping its waste in it. If the firm were to employ 10 per cent of it labour for to dispose of its waste in an alternative, non-polluting manner, the firm would produce a smaller output of £90million a year. Which course of action would appear to be more 'productive'?

✔ Answer 2.26

If the firm decides to pollute rather than not to pollute, its contribution to GDP will be larger (£100 million instead of £90 million) because no system or procedure currently exists in the National Income Accounts to attach a value to a clean river. Ideally the economic costs of environmental degradation should be subtracted when calculating a firm's contribution to domestic output; while the economic benefit of environmental protection should be added to the value of the output of activities that improve the environment. For example, the economic value of the output of a wildlife park or nature reserve is more than the leisure services they provide, as measured by the value of the tourist industry they sustain.

These 'measurement' issues are less theoretical and abstract than one may think. GDP figures and similar statistics are constantly referred to in political debates and economic analysis; they do have a significant impact on the shaping of government economic policies. If not remedied, shortcomings must at least be exposed. This is also particularly worrying for developing economies. Poorer countries' governments, caught up in the frenzied race towards faster growth that characterizes industrialized economies, strive to raise measured GDP as quickly as possible, often to satisfy international bodies of the soundness of their economies and their credit worthiness. Those who succeed often do so by overexploiting their natural resources and polluting their environment. The development of more subtle national accounting procedures, which take into account the environmental resources of an economy and quantify their depletion, would therefore represent a real step forward towards their protection.

Progress has been made in this direction by the recent collection and publication of environmental effects of production by the Office for National Statistic in Britain, as the Tables 2.12 and 2.13 show.

The UK environmental account aims to give an industrially disaggregated assessment of pressures on the environment from economic activity. It is a 'satellite account', which means that it uses alternative concepts to record effects of economic activity, that the main national accounts do not capture.

Human Development Index (HDI)

The **Human Development Index (HDI)** is an alternative measure introduced by the United Nations in

Table 2.12   UK environmental account, 1993

				Emissions by industry group								
	Agriculture	Mining and quarrying	Manufacturing	Electricity, gas and water supply	Construction	Wholesale and retail trade	Transport and communication	Financial intermediation	Public administation	Education, health and social work	Other services	Total
Emissions by theme												
Greenhouse gases[1] (million tonnes)	30	34	139	178	3	13	50	3	9	11	43	513
Carbon dioxide (CO_2) (million tonnes)	3	21	119	169	3	13	50	3	9	11	3	404
Methane (CH_4)	1107	637	8	380	—	1	2	—	—	1	1891	4027
Nitrous oxide (N_2O)	10	—	64	2	—	—	1	—	—	—	—	77
Acid rain precursors[2]	553	152	912	2500	13	55	552	8	58	57	23	4883
Sulphur oxides (SO_x)	13	35	735	2095	5	14	135	4	26	48	13	3123
Nitrogen oxides (NO_x)	19	168	255	582	11	60	600	6	47	13	14	1775
Ammonia (NH_3)	280	—	—	—	—	—	—	—	—	—	—	280
Air quality emissions[3,4]												
Blacksmoke	3	3	34	21	4	22	123	2	4	2	45	263
Carbon monoxide (CO)	6	48	85	23	3	24	176	2	19	3	52	441
Non-methane volatile organic compounds	81	94	673	24	27	140	55	1	3	1	33	1132
Benzene	—	—	9	—	—	2	—	—	—	—	—	11
Lead (tonnes)	3	2	770	46	4	25	141	2	10	—	108	1111

Source: ONS, Blue Book, 1997

1 Greenhouse gases aggregated by summing emissions of CO_2, CH_4 and N_2O according to their global warming potentials at 100 years.
2 Acid rain precursors aggregated by summing SO_x, NO_x, and ammonia according to potential hydrogen ions production.
3 Emissions from private use of cars, and gas use within the home.
4 Most unattributed emissions are from non-private household use of cars and use of light goods vehicles.
5 Totals may not sum due to rounding.

Table 2.13 UK emissions by final demand

	Consumers' expenditure	General government final consumption	GDFCF	Change in stocks	Exports	Total	Unattributed	Total
				Emissions by final demand				
Emissions by theme								
Greenhouse gases								
(million tonnes)	154	—	—	—	—	154	24	689
Carbon dioxide (CO_2)								
(million tonnes)	151	—	—	—	—	151	23	577
Methane (CH_4)	70	—	—	—	—	70	6	4103
Nitrous oxide (N_2O)	4	—	—	—	—	4	1	82
Acid rain precursors	600	—	—	—	—	600	205	5686
Sulphur oxides (SO_x)	127	—	—	—	—	127	17	3264
Nitrogen oxides (NO_x)	679	—	—	—	—	679	161	2615
Ammonia (NH_3)	—	—	—	—	—	—	40	320
Air quality emissions								
Blacksmoke	153	—	—	—	—	153	36	452
Carbon Monoxide (CO)	4094	—	—	—	—	4094	793	5328
Non-methane volatile								
organic compounds	688	—	—	—	—	688	470	2290
Benzene	24	—	—	—	—	24	6	41
Lead (tonnes)	1270	—	—	—	—	1270	382	2763

Source: ONS, *Blue Book*, 1997

1990 to measure the relative socioeconomic progress of nations.

Less ambitious than the MEW in what it aims to take into account and calculate, the HDI is a composite index which incorporates three important components of human welfare: life expectancy at birth, knowledge and standard of living. Life expectancy is measured as the number of years a newborn baby would live given the prevailing patterns of mortality for the country. Knowledge is measured as a combination of adult literacy and years spent in education. Standard of living is measured by real per capita income adjusted for cost of living. The HDI is expressed as a value between 0 and 1: the closer the value is to 1, the better the living conditions.

Table 2.14 shows HDI value for selected countries and their ranking on the basis of HDI and GDP per capita (PPP). As the data show, there is a general positive correlation between HDI and per capita GDP ranking. In some cases, however, this correlation breaks down. It would seem that countries with an HDI ranking higher than their per capita GDP ranking show greater concern for balanced development. The opposite can be said for, among others, countries like Switzerland, Germany, Singapore, Malaysia and South Africa.

HOW TO FIND RELEVANT STATISTICS AND SOURCES OF INFORMATION

Throughout this chapter we have discussed important conceptual and practical issues involved in measuring the macroeconomy. You now understand the importance of the information contained in the national income accounts. But who is responsible for collecting and publishing these data and where do you find them? If you need data on an international economy, say, the rate of inflation in India during the past ten years, where do you look? Here is some information on available sources of statistical information which should help you.

First, at the following address on the Internet:

http://www.elsevier.nl:80/econbase/othergo-phers/ you will find a useful list of resources, such as statistics, department working papers, etc., available on the Net to economists and other interested business users.

The last four pages of *The Economist*, which is published every week, provide up-to-date information on rate of growth of GDP, rate of inflation, unemployment,

Table 2.14 HDI and GDP ranking

	HDI value	HDI rank	GDP rank per capita (PPP$)
Industrial countries			
Canada	0.950	1	8
USA	0.937	2	1
Japan	0.937	3	8
Netherlands	0.936	4	20
France	0.930	8	11
Sweden	0.929	10	17
Switzerland	0.925	13	2
Germany	0.921	15	6
Denmark	0.920	16	12
UK	0.916	18	23
Italy	0.912	20	19
Hungary	0.856	50	50
Poland	0.855	51	71
Developing countries			
Argentina	0.883	30	39
South Korea	0.882	31	38
Singapore	0.878	35	16
Mexico	0.842	53	47
Malaysia	0.822	59	45
Brazil	0.804	63	64
South Africa	0.705	95	80
Romania	0.703	98	104
Indonesia	0.637	104	99
China	0.597	111	123
India	0.439	134	141
Zambia	0.425	136	142
Uganda	0.329	158	154

Source: United Nations, *Human Development Report,* 1995

exchange rates, interest rates, balance of trade, money supply of a large number of countries.

UK data

Office for National Statistics

The Office for National Statistics (ONS) is the government agency responsible for compiling, analysing and disseminating many economic, social and demographic statistics on the UK, including the retail price index, trade figures and labour market data, as well as the periodic census of the population and health statistics.

The ONS was formed in April 1996 from a merger of the Central Statistical Office and the Office of Population Censuses and Surveys. The agency is independent of any other government department and accountable to the Chancellor of the Exchequer. The ONS works in partnership with others in the government statistical service (GSS) located throughout many different government departments. It brings together its wealth of statistics in its main publications and data-

bases. These publications form an invaluable tool for any business person or economist interested in the state of the economy.

EU data

Eurostat, which is published annually, provides a wealth of EU statistics.

US data

- *Statistical Abstract of the United States,* published annually by the US Department of Commerce, Bureau of Economic Analysis. It is an excellent source of statistical information on a wealth of macroeconomic variables. Internet address (access by subscription only): http://www.bea.doc.gov/bea/otherpub.html
- *Survey of Current Business,* published monthly by the US Department of Commerce, Bureau of Economic Analysis.
- *Economic Report of the President,* published by the US Government Printing Office, Washington DC and written by the Council of Economic Advisers, provides a good discussion of current and past trends of most macroeconomic variables.

Data on other countries

An excellent source of international statistical information is provided by the Organization for Economic Cooperation and Development (OECD), set up after World War II and located in Paris. The OECD regularly publishes the following:

- *OECD Economic Outlook,* published twice a year. It includes a wealth of data for many macroeconomic variables for most of the rich countries of the world.
- *OECD Employment Outlook,* published once a year. It focuses specifically on labour market conditions in OECD countries.
- The OECD also periodically publishes individual country studies, which offer a comprehensive, albeit short term, analysis of OECD countries' economies.
- *OECD Historical Statistics* are a valuable source of information. The most recent, published in 1995, provides data for the period from 1960–93.
- The OECD data are also available on disk and the organization's Internet address is: **http: //www.oecd.org/**

An equally valuable source of international statistics and macroeconomic analysis is provided by the publications of the International Monetary Fund (IMF) based in Washington DC. Four periodical publications of the IMF are particularly useful:

■ *IMF, World Economic Outlook*, published every two years, describes major macroeconomic trends which have taken place worldwide and in specific countries.
■ *IMF, International Financial Statistics (IFS)*, published monthly, with data for individual countries usually going back a few years.
■ *IMF International Statistics Yearbook*, published annually, covers the same countries as the IFS but provides annual data going back 30 years.
■ *IMF, Government Finance Statistics Yearbook*, published annually, with data on each country's budget, with data going back ten years.

The IMF Internet address is: gopher://gopher.imf.org

Eastern European data

Many Eastern European countries are not yet included in IMF statistics, although many are now members of the IMF. To complement IMF and other OECD statistics, you can usefully consult the following:

■ *The Annual Transition Report*, published by the European Bank for Reconstruction and Development (EBRD) based in London.
■ *OECD, Short-term indicators: Central and Eastern Europe*, which is a quarterly publication.

MILTON FRIEDMAN: PERSONAL PROFILE

Milton Friedman, the son of Jewish immigrants from what is now Ukraine, was born in New York City on 31 July 1912. He studied economics at the University of Chicago, where he started his academic career. Friedman made his mark on the academic world even before the outbreak of World War II, with his contribution to statistical analysis, while he was working in the Treasury's department of tax research. Thanks to Friedman's influential work, statistical analysis became an essential component of economics. In 1946 Friedman went back to the University of Chicago, where he worked until retirement in 1979. During these years he became increasingly influential in the so-called Chicago School, which became the focal point and liveliest testing ground for Friedman's own approach to economics.

The Chicago School came to stand for an approach to economic thinking which was radically antagonistic

to the Keynesian approach prevailing in most academic and political circles. In microeconomics, Friedman's approach came to signify the belief that capitalist markets free from government regulation bring about the best possible allocation of the economy's scarce resources and the largest possible output.

In macroeconomics, the Chicago School under Friedman provided a theoretical counter-example to the Keynesian model of how the economy works. This approach is often referred to as the **monetarist model** and the Chicago School as the Monetarist School.

While Keynes argued that the strength of demand for the economy's output ultimately determines how much the economy produces and how much employment is generated, Friedman argued that a policy aimed at stimulating aggregate demand would only result in higher prices and not in larger output and more employment. This was the fundamental tenet of what became to be known as **monetarism**, expounded in Friedman's most influential theoretical work, *The Quantity Theory of Money: A Restatement* (1956).

Keynes used the experience of the world depression in the inter-war period as an example of how economies left to themselves without government intervention could be condemned by weak aggregate demand to remain stuck at the bottom of the cycle without hope of recovery. Keynes used the experience of prolonged recessions to prove, in other words, the fallacy of economic liberalism dominant at the time (the so-called classical theory), and the need for governments to stimulate aggregate demand with the use of predominantly fiscal measures.

In another seminal book, written in collaboration with Anna Schwartz in 1963, *A Monetary History of the United States, 1867–1960*, Friedman argued, using copious factual monetary data from the Federal Reserve, that the prolonged recession experienced by USA in the inter-war period was due not to a depressed aggregate demand, but to a too sudden and drastic reduction in the quantity of money in circulation in the US economy. In other words, Friedman and Schwartz attributed the depression to the wrong money supply policy on the part of the American government and not to an inherent weakness of the macroeconomic system or to the role played in it by aggregate demand.

Friedman displayed the same skilful combination of economic modelling, empirical evidence and statistical analysis in his theory of consumer behavior. His *Theory of the Consumption Function* (1957) aimed to identify and distinguish between the effect that increases in personal disposable income have on people's consumption behaviour.

Friedman's ideas took off in a big way and became the dominant theory in the 1970s and 1980s, when the experience of stagflation seemed to provide a final counter-example to the Keynesian demand management model. Friedman became a celebrity and his ideas were debated in books, newspapers, conferences, radio and television programmes. Friedman was finally awarded the Nobel Prize for economics in 1976 in recognition for his achievement in the fields of monetary history and theory and his demonstration of the complexity of stabilization policy.

His economic liberalism and advocacy of deregulation appealed to the political right and conservative parties. Margaret Thatcher and Ronald Reagan were among his most staunch supporters. He preached the virtues of economic liberalism, rolling back the frontiers of the state, freeing the forces of the market from government intervention, the abandonment of any attempt at stimulating the economy and reducing unemployment, the need for the economy and unemployment to find their 'natural' levels, the virtue of price stability and monetary 'wisdom'.

His fame and fortune have somewhat faded in the unemployment-ridden 1990s, although monetarism maintains a strong hold on government policymaking, particularly in the European Union. Inflation has been brought under control, but at a huge price in terms of unemployment. Economists and government officials alike have been left still searching for an answer.

☆ **For revision of this chapter, see the Chapter Summaries at the end of the book, starting on page 411.**

3 The circular flow model and macroeconomic equilibrium

Objectives

After studying this chapter, you will be able to understand:

- the concept of macroeconomic equilibrium;
- the concept of circular flow of income, output and expenditure;
- the difference between potential and actual output;
- the meaning and effect of withdrawals and injections;
- what is meant by saving and investment;
- the role of taxes and government spending;
- what is meant by imports and exports;
- the consequences of macroeconomic disequilibrium.

INTRODUCTION

Having learnt how to measure the level of economic activity through the system of national income accounting, we now want to develop a model which explains how the 'parts' of the economic system fit together to produce a macroeconomic outcome, measurable in terms of growth, employment, price stability and external balance. We want a model that can explain why the macroeconomic outcome is what it is; a model that can explain why the level of output, prices and employment are what they are. It is at this point that views begin to differ.

The debate in macroeconomic used to be characterized as one between **demand-side** economists who, with Keynes, stress the role of aggregate demand – the total amount of goods and services the economy as a whole wishes to buy – as the main determinant of output and employment; and **supply-side** economists who, with Friedman, focus on supply side conditions and dismiss demand management. This school of thought favours a government policy aimed at tight control of monetary conditions, sound finances and lower taxation, leaving the aggregate outcome of the

economy's output and employment to be determined by the free forces of competition. Nowadays a more eclectic approach seems to prevail in economic thinking. Such an approach recognizes that the economy's output, employment and price levels are in fact determined by the interaction of demand and supply conditions. The correct policy stance for a government would therefore be to stimulate aggregate demand, while at the same time affecting the 'supply' decisions of firms and businesses through the provision of adequate microeconomic incentives.

The outcome of the debate can be summarized quite succinctly, as we have just done. To be able really to understand the issues involved and to be able to appreciate the policy implications takes much longer; it will take, in fact, the best part of this book.

As we shall see, much of the debate centres around the relationship between expenditure, output and income, illustrated by the circular flow model. The crucial question that the model leaves unanswered is one of **causality**: what determines what. Therefore we need to go back to the model and tease out of it some causal and dynamic concepts, by asking the following questions:

- What determines the level of output in the economy? Is it, as Figure 3.1 shows, how much people want to buy, that is the level of aggregate demand or total desired expenditure, so that as more is demanded, more is produced and as more is produced, more is earned by the factors of production (Figure 3.1)?

■ Or is it the other way round as Figure 3.2 shows? Is it the level of output that determines the level of income, which in turns determines demand?

According to the **demand-side** model, aggregate demand determines how much is produced, aggregate supply, and therefore also the level of employment. According to the **supply-side** model, aggregate supply 'creates its own demand', as the classical **Say's Law** maintained, by determining people's incomes and therefore their demand.

Although these two explanations may appear to be saying the same thing in the end, the different order of causality which they imply makes a very big difference when it comes to dictating macroeconomic policies for the general management of the economy and for the reduction of unemployment in particular.

We start now to take a closer look at the Keynesian model of the macroeconomy. As a preliminary step, however, it is useful to go back to the circular flow of income and output model introduced earlier and with its help to explore not macroeconomic accounting identities, but issues of dynamics and causality. The circular flow model will be our back door to the Keynesian model of the economy. We'll see that the use of even this simple conceptual tool will enable us to put forward a first explanation of what causes inflation, unemployment and growth.

CIRCULAR FLOW MODEL AND MACROECONOMIC EQUILIBRIUM

Let's go back to the circular flow model of Chapter 2. We do not need to worry here about the various meas-

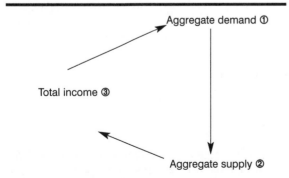

Figure 3.1   Demand-side model

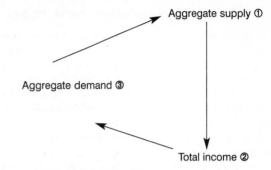

Figure 3.2   Supply-side model

ures of national income discussed in that chapter. What we now focus on is the real income of the economy, by which we mean the output of the economy and the incomes generated by its production. Income and output are synonymous and are denoted by the same symbol Y.

The important point that the simple circular flow model helped us to establish was that if (**assumptions**):

■ all factors are fully rewarded
■ all factors income is spent
■ all goods produced are sold

then:

total income ≡ total expenditure ≡ total output

or

$$Y \equiv E$$

where Y denotes real income and output. Given our assumptions, this is an axiomatic conclusion. This is why we use the symbol ≡, which denotes 'equivalence by definition'. Such equations are called **identities**.

A situation where people use all their incomes to buy all the goods produced in the economy over a given period of time, say a year, is also quite clearly a situation of **equilibrium**. Equilibrium is defined as a state of things that will be maintained for ever if nothing intervenes to change it from outside.

If producers sell all they produce and there are no unwanted stocks of unsold goods piling up in warehouses, and if consumers spend all their incomes in the process, the economy is in equilibrium and there is no reason for anything to change, that is, for producers to produce more or consumers to consume more. We can therefore look at:

$$Y = E$$

as an **equilibrium condition**, rather than a definitional identity. For the economy to be in equilibrium, it must be that all that is produced is sold and all income is spent:

total income = total expenditure = total output.

It is worth noting here an important link between level of output and unemployment. To produce goods and services, firms will employ people. For a given state of technology and amount of capital, and assuming also that wages paid by firms remain constant, the number of people that firms employ will depend on the firms' level of production and increase or decrease with it. Assuming no change in productivity or technology, the greater the economy's output, the greater the demand for labour by firms, the greater the employment level. This is what economists mean when they say that the demand for labour is a 'derived demand'; in other words, it depends on the level of production. If firms wish to expand production, everything else being constant, they will take on more people; if they want to reduce their output, they will eventually make some people redundant.

✍ Activity 3.1

What kind of assumptions are we making when we say that firms wishing to expand production will do so and in particular will take on more people?

✓ Answer 3.1

We are making two important assumptions:

1 We are assuming that there are 'unused resources', in particular labour, which can be used and drawn into production by firms in order to produce more.
2 We are also assuming that wages are constant and do not increase as more labour is demanded.

If wages did increase, in particular in line with the increase in the price of other goods, firms faced by increasing wage demands would be unwilling to respond to an increase in demand by stepping up production. To keep things simple, however, we deliberately postpone these complicated issues of relative changes in prices and wages to a later stage, and assume for the time being that prices and wages do not change in response to a change in demand conditions.

If firms in the economy are capable of producing more, it must mean that more can be produced, that aggregate production has not reached full capacity. This concept is expressed by the distinction between actual output and potential output or full employment level of output. **Actual output** is the output level which the economy is currently producing. **Potential output** is the maximum level of output which the economy is capable of producing at a certain moment in time, given its productive resources of land, labour and capital. It implies full use or full employment of all its productive resources, including labour.

So, if the economic system is producing at full employment, if it is using up all the productive resources available including labour, and total income and output equal total expenditure (that is, all the incomes generated by the system are entirely spent back to buy up its output), then the system will be in a state of full employment equilibrium.

✍ Activity 3.2

Distinguish between equilibrium level of output and full employment equilibrium level of output. Can the two differ? What do you think would happen if they did?

✓ Answer 3.2

The equilibrium level of output is that level of output whose production creates total spending just sufficient to purchase the output itself. The aggregate supply of the economy, the total quantity of goods and services produced, is just equal to aggregate demand – the total quantity of goods and services people are willing to buy. The annual rate of aggregate production (output) and spending (expenditure) are in balance. There is neither overproduction – stocks of unwanted goods piling up – nor excess demand, which by running down inventory levels gives firms an incentive to increase the rate of production. The full employment equilibrium level of output is the level of output achieved when all the productive resources available are fully used up, including labour; this also just equals aggregate demand. The classical economists who preceded Keynes believed that the economy would always operate at full employment and would always be in equilibrium. The prolonged recession of the 1920s and 1930s seemed to prove them wrong. According to Keynes, economies could find themselves stuck in an 'equilibrium' position – from which they would not spontaneously move – at less than full employment. In that situation unemployment would become permanent and not temporary, as classical economists believed. Only government intervention could then help the economy out of its permanent disequilibrium.

✍ Activity 3.3

Look at Table 3.1 and Figure 3.3 and comment on their significance.

✓ Answer 3.3

The minus (–) sign in front of most of the figures presented in Table 3.1 indicates the existence of output gaps. A plus (+) sign indicates that the economy's per-

Table 3.1 Output gaps, selected OECD countries, 1981–98 (deviations of actual GDP from potential GDP as a percentage of potential GDP)

	1981	1982	1983	1984	1985	1986	1987	1988	1989	1990	1991	1992	1993	1994	1995	1996	1997	1998
USA	−1.1	−5.5	−3.8	−0.2	+0.2	+0.1	+0.1	+1.2	+2.1	+1.1	−1.8	−1.0	−0.8	+0.3	−0.3	−0.3	+0.9	+0.6
Japan	+0.9	+0.3	−1.0	−0.9	−0.8	−2.0	−1.9	+0.2	+1.2	+2.8	+3.3	+1.4	−1.0	−2.7	−3.9	−2.8	−3.1	−2.9
Germany	−0.4	−3.2	−3.3	−2.2	−1.8	−1.4	−1.9	−0.6	+0.1	+2.1	+2.7	+2.7	+0.9	−0.6	−0.9	−1.4	−1.2	−0.8
France	−0.8	+0.6	−0.9	−1.9	−2.4	−2.2	−2.3	−0.4	+1.4	+1.5	+0.2	−0.7	−3.6	−2.6	−2.4	−2.8	−2.3	−1.6
Italy	+1.6	−0.9	−2.3	−2.7	−2.2	−1.6	−0.7	+0.5	+1.8	+1.8	+1.2	−0.1	−2.1	−1.7	−0.6	−1.6	−2.3	−2.3
UK	−3.7	−3.8	−2.1	−2.0	−0.8	+1.0	+3.5	+5.9	+5.7	+3.7	−0.6	−2.9	−3.2	−1.6	−1.3	−1.4	−0.6	0.0
Canada	+0.4	−6.0	−5.7	−2.4	−0.3	+0.1	+1.6	+3.8	+3.6	+1.4	−2.5	−3.8	−3.7	−1.9	−1.9	−2.7	−1.7	−1.1
Total of above countries	−0.6	−3.3	−2.9	−1.1	−0.7	−0.7	−0.4	+1.1	+2.0	+1.8	0.0	−0.3	−1.4	−1.0	−1.4	−1.3	−0.7	−0.7

Source: OECD, *Economic Outlook*, July 1997. Forecasted values for 1998.

formance is above trend and is in fact producing more than its estimated potential output, with actual GDP greater than potential.

Table 3.1 and Figure 3.3 show that in a number of countries, notably the USA and UK, as well as Australia, New Zealand and some smaller northern European countries, cyclical expansions are mature and reaching their peak, with margins of spare capacity having either been largely eliminated or rapidly declining. The UK data are particularly interesting. The UK output gap values appear to reflect the cyclical performance of the UK economy: the output gap is positive and has its largest value for the whole 28-year period, from 1980 to 1997, in 1988, with a value of 5.9 per cents, when the economy reached the peak of 'Lawson's boom'. Actual output (actual GDP value) in that year appears to have exceeded potential GDP (trend value) by approximately 6 per cent. Output gap values remain positive but declining until 1990, to turn negative as the UK economy enters a contractionary phase in 1991, and worsening as the economy falls deeper into the recession of the early 1990s. The output gap between actual output and potential output is narrowing again as the UK economy is expanding once more, with equilibrium between actual output and potential output forecasted to be reached in 1998 (output gap value equal to 0).

These are very interesting data, which prompt us to reflect on some other important, related issues.

✍ Activity 3.4

What other questions spring to your mind, as you reflect on these findings?

✓ Answer 3.4

Two main issues seem to emerge:

■ If the UK economy operated at more than full

capacity in 1988–90 and if it is estimated to reach equilibrium output in 1998, how can we reconcile this situation with a rate of unemployment which went from 7.8 per cent in 1988 to 5.8 per cent in 1990, when the economy was allegedly producing above capacity? How can we reconcile an equilibrium between actual output and potential output, i.e. the economy producing its full employment level of output in 1998, with an unemployment rate of 5.6 per cent? This must surely force us to reflect on our definition of full employment and our understanding of what constitutes a fully employed economy. This will be the topic of a later chapter. It may suffice at this stage to make a mental note of the fact that increasingly economists refer to an unemployment rate of 5.6 per cent for the UK as 'effective' full employment.

■ The second issue of great importance that these statistics raise is related to the calculation of potential output. How can economists know what the potential output for an economy is? The case study at the end of the chapter provides an answer to this question.

SOME ISSUES OF DYNAMICS

For the economic system to be in equilibrium, the set of assumptions specified earlier must hold. Now we must ask ourselves: what happens if those assumptions do not hold? What happens in our highly simplified model of the economic system:

■ if households do not spend all their income;
■ if firms produce for other firms and not just for households' consumption;
■ if firms do not sell all their outputs?

Figure 3.3   Selected OECD countries: (a) estimated output gaps, 1998; (b) projected output gaps, 1999

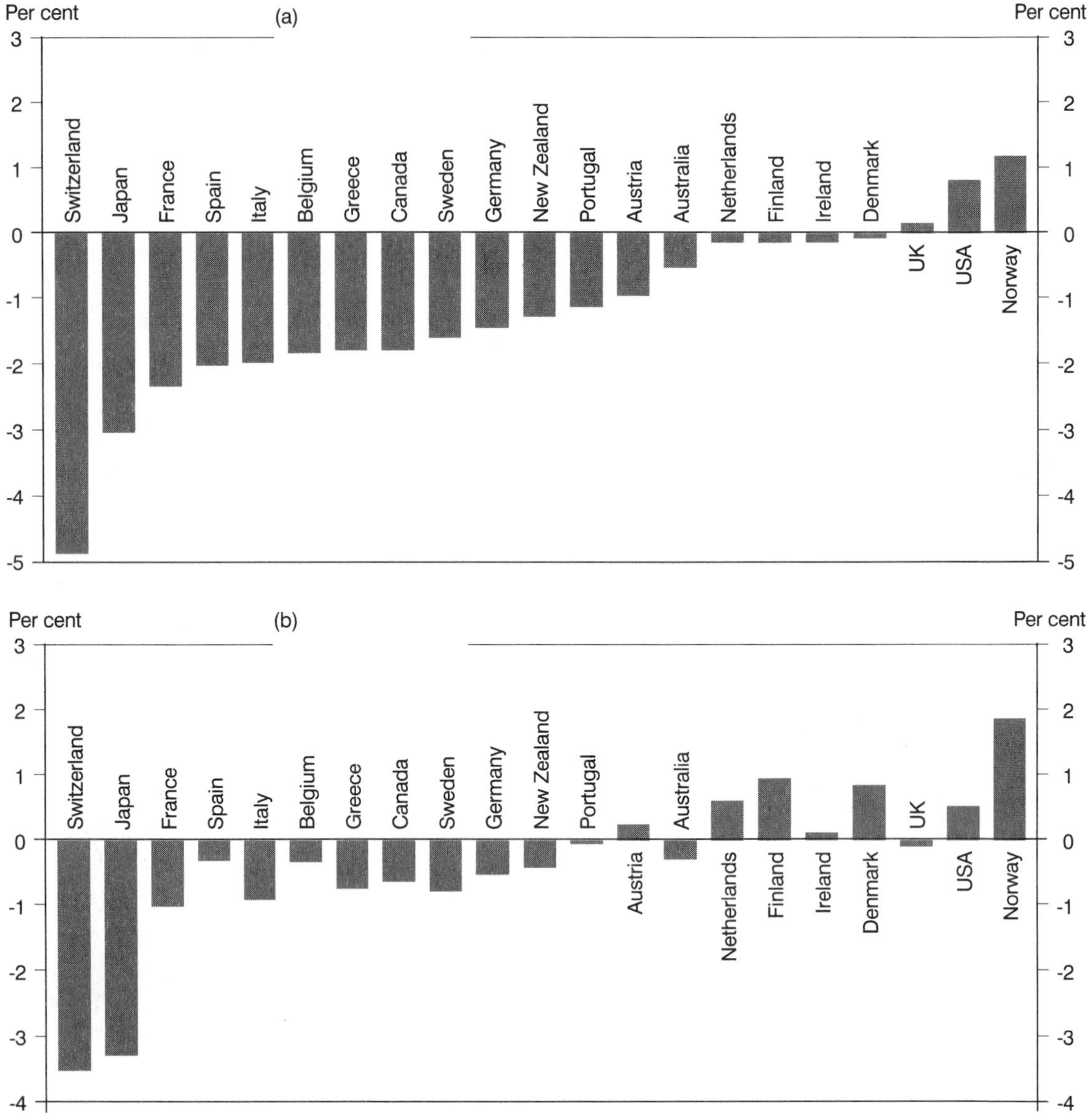

Source: OECD, 1997

The simple circular flow model we introduced earlier describes the situation of an economy that does not trade with the outside world: what economists call a **closed economy**. Can our model be adapted to take into account the fact that economies are **open**, that is that they buy and sell goods and services to and from each other? What happens:

■ when people buy foreign goods and services?
■ when foreigners buy our goods and services?

Our simple model, as it stands, does not take into account the role of government, with its power to tax and to spend. This too needs to be incorporated into our simple analysis. We need to ask the following questions: what happens to the circular flow of income and output:

■ when the government taxes people's incomes;
■ when the government spends money buying goods and services produced by firms?

We must develop our model a step further and introduce the concepts of saving and investment, government spending and taxation, and import and export.

SAVING AND INVESTMENT IN THE CIRCULAR FLOW MODEL

Not all firms produce consumption goods destined for consumers like you and me. Some firms specialize in the production of what economists call **capital** or **investment goods**, like machinery and equipment, which other firms in the economy need in order to produce final consumption goods. When firms buy capital goods from other firms they are making what economists call an act of **investment**.

But where do firms get the money to finance their investments? Investment expenditure by firms is not financed out of the firms' current sales revenue. This is shared out among the factors of production employed, as a reward for services – which must be done if they want to retain those services. Therefore the firms' investment expenditure – as it does not come from the current flow of expenditure paid into firms – represents an **injection** of extra money into the circular flow of income. But where does this extra money to purchase capital goods come from? It must come from the firms' own past savings, which have been held in a bank account and are now reinjected to finance the investment; or it must come from money borrowed from financial institutions. Financial institutions, in turn, will use their depositors' money – including households' savings – to give new loans to firms.

Just as it is obvious that firms produce goods both for household consumption and for other firms' use, it is also quite clear that people do not spend their entire income buying goods and services. People save as well. Beyond a level of income which is too low to allow any saving and is just sufficient to finance current consumption, people tend to spend only part of their income, while saving the rest. That part of people's income which is saved is money that leaks out of the circular flow system. Money which is saved is not spent to buy goods and services; it does not return to the firms as their sales revenue. Will firms' sales revenues on the whole fall short as a result? Not necessarily, because not all firms produce consumption goods. Some produce investment goods not destined for household consumption. The capital goods industries – as opposed to the consumption goods industries – employ people and generate households' incomes but do not produce for household consumption. The total value of consumption goods produced by an economy is smaller than the total value of household incomes. So provided the amount the economy saves (S) is compensated and equal in value to the amount firms in the economy wish to invest in buying capital goods (I) the economy will remain in equilibrium. The amount of money which leaks out in the form of saving may be injected back as investment spending.

To see this point more clearly, let's assume initially that all firms produce £10,000 worth of goods and services for household consumption. The value of the economy's output is £10,000 a year. Total income is also £10,000 as the factors of production, land, labour and capital, used by firms for the production of goods and services are fully rewarded and receive incomes, rents, interest and profit:

total output (£10,000) = total income (£10,000).

Let's now assume that households wish to save 20 per cent of their income either towards a pension or for future expenditures. Households will only be willing to spend £8,000 on buying up the economy's output of consumer goods.

✍ Activity 3.5

What is likely to happen to the economy as a result of this situation?

✓ Answer 3.5

The firms which have produced £10,000 worth of goods and services will find that £2,000 worth remains unsold. Stocks of unwanted, unsold consumption goods will start piling up in warehouses. **Total expenditure** is not equal to total **output** and **income**. Total expenditure (£8,000) is smaller than output and income (£10,000):

$$Y \neq E$$

where the sign $\neq$ means 'not equal to'. **This is not an equilibrium situation.**

✍ Activity 3.6

Something will have to change in our system to restore equilibrium, but what?

✓ Answer 3.6

Economists give a different answer to this crucial question according to which school of thought they belong: Keynesian or monetarist. What follows is a very simplified version of Keynes's answer. The classical and monetarist view is examined in Chapter 9. So Keynes's answer to the question, 'What will happen if desired expenditure is smaller than firms' current output?' is that firms' output and consequently the level of employment in the economy will change. As firms see stocks of unwanted goods piling up unsold, they will adjust their output plans for the next period, say the following year. Everything else being equal, they will cut down on production and consequently on employment. The economy's output will fall and unemployment will rise. If expenditure is less than total income and output, output will fall and with it employment.

Let's now drop the assumption that only goods for household consumption are produced in this economy and allow for the fact that some firms produce **capital goods** – equipment and machinery – that they sell to other firms. The economy is still producing £10,000 worth of output, of which only £8,000 is made up of **consumption goods** – goods and services for household consumption – while the remaining £2,000 is made up of capital goods:

$$\text{total output} = £10,000.$$

Total income of the economy is still £10,000, as firms in the capital goods industry also need fully to reward the factors of production – their employees and the capital and land resources they use – if they want to retain them. They generate incomes in the same way as firms in the consumption goods industry:

$$\text{total income} = £10,000.$$

Households once more wish to save 20 per cent of their income. They spend £8,000 to purchase the goods and services they need and save £2,000. The money saved leaks out of the circular flow of income and output. It is tucked away somewhere safe, in bank accounts, building societies or under people's mattresses, and does not flow back to firms in exchange for goods. It does not become firms' sales revenue, although it is money that came from them in the first place as factors of production's income, reward paid by the firms to their employees, etc. We can summarize this situation as follows, using Y to denote income, S to denote saving and C to denote consumption expenditure, or consumption for short.

$$Y = C + S$$

where saving is defined as 'that part of income which is not spent on consumption'. In symbols this is:

$$S \equiv Y - C.$$

In our example, total income is £10,000, consumption is £8,000 and saving is £2,000:

$$£10,000 \ (Y) = £8,000 \ (C) + £2,000 \ (S).$$

Saving in this model is a **leakage**. It is money that households withdraw from circulation, not using it to buy goods and services from firms. Out of a total income of £10,000, consumption expenditure is only £8,000, as £2,000 leaks out of the system in the form of saving. But the economy has produced £8,000 worth of goods and services for household consumption and £2,000 worth of capital goods not for household consumption. So the amount households spend on consumption of goods and services (C), which is £8,000, is exactly equal to the amount of such goods produced in the economy.

So if, and this is a big 'if', firms in the economy are willing to invest £2,000 in buying up the capital goods that other firms in the capital goods industry have produced, the system will be in equilibrium and nothing will have to change. Total expenditure (E) which includes consumption expenditure on goods and services (C) and investment expenditure on capital equipment (I), will be just equal to total income and output (Y). In symbols, this can be summarized as follows:

$$E = C + I.$$

But the system is still in equilibrium as:

$$Y = E.$$

✍ Activity 3.7

Check again how this works, using the figures provided in the example.

✓ Answer 3.7

The value of total income and output (Y) is £10,000. Total expenditure (E) is equal to £8,000 of consumption expenditure (C) on goods and services by households and £2,000 of investment expenditure by firms. So $E = £10,000$, which is equal to Y. In other words, the system is in equilibrium if investment equals saving or:

$$I = S.$$

This is a new way of expressing the equilibrium condition for the economy as a whole, which we were previously expressing as:

$$Y = E.$$

✍ Activity 3.8

The equilibrium condition above can be derived from the equations we have introduced so far.

✓ Answer 3.8

We started off with the circular flow **equilibrium condition** which stated that all income (Y) is spent (E) on purchasing the output of the economy. This we expressed as:

$$Y = E. \qquad (1)$$

Income is equal to expenditure. However, part of the income is saved. So:

$$Y = C + S. \qquad (2)$$

Expenditure, on the other hand, comprises consumption expenditure by households and investment expenditure by firms. So:

$$E = C + I. \qquad (3)$$

From (1)–(3) we obtain:

$$C + S = C + I. \qquad (4)$$

If we simplify this, it gives:

$$S = I \qquad (5)$$

as our **new equilibrium condition**.

But where do firms get the money to finance their investment expenditure? Firms receive £8,000 from the sale of consumption goods, which is then given out as wages, rents, interest and profit to the factors of production. Where does the extra £2,000 come from to finance investment spending in capital goods?

As we said before, investment is an **injection** of money into the circular flow. This money comes from outside the system; it does not flow automatically inside it. What exactly do we mean by this?

Firms wishing to maintain or expand their productive capacity and to invest in capital equipment will typically take up a loan from a bank. Banks and financial institutions will again typically be the places where households place their savings. So in a sense it is true to say that the savings that flow out of the system are channelled back, through financial institutions, into the system as investment. However, there is no automatic link or direct mechanism to guarantee that this will happen, when it will happen, or that the amount people wish to save will be exactly equal to the amount firms wish to invest.

Households and firms represent two quite distinct groups of economic agents, with a totally different set of priorities guiding their economic behaviour. Nothing guarantees that planned investment will be equal to planned saving. If they are not, however, the economy is not in equilibrium. Something will happen in the economy to restore equilibrium and it will always be true that in equilibrium actual savings equal actual investment. We will explain the distinction between planned and actual savings and investment in the next chapter. For the moment, we restate the important conclusion that the economic system will be in equilibrium if savings, which are a leakage or withdrawal of funds from the circular flow, are compensated by an equal amount of investment, which is an injection of funds into the circular flow. This situation can be shown by changing our initial model, as illustrated in Figure 3.4. In Figure 3.4 $S = I$: the system is in equilibrium.

✍ Activity 3.9

Using the hypothetical data in Table 3.2, determine the equilibrium level of output. Note that **unintended changes in inventory investment** occur in the economy when:

total desired expenditure $\neq$ total output

or, which is the same, when:

aggregate demand $\neq$ aggregate supply.

Inventories increase (+) when:

$$E < Y$$

and decrease (–) when:

$$E > Y.$$

Changes in inventory investment (whether firms are adding to stocks or destocking) are therefore an important indicator of the behaviour of aggregate demand and overall equilibrium in the economy.

State what is the value of savings, investment and consumption at the equilibrium level of output.

Table 3.2 Savings and investment

Savings billions £	Investment billions £	Aggregate demand (C + I), billions £	Unintended changes (+) or (–) in inventories £
0	20	410	–20
5	20	425	–15
10	20	440	–10
15	20	455	–5
20	20	470	0
25	20	485	+5
30	20	500	+10
35	20	515	+15

Figure 3.4 The circular flow with saving and investment

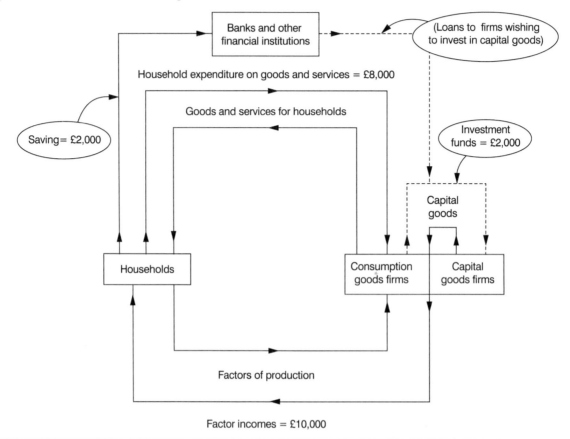

Factor incomes = £10,000

✓ Answer 3.9

Equilibrium occurs in the economy when unintended changes in inventories are equal to zero. This occurs when total output is £470 billion which is also equal to total expenditure or aggregate demand: $C + I$. At this equilibrium position, savings are £20 billion and investment is £20 billion. So our equilibrium condition is satisfied:

$$saving = investment$$

or:

$$S = I.$$

If in equilibrium total expenditure or aggregate demand is £470 and investment is £20 billion, it must be that consumption expenditure is £450 billion.

✎ Activity 3.10

Look at Figure 3.5, which charts the behaviour income, consumption and saving of the UK economy since 1956 and comment on what it shows.

✓ Answer 3.10

As Figure 3.5 shows, personal saving ratio (saving as a percentage of disposable income) was very low in the immediate post-war period. However, it rose during the 1960s and 1970s. This was due to two reasons: the 1970s were characterized by high inflation in Britain, which required people to save more simply to maintain the real value of their savings. At the same time, higher unemployment led to greater job insecurity and higher precautionary saving. The saving ratio peaked in 1980 at 13.5 per cent.

In the second half of the 1980s the saving ratio fell sharply, as consumers' expenditure accelerated due to laxer government fiscal and monetary policies, lower oil prices and financial liberalization, which in turn meant easier credit. Between 1986 and 1988, consumer spending increased at an average rate of 6.5 per cent a year, and the saving ratio fell to 6 per cent in 1988. There was a boom in the housing market, with prices increasing by around 90 per cent between 1986

Figure 3.5 UK private sector consumption, income and saving, 1956–96

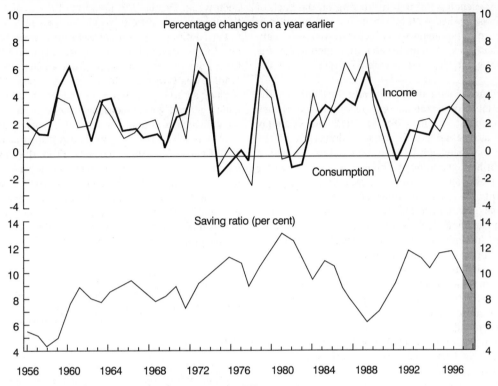

Source: HM Treasury, *Financial Statement and Budget Report*, July 1977

Figure 3.6 Whole UK economy investment–GDP ratio,[1] 1960–96

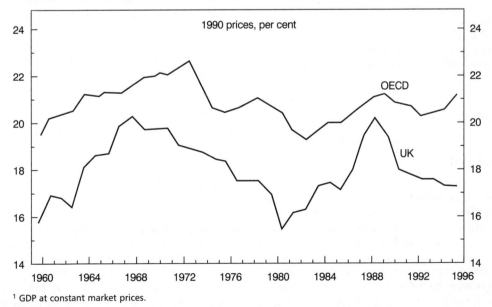

[1] GDP at constant market prices.

Source: OECD statistics, 1997

and 1989, and many homeowners financed their consumption spending through borrowing on the back of rising house prices. With falling saving and increase in house purchases, the personal sector moved into financial deficit (consumption greater than income) in the late 1980s for the first sustained period since the 1950s.

Conditions changed dramatically in 1988 as the small bubble of economic expansion of the British economy burst. From 1988 to 1992 the economy entered a recession, with a sharp downturn of the housing market which left the personal sector with a high debt burden and many homeowners with negative equity (the value of their outstanding mortgages exceeding the market value of their properties). Consumer expenditure fell by 3.5 per cent from peak to trough and house prices fell on average by almost 13 per cent. In 1992, the saving ratio reached its peak at almost 13 per cent, despite relatively low inflation, and has remained at a high level since then. This in part reflects increased caution after the experience of the late 1980s. Since 1996 the saving ratio, although still high, has started to come down, reflecting higher consumer spending.

Consumer spending is by far the largest expenditure component of GDP, accounting for approximately 70 per cent of its total. Consumer spending increased by about 2 to 3 per cent a year between 1993 and 1995 and by 3.5 per cent in 1996, increasing further to an annual growth rate of about 4 per cent in the first part of 1997. Consumer credit and consumer confidence seemed to be back to levels last reached in 1988.

Real disposable income also grew strongly by nearly 4 per cent in 1996, well above its long-term trend rate of around 2.5 per cent, due to income tax cuts, rising employment, higher real average earnings growth and dividend receipts growth.

✍ Activity 3.11

Look at Figure 3.6 and comment on what it shows.

✓ Answer 3.11

The UK's relatively weak growth performance over the past 25 years partly reflects underinvestment. The UK ratio of investment to GDP is low by both historical and international standards. The ratio of the whole economy fixed investment to GDP has consistently been well below the OECD average since 1960, and the gap has been widening in recent years. Since 1960 the investment–GDP ratio for the OECD as a whole has averaged around 21 per cent, compared with a UK average figure of about 18 per cent.

The investment recovery from 1992 to 1997 has been weak. Despite the upswing of the economy over those years, the ratio of whole investment to GDP has fallen continuously, in contrast with the 1980s recovery. In the 1990s, however, it has fallen from an historic high rather than rising from an historic low. In 1996 it was lower than for most of the past 30 years.

Sluggish whole economy investment mainly reflects falling general government investment. Business investment, which accounts for around 65 per cent of the total, has been stronger, but it has grown at a slower pace than in the 1980s recovery. From the through of output, total business investment has increased by 17.5 per cent, compared to the increase in GDP of about 15 per cent. In contrast, while GDP increased by around 15 per cent in the first five years of the last upswing – between early 1981 and the end of 1985 – the increase in business investment was about 23.5 per cent.

WITHDRAWALS AND INJECTIONS: THE COMPLETE PICTURE

Withdrawals

As we have just seen, not all income generated by production within the domestic economy gets 'passed round' and becomes expenditure. Some is withdrawn and leaks out in the form of saving. At the same time, money is injected into the circular flow of households' income and expenditure from 'outside' to finance investment expenditure. But saving and investment are not the only leakages from and injections into the system. Government and the international sector both add leakages and injections to the internal flow of income and expenditure of the domestic economy.

✍ Activity 3.12

To understand how we can incorporate 'government' into our circular flow model, try and make a list of the main macroeconomic functions of governments.

✓ Answer 3.12

The government is:

- ■ a consumer of goods and services produced in the economy. This is what we call **government expenditure** and we denote it with the symbol G. When the government decides to expand the National Health Service and, say, have more hospitals built, it signs contracts with private firms to carry out the works. Government spending will add to private demand for those firms' output. G is money directly spent by the government on purchasing part of the economy's output.

- a producer of capital goods and consumption goods, through nationalized industries. The government also acts as a firm, producing output and employing factors of production.
- an employer of factors of production. Government has government employees in its various departments, etc. The amount of money that it decides to pay its employees will have an effect on the broader economy.
- a wealth reallocator through its taxes (direct and indirect) and transfer payments to households (such as child benefit, unemployment benefit, income supplement, pensions, etc.). Taxes reduce people's disposable income and therefore their expenditure, while benefits increase them.

Let's now look at the various forms of withdrawals from the circular flow.

1 The first category of withdrawals we have looked at is **savings** (S). Savings are the income that households choose not to spend, but rather to put aside somewhere safe. They represent a withdrawal from the circular flow. Firms also save: they save when they choose not to pay out profits as dividends to shareholders or to pay out only part of the profits, retaining some for future investments.

2 The second category of withdrawals of funds from the circular flow of income and output is represented by **taxes** (T). Taxes reduce people's disposable income (Y_D) and consequently their expenditure. Some taxes are paid out of households' incomes directly to the government, like PAYE (income tax) and National Insurance contributions. Some taxes are paid out of firms' incomes, like corporation tax. By imposing taxes, whether direct or indirect, the government withdraws funds from the economy, reducing the flow of expenditure.

3 The third category of withdrawals is represented by **import expenditure** (M). In the real world, economies trade with one another. British people may wish to spend some of their money on American Harley Davidson motorcycles, Italian wine or a holiday in Australia. However, when they do so they are withdrawing from the domestic circular flow of income and expenditure some of the income they have earned producing goods or services in the domestic economy (assuming no property income from abroad). Part of the domestically generated income leaks out into foreign economies, rather than flowing round in the domestic economy

through purchases of domestic goods. Likewise firms also import when they buy raw materials, machinery and partly finished goods from abroad.

Total withdrawals are the sum of savings, taxes and imports. Using symbols this becomes:

$$W = S + T + M.$$

Injections

Only part of the money flowing to firms as sales revenue comes from household expenditure; part comes from outside sources. There are three main sources or forms of injection:

1 The first category of injections is represented by **investment expenditure** (I). By investment, economists mean the purchase of capital equipment, plant, etc. Firms finance investment expenditure not out of current sales revenues but rather from loans or past savings (unshared profits).

2 The second category of injections is represented by **government expenditure** (G). As we have seen, this can take various forms:

- direct government expenditure on goods and services, that is, money spent on roads, hospitals, education, etc.;
- wages to government employees;
- indirect government expenditure in the form of subsidies and grants to firms. This form of government expenditure is indirect because the actual spending is eventually done by the firms receiving the subsidy.
- indirect government expenditure in the form of transfer payments to households, like pensions, child benefits, etc. Again, we call this form of government expenditure 'indirect' because the actual decision on how much to spend of the government benefit payments is ultimately made by the individuals receiving them and not by the government.

3 The third category of injections into the circular flow of income, output and expenditure is represented by **export expenditure**. This is income generated outside the domestic economy which is spent by foreigners to purchase British-made goods or services. Money flows into the circular flow from abroad when:

- foreigners buy UK exports;
- foreigners invest in the UK;
- UK households receive money from abroad in the form of dividends earned on foreign shares.

Total injections into the circular flow of income and expenditure are the sum of investment, government expenditure and exports. Using symbols this becomes:

$$J = I + G + X$$

where J is injection, I is investment, G is government spending and X is export. Figure 3.7 incorporates all these categories of withdrawals and injections into the circular flow model.

✍ Activity 3.13

Look at Table 3.3 and Figure 3.8 and comment on what they show.

✓ Answer 3.13

Table 3.3 shows the components of expenditure undertaken by the UK government and the ways in which revenue has been raised in order to finance those expendi-

Figure 3.7 Withdrawals and injections into the circular flow model

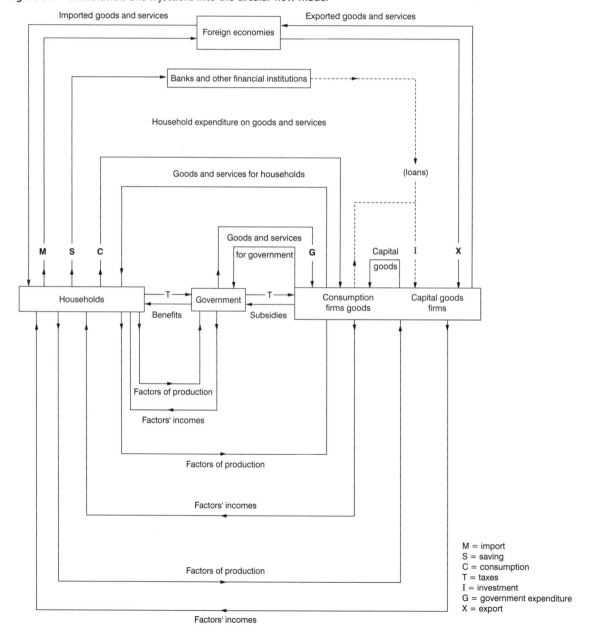

M = import
S = saving
C = consumption
T = taxes
I = investment
G = government expenditure
X = export

Table 3.3 Government expenditure and receipts, 1965–95 (£m at current prices)

	1965	1970	1975	1980	1985	1990	1991	1992	1993	1994	1995
Current expenditure											
Military defence	2062	2417	5096	11 327	17 857	22 897	23 211	24 391	24 552	23 946	23 150
National Health Service	1056	1735	4917	11 280	17 212	27 766	31 150	34 999	36 765	38 749	40 844
Education spending by local authorities	1052	1857	5323	9864	13 314	19 849	21 668	22 983	21 064	21 284	22 015
Other final consumption	1841	3029	7781	17 513	26 884	42 422	48 076	49 502	55 700	60 135	63 465
Total	6011	9038	23 117	49 984	75 267	112 934	124 105	131 875	138 081	144 114	149 474
Gross domestic fixed capital formation	1493	2447	4986	5499	6872	12 659	12 143	12 506	11 803	12 290	12 453
Value of physical increase in stocks	23	45	90	43	450	156	151	–17	–24	–251	–154
Transfer payments											
Subsidies	571	884	3771	5719	7225	6066	5995	6737	7203	7060	6966
Current grants to personal sector	2596	4330	10 278	25 524	45 351	58 939	69 287	80 066	88 384	92 574	96 480
Current grants abroad	177	169	337	1780	3427	4596	1083	4834	4969	5135	7180
Capital grants	182	796	1204	2193	3319	10 148	7939	7680	8602	7934	7498
Total net lending	944	1229	3740	3551	–1733	–8651	–9300	–6217	–4247	–5582	–989
Debt interest	1348	2025	4127	10 873	17 586	18 696	16 936	17 039	18 427	22 144	25 800
Total, all expenditure items	13 345	20 963	51 650	105 166	157 764	215 543	228 339	254 503	273 198	285 418	304 708
Total as % of GDP	37.0	48.8	48.8	45.4	44.1	39.1	39.7	42.6	43.3	42.7	43.5
Implicit deflator, gen. govt final consumption	8.3	11.4	24.7	49.5	71.6	100.9	107.1	113.8	118.6	121.9	124.9
Taxes on incomes	4099	7410	16 758	31 002	51 598	76 875	75 178	73 716	73 232	80 670	90 672
Taxes on expenditure	4922	8352	14 036	36 474	56 667	78 298	85 416	87 521	90 336	96 138	103 597
Social security contributions	1685	2655	6848	13 939	24 210	34 457	36 216	36 975	39 499	41 943	44 251
Community charge	0	0	0	0	0	8629	8128	7907	8038	8450	8989
Rent, dividends, interest	883	1606	3625	8205	11 718	10 621	10 210	9975	9999	10 598	10 823
Taxes on capital	290	673	797	1178	2371	3806	3763	3603	3679	3837	4129
Other	343	522	977	2088	2866	516	509	625	816	1194	1332
Total receipts	12 222	21 218	43 041	92 886	149 430	213 202	219 420	220 322	225 599	242 830	263 793
PSBR	1170	–51	10 161	11 786	7445	–2506	8077	28 794	47 549	40 273	40 073

Source: ONS, *Blue Book*, 1997

Figure 3.8 Government expenditure by category, 1980–95 (£m, deflated to constant 1990 prices)

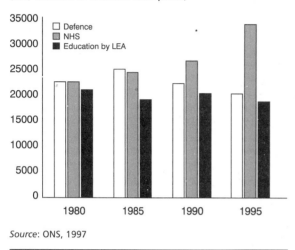

Source: ONS, 1997

tures. During the 1980s and 1990s the government has made conscious attempts to reduce the degree of its involvement in the economy. This was done partly through privatization, which transferred into private sector hands many state-run industries and enterprises; partly through reduction of government's direct and indirect expenditures. Table 3.3 shows that the government has achieved only a limited success in its endeavour. Total government expenditure represented a larger share of GDP in 1995 than it had done in 1965 and only a slightly smaller share than in 1980. We have to wait until we reach Chapter 5, where we discuss government and fiscal policy fully to explain this result.

In interpreting these data you must also remember that the measurements are in *current*, as opposed to *constant prices*. To convert the data into real terms for the purpose of comparisons over time, you need to use the implicit deflators of general government final consumption provided in Table 3.3. Real spending on defence, education and health in real, as opposed to nominal, terms is shown in Figure 3.8, where the data in Table 3.3 are transformed using the deflators provided.

✍ Activity 3.14

Look at Table 3.4 below and comment on what its shows.

✓ Answer 3.14

For an open economy, i.e. a country trading with other countries, it is very important to be able to monitor the international transactions that take place. If the value of the goods bought by Britain and imported into the country is greater than the value of the goods sold by Britain and exported to other countries in the world, the difference needs to be financed in some way. This can be done either by using foreign exchange reserves (i.e. reserves of foreign currencies used in international transactions) accumulated from past surpluses, by selling UK assets to foreigners, or by acquiring more foreign currency on foreign exchange markets in exchange for domestic currency, allowing the value of the domestic currency to depreciate.

The **balance of payments** is the set of accounts in which all such international transactions are recorded, including transaction in financial assets. The accounts show three main categories of transactions: transactions in goods, transactions in services and transactions in financial assets and liabilities. The **visible balance** shows the balance of trade between exports and imports of **goods**. As Table 3.4 shows, the balance of trade has been consistently negative in recent years, indicating that the UK has been buying more goods from abroad than it sells. The **invisible balance** shows the trade balance on **services**, including interest, profit, dividends and transfer payments. This balance is typically positive for the UK. The visible and invisible balance together account for the **current account** of the balance of payments. Transactions in UK assets and liabilities are recorded by the **capital account** of the balance of payments. They include both private and government transactions. When the central bank intervenes on foreign exchange markets to support the value of the currency by selling foreign currency, its transactions would be reflected in these figures. If all transactions were observed and recorded with total accuracy, the current and the capital account of the balance of payments would always exactly match each other. In practice, however, this does not happen, because the information comes from so many different sources. This mismatch between identified current transactions and their capital account financing is called the **balancing item**. The balancing item is needed to make sure that everything adds up properly. The total **balance of payments** is always equal to zero by definition. This balance can be achieved in different ways: either both accounts are in equilibrium, or a current account deficit is balanced by a capital account surplus or vice versa.

RELATIONSHIP BETWEEN WITHDRAWALS AND INJECTIONS

There are obviously some indirect links between the various categories of withdrawals and injections, that

Table 3.4 UK balance of payments, 1971–96 (£m at current prices)

Year	Exports (fob)	Imports (fob)	Visible balance	Invisible balance	Current balance	Net transactions in the UK assets and liabilities	Other recorded transactions	Balancing item
1980	47 149	45 792	1357	1487	2844	–3940	180	916
1981	50 668	47 416	3252	3496	6748	–7436	158	530
1982	55 331	53 421	1910	2741	4651	–2519		–2132
1983	60 700	62 237	–1537	5066	3529	–4562		1033
1984	70 265	75 601	–5336	6817	1481	–8534		7053
1985	77 991	81 336	–3345	5583	2238	–3720		1482
1986	72 627	82 186	–9559	8688	–871	–3820		4684
1987	79 153	90 735	–11 582	6769	–4813	7410		–2597
1988	80 346	101 826	–21 480	5005	–16 475	14 917		1558
1989	92 154	116 837	–24 683	2285	–22 398	18 176		4222
1990	101 718	120 527	–18 809	62	–18 746	16 543		2203
1991	103 413	113 697	–10 284	2331	–7954	7445		509
1992	107 343	120 447	–13 104	2972	–10 133	4965		5168
1993	121 398	134 858	13 460	2706	–10 756	13 080		–2324
1994	134 666	145 497	–10 831	8411	–2419	–2650		5069
1995	153 075	164 659	–11 584	7841	–3743	512		3231
1996	166 092	178 320	–12 228	12 214	–14	–2947		2961

Sources: ET, April 1997; UKEA, MDS, April 1997
Note: Series for visible and current balances and the balancing item are calculated from other items in the table, so there may be minor rounding differences with the published series.

is, between savings and investment, taxation and government expenditure, imports and exports.

Increased savings will make more funds available to financial institutions, which in turn will make them keener to grant loans to firms. However, this does not guarantee that firms will want to borrow money to invest. If anything, Keynes argued, it will make them less willing. The decisions to save and to invest are made by different groups of people, for different reasons. If households start cutting down on consumption in order to save more (depositing funds within the banking system), this is likely to discourage firms from borrowing in order to expand their businesses. After all, what business would want to expand when market demand is falling?

Equally, governments finance their spending mostly through taxation. This is not to say, however, that governments will always inject back into the economy the exact amount of money they take out of it in the form of taxes (T). Government policies differ widely on the topic of taxation and government budgets.

When the amount of government spending (G) is just equal to tax revenues, the government is said to have a **balanced budget**. When government expenditure exceeds tax revenues ($G > T$), the budget is in deficit. A **budget deficit** represents a net injection into the circular flow. The government injects more into the circular flow, through its expenditure, than it takes out in the form of taxes. When the opposite is true and tax revenues are greater than government expenditure ($T > G$), the government has a **budget surplus**. A budget surplus represents a net withdrawal from the circular flow, as $T > G$.

✍ Activity 3.15

Look at Table 3.5 and comment on what it shows in relation to British government financial balances over the period, compared with the average for the main OECD countries.

✓ Answer 3.15

Table 3.5 shows that for the period from 1981 to 1992 the UK government's deficit represented a lower percentage of nominal GDP than the average of the main OECD countries; since 1992 the opposite has been true as UK budget deficits, measured as a percentage of nominal GDP, have been larger.

The amount of government spending and taxation is determined by a policy decision taken by the government and there is no automatic mechanism that guarantees that G will always be equal to T. Equally, there is no straightforward link that ensures that the withdrawal from the circular flow represented by imports is exactly balanced by the injection represented by exports. While relative rates of inflation and exchange rates will affect both imports and exports, decisions to import will also largely depend on the rate of growth of the domestic economy, while exports will be affected by the state of the world economy and world demand for our goods. So it may very well be the case that **planned injections** are not equal to **planned withdrawals**.

✍ Activity 3.16

What do you think will happen as a result of this, according to the model presented so far?

✓ Answer 3.16

If withdrawals from the circular flow are greater than injections, if savings are greater than investment, taxes higher than government spending and/or imports greater than exports, then total demand in the economy will fall short of the current level of output. Unwanted inventories will develop, unsold goods will pile up in warehouses. Assuming no changes in prices and wages, firms will react by cutting down production and laying off workers. The output of the economy, together with its level of employment, will fall.

Summary

What the circular flow model helps us to see is that the economic system is in equilibrium if all the income generated by the system in the process of producing its output is spent on buying the output itself, whether it consists of consumption goods or capital goods. We defined this equilibrium condition as:

$$E = Y.$$

For the economy to be in equilibrium, expenditure has to equal income and output. If expenditure falls short of output, that is, if not all that has been produced finds a buyer, output will fall.

Here we have reached the cornerstone of Keynes's model. The underlying principle is simple, but extremely powerful. It is the level of total expenditure or aggregate demand that determines the level of output and ultimately of employment. In Keynes's model, output and income are demand determined.

EQUILIBRIUM CONDITION REDEFINED

This important conclusion applies also to our extended model, which takes into account withdrawals and

Table 3.5 General government financial balances, 1980–96 (surplus (+) or deficit (–) as a percentage of nominal GDP)

	1980	1981	1982	1983	1984	1985	1986	1987	1988	1989	1990	1991	1992	1993	1994	1995	1996	Projections 1997	Projections 1998
USA	-1.4	-1.1	-3.5	-4.1	-3.0	-3.2	-3.5	-2.6	-2.1	-1.7	-2.7	-3.3	-4.4	-3.6	-2.3	-2.0	-1.6	-1.1	-1.2
Japan	-4.4	-3.8	-3.6	-3.6	-2.1	-0.8	-0.9	0.5	1.5	2.5	2.9	2.9	1.5	-1.6	-2.3	-3.7	-4.4	-3.1	-2.3
Germany[a]	-2.9	-3.7	-3.3	-2.6	-1.9	-1.2	-1.3	-1.9	-2.2	0.1	-2.1	-3.3	-2.8	-3.5	-2.4	-3.6	-3.8	-3.2	-2.7
France[b]	-0.0	-1.9	-2.8	-3.2	-2.8	-2.9	-2.7	-1.9	-1.7	-1.2	-1.6	-2.0	-3.8	-5.6	-5.6	-5.0	-4.2	-3.2	-3.0
Italy	-8.6	-11.5	-11.4	-10.7	-11.7	-12.6	-11.7	-11.0	-10.7	-9.9	-11.0	-10.2	-12.1	-9.7	-9.6	-7.0	-6.7	-3.2	-3.8
UK	-3.4	-2.6	-2.5	-3.3	-3.9	-2.8	-2.4	-1.6	0.7	1.0	-1.2	-2.5	-6.3	-7.8	-6.8	-5.5	-4.4	-2.8	-1.8
Canada	-2.8	-1.5	-5.9	-6.9	-6.5	-6.8	-5.4	-3.8	-2.5	-2.9	-4.1	-6.6	-7.4	-7.3	-5.3	-4.1	-1.8	-0.2	0.5
Total of above countries	-2.7	-2.8	-4.0	-4.4	-3.6	-3.4	-3.4	-2.5	-1.9	-1.2	-2.1	-2.7	-4.0	-4.3	-3.6	-3.4	-3.1	-2.1	-1.9
Australia	-1.7	-0.7	-0.5	-3.9	-3.3	-2.8	-3.0	-0.3	1.0	1.0	0.6	-2.7	-4.0	-3.8	-4.0	-2.0	-1.4	-1.0	-0.1
Austria	-1.7	-1.8	-3.4	-4.0	-2.6	-2.5	-3.7	-4.3	-3.0	-2.8	-2.2	-2.7	-1.9	-4.2	-4.8	-5.3	-3.9	-3.0	-3.4
Belgium	-8.8	-12.9	-11.0	-11.6	-9.5	-9.0	-9.5	-7.7	-7.0	-6.4	-5.6	-6.5	-7.2	-7.5	-5.1	-4.1	-3.4	-2.8	-2.7
Denmark	-3.3	-6.9	-9.1	-7.2	-4.1	-2.0	3.4	2.4	0.6	-0.5	-1.5	-2.1	-2.9	-3.9	-3.4	-1.9	-1.6	0.0	0.7
Finland	2.8	3.5	1.9	0.6	3.0	2.9	3.4	1.0	4.1	6.3	5.4	-1.5	-5.8	-7.9	-6.2	-5.1	-2.6	-2.0	-1.4
Greece[c]	-2.6	-8.3	-6.3	-7.1	-8.4	-11.5	-10.3	-9.5	-11.5	-14.4	-16.1	-11.5	-12.3	-14.2	-12.1	-9.2	-7.4	-5.2	-4.0
Iceland	1.3	1.3	1.7	-2.0	2.2	-1.7	-4.1	-0.9	-2.0	-4.6	-3.3	-2.9	-2.8	-4.5	-4.7	-3.1	-1.8	-1.1	-0.7
Ireland	-12.3	-13.0	-13.4	-11.4	-9.5	-10.9	-10.7	-8.6	-4.5	-1.8	-2.3	-2.4	-2.5	2.5	-1.8	-2.1	-0.9	-1.2	-1.0
Korea	0.1	0.5	1.7	1.7	1.5	1.2	1.7	2.7	3.7	3.6	3.7	2.0	1.5	2.8	3.4	4.0	4.0	3.8	3.9
Netherlands	-4.2	-5.4	-6.6	-5.8	-5.5	-3.6	-5.1	-5.9	-4.6	-4.7	-5.1	-2.9	-3.9	-3.2	-3.4	-4.1	-2.4	-2.3	-1.7
New Zealand	—	—	—	—	—	—	-6.8	-2.5	-5.1	-4.2	-5.4	-4.1	-3.6	-1.2	3.0	3.2	3.1	2.8	2.9
Norway	5.2	4.4	4.0	3.7	7.4	9.9	6.2	5.1	2.7	1.8	2.6	0.1	-1.7	-1.4	0.4	3.3	5.9	6.7	7.1
Portugal	5.6	-10.7	-7.7	-10.2	-7.1	-7.5	-6.4	-5.6	-3.6	-2.5	-5.6	-6.7	-3.6	-6.8	-5.7	-5.0	-4.0	-2.9	-2.8
Spain	-2.0	-3.5	-5.2	-4.4	-5.0	-6.8	-5.8	-3.0	-3.0	-2.5	-3.8	-4.4	-3.6	-6.8	-6.3	-6.6	-4.5	-3.0	-2.6
Sweden[d]	-4.0	-5.3	-7.0	-5.0	-2.9	-3.8	-1.2	4.2	3.5	5.4	4.2	-1.1	-7.8	-12.3	-10.3	-7.7	-3.6	-2.1	-0.2
Total of above smaller countries	-2.0	-3.7	-4.0	-4.2	-3.4	-3.6	-3.3	-1.9	-1.4	-1.2	-1.7	-2.9	-3.6	-4.6	-3.8	-3.1	-1.7	-1.0	-0.5
Total of above OECD countries	-2.6	-2.9	-4.0	-4.3	-3.5	-3.4	-3.3	-2.4	-1.8	-1.2	-2.1	-2.7	-3.9	-4.3	-3.6	-3.3	-2.9	-1.9	-1.7
Memorandum item																			
Total of above European Union countries	-3.4	-5.1	-5.3	-5.1	-4.9	-4.9	-4.5	-3.9	-3.4	-2.5	-3.8	-4.4	-5.6	-6.5	-5.8	-5.2	-4.4	-3.0	-2.6

Source: OECD, Economic Outlook, 1997

injections. We can now say that the economy will be in equilibrium if:

$$withdrawals = injections.$$

This does not mean, of course, that savings must be exactly equal to investment, that taxes must be exactly equal to government expenditure or that imports must be exactly equal to exports. It means that an overall balance must be reached in the economy between the level of total aggregate expenditure and output, taking into account injections and withdrawals, for the economy to be in equilibrium.

For the economy to be in equilibrium, an overall balance must be reached between withdrawals and injections:

W	=	J
S		I
T		G
M		X

between savings, taxes and imports, on one hand, and investment, government spending and export, on the other. If:

$$W \neq J$$

and total expenditure is not equal to the economy's output, the latter will change to adjust to the former. **The level of the economy's output adjusts to the level of aggregate expenditure.**

✍ Activity 3.17

To practise the concept of injections and withdrawals just introduced, state which of the following are changes in injections and which are changes in withdrawals in the UK circular flow of income. In each case, assume ceteris paribus, i.e. that nothing else changes at the same time. Specify whether the change is an increase or a decrease and its effect on the economy's income, output, and employment:

(a) Local council funds a new metro project for the city.
(b) Government raises tax allowances.
(c) Government reduces child benefit.
(d) A leading UK company wins a major overseas contract.

(e) Firms borrow more money in order to increase capacity in preparation for anticipated rise in consumer demand.

Answer 3.17

(a) Increase in injection. The local council pays private firms to carry out the works. As a result of the works carried out, more goods and services are needed, firms step up their production: output, income and employment will all rise.
(b) Reduction in taxes, which are a withdrawal, acts as a stimulus. More disposable income will induce people to spend more, demand more goods and services; firms will expand production, create new jobs, taking on more people. As a result output, income and employment will all rise.
(c) This is a reduction of an injection as government indirect expenditure is reduced. Parents receiving a smaller child benefit payment will have less income to spend. This will reduce their demand for goods and services, which in turn will cause firms to cut down on production of goods and services. As a result, output and employment will fall.
(d) This is an increase in export, which represents an increase in injection. Foreign demand for domestically produced goods and services increases, inducing British firms to produce more: output, income and employment will all rise as a result.
(e) This is an increase in investment, which represents an increase in an injection: output, income and employment will all rise as a result.

STABILITY OF EQUILIBRIUM

What happens if something intervenes to upset the equilibrium of the economic system? What happens if the withdrawals planned by some groups of people in the economy are greater or smaller than the injections planned by other economic agents? Will the economy be in **disequilibrium** forever, or will it find its equilibrium again? What happens when the economy is in disequilibrium?

The answer to this question is that the economy will eventually reach a new equilibrium, at a higher or lower level of income and output accordingly. This is what we mean when we say that the **economic system is stable**. It will not carry on being off-course for ever. But how?

If withdrawals exceed injections, then the level of national income and output will begin to fall. When will it stop falling? As output and income fall, withdrawals fall too. This is because the level of withdrawals is directly related to the level of income. The falling level of income will reduce the size of the withdrawals, until withdrawals are equal to injections once more and the economy's equilibrium is restored.

Why this is so can be easily explained: people's savings are determined by their income. Savings, remember, represent a withdrawal of funds from the circular flow. As income falls, so do people's savings: withdrawals will be reduced. As income levels fall, so do taxes: the government will collect lower income taxes, as fewer people have jobs and incomes are generally lower; expenditure taxes, like VAT, will also be lower as people consume less. So, withdrawals represented by taxes will fall. As income falls, so do imports, as people cannot afford expensive holidays or fashionable foreign goods and firms do not need to import quite as many raw materials and other inputs for their production as before, as they are cutting down on production levels.

So in the end the economy will find its equilibrium again, where **actual** (as opposed to planned) **withdrawals** are equal to **actual injections**, but at a lower level of income and output. The same applies, but in reverse, when the economy expands as a result of planned injections being greater than planned withdrawals.

To appreciate fully these important points, we need to develop Keynes's model further and leave behind the simple circular flow model, which is what we do in the next chapter. The circular flow model has fulfilled its function:

- It has helped us to understand that the equivalence between expenditure, output and income determines overall equilibrium in the economy.
- It has further helped us to understand how that equilibrium is affected by withdrawals and injections.
- It has also helped us to understand that, according to Keynes, the level of output and employment alters and adjusts to changes in the level of total expenditure. In the next chapter we develop our analysis of these points using a different theoretical tool, the **Keynesian-cross model** or **aggregate demand model**.

✍ Activity 3. 18

Look at Table 3.6 and explain what it shows.

Table 3.6 UK demand and output, 1994–9 (percentage changes from previous period, seasonally adjusted at annual rates, volume, 1990 prices)

	1993 current prices billion £	1994	1995	1996	1997	1998	1999
Private consumption	406.4	2.6	1.9	3.0	3.8	3.4	2.3
Government consumption	137.8	1.7	1.5	0.8	1.1	1.0	1.2
Gross fixed investment	94.3	2.9	−0.1	1.0	4.1	5.6	3.5
Public[a]	16.7	1.7	−6.9	−18.6	−9.5	0.9	0.8
Private residential	17.1	3.5	0.7	0.3	8.7	7.3	5.1
Private non-residential	60.5	3.2	1.8	6.9	5.8	6.1	3.5
Final domestic demand	638.5	2.4	1.5	2.2	3.3	3.3	2.3
* stockbuilding	0.3[b]	0.5	0.1	−0.2	−0.2	0	0
Total domestic demand	638.8	2.9	1.5	2.0	3.2	3.4	2.3
Exports of goods and services	160.0	9.2	8.0	6.3	6.0	5.3	5.1
Imports of goods and services	167.9	5.4	4.4	7.8	6.6	7.4	5.4
* net exports	−7.9[b]	0.9	0.9	−0.4	−0.3	−0.7	−0.2
* compromise adjustment	0.0[b]	0.0	0.0	0.6	0.1	0.0	0.0
GDP at market prices[c]	630.9	3.8	2.5	2.1	3.0	2.7	2.1
Industrial production[d]	—	4.2	2.2	0.3	1.9	2.3	2.0

Source: OECD, 1998. Estimated values for 1999.
* Contributions to changes in real GDP (as a per cent of real GDP in the previous period).
(a) Including nationalized industries and public corporations.
(b) Actual amount.
(c) Data for GDP in the past are based on a compromise estimate which is the average of the expenditure, output and income estimates of GDP, the company adjustment is the difference between compromise GDP and the expenditure estimate of GDP.
(d) Manufacturing production.

✓ Answer 3.18

Table 3.6 provides a summary of the economic situation in the UK between 1998 and 1999. While the economy continued to expand (percentage changes of GDP at market prices reached highest growth rate in 1997, when GDP grew at 3.4 per cent), growth slowed down considerably to a more sustainable rate of 2.1 per cent in 1999 – pressure of domestic demand too eased up in 1998–9.

CASE STUDY: HAS THE BRITISH ECONOMY REACHED FULL CAPACITY?

Was Britain producing at full capacity its full-employment level of output, its **potential output**, in 1997? If it was, it would have been pointless and in fact quite inflationary to try and stimulate aggregate demand further. The government should have tried to control demand instead. But was it?

The **output gap** – as defined by HM Treasury in the *Financial Statement and Budget Report*, July 1997 – is 'the difference between actual output and a measure of potential or trend output'. The words 'potential' and 'trend' refer to the two different methods of calculating the output gap, which we discuss below.

The output gap – the difference between the maximum level of output the economy can produce and the level of output actually produced – can be used as a measure of demand pressure, i.e. as a measure of the degree of under- or over-heating in the economy. The stronger the economy's performance, the smaller the output gap. If the output gap were to close and be above trend for a sustained period of time, experience suggests that there would tend to be upward pressure on inflation.

This leads economists to redefine **potential output** as **the maximum output the economy can produce consistent with a non-accelerating rate of inflation**. Although we do not want to bring price changes into our discussion as yet, to keep things simple for the moment, we must also be aware of the fact that as the economy approaches its full-employment level of output and the output gap closes, prices will tend rise. This increase in prices merely reflects the fact that the factors of production have become almost fully employed and therefore relatively scarce: to obtain their use firms will have to pay a higher price. While actual GDP in excess of potential GDP can cause inflation to accelerate, as it did in the UK in 1988, actual GDP below potential GDP represents a waste of the economy's resources, as they are not being fully utilized. An output gap of either sign, positive or negative, is likely to cause problems for the economy. It is important, therefore, particularly for policymakers, to be able to estimate the value of potential GDP as accurately as possible. By how can this be done?

How is potential output calculated?

The methods followed to estimate potential GDP are mainly: the **trend method** and the **production function method**.

1 The **trend method** consists of extrapolating a trend growth for the economy from past data. Economists do this by using regression analysis. This method can also be explained graphically. To do so, let's refer back to Figure 1.5, which shows the annual rate of change of UK GDP over the past twenty years. As you can see the growth rate displays a cyclical pattern over the period, with ups and downs associated with booms and recessions. The trend rate is calculated as a straight line that runs across the ups and down of the figure. The straight trend rate line represents potential output, while the other line measures the changes in the rate of growth of actual GDP. When the actual GDP is above the trend line, the economy has a positive output gap and might experience inflation. When the line for actual GDP is below the trend line, the output gap is negative and the economy is producing at below capacity.

2 The **production function method** measures potential output with reference to capacity utilization, that is to changes in available factor resources, such as capital and labour, and their utilization rate. The main factors that need to be taken into account in this calculation are:

■ an estimate of the growth of productive factors such as labour, capital and energy sources;

■ an estimate of the utilization level of these inputs which is consistent with a non-accelerating inflation;

■ an estimate of the productivity of these factors of production, in order to derive an estimate of total factor productivity growth;

■ all these estimates are then combined to obtain an estimate of the potential growth of the economy's output.

As you can well appreciate, it is impossible to measure the output gap with any degree of certainty. Business surveys of capacity utilization provide an indication of short-term capacity pressures in product markets. Surveys of skilled labour shortages, together with other labour market indicators such as unemployment, vacancies and average earnings, can be used to estimate the degree of slack in the labour market. The two then need to be put together to decide whether the economy is exceeding its 'speed limits', whether the red light should flash and brakes be applied. Let's look at what the data tell us about the existence of spare capacity in the UK economy in the second part of the 1990s. We look first at capacity utilization indicators and then at labour market indicators.

✍ Activity 3.19

Look at the results of the CBI survey of capacity utilization in manufacturing plotted in Figure 3.9 and briefly explain its findings.

✓ Answer 3.19

The CBI measure of capacity utilization has been just above its long-run average since mid-1994. However, this refers only to the manufacturing sector. It is unlikely that the economy as a whole was above trend in 1994, so soon after the recession of the early 1990s.

✍ Activity 3.20

Now look at the results of two more surveys of capacity utilization in the UK services and construction industries since the mid-1980s, as shown in Figures 3.10 and 3.11, and comment on their significance.

✓ Answer 3.20

The surveys in Figures 3.10 and 3.11 suggest that capacity utilization may be tighter in the service sector. The British Chambers of Commerce (BCC) survey shows that capacity utilization has continued to rise in services in 1997 and is now above its 1989 level, when demand pressure was undoubtedly high. The Building Employers' Confederation (BEC) survey indicates that capacity utilization is also slightly above its long-run average in construction.

continued opposite

HAS THE BRITISH ECONOMY REACHED FULL CAPACITY?

Figure 3.9 CBI survey of capacity utilization in manufacturing, 1972–96

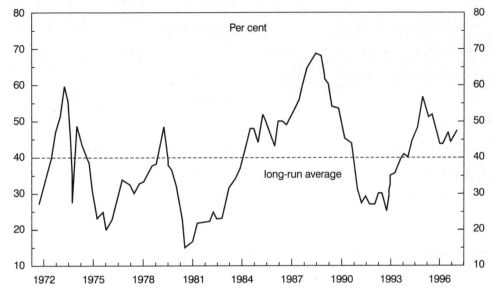

Source: HMT, *Financial Statement and Budget Report,* July 1997

Figure 3.10 BCC survey of capacity utilization in services, 1989–97

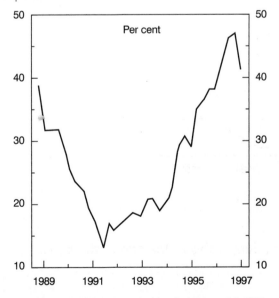

Source: HMT, *Financial Statement and Budget Report,* July 1997

Figure 3.11 BEC survey of capacity utilization in construction, 1984–96

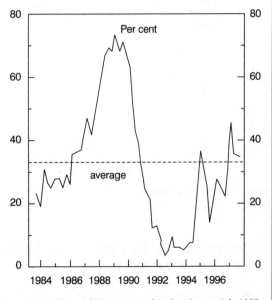

Source: HMT, *Financial Statement and Budget Report,* July 1997

continued overleaf

HAS THE BRITISH ECONOMY REACHED FULL CAPACITY?

Red lights?

Combining these findings on capital and labour utilization, what conclusion should one reach? Has the UK economy reached its speed limits in 1997, with a rate of unemployment of 5.6 per cent? For reasons that will become clearer when we discuss inflation, it is possible for inflation to rise even with a negative output gap, i.e. with the economy operating below its supply potential and unemployed labour, if the economy is growing very fast. This is what economists call the **speed limit effect**.

✍ Activity 3.21

The analysis developed so far can be turned on its head. To do this, try and consider what high levels of capacity utilization may also reflect.

✓ Answer 3.21

High levels of capacity utilization are reached when firms are producing as much as they can, given the equipment, capital and labour available. Firms produce at full capacity when spending is high and orders for prod-

ucts pour in. Hence high levels of capacity utilization are certainly an indication of the pressure of demand. However, they also reflect – and this is when we turn the analysis on its head – the weakness of firms' capital investment in recent years. Capacity in a business sector can be easily reached if capacity is very limited because additions to capital stock have been limited. This has been the case in the manufacturing sector in recent years. Since manufacturing growth has slowed, but the service sector output has accelerated, this has been reflected in the acceleration in service sector earnings and an unbalanced growth. We discuss the UK unbalanced growth problem in the case study at the end of Chapter 4.

The output gap: a conclusion

To conclude, as shown in Figure 3.12 below, the UK economy has been running into speed limits in the service and, albeit less so, in the manufacturing sector in 1997. However, this result on its own is not enough to imply that the output gap in the economy as a whole has turned positive. The evidence overall suggests that the output gap is now close to zero.

Figure. 3.12 Actual and trend output growth, 1990–97

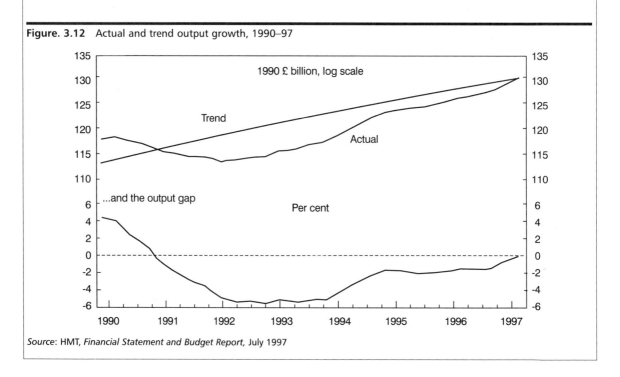

Source: HMT, *Financial Statement and Budget Report*, July 1997

☆ **For revision of this chapter, see the Chapter Summaries at the end of the book, starting on page 411.**

4 Demand-side economics: Simple Keynesian model

Objectives

After studying this chapter, you will be able to:

- understand the role of aggregate demand in the Keynesian model;
- explain what is meant by aggregate demand and what its components are;
- explain what affects the demand for consumption goods;
- explain what affects investment demand;
- understand how investment affects economic growth;
- understand what is meant by the multiplier effect;
- understand how overall economic equilibrium is achieved;
- understand how monetary conditions affect the economy;
- explain inflation and unemployment within the simple Keynesian model.

FROM THE CIRCULAR FLOW TO THE KEYNESIAN MODEL

Before we move on, let's summarize what we have learnt so far.

- We have learnt to describe our economy through a set of **data**. We measure the level of economic activity through a system of **national accounts**, compiled in three alternative ways. We also know the limitations of those figures.
- We understand what we want to explain with the help of macroeconomic theory. We want to explain how economies can reach and maintain a state of equilibrium, where the greatest possible output is produced, full employment is achieved together with price stability, and external balance, a balance of payments equilibrium, is also maintained. This is an enormous undertaking.
- The circular flow model has helped us to give substance to the abstract notion of equilibrium. We now understand that the economic system can only be in equilibrium when:

total output = total expenditure = total income.

If that is not the case, something will have to change and the situation cannot be described as one of equilibrium.

- We can express this using symbols and can write the condition for macroeconomic equilibrium as:

$$Y = E.$$

- We now also know that there are different categories of spending that make up total expenditure (E) based on the economic agents who do the spending, that is, households, firms, government and foreigners:

$$E = C + I + G + (X - M)$$

- **Leakages** or **withdrawals** of money from the circular system of the economy cause the flow of expenditure to be less than output. The money spent buying domestically produced goods and services is not enough to pay for all the goods and services produced; some will remain unsold. If this happens, producers will have to review their production plans and adjust them accordingly. These

reductions in the flow of spending (leakages or withdrawals) occur when:
— people save some of their income (S for saving);
— the government imposes direct or indict taxes (T for taxes);
— British people, firms, government, buy foreign goods and services (M for imports).

■ At the same time, however, there are injections of fresh money into the economy, which is used to purchase the economy's output, in addition to consumption expenditure (C), which is financed by households' current income. These injections are:
— money that firms use to finance their **investments** in capital equipment (I), which they either had put aside as past saving or borrow from financial institutions;
— money that the government **spends** in various forms on the economy (G);
— money that people in other countries spend to purchase British-made goods (X).

■ So despite the fact that leakages out of the circular flow of the domestic economy reduce expenditure and threaten overall equilibrium, this equilibrium can be restored or maintained if injections of money into the flow are of the same magnitude as the withdrawals, and sustain total expenditure.

■ Equilibrium in the economy can then also be thought of as equilibrium between injections and withdrawals. If the money injected into the flow equals the money that leaks out, there will be no 'shortage of spending', total expenditure will still be equal to total output and nothing will have to change.

Instead of writing:

$$E = Y$$

as our equilibrium condition, we can equally write:

$$W = J$$

as our equilibrium condition, remembering that:

W = J	
S	I
T	G
M	X

where it is the overall balance between withdrawals and injections in the economy that matters rather than

the individual balancing of saving with investment, tax revenue with government expenditure and imports with exports.

ROLE OF DEMAND IN THE MACROECONOMY

We have reached an important point. We are now in a position to say what **maintains equilibrium** in the economy: it is the equivalence between spending and production. For the system to be in equilibrium, total spending must be equal to total output, or aggregate demand must be equal to aggregate supply:

$$E = Y$$

or:

$$AD = AS.$$

This is the economy's **equilibrium condition**. Remember how we defined equilibrium earlier: equilibrium is a situation which, once reached, will be maintained unaltered unless something intervenes to change it from the outside. But if the system is not in equilibrium and not all output produced finds a buyer, if $E < Y$ something will have to change. What will change, according to Keynes, is the level of output.

It is worth remembering at this point the assumption that we made at the beginning, which we will eventually drop, namely that prices do not change. Prices do not increase, despite the fact that firms supply more, as we assume that the firms' costs do not go up (which is not a very realistic assumption sustainable in the long run); nor do prices fall, when firms see their stocks of unsold goods piling up in warehouses. This simplifying assumption forces us to focus on the role of demand in the determination of output. This is an assumption which is possibly correct only in the short run, before prices have had time to change and react to changes in demand. The Keynesian model we are developing here is more likely therefore to be relevant for changes in output in the short run.

The monetarists, like the classical economists before them, disagree with this model. Their objections, which are examined in Chapter 9, rest on the effect that changes in demand have on both prices and firms' costs. Their approach therefore seems more suitable to explain how output is determined over a longer period, say of ten years or more.

For the moment, we concentrate on Keynes's explanation of what determines the level of output of an economy. According to his model, if the level of total spending is less than the level of output, level of output will change.

✍ Activity 4.1

Try and explain why this might be the case.

✓ Answer 4.1

If total expenditure is not equal to total output, there are only two possibilities:

- total expenditure is smaller than current output;
- total expenditure is greater than current output.

Let's look first at what happens if expenditure is smaller than income and output.

Case One: expenditure is smaller than output ($E < Y$)

This means that not all the output produced is being bought. Stocks of unwanted goods pile up in warehouses, orders to firms fall and firms cut down on their planned production for the following year. To produce less, they will need to employ fewer people and use up less inputs of raw materials and partly finished goods. The firms selling those products to other firms will also experience a reduction in the number of orders placed with them. They too will start to cut down on production. Those made redundant will cut down on their current consumption of goods and services, as they cannot afford as much as before. This will cause a further reduction in expenditure, which will in turn cause a further reduction. The economy will be caught in a process of spiralling contraction, at the end of which total **output** of the economy, total **income** and total **employment** will be **smaller**. The system will eventually stabilize in a position of equilibrium when output has contracted enough to be equal to expenditure once more, but at a lower level. We can summarize this situation in symbols:

$$E < Y \rightarrow Y \downarrow$$

which we can read as follows: if aggregate expenditure is smaller than income and output, then income and output will fall.

Case Two: expenditure is greater than output ($E > Y$)

In a situation where desired expenditure is greater than the current level of output, people will demand goods and services in excess of what is currently available. Existing stocks of wanted goods will be run down and new orders will be placed with firms. Encouraged by new orders which they find difficult to satisfy, firms will plan to increase production for the following period.

This is only possible, however, if there are still unemployed resources in the economy (in terms of people available for work, raw materials and partly finished goods, etc.) that firms can draw into production, to increase their output. They will take on more people and in turn place orders with other firms for more raw materials and other inputs needed. Capital goods industries will in turn expand production and take on more people.

People who have now got jobs, will be better off than before and consume more. The demand for goods and services will increase further, in a virtuous circle of greater demand and greater spending, greater output, income and employment. The economy's output will grow to accommodate the increase in demand, provided there are unused resources in the economy that can be put to some use. If this is not the case and the economy has already reached its full-employment level of output, the excess of aggregate demand over aggregate supply will only cause prices to rise. To summarize this situation in symbols, we can say that if:

$$E > Y \rightarrow Y \uparrow$$

assuming unused resources in the economy, particularly labour, and assuming that for the moment prices and wages do not change.

This is a very important point, which represents the cornerstone of the entire Keynesian model. The conclusion we have reached is that output and income are demand determined. The level of aggregate demand in the economy, or total desired expenditure, determines the level of supply, how much the economy is producing:

- What determines the level of output of an economy?
- Why do some economies expand faster than others?

The answers would seem to be: given the availability of resources, the strength of the economy's aggregate demand determines how much the economy will actually produce. **Supply adjusts to demand**.

This is a very powerful statement. An equally powerful conclusion follows from it. To produce output firms need resources, in particular labour. The greater the output produced, the greater the employment or the lower the unemployment in the economy. If the level of expenditure in the economy, the economy's aggregate demand, determines the level of output – how much the economy produces – then it is demand that also determines the level of employment.

If this is so, then we have found an answer, or perhaps just the beginning of an answer, to the other crucial question which macroeconomics wants to settle: what determines the level of employment or, more appropriately, of unemployment in an economy? What causes unemployment? The answer can be presented as a syllogism. The demand for labour, the number of jobs created in an economy, depends on the level of output produced. This, in turn, depends on the level of demand. Hence, the level of employment (or unemployment) depends on the level of demand.

To find the cure from an illness, the doctor needs to understand what is causing the illness in the first place. Similarly with unemployment, Keynes thought he had identified its cause: lack of demand in the economy. From that, the cure follows: stimulate demand. If people bought more goods and services (consumption expenditure), if firms bought more machinery and equipment (investment expenditure), if governments built more hospitals and schools (government expenditure), if foreigners came to Britain on holiday in greater numbers and spent more money on British goods and services (export expenditure), more jobs would be created to satisfy all those increased demands. Essentially, Keynes's cure for the problem of unemployment seemed very straightforward: increase demand and output and employment will rise. **Output is demand determined**.

Activity 4.2

Using symbols, briefly state the condition of equilibrium for the economy. Explain what would happen, according to Keynes, if the equilibrium condition is not met.

Answer 4.2

Equilibrium condition: total expenditure is equal to total output. All that is produced is also bought.

$$E = Y$$

if $E \neq Y$ and $E < Y \rightarrow Y \downarrow$

if $E \neq Y$ and $E > Y \rightarrow Y \uparrow$

assuming the economy is not already employing all the productive resources available. We can express the same in terms of withdrawals and injections. To say that $E < Y$ is the same as saying that $W > J$

if $W > J \rightarrow Y \downarrow$ (output $\downarrow$ income $\downarrow$ employment $\downarrow$)

if $W < J \rightarrow Y \uparrow$ (output $\uparrow$ income $\uparrow$ employment $\uparrow$).

✍ Activity 4.3

Why are we concerned with the level of savings, taxes and imports in our economy?

✓ Answer 4.3

We are concerned with the levels of savings, taxes and imports because savings, taxes and imports represent withdrawals of money from the circular flow of the economy and mean a reduction in total expenditure. An increase in withdrawals from the circular flow reduces aggregate demand and consequently also output and employment.

COMPONENTS OF AGGREGATE DEMAND

In the Keynesian model, the level of aggregate demand or total expenditure in the economy determines the level of output and employment. If demand is strong, output grows and so does employment. If that is so, it then becomes very important to be able to control the level of aggregate demand. To control it, we must understand it. To understand what affects the level of aggregate demand or expenditure becomes crucial.

We know what the **components** of aggregate demand or total expenditure are. We now want to explain **what affects each component**, in order to be able to stimulate or reduce aggregate demand, as the case might be, to maintain equilibrium in the economy. We start off once more from the equilibrium condition:

$$E = Y$$

E is made up of the following components:

$$E = C + I + G + (X - M).$$

To manipulate E, we need to understand what affects each component in turn. We need to understand what affects consumption and investment decisions to be able to change their level. We need to understand what affects government decisions about spending and taxation. We need to understand what affects import and export expenditure so we can restore the external balance or reduce an import leakage.

In the rest of this chapter we focus on the analysis of consumption and investment decisions. We look at government policies in Chapters 5, 6 and 7 and at the international sector in Chapter 10. Even without explaining what determines them, by the end of this chapter we will be able to incorporate government spending and international transactions into our analysis, to determine the economy's equilibrium output.

In the slightly more formal Keynesian model developed here, two important assumptions hold, unless otherwise stated. We assume that prices remain constant and that there are unemployed resources, in particular unemployed labour, in the economy.

Because we are assuming for the moment that prices to not change in response to changes in aggregate demand or aggregate supply conditions, we continue to develop our analysis of the macrosystem using the concepts of total expenditure and total output. As we said at the beginning of this chapter, total expenditure is the economy's aggregate demand for a given price level, just as total output is the economy's aggregate supply for a given price level. We relax the assumption that prices do not change in Chapter 10, where we look at what happens to output and employment when demand and supply conditions change, together with prices. At that point we cease to use the concepts of total expenditure and total output and refer instead to aggregate demand – the total amount of output the economy demands at each price level – and aggregate supply – the total amount of output firms in the economy as a whole are prepared to supply at each price level.

✍ Activity 4.4

Interpret the data provided by Tables 4.1 and 4.2 and Figure 4.1.

✓ Answer 4.4

Total expenditure is made up by consumers' expenditure, gross fixed investment, government consumption and exports. As Table 4.1 shows, half of total expenditure of the UK economy in 1997 was accounted for by consumers' expenditure (49.7 per cent). So consumers' expenditure is the single largest component of aggregate demand. Gross fixed investment accounts for 12 per cent of total expenditure, with private sector investment representing 10.9 per cent of gross fixed

investment. The second largest category of expenditure is exports, which represents 22.3 per cent of total expenditure. However, net exports, as shown in Table 4.2, are often negative. Government expenditure on goods and services represents 16 per cent of total expenditure.

As figures in Table 4.2 show, domestic demand, sustained by consumers' expenditure and in turn fuelled by building societies' windfall gains, grew by one percentage point in one year, jumping from 2¾ per cent in 1996 to 3¾ in 1997, to slow down marginally to 3¼ per cent in 1998. The increase in consumers' expenditure compensated for the decrease in government expenditure, which actually decreased in real terms in 1997 and 1998. Export demand, which had grown very strongly in 1994 (+ 9 per cent) thanks to the relative weakening of sterling, has also slowed down, increasing by 5 per cent in 1998. The share of total final expenditure of both private and public investment recovered from the 1995 low (+1 per cent), showing a rate of growth of 6 per cent in 1998. In 1998, total final expenditure grew by 3 per cent, while the growth in export demand was more than compensated by the growth in imports of goods and services (+ 7¾)

CONSUMPTION DEMAND

Households buy the goods and services they need to use, to consume. They perform what economists call

Table 4.1 UK GDP and shares of expenditure, 1991–7

Annual	Gross domestic product at current factor cost	Total final expenditure (current market prices) (£mn)	Percentage share of total expenditure					
			Consumers' expenditure	General government consumption	Gross fixed investment			Exports
					General government	Public corporations	Private sector	
1991	495 900	716 131	51.0	17.3	1.7	0.5	11.4	18.7
1992	516 458	747 111	51.1	17.7	1.7	0.6	10.2	19.0
1993	547 870	799 411	50.8	17.2	1.5	0.6	9.7	20.0
1994	580 135	852 024	50.2	16.9	1.5	0.6	9.8	20.8
1995	608 090	908 536	49.1	16.4	1.4	0.6	10.0	22.0
1996	642 916	963 928	49.1	16.2	1.1	0.5	10.3	22.5
1997	665 064	988 340	49.7	15.9	0.8	0.4	10.9	22.3

Source: ONS, *Economic Trends*, various years

Table 4.2 UK GDP and its components, 1994–2000 (£billion at 1990 prices, seasonally adjusted)

	Consumers' expenditure	General government consumption	Total fixed investment	Stock-building	Domestic demand	Exports of goods and services	Total final expenditure	*Less* imports of goods and services	*Less* adjustment to factor cost	*Plus* statistical discrepancy[1]	GDP at factor cost
1994	358.2	118.3	99.5	2.6	578.6	154.9	733.6	161.9	74.9	–0.5	496.3
1995	366.7	119.1	100.5	3.8	590.1	163.9	754.0	168.0	76.7	0.1	509.3
1996	376.6	122.4	104.1	2.6	605.8	179.8	785.6	184.7	77.2	0.8	524.5
1997	394.5	120.5	108.7	2.2	625.9	193.9	819.8	201.6	79.8	2.1	504.5
1998	409.5 to 410.8	122.0	114.0 to 114.3	1.2 to 1.5	646.7 to 648.7	200.1 to 200.8	846.8 to 849.5	216.8 to 217.5	80.5 to 80.7	2.3	551.9 to 553.6
1999	416.6 to 420.0	124.6	117.2 to 118.1	2.4 to 3.4	660.7 to 666.1	209.2 to 210.9	869.9 to 877.0	228.6 to 230.4	81.9 to 82.6	2.3	516.7 to 566.3
2000	425.6 to 430.5	127.0	120.0 to 121.4	2.8 to 4.4	675.5 to 683.3	221.7 to 224.3	897.2 to 907.6	241.2 to 244.0	83.8 to 84.8	2.4	574.6 to 581.3
					Percentage changes on a year earlier[2]						
1994	3	2	3	0.5	3	9	4	5	3	0	4
1995	2	1	1	0	2	6	3	4	3	0	3
1996	3½	2½	1¾	–¼	2¾	7	3½	8½	1½	¼	2½
1997	4½	–½	4¾	0	3½	8	4½	9¼	4½	¼	3
1998	3¾ to 4	1¼	4¾ to 5¼	–¼	3¼ to 3¾	3¼ to 3½	3¼ to 3½	7½ to 8	¾ to 1¼	0	2 to 2½
1999	1¾ to 2¼	2	2¾ to 3¼	¼	2¼ to 2¾	4½ to 5	2¾ to 3¼	5½ to 6	1¾ to 2¼	0	1¾ to 2¼
2000	2¼ to 2½	2	2½ to 2¾	0 to ¼	2¼ to 2½	6 to 6¼	3¼ to 3½	5½ to 5¾	2¼ to 2¾	0	2¼ to 2¾

Sources: HMT, *Financial Statement and Budget Report*, November 1995, March 1998

[1] Expenditure adjustment

[2] For stockbuilding and the statistical discrepancy, changes are expressed as a percent of GDP.

Figure 4.1 UK shares of expenditure

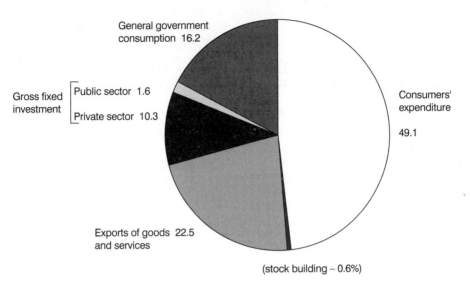

Total final expenditure

Share at current market prices, 1996

General government consumption 16.2

Gross fixed investment

Public sector 1.6

Private sector 10.3

Consumers' expenditure

49.1

Exports of goods 22.5 and services

(stock building – 0.6%)

Source: ONS, *Economic Trends*, July 1997

an act of **consumption expenditure**, they take consumption decisions. We want to understand what affects consumption decisions by households. To do this we develop what economists call a **theory of the consumption function** which explains what affects consumption decisions, and what consumption expenditure is a function of.

The analysis of the consumption function and the multiplier effect are at the core of the Keynesian model. The consumption function presented here is what is known as Keynes's **absolute income hypothesis**. Since 1936, when the *General Theory* was written, consumption behaviour has been the subject of a huge amount of study and empirical testing. More refined versions of Keynes's original theory have subsequently been put forward: the 'relative income hypothesis' by J S Duesenberry in 1947; the 'permanent income hypothesis' by M Friedman in 1957, and the 'life-cycle hypothesis' developed by Ando and Modigliani, provide explanations of consumption behaviour. However, they do not alter Keynes's fundamental analysis.

✍ Activity 4.5

What in your view determines people's consumption?

✓ Answer 4.5

The main behavioural assumptions made by Keynes about people's consumption decisions are the following:

1 Consumption is a function of current disposable income, of income after tax. Let's assume for the moment that there are no taxes in our system. So we can simply say that consumption is a function of income. In symbols, we can express this as follows:

$$C = f(Y).$$

We can also add that consumption is a positive function of income: as income rises, so does consumption.

2 People consume (the economy consumes) goods and services to remain alive, also when their income is zero. To do so they use up past savings, other people's savings (charities), or other people's incomes (that part that is taxed away by the government and given, in the form of benefits, to those in need).

3 Beyond a certain level of income, people will not consume all their income, but only part of it. They will save the rest. We can summarize our assumptions in the following equation:

$$C = a + bY$$

where a is the amount of consumption people do

regardless of their income, even when their income is zero, in order to stay alive, and b is what we call the **marginal propensity to consume**; b measures how much is spent on consumption out of any additional £1 of income.

✍ Activity 4.6

Where does this model of consumption behaviour come from? How can we explore this functional relationship?

✓ Answer 4.6

The relevance of this model of consumers' behaviours can be tested by collecting and examining data on consumers' expenditure and income. Such data are shown in Tables 4.3 and 4.4. They show a sharp upward trend in the demand for consumer durables and services. Another way of looking at the data is to plot disposable income against consumers' expenditure for each year over a longer period (10 or 20 years). If we do that we find the pattern formed displays a considerable regularity, which is explained by the theory.

Figure 4.2 illustrates graphically the assumptions we have just made about the consumption function. First we put in the 45° line. The 45° line, bisecting the right angle, shows us the set of points where the quantity measured on the vertical axis is exactly equal to the quantity measured on the horizontal axis. In Figure 4.2 the 45° line proves a useful device as it indicates the points where consumption is exactly equal to income.

The consumption function shows the desired level of aggregate consumption at each level of aggregate income. With zero income, consumption is the amount indicated by the intercept **a**. This is what we call **autonomous consumption**, because it is not related to the level of income.

The consumption function slopes upwards. This illustrates the fact that as Y goes up, so does C. Consumption is a positive function of income. As income increases, consumption increases too by **b** of **Y**; **b** is the marginal propensity to consume. Let's assume $b = 0.7$. This means that out of each extra £1 of income, 70 pence is consumed.

✍ Activity 4.7

Assuming that the marginal propensity to consume b, is 0.75, calculate the rise in consumption expenditure when income rises by £40 billion.

✓ Answer 4.7

When income rises by £40 billion, consumption rises by $0.75 \times £40$ billion = £30 billion.

Let's pause and note a few points.

■ Consumption is a function of income; it is determined by the level of income. But income is itself determined within our model, by the level of aggregate demand. So we say that consumption is an **endogenous variable**. Its value is determined within the model, by it. Models have two types of variables: **endogenous and exogenous variables**. When variables depend on other variables within the model and are explained by them, we call them endogenous variables. Other variables are not explained within

Table 4.3   UK personal disposable income and consumption, 1991–7

| | £ million, current prices | | | | | £ million 1990 prices | | |
| | Personal income before tax | | | | | | | |
	Total	of which: Wages, salaries and forces' pay	Total personal disposable income	Consumers' expenditure	Personal saving ratio (percentage of personal disposable income)	Real personal disposable income	Total consumers' expenditure	Real personal disposable income at 1990 prices (1990 = 100)
1991	516 470	290 256	405 831	364 972	10.1	377 969	339 915	99.9
1992	547 656	301 239	381 715	381 715	12.2	386 804	339 537	102.2
1993	570 947	308 332	405 462	405 462	11.4	393 125	348 447	103.9
1994	594 371	318 413	427 545	427 454	9.4	396 181	358 230	104.7
1995	636 097	333 558	505 401	446 169	11.7	412 376	364 046	108.9
1996	672 406	348 778	537 677	473 509	11.9	427 690	376 648	113.0
1997	689 132	363 544	547 948	490 764	10.4	430 656	385 712	113.7

Source: Adapted from ONS, *Economic Trends*, July 1995–7

Table 4.4 UK real consumers' expenditure at constant 1990 prices, component categories, 1994–7

	Total consumers' expenditure	Durable goods			Non-durable goods						Services					
		Total	Vehicles	Other durables	Total	Food (household expenditure)	Alcohol and tobacco	Clothing and footwear	Energy products	Other goods	Total	Rent, rates and water charges	Catering	Transport and communi-cation	Monetary services	Other services
Annual																
1994	357 845	36 156	17 259	18 897	159 076	43 458	27 695	23 854	22 720	41 349	162 613	40 803	28 386	36 007	13 795	43 622
1995	364 046	37 664	17 582	20 082	159 380	43 581	27 044	24 852	22 198	41 705	167 002	41 403	29 126	37 060	14 024	45 389
1996	376 648	40 414	18 666	21 748	164 843	44 862	27 559	26 516	23 122	42 784	171 391	41 868	30 712	37 846	15 063	45 902
1997	385 712	41 944	18 772	23 172	168 300	45 932	27 560	27 244	22 632	44 932	175 468	41 136	31 620	37 936	15 888	47 888

Source: Adapted from ONS, Economic Trends, 1997

Figure 4.2 The consumption function

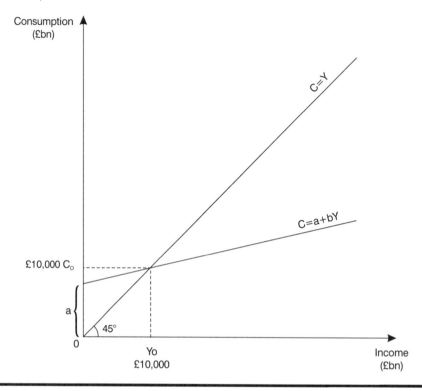

the model, but instead they are taken as given. We call these variables exogenous. Withdrawals such as savings, taxes and imports, as we see, are also a function of income. They too are endogenous variables. Injections, on the contrary, as the word suggests, are determined **outside the system**. Their value is determined by other factors, and not by income. They are what we call **exogenous variables**.

■ Looking at Figure 4.2, we see that when income levels are low the consumption function lies above the 45° line. This means that aggregate consumption is in excess of aggregate income. This represents a situation in which people with very low income levels may find themselves, having to spend more than they earn merely to survive, either using some of their own past savings (dissaving or negative saving) or borrowing from other people. A country whose national product and income is insufficient to feed its population is in this position of the consumption function. To keep its people alive, the country has to borrow internationally and accumulate international debt; its aggregate level of consumption is greater than its income and output. This is a problem common to many developing countries since the early 1970s.

■ At a given level of income, the consumption function crosses the 45° line. At this point:

$$C = Y.$$

The country consumes all that it produces. Consumption expenditure equals income and output.

■ Beyond this point consumption is less than Y. Part of some people's incomes will go towards savings, payments of taxes and imports. The higher the level of income, the larger the proportion that will go into savings, payment of taxes and imports, the smaller the proportion that will be consumed.

■ From these observations, it follows that the slope of the consumption function is less than the 45° line. The slope is given by the **marginal propensity to consume** (MPC).

■ The **MPC** is the **proportion of any increase in national income that goes on consumption**:

$$MPC = \Delta C / \Delta Y.$$

If an increase in income of £10 leads to an increase in consumption of £8, then it must be that the marginal propensity to consume is 8/10 or 0.8. The mpc determines the slope of the consumption function. Being a straight line, the consumption function has a constant slope, hence the mpc is also constant. No matter whether income is high or low, for every £1 that income rises (measured horizontally), consumption rises by 80p (measured vertically).

■ The **APC** is the **proportion of total national income that is consumed**. The formula is:

$$APC = \frac{C}{Y}.$$

If when Y = £100 billion, C = £90 billion, then apc = 90/100 = 0.9.

The consumption function of Figure 4.3 shows an economy's aggregate consumption derived from the equation:

$$C = 100 + 0.75\, Y.$$

This function shows that when income is zero, aggregate consumption is £100bn. As income rises, so does consumption: for every £100bn increase in income, consumption rises by £75bn. The slope of the line is 0.75.

 Activity 4.8

What factors other than people's current income might affect their consumption?

✓ Answer 4.8

People's consumption of goods and services is also affected by the following:

1 **stock of wealth**: i.e. the value of assets they hold, such as properties, shares, etc. The greater the value of people's wealth, for a given level of income, the greater their consumption. For example, suppose you learn that an oil painting you had kept in the loft for many years, is in fact worth £5,000. You sell it at auction and deposit the money in your bank account. How does this sudden increase in your wealth affect your consumption behaviour? The effect of this windfall gain of £5,000 is the same as if you had received a bonus payment at work: you will probably use some of it to buy yourself some new clothes, some CDs, or something for the house. Generally, when wealth increases, there is less need to save for the future out of current income. Hence an increase in wealth raises current consumption and lowers current saving. In macroeconomic terms, the result is the same. An increase in aggregate wealth increases aggregate consumption. Similarly, if wealth decreases, desired consumption will fall.

2 **government benefits**: the higher the benefit payment, the higher consumption and vice versa. The

Figure 4.3 A consumption function

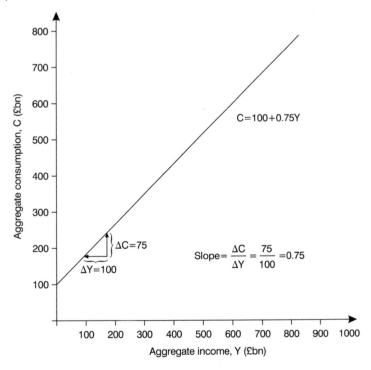

change in benefit payments is equivalent to a change in income and affects consumption demand.

3 **availability and cost of credit**: the greater the availability of credit, the lower its cost, the greater consumption. Lower interest rates also tend to discourage saving, therefore increasing consumption.

4 **expectations of future price changes** or of **future income changes**: expectations of increases will lead, in both cases, to increased consumption and vice versa;

5 **distribution of income**: a redistribution of income from the rich to the poor will increase aggregate consumption as the marginal propensity to consume (mpc) of people on lower income is higher than that of people in higher income brackets. (This is shown by a change in the slope of the consumption function, which becomes steeper.)

6 **tastes and attitudes**: as empirical research demonstrates, people in some economies are more spendrift than in others. Social attitudes are also subject to change.

With the exception of 2, 3 and 5, changes in any of these other non-income factors, will cause a change in consumption that is shown by a **shift** of the consumption function, up or down, as in Figure 4.4. Movements along the curve show the effects on consumption of changes in disposable income.

✍ Activity 4.9

Using Figure 4.4 as a reference, show the effect of the following on the consumption function (consider the initial effects only):

(a) decrease in child benefits paid by government;
(b) 1% cut in the interest rates;
(c) policy of income redistribution from the rich to the poor.

✓ Answer 4.9

(a) Movement along the consumption function: C↓.
(b) This will have two effects. It will increase the incomes of people with mortgages. Therefore their consumption will increase (movement up along a given consumption function). But it will also discourage saving and make buying by credit easier, hence increasing consumption (this changes the slope of the consumption function, which becomes steeper).
(c) Change in the slope of the consumption function, which becomes steeper: C↓.

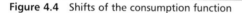

Figure 4.4   Shifts of the consumption function

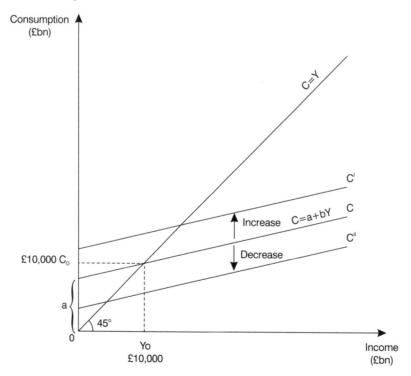

SAVING FUNCTION

If, beyond a certain level of income, not all income is consumed, then it must be saved. The more people spend on consumption, the less they will save and vice versa. There are two points that need to be stressed here:

1 Saving in this model is a withdrawal. It is income not spent on consumption, which is withdrawn from circulation and does not flow back to firms to finance further production.

2 How much saving a person does is automatically decided by that person's consumption. For example, when you are presented with your birthday cake and asked to cut the first slice for yourself, how big you make your own slice determines how much is left for the others. Once consumers have chosen how much to consume out of their current income, they have also by default chosen how much to save, and vice versa. If people's consumption decisions are determined by their disposable income, then so are their saving decisions. Therefore, if saving is defined as the part of income that is not consumed, saving can be said to be a function of income. The saving function is shown in Figure 4.5.

The saving function shows the amount of desired savings at each income level. Since we are assuming that all income is either saved or spent on consumption, the saving function can be derived from the consumption function and vice versa. We define households' saving as that part of their income which is not spent on consumption:

$$S \equiv_{Def} Y - C \tag{1}$$

and since:

$$C = a + bY \tag{2}$$

by substituting equation (2) in (1), we can derive the function for saving as follows:

$$S = Y - (a + bY) \tag{3}$$

$$S = a - bY + Y \tag{4}$$

$$S = -a + (1 - b)Y. \tag{5}$$

The **marginal propensity to save** (**mps**) is the proportion of an increase in income that is saved. It tells us how much people save out of an additional unit of income:

$$MPS = \frac{\Delta S}{\Delta Y}.$$

Consumption and saving decisions are like a cake in two slices. If 1 represents the whole cake and b the

Figure 4.5 The saving function

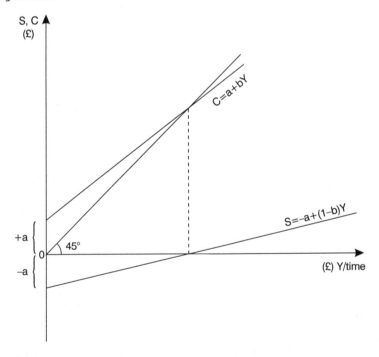

part you eat, $(1-b)$ is the part you save. It follows from what we have said about the 'residual' nature of the saving (or consumption) decision that if b is the marginal propensity to consume, $(1-b)$ must be the marginal propensity to save. The assumption made earlier about the value of the marginal propensity to consume, b, being between zero and one, means that the marginal propensity to save, $(1-b)$, is also between zero and one.

If the mpc is 0.8, the mps is $(1-0.8) = 0.2$. The mps is given by the slope of the saving function, as shown in Figure 4.5.

✍ Activity 4.10

This involves a little algebra.

Let C be consumption, S savings and Y disposable income. Suppose the consumption function is as follows:

$$C = 200 + 2/3\ Y.$$

(a) What would the formula be for the savings function?
(b) When would savings be zero, or at which level of income would consumption be equal to income (nothing left to save)?

✓ Answer 4.10

Remember that the savings function $S = -a + (1-b)\ Y$ is derived from the definition of savings as that part of income not spent on consumption:

$$S \equiv_{Def} Y - C. \qquad (1)$$

If we substitute the consumption function given above into (1), we obtain:

$$S = Y - (200 + 2/3\ Y). \qquad (2)$$

Rearranging (2) we obtain:

$$S = -200 + (1 - 2/3)\ Y \qquad (3)$$

$$S = -200 + 1/3\ Y \qquad (4)$$

which is the answer to (a). The answer to (b) is obtained by equating (4) to zero:

$$0 = -200 + 1/3\ Y \qquad (5)$$

$$1/3\ Y = 200 \qquad (6)$$

$$Y = 600. \qquad (7)$$

Saving is zero when income is 600. At that level of income, all income is consumed.

The paradox of saving

Keynes's view of saving, which we have just introduced, is more powerful than it might seem at first.

Let's try and understand its implications, together with the famous paradox to which it leads.

In the Keynesian model saving is a withdrawal. The more we save, the less we consume; the less we consume, the less the economy demands, the less is produced. If less is produced, less employment is generated, together with lower incomes and outputs, which leads to a vicious circle of further contraction.

In the old days of the classical economists saving was regarded as a virtue to be encouraged, good for the individual and the economy alike. Keynes's view of saving as a withdrawal represents a radical departure from the view held by the classical economists who preceded him. Classical economists held what is known as the 'loanable fund theory of investment'. According to this theory saving is a function of the interest rate and not of income. The higher the interest rate, the more people save. The more they save, the more funds they make available to financial institutions, who will then consequently lend at a lower price, charging a lower interest rate. The lower interest rate will encourage people to take up loans and firms to borrow to finance their investments. Investment will therefore increase as well, as a result of increased saving. The economy will not contract. Output and employment will be the same as before, as the increase in saving will be automatically compensated by an equivalent increase in investment: the system will always be in equilibrium.

This analysis might have applied in the old days of sole traders and single entrepreneurs, whose act of saving (profits not consumed but ploughed back into the business) was also directly an act of investment. This analysis is no longer relevant; in fact is positively misleading when applied to contemporary economies where the act of saving and the act of investment are performed by different economic agents for different reasons. Increased saving does not lead to an increase in investment, if anything it has the opposite effect, argued Keynes. The decision 'not to have dinner tonight' reduces the demand for dinner tonight and reduces the business of providing dinner tonight, but does not add to the demand for dinner tomorrow. First, increased saving causes a reduction in demand, which is likely, if anything, to cause a reduction and not an increase in investment. Second, as the paradox of thrift shows, although the proportion of income that people wish to save may have increased, it does not follow that increased actual saving will be forthcoming. Desired saving increases, but actual saving remains the same, as income falls as a result. Third, even assuming that actual saving increased and people succeeded in saving more as a whole, speculation and uncertainty on the stock market may prevent interest rates from falling far enough and fast enough to cause a compensating increase in investment. Fourth, as we already stressed, the investment decision on the part of firms, is made not only on the basis of interest rates, but also on the state of confidence in demand and the economy, which an increase in saving could only cause to contract.

The classical economists believed that what is good for the individual must also be good for the economy as a whole. What is good for the individual – argued Keynes instead – is not good for the economy as a whole; what is more, it may not be possible. If everyone at a crowded football match stands on tiptoe to get a better view; nobody will be able to see any better and everybody will be more uncomfortable. The same applies to saving: one individual may succeed in saving more and consuming less out of his or her income, but if everyone tried to do that nobody would succeed in saving more; in the end all might end up saving less. Hence the paradox, but how do we explain it?

Suppose that at a given level of income consumers decide to save more. What will happen to output and saving? In order to save more at their initial level of income, people cut down on their consumption. Decreased consumption in turn decreases demand, which decreases production. What will happen to saving? As people are now saving more at any level of income, this will tend to increase saving. But on the other hand, the decreased consumption lowers income and this will lower saving. Can we say what the net effect will be? Remember what we said in Chapter 3 about the economy's equilibrium condition. The economy will settle at that level of output where aggregate demand equals aggregate supply, or where saving equals investment:

$$E = Y$$

or:

$$S = I.$$

Nothing has happened to change the level of investment which, for the time being at least, is the same. If consumption decreases as people save more, it must follow that income falls. As income falls, the actual amount saved (not the proportion of income saved) also falls. Actual saving remains equal to actual investment, but at a lower level of income. Desired saving, however, represents a larger proportion of people's current income. Attempts by people to save more lead both to a decline in output and to unchanged saving. This result is known as the **paradox of thrift**. We can show this result using a numerical example and also a diagram.

✎ Activity 4.11

The data given below refer to an hypothetical economy. The three stages represent changes through time. Study the data and explain these results.

Stage One	Stage Two	Stage Three
MPS = 20%	MPS = 25%	MPS = 25%
Y = 100	Y = 80	Y = 60
C = 80	C = 60	C = 45
I = 20	I = 20	I = 15
S = 20	S = 20	S = 15

✓ Answer 4.11

When the economy is at Stage One, the initial level of income and output is 100, consumers consume 80 (MPC = 0.8) and save 20 (MPS = 0.2), while investment is given at 20. At Stage Two people decide they want to save more: instead of saving 20 per cent of their income, they now want to save 25 per cent (MPS = 0.25). They cut down on consumption (MPC = 0.75) and as a result, given that the injection represented by investment is fixed at 20, output and income will fall to 80. When income is 80, withdrawals are equal injections once more, as saving (25 per cent of 80 = 20) is equal to investment (20). People succeed in saving a larger percentage of their income, 25 per cent, but because income has fallen from 100 to 80 the actual amount they save remains the same, 20 as before, but at a lower level of income. Remember the effect of tiptoeing at a football match: everybody is more uncomfortable and nobody gets a better view. You may think that the result of saving remaining unchanged has something to do with the assumption that investment is fixed. If we relax that assumption in Stage Three and allow the investment level to change, do you think investment will increase? If we allow investment to change with output we obtain a result which is even more dramatic. Attempts by people to save more lead to a fall in demand and output. In Stage Three, faced with falling demand and output, firms will cut down their investment expenditure from 20 to 15, causing a further fall in output and income (60) and consequently a *decrease* in saving (15).

Does saving have a negative effect on the economy? Contrary to common belief, higher saving does depress demand and causes recessions in the short run. Over a longer period of time, more complex mechanisms come into play which might lead to higher saving causing higher income. In the short run, however, the paradox does seem to apply.

■ If saving increases as income increases, to maintain equilibrium in the economy at a higher level of income, investment must also increase. But is this certain to happen, given that investment is not a function of income and does not increase as income increases? If it does not, is there another component of aggregate demand that could increase instead, to balance out the withdrawal represented by increased saving? Can governments intervene? We shall soon need to revisit our initial equilibrium condition.

✍ Activity 4.12

Study Figure 4.6 and explain what it shows.

✓ Answer 4.12

Figure 4.6 is based on empirical data for income, consumption and saving for the period from 1965 to 1997 which are shown as percentage changes on a year earlier. A forecast is offered for 1998–2000. The rate of consumption is forecast to fall throughout 1998 and 1999 to pick up again marginally in the year 2000.

As Figure 4.6 shows, 1997 saw strong growth in personal spending. Aggregate consumers' expenditure grew by about 4 per cent, well above its long-run average and more than enough to account for the growth of GDP in 1997. Spending on consumer durables grew by almost 11 per cent. The rapid growth in consumers' expenditure can be explained by changes in income and

wealth, as personal disposable income grew by about 4 per cent in 1997, driven by greater employment, higher average earnings and personal sector financial wealth growth of £375bn (a 25 per cent increase) due to a buoyant equity market, to which windfall payments received by households during 1997 from the flotation of building societies and insurance companies added another £35 billion. Higher interest rates contributed to the slowing down of consumers' expenditure in 1998. The major uncertainty for 1998 and 1999 was the degree to which consumers cushioned spending through lower saving as income growth slowed.

The persistence of high personal sector saving was one of the major features of the upswing in 1996–7. This contrasts with the 1980s when the saving ratio, as a percentage of disposable income, fell sharply. The saving ratio in Britain is expected to be at around 9 per cent by 2000. As Table 4.5 shows, this is the third lowest, after Canada and the USA among the Group of 7 most industrialized countries. In Europe, the UK has the lowest saving rates after Finland and Hungary.

TOTAL EXPENDITURE

If we ignore government expenditure (G) and net export ($X - M$) for the time being, we can define total

Figure 4.6   UK personal sector consumption, income and saving, 1965–97

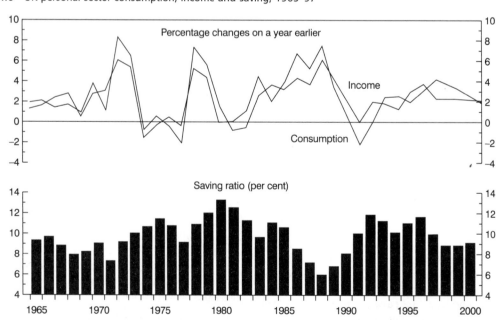

Source: HMT, *Financial Statement and Budget Report*, 1998

Table 4.5 Household saving rates, selected OECD countries, 1980–96 (Percentage of disposable household income)

	1980	1981	1982	1983	1984	1985	1986	1987	1988	1989	1990	1991	1992	1993	1994	1995	1996	Estimates and projections 1997	1998	1999
USA	8.8	9.6	9.3	7.1	9.0	7.4	6.7	5.5	5.7	5.3	5.5	6.1	6.0	5.4	4.5	5.1	4.4	4.0	4.2	4.4
Japan	17.9	18.4	16.7	16.1	15.8	15.6	15.6	13.8	13.0	12.9	12.1	13.2	13.1	13.4	13.3	13.1	11.9	11.2	11.1	11.5
Germany	12.8	13.6	12.7	10.9	11.4	11.4	12.3	12.6	12.8	12.4	13.8	12.9	12.8	12.2	11.6	11.3	11.4	11.0	11.0	11.3
France	17.6	18.0	17.3	15.9	14.5	14.0	12.9	10.8	11.0	11.7	12.5	13.2	13.6	14.1	13.6	14.5	12.8	13.6	13.4	13.2
Italy	23.4	22.4	20.8	23.3	21.5	19.8	19.0	18.3	17.3	15.9	17.4	17.6	17.3	15.5	15.1	14.7	12.9	11.7	11.3	10.9
UK	13.4	12.6	11.3	9.7	11.1	10.7	8.6	7.3	6.2	6.9	8.2	10.1	12.0	11.5	10.4	11.7	11.9	10.8	10.1	10.1
Canada	13.6	15.4	18.2	14.8	15.0	13.3	10.7	9.2	9.7	10.4	9.7	9.9	10.3	9.6	7.6	7.0	4.6	1.4	1.7	2.3
Australia	10.8	9.7	8.3	8.6	9.9	7.4	7.1	58	6.2	6.3	6.6	5.0	4.4	2.7	3.5	3.9	4.9	4.7	4.6	4.3
Austria	11.5	9.4	10.4	8.3	8.2	8.6	10.5	12.1	10.1	11.1	12.2	13.2	10.2	9.1	10.1	10.2	8.5	8.5	9.0	9.5
Belgium	18.3	18.9	15.8	16.1	15.1	13.1	14.6	13.5	14.4	16.4	16.3	18.1	18.8	20.6	18.4	17.6	16.3	16.3	16.3	16.4
Denmark	—	—	—	—	—	—	—	—	7.5	8.5	11.3	11.0	9.8	8.6	4.8	59	5.3	4.2	5.0	4.6
Finland	5.4	4.5	5.2	5.8	4.5	3.8	2.5	2.9	-1.2	-0.6	0.4	5.1	7.1	5.2	0.4	3.6	1.3	0.8	0.3	0.6
Greece	—	—	—	—	—	—	—	—	—	—	—	—	—	—	—	—	—	—	—	—
Hungary	—	—	—	—	—	—	—	—	—	—	—	—	—	8.1	10.0	11.0	11.8	13.0	12.8	12.8
Ireland	17.2	19.2	21.0	19.4	19.7	17.9	16.3	17.1	13.0	11.4	12.6	13.1	12.3	13.7	10.5	9.8	9.4	8.2	8.3	8.4
Korea	9.1	9.1	11.0	10.8	13.7	13.5	18.5	21.8	23.4	21.7	19.8	21.9	20.2	18.6	17.9	18.0	17.8	18.0	16.5	15.2
Netherlands	1.8	3.3	3.4	-0.4	-0.6	0.1	2.8	2.3	2.2	4.0	5.8	1.1	2.3	0.8	1.0	0.8	1.2	0.9	1.2	1.3
New Zealand	10.6	11.8	9.0	6.9	6.6	5.7	5.2	8.0	6.5	6.3	4.2	6.5	4.1	2.7	1.3	1.4	3.0	3.8	3.6	3.5
Norway	2.7	5.3	4.4	4.2	5.0	-1.8	-4.6	-4.6	-1.0	1.1	2.2	4.1	5.8	6.8	6.0	5.6	6.1	6.6	5.9	5.4
Portugal	24.3	24.1	24.1	22.4	23.2	24.3	21.8	21.4	17.3	16.1	17.3	17.2	14.8	12.4	12.4	12.2	10.9	10.8	10.8	10.5
Spain	11.3	12.2	13.2	12.7	11.8	11.6	11.7	9.0	10.3	8.6	10.9	12.1	10.2	13.2	10.9	12.8	12.4	12.5	12.1	11.7
Sweden	6.7	5.1	1.7	2.4	2.1	2.3	1.3	-2.8	-4.8	-4.9	-0.6	3.1	7.7	8.3	8.0	6.5	4.7	2.6	2.4	3.0
Switzerland	0.5	2.2	3.3	2.9	3.4	3.5	4.4	5.8	8.0	9.6	11.2	11.6	11.0	9.9	8.4	8.5	6.5	5.5	5.5	5.7

Source: OECD, Economic Outlook, December 1997

expenditure as the total amount that households wish to spend on consumption goods and services, at each level of income, and that firms wish to spend on investment goods:

total expenditure = consumption + investment.

Investment demand consists of firms' desired or planned additions both to their physical capital (factories and machines) and to their inventories. Inventories are stocks of goods being held for future production or sale. To keep our model as simple as possible, we assume that there is no close connection between the current level of income and output and firms' investment decisions. We say that **investment is autonomous** and we put a bar on the symbol I to remind us of the fact that we take investment as a given amount. We will develop a theory of what determines investment later on in this chapter. There we will discuss the plausibility of this assumption. It is not hard to see that if firms increase their production to meet an increase in demand, they may also decide that they need more machines and so increase their investment in order to do so. For the moment, however, we simply say that investment is a certain amount of spending on

capital by firms which is independent of the level of current income.

Investment expenditure is an exogenous variable: a given amount determined elsewhere, by other factors:

$$I = \bar{I}_o.$$

If we add together the consumption demand and investment demand shown in Figure 4.7 as a straight line, a constant amount I_o, we obtain the economy's aggregate demand or total expenditure function. This expenditure function shows us the behaviour of aggregate demand. Aggregate demand, or total spending rises as income rises, because consumption demand by households, which is part of it, increases as income rises. Aggregate demand, however, also comprises a certain amount of investment expenditure. We still cannot say what affects investment expenditure. We know it is not the current level of income, which is why we show the investment component of aggregate demand as a straight line, a given amount I_o. What we can say, however, is that if investment expenditure increases, so does aggregate demand and vice versa. So the aggregate demand or total expenditure function, leaving government and

Figure 4.7 The total expenditure function

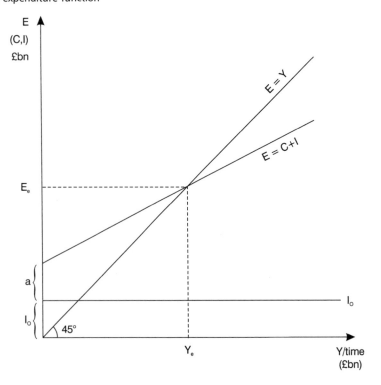

international trade aside for the moment, can be written as follows:

$$E = C + I \qquad (1)$$
$$C = a + bY \qquad (2)$$
$$I = I_o \qquad (3)$$
$$E = a + bY + I_o. \qquad (4)$$

Figure 4.7 shows the total expenditure function as a function of income (Y), where Y_e stands for 'equilibrium level of output' and E_e for 'equilibrium level of expenditure'. Y_e and E_e are at an 'equilibrium level' because at those levels they are equal: $E = Y$. We know they are equal because at those values the total expenditure function crosses the 45° line.

Movements along and shifts of the total expenditure curve

The aggregate demand or total expenditure curve is shown here as a straight line whose position depends on its intercept, the point it starts on the vertical axis, and its slope. The **intercept** is the total amount of autonomous spending: autonomous consumption plus autonomous investment spending. The **slope** is given by the marginal propensity to consume (mpc). For a given level of autonomous demand, changes in income lead to increases in aggregate demand shown as **movements along** a given aggregate demand. All other changes are shown by shifts.

As Figure 4.8 shows, an increase in investment will shift the whole aggregate demand curve up by the same amount. The economy was previously in equilibrium at A, where total expenditure, E_e, measured on the vertical axis, was equal to Y_e, income and output, measured on horizontal axis. We know that at A:

$$E = Y$$

because A is the only point where the aggregate demand curve crosses the 45° line. The 45° line is the set of values of E and Y where $E = Y$. So at A:

$$E = Y.$$

If investment expenditure increases, E is greater than Y by the amount of the increase in investment. The aggregate demand curve shifts up by that amount.

As $E > Y$, assuming that prices are stable and there are unused resources in the economy, output will

Figure 4.8 Effect of an increase in investment on aggregate demand

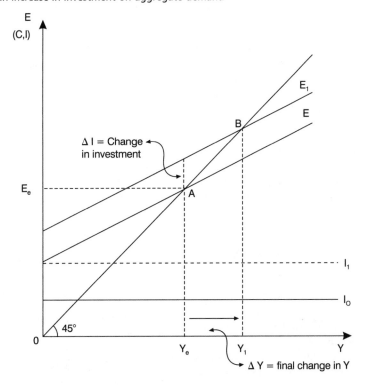

increase and so will income and employment. The economy will grow from Y_e to Y_1, from A to B, where it reaches a new equilibrium point.

The increase in output and income from Y_e to Y_1, ΔY_1, far exceeds the initial increase in investment, ΔI. The injection of new investment causes a greater expansion of output and income. This fact is explained by Keynes with the theory of the multiplier.

THE MULTIPLIER

The multiplier effect, as the name implies, refers to the fact that any injection of expenditure, whether investment, government spending or exports, causes income and output to grow more than the injection itself. This apparently surprising result rests on the assumption that if there are unemployed resources, particularly unemployed labour, in the economy then when expenditure rises and people demand more goods, output also does, as firms step up production to meet the increased demand. So if there is an increase in investment spending, say by £1bn, that money is spent directly to buy capital goods and will end up in the hands of whoever has produced those capital goods. Those firms will be able to produce and sell more than before. They will do so by employing more people. People just taken on will see their income rise; as their income goes up, so will their consumption. As we have just learnt, consumption is a function of income. As better-off workers now demand more goods and services, more will be produced, and so on. By how much Y will grow in the end, as a result of an initial injection, will depend on the marginal propensity to consume: the greater the marginal propensity to consume, the greater the multiplier effect. We can explain this point better with a numerical example.

Suppose a consortium of private firms raise £10mn to invest in a major redevelopment project along the River Thames. At completion of the project, £10mn will have been spent (initial injection) on steel, cement, bricks, timber, tiles, glass, pipes, etc., and construction workers, engineers, plumbers, electricians, consultants, architects, surveyors – all that goes into turning a development project into a built reality. The steel, cement, brick, timber and glass producers or distributors and all the people involved in the realization of the project, who received between them £10mn, will be £10mn better off than before as a group. Their group income has risen by £10mn. We have learnt from studying people's consumption behaviour (the consumption demand) that when their incomes go up they consume part of the increase (mpc × increase) and

save some (mps × increase). Suppose that the marginal propensity to consume is 0.8. In this case, the increase in income of £10mn for the construction people involved in the project will generate a further increase in consumption of £8mn and an increase in saving of £2mn. These people will decide they can now afford to redecorate their houses, buy new kitchens, go on holiday, buy granny an expensive present, and so on. Someone else in the economy will be receiving the extra £8mn now spent: for example, in the furnishing sector, kitchen manufacturers, tour operators, gift shops. They will see their income go up and in turn will consume an extra £6.4mn (0.8 × £8mn, which is the mpc times their increase in income) on other consumption goods, and so on.

The £10mn injected at the beginning by the redevelopment project creates a ripple of extra demand and extra spending in many other sectors of the economy, not just in the construction industry, as people consume part of their income increases on consumption goods. The ripple effect gets smaller and smaller because at each stage of the income expenditure process only part (mpc × increase) of the increase in income is spent. Each increase in income generates a successively smaller increase in consumption.

We need to make three important points here:

1   The increase in expenditure that triggers the whole expansion process, the multiplier effect, does not have to be investment. It can equally be a increase in government spending or an increase in export spending by foreigners; in other words, any injection of autonomous spending.

2   The multiplier process works not only for injections and expansions but also in exactly the same way, in reverse, for withdrawals and contractions. A reduction in investment, for instance, will cause a greater reduction in income and output, because of the multiplier effect.

3   Finally, once we have understood the multiplier effect, we can use a formula to calculate the final change in income, brought about by an initial injection or withdrawal, without having to work through the successive increases or decreases, as we have done in Table 4.5.

The formula to measure the multiplier effect of any injection or withdrawal is as follows:

$$\Delta Y = k\Delta J \ \text{ or } \ \Delta Y = k\Delta W$$

where k is the 'multiplier', a numerical coefficient which is equal to:

$$k = \frac{1}{1-MPC} \ \text{ or } \ k = \frac{1}{MPS}.$$

Figure 4.9 The multiplier effect of an increase in investment

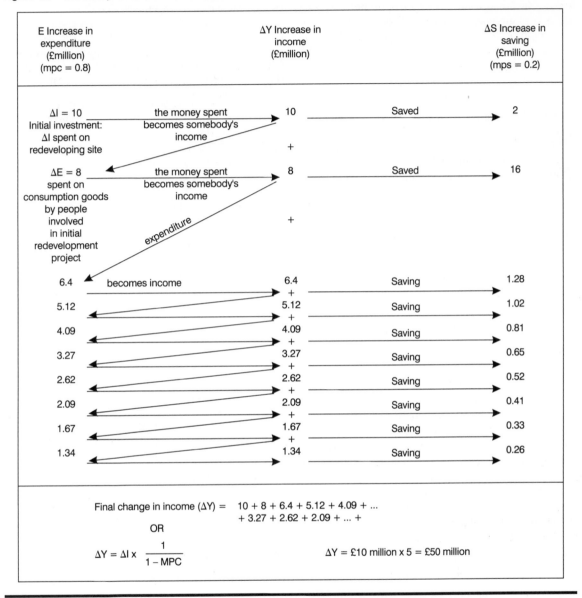

The multiplier is the numerical coefficient used to calculate the final change in income caused by an initial change in any autonomous component of aggregate demand. To calculate the value of the multiplier, you need to know either the value for the marginal propensity to consume or the value of the marginal propensity to save. If, as in our example in Table 4.1, the mpc = 0.8 then the value of the multiplier is calculated as follows:

$$k = \frac{1}{1-MPC} = \frac{1}{1-(0.8)} = \frac{1}{0.2} = 5.$$

To calculate the multiplier effect of the initial injection of £10mn worth of investment, we multiply the injection by 5.

$$\Delta Y = k\Delta I \text{ in our example becomes}$$

$$\Delta Y = 5 \times £10\text{mn} = £50\text{mn}.$$

The final increase in income caused by the initial increase in investment of £10mn is £50mn. We can look at the multiplier the other way round and define it as the ratio of the change in equilibrium output to the change in autonomous spending that causes the change in output:

$$k = \frac{\Delta Y}{\Delta I}.$$

But this is no different from what we said earlier:

$$\Delta Y = k\Delta I.$$

If you knew that the initial change in investment was £10mn and the final change in output was £50mn, then you could calculate the value of the multiplier as:

$$k = \frac{\Delta Y}{\Delta I} = \frac{50}{10} = 5.$$

But remember, the multiplier is more commonly used to calculate the final change in output and income, given an initial change in expenditure. To do that you must multiply the initial change in expenditure by the multiplier:

$$\Delta Y = k\Delta J \text{ or } \Delta Y = k\Delta W$$

where:

$$k = \frac{1}{1-MPC} \text{ or } \frac{1}{MPS}.$$

Until now, for simplicity's sake, we have assumed that income can only be consumed and saved. Saving is the only leakage we have taken into account. We know from our earlier analysis, however, that income also leaks out of the flow of expenditure as taxes or imports. These further leakages, by reducing the ripple effect of successive income increases, reduce the size of the multiplier. The size of the multiplier is reduced by 'withdrawals' (saving, taxation, imports). For a closed economy with no taxes, the basic multiplier is:

$$k = \frac{1}{1-MPC} \text{ or } \frac{1}{MPS}.$$

Taking into account also the possibility of the other leakages, the multiplier becomes smaller:

$$k = \frac{1}{MPS + MPM + MPT}$$

where *MPM* is the marginal propensity to import and *MPT* is the marginal propensity to tax.

📝 Activity 4.13

The value of the multiplier is of vital importance for government stabilization policies, as we shall see in Chapter 5. The value of the multiplier in Britain is calculated on the basis of empirical estimates. In 1990, the mpc of disposable after-tax income was estimated to be 0.75. Every £1 of additional GDP generated approximately 67 pence of disposable income (mpt = 0.33) and the marginal propensity to import was 0.34 (imports in that year were 34 per cent of GDP).

(a) On the basis of these estimates, calculate the value of the multiplier for the British economy in 1990.

(b) In 1970, the marginal propensity to import was 0.25. What would the value of the multiplier be if that rate still applied today?

✓ Answer 4.13

(a) In 1990, the multiplier in the UK was just above 1, which is rather small (1.08).

$$k = \frac{1}{MPS + MPT + MPM} = \frac{1}{0.25 + 0.33 + 0.34} = \frac{1}{0.92} = 1.08.$$

On the basis of this result, we know that £10 worth of injection would generate an increase in income and output equal to £10.8. A very small multiplier effect.

(b)

$$k = \frac{1}{0.25 + 0.33 + 0.25} = \frac{1}{0.83} = 1.20.$$

The multiplier would be greater. An injection of £10 would generate an increase in income and output of £12.00. A lower marginal propensity to import (mpm =0.25 while in case (a) MPM =0.34) increases the size of the multiplier (*k* = 1.20 larger than *k* = 1.08).

📝 Activity 4.14

Suppose the government decides to increase its expenditure by £50bn. What effect will this have on GNP if the marginal propensity to consume is 0.75?

✓ Answer 4.14

Initial injection: ΔG = £50 billion. MPC = 0.75.

$$\text{Multiplier } k = \frac{1}{1-MPC} = \frac{1}{1-(0.75)} = \frac{1}{0.25} = 4.$$

📝 Activity 4.15

By how much must investment rise to bring about a £300mn change in output and income if MPC = 0.80?

✓ Answer 4.15

We need to find the value of initial injection: ΔI = ?

$$\text{Multiplier } k = \frac{1}{1-(0.80)} = \frac{1}{0.2} = 5$$

given that:

$$\Delta Y = k\Delta I$$

$$\Delta I = \frac{\Delta Y}{k}$$

$$\Delta I = \frac{300}{5} = 60.$$

Investment must rise by £60mn.

Let's stress again that the analysis developed so far applies to any change in injections or withdrawals, to a reduction in investment expenditure as well as to an increase: the multiplier analysis still holds, but negatively. A reduction in investment spending, shown by a shift down of the aggregate demand or total expenditure curve, causes a greater reduction in income and output from Y_0 to Y_1. This, again, is shown in Figure 4.10.

OTHER DETERMINANTS OF AGGREGATE DEMAND

The formal analysis of aggregate demand we have developed so far would equally apply, unchanged, if we intro-

duce government spending and net export. Both these two categories of expenditure do not depend on current income. Government decisions about how much to spend on goods and services might be dictated by political considerations or by the size of the budget deficit, while spending by foreigners might be affected by the price competitiveness of British-made goods or the buoyant state of economies abroad. In either case, it does not depend on domestic income. We can, therefore, show both government spending (G) and net export ($X - M$) as a given amount that adds to consumption and investment expenditure in exactly the same way as investment did, to give us the economy's total expenditure or aggregate demand. This is shown in Figure 4.11.

An increase in G or ($X - M$) is shown by a shift up of the aggregate demand curve by the same amount. The resulting increase in output and income (Y), is greater than the original injection because of the multiplier effect. This analysis also applies in the case of a reduction of G and net export. In this case Y will fall by more than the initial reduction in autonomous expenditure.

✍ Activity 4.16

Using the Keynesian income expenditure model as shown in Figure 4.12, and assuming constant prices

Figure 4.10   Effects of a reduction of investment on Y

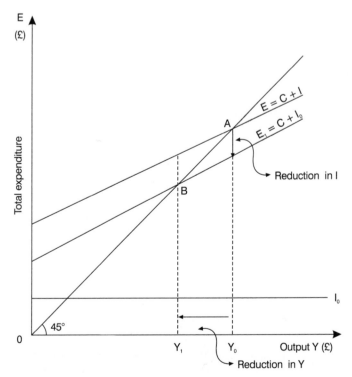

Figure 4.11   Aggregate demand or total expenditure

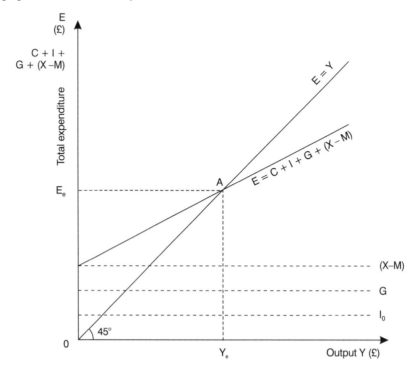

Figure 4.12   Change in aggregate demand or total expenditure

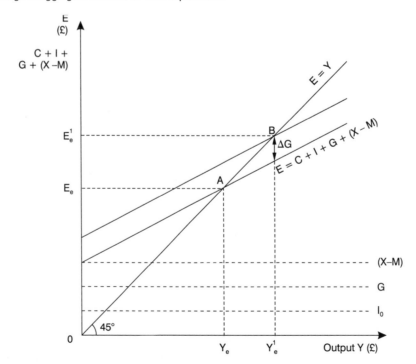

and unused resources, show the effect of the following on the equilibrium level of income and output:

(a) rise in exports;
(b) fall in the marginal propensity to save;
(c) increase in the level of consumption;
(d) new road building plan undertaken by the government;
(e) increase in interest rates causing investment to fall.

✓ Answer 4.16

(a) Shift up of aggregate demand curve: income and output will rise: $Y\uparrow$.
(b) This is equivalent to an increase in the mpc. The mpc determines the slope of the aggregate demand curve. A greater mpc will mean a steeper aggregate demand curve than before and a greater Y as a result: $Y\uparrow$.
(c) Shift up of aggregate demand curve: $Y\uparrow$.
(d) Shift up of aggregate demand curve: $Y\uparrow$.
(e) $I\downarrow$ Shift down of aggregate demand curve: $Y\downarrow$.

INVESTMENT DEMAND

We discuss what affects government expenditure and government's general fiscal policy in Chapter 5 and what affects export expenditure in Chapter 10. Here we complete our analysis by focusing on what determines investment expenditure or investment demand.

Total investment spending comprises investment in fixed capital and working capital. Investment in **fixed capital** includes the purchase of factories, houses, plant and machinery for production purposes.

Working capital consists of additions to stocks and inventories. Total investment, which we call I, only includes **private investment**. It does not include **public investment**, which comprises general government investment normally treated as part of government spending (G) and investment by public corporations. Some statistics, however, do include government spending on investment as part of gross investment.

✍ Activity 4.17

State which of the following constitutes investment from an economist's point of view:

(a) a company builds a new factory;
(b) a private individual buys BT shares;
(c) a jeweller buys gold;
(d) a company buys a new car for one of its sales persons;
(e) an individual buys a new car to get to work.

✓ Answer 4.17

(a) Yes;   (b) No;   (c) Yes;   (d) Yes;   (e) No.

✍ Activity 4.18

The official figures for investment distinguish between private investment in fixed assets, public investment in fixed assets (which has been steadily declining) and stock building (which has shown to be very volatile). Look carefully at the statistics in Tables 4.6 and 4.7 and Figure 4.13 comment on their significance.

✓ Answer 4.18

Table 4.6 provides data on gross domestic fixed capital formation divided by sectors, whether private, government or public corporation and by type of asset (dwellings, other building works, vehicles, plant and machinery).

As Figure 4.13(a) shows, in real terms gross domestic capital formation in the UK took a sharp drop in 1989, when the economy entered a severe recession and had not recovered the 1989 level by 1996. As Figure 4.13(b) shows, over the last decade the proportion of private sector gross fixed capital formation has also changed very little, remaining at around 80–85 per cent of the total. Private sector investment in 1996 at around 86 per cent edged closer to its share of total investment in the late 1980s, after remaining at around 80 per cent during the years 1992–4. These data confirm the importance of private investment in the UK economy.

As far as the type of assets in which UK firms have currently invested, as Figure 4.13(c) shows, construction industry products (dwellings and new buildings and works) represent an important element of fixed investment accounting for some 55 per cent of the total in 1996. Plant and machinery make up another 36 per cent of the assets purchased, the remainder being vehicles. Finally, as Figure 4.13(d) shows, stockbuilding continued in real terms during 1996 in the British economy, after three years of destocking in the early 1990s. While the level of stockbuilding was respectable, at £2.6bn in 1996, it was nonetheless much lower than the level seen in 1988 when it stood at over £5 billion.

✍ Activity 4.19

While the preceding statistics gave us an idea of the components of gross domestic investment by sectors and type of assets, the following statistics look at the behaviour of investment in the UK and convey different

Table 4.6 UK gross domestic fixed capital formation, 1988–97 (£ million, 1990 prices)

| Annual | Analysed by sector | | | Dwellings | | Analysed by type of asset | | | | Total gross domestic fixed capital formation |
	Private sector	General government	Public corporations	Private	Public	Total	Other new building and works	Vehicles, ships and aircraft	Plant and machinery	
1988	92 481	7579	5104	21 741	3506	25 247	35 775	10 372	33 770	105 164
1989	95 745	10 054	5671	20 643	4136	24 789	37 525	11 231	37 925	111 470
1990	89 963	12 659	4954	17 212	4227	21 439	39 110	10 266	36 762	107 577
1991	80 896	12 643	3864	15 083	2836	17 919	37 521	8008	33 955	97 403
1992	77 225	13 787	4961	15 524	2811	18 335	37 249	7787	32 602	95 973
1993	77 268	14 051	5267	16 448	3213	19 661	36 449	8727	31 749	96 586
1994	81 201	14 434	5143	17 047	3324	20 371	36 828	9874	33 705	100 778
1995	84 085	13 374	4790	17 407	2915	20 322	36 125	9450	36 352	102 249
1996	89 388	10 421	4312	17 592	2514	20 106	37 205	9727	37 083	104 121
1997	94 994	7877	3874	13 896	1619	20 344	47 343	8278	37 780	106 903

Source: ONS, Economic Trends, 1997

Table 4.7 UK gross domestic fixed capital formation, percentage changes 1997–2000

Percentage changes on a year earlier Forecast	1997	1998	1999	2000
Whole economy	4¾	4¾ to 5¼	4¾ to 5¼	4¾ to 5¼
of which				
Business[1]	7¾	4½ to 5	4½ to 5	4½ to 5
Housing	7½	4¼ to 4½	4¼ to 4½	4¼ to 4½
General government	−15¾	14	14	14

[1]Private sector and public corporations (except National Health Service Trusts) non-residential investment. Includes investment under the Private Finance Initiative.
Source: HMST, Financial Statement and Budget Report, 1998

Figure 4.13 UK investment at a glance, 1986–96

(a) Gross domestic fixed capital formation (at constant 1990 prices)

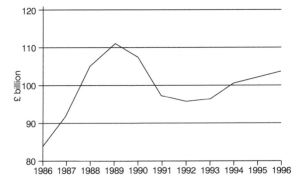

(c) Capital formation by asset 1996 (at constant 1990 prices)

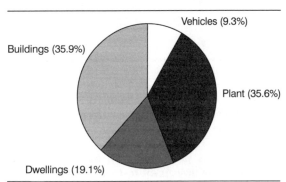

(b) Gross domestic fixed capital formation (at constant 1990 market prices)

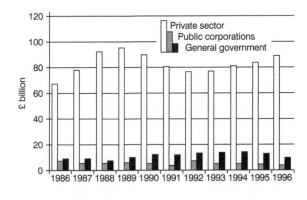

(d) Value of physical increase in stocks and work in progress (at constant 1990 market prices)

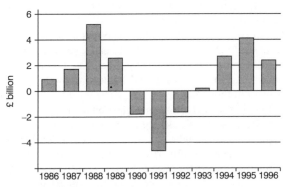

Source: ONS National Accounts, 1997

Figure 4.14   UK investment, GDP ratio 1948–98

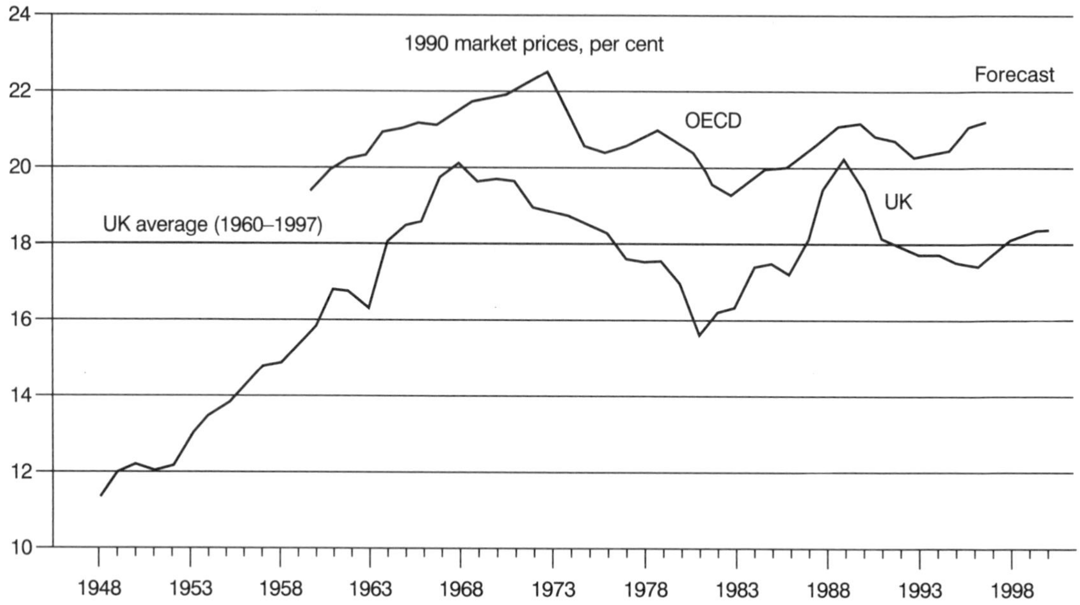

Source: OECD, 1998

information. Take a look at Figure 4.14 and to Tables 4.8 and 4.9 and explain what they show.

✓ Answer 4.19

As the statistics presented show, the UK's ratio of whole economy investment to GDP has been low by international standards. Although non-residential and business investment ratios have been more on a par with other major economies, the UK has invested out of a lower level of GDP per head. Consequently, UK investment per worker has been relatively low, leading to a deficient capital stock per worker. This is one key factor in explaining why the UK has a lower level of labour productivity than other major economies, as we shall see in Chapter 9. In order to catch up with major competitors in terms of GDP per head, as Figure 4.15 shows, higher investment and higher productivity are needed in the UK.

But how can they be brought about? Even during the UK economy's upswing of the late 1990s, investment remained subdued, having fallen considerably in the first part of this decade. Business investment which had been rising as a share of GDP since 1994, compensating further reductions in general government investment, was negatively affected by the appreciation of the pound in the first part of 1998 and by the slowing down of demand. The prospects for investment in the UK remain uncertain. On the one hand, as we shall discuss later on, there is widespread evidence of capacity constraints in the UK economy. This means that all the capital stock currently available in the UK is used. To produce at a faster rate, the UK would need more investment in capital stock. On the other hand, the strength of consumer demand in 1997, which should have encouraged investment, has instead led to higher interest rates, in an attempt by the Bank of England to contain inflationary pressures. But, as we explain below, higher interest rates discourage investment expenditure. The UK economy is now faced with a dilemma.

As UK Chancellor Gordon Brown acknowledged in his 1998 budget, the scale of the challenge facing the UK economy is highlighted by the extent to which the UK is currently lagging behind other major industrial countries. As figure 4.15 shows, output per head in the UK is around 50 per cent lower than in the USA. This **output per head gap** reflects a number of factors, including:

■ **low employment rate**: As we explain in Chapter 8, around one in four of the working-age population is either unemployed or economically inactive. Around one in five working-age households has no one in work, double the level in 1979 and higher than most other developed economies.

Table 4.8 Gross fixed capital formation in the EU economy at 1990 prices, 1961–97 (Annual percentage change)

	B	DK	D	EL	E	F	IRL	I	L	NL	A	P	FIN	S	UK	EUR15	USA	JAP
1961	12.4	13.9	6.5	8.1	17.9	10.9	16.9	11.6	9.0	6.0	12.6	6.7	9.2	8.0	9.8	9.8	1.3	23.4
1962	5.9	6.7	3.8	8.4	11.4	8.5	14.8	9.8	7.8	3.4	2.7	1.7	0.5	6.2	0.7	5.7	7.1	14.1
1963	0.1	-2.4	1.2	5.5	11.4	8.8	12.0	8.1	14.2	1.1	3.4	15.3	-3.0	6.8	1.4	4.7	7.4	11.9
1964	14.7	23.5	11.2	20.7	15.0	10.5	10.8	-5.8	22.1	19.2	9.6	4.0	6.1	7.6	16.6	9.4	8.1	15.7
1965	4.1	4.7	4.7	12.8	16.4	7.0	10.5	-8.4	-13.9	5.3	5.2	10.3	10.4	4.0	5.2	4.1	8.6	4.6
1966	6.8	4.3	1.2	3.2	7.3	7.3	3.0	4.3	-5.1	8.0	8.8	17.9	3.9	4.6	2.6	4.9	4.2	14.0
1967	2.9	5.4	-7.0	-1.6	6.0	6.0	6.8	11.7	-7.9	8.5	0.1	5.2	-1.2	5.3	8.7	3.7	-1.6	18.1
1968	-1.3	1.9	3.3	21.4	9.5	5.5	13.2	10.8	-4.2	11.2	2.9	-9.3	-5.2	0.6	6.3	5.9	5.8	20.5
1969	5.3	11.8	9.6	18.6	10.0	9.2	20.5	7.8	10.5	-2.2	4.9	8.1	12.7	4.3	-0.6	6.9	2.7	18.9
1970	8.4	12.2	8.9	-1.4	3.4	4.6	-3.3	3.0	7.5	9.2	9.8	11.4	12.5	3.3	2.5	5.3	-3.4	16.9
1961–70	5.8	7.0	4.2	9.3	11.3	7.8	9.6	5.1	3.4	6.8	5.9	6.9	4.4	5.1	5.2	6.0	3.9	15.7
1971	-1.9	1.9	5.9	14.0	-3.0	7.3	8.9	-0.8	10.7	0.7	13.8	10.2	3.8	-0.6	1.8	3.4	5.4	4.7
1972	3.4	9.3	2.7	15.4	14.2	6.0	7.8	0.9	7.0	-3.0	12.1	14.0	6.5	4.2	-0.2	4.1	8.9	10.1
1973	7.0	3.5	-0.3	7.7	13.0	8.5	16.2	8.4	11.8	4.6	0.3	10.3	8.5	2.7	6.5	5.9	7.0	11.6
1974	6.9	-8.9	-9.7	-25.6	6.2	1.3	-11.6	1.9	-7.0	-3.0	4.0	-6.1	3.5	-3.0	-2.4	-2.2	-6.0	-8.5
1975	-1.9	-12.4	-5.4	0.2	-4.5	-6.4	-3.6	-7.1	-7.4	-4.1	-5.0	-10.6	5.9	3.1	-2.0	-4.8	-10.9	-0.7
1976	4.0	17.1	3.6	6.8	-0.8	3.3	10.1	-1.0	-4.2	-3.3	3.8	1.3	-8.8	1.9	1.7	1.7	7.4	2.9
1977	0.0	-2.4	2.6	7.8	-0.9	-1.8	4.8	1.4	-0.1	9.9	5.1	11.5	-2.7	-2.9	-1.8	-1.0	12.1	2.8
1978	2.8	1.1	4.1	6.0	-2.7	2.1	18.3	0.6	1.1	2.4	-4.1	6.2	-7.2	-6.8	3.0	1.7	9.3	7.9
1979	-2.7	-0.4	6.7	8.8	-4.4	3.1	14.5	5.2	3.8	-1.5	3.5	-1.4	2.6	4.5	2.8	3.2	4.2	5.9
1980	4.6	-12.6	2.2	-6.5	0.7	2.6	-3.7	8.4	12.7	-0.2	3.0	8.5	11.0	3.5	-5.4	1.9	-6.7	-0.4
1971–80	2.2	-0.8	1.2	2.8	1.6	2.5	5.7	1.7	2.6	0.2	3.5	4.1	2.1	0.6	0.4	1.6	2.8	3.5
1981	-17.7	-19.2	-5.0	-7.5	-1.9	-1.9	7.3	-3.1	-7.4	-9.9	-1.4	5.5	1.3	-6.0	-9.6	-4.8	0.6	2.3
1982	-1.6	7.1	-5.4	-1.9	2.1	-1.4	-3.4	-4.9	-0.5	-4.2	-8.2	2.3	5.1	-0.4	5.4	-1.8	-7.2	-0.2
1983	-4.2	1.9	3.1	-1.3	-2.4	-3.6	-9.0	-1.0	-11.8	2.5	-0.6	-7.1	3.7	1.7	5.0	0.0	5.8	-1.1
1984	1.9	12.9	0.1	-5.7	-6.9	-2.7	-2.7	3.4	0.1	5.8	2.1	-17.4	-2.1	7.2	8.9	0.8	14.7	4.3
1985	0.7	12.6	-0.5	5.2	6.1	3.2	-7.8	0.5	-9.5	7.0	5.0	-3.5	2.2	6.1	4.2	2.4	5.5	5.0
1986	4.5	17.1	3.3	-6.2	9.9	4.5	0.0	2.0	31.2	6.9	3.7	10.9	-0.4	1.0	2.6	3.9	0.6	4.8
1987	5.6	-3.8	1.8	-5.1	14.0	4.4	-2.3	4.4	14.7	0.9	3.1	16.9	4.9	7.9	10.3	5.4	1.0	9.1
1988	15.7	-6.6	4.4	8.9	13.9	9.6	-1.6	6.9	14.1	4.5	6.0	11.5	9.8	6.0	13.9	8.5	3.7	11.5
1989	11.6	1.0	6.3	7.1	7.9	7.9	13.8	4.4	8.9	4.9	6.2	4.5	14.8	11.7	6.0	7.2	1.4	8.2
1990	12.0	-1.7	8.5	5.0	6.6	2.8	11.1	3.6	2.5	1.6	5.7	7.8	-4.1	0.7	-3.5	3.6	-0.6	8.5
1981–90	2.4	1.6	1.6	-0.3	5.2	2.3	0.3	1.6	3.5	1.9	2.1	2.7	3.4	3.5	4.1	2.4	2.4	5.2
1991	-5.0	-5.7	6.0	4.8	1.6	0.0	-7.4	0.8	9.8	0.2	6.3	2.9	-20.3	-8.4	-9.5	-0.4	-5.3	3.3
1992	1.8	-4.2	-0.6	-1.4	-4.2	-2.8	-2.5	-1.8	-2.1	0.6	1.7	5.4	-16.9	-10.8	-1.5	-1.9	-5.8	-1.5
1993	-5.0	-4.7	-10.0	-2.8	-10.6	-6.7	-2.1	-12.8	3.9	-2.8	-1.6	-4.8	-19.2	-17.2	0.6	-7.7	11.9	-2.0
1994	0.3	3.0	-0.1	0.5	1.3	1.4	8.7	0.2	0.1	1.6	6.8	3.9	0.2	-0.2	3.7	1.4	12.3	-1.0
1995	3.0	10.2	1.5	6.3	8.2	2.8	10.1	5.9	3.5	6.7	6.0	2.8	7.7	10.6	-0.1	2.5	5.3	0.6
1996	3.3	4.9	-1.4	8.3	2.6	-0.3	9.9	1.8	6.0	3.2	1.2	4.0	4.9	12.0	3.7	1.5	5.7	8.6
1997	5.0	5.3	1.2	8.6	4.8	2.2	7.7	2.5	4.0	3.0	1.6	5.2	8.5	2.7	5.6	3.1	3.9	1.8

Source: European Economy, *Annual Economic Report*, 1997

Table 4.9 Stockbuilding in the EU economy, 1960–97 (Percentage of gross domestic product at market prices)

	B	DK	D	EL	E	F	IRL	I	L	NL	A	P	FIN	S	UK	EUR15	USA	JAP
1960	-0.1	4.4	3.0	-0.4	-0.5	3.0	2.0	2.1	2.4	3.3	3.2	1.4	1.0	2.6	2.2	2.4	0.7	3.9
1961	0.5	1.9	2.0	1.8	1.7	1.7	1.4	2.3	2.2	2.7	2.2	3.9	1.2	1.6	1.0	1.7	0.4	5.0
1962	0.0	2.9	1.6	1.1	3.6	2.3	1.6	1.7	5.6	1.5	0.4	1.8	0.4	1.0	0.0	1.4	1.1	2.0
1963	0.4	0.8	0.7	2.1	3.4	1.5	0.9	1.0	-0.1	1.1	-0.2	2.0	-0.8	0.2	0.5	1.0	0.9	2.2
1964	1.5	1.7	1.5	4.7	2.7	2.4	1.2	0.5	-1.2	3.0	1.6	3.3	1.7	2.5	2.1	1.8	0.7	2.9
1965	0.8	2.3	2.3	4.7	3.0	1.6	2.3	0.7	2.1	1.9	0.7	4.4	2.0	1.1	1.3	1.7	1.2	2.1
1966	1.0	0.8	1.1	0.6	2.9	2.0	0.8	0.8	1.7	1.3	2.0	1.8	0.7	0.2	0.8	1.3	1.5	2.1
1967	0.4	0.0	-0.1	2.0	1.4	1.8	-0.4	1.1	-3.0	0.9	1.0	0.6	-0.2	0.3	0.7	0.8	1.2	3.4
1968	0.9	0.6	2.1	-0.1	0.8	1.8	1.1	0.0	-1.9	0.6	1.7	3.1	1.3	1.3	1.0	1.2	1.0	3.6
1969	1.9	1.3	2.9	1.3	2.5	2.6	2.4	0.7	-1.2	1.6	2.0	1.8	1.1	3.1	1.1	1.9	1.1	3.1
1970	1.6	1.0	2.1	4.5	0.8	2.5	1.7	2.6	2.7	1.6	3.9	5.9	3.5	1.3	0.7	2.1	0.1	3.5
1961–70	0.9	1.3	1.6	2.3	2.3	2.0	1.3	1.1	0.7	1.6	1.5	2.9	0.9	1.3	0.9	1.5	0.9	3.0
1971	1.4	0.6	0.6	2.7	0.9	1.5	0.3	0.8	1.3	0.4	1.8	3.2	2.3	-0.1	0.2	0.9	0.7	1.5
1972	0.5	0.2	0.5	1.8	0.9	1.6	1.4	0.6	0.7	0.2	0.4	3.6	-0.6	-0.5	0.0	0.7	0.7	1.4
1973	1.3	1.3	1.3	7.8	0.8	2.0	1.6	2.0	-0.2	1.0	2.4	5.9	-0.1	2.4	2.1	1.7	1.2	1.7
1974	2.2	1.2	0.4	7.1	2.2	2.3	4.4	4.0	-3.4	2.1	2.7	5.2	4.7	3.3	1.2	2.0	0.9	2.5
1975	0.6	-0.2	-0.6	6.2	2.1	-0.7	0.0	-1.1	-4.8	-0.2	-0.7	-3.3	2.3	2.3	-1.3	-0.3	-0.3	0.3
1976	0.2	1.0	1.4	5.1	2.0	1.4	0.5	2.9	-2.2	1.0	1.3	1.8	-1.2	-0.6	0.7	1.5	0.9	0.7
1977	0.3	0.8	0.6	3.5	1.1	1.5	3.1	1.2	-4.7	0.6	1.1	2.5	-1.4	-1.8	1.3	1.0	1.3	0.7
1978	0.1	-0.2	0.6	3.7	0.2	0.8	1.5	1.2	0.9	0.4	0.4	2.6	-1.9	0.2	1.1	0.6	1.3	0.5
1979	0.7	0.5	1.7	4.3	0.8	1.3	2.3	1.7	-2.3	0.4	1.4	2.9	2.3	1.1	1.1	1.3	0.6	0.8
1980	0.7	-0.3	0.8	4.4	1.0	1.2	-1.2	2.6	-1.9	0.8	2.8	4.2	3.5	0.7	-1.1	1.0	-0.2	0.7
1971–80	0.7	0.5	0.7	4.6	1.2	1.3	1.4	1.6	-1.7	0.7	1.4	2.9	1.0	0.2	0.5	1.0	0.7	1.1
1981	-0.1	-0.2	-0.7	3.1	0.0	-0.2	-1.1	0.9	-0.9	-0.3	1.0	3.7	1.0	-0.7	-1.1	-0.2	1.0	0.6
1982	0.1	0.2	-1.0	1.2	0.6	0.5	1.4	1.2	-0.1	-0.5	-0.2	3.0	0.8	-1.0	-0.4	0.0	-0.4	0.4
1983	-0.7	0.0	-0.1	1.6	0.7	-0.4	0.7	0.8	3.1	0.2	-0.5	-0.9	0.0	-1.4	0.5	0.1	0.0	0.1
1984	0.4	1.2	0.3	1.0	1.0	-0.3	1.4	1.8	4.7	0.2	1.6	-1.3	0.5	-1.0	0.4	0.5	1.9	0.3
1985	-0.7	0.8	0.1	2.2	0.0	-0.4	0.9	1.8	-1.0	0.3	0.8	-1.2	-0.1	-1.0	0.2	0.3	0.7	0.7
1986	-0.6	0.8	0.2	1.4	0.5	0.3	0.6	1.3	-0.8	0.9	0.7	-1.0	-0.6	-0.6	0.2	0.4	0.4	0.5
1987	0.2	-0.7	0.0	0.5	0.7	0.4	0.1	1.5	-2.4	-0.1	0.9	0.7	-0.2	-0.5	0.3	0.4	0.6	0.2
1988	0.4	-0.2	-0.5	0.6	1.0	0.7	-0.2	1.4	-2.7	0.1	1.0	2.1	0.7	-0.3	0.9	0.7	0.2	0.7
1989	0.4	0.2	0.7	-0.2	1.0	1.0	1.0	1.2	-0.1	1.1	0.8	1.3	1.3	0.0	0.5	0.8	0.7	0.6
1990	0.0	-0.1	0.5	-0.3	0.9	1.1	2.6	0.8	-1.1	1.3	1.0	1.1	0.6	0.6	-0.3	0.6	0.7	0.5
1981–90	-0.1	-0.1	0.0	1.1	0.6	0.3	0.7	1.3	-0.1	0.3	0.7	0.8	0.7	-0.5	0.1	0.4	0.5	0.8
1991	0.1	-0.3	0.6	0.9	0.8	0.3	2.2	0.8	-0.3	1.0	0.5	0.6	-1.9	1.1	-0.9	0.3	0.0	0.8
1992	0.0	-0.8	-0.1	0.7	0.8	-0.4	-0.3	0.3	-0.8	0.6	0.3	0.9	-1.2	-1.5	-0.3	0.0	0.1	0.3
1993	0.0	0.0	-0.5	0.8	0.0	-1.4	-0.4	0.0	-0.6	0.6	0.5	0.7	-0.8	-0.5	0.1	-0.4	0.3	0.0
1994	0.1	1.3	0.5	0.9	0.3	0.0	-0.6	0.5	-0.3	1.0	1.5	0.3	1.3	-1.0	0.5	0.2	0.0	0.8
1995	0.0	0.8	1.5	1.7	0.4	0.2	0.2	0.8	-0.8	0.6	0.5	0.6	-1.9	0.6	-0.9	0.0	0.1	0.3
1996	0.3	-0.1	0.6	1.3	0.6	-0.4	0.5	1.1	0.7	0.0	1.5	1.0	0.1	-0.2	0.1	0.4	0.3	0.2
1997	0.4	0.1	0.9	1.2	0.7	0.1	0.4	1.0	-0.3	0.3	1.9	1.4	0.1	0.0	0.3	0.6	0.1	0.3

Source: European Economy, *Annual Economic Report*, 1997

Figure 4.15   GDP per head: major OECD economies, 1997

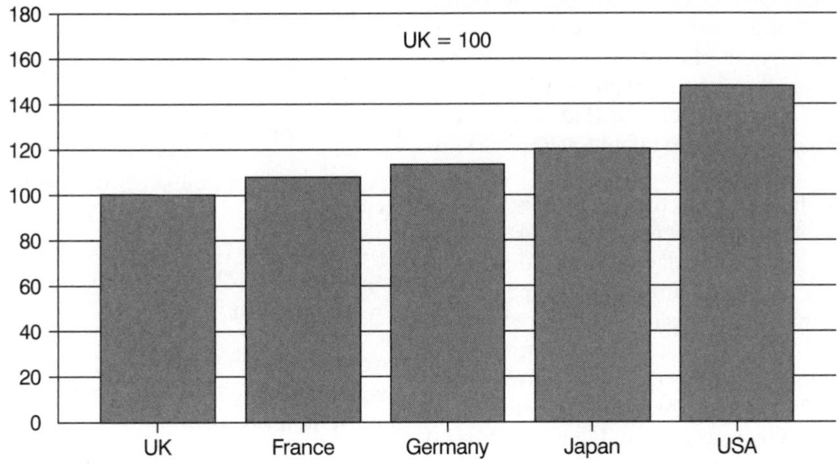

Source: OECD, 1998

■ **low investment**: which translates, as we have just seen, to a capital stock per employee which is as much as 50 per cent lower than in other leading economies such as Japan, Germany and the USA. Investment can be in machinery and building, but also includes investment in human capital and research and technology. Low investment therefore reflects in business enterprise **research and development** (R&D), which also fell in the UK relative to almost every other G7 country between 1981 and 1995, according to OECD statistics published in 1997.

So we return now to the important question of private investment and to the factors that influence decisions to invest. Higher investment will not come about of its own accord; there must be the incentive to invest more.

✍ Activity 4.20

Why do firms invest?

✓ Answer 4.20

Firms add to their plant and equipment for the following reasons:

■ because they foresee profitable opportunities that can be gained by expanding their output;
■ to reduce their costs, and hence increase their profits, by moving to more capital intensive production methods.

In each case, the firm has to weigh the **benefits** it will derive from new plant and equipment against the

cost of the investment. The investment will only be worthwhile for the firm if the future returns outweigh the cost of forgone current consumption.

This is where the interest rate comes in. To finance its investment in capital and equipment, the firm will typically arrange for a loan from a financial institution which it will need to pay back with interest. The interest rate represents the cost of borrowing money, which will add to the cost of the investment. Suppose you borrow £1,000 from a bank for a year, at the end of which period you agree to pay back £1,100. The extra £100 you pay represents a 10 per cent interest rate. Suppose the bank imposed a 20 per cent interest rate on the loan. After a year you would have to pay £1,200 back; in other words, the higher the interest rate the more the loan will cost you and vice versa.

✍ Activity 4.21

If a firm does not need a loan from a bank to finance its investment project, but rather uses 'internal funds' previously accumulated (past unshared profits), can we still say that the interest rate has an effect on a firm's investment decision?

✓ Answer 4.21

Yes, in this situation the interest rate measures the opportunity cost to the firm of using up its funds to buy capital equipment. This is the interest the firm forgoes by not lending its money on the market; so the higher the interest rate, the higher the cost of the investment project.

The firm will have to calculate whether the investment will return enough extra profits to pay back with interest the loan used to finance it. In the same way, if the project is financed out of existing profits, the firm has to ask whether the new investment will yield a return at least as great as the one that could have been earned by lending the money out at the current interest rate.

The higher the interest rate, the larger must be the return on a new investment before it will match the opportunity cost of the funds tied up in it. To see this point more clearly, let's work through an example.

Let's assume that three business studies students have been asked to present an investment project based on a business idea, showing costs and expected returns from the investment. All three students have £1,000 available to buy a secondhand van, which represents the bulk of their investment.

The three students decide to use the secondhand van for different purposes. Jack wants to set up a fast delivery courier service. Gill wants to set up a business providing meals on wheels, and Paolo wants to sell ice-cream.

Let's further assume that the yield of these three different business ideas accrues entirely within the same year and that there are no other costs involved other than repaying the loan after the first year. Let's also assume that the vans are fully depreciated at the end of the year and have no scrap value. Jack expects total revenues of £10,000 over the period. Gill expects total revenues of £5,000 over the period, while Paolo expects total revenues of £1,200 over the period.

✍ Activity 4.22

Assuming a 10 per cent interest rate, calculate the profitability of these investment projects. Should the students go ahead with them? Assume now that the interest rate has gone up to 20 per cent. In what way does this affect your conclusion about the viability of the three investment projects?

✓ Answer 4.22

Fast delivery service r = 20 per cent	r = 10 per cent	
Investment cost (£)	1,100	1,200
Expected revenue	10,000	10,000
Return on investment	8,900	8,800

The project is profitable (> 0) at either interest rate and should be undertaken.

Meals on wheels r = 20 per cent	r = 10 per cent	
Investment cost (£)	1,100	1,200
Expected revenue	5,000	5,000
Return on investment	3,900	3,800

The project is profitable (> 0) in either case. It should be undertaken.

Ice-cream r = 20 per cent	r = 10 per cent	
Investment cost (£)	1,100	1,200
Expected revenue	1,150	1,150
Return on investment	50	– 50

The project is marginally profitable (+ £50) and could be undertaken only when interest rate is at 10 per cent. This investment project becomes unprofitable (– £50) at the higher interest rate of 20 per cent and should not be undertaken.

This example shows that at higher interest rates fewer investment projects are profitable. Those becoming unprofitable are dropped and not undertaken. So we can conclude that: the higher the interest rate, the higher the **cost** of the investment project, the lower the total level of investment undertaken in the economy as investment projects that become unprofitable are not undertaken.

We can summarize the relationship between investment and the interest rate by saying that investment is a negative function of the interest rate: the higher the interest rate, the lower the amount of investment undertaken in the economy:

$$I = f(r)$$

where I denotes investment, f means 'it is a function of' and r denotes the interest rate.

To sum up, the higher the interest rate, the higher the cost of the investment, the lower the total amount of investment undertaken. There is, however, another important reason that explains the negative relationship between investment and interest rates, which relates to the **revenue** side of the investment calculation rather than to its cost. As we have just seen, the higher the interest rate, the higher the cost of the investment (costlier to borrow funds, higher opportunity cost), the smaller the amount of investment. However, it is also the case that the higher the interest rate, the lower the discounted value of the expected return from the investment, the smaller the total amount of investment.

We can reason this in the following way. In the example of the three investment projects we have just used, to keep matters simple we assumed that the returns on the investment were all to be obtained by the end of the year and nothing else after that. In real life situations, however, returns on investments occur in the future and typically are spread over a number of years, while the costs of the investment are all incurred the moment the investment spending is done in the present. To decide whether an investment project is profitable, therefore, firms need to compare returns and costs now, to be able to calculate the profitability of investments.

In order to do so, firms calculate the present discounted value (PDV) of a project. The interest rate, also referred to as the rate of discount, is used in PDV calculations to evaluate how much any **future** return is **worth now**.

To calculate the PDV of an investment project, a firm weighs the **stream of future income returns**, R_t, from the project, discounted by the rate of interest:

$$R_t + \frac{R_{t+1}}{1+r} + \frac{R_{t+2}}{(1+r)^2} + \ldots\ldots + \frac{R_{t+n}}{(1+r)^n}$$

using the formula:

$$PDV_t = -C + R_t + \frac{R_{t+1}}{1+r} = \frac{R_{t+2}}{(1+r)^2} + \ldots\ldots + \frac{R_{t+n}}{(1+r)^n}$$

where C is costs and R_t returns expected in year t, R_{t+1} are returns expected in year $t + 1$, etc.

In this calculation of the present value of the future income stream, the interest rate (r) is used in evaluating, **in the present**, the 'worth' of each future return.

If, for example, Paolo were to offer Gill £104, payable in one year, in exchange for cash now, Gill would have to decide how much that £104 in a year's time is worth to her now. If she knew that she could lend money in the market, that is put it in a bank, and receive a 4 per cent return, she would decide that £104 in one year's time is worth £100 now. Therefore, Gill would give Paolo £100 now in exchange for £104 in a year. This is the way of **valuing future payments at the present time** and can be expressed mathematically:

$$\text{PDV of £104 now: } PDV_t = \frac{R_{t+1}}{1+r} = \frac{£104}{1.04}$$

If the money were to be returned in two years, the PDV of this repayment would be:

$$PDV_t = \frac{R_{t+2}}{(1+r)^2} = \frac{£104}{(1.04)^2} = £96$$

and so on.

If £104 were to be repaid back in three years, it would be worth £92 now, etc. It can be seen that the further in the future Gill expects to be paid, the less the payment is worth to her now.

Firms can rank their various projects in order of their PDVs as shown in Figure 4.16.

i_0 is the total amount of investment firms wish to undertake when the interest rate is r_0. i_1 is the smaller amount of total investment firms wish to undertake when the interest rate is r_1, higher than r_0.

Assuming that firms have investment funds, they will invest in all projects with PDV ≥ 0, in other words in all the projects which have positive net returns. This would push the level of investment to i_0. If a firm had only limited investment funds it would invest them in the most productive projects (highest PDVs) until its funds ran out, at a point somewhere to the left of i_0.

Thus, applying the PDV formula of equation 2 to its potential investment projects using r_0, the firm comes to an investment level I_0. If the r were higher, **all the entries** in the PDV formula for each project would have a larger denominator, so the PDV of each project would be smaller. As interest rates rise, all PDVs fall and the PDV_0 curve shifts down to PDV_1 reducing the level of planned investment from i_0 to i$_1$. This once more gives us the simplest investment model obtained before, where $i = f(r)$. Investment is inversely related to the interest rate.

The investment demand curve shows how much investment firms wish to make at each interest rate

Figure 4.16 Present discounted value of investment projects

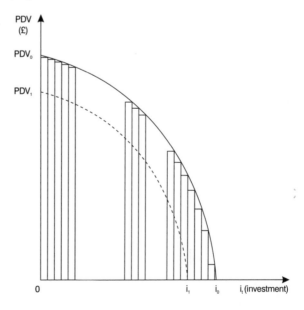

(Figure 4.17). If the interest rate rises from r_0 to r_1, fewer investment projects will have a positive PDV and will cover the opportunity cost of the funds tied up in them, and desired investment will fall from I_0 to I_1.

What determines the height of the curve? There are two main factors:

- cost of new machines;
- stream of profits to which new machines give rise.

For a given expected income stream from an investment, an increase in the purchase price of new capital goods will reduce the rate of return earned on the money tied up in investment. If firms are less optimistic about future returns from investments or if the economic climate is less optimistic, firms will revise downward their **expected** returns. Total investment demand will fall. For a given cost of new capital goods, the expected return on each project will be lower, hence the total amount of planned investment will also be lower.

✍ Activity 4.23

Suppose an investment costs £12,000 and yields £5,000 per year for three years. At the end of the three years the equipment has no value. Calculate whether the investment will be profitable if the rate of interest (or rates of discount) is 5 per cent, 10 per cent and 20 per cent.

Figure 4.17 Investment function

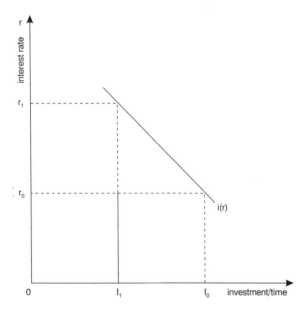

✓ Answer 4.23

At r = 5 per cent: $PDV_t = -12{,}000 + 5{,}000 + \dfrac{5{,}000}{1.05} + \dfrac{5{,}000}{(1.05)^2} = £2{,}297.$

At r = 10 per cent: $PDV_t = -12{,}000 + 5{,}000 + \dfrac{5{,}000}{1.10} + \dfrac{5{,}000}{(1.10)^2} = £1{,}677.$

At r = 20 per cent: $PDV_t = -12{,}000 + 5{,}000 + \dfrac{5{,}000}{1.20} + \dfrac{5{,}000}{(1.20)^2} = £639.$

OTHER DETERMINANTS OF INVESTMENT

Although Keynes recognized the fact that investment demand is affected by interest rates in the way we have just described, he also maintained that:

1 Investment decisions are not particularly responsive to interest rates. This view was later supported by not totally uncontroversial empirical evidence. If this is the case, reducing interest rates is not the most effective or the most direct way of increasing the level of investment.
2 Investment decisions are affected by other factors as well such as:

- the cost and efficiency of capital equipment;
- expectations about future market conditions.

Keynes stressed in particular the role of expectations about future market conditions and about consumer demand as being very important in determining the level of investment. Expectations are very volatile and their influence also makes investment behaviour volatile. This aspect of investment behaviour is best explained by the 'accelerator model of investment', where investment is seen as a function of expected future sales, based in turn on growth of sales in the current period. What the accelerator model suggests is that investment spending is very volatile, since small changes in Y produce much larger changes in net investment I. This would once more point at the need for direct government intervention, through spending, to steady the economy and encourage faster growth. The accelerator theory of investment and its relationship to the business cycles is further explored in Chapter 9.

The volatility of consumption and investment: a comparison

Now that we have looked in depth at consumption and investment, we are in a position to draw some conclusions on the differences and similarities of their behaviours. We can also attempt to expand our analysis and reflect on the impact that **expectations** have on both consumption and investment behaviour.

Although consumption and investment are affected by different economic factors, we can also see similarities in the way in which they respond to changes in the economic environment. As we said at the beginning of this chapter, consumers decide the amount of their consumption on the basis of their current income. However, it can be argued – although recent empirical evidence from the British economy would seem partly to disprove it – that consumers adjust their consumption decisions to current changes in income by less if they perceive such changes to be temporary rather than permanent.

Equally, firms' investment decisions are affected by their perception of changes in sales as being temporary rather than permanent. If a firm does not expect a current increase in sales to last, it will not be willing to expand in response to it, buying new machines, building new factories or renting new offices. This is why the upsurge in UK sales in the summer of 1997, caused by large building societies share ownership windfall gains, was not followed by an equal upsurge in investment.

There are, however, some fundamental differences in the way in which consumption and investment respond to changes in the economy, which account for the much greater volatility of investment decisions compared with consumption decisions.

The theory of consumption developed in this chapter tells us that when consumers experience an increase in their income which they regard as sufficiently permanent, they respond to it by increasing their consumption by an amount which is at most as big as the increase in income, but not bigger. If it were bigger, this would imply that consumption would have to decrease at some point in the future.

There is no reason for this constraint to hold for firms. If a firm is faced by an increase in sales regarded to be permanent and not short lived, it will consider expanding its productive capacity, buying new machinery or building a new factory. This investment expenditure is likely to be large, short lived and to exceed the value of the current increase in sales. This point can be seen more easily with an example.

Suppose a firm has a ratio of capital to annual sales equal to 3. This means that to be able to accommodate an expected increase in sales of £10mn the firm has to spend £30mn in additional capital equipment. Now suppose that the firm expects its sales to increase by £10mn. If the firm goes ahead with the necessary investment to meet such an increase in demand and buys £30mn worth of capital, its investment spending this year will be equal to three times the expected

increase in sales. Once the adjustment in capital stock is made, however, it does not need to be altered any further and the firm will return to its normal pattern of annual investment, which will include only the replacement investment needed to keep its capital stock constant. So, in response to a permanent increase in sales, investment may increase a lot initially and return to normal over time. Investment is therefore more volatile than consumption.

This point can be seen by comparing yearly rates of change in UK consumption and investment since 1970, which you can do using the statistics provided in this chapter. You will notice two main points:

- First, consumption and investment tend to move together. They both tend to decrease during recessions and increase during expansions, with changes in consumption preceding those in investment.
- Second, you can clearly see that investment is much more volatile than consumption. Relative movements in consumption range from only plus or minus 2 or 3 per cent, while relative movements in investment range from plus or minus 6 or 8 per cent.

The volatility of investment behaviour is more accurately modelled, along the principles described above, by the **accelerator theory of investment**, mentioned before. However, the accelerator theory of investment has not proved particularly useful in predicting investment behaviour. For the moment, therefore, we continue to use the model of investment behaviour introduced in this chapter, which stresses the relationship between investment and the rate of interest.

MONEY, INTEREST RATES AND AGGREGATE DEMAND

From the negative, functional relationship between investment and the interest rate, we derive the conclusion that a fall in interest rates increases investment demand. A fall in interest rates will also increase consumption demand if we include wealth, and not simply current income, in the consumption function as one of the factors affecting it. Now we know how to stimulate aggregate demand. To increase investment demand, interest rates must be lowered.

But what brings down the interest rates? The increase in the money supply brings down interest rates. We have reached an important point, which we are going to explore further when we study the money supply in Chapter 6. What we want to stress now is the fact that we have at last found a clear **transmission mechanism** through which an increase in the money supply, via its effect on the interest rate and investment, has an impact on the output of the economy. The transmission mechanism works as follows:

- An increase in the money supply, ceteris paribus, lowers interest rates.
- Lower interest rates stimulate investment demand.
- Investment is an injection of funds that increases aggregate demand and, via the multiplier, causes output, income and employment to increase.

✍ Activity 4.24

Why is it that when aggregate demand $(C + I + G + (X - M))$ exceeds aggregate supply, assuming constant prices and unused resources in the economy, the effect is to increase employment?

✓ Answer 4.24

The level of demand determines the level of output in the economy. Firms will adjust to market conditions (demand) and produce more if more is demanded. In the process, incomes will rise, together with employment.

Investment and economic growth

Before we reconsider the general equilibrium of the economy in the light of what we have learnt so far about the factors affecting aggregate demand, there is one more point which is worth making about investment: its effect on economic growth. Until now we have talked about investment as a 'component of aggregate demand'. We have stressed that spending by firms on capital equipment, etc. adds to the demand for such goods, causing firms producing capital goods to expand their production. This, ceteris paribus, creates more employment, more income and eventually more output via the multiplier effect. What we are describing here is simply the effect that increased **investment demand**, increased **spending on capital goods**, has on the economy, including its multiplier effect. However, this is not the whole story concerning investment.

Investment spending also contributes to the growth of output because the capital goods bought actually add to the productive capacity of the system: firms will be able to produce more than before as a result of their investment spending, or more efficiently than before. Hence, investment spending affects the **supply side** of the economy as well, and not just the **demand side**, by increasing the output capacity or potential output of the economy. This is because higher investment spending on capital and equipment:

- increases the quantity of goods a firm can produce in a period of time;
- increases the efficiency (lower inputs of other factors, better use of resources) of production;
- has further positive, growth enhancing, spillover effects by encouraging the development of new technologies, knowledge-based industries and tertiary education.

In other words, investment in physical and human capital, not only adds to the **demand** for the output of the economy, therefore stimulating its production, but also to the **supply** of the output by inducing increases in productivity. This is what recent theories of growth have focused on: the possibility that investment in human and physical capital raises the growth rate of the economy. Nobody questions the fact, however, that a rise in the investment–GDP ratio, the proportion of spending on investment goods out of total spending, could significantly raise the growth rate of GDP for a protracted period, even if not permanently, as the economy goes through the transition to the higher GDP path.

To produce more goods, more output, you need more inputs, more factors of production, such as raw materials, labour and capital. The proportions in which those inputs are needed to produce one more unit of output will vary according to the technical requirements of production. Technical conditions of production will also determine the **capital–output ratio**, in other words, how much capital is needed to produce one unit of output. For a given capital–output ratio, to increase the output you will need to increase the capital needed as well, i.e. you need more investment. The amount of extra investment, the extra capital goods purchased, has to take into account the need to replace worn-out capital, used up machinery (depreciation). For the economy to grow and produce more output, investment also has to grow: more capital goods are needed to produce more. Stated rather more formally, given capital–output ratio, the investment ratio required to sustain steady output growth needs to be sufficient to expand the capital stock at the same rate as output after covering for depreciation.

Let's take the UK economy as an example and look at its investment–GDP ratio and growth prospects. As we have learned from the relevant statistics earlier on in this chapter, in 1997 the ratio of investment to GDP in the UK was around 12 per cent for business investment and the ratio of the business sector capital stock to GDP was of the order of 2.5:1. Consequently it can be calculated that if capital productivity were unchanged (i.e. constant capital–output ratio), then the current investment ratio would be sufficient to sustain trend GDP growth of 2.25 per cent a year only if the depreciation rate of the business sector capital stock were no more than around 2.5 per cent a year. The depreciation rate is in fact likely to be much more. If that is the case, more investment is be needed (i.e. a higher investment–GDP ratio than the current 12 per cent) even to support the current unspectacular trend growth of 2.25 per cent a year, unless capital productivity increases. If the UK economy is to grow faster and catch up with other major industrialized countries in terms of output per head (in 1997 the UK ranked fifth, with Italy, in the world league of GDP per head, after the USA, Japan, Germany and France), then from what we have just said, it seems certain that it will need a higher rate of investment.

So, what we have established is that investment affects the output capacity of the economy, how much the supply side of the economic system can produce: the investment rate determines, among other factors, the growth rate of the economy. However, a higher investment and a higher investment–GDP ratio will not come about of their own accord. That's were we go back to our theory of investment, to determine what affects investment demand.

For firms to invest more, there must be incentive. It will only be worthwhile for businesses to invest more if the future returns outweigh the cost of forgone current consumption, i.e. the cost of the investment project. Lower cost of capital, in other words, lower interest rates, together with greater total factor productivity growth, i.e. greater expected returns, will encourage investment. This takes us back to the transmission mechanism: it is the government's monetary policy that determines the rate of interest hence, ceteris paribus, the amount of investment spending. It is to the determinants of monetary policy that we then need to turn.

Equilibrium condition revisited

At the end of this analysis of consumption, saving and investment, it might be useful to revisit our earlier discussion of equilibrium in the macro economy. We have talked earlier of equilibrium in terms of equality between the aggregate demand for goods and the aggregate supply or production. An alternative way of thinking about equilibrium focuses on investment and saving. This can be done starting from our equilibrium condition and using algebra, as follows:

$$Y = E \tag{1}$$

$$E = C + I \tag{2}$$

$$Y = C + I \tag{3}$$

$$S \equiv Y - C \tag{4}$$

$$Y = S + C \tag{5}$$

from (3) and (5):

$$C + I = S + C \tag{6}$$

$$I = S. \tag{7}$$

CASE STUDY: AGING POPULATION AND AGGREGATE SAVING IN EUROPE

In the next 40 years an ageing population in Europe will cause large changes in the demand for a wide range of products and services, provided both privately and publicly. In the savings behaviour in particular this demand change will be especially large, with a consequent macroeconomic impact of large proportion. This case study helps you to focus on the main macroeconomic implications of this important demographic change.

An ageing European population

As the post-war baby boom generation ages, Europe is becoming more middle-aged. Recent calculations show that the largest age group in western Europe at present is the 15–29 year olds. In ten years time, however, as Figure 4.18 shows, the 50–64 age group will be the largest. This group will continue to be the largest until 2035, after which date those beyond retirement age will begin to dominate numerically.

This demographic shift will not occur evenly across all European countries. Support ratios – the ratio of working age population to the elderly – will fall to much lower levels in Italy, Spain and Germany than in the UK or Norway. Nor will the shift occur with equal speed; some countries such as the Netherlands will experience significant demographic changes in the next 25 years, while others such as Spain, will be unaffected until much later (see Figure 4.19).

The impact on aggregate saving

The long-term impact of an older population is to reduce aggregate saving. Retired people typically dissave, i.e. they live on past savings, while people in employment are generally adding to saving. A declining ratio of working age people to retired people will therefore mean a declining amount of net saving.

The savings impact of the demographic shift will vary across countries. Most European countries have not yet reached the point of declining saving. In fact, the growing preponderance of the middle aged, who at the peak of their earning potential are the largest savers, implies higher rather than lower saving rates in the early years of the next century. If one

assumes, in line with the life-cycle hypothesis of consumption behaviour, that the average person tends to smooth their consumption over their expected lifetime, one can build a model to estimate the spending and saving patterns of people in the EU over their lifetime. The results of such a model suggest that the effect of the impending demographic change will be to raise saving rates in European countries in the coming years, before depressing them in 20 to 30 years time.

Because of the differing speed and degrees of demographic change, this predicted impact on saving will vary across countries. The largest effects are likely to be felt in Italy, Spain and the Netherlands and the smallest in France and Germany, with the UK somewhere in the middle.

The public pension crisis

The ageing European population is also likely to put a strain on public pension systems. As a result, public pensions are likely to become less generous, either by limiting provisions to the less well off or by offering less favourable payments indexation. The impact of this change is likely to be large. European public pension schemes, which for years enjoyed surpluses as a result of the large middle-aged group of payees, are now faced by a situation of growing deficits as the contributions of the ageing baby boom generation begin to shrink, relative to payments. For most European countries the peak in pension payments will occur around the year 2040 while the average increase in payments from now to the peak is calculated to be equal to about 6 per cent of GDP.

Faced by these growing deficits in the public pension schemes – which should be regarded as public debt – the European governments have, it seems, three policy options:

- They can do nothing, but this will result in huge public sector deficits in most countries, which are against the Maastricht conditions for EMU growth and stability.
- They can raise tax rates or social security contribution rates. However, in many countries these rates are already high by international standards. This may reduce EU international competitiveness.

Figure 4.18   EU population by age group, 1995–2045

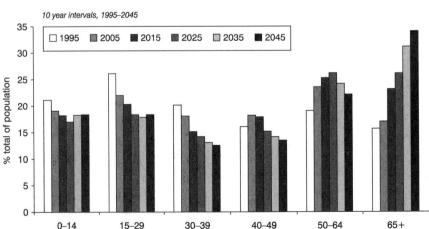

10 year intervals, 1995–2045

Legend: ☐ 1995 ▨ 2005 ■ 2015 ▨ 2025 ▨ 2035 ■ 2045

y-axis: % total of population (0–35)
x-axis groups: 0–14, 15–29, 30–39, 40–49, 50–64, 65+

Source: Lloyds Bank Economic Bulletin, August 1997

AGING POPULATION AND AGGREGATE SAVING IN EUROPE

Figure 4.19   EU support ratios, 1995–2040

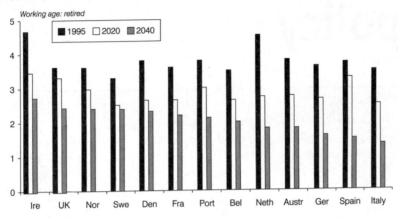

Source: Lloyds Bank Economic Bulletin, August 1997

■ They can make public pensions less generous, either restricting eligibility to the least well off or reducing the real value of pensions. Given the difficulty associated with the first two options, most governments will probably be forced to choose the third one.

The macroeconomic impact of the saving cycle

Saving in Europe as a whole is therefore likely to swing in coming years, as a result from its ageing population, first rising sharply and then falling equally sharply. The extent of this swing will vary from country to country. It is estimated to be rather modest in the UK, with saving rates rising to 4 per cent above current levels in the first few years of the new millenium and eventually falling to 4 per cent below current levels. Swings in other countries, particularly Spain and Italy, are likely to be much more pronounced, in the region of plus and then minus 8 per cent.

The saving swing will have profound macroeconomic effects. The initial upturn in saving is likely to lead to a prolonged period of depressed consumer demand, which will result in slow growth and possibly a recession, with the biggest slow down recorded in Germany, Italy, Spain and the Netherlands. France and the UK will be less affected. Inflation and interest rates will fall further from current levels.

Because the USA and Japan will be experiencing a similar saving upturn, the world cost of capital is likely to fall. Given the weak demand condition prevailing, the reduced cost of capital will be unlikely to encourage investment in most industrialized countries. Because of the domestic saving rise relative to investment, most industrialized countries will be likely to run sizeable current account surpluses with the rest of the world. Less developed countries, or newly industrialized countries, with much younger populations, will be able to benefit from the reduced cost of capital. They will need to import capital from abroad to finance their investment. As Foley (1997) concludes: 'A major challenge for world capital markets will be to finance these deficits, from the developed world's increased savings, in ways that do not create the conditions for a repeat of the debt crisis.'

☆ **For revision of this chapter, see the Chapter Summaries at the end of the book, starting on page 411.**

5 Government and fiscal policy

Objectives

After studying this chapter, you will be able to:

- understand the nature of fiscal policy and of countercyclical measures;
- distinguish between budget deficit, budget surplus, balanced budget, PSBR, PSDR, national debt and public sector debt;
- understand the difference between automatic and discretionary fiscal policy;
- understand the notion of structural and cyclical deficits;
- explain the process of 'fiscal drag';
- distinguish between the four multipliers: government expenditure multiplier, tax multiplier, transfer payment multiplier, balanced budget multiplier;
- calculate the changes in government expenditure and taxation necessary to achieve a certain level of national income;
- describe the practical problems and the possible adverse effects of fiscal policy.

INTRODUCTION

The various parts of the economy begin to fall into place quite neatly once we have understood the main points of the Keynesian model. It should be clear why we now move on to talk about government. We are still following the theoretical thread which Keynesian theory has given us. Let's repeat it.

We started off by asking ourselves what could be done, if anything, to increase the economy's output, so that we could all have more goods and services, we could all be richer and healthier and we could all be in employment if we wanted. Keynes thought he knew what could be done to achieve this: stimulate aggregate demand. If more goods and services are demanded, provided the economy can produce more, more will be produced; if more is produced, income and employment will rise. So why don't we all demand more? This is exactly what we set out to discover, identifying first of all who is doing the demanding of goods and services. We listed them as **categories of expenditure**:

$$E = C + I + G + (X - M).$$

There are the consumers, of course. They buy goods and services, but only if they have the money. They won't buy more if they don't earn more and they can only earn more if the economy is producing more.

There are the firms, of course; they buy capital goods. Why don't they buy more capital goods? Well, they will try to work out if it is profitable for them to expand and invest in capital, machinery, etc. They will certainly think twice if loan interest is very high. How can they be sure that they will be able to sell more afterwards to repay the loan? It's a very risky decision, particularly when interest rates are high.

Then there is the government. If consumers cannot consume more because their incomes are not rising; if business people are not investing more because they do not know what the future of the economy will hold and cannot afford high interest repayments, why can't the government increase its spending? If the government adds to the demand for goods and services by spending more, more will be produced, new jobs will be created, people's incomes will rise, so they too will demand more goods and services. The government in this way can pump prime the economy. The government has all the money it collects in tax revenues, can't it use that? If that is not enough, the government can always print new money, can't it? The Bank of England is its agent. So can't the government tell the Bank of England to print more money to pay for the goods and services, etc? If this 'printing of new money' is frowned upon and heads are shaken in disapproval in case it causes inflation, the government can always borrow. Isn't this what government ministers and the press are always worrying about: that the government debt is too big and should be reduced? But if the money the government borrows is spent on the economy to create jobs and more real wealth, won't the government spend less on unemployment benefits and get more in tax revenue? Won't that reduce the debt then? But when the government borrows money, who does it borrow it from? What would the people who lent their money to the government have done with it, had they not lent it to the government? Who else, if not the government, could have borrowed it?

There are many questions, here, as you can see. Let's try and unravel them first and then answer them.

FISCAL POLICY: SOME DEFINITIONS

Governments have a wide variety of regulatory powers that affect the microeconomy and the conduct of our lives and our businesses. From a purely macroeconomic point of view, governments affect the economy through two broad policy areas: fiscal policy and monetary policy.

Monetary policy affects the economy through changes in the money supply, regulated in the UK by the Bank of England, which determines the liquidity conditions of the economic system.

Fiscal policy is the general name given to government policies aimed at influencing the level of aggregate demand and economic activity by varying the level of government expenditure and taxation. Fiscal policy can be implemented in three distinct areas:

- **Policies related to the purchases of goods and services** by the government. This is a **direct spending** by the government, which we have called G.
- **Policies related to transfer payments,** such as unemployment benefits, child benefit, social security benefits, welfare payments, etc. that the government makes to households. This is **indirect government spending**. The government gives out money to some people, who will then go out and do the spending themselves, if they wish. These payments are also included in G.
- **Policies related to taxes**, whether direct taxes (income taxes) or indirect taxes (expenditure taxation). **Net taxes** (T) is equal to the tax payments made to the government by households and firms, minus transfer payments made by the government to households and firms.

Activity 5.1

Look at the pie chart of the UK general government expenditure for 1997–8 presented by the Chancellor in the July Budget of 1997 (Figure 5.1). Translate the

Figure 5.1 General government expenditure by function, 1997–8

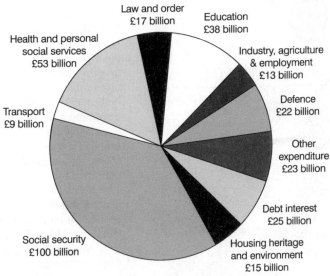

GGE (X) = £315 billion.

Source: HMSO, *Financial Statement and Budget Report, 1997*

value shown in percentages of total expenditure and say which is the largest item of expenditure.

✔ Answer 5.1

Government expenditure for 1997–8 was divided up as indicated in Table 5.1, which also shows government expenditure allocations by the previous 1996–7 budget. You can work out the budgetary changes, if any, of the first Labour government in the UK for 19 years. One should also add, however, that the Labour government had only been in government for two months when its first partial July budget 1997 was published. The first full-scale budget, published in March 1998, presented some important innovations which we discuss further on.

The government spent £100b on social security in 1997–8, out of a total government spending of £315b. This is the largest amount, which represents nearly 32 per cent of total government spending.

🖒 Activity 5.2

Look at the pie chart of UK government revenues as presented by the Chancellor in the July budget for 1997–8 (Figure 5.2). Calculate the values in percentages and say which is the largest source of revenue for the government. What percentage does borrowing represent?

✔ Answer 5.2

Table 5.2 shows the government revenues in 1997–8, expressed as percentages of total government revenues. The largest source of government revenue is income tax, which represents 22.8 per cent of total government revenue. The amount the government borrows represents 6 per cent of total revenues, 1.3 per cent less than in 1996–7.

Table 5.1 UK government expenditure, 1996–7, 1997–8

	Labour government budget 1997–8 %	Conservative government budget 1996–7 %
Health	16.8	16.6
Law and order	5.3	5.2
Education	12.06	12.4
Industry	4.1	4.2
Defence	6.9	6.8
Other	7.3	7.5
Debt interest	7.9	7.1
Housing	4.7	5.2
Social security	31.7	31.0
Transport	2.8	2.9

Table 5.2 UK government revenues, 1996–7, 1997–8

	1997–8 %	1996–7 %
Income tax	22.8	22.8
VAT	16.1	15.6
Corporation tax	8.5	8.8
Excise duties	10.7	10.1
Other taxes	7.6	10.1
Business rates	4.7	4.9
Social security contributions	15.5	15.3
Borrowing	6.0	7.3
Other	4.1	4.9

The government finances its expenditures by using **tax revenues**.

■ If government expenditure (G) exceeds tax revenues (T) the government runs a **budget deficit**:

$$G > T.$$

■ If government expenditure (G) is equal to tax revenue (T) the government has a **balanced budget**:

$$G = T.$$

■ When tax proceeds (T) exceed government expenditure, the government has a **budget surplus**:

$$T > G \text{ or } G < T.$$

The excess of government spending over tax revenues, the government **deficit**, has to be financed somehow. As we see later in this chapter, it can be financed in two way:

1 the government can **borrow from the public**, through what are known as **open market operations (OMO)**. This system of financing a government deficit tends to push up interest rates, which in turn reduce private investment (this effect is often referred to as the **crowding out effect** of a budget deficit). As a result of this borrowing, the government builds up its debt to the public. While the budget deficit refers to the debt which the government incurs in one year, the **national debt** is the **stock** of accumulated, outstanding government debt over the years.

2 The government could, until recently, also automatically **borrow from the Bank of England** which in turn 'printed' more money as a result (in fact it simply credited the government balances at the BoE with an equivalent amount of sterling). This form of financing the government deficit increases the money supply and can be inflationary. To meet the Maastricht conditions for the introduction of

Figure 5.2 The financing of general government expenditure (X), 1997–8

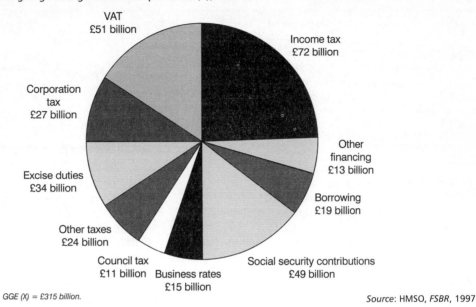

VAT
£51 billion

Income tax
£72 billion

Corporation
tax
£27 billion

Other
financing
£13 billion

Excise duties
£34 billion

Borrowing
£19 billion

Other taxes
£24 billion

Council tax
£11 billion   Business rates
£15 billion

Social security contributions
£49 billion

GGE (X) = £315 billion.

Source: HMSO, *FSBR*, 1997

the single currency and the European Central Bank, EU governments were required to guarantee a certain measure of national central banks independence. This led to important reforms in all EU countries, including Britain, in the conduct of their monetary policy in 1997. EU central banks can no longer automatically paper over government deficits. We discuss this more fully in Chapters 6 and 7.

A word of warning at this point about terminology and data. When we talk about **budget deficits**, **budget surpluses** and **national debt** we are referring to the budget and debt position of **central government** only.

When we talk about the **public sector borrowing requirement** (PSBR), the **public sector debt repayment** (PSDR) and **net public sector debt**, we are referring to the budget and debt position of the **entire public sector**, which includes central and local government as well as public corporations.

The new system of national accounts adopted in the UK in September 1998 in accordance to the European System of Accounts, ESA95, introduced some changes to public finance statistics and national accounting conventions. In relation to the concepts introduced here, the main new measure used in the European accounts is that of **general government**, which includes central and local government but excludes public corporations. Similarly, the **general government financial deficit/surplus (GGFD/GGFS)** which exclude the financial deficit or

surplus of public corporations, is the most internationally comparable measure of the budget deficit/surplus. **General government gross debt** is the stock analogue of the GGFD and is the measure used in the EU for accumulated general government debt. As a general government measure, it excludes the debt of public corporations. These distinctions are summed up in Table 5.3. Finally, the **general government expenditure (GGE)** is a broad measure of government spending which includes: current expenditure as well as capital expenditure and net lending to the private sector and abroad and central government lending to public corporations. GGE(X), on the other hand, differs from GGE in that it excludes privatization proceeds and lottery-financed expenditure and nets off interest and dividends receipts.

All these accounting conventions, although important, do not alter the economics of fiscal policy, which is our focus. To this effect we will not attempt to maintain the distinction between central government and general government in our discussions, except where official statistics are referred to.

✍ Activity 5.3

Study Table 5.4 which shows the public sector borrowing requirement estimated to the year 2002. They answer:

(a) How are figures for the general government borrowing requirements obtained?

Table 5.3   General government and public sector

Central government	Budget deficit G>T	Budget surplus G<T	National debt
General government: Central and local government	General government financial deficit (GGFD)	General government financial surplus (GGFS)	General government gross debt (GGGD)
Public sector: Central government, Local government and public corporations	Public sector borrowing requirement (PSBR)	Public sector debt repayment (surplus) (PSDR)	Net public sector debt (NPSD)

(b) How are PSBR figures obtained?

(c) What is the projected trend for PSBR?

(d) What do the top and bottom halves of Table 5.3 show?

(e) Why are the figures shown in the bottom half important?

✓ Answer 5.3

As we can see from Table 5.4:

(a) The general government borrowing requirement (GGBR) is obtained by subtracting general government receipts from general government expenditure.

(b) The public sector borrowing requirement (PSBR) figures are obtained taking into account the bor-

rowing requirement of public corporations. Negative borrowing requirements indicate receipts in excess of expenditures from public corporations; hence the PSBR for 1996–7 and 1997–8 is smaller than the GGBR.

(c) The public sector borrowing requirement (PSBR) is projected to decrease steadily over the next few years, with budget balance achieved by the year 2000 and a surplus recorded thereon.

(d) The top half of table shows general government expenditure, receipts, borrowing requirement and PSBR in £bn for the period from 1995 to 2002. The bottom half of the table shows the same items, but expressed as percentages of nominal GDP for the same period.

Table 5.4   Public sector borrowing requirement[1]

	Outturn	Forecast		Projection[2]			
	1995–6	1996–7	1997–8	1998–9	1999–2000	2000–01	2001–02
£billion							
General government expenditure	303.0	308.5	319.0	327	336	345	353
General government receipts	269.2	280.9	299.4	315	333	352	370
General government borrowing requirement	33.8	27.7	19.6	12	4	–7	–18
PCMOB[3]	–2.2	–1.3	–0.4	0	0	0	0
PSBR	**31.7**	**26.4**	**19.2**	**12**	**3**	**–8**	**–18**
Per cent of money GDP							
General government expenditure	42¾	41¼	40½	39½	39	38¼	37½
General government receipts	38	37¾	38	38	38½	39	39¼
General government borrowing requirement	4¾	3¾	2½	1½	½	–¾	–2
PCMOB[3]	–¼	–¼	0	0	0	0	0
PSBR	4½	3½	2½	1½	½	–¾	2
Money GDP – £billion	708.5	745.7	786.9	826	864	903	943

Source: HMSO, *FSBR*, 1997 (figures rounded up to next integer)
[1] Constituent items may not sum to totals because of rounding.
[2] Projections are rounded to the nearest £1 billion from 1998–9 onwards.
[3] Public corporations' market and overseas borrowing.

(e) The bottom half of this table is important because it shows the relative size of the deficit and PSBR, in terms of the output of the economy (GDP). It also shows that by 1997–8 Britain was able to meet one of the criteria set out in the Maastricht Treaty for membership of the European Monetary Union (EMU), which is a PSBR not greater than 3 per cent of GDP.

✍ Activity 5.4

Study Figure 5.3 and explain briefly what it shows.

✓ Answer 5.4

Figure 5.3 shows in a bar chart the same information provided by the bottom half of Table 5.4, that is, PSBR as a percentage of nominal GDP; this time, however, from 1973 to the year 2002 (estimated). By early 1998 the PSBR was well within the 3 per cent reference level for deficits used in EU calculations and was projected to fall substantially below that level in subsequent years, ending in surplus (PSDR) after the year 2000. The projected fall in the PSBR over time is driven by continued

control over public spending and gradual increase in receipts as percentage of GDP. The increase in receipt is envisaged to come from increasing road fuel and tobacco duties. The difference between general government expenditure and receipts measures the general government deficit. General government in the UK should reach a balanced budget position by the year 2000.

✍ Activity 5.5

Study Table 5.5 and explain clearly what it shows, comparing it with Table 5.4.

✓ Answer 5.5

Table 5.5 sets out projections for two different measures of government and public sector debt. **Net public sector debt** is the stock analogue of the PSBR. It measures the public sector's financial liabilities to the private sector and abroad, net of short-term financial assets, both in current figures and as a percentage of GDP.

Gross general government debt is the measure of debt used in the EU's excessive deficits procedure. As

Figure 5.3   UK public sector borrowing requirements and current deficit

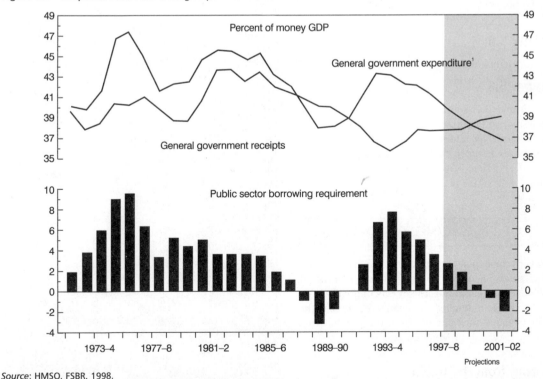

Source: HMSO, FSBR, 1998.
[1] GGE (X). General government expenditure excluding privatisation proceeds and lottery financed spending, and net of interest and dividend receipts.

Table 5.5   UK public sector debt

	1996–7	1997–8	Forecast 1998–9	1999–2000	2000–01
Net public sector debt					
£ billion	350	355	359	366	354
-per cent of GDP	45.0	43.5	42.1	41	38
General government gross debt					
-£ billion	409	413	421	426	414
-per cent of GDP	54.3	51.9	50.5	47	44

Source: HMSO, FSBR, 1998

a general government measure, it excludes the debt of public corporations. It measures general government's total financial liabilities before netting off short-term financial assets. However, this level of technical detail goes beyond what is necessary for us here. It is more important to focus on the percentage of GDP represented by the net public sector debt, which measures the value of the public sector accumulated debt. Net public sector debt is now forecast to fall from 45 per cent of GDP by March 1999. General government gross debt was 53.4 per cent in December 1997, compared with the Maastricht criterion of 60 per cent, and is forecast to fall to 50.5 per cent of GDP by March 1999.

✍️Activity 5.6

Study and briefly comment on Tables 5.6 and 5.7.

✓ Answer 5.6

Tables 5.6 and 5.7 show a historical series for the PSBR and its main components which allows us to see the PSBR trend over a longer period of time.

We now look in more detail at how the government finances the deficit between its revenues and its spending.

WAYS OF FINANCING THE DEFICIT

If the government spends more than it receives, the difference, its debt, needs to be financed in some way. A heated debate still surrounds the effects of government deficits and their financing. To finance its deficit, the government can either borrow from the public, from the Bank of England, or from abroad.

Borrowing from the public

When the government borrows from the public, it does

Table 5.6   Historical series for the PSBR and its components, 1965–2002 (figures rounded up to next integer)

	Per cent of money GDP			
	GGE	General government receipts	Public corporations' market and overseas borrowing	PSBR
1965–6	38	35	0	3
1966–7	39	36	0	3
1967–8	43	38	0	5
1968–9	41	41	0	1
1969–70	41	42	0	−1
1970–1	41	40	0	1
1971–2	42	40	0	2
1972–3	41	38	0	4
1973–4	43	38	1	6
1974–5	49	40	1	9
1975–6	49	40	0	9
1976–7	47	41	1	6
1977–8	43	40	0	3
1978–9	44	39	0	5
1979–80	44	39	0	5
1980–1	46	41	0	5
1981–2	47	44	0	3
1982–3	47	44	0	3
1983–4	46	43	0	3
1984–5	46	43	0	3
1985–6	44	42	0	1
1986–7	43	41	0	1
1987–8	41	41	0	−1
1988–9	38	40	0	−3
1989–90	39	40	0	−1
1990–1	39	39	0	0
1991–2	41	38	0	2
1992–3	43	37	0	6
1993–4	43	36	0	7
1994–5	42	37	0	5
1995–6	42	38	0	4
1996–7	41	38	0	3
1997–8	40	38	0	2
1998–9	39	38	0	1
1999–00	38	39	0	0
2000–01	38	39	0	−1
2001–02	38	39	0	−2

Source: HMSO, FSBR, 1998

Table 5.7 Historical series for government receipts, 1965–2002

	Per cent of money GDP		
	General government receipts	Non-North Sea taxes and NICs[1]	Public sector current receipts
1965–6	35	32	37
1966–7	36	32	38
1967–8	38	34	40
1968–9	41	36	42
1969–70	42	37	44
1970–1	40	37	43
1971–2	40	35	41
1972–3	38	33	39
1973–4	38	34	40
1974–5	40	36	43
1975–6	40	37	43
1976–7	41	36	44
1977–8	40	35	42
1978–9	39	35	41
1979–80	39	35	42
1980–1	41	36	43
1981–2	44	39	46
1982–3	44	38	46
1983–4	43	38	45
1984–5	43	38	44
1985–6	42	37	44
1986–7	41	38	43
1987–8	41	38	42
1988–9	40	37	41
1989–90	40	37	41
1990–1	39	37	40
1991–2	38	37	39
1992–3	37	35	37
1993–4	36	34	36
1994–5	37	35	37
1995–6	38	36	39
1996–7	38	36	38
1997–8	38	36	39
1998–9	38	37	39
1999–00	39	37	39
2000–01	39	37	39
2001–02	39	38	40

Source: HMSO, FSBR, 1998
[1]As a per cent of non-North Sea GDP.

so by selling government securities: treasury bills, which are short-term loans to the government (three months) and government bonds, which are long-term loans.

Government bonds are financial assets promising to pay a fixed amount or yield until they reach their maturity date, when they are repurchased back by the government at their face value and not their market value. To persuade people to buy more of these bonds, the government has to pay a higher interest than the current market rate, or it must sell them at a lower price, that is, below their redemption value. We discuss gov-

ernment bonds in more detail in Chapter 6, when we study the monetary sector. It is enough for you to remember here that **open market operations (OMO)** used by the government to raise money from the public for a certain period of time at particular interest rates, tend to push up interest rates. This in turn may put off private investment which then falls as a result. The monetarists therefore argue that government expenditure financed by OMO does not represent a net addition to aggregate demand as it simply displaces another component of it, namely investment. Given that aggregate expenditure (E) is:

$$E = C + I + G + (X - M)$$

if $G\uparrow$ but $I\downarrow$ by the same amount, E will remain the same. This effect is known as the 'crowding out' effect of government expenditure, financed by OMO.

✍ Activity 5.7

What may get crowded out by government expenditure financed by borrowing from the public and why?

✓ Answer 5.7

As we saw earlier, private investment might be crowded out, as OMO raises interest rates and higher interest rates then tend to reduce investment. The Keynesians would argue, however, that since investment does not seem to be very responsive to interest rates on the basis of empirical evidence, it is not likely to be displaced by government borrowing and will not decline as a result. An increase in government expenditure financed by OMO would then, in their view, represent a net addition to aggregate demand.

Borrowing from the Bank of England

If the entire sum the government needs to borrow to pay for its deficit spending, that is, the difference between tax revenues and spending, is not raised in the form of loans from the public, the Bank of England is no longer obliged – as it used to before the 1997 reforms – to make up the difference by buying the remaining unsold government bonds. When the Bank of England bought government bonds, it paid the government money in exchange, effectively giving the government a loan for a certain period of time. This policy increases the money supply and can be inflationary. According to recent empirical studies, little clear correlation can be found between inflation rates and government deficits over time. The empirical evidence does seem to disprove the connection between budget deficits and inflation (more on this in later chapters).

FISCAL POLICIES AND BUSINESS CYCLES

The main objective of fiscal policies is to control aggregate demand and stabilize the economy. Even when economies expand and their output grows over time, they do not do so smoothly. This was true at the time when Keynes was writing just as much as it is true today. Economies go through what are known as **business cycles**, lasting for eight to ten years each. During this time, economies go through four phases: expansion, levelling off (peak), contraction, depression (bottom); and the recovery and expansion again, peak, contraction, and so on. The terms often used to refer to this pattern of behaviour of the economy is **boom and bust**.

During an **expansion** – the so-called booms – everything grows: output and employment, but also prices, wages and balance of trade deficits. Businesses encouraged by buoyant demand express their optimism by investing to expand production. As the upswing continues, however, obstacles begin to occur which impede further expansion. Production costs begin to increase, shortages of raw materials may further hamper production; interest rates rise, making further investments more costly; prices rise and consumers react by buying less. As consumption starts to lag behind production, inventories accumulate, causing a slowing down in price rises. Manufacturers begin to retrench. The expansionary phase has reached its **peak**. Once reached, typically after two or three years, the expansion levels off for about two years and then the economy begins to contract. During a **contraction** or **recession** the rate of growth of output begins to fall, workers are laid off, unemployment rises, businesses lose confidence in the state of the economy and investment falls as inflation slows down and profits drop; current account problems ease up. The recessionary phase also lasts typically two to three years, until the economy reaches the **bottom** of the recession, which is characterized by low inflation and current account surpluses, but also low output and high unemployment. Production cutbacks are severe; factories shut down; there is excess capacity and capital lies idle; unemployment becomes widespread. The economy is in a **depression**.

Recovery eventually begins and may be initiated by several factors, including a resurgence in consumer demand, the total running down of inventories, or government action to stimulate demand. Often generally slow and uneven at the start, recovery soon gathers pace. Prices start rising once more, faster than costs,

giving businesses an incentive to expand production. Employment increases, providing people with more income, hence reinforcing demand for consumer goods. To meet the increased consumer demand investment in capital goods increases, as firms want to expand capacity. Capital goods industries also expand, generating further employment. A mood of optimism pervades the economy once more and businesses' desire to speculate on new business ventures triggers further expansions. A new cycle is under way.

In real life, business cycles do not always behave quite as neatly and can vary considerably in severity and duration. The most severe and widespread of all economic depressions occurred between 1929 and 1932; it started in the USA, spread to Europe and lasted for almost a decade. It was precisely the need to find a way out of the Great Depression that prompted Keynes to develop his model of the macroeconomy, which advocates the need for government intervention.

However, since World War II most industrialized economies have been growing, despite experiencing economic cycles. This has meant that every peak reached by the economy during a boom has been at a higher level of output than the previous one. When the economy contracted, the output level remained higher than that of the previous contraction. Overall the output trend over time remained positive, despite its large fluctuations. Governments' stabilization policies are therefore aimed at achieving two goals:

- bringing the economy's **actual output** as close as possible to its **potential output** or **full-employment output**;
- reducing actual output's cyclical fluctuations by means of counter-cyclical policies.

This situation is illustrated in Figure 5.4. Actual output as shown in Figure 5.4 is consistently below potential output. The first aim of stabilization policies is therefore to shift up actual output in line with the potential output of the economy. The second aim is to smooth out its path and reduce the size of its fluctuations. The phases of the cycles of actual output are numbered 1, 2, 3 and 4. The number 1s denote the bottom of the recessions. Recessionary phases are characterized by low inflation and current account surpluses, but low output growth and high unemployment. Note that successive number 1s are at higher levels of national output. The number 2s denote the transition phases out of recessions and into expansions. The 3s denote the points at which expansions reach their peak level. Boom periods are characterized by high output and low unemployment, but also high inflation and current account deficits.

Figure 5.4 Actual output and potential output

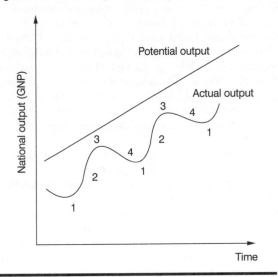

where the **inflationary gap** measures the excess of aggregate demand over the full employment level of output. People demand more goods than the economy is capable of producing in the short run, as the economy is already using all the resources available, including labour. This excess demand will only cause prices to rise (inflation), as no more goods can be produced in the short term. In a situation of demand overexpansion or overheating, the government should aim to run a **budget surplus**, increasing taxes to reduce people's demand and cutting down on its own expenditure.

During recessions, when aggregate demand falls short of what the economy can produce at full employment, the **deflationary gap** measures the shortage of demand, i.e. by how much demand would need to increase to bring about the production of a full employment level of output. The deflationary gap shows the gap in effective aggregate demand that needs to be filled by the government's **budget deficit**, which can be a combination of reduced taxation and increased spending, in order to bring about potential, full employment levels of output.

To smooth out these fluctuations, the government should use **counter-cyclical fiscal policies**: **expansionary policies** ($G > T$) when the private sector of the economy shows signs of slowing down and entering into a recession; **contractionary policies** ($T > G$) when the opposite is true and the economy shows signs of overexpansion. This situation is illustrated in Figure 5.5

✍ Activity 5.8

Assuming these counter-cyclical fiscal policies are successful in smoothing out the path of actual output and expenditure, what can you say about the government budget over the course of the cycle?

Figure 5.5 Counter-cyclical stabilization policies

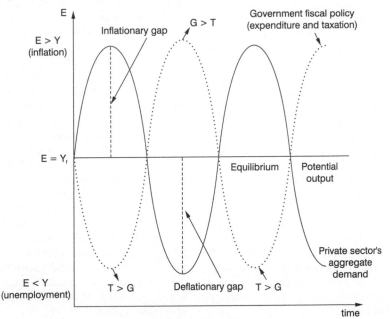

✓ Answer 5.8

These policies are meant to be countercyclical. Therefore, the government budget position will deteriorate during recessions (budget deficits) and improve during booms (budget surpluses), as the government increases spending and reduces taxes, in order to reduce recessions and reduces spending and increases taxes during booms, to reduce overheating.

As Figure 5.5 shows, the **timing of counter-cyclical policies** is crucial as mistimed policies might result in greater rather than smaller fluctuations. Delay in the implementation of a policy designed to reduce demand to prevent the economy from overheating might mean that government contractionary policies begin to bite when the economy is already slowing down and about to enter a recession of its own accord. In this case, government policies aimed at preventing an overexpansion would result in further deepening the recession.

AUTOMATIC FISCAL POLICY

A budget deficit, when government expenditure exceeds tax revenues, does not necessarily indicate that the government is debt financing an expansionary fiscal policy; just as a budget surplus does not necessarily mean that the government is deliberately pursuing a contractionary fiscal policy. Budget **deficits**, like budget **surpluses** can develop automatically, as a result of changing economic circumstances, and not necessarily or always as a result of a deliberate act of fiscal policy on the part of the government.

When the economy enters into a recession and unemployment rises, the government has to spend more on social security, principally through unemployment related benefits, and receives less in taxes, both in direct taxes as people's incomes fall and in indirect taxes like VAT, as people consume less. A budget deficit ($G > T$) might therefore develop automatically as a result of a recession. If we simply looked at a swelling government deficit, we might conclude that the government policy is unduly expansionary and recommend a cut in spending or an increase in taxation. This would be a good example of wrong assumptions leading to disastrous conclusions, as the right policy prescription during a recession, at least according to Keynes, would be for government spending to increase, making the deficit worse. By boosting demand, a larger government deficit would help the economy out of its recessionary hole; reducing government expenditure, with a view to balancing the budget, would not help.

In very much the same way, a budget surplus ($T > G$) can develop automatically when the economy is expanding. During a boom, unemployment is low and income high. Consequently, the amount of money which the government has to spend on unemployment benefits falls, while the amount of money it receives through direct and indirect taxation increases, as people's incomes and consumption are both higher. So the high-growth phase of the cycle is usually characterized by higher tax receipts and falls in spending on social security.

So **taxes**, whose revenue rises as national income rises, and government expenditure that falls as national income rises are called **automatic stabilizers**. They are automatic because their value changes as a result of changes in income and not as a result of deliberate government policy decision. They act as stabilizers of the economy because they tend to reduce its fluctuations. Virtually all taxes fall into the category of automatic stabilizers, but not all government expenditure is income related.

A recession causes a **budget deficit** to develop automatically. A budget deficit ($G > T$) represents a **net injection** of money by the government – the government is giving out more in benefits than it is taking out in taxes, which reduces the severity of the recession, the size of the contraction of the economy. A boom situation may cause an automatic **budget surplus**. A budget surplus ($T > G$) represents a **net withdrawal** of funds by the government. The government takes away through taxation more than it is giving out in benefits; this reduces the size of the expansion and dampens the overheating of the economy.

Summing up, the economic cycle is one of the most important short-term influences on government finances and government budgets. In turn, government automatic fiscal policy contributes to reduce the severity of cyclical fluctuations. The automatic changes we have just described help to stabilize the economy by automatically putting more money into the economy when demand is weak, and reducing it when demand is too strong. The effect of automatic stabilisers will be stronger, the larger the government sector, the more progressive the tax system and the more generous the unemployment benefit system. Cyclical fluctuations in public finances, however, can make it more difficult to distinguish underlying trends. This is why recent government official statistics separate budgets' cyclical components from the main budget figures. The operation of automatic fiscal stabilizers is explained more formally in the following pages, which can be omitted by the non-specialist student.

GOVERNMENT TAX AND EXPENDITURE FUNCTIONS

The following tax function summarizes what we have said so far:

$$T = t_0 + t_1 Y.$$

T represents tax revenues. Tax revenues are made up by a certain amount which is fixed (t_0), in the sense that it does not depend on national income; and by an amount that varies with income by t_1 of Y. The bulk of tax revenue is a function of income: it increases as income increases and falls as income falls. The amount by which tax revenues increase as income increases is represented by t_1, which is the **marginal propensity to tax**; t_1 measures the amount tax revenue changes for every £1 change of national income; t_1 determines the slope of the tax function.

The height of this function, just like its slope (t_1), is determined by a policy decision taken by the government. This is where the government uses its discretion. We see this happening every year in the April budget, when the Chancellor of the Exchequer changes the rate of tax for certain categories of people, exempts certain goods from VAT or imposes it on others. The total tax revenue will depend, however, on national income and will rise or fall with it, unless the government intervenes with an act of **discretionary fiscal policy** to change either t_0 or t_1.

The following government expenditure function describes what we have said so far:

$$G = g_0 - g_1 Y$$

where G stands for government expenditure, comprising both direct government spending on goods and services and transfer payments, like unemployment benefits, etc. g_0 represents that amount of government expenditure that does not depend on income, but rather reflects autonomous government spending decisions, like building hospitals, roads, schools, etc. g_1 represents that part of government expenditure which does depend on income, like unemployment benefits or income support benefits, which decreases when income rises, as less is paid out; fewer people are unemployed and fewer receive income support benefits.

If we combine the analysis of government spending and taxation in a single diagram, we can show very clearly the government budget position and how it is influenced, ceteris paribus, by the level of national income, as in Figure 5.6.

When national income is Y_0 the government has a balanced budget ($G = T$). At levels of income below Y_0,

Figure 5.6 Public sector deficit and national income

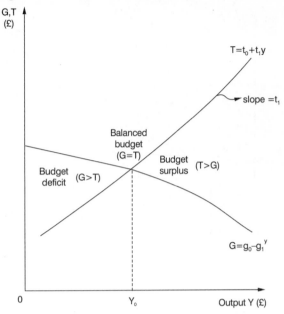

T is the tax function, while G is the government expenditure function.

the government has a budget deficit ($G > T$); at income levels greater than Y_0, the government has a budget surplus ($T > G$).

✍ Activity 5.9

Referring to Figure 5.6, explain in what way G and T act as automatic stabilizers.

✓ Answer 5.9

First of all we need to understand what we mean by 'stabilizers' and 'stabilization'. G and T will act as stabilizers of the economy as they tend to bring the economy back to the equilibrium level of output and income the economy was at before.

If something intervenes to push the economy away from its equilibrium position Y_0 (where $E = Y$), say a reduction in exports or a reduction in investment expenditure, causing the level of income to fall below Y_0, G and T will act as stabilizers. Ceteris paribus, they will tend to bring the economy back to its original equilibrium position Y_0. If, on the other hand, an increase in exports or investment were to push the level of income beyond its current equilibrium value at Y_0, the same would apply, but in the opposite direction. G and T would again act as automatic stabilizers: G and T will

Figure 5.7   Automatic stabilizers

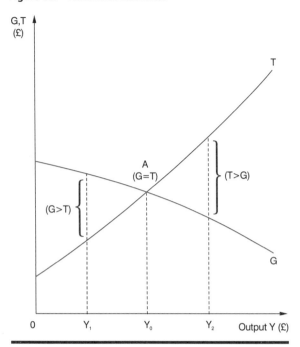

Figure 5.8   Effects of boom and recession

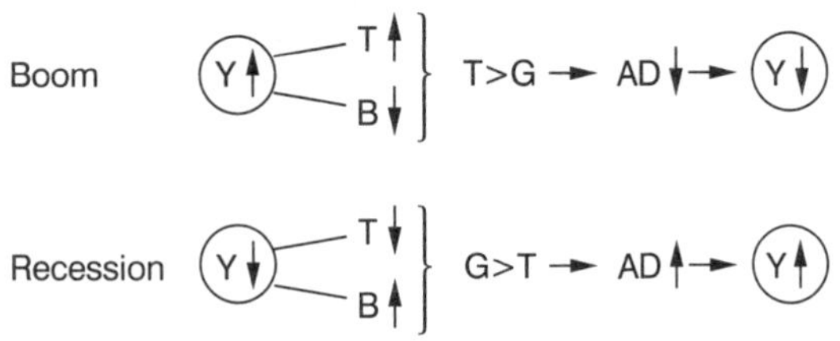

automatically act as 'brakes' and tend to push the economy back to its old equilibrium position. (See Figure 5.7.)

Assume the economy is in equilibrium at Y_0 where it is also the case that $G = T$: the government runs a balanced budget. Assume now that a decrease in exports pushes the economy away from Y_0 to Y_1. At Y_1, however, $G > T$; this represents a **net injection**. The government is putting more money into the economy than it is taking away. This adds to demand and will push the economy back to Y_0 (as only at Y_0: G stops being greater than T, and $G = T$ once more). If, on the other hand, an increase in, say, export demand, adding to aggregate demand, stimulates the economy and as a result output (and income) grow from Y_0 to Y_1, an opposite situation will develop. At Y_2, $T > G$, the government collects more in taxes than spending back on the economy. This causes a **net withdrawal** of funds from the economy, which will reduce aggregate demand and push the economy back to its previous equilibrium level, Y_0. (See Figure 5.8.)

So the withdrawal, represented by taxes, increases as income increases and acts as a brake on expansion. The reasons this happens is partly due to the fact that when more people earn more, there is more income to be taxed. This is also due partly to the fact that, with progressive tax systems, as people earn

more they move up into higher tax brackets and the tax rate they pay increases. This process is often referred to as **fiscal drag**. The name refers to the fact that the increase in average tax rates that results when people move into higher brackets acts as a 'drag' on the economy.

Inflation alone often pushes people into higher income brackets; and inflation often accompanies expansions. Assume you had been given a better job and received a 10 per cent increase in your income, but that at the same time prices also rose by 10 per cent. You would not be better off at all **in real terms** because, although you have 10 per cent more money than before at the end of the month, you have to pay 10 per cent more for all the goods you buy. But when it comes to filling in your tax return, your income, **in nominal terms**, will appear to be higher. If the tax brackets are not adjusted periodically for inflation, you might end up paying more taxes and being worse off than before as a result.

Summing up, fiscal drag is the negative effect that occurs when average tax rates increase because taxpayers have moved into higher income brackets during an expansion. As the economy expands and income increases because more people earn an income and more people earn higher incomes, the automatic tax increase mechanism built into the tax system gets into action and, by reducing after-tax incomes, slows down expansion.

This can be clearly seen by comparing the reaction of two economies with different marginal rates of taxation, one higher and one lower, to the same increase in government expenditure.

✍ Activity 5.10

Look at the Figure 5.9, where G_1 represents the original level of government expenditure and G_2 represents a new increased level of government spending due to an independent decision taken by the new Chancellor of the Exchequer. T_1 represents the tax function of Country A and T_2 represents the tax function of Country B. Which country has the 'heavier' tax sys-

Figure 5.9 Effects of different marginal rates of taxation on income and output

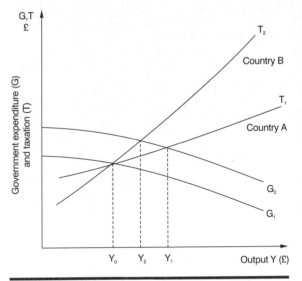

government therefore has to intervene with deliberate fiscal measures.

Discretionary fiscal policies are deliberate changes in tax rates or the level of government expenditure, to control the level of aggregate demand. They occur when the government increases or decreases the level and composition of its spending and/or the tax rates it imposes.

In real life, however, the distinction between automatic fiscal policy and discretionary fiscal policy is not as sharp as economic theorists make out. The British government adjusts its fiscal policies on a regular basis. In the Chancellor's 'autumn statement' the **changes in expenditure** are announced for the next financial year from April to March. In the spring budget statement, **changes in taxation** are announced.

📖 Activity 5.12

Study Table 5.8 carefully and calculate the estimated percentage change in spending plans in 1998–9 with respect to 1997–8. Calculate the percentage change in PSBR in 1997–8 from the previous year.

✓ Answer 5.12

The main expenditure changes, in percentage terms, of the 1998–9 budget with respect to the 1997–8 budget appear to be the following:

General government expenditure percentage changes from previous plan, 1998–9

Social security	1.2
Health	0.4
DOE – local government	0.0
DOE – other	–0.3
Scotland, Wales and Northern Ireland	–0.3
Defence	–0.4
Education	–1.0
Home Office	0.1
Transport	0.1
Other departments	0.3
Local authority	0.3
Reserve	–2.5
Total	**–1.9**
Cyclical social security	–0.4
Central government debt interest	0.4
Accounting adjustments	0.2
GGE(X)	**–1.8**

What is also interesting to note is the fact that the cyclical component of social security payments – that is, the social security payment changes, mainly job-

tem? Compare the effects of the government expenditure change on the two economies.

✓ Answer 5.10

Country A has a lower marginal rate of taxation than Country B; A has smaller **mpt**, hence a flatter slope of its tax function. The same increase in government spending from G_1 to G_2 causes a greater output and income expansion from Y_0 to Y_1 in Country A, which has a lower tax rate than Country B, with the higher tax rate. Taxes act as bigger automatic stabilizers and reduce growth, in this case, rather more in country B (from Y_0 to Y_2) than in country A (from Y_0 to Y_1).

📖 Activity 5.11

Repeat Activity 5.10 and look at the effect in the two countries of a reduction in government expenditure.

✓ Answer 5.11

A reduction in government expenditure is shown by a shift down of the government expenditure function. It causes a greater output contraction in Country A than in Country B.

DISCRETIONARY FISCAL POLICY

Although automatic fiscal stabilizers reduce the size and length of recessions, they also prevent expansions in the long run. To allow the economy to grow, the

Table 5.8   The public finances, 1998–2000

General government expenditure

	£ billion	New Plans	
	1997–8	1998–9	1999–2000
Control total by department			
Social security[1]	79.7	82.9	86.2
Health	34.9	35.4	36.1
DOE – local government	31.4	31.7	31.6
DOE – other	7.6	7.6	7.0
Scotland, Wales and N Ireland[1]	29.5	29.6	29.8
Defence (excluding sale of married quarters)	21.8	22.2	22.8
Education and employment[2]	14.0	14.0	14.0
Home Office	6.8	6.8	6.9
Transport	5.2	4.6	4.3
Other departments	19.5	20.1	20.3
Local authority self-financed expenditure	13.7	13.7	14.3
Reserve	2.5	5.0	7.5
Control total	266.5	273.7	280.9
Cyclical social security	14.1	14.3	14.7
Central government debt interest	24.8	24.4	24.0
Accounting adjustments	9.2	9.8	11.0
GGE(X)[3]	314.7	322.2	330.6
Real growth (per cent)			
Control total	¼	¾	½
GGE(X)	¼	½	½
GGE(X) as per cent of GDP	40	39	38¼

[1] Excluding cyclical social security.
[2] Does not include local authority Total Standard Spending on education.
[3] General government expenditure excluding privatisation proceeds and lottery-financed spending and net of interest and dividend receipts.

Public sector borrowing requirement

	£ billion		
	Outturn 1996–7	Estimate 1997–8	Forecast 1998–9
General government expenditure	301.1	317.1	332.5
General government receipts[1]	286.4	313.1	330.1
General government borrowing requirement	22.7	3.9	2.4
PCMOB[2]	0.0	−1.4	−0.1
PSBR			
£ billion	22.7	2.6	2.3
PSBR excluding windfall tax[3]	22.7	5.0	3.9
per cent of GDP	3.0	0.6	0.5

[1] On a cash basis.
[2] Public corporations' market and overseas borrowing.
[3] PSBR excluding windfall tax receipts and associated spending.

Source: HMSO, *FSBR*, 1998

General government receipts

£ billion

	Outturn 1996–7	Estimate 1997–8	Forecast 1998–9
Inland Revenue			
Income tax (gross of tax credits)	71.5	79.4	86.1
Income tax credits	–2.4	–2.7	–1.8
Corporation tax	27.8	30.5	30.0
Windfall tax		2.6	2.6
Petroleum revenue tax	1.7	1.1	0.5
Capital gains tax	1.1	1.4	2.2
Inheritance tax	1.6	1.7	1.9
Stamp duties	2.5	3.4	4.6
Total Inland Revenue (net of tax credits)	**103.7**	**117.4**	**126.1**
Customs and Excise			
Value added tax	46.7	51.0	53.3
Fuel duties	17.2	19.1	21.5
Tobacco duties	8.0	8.3	8.9
Spirits duties	1.6	1.5	1.6
Wine duties	1.3	1.4	1.5
Beer and cider duties	2.8	2.8	2.9
Betting and gaming duties	1.4	1.5	1.6
Air passenger duty	0.4	0.5	0.7
Insurance premium tax	0.7	1.0	1.3
Landfill tax	0.1	0.4	0.4
Customs duties and levies	2.3	2.3	2.0
Total Customs and Excise	**82.4**	**89.9**	**95.6**
Vehicle excise duties	4.2	4.6	4.6
Oil royalties	0.7	0.5	0.3
Business rates	14.7	14.7	15.0
Social security contributions	47.1	50.5	53.7
Council Tax	10.1	11.1	11.6
Other taxes and royalties	7.9	7.6	7.2
Net Taxes and Social Security Contributions	**270.7**	**296.1**	**314.1**
Interest and dividends	5.2	5.1	4.5
Gross trading surpluses and rent	4.9	4.8	4.9
Other receipts and accounting adjustments	5.6	7.1	6.6
General Government Receipts	**286.4**	**313.1**	**330.1**
North Sea revenues[1]	3.6	3.4	2.6

[1] North Sea corporation tax, petroleum revenue tax and royalties.
Source: HMSO, FSBR, 1998

seeking allowances due to the cycle – is accounted for separately and falls slightly, in line with the current positive cyclical position of the economy. This indicates that the non-cyclical increase in social security payments of 1.2 per cent is structural: i.e. due to an increase in the 'natural' rate of unemployment. The concept of natural and structural rate of unemployment will be explained in Chapter 8.

The PSBR in 1997–8 was £5bn, down by nearly 78 per cent. This reflect the shortfall in general government expenditure analysed above, higher government receipts and an unexpected repayment of debt by public corporations.

BUDGET DEFICIT AND FISCAL STANCE

As we have seen, the condition of the economy affects the budget position: budget deficits may develop as a result of a recession and budget surpluses as a result of an expansion. Looking at the size of the deficit gives no indication about the government fiscal stance, whether it is expansionary or contractionary. We therefore need a benchmark for evaluating fiscal policy. This benchmark is provided by the **full-employment budget**, that is, the budget consistent with a situation of full employment. Let's explain this concept with an example.

Suppose the economy is in a recession and the budget deficit is £250bn. Suppose also that the deficit would be £75bn if the economy were to be at full employment. The £75bn deficit represents the **structural deficit**, the deficit that would remain despite full employment because of deliberate spending programmes and tax policies of the government. The structural deficit is the deficit of the full employment budget. The remaining £175bn (250 – 75) can therefore be seen as the **cyclical deficit**, that part of the deficit which is caused by the fact that the economy is in a recession.

✍ Activity 5.13

Look at Tables 5.9 and 5.10 and comment on the information they provide.

✓ Answer 5.13

Tables 5.9 and 5.10 provide data on the structural deficit of the general government of some OECD groups of countries. By subtracting those data from those government financial balances, we can obtain the size of cyclical deficits, as percentage of nominal GDP.

MULTIPLIER EFFECT OF FISCAL POLICY

Fiscal policy is the attempt by the government to smooth out aggregate demand fluctuations by varying counter-cyclically its spending (G) and its taxes. If the government expects the economy to enter a recession, it will increase its expenditure G and/or lower taxes. If, on the other hand, a boom is anticipated, where the economy is likely to overheat with aggregate demand exceeding what the economy is currently capable of producing (the output gap is already closed), the government will want to reduce AD by lowering spending or increasing taxation.

Government expenditure multiplier

By how much should the government increase or decrease its target spending or taxation to achieve the desired level of output? The government must calculate the size of the increase or decrease of G and T necessary to achieve its target levels of output. To make this calculation the government must know the size of the multiplier effect of its own actions.

Suppose you are the chief economic adviser to the Chancellor of the Exchequer and that the economy has settled for some time at an 'equilibrium' output and income of £450bn a year. The government is spending £50bn on goods and services per year and is financing this expenditure by raising £50bn per year in taxes. The government's budget is balanced. Investment spending is £50bn a year. Suppose further that the Chancellor of the Exchequer wants to reduce unemployment by increasing output and income by £100bn, bringing it to a total of £550bn.

✍ Activity 5.14

By how much must G rise to achieve that? The Chancellor does not wish to increase taxes.

✓ Answer 5.14

You might be tempted to say that in order to increase income by £100bn the government should increase its spending by £100bn. But this would be wrong, because you would be forgetting the multiplier effect of any injection. The injection of government spending would add to demand. $E > Y \rightarrow Y \uparrow$. Desired expenditure would be greater than output, inventories would run low, firms would increase output, by taking on more people. Some of the newly employed people will have more income and increase their spending. Firms will respond again to the new consumption spending, by producing more, etc., etc. So to calculate the size of the increase in G needed to bring about $\Delta Y = £100$bn, we need to know the MPC in order to calculate the multiplier.

If MPC = 0.75, then $k = \dfrac{1}{1 - MPC} = \dfrac{1}{0.25} = 4$.

So if $\Delta Y = k\Delta J$:

$$\frac{\Delta Y}{k} = \Delta J \text{ so } \frac{100}{4} = 25.$$

Where the marginal propensity to withdraw MPW = MPS + MPT + MPM.

The government would need to increase its spending by £25bn to obtain an increase in Y of £100bn. So the government expenditure multiplier is just like the multiplier already defined:

$$\frac{1}{MPW} \text{ or } \frac{1}{1 - MPC}.$$

Table 5.9   Selected OECD countries: general government financial balances, 1981–99 (surplus (+) or deficit (–) as a percentage of nominal GDP)

	1981	1982	1983	1984	1985	1986	1987	1988	1989	1990	1991	1992	1993	1994	1995	Estimates and projections			
																1996	1997	1998	1999
USA	-1.1	-3.5	-4.1	-3.0	-3.2	-3.5	-2.6	-2.1	-1.7	-2.7	-3.3	-4.4	-3.6	-2.3	-1.9	-1.1	0.0	0.1	0.0
Japan	-3.8	-3.6	-3.6	-2.1	-0.8	-0.9	0.5	1.5	2.5	2.9	2.9	1.5	-1.6	-2.3	-3.7	-4.4	-2.8	-2.6	-2.4
Germany	-3.7	-3.3	-2.6	-1.9	-1.2	-1.3	-1.9	-2.2	0.1	-2.1	-3.3	-2.8	-3.2	-2.4	-3.3	-3.4	-3.0	-2.6	-2.3
France	-1.9	-2.8	-3.2	-2.8	-2.9	-2.7	-1.9	-1.7	-1.2	-1.6	-2.0	-3.9	-5.7	-5.7	-5.0	-4.1	-3.1	-3.0	-2.7
Italy	-11.5	-11.4	-10.7	-11.7	-12.6	-11.7	-11.0	-10.7	-9.8	-11.1	-10.1	-9.6	-10.0	-9.6	-7.0	-6.7	-3.0	-3.0	-2.7
UK	-2.6	-2.5	-3.3	-3.9	-2.8	-2.4	-1.6	0.7	1.0	-1.2	-2.6	-6.3	-7.9	-6.9	-5.6	-4.7	-2.3	-1.1	-0.6
Canada	-1.5	-5.9	-6.9	-6.5	-6.8	-5.4	-3.8	-2.5	-2.9	-4.1	-6.6	-7.4	-7.3	-5.3	-4.1	-1.8	0.4	1.0	1.5
Total of above countries	-2.8	-4.0	-4.4	-3.6	-3.4	-3.4	-2.5	-1.9	-1.2	-2.1	-2.7	-3.8	-4.2	-3.6	-3.3	-2.9	-1.5	-1.3	-1.1
Australia	-0.7	-0.5	-3.9	-3.3	-2.8	-3.0	-0.3	1.0	1.0	0.6	-2.7	-4.1	-3.7	-3.9	-2.1	-1.2	-0.8	-0.1	0.6
Austria	-1.8	-3.4	-4.0	-2.6	-2.6	-3.8	-4.4	-3.3	-3.1	-2.4	-2.6	-1.8	-4.1	-4.8	-5.0	-4.0	-2.9	-2.8	-2.5
Belgium	-12.8	-10.9	-11.5	-9.4	-8.9	-9.4	-7.6	-6.8	-6.2	-5.5	-6.3	-6.9	-7.1	-4.9	-3.9	-3.2	-2.5	-2.2	-2.1
Denmark	—	—	—	—	—	—	—	1.5	0.3	-1.0	-2.4	-2.2	-2.8	-2.7	-1.8	-1.1	0.5	1.6	2.6
Finland	3.5	1.9	0.6	3.0	2.9	3.4	1.0	4.1	6.3	5.4	-1.5	-5.7	-7.9	-6.2	-5.2	-3.2	-1.3	-0.2	0.3
Greece	-8.3	-6.5	-7.1	-8.4	-11.5	-10.3	-9.5	-11.5	-14.4	-16.1	-11.5	-12.8	-13.8	-10.3	-9.8	-7.6	-5.0	-3.9	-4.5
Iceland	1.3	1.7	-2.0	2.2	-1.7	-4.1	-0.9	-2.0	-4.6	-3.3	-2.9	-2.8	-4.5	-4.7	-3.0	-1.4	-0.7	-0.6	-0.5
Ireland	-13.0	-13.4	-11.4	-9.5	-10.9	-10.8	-8.6	-4.5	-1.8	-2.3	-2.4	-2.5	-2.5	-1.6	-1.9	-0.5	-0.2	0.3	0.6
Korea	0.5	1.7	1.7	1.5	1.2	1.7	2.7	3.7	3.6	3.7	2.0	1.5	2.8	3.4	4.7	4.9	3.9	3.7	3.5
Netherlands	-5.4	-6.6	-5.8	-5.5	-3.6	-5.1	-5.9	-4.6	-4.7	-5.1	-2.9	-3.9	-3.2	-3.8	-3.7	-2.3	-2.0	-1.9	-1.6
New Zealand	—	—	—	—	—	-6.9	-2.5	-5.1	-4.2	-5.4	-4.1	-3.6	-1.2	3.0	3.2	3.0	1.7	1.0	1.2
Norway	4.8	4.0	6.1	7.0	9.9	5.9	4.6	2.7	1.8	2.6	0.1	-1.7	-1.4	0.4	3.3	5.9	7.3	8.0	8.7
Portugal	-10.7	-7.7	-10.2	-7.1	-7.5	-6.4	-5.6	-3.6	-2.5	-5.6	-6.7	-3.6	-6.1	-6.0	-5.8	-3.2	-2.9	-2.6	-2.1
Spain	-3.5	-5.2	-4.4	-5.0	-6.8	-5.8	-3.0	-3.0	-2.5	-3.8	-4.4	-3.6	-6.8	-6.3	-6.5	-4.5	-2.9	-2.4	-2.2
Sweden	-5.3	-7.0	-5.0	-2.9	-3.8	-1.2	4.2	3.5	5.4	4.2	-1.1	-7.8	-12.3	-10.3	-7.0	-3.3	-1.5	0.2	0.1
Total of above smaller countries	-3.6	-3.8	-4.0	-3.4	-3.7	-3.6	-2.1	-1.4	-1.1	-1.7	-2.9	-3.5	-4.5	-3.8	-2.9	-1.5	-0.8	-0.3	-0.1
Total of above EU countries	-5.0	-5.2	-5.1	-5.0	-4.9	-4.6	-4.0	-3.3	-2.5	-3.8	-4.3	-5.2	-6.4	-5.8	-5.1	-4.3	-2.7	-2.3	-2.0
Total of above OECD countries	-2.9	-4.0	-4.3	-3.5	-3.4	-3.4	-2.4	-1.8	-1.2	-2.1	-2.7	-3.8	-4.4	-3.6	-3.3	-2.7	-1.4	-1.1	-1.0
Memorandum items																			
General government financial balances excluding social security																			
USA	-0.9	-3.3	-4.1	-3.1	-3.5	-3.8	-3.1	-2.9	-2.7	-3.7	-4.2	-5.2	-4.3	-3.1	-2.8	-2.0	-1.1	-1.1	-1.2
Japan	-6.6	-6.3	-6.3	-4.8	-3.9	-4.0	-2.3	-1.7	-0.8	-0.7	-0.8	-1.9	-4.7	-5.0	-6.6	-7.3	-5.5	-5.0	-4.8

Source: OECD, 1997

Table 5.10   Selected OECD countries: general government structural balances, 1981–99 (surplus (+) or deficit (−) as a percentage of potential GDP)

	1981	1982	1983	1984	1985	1986	1987	1988	1989	1990	1991	1992	1993	1994	1995	Estimates and projections 1996	1997	1998	1999
USA	−0.7	−1.5	−2.6	−2.8	−3.3	−3.5	−2.6	−2.5	−2.4	−3.2	−3.3	−4.0	−3.3	−2.3	−1.8	−0.9	−0.3	−0.3	−0.2
Japan	−4.2	−3.7	−3.1	−1.6	−0.3	0.1	1.5	1.6	2.1	1.8	1.9	1.0	−1.2	−1.4	−2.4	−3.7	−1.5	−1.1	−0.9
Germany	−3.5	−1.6	−0.8	−0.8	−0.2	−0.6	−0.9	−1.8	0.1	−3.1	−4.6	−4.5	−2.9	−2.2	−2.9	−2.6	−2.3	−2.1	−2.0
France	−1.5	−3.0	−2.7	−1.7	−1.6	−1.5	−0.7	−1.4	−1.9	−2.4	−2.1	−3.6	−3.8	−4.3	−3.8	−2.7	−1.8	−2.1	−2.0
Italy	−12.0	−11.1	−9.8	−10.7	−11.8	−11.0	−10.7	−10.9	−10.5	−11.8	−10.6	−9.6	−9.2	−9.0	−6.7	−6.1	−2.3	−2.4	−2.4
UK	−1.6	−1.1	−2.7	−3.4	−2.8	−3.3	−3.4	−1.9	−1.6	−2.9	−2.3	−4.8	−6.1	−6.0	−5.1	−4.3	−2.3	−1.1	−0.6
Canada	−1.6	−2.9	−3.9	−5.2	−6.6	−5.4	−4.5	−4.3	−4.7	−4.8	−5.3	−5.3	−5.2	−4.2	−3.1	−0.5	1.2	1.5	1.7
Total of above countries	−2.6	−2.8	−3.1	−3.0	−3.0	−3.0	−2.3	−2.3	−2.0	−2.9	−3.0	−3.7	−3.6	−3.2	−2.8	−2.3	−1.1	−1.0	−0.8
Australia	−1.1	0.1	−2.1	−2.5	−2.9	−2.7	−0.1	0.9	0.7	0.6	−1.4	−2.3	−2.4	−3.6	−2.1	−1.2	−0.6	0.1	0.8
Austria	−1.2	−2.5	−3.5	−1.3	−1.4	−2.9	−3.5	−3.0	−3.8	−3.6	−3.8	−2.2	−3.3	−4.4	−4.6	−3.4	−2.3	−2.6	−2.6
Belgium	−13.4	−11.2	−10.7	−8.7	−7.6	−7.8	−6.0	−6.5	−6.6	−6.4	−6.9	−7.2	−5.4	−3.6	−2.8	−1.9	−1.4	−1.6	−1.8
Denmark	—	—	—	—	—	—	—	1.7	1.3	0.3	−0.9	−0.4	−0.6	−1.3	−0.9	−0.5	0.5	1.4	2.2
Finland	3.6	2.0	0.8	3.2	2.9	3.6	0.7	2.5	3.3	3.2	0.9	−0.6	−2.0	−2.3	−3.4	−2.0	−1.2	−0.7	−0.3
Greece	−8.9	−6.2	−6.0	−7.6	−11.1	−9.9	−8.4	−11.6	−15.3	−16.0	−11.8	−12.5	−12.2	−8.7	−8.1	−6.4	−4.2	−3.4	−4.2
Ireland	−12.3	−12.4	−8.9	−8.0	−9.6	−8.1	−6.6	−3.5	−2.1	−4.2	−2.1	−1.1	0.3	0.8	−1.1	0.0	−0.1	0.2	0.6
Netherlands	−4.8	−4.5	−4.0	−5.1	−4.1	−5.6	−5.6	−4.0	−5.2	−6.3	−3.7	−4.3	−2.4	−3.4	−3.2	−2.0	−1.9	−2.1	−2.0
New Zealand	—	—	—	—	—	−7.3	−2.8	−4.7	−3.6	−4.1	−1.7	−0.9	0.2	3.2	3.2	3.2	2.2	1.2	1.3
Norway	−4.1	−4.1	−1.9	−2.1	−0.2	1.8	1.5	1.7	0.4	−0.6	−3.5	−5.4	−6.1	−5.0	−2.0	−0.3	0.9	1.6	2.0
Portugal	−11.8	−8.6	−10.1	−5.3	−5.5	−4.8	−5.1	−3.8	−3.2	−7.1	−8.2	−4.8	−6.3	−5.3	−4.8	−2.3	−2.3	−2.3	−2.0
Spain	−1.8	−3.8	−3.0	−3.5	−5.5	−5.0	−3.7	−4.9	−5.3	−6.9	−7.0	−4.7	−5.6	−5.0	−5.2	−2.8	−1.6	−1.6	−2.0
Sweden	−4.6	−6.0	−4.3	−4.1	−5.3	−3.2	1.4	0.2	1.8	1.1	−2.4	−7.3	−9.1	−8.5	−6.6	−2.3	−0.2	1.0	0.8
Total of above smaller countries	−4.4	−4.4	−4.3	−4.0	−4.6	−4.5	−3.2	−3.0	−3.4	−4.3	−4.6	−4.5	−4.6	−4.3	−3.8	−2.1	−1.3	−1.0	−1.0
Total of above EU countries	−4.7	−4.4	−4.1	−4.0	−4.2	−4.2	−3.8	−3.9	−3.5	−5.0	−5.0	−5.3	−5.2	−4.9	−4.4	−3.5	−2.0	−1.8	−1.7
Total of above OECD countries	−2.8	−3.0	−3.3	−3.2	−3.2	−3.2	−2.4	−2.4	−2.1	−3.1	−3.2	−3.8	−3.7	−3.3	−3.0	−2.3	−1.1	−1.0	−0.9

Source: OECD, 1997

The final government expenditure multiplier effect is equal to:

$$\Delta Y = \frac{1}{MPW} \times \Delta G.$$

Autonomous tax multiplier

Now imagine that the Chancellor wishes to obtain the same result of increasing aggregate income by £100bn, but this time decreasing taxes rather than increasing government expenditure. What will be the size of the tax cut needed to achieve that? To answer this question you need to know the tax multiplier. In order to derive that, you need to reflect on an important point first.

When the government increases its spending, G, the effect on the economy's aggregate spending is immediate and direct: it is direct spending, G, done by some government department. It is money spent, pound for pound, to pay for works commissioned, projects financed, etc., which adds directly to the demand for goods, services and capital goods produced by the private sector of the economy.

When the government cuts taxes, however, the impact on spending is indirect. The spending is not done directly by the government, but by the people, whose disposable income increases as a result of the tax cut. We know from the analysis of consumption demand in Chapter 4 that if people's income increases, they will consume more. So a tax cut, which increases the amount of money people have left in their wallets after they have paid their income taxes, will increase demand.

✍️ Activity 5.15

Will demand increase by the same amount as the tax cut?

✓ Answer 5.15

Remember what we said about people's consumption behaviour. People tend not to consume all their income: they save some. So of the increase in disposable income brought about by a tax cut, only part will be consumed and will add to aggregate demand, the other part will be saved. The addition to consumption demand will be given by the marginal propensity to consume multiplied by the change in taxes.

✍️ Activity 5.16

Suppose the government decides to cut taxes by £1. By how much will aggregate demand increase?

✓ Answer 5.16

The marginal propensity to consume (MPC) tells us by how much consumption expenditure increases as

income increases. If we know that the MPC = 0.75, which is a fairly realistic value, then we also know that £1 cut in taxes, which is equivalent to £1 extra in people's pockets, will result in only 75p increase in consumption, as 25p is saved.

To find out the final impact on aggregate demand of a tax cut, remember what we have just said about the effect of an increase in government spending. When government spending increases by £1, the final effect on aggregate demand is given by the multiplier times the full initial increase in aggregate expenditure:

$$\Delta Y = \frac{1}{MPW} \times \Delta G.$$

To work out the tax multiplier you follow the same reasoning. The final effect on aggregate demand (ΔY) will be given by the multiplier $\frac{1}{MPC}$ times the initial increase in aggregate expenditure. So we need to ask what that initial increase would be, in the case of a tax cut. And you know the answer to that now: it is the MPC times the change in taxes ($MPC \times -\Delta T$). If this is the initial injection, to obtain the final effect on aggregate expenditure and output ΔY, we multiply that by the multiplier $\frac{1}{MPC}$

$$\Delta Y = (-\Delta T \times MPC) \times \frac{1}{MPW}$$

$$\Delta Y = -\Delta T \times \frac{MPC}{MPW}.$$

Summing up, the autonomous tax multiplier is:

$$\text{Autonomous tax multiplier} = -\frac{MPC}{MPW}.$$

Since a **tax cut** causes an **increase** in consumption expenditure and output and a **tax increase** causes a **reduction** in consumption expenditure and output, the autonomous tax multiplier is negative.

✍️ Activity 5.17

In the light of what we have said, how would you define the tax multiplier?

✓ Answer 5.17

The tax multiplier is the ratio of the change in income and output to the change in taxes that has brought about the change in income and output. The multiplier for a change in autonomous taxes is not the same as the multiplier for a change in government spending.

✍️ Activity 5.18

Assuming that MPC = 0.75, calculate the size of the autonomous tax multiplier and compare it with the size of the government expenditure multiplier.

✓ Answer 5.18

If the MPC = 0.75, then using the formula for the tax multiplier given above we obtain: $\left(-\dfrac{MPC}{MPS}\right)$

$$-\frac{0.75}{0.25} = -3.$$

The government expenditure multiplier was the full multiplier: $\dfrac{1}{MPW} = \dfrac{1}{0.25} = 4.$

The tax multiplier is smaller than the government expenditure multiplier.

✍ Activity 5.19

Now try and answer the question posed by the Chancellor. To increase aggregate output and income by £100bn, what size tax cut should be implemented?

✓ Answer 5.19

We use the autonomous tax multiplier formula:

$$\Delta Y = -\Delta T \times \frac{MPC}{MPW}.$$

We have already calculated

$$\frac{MPC}{MPW} = 3 \quad \frac{£100bn}{3} = -\Delta T.$$

The tax cut needed is £33bn.

We have obtained an interesting result. To achieve an increase in expenditure and output of £100bn, the government needs to cut taxes by £33bn. While to obtain the same increase in expenditure and output, the government needed to increase G by £25bn. To stimulate demand and output by a reduction in taxation rather than by an increase in government spending would cause a larger budget deficit (£8bn more). However, we could ask: how is the government going to finance its spending G. If through OMO this will affect the interest rate and possibly reduce investment, which is a component of aggregate demand. To measure the net effect on aggregate expenditure and output of an increase in direct government expenditure financed by OMO, we would also have to calculate the possible displacement of private investment. If, on the other hand, an increase in direct government expenditure G were financed by the Bank of England, which can in theory at least resort to the printing press and print more money, then there would be no displacement of private investment. In fact, the opposite might be true: an increase in the money supply lowers the interest rate, as we see in Chapter 6, which in turn stimulates investment and further adds to aggregate expenditure. There are, alas, other problems associated with an increase in the money supply, which make this policy choice less appealing than it appears to be.

Transfer payments multiplier

Now imagine that the Chancellor wishes to obtain the same result of increasing aggregate income and output by £100bn, but this time by increasing benefits, like pensions, child allowances, etc., rather than cutting taxes or increasing its direct expenditure. By how much should the Chancellor increase the benefits?

Again, to answer this question you need to know by how much aggregate income and output will increase as benefits are increased. You need to calculate the transfer payment multiplier.

✍ Activity 5.20

How would you define a transfer payment multiplier?

✓ Answer 5.20

The transfer payment multiplier is the ratio of the change in aggregate income and output to the change in transfer payments that has brought it about. Alternatively, we can say that the transfer payments multiplier is the amount by which a change in transfer payments must be multiplied to obtain the change in equilibrium income and output that it generates.

To understand the effect of changes in transfer payments on aggregate expenditure and output, you must remember that a change in transfer payments means a change in income for those who receive the payment. If benefits are increased, the income of those who receive them goes up. From the theory of consumption we studied in Chapter 4, we know that those people's consumption will also go up as a result, but not by the full amount of the increases in benefit, as part of the increase will be saved. The amount by which individual consumption and total aggregate expenditure goes up therefore depends on the marginal propensity to consume (MPC). If MPC = 0.75, a £1 increase in transfer payments increases consumption by 75p and saving by 25p. The analysis is exactly the same as the one we developed for a reduction in taxes. So an increase in benefit, ΔB, will increase aggregate expenditure by $\frac{MPC}{MPW}$.

✍ Activity 5.21

Work out the amount the Chancellor should increase benefits by to bring about a £100bn increase in income and output, assuming MPC = 0.75.

✓ Answer 5.21

The calculation is in fact identical to the one we did for the autonomous tax multiplier. The only difference is that the transfer payment multiplier is not negative. So we apply the formula:

$$\Delta Y = \Delta B \times \frac{MPC}{MPW}.$$

We have already calculated the multiplier:

$$\frac{MPC}{MPW} = \frac{0.75}{0.25} = 3.$$

We want ΔY to be £100bn, so:

$$£100bn = \Delta B \times 3$$

$$\Delta B = \frac{100}{3} = £33bn.$$

The Chancellor must increase benefits by £33bn.

Balanced budget multiplier

Let's go back to our Chancellor once more. He still wants to increase aggregate expenditure, output and income by £100bn. We now know that there are various ways in which he can achieve that:

- He can increase government expenditure, leaving taxes unchanged. He must spend £25bn on the economy, building hospitals, schools, motorways, etc.
- He can reduce autonomous taxes by £33bn.
- He can increase benefits by £33bn.

However, these three methods leave another question open: how is the Chancellor to finance the budget deficit caused by these measures? Is there a way in which the Chancellor could achieve his target of increasing expenditure and output **without** increasing his budget deficit, with a balanced budget?

The answer is 'yes'. To understand why, we need to work through the balanced budget multiplier step by step.

First of all remember that the government has a balanced budget when $G = T$. So to maintain a balanced budget it must be that the increase in government spending G is exactly matched by an increase in T. So let's assume that the increase in G of £100bn is entirely financed by an increase in T of £100bn:

$$\Delta G = 100 \quad \Delta T = 100.$$

Now we need to answer two separate questions:

(a) By how much will aggregate expenditure and output increase as a result of an increase of government spending by £100? $\Delta G = 100 \rightarrow \Delta Y$?

(b) By how much will aggregate expenditure decrease as a result of an increase in taxes of £100? $\Delta T = 100 \rightarrow \Delta Y$?

If the MPC = 0.75 we can work out the answer to (a) and (b) quite easily.

(a) $\Delta Y = \Delta G \times \dfrac{1}{MPW}$

$$\Delta Y = 100 \times \frac{1}{0.25} = 400.$$

The increase in government spending of £100 will cause an **increase** in aggregate expenditure and output of £400 billion.

(b) $\Delta Y = -\Delta T \times = \dfrac{MPC}{MPW}$

$$\Delta Y = -100 \times \frac{0.75}{0.2} = -300.$$

The increase in taxes of £100 will cause a **decrease** in expenditure and output of £300bn.

Then we need to ask: what will be the **net** effect on expenditure and output of these two measures taken together?

$$\Delta Y = +400 - 300 = 100.$$

Total expenditure and output will increase by £100bn, which is exactly equal to the initial injection of government expenditure, and also what the Chancellor wanted to achieve.

The balanced budget multiplier **must always be equal to one**. This result follows from the fact that in the implementation of these two policy measures there are two multipliers at work:

the government expenditure multiplier = $1/MPW$ and the tax multiplier = $-MPC/MPW$. Adding these two together gives the **balanced budget multiplier**, which applies every time changes in government expenditure G and changes in autonomous taxes (T) are the same.

Balanced budget multiplier = $\dfrac{1}{MPW} - \dfrac{MPC}{MPW} = \dfrac{1-MPC}{MPW}$.

But $1 - MPC = MPW$ so substituting this into the numerator gives:

Balanced budget multiplier = $\dfrac{MPW}{MPW} = 1$.

So if the government increases its expenditure on goods and services and increases autonomous taxes by the same amount, maintaining therefore a balanced budget, $G = T$, the net effect on the economy is to increase aggregate expenditure, output and income by the same amount. This result is very important, as it shows that the government can stimulate aggregate demand without running a deficit. It can do so maintaining a **balanced budget**. (See Table 5.11.)

✍ Activity 5.22

Is the multiplier effect of government transfer payments such as child benefit, unemployment benefit and pensions the same as the multiplier effect of government expenditure on goods and services?

✓ Answer 5.22

As we can see from Table 5.11, the answer is no. The multiplier effect of transfer payments is smaller than that of direct government spending as the transfer payment multiplier is smaller:

$$\frac{MPC}{MPW} \text{ and not the full multiplier } \frac{1}{MPW}.$$

This is because only part of the change in transfer payment is spent (MPC of ΔB), and part of it is saved.

FISCAL POLICY AND AGGREGATE EXPENDITURE

The analysis of the effect of fiscal policy on the equilibrium level of income and output developed so far can be also shown graphically using the Keynesian income-expenditure model we developed in Chapter 4. We know that equilibrium in the economy occurs when aggregate expenditure is equal to total output and income:

$$Y = E$$

or:

$$Y = C + I + G + (X - M).$$

For simplicity we assume, as we have done in our discussion of the multipliers, that taxes are autonomous and not a function of income, a fixed amount T. The consumption function, given the existence of taxes, now becomes:

$$C = a + b\,(Y - T)$$

where consumption is a function of disposable income or income after tax. (See Figure 5.10.)

Figure 5.10 An increase in government expenditure

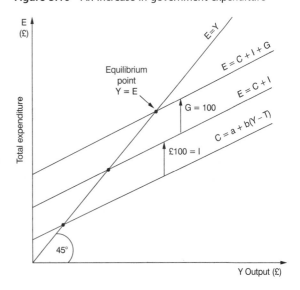

Table 5.11   Summary of fiscal policy multipliers

	Policy	Multiplier	Final impact on equilibrium Y
Government spending multiplier	ΔG	$\dfrac{1}{MPW}$	$\Delta Y = \Delta G\,\dfrac{1}{MPW}$
Autonomous tax multiplier	ΔT	$-\dfrac{MPC}{MPW}$	$\Delta Y = \Delta T - \dfrac{MPC}{MPW}$
Transfer payment multiplier	ΔBenefit	$\dfrac{MPC}{MPW}$	$\Delta Y = \Delta B\,\dfrac{MPC}{MPW}$
Balanced budget multiplier	$\Delta G = \Delta T$	1	$\Delta Y = \Delta G \times 1$

Since *I* is an autonomous expenditure, whose value is not determined by income, we show it here as a fixed amount of investment, say *I* = £100, which pushes up the aggregate expenditure function by £100 billion. We now add *G*, government expenditure, in very much the same way, as a further autonomous component of aggregate expenditure. The aggregate expenditure function shifts up by the amount *G*.

- An increase in government expenditure, *G*, is shown by a shift up of the aggregate expenditure function.
- A decrease in government expenditure will be shown, therefore, by a shift down of the aggregate expenditure function.

Changes in taxes and benefits will change disposable income and therefore affect consumption.

✍ Activity 5.23

The government wants to stimulate output and income to reduce the unemployment level. Let's assume that the current equilibrium level of income and output is £400bn, and that the government wishes to raise it by increasing its spending on infrastructure by £100bn. Assuming that MPC = 0.75, by how much will the economy grow and why? Show your result by the use of a Keynesian income–expenditure diagram.

✓ Answer 5.23

$Y = 400; \quad \Delta G = 100; \quad MPC = 0.75$

$$MPW = 1 - MPC = 0.25$$

$$\Delta Y = \Delta G . \frac{1}{MPW}$$

$$\Delta Y = 100 \frac{1}{0.25}$$

$$\Delta Y = 100 \times 4$$

$$\Delta Y = 400.$$

Equilibrium output = 400 + 400 = £800bn. As a result of increased government spending by £100bn, income and output will grow by £400bn and reach a new equilibrium point at £800bn. The change in income and output is greater than the initial injection of government spending because of the multiplier effect. The increase in government expenditure shifts up the whole aggregate expenditure curve. The new equilibrium is at £800bn output and income.

FISCAL POLICY IN PRACTICE

These results are very interesting, particularly the last one. They point to the fact that the government, with the use of fiscal policy, could control the level of aggregate demand and stabilize the economy around its full employment level of output. In practice, however, as experience in the 1950s and 1960s has taught us, the use of fiscal policies for 'fine tuning' of the economy is difficult. This is due to the existence of the following problems:

- time lags;
- estimated variables and forecast errors;
- shocks, unforeseen events, international factors;
- displacement of other components of aggregate demand.

Time lags

There is the problem of time lags, which are considerable when we try to implement fiscal policy changes. It takes a long time for the government machinery to produce outcomes, because of the legislative process, the bureaucracy and red tape involved. A year or more is often the estimated time lag. A year is a long time for an economy and mistimed government policies may end up having a destabilizing effect rather than a stabilizing one. Three types of time lags are involved in this process: recognition lags, implementation lags and response lags.

Recognition lags

It takes time for policymakers to recognize the existence of a boom or slump. Data need to be collected and elaborated, which takes time. Main data on national income and national product are available only quarterly. They are only preliminary and their interpretations are rather difficult.

Implementation lags

Once the onset of a recession or of a boom has been established and identified, it takes time to agree on which policy to choose to rectify the course of the economy and to implement it.

Response lags

After a problem situation like a recession or a boom has been identified and adequate policy measures taken, it still takes time for the economy to respond. Meanwhile, the problem situation will persist. It takes time, for instance, for the multiplier effect of government spending to develop fully. Firms need time to adjust to increased orders. They will first do so using up stocks of finished goods and raw materials. They will not rush immediately to place orders and buy more from other firms. The whole process may take months, with neither individuals nor firms raising their spending plans immediately. As a result of time lags, an expansionary policy that should have started to have effect at point A might start to have effect at point B. The result of this will be to increase the fluctuation overheating in the economy as shown by Figure 5.11.

A government trying to use fiscal policy to stabilize the economy is compared by Milton Friedman to 'a fool in the shower'. The fool in the shower turns the water on. As the water is cold, the fool turns it on hot. The water does not get hot immediately. He then turns it on hot a bit more. As a result, he gets scalded. He then turns it down to cold. As it is still too hot, he turns it down further until he freezes because the water is too cold, and so on and so forth.

Estimated variables and forecast errors

Budget deficits and surpluses are obtained by subtracting two large aggregates of spending and receipts; their forecasts are inevitably subject to wide margins of error. To give you an idea, over the past five years, the average absolute errors in the spring and summer forecasts (six months apart) of the PSBR for the financial year ahead have been in the order of about 0.75 per cent of GDP, plus or minus £6bn. Errors also tend to grow as the forecast horizon lengthens.

Projections of the public finances are critically dependent on the path of the economy, as most tax revenues and some government expenditure, especially cyclical social security, vary automatically with the economic cycle. If GDP growth were 1 per cent higher or lower over the coming financial year than has been assumed, the PSBR might be higher or lower by around 0.25 per cent of GDP, roughly equivalent to £2bn in the first year, increasing in subsequent years. For this reason the economic fundamentals on which the budget is formulated are subject to an independent economic audit. The fact remains, however, that the data used are only estimates and estimates can be wrong. The effect of government policies also rests, as we have seen, on the size of the multiplier, but that too is only an estimate. Its value depends on the value of the MPC, which might fluctuate.

Unforeseen events

There are events that cannot be foreseen but which can blow the economy off course. The fiscal policies being implemented at the time may turn out to be the wrong ones to deal with changed circumstances. The oil price shocks of 1973 and 1979 are two good examples. Most recently, the economic and financial turmoil in Asia, which has sent shock waves and affected growth rates across the world, is another good case in point. The severity of Asia's financial difficulties has taken nearly everybody by surprise. Following the abandonment by the authorities in Thailand of the baht's 13-year peg to the US dollar in July 1997, turbulence in Asian financial markets spread rapidly across South East Asia, and then to North East Asia in the second part of 1997. Large financial packages from the international community were quickly put in place in support of programmes of reform. The far-reaching effect of Asian financial turmoil has been to lower both growth and inflation in the major economies and to reduce trade in the wider global economy. It is estimated that financial turbulence in Asia has reduced UK GDP by 0.5 per cent in 1998.

Displacements of other components

Fiscal policy may, at least partly, displace other components of aggregate demand. If the government does not increase the money supply to finance its deficit, open market operations will cause interest rates to go up and this in turn will crowd out private investment. However, it might be difficult to predict the size of this displacement. This in turn makes it difficult for the government to estimate the impact of its fiscal policy on demand.

Figure 5.11   Time lags and possible destabilizing effects of fiscal policies

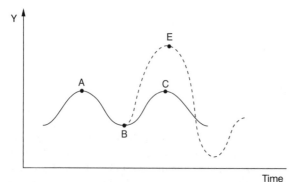

FISCAL POLICY: THE DEBATE IN HISTORICAL PERSPECTIVE

These difficulties of implementation have resulted in often sharply diverging views on the usefulness of fiscal policies. Let's first of all summarize Keynes's position once more. Contrary to what the classical economists had thought, according to Keynes there is no guarantee that the economic system will always work 'at full employment', producing the greatest possible output, employing all the resources available and all the people capable and willing to work. On the contrary, the experience of the Great Depression of 1929–31 and of the years that followed proved that economies can remain stuck, year after year, in a situation of equilibrium at less than full employment, in other words, in a situation of fundamental disequilibrium. The supply side of the economy, according to Keynes, adjusts to demand: the level of output reflects how much people, firms, governments and foreigners all taken together want and consume. If what they want collectively, the aggregate demand of the economy, is not enough to require for its production the employment of the entire labour force of a country, unemployment will be the inevitable outcome. To reduce unemployment, demand must be stimulated, which is precisely what governments should do, given that they are in a position to achieve it. Governments can stimulate demand by altering the amount of their spending and taxation, through the use of fiscal policy. But can they really? For a long time after World War II, governments in Europe and the USA thought they could and in fact they did. They used fiscal policy according to Keynesian prescriptions and unemployment was defeated.

Keynesian prescriptions typically advocated budget deficits. Balancing the budget, keeping government expenditure in line with tax revenue, had been a firm tenet of treasuries in the 1920s and 1930s. This view was abandoned after World War II and Keynesian policies of budget deficits were increasingly used. The rationale was simple: for the government to stimulate demand it must be that the money it injects into the economy as expenditure (G) is greater than the money it withdraws from it as taxes. Governments must run budget deficits: $G > T$.

The main problem with which western world governments were faced in the 1970s ceased to be one of unemployment and became one of inflation. The monetarists blamed inflation on government policies, as well as on deficit financing of government expenditure by resorting to the use of the printing press. The monetarists, who found two enthusiastic followers in Ronald Reagan in the USA and Margaret Thatcher in the UK in the early 1980s, claimed that government deficits were inflationary and advocated a reduction of government intervention. Rolling back state frontiers through radical programmes of public utilities privatizations, tight control of money supply, sound finances and balanced budgets became, and remained for almost two decades, the main objectives of many western governments. At the same time unemployment levels soared.

Priorities are only very gradually beginning to change once more in western government agendas, as the world enters the new millennium. Commonsense and nearly half a century of attempts at macroeconomic management seem to suggest the need to strike a compromise between short-term, demand-side government macroeconomic policies, aimed at sustaining demand to reduce unemployment, and long-term, supply-side microeconomic measures aimed at increasing the output potential of the economy, within a context of sound, anti-inflationary monetary management.

✍ Activity 5.24

The following extracts are taken from the government budget that the Chancellor of the Exchequer, Gordon Brown, laid before the House of Commons in March 1998. Read them carefully. Would you say that the Chancellor is following Keynesian policy prescriptions? What kind of story do the projections of PSBR into the year 2003, shown in Figure 5.12, tell us?

The budget sets new and long-term ambitions for Britain and responds to the major challenges facing the economy. It is a budget to ensure economic stability, reward work, encourage enterprise and promote fairness:

- the Government's macroeconomic policies will secure **economic stability** based on low inflation and sound public finances;
- an extension of the New Deal programmes, radical tax and benefit reforms and a skills package will **promote employment and make work pay**;
- a package of **enterprise reforms**, including major corporation tax changes and support for small and growing business, underline the Government's commitment to promote a more dynamic business sector; and
- the **fairness** measures will help to support families with children, tackle child poverty, improve public services and the environment and ensure that people and companies pay a fair share of tax by tackling avoidance. (p. 5)

The UK economy faces a number of major challenges as we approach the 21st Century … Government policy can help companies respond flexibly and quickly to market opportunities by:

■ promoting economic stability, which will provide the platform for firms to invest in new products and equipment;
■ fostering an enterprise culture in which dynamic firms can grow;
■ ensuring that the workforce has flexible and up-to-date skills. (p. 7)

The UK economy continues to suffer from a number of underlying structural weaknesses … the Government is now set on providing the economic framework and opportunities to raise the economy's sustainable rate of growth. However, at the same time as putting in place policies aimed at improving the country's long-term performance, the Government has had to address the short-term pressures facing the economy. By the middle of last year the economy had largely used up its spare capacity and output was growing at an unsustainable rate, putting upward pressure on inflation. Both the monetary and fiscal policy action which has been taken since last May should ensure that domestic demand will slow down … putting the economy back on track for more sustainable growth. (p. 83)

✓ Answer 5.24

The views expressed by the Chancellor in his autumn statement are rather more in line with monetarist than Keynesian policy prescriptions. They can be summed up as follows:

1 Long term growth is achieved through **structural policies** (supply side policies) to improve the long-term performance of the economy and not through aggregate demand management.
2 Tight control of public spending.
3 Monetary and fiscal policies are directed at maintaining low inflation on a permanent basis, rather than to achieve full employment. However, Gordon Brown's approach appears to be slightly more interventionist, along Keynesian lines, than monetarists would possibly like it, by envisaging a counter-cyclical use of demand side instruments.

Figure 5.12 well illustrates the outcome of these policies and the Chancellor's commitment to balanced budgets: a consistent, downward trend of the ratio of PSBR to GDP well into the new millennium, with the overall budget moving into surplus by 1999–2000.

Is the UK Chancellor isolated or at odds with other European and world governments in his approach towards sound public finances and balanced budgets? As Table 5.10 showed us earlier on, a similar clear trend towards reduction of government deficits is present in most OECD countries. It is useful, however, at this point, to conclude the chapter by focusing more specifically on government attitudes towards fiscal policy in the EU.

Figure 5.12 Projections of UK public sector borrowing requirement[1]

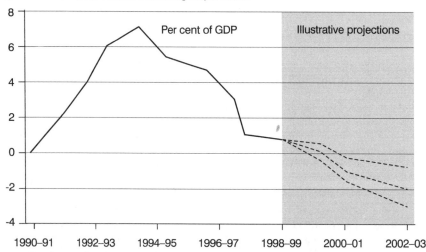

Source: HMSO, FSBR, 1998
[1] Excluding windfall tax and associated spending.

THE CHANGING BALANCE BETWEEN PUBLIC AND PRIVATE SECTOR

Attempts to reduce public spending have lead governments throughout the 1990s to:

- the privatization of public utilities, which has substantially reduced the size of their public sector, with questionable gains, however, in terms of competition, efficiency, investment and social welfare;
- attempts to involve the private sector in the provision of public services, by 'contracting out' services such as hospital/school cleaning, catering, etc., to cost-efficient private firms;
- attempts to involve the private sector in the provision of capital spending in public services: such a scheme was introduced in Britain under the Private Finance Initiative (PFI) in 1993.

These policies affect both the overall level of activity in the economy and the balance between the public and private sector; in other words, they affect not only the value but also the composition of public expenditure. By themselves, public expenditure figures can therefore give a misleading impression, particularly in relation to capital spending. In analysing them, care needs to be taken to establish what they really comprise: how large is the public sector, which utilities are privatized in each country, which major services are contracted out, and the extent of private capital funding of public services.

The effect of privatization

If we look at the UK, for example, we see that direct public capital spending has fallen since 1979. This date marks the beginning of the first Thatcher government, together with the introduction in Britain of a privatization programme. As Table 5.12 shows, the programme of privatization did not take off on a large scale from the start, but it certainly gathered momentum and scope from 1983 onwards, when all the major public utilities such as gas, water, telecommunications, electricity, steel and the railways were sold off. Only the Post Office and a much downsized British Coal remain in public hands. The large fall in direct public spending shown by the statistics is therefore not surprising given the extent of privatization over the period and the further shifting of investment from public to private hands through PFI.

✍ Activity 5.25

Study Figure 5.13 and try to explain what it shows.

Figure 5.13 UK aggregate capital spending, 1979–99

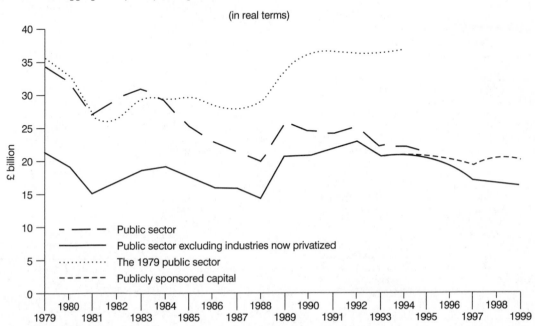

(in real terms)

£ billion

- – — – Public sector
- ——— Public sector excluding industries now privatized
- ············ The 1979 public sector
- – – – – Publicly sponsored capital

Source: HMSO, FSBR, 1998

Table 5.12   UK privatizations, 1979–97

Year	Company name	Business sector	Proceeds (£m)
1979	British Petroleum (1st part)[1]	Oil	276
	ICL[1]	Computers	37
1980	Fairey	Construction	22
	Ferranti[1,2]	Hi-tech industrial	55
	Motorway service stations (Dept of Transport)[2]	Motorway services	28
1981	British Aerospace (1st part)	Aerospace	149
	British Sugar Corporation[1]	Sugar refining	44
	Cable and Wireless (1st part)	Telecommunications systems	224
1982	Amersham International	Radio-chemicals	64
	National Freight Corporation[3]	Road haulage	54
	Britoil (1st part)	Oil	548
1983	Associated British Ports (1st part)[1,2]	Seaports	−34
	International Aeradio[2]	Aviation communications	60
	British Rail Hotels[2]	Hotels	51
	British Petroleum (2nd part)[1]	Oil	543
	Cable and Wireless (2nd part)	Telecommunications systems	275
1984	British Gas (onshore)[2]	Oil	82
	Associated British Ports (2nd part)[1,2]	Seaports	48
	Enterprise Oil	Oil	380
	Sealink[2]	Ferries	66
	Jaguar	Cars	297
	British Telecom (1st part)	Telecommunications	3916
	Inmos[2]	Computer systems	95
1985	British Aerospace (2nd part)	Aerospace	363
	British Shipbuilders (1st part)[2,3]	Various shipyards	220
	Britoil (2nd part)	Oil	449
	Cable and Wireless (3rd part)	Telecommunications systems	900
1986	British Shipbuilders (2nd part)[3]	Various shipyards	67
	Royal Ordnance (1st part)[2]	Weapons manufacture	11
	National Bus Company	Bus and coach carriers	260
	BA Helicopters[2]	Helicopter carriers	135
	British Gas	Gas	5400
1987	Unipart[3]	Car parts	30
	Leyland Bus[3]	Bus manufacture	4
	British Airways	Airline	900
	Royal Ordnance (2nd part)[2]	Weapons manufacture	190
	British Rail Doncaster Wagon Works[3]	Rolling stock manufacture	7
	Rolls-Royce	Aero engines	1080
	British Airports Authority (BAA)	Airports	1281
	British Petroleum (3rd part)[1]	Oil	7200
1988	British Steel	Steel	2500
	Rover Group (sold to British Aerospace)[2]	Car manufacture	−435
1989	Water companies (10)	Water supply and sewage treatment	3500
1990	Regional electricity companies (12)	Electricity supply and national grid	5300
1991	National Power and Power Gen (1st part)	Electricity generation	3200
	Scottish Electric	Electricity generation and supply	2200
	British Telecom (2nd part)	Telecommunications	11 100
1994	British Coal (part)	Mines	800
1995	National Power and Power Gen (2nd part)	Electricity generation	1800
1996	Various train operating companies[4]	Trains	0
	Railtrack	Railway infrastructure	1930
	British Energy	8 nuclear power stations	2500
	Total privatization proceeds		64 000

[1] In these cases the companies were only partly government owned in the first place.
[2] These were private sales to other companies.
[3] These were management and/or worker buyouts.
[4] Subsidies paid.

Sources: ONS, *Financial Statistics*, 1997

✓ Answer 5.25

If public capital expenditure is adjusted to exclude those industries now privatized, a rather different picture emerges. Figure 5.13 shows three different graphs: the dashed line traces public sector capital spending. As you can see, it shows a sharp drop between 1979–81 and 1983–8, when major privatizations were taking place, and indicates an overall downward trend over the whole period. The solid line shows public sector capital spending excluding the industries now privatized, in order to trace the government actual capital spending in all the other areas which have remained in public hands. What the solid line shows us is that, excluding privatized industries, capital spending rose in real terms towards the end of the 1980s and remained consistently higher from 1989–90 to 1996–7 than it was during the 1980s. The dotted line that starts off in 1993–4 shows the increase in PFI and corresponding reduction of public sector capital spending. In other words, private sector capital funding through PFI has simply displaced an equivalent amount of public sector capital spending. This is an interesting insight into the changing balance between public and private sectors in Britain and a useful example of the 'displacement' of components of aggregate demand which we were explaining earlier on. In this case, however, private investment demand, under the Private Finance Initiative (PFI) is replacing public capital spending, rather than the other way round; government expenditure 'crowding out' private investment demand. What matters for the economy as a whole, however, in the short run at least, is whether the overall level of aggregate demand increases as a result. In this case it clearly has not, as public sector capital expenditure has been falling, while PFI spending has been rising by an equal amount.

What would remain to be investigated, however, to complete this picture, is the impact of privatization on capital spending by privatized utilities, which is not shown in the Figure 5.13. In other words, has overall investment in now privatized ex-public utilities such as gas, water, electricity, etc. increased as a result of their private ownership? What the data show (the tiny dots line called 'the 1979 public sector' which includes capital expenditure in the utilities and transport and communications industries added to that in the public sector and including all health and education capital expenditure, shown in Figure 5.13) is that there was an overall substantial drop between 1979 and 1981 in the aggregate level of capital expenditure, only compensated in the latter part of the 1980s by a substantial increase. However, this increase, recorded between 1988 and 1990, just managed to restore the level of aggregate spending, in real terms, in public utilities by the public and private sector roughly back to its 1979 pre-privatization level; that level has remained stationary, without showing signs of any vigorous upward trend in the 1990s. What this seems to indicate is that the **privatization** of public utilities has:

■ **failed** to bring about substantial amounts of fresh capital spending by privatized utilities, which have been trading in long-term growth for short-term increases in shareholders' returns;

■ **failed** to increase the overall aggregate public capital spending level, as public capital spending has simply been displaced by private capital spending in the privatized utilities, with a broadly unchanged overall balance. (See Table 5.13 which shows that the total of publicly sponsored capital expenditure estimated for 1998–9 (£20.9bn), is less than the 1992–3 total, £21.6bn.

Effect of the Private Finance Initiative (PFI)

The PFI is a policy designed to harness private sector capital and management in the delivery of public services. Under the PFI, the public sector does not have to buy capital assets to deliver certain goods or services to the public. Instead it buys in private sector services, which will in turn acquire the capital asset instead. Contracts under the PFI involve capital investment by the private sector which would traditionally have been undertaken by the public sector acquiring capital assets itself. An example is provided by the Prisons Service's contract for custodial services at Bridgend, rather the acquisition of a prison building by the government.

Expenditure under the PFI is increasing in Britain. Projects with a combined capital value of more than £12bn in areas such as schools, colleges, hospitals, local authorities, defence, IT and property management are expected by the year 2001 (Table 5.13).

Although the investment is carried out by the private sector, it needs to be taken into account when assessing the total level of investment 'sponsored' by the public sector. Table 5.14 shows how total publicly sponsored investment is expected to remain through to 1999 just below its 1992–3 levels, but well below its 1979 level.

Table 5.13   Private Finance Initiative (PFI): estimated capital spending by the private sector in the UK, 1997–2001

	£ million			
	1997–8	1998–9	1999–2000	2000–01
Defence	200	340	300	220
Foreign Office and Overseas Development	0	20	30	0
Agriculture[1]	10	20	20	20
Trade and Industry	10	30	60	20
Environment, Transport and Regions[2,3]	920	1070	1520	1380
Education and Employment[4]	0	30	20	20
Home Office	170	183	330	330
Legal Departments	10	30	20	20
Culture, Media and Sport	10	10	20	10
Health	50	320	590	790
Social Security	10	70	270	150
Scotland	70	360	540	300
Wales	10	90	70	70
Northern Ireland	0	50	100	80
Chancellor's Departments	20	50	40	40
Local authorities[5,6]	10	300	300	150
Total	**1500**	**2970**	**4230**	**3600**

Source: HMSO, FSBR, 1998
[1] Includes Forestry Commission.
[2] Includes the private sector capital investment in CTRL which is currently the subject of further negotiations.
[3] In addition, substantial private investment is levered in through housing, urban regeneration and other programmes.
[4] Excludes private finance activity in education institutions classified to the private sector. Estimated total capital values for these are £189 million in 1997–8 and £92 million in 1998–9.
[5] Figures represent spending on projects signed, and expected to be signed, up to the end of 1998–9 only.
[6] PFI activity in local authority schools is included in the local authorities line.

Table 5.14   UK public sector capital expenditure, 1992–9

	1992–3	1993–4	1994–5	1995–6	1996–7	Estimate 1997–8	Forecast 1998–9
Central government	10.9	9.8	9.1	8.6	6.5	6.0	6.0
Local authorities	7.2	6.7	7.3	7.2	6.4	6.4	7.0
Public corporations[1]	3.6	3.4	4.2	4.2	4.4	4.6	4.6
Notional allocation of the reserve							0.3
Total public sector capital expenditure	21.6	19.9	20.6	20.0	17.3	17.0	17.9
Estimated capital expenditure under the private finance initiative		0.1	0.2	0.4	1.1	1.5	3.0
Total publicly sponsored capital expenditure	21.6	20.0	20.8	20.4	18.4	18.5	20.9
Memo public sector capital spending[2]							
gross of depreciation	23.5	21.3	21.7	20.8	17.4	17.0	17.9
net of depreciation	14.1	11.7	11.6	10.0	6.8	6.4	7.0

Source: HMSO, FSBR, 1998
[1] Excluding the capital expenditure of privatized industries.
[2] Including industries, now privatized, while they were in the public sector.

CASE STUDY: PUBLIC FINANCES IN THE EUROPEAN UNION

One of the conditions set out at Maastricht for European Union membership and the introduction of the single currency was (and still is) a general government deficit of not more than 3 per cent of GDP and gross public debt not greater than 60 per cent of GDP by 1999. Many Community members do not currently meet those requirements (Table 5.15). A reduction of EU government deficits is seen as an indispensable **macroeconomic** and **structural** requirement for virtually all member states.

Reducing government deficits is seen among Community officials as 'the condition for a strong and durable expansion of investment, output and employment over the short and medium term', while reducing public ownership in the economy is seen as a way not only of reducing government indebtedness, but also of creating an environment more conducive to business activity, competitiveness and specialization. Smaller government means, in other words, lower taxes and lower interest rates, which – in the eyes of the Commission – is all that businesses want.

In fact businesses want much more: they also want economic growth, as well as stability, and a strong and sustained demand, which may only be achievable through government intervention to stimulate demand. But it should be clear by now which school of economic thought influences the European Commission's thinking.

Long-term trends in Community public finances

The current large deficits and debts of Community members are the result of long-term trends in spending and taxation which have been more or less common to nearly all member states. We need therefore to look at the sources of government spending and taxation in the EU over the past four decades or so.

Government spending

Government spending has been increasing steadily in the Community over the last 35 years, growing from an average of 34 per cent of GDP in 1961 to more than 52 per cent in 1993, before beginning to fall somewhat in the second part of the 1990s.

✍ Activity 5.26

Look at Table 5.16 and comment on what it shows.

✓ Answer 5.26

While government expenditure, as a percentage of GDP, has grown in the USA and Japan since 1961, its growth was far more marked in the Community than in its major trading partners. In 1996 government expenditure represented 36.7 per cent of GDP in the USA and 36.6 per cent of GDP in Japan, against 50.6 per cent in the Community.

✍ Activity 5.27

Look at Table 5.17 and explain what accounted for the rapid growth of government spending in the Community.

✓ Answer 5.27

Table 5.17 provides data for the five components of government expenditure in the Community: current transfers to households and to firms, interest payments, public consumption, net capital transfers and gross capital formation from 1961 to 1996. The fastest growing spending

Table 5.15 Gross public debt, EC countries (% of GDP)

	Level					Change	
	1993	1995	1996	1997	1998	1995/93	1998/95
B	137.0	133.7	130.6	127.0	123.9	−3.3	−9.8
DK[1]	80.1	71.9	70.2	67.8	65.5	−8.2	−6.4
D	48.2	58.1	60.8	61.9	61.9	9.9	3.8
EL[2]	111.8	111.8	110.6	109.3	107.2	0.0	−4.6
E	60.5	65.7	67.8	67.1	65.8	5.2	0.1
F	45.6	52.8	56.4	58.1	59.2	7.2	6.4
IRL[2]	94.5	81.6	74.7	70.0	65.4	−12.9	−16.2
J	119.3	124.9	12.4	122.3	119.4	5.6	−5.5
L	6.2	6.0	7.8	8.8	9.2	−0.2	3.2
NL	80.8	79.7	78.7	76.8	75.1	−1.1	−4.6
A	62.8	69.0	71.7	72.2	72.2	6.2	3.2
P	68.2	71.7	71.1	69.0	67.8	3.5	−3.9
FIN	57.3	59.2	61.3	61.5	61.7	1.9	2.5
S	76.0	78.7	78.1	77.6	74.9	2.7	−3.8
UK[2]	48.5	54.1	56.2	57.0	56.5	5.6	2.4
EUR	66.1	71.3	73.5	73.7	72.9	5.2	1.6

Source: European Commission, *European Economy*, 1997

continued overleaf

PUBLIC FINANCES IN THE EUROPEAN UNION

Table 5.16 Size of public finances in the EC, USA and Japan, 1961–96 (% of GDP)

	1961	1973	1982	1996
Total expenditure				
EUR	33.6	38.7	49.3	50.6
USA	30.3	32.9	38.9	36.7
JAP	17.3	22.3	33.6	36.6
Total current receipts				
EUR	34.3	38.2	44.3	46.2
USA	29.5	33.2	35.0	34.6
JAP	19.7	22.8	30.0	31.6
Net lending (+)/(−)				
EUR	0.7	−0.6	−5.1	−4.4
USA	−0.6	0.3	−3.9	−2.2
JAP	2.4	0.5	−3.6	−5.0

Source: European Commission, *European Economy*, 1997

category since early 1960s has been current **transfer payments**, which have accounted for more than half of the increase in the total government spending ratio of the Community. At present transfer payments represent the largest spending category, representing almost one-quarter of GDP and about half of total government expenditure (23.7 out of 50.6 per cent of GDP in 1996). The rapid increase in current transfers has

been almost entirely due to increased benefits to households, while subsidies to firms have remained fairly stable at around 3 per cent.

This growth in government spending in the community reflects the growth of the welfare state in three major social policy areas:

- pensions;
- healthcare;
- unemployment benefit.

The expansion of the welfare state in the 1960s and 1970s was characterized in turn by:

- broadening of the coverage of programmes;
- widening of eligibility criteria;
- increase in the level of benefits.

The expansion, coupled with demographic and economic changes, such as increased unemployment, an ageing population and rising costs, contributed to the swelling of government expenditure and deficits. To reduce their deficits, Community governments are now faced with the difficult task of reforming their welfare states.

The more the government borrows, the more it has to pay in interest to lenders. If old outstanding debt is not gradually repaid and instead the government continues to borrow, the interest burden gets bigger and bigger. As you can see from Table 5.14, **interest payments** on outstanding public debt have been another important component of the rise in government spending and have rise from 3.1 per cent of GDP in 1961 to 5.4 per cent in 1996. Interest rate increases, of course, make the burden of debt servicing greater. **Public consumption** grew by about 6 per cent over the period, finally to stabilize at about 19 per cent of GDP. **Public investment**, as a share of GDP, has been falling steadily over the last 35 years.

Table 5.17 Receipts and expenditures of general government, EUR[1] (% of GDP)

	Levels						Changes				
	1961	1973	1982	1989	1993	1996	1973/61	1982/73	1989/82	1993/89	1996/93
Total expenditure of which	33.6	38.7	49.3	47.2	52.4	50.6	5.1	10.6	−2.1	5.2	−1.8
1. Current transfers of which	11.5	16.0	21.6	20.7	23.7	23.3	4.5	5.6	−0.9	3.0	−0.4
Households	—	13.0	17.9	17.1	19.9	19.8	—	4.9	−0.8	2.8	−0.1
2. Actual interest payments	3.1	1.7	4.1	4.6	5.4	5.4	−1.4	2.4	0.5	0.8	0.0
3. Public consumption	13.7	16.4	19.6	18.2	19.6	18.9	2.7	3.2	−1.4	1.4	−0.7
4. Net capital transfers	0.8	0.9	1.0	0.9	1.1	0.6	0.1	0.1	−0.1	0.2	−0.5
5. Gross capital formation	4.5	3.7	2.9	2.8	2.8	2.4	−0.8	−0.8	−0.1	0.0	−0.4
Current receipts of which	34.3	38.2	44.3	44.8	46.3	46.2	3.9	6.1	0.5	1.5	−0.1
6. Indirect taxes	13.9	12.9	13.2	13.5	13.6	14.0	−1.0	0.3	0.3	0.1	0.4
7. Direct taxes	8.7	10.7	12.4	13.3	12.9	12.8	2.0	1.7	0.9	−0.4	−0.1
8. Social security contributions	10.2	11.8	14.7	14.6	16.0	16.1	1.6	2.9	−0.1	1.4	0.1
9. Other current receipts	1.5	2.8	4.0	3.4	3.7	3.4	1.3	1.2	−0.6	0.3	−0.3
Memory items											
10. Gross saving	6.0	4.1	−1.0	1.2	−2.5	−1.3	−1.9	−5.1	2.2	−3.7	1.2
11. Net landing (+)/borrowing (−)	0.7	−0.6	−5.1	−2.4	−6.3	−4.4	−1.3	−4.5	2.7	−3.9	1.9
12. Gross public debt[2]	65.2	35.3	45.6	54.1	66.1	73.5	−29.9	10.3	8.5	12.0	7.4

Source: European Commission, *European Economy*, 1997
[1] 1961: EUR 15 excluding Greece, Portugal, Austria, Sweden and Finland; 1973: EUR 15 excluding Luxembourg, Greece and Portugal.

PUBLIC FINANCES IN THE EUROPEAN UNION

Its present share of 2.5 per cent of GDP is just above half the 1961 level. The reduction in public consumption over the period can be explained by many factors:

- completion of major infrastructure system;
- easier to constrain public investment than to control current spending;
- privatization of public utilities.

Savings on public investment have a long-term cost, as public investment, particularly in infrastructure, affects the growth in productivity of the private sector.

Government receipts

The growth of public expenditure in the Community has gone hand in hand with an increase in the overall tax burden (the sum of indirect taxes like VAT, direct taxes on income and social security contributions). Over the last 35 years government receipts, as a share of GDP, have grown by 12 percentage points, to reach 46 per cent in 1996. The bulk of the rise occurred in the period from 1961 to 1982 and then again in the early 1990s, due to the need to finance the sharp increase in unemployment benefits because of the severe economic downturn experienced by the Community in the early 1990s.

Governments in the Community are now increasingly reluctant to increase taxation further for the following reasons:

- taxation distorts prices and competition;
- taxation reduces work incentive and increases unemployment;
- taxation creates political resistance.

Attempts by Community governments to reduce taxation have only been very moderately successful.

✍ Activity 5.28

Look at Tables 5.18 and 5.19 and explain what they show.

✓ Answer 5.28

Tables 5.18 and 5.19 provide data on the budgetary and debt position of the 15 EU countries. The data confirm what has already been explained in aggregate terms. Efforts to reduce deficits to 3 per cent and debts to 60 per cent of GDP have been stepped up recently throughout the Community, in an effort to meet the Maastricht criteria. Eleven countries have since met those criteria and have adopted a single currency in 1999. The UK did meet the criteria but has opted not to join the single currency in the first wave of membership. Reductions in deficits have largely been achieved through reduction in public spending rather than through increases in taxation.

A return to the use of counter-cyclical fiscal policy?

The reduction in government deficits and debts to more manageable proportions is likely to restore the use of fiscal policy for the counter-cyclical management of demand, at least in those countries which had favoured their use in the past. In order to ensure that budgetary discipline, once restored, is maintained, the Maastricht Treaty stipulates that the budget deficit in participating countries is not allowed to exceed 3 per cent of GDP except in 'exceptional and temporary' circumstances. Such circumstances do not include normal cyclical downturns.

Table 5.18 Single EU government budgets, 1995–8 (% of GDP)

	Receipts				Expenditures			
	1995	1996	1997	1998	1995	1996	1997	1998
B	50.3	50.5	50.1	49.7	54.5	53.8	53.0	52.1
DK	58.1	58.8	58.0	56.4	59.7	60.3	58.2	56.7
D	46.3	45.7	46.0	45.9	49.9	49.7	48.9	48.2
EL	37.6	38.0	38.4	38.7	46.7	46.0	44.9	44.0
E	39.7	40.3	40.5	40.2	46.3	44.8	43.5	43.0
F	49.5	50.6	50.5	50.2	54.3	54.7	53.5	53.1
IRL	35.4	34.7	34.3	33.9	37.4	36.3	35.2	34.3
I	44.8	46.3	47.7	47.1	51.8	52.9	51.0	50.1
L	40.8	41.7	41.2	40.8	40.0	40.7	40.7	39.9
NL	49.1	48.3	47.7	47.0	53.2	50.9	50.1	49.0
A	46.9	48.2	48.7	48.3	52.8	52.5	51.7	51.2
P	40.1	40.4	41.3	41.1	45.3	44.5	44.3	44.0
FIN	53.3	55.3	54.3	53.9	58.8	58.7	56.5	55.3
S	60.1	63.0	61.7	60.5	68.2	66.9	64.6	61.5
UK	37.8	37.6	37.7	38.0	43.5	42.3	41.3	40.2
EUR	45.8	46.2	46.4	46.1	50.9	50.6	49.4	48.5

Source: European Commission, *European Economy,* 1998

continued overleaf

Table 5.19 Government expenditures, EU (changes in % of GDP)

	Public consumption		Public investment		Transfers to households		Transfers to companies		Capital transfers		Interest payments		Total	
	1997/95	1998/97	1997/95	1998/97	1997/95	1998/97	1997/95	1998/97	1997/95	1998/97	1997/95	1998/97	1997/98	1998/97
B	-0.4	-0.3	0.0	0.0	-0.3	-0.3	-0.3	-0.1	0.1	0.0	-1.0	-0.2	-1.5	-0.9
DK	-0.3	-0.4	0.0	0.0	-1.2	-0.7	-0.6	-0.1	1.0	0.0	-0.8	-0.3	-1.5	-1.5
D	-0.2	-0.04	-.04	-0.1	0.1	-0.1	-0.3	0.0	-0.1	0.0	0.2	0.0	-1.0	-0.7
EL	0.2	-0.1	-0.1	0.1	0.3	-0.1	-0.1	0.0	-0.2	-0.1	-1.9	-0.6	-1.8	-09
E	-0.9	-0.3	-0.9	0.1	-0.6	-0.2	-0.2	0.0	-0.2	0.0	-0.1	-0.1	-2.8	-0.5
F	-0.2	-02	-0.3	0.0	-0.1	-0.3	0.3	-0.1	-0.5	0.4	0.1	0.0	-0.8	-0.4
IRL	-0.7	-0.2	0.0	0.0	-0.9	-0.3	-0.3	-0.1	-0.1	0.0	-0.8	-0.3	-2.2	-0.9
I	0.0	-0.2	-0.1	0.1	0.8	0.1	-0.7	0.1	0.3	0.4	-1.6	-1.5	-0.8	-0.9
L	0.4	-0.2	0.2	0.1	0.0	-0.4	-0.2	-0.2	0.0	0.0	0.1	0.0	0.7	-0.8
NL	-0.4	-0.1	-.01	0.0	-1.7	-0.8	-0.2	-0.1	-0.2	0.0	-0.6	-0.1	-3.1	1.1
A	-0.6	-0.3	-0.1	0.0	-0.4	-0.3	-0.4	-0.1	-0.1	0.0	0.3	0.1	-1.1	-0.5
P	0.8	-0.2	0.5	0.3	0.6	0.1	-0.1	0.0	-0.5	-0.1	-1.1	-0.3	0.2	-0.2
FIN	-0.4	-0.5	0.2	0.0	-1.7	-0.8	-0.2	-0.1	-0.5	-0.1	0.4	0.0	-2.3	-1.2
S	-0.6	-0.7	-0.2	-0.1	-1.8	-1.0	-0.7	-0.2	-0.1	0.0	-0.1	-0.8	-3.6	-3.1
UK	-0.9	-0.4	-0.4	-0.1	-0.5	-0.4	0.0	-0.1	-0.4	-0.1	0.2	0.0	-2.2	-1.1
EUR	-0.4	-0.3	-0.3	0.0	-0.2	-0.3	-0.2	0.0	-0.2	0.1	-0.1	-0.3	-1.5	-0.9

Source: European Commission, European Economy, 1998

☆ **For revision of this chapter, see the Chapter Summaries at the end of the book, starting on page 411.**

6 Money and financial markets

Objectives

After studying this chapter, you will be able to understand:

- what money is and what functions it fulfils;
- main official definitions of money in the UK;
- how commercial banks create money;
- how the Bank of England controls the money supply;
- what is meant by open market operations;
- what is meant by the demand for money;
- what affects the demand for money;
- what determines bond prices and bond yields;
- what affects the stock market;
- how interest rates are determined.

DETERMINATION OF INTEREST RATES

In this Chapter and Chapter 7 we look at the special role that money plays in the economy. The quantity of money in circulation, as we shall see, can affect the level of employment and the rate of economic growth, as well as inflation, interest rates, the exchange rate and balance of payments.

Before we move on, however, let's remind ourselves of where we are. At the beginning of this book, we set ourselves the task of understanding what determines the level of output and employment in the economy and what affects its rate of growth. We started by using Keynes's model of the macroeconomy. According to Keynes, the level of aggregate demand determines the level of output, income and employment and ultimately the rate of growth. But what determines the level of aggregate demand? To find an answer to this question we looked at the components of aggregate demand: consumption, investment, government spending and net export demand and asked the same question again, in relation to each individual component:

$$E = C + I + G + (X - M).$$

With the exception of export demand, which we exam-

ine in a later chapter, we know a lot about what determines each component. We understand the constraints affecting government spending decisions and we appreciate the fact that it is very much a policy decision by the government whether to aim at reducing unemployment by increasing its deficit spending or whether to reduce inflation by pursuing a policy of balanced or surplus budgets. We understand that consumption expenditure is affected by the level of current disposable income. We understand that investment expenditure is inversely affected, among other things, by the interest rate: the lower the interest rate, the higher desired investment. What we have not explained, however, is what determines the interest rate.

This becomes our next crucial link in the task of stimulating aggregate demand to a level consistent with full employment. Aggregate demand can be stimulated by increasing investment demand. To increase investment demand, we need to lower interest rates. But how do we do that? Who decides what the interest rate should be? How is the rate of interest determined? This is what we are going to find out now.

What we will discover in the course of this chapter is that the interest rate is determined by the interaction of the supply of money with the demand for money. The interest rate is determined by the money supply, given the demand for money in the economy.

This does not mean anything to us at the moment, and we shall spend most of this chapter clarifying the answer. What is clear, however, is that to explain what determines the interest rate we need to refer to the money market, in other words, to the **supply of money** and to the **demand for money**. In particular, we need to explain:

- what we mean by money supply;
- what affects the money supply;
- what we mean by demand for money;
- what affects the demand for money.

We can put supply and demand together and show how interest rates are determined.

In the next chapter we move on to examine the operation and effectiveness of monetary policy. We will discuss how money supply and interest rates are controlled by the monetary authorities and the effect that this has on the economy.

As we explain these concepts, many other underlying questions related to money will become clear. What is money? Why do we use money? What do commercials banks do? What is their function? How do they make money? What is the function of the central bank ? Who decides how much money to print? Does it make any difference if we pay by cash, cheque or credit card? Does it matter if we keep our savings under the mattress or in a bank high rate deposit account?

✍ Activity 6.1

Think about possible answers to these questions in your own words.

✓ Answer 6.1

Throughout the chapter, we will be identifying answers to these questions.

MONEY: DEFINITION AND FUNCTION

What is money? Money is anything, from shells and cigarettes to gold coins, that fulfils three functions:

- a **generally accepted medium of exchange**;
- a **store of value**;
- a **measure of value** or **unit of account**.

The first important point we are making here is that it does not really matter what money is in physical terms. Of course it helps, if whatever it is that we call money also possesses the following physical characteristics:

- it has a high value for its weight, so that it is not too bulky to carry around;
- it is not readily counterfeitable;
- it is divisible, to facilitate exchange of goods of different value.

What does matter, however, is that whatever we call money is a **generally accepted medium of exchange**. What matters is that we all agree on accepting whatever it is that we call money, a piece of brown paper or shiny metal, to settle our transactions.

✍ Activity 6.2

How would we buy goods if we didn't have money?

✓ Answer 6.2

If we wanted to exchange goods on the marketplace and we didn't have money, we would have to go back to bartering. Suppose I wanted to exchange my CD for some wine: I would go to the market. Suppose I only found someone who would give me ten packets of cigarettes for it, I would still need to find someone with wine who wanted my cigarettes. Barter is a very cumbersome, lengthy and inefficient way of carrying out exchanges as it requires a double coincidence of needs and wants. You not only need to find someone who wants what you have got to sell, but that person must also happen to sell what you want to buy. Money simplifies matters and is therefore efficient. You only need to find someone who wants what you have and is willing to pay you money for it. Once you have the money, you can find someone else who is selling what you want and will accept your money in exchange for it.

This brings us to the second function fulfilled by what we call money, that is, a **store of value**. After I have exchanged my CD for money, I do not have to rush and immediately exchange the money for the wine I want. I can do so tomorrow, in a month's time or in a year's time: the money will maintain its purchasing power unchanged, assuming zero inflation, of course. The money will store the value of the good I have exchanged for it and allow me to carry out the second exchange – money for good – at any other time. Money is a claim on goods that we can exercise at some unspecified future date. This is another very convenient property. But again, to be a satisfactory store of value money must have a stable value, that is, prices should be stable.

Finally, whatever we call money should serve as a **measure of value** or **unit of account**: an agreed measure for stating the prices of goods, a common denominator by which the prices of all goods can be understood. Our CD might have been worth ten packets of cigarettes, but how many packets of cigarettes are ten litres of wine worth, and how many CDs would we pay for a coat, a car or a haircut? For the money to fulfil its function as a medium of exchange, it must also be possible to express the value of goods as so many **units of money**. A CD is worth £10, a haircut is worth £8, a litre of ordinary wine £4.

MONEY IN BRITAIN TODAY

Money, we have just learnt, is anything that fulfils the three functions of being a generally accepted medium of exchange, a store of value and a measure of value. So to answer the question what is money in Britain today, think about what we use every day to pay for what we buy.

✍ Activity 6.3

What do you think money is in Britain today? Think of what you use to settle your purchases and make a list. I'll do the same and then we can compare answers.

✓ Answer 6.3

If I look in my wallet, I find metal coins of little intrinsic value and some pale coloured pieces of paper, with the sign £5, £10 or £20 printed on them. This is the **cash** I carry, usually not much. I use cash to pay for the newspaper and a pint of milk in the morning, to buy my cappuccino at lunchtime or some fresh vegetables on the way home. When I get petrol for my car I use a credit card. I receive a credit card bill once a month and it is always a shock. I settle it by writing out a cheque to the bank which holds my account. If I buy a jumper at Marks & Spencer, I cannot use my credit card; they won't accept it. However, they'll take my Barclays Connect card instead, which is a debit card and not a credit card. If I go into Principles or the House of Fraser I can use their own credit card and walk out with goods. If I try to use these cards elsewhere, I cannot. However, I can use my debit or credit cards at a cash machine and get cash at the press of a button. If I walk into the bank to deposit a cheque for £40 in exchange for cash I won't succeed as it takes the banking system five working days to clear a cheque. On the other hand, I can pick up the phone and transfer £5,000 from a high rate deposit account to a current account which is instantly credited. With a second phone call I can book a skiing holiday in Canada and just dictate my credit card number over the phone.

I recently bought a house. To pay for it I used the sale proceeds of company shares I held abroad, which I transferred from France into a foreign currency account I hold here in London. As my share holdings were liquidated in two separate tranches, I had to hold some of the funds in different forms for a few months. I left some in a current account I have with a French bank, some on a high rate deposit account, again in France. With the remaining part I bought French government bonds which I held, together with shares in the French electricity company, in my asset portfolio at another French bank. When the second tranche of funds became available, I liquidated everything, transferred the proceeds into my ordinary current account here in London and wrote a cheque to the house vendor's solicitor.

So, what is money then? Notes and coins, bank credit and debit cards, individual shop credit cards, current accounts, high rate deposit accounts, foreign currency accounts held in Britain, foreign currency accounts held abroad, saving accounts held abroad, all of that? Not quite, although all of those ways were instrumental in settling transactions. We need to look at what really settled them. Let's look at each of these different forms of payment.

Notes and coins

Notes and coins are obviously money as they satisfy the three functions described above. Money used to be made out of gold itself or alternatively used to be pieces of paper (paper money) which were backed and fully convertible with gold. People could go to a bank and ask for their paper money to be exchanged for gold and the bank would oblige. People would readily accept paper money in transactions because it was as good as gold. When convertibility was permanently abandoned in the UK in 1931 and paper notes ceased to be convertible with gold, they remained as fiat money, an intrinsically worthless commodity which nonetheless fulfils the function of money. Nowadays even coins are fiat money as they do not contain any precious metal. People are willing to accept fiat money in exchange for goods because they know that in turn it is accepted by other people when they are buying goods and services. The term 'fiat' means by government order.

Plastic cards of any type

Plastic cards are not money; they are a convenient way of accessing money which is held in an account. The money is not the piece of plastic, but the deposit itself which has been made with a bank or building society.

When you use a debit card like Access or Barclays Connect card you are simply directly accessing money you have in your account at the bank. Your account is immediately debited with the amount of the transaction. When you use a credit card or a particular shop's plastic card, you are simply given credit by the bank or shop which you then have to pay back at the end of the month by writing a cheque against money that you hopefully hold in a bank or building society account. Credit cards only temporarily increase your potential spending power over and above the money you have in your bank account. Ultimately, the money you hold in your account and not the piece of plastic settles your transactions.

Deposit accounts of any description

Big changes have occurred in this area in the last decade or so. In the 1970s, there was a clear distinction between two types of deposits or accounts: current accounts, also called sight or chequeable accounts, and deposit or time accounts. The current accounts paid no interest. People used them to keep their money safe in a bank, knowing that they could withdraw it at any time and that they could write out cheques against it to settle their transactions. Cheques are simply a claim on a certain amount of money held by the bank in someone's account, which people exchange among themselves.

Deposit or saving accounts, often also referred to as time deposit accounts, paid interest, but your money was tied up; you could not withdraw it when you wanted, not before certain dates; you could not write cheques against your accounts and you could not use them to settle your transactions directly. To do that you had to transfer your money from the saving account or time deposit account to your sight or current account; but that would take time, a month, three months, six months or possibly longer. Money kept in these accounts was not as liquid as cash money or money kept in current accounts.

Government deregulation of financial services in the 1980s removed most of these distinctions. Competition between banks and building societies intensified. Building societies started paying interest on their deposits, which became chequeable, that is, you could write a cheque against the money deposited at a building society and use it to settle your transactions. Banks had to follow suit. Certain deposits nowadays pay interest and also allow instant access to your money. A phone call allows instant access to the money in your high rate deposit account, which is transferred to your current account and then again instantly accessed

using your debit card over the phone. There is no clear distinction any more between current and time deposits. The difference is only in the rates of interest paid on the different accounts, which varies inversely with the ease with which money can be withdrawn: the longer it takes to withdraw the money, the less liquid the deposit, the higher the interest rate; but the liquidity of the whole range of deposits has increased.

The institutions themselves have become more alike and the traditional distinction between banks and building societies is totally blurred. Banks now give mortgages for the purpose of house buying and building societies grant loans for almost any purpose. Some building societies, like Abbey National, have turned themselves into banks. Even major food stores such as Sainsbury's and Tesco are turning into financial institutions. When you pay for your food with a credit or debit card, they offer you a 'cash back' facility. They debit your account for more than the amount you have spent on food and give you the difference in cash. At one time, you used to have to make a special trip to the bank during opening hours to get cash. Marks & Spencer, Debenhams, Sainsbury/Homebase, Tesco and Asda are now competing with more established retail banks, offering personal loans and a whole range of financial services.

To sum up our discussion, what is money today in Britain? It is notes and coins, quite clearly; it is also money deposited with a broad spectrum of financial institutions. There is no single correct definition of money and there are many liquid assets which are not included in any of the major monetary aggregates of an economy, but which nevertheless need to be taken into account when interpreting monetary conditions. We are now in a position to understand the official definitions of money used in the UK.

Official definitions

It is very important, for reasons that will be explained in Chapter 7, to have an idea of the amount of money available in the economy, as monetary aggregates play a central role in the formulation of monetary policy. Remember, by money we mean not only notes and coins; but also a variety of deposits, as they too can be indirectly used as a medium of exchange, liquidity for spending. Various official measures of the money stock have been used in Britain in recent years. Changes in the official measures in part reflect the changes in banking practices which have followed deregulation in the 1980s; they also reflect a changed attitude towards the use of monetary instruments for the management of the economy.

A specific growth of the money supply represented an intermediate target in the 1970s; it was seen as the link between changes in monetary instruments (interest rates) and changes in the final economic variable (nominal income), which was the real target. More recently the monitoring ranges (since 1993) in the growth of money supply have been treated as useful timely indicators of inflationary pressures.

The official measures of the money stock currently used in the UK are **M0** and **M4**, while M2, used with M0 and M4 until 1996, has now been dropped as a major liquidity indicator. M0 includes the cash held by the public, but also includes the cash held by the banking system, by commercial banks and building societies, and the cash held by the Bank of England, as commercial banks and financial institutions bank at the Bank of England, that is, they deposit some of their cash there. So M0 really measures the monetary base, the high-powered currency or actual amount of physical notes and coins in circulation, whether it is in the hands of the public or in banks' vaults.

Official definition of M0

- cash held outside the Bank of England by banks, building societies and the public;
- banks' operational deposits at the Bank of England.

The problem with this measure of money is that, according to the definition of money as a medium of exchange, it includes some cash that is not really money, while it does not include something else which is not cash but, in fact, is money. As it is important for the government to have a measure of the amount of money in the economy, M0 is not a very satisfactory measure.

✍ Activity 6.4

What does M0 include that is not money? What does it not include that is money?

✓ Answer 6.4

M0 includes the cash balances held by the banking system, which the public cannot get access to and spend, and these cannot therefore count as money. So part of M0 is not really money, according to our definition. Because M0 only measures notes and coins, it fails to measure other types of money, most notably current accounts and other chequeable sterling deposits that people have at banks and building societies and can use as a medium of exchange, by writing cheques against them.

M2 rectified these drawbacks and included all cash held by the public, but not that held by the banking

system, and all chequeable deposits, whether earning interest or not and whether at commercial banks or building societies. M2 also included sterling non-chequeable deposits of up to £100,000 which allowed instant withdrawal subject to a small penalty. In these cases, although people are not allowed to withdraw their money for up to, say, a month, the bank may allow instant withdrawal of a certain sum, claiming back part of the interest earned in the previous month. So it can be argued that even non-chequeable deposits of this kind can be used as money.

Official definition of M2

- cash held by the public;
- non-interest bearing sterling bank deposits;
- other retail sterling deposits at banks;
- retail sterling deposits at building societies.

As a measure of liquidity of the economic system, M2 was open to criticism and was finally dropped in 1992.

✍ Activity 6.5

What do you think were the criticisms of M2?

✓ Answer 6.5

Some economists disputed the inclusion in M2 of non-chequeable deposits (up to £100,000). Others argued the opposite, stating that it was too restrictive because it only included them up to £100,000 and therefore was not very meaningful as a measure of what really goes on in the economy. Since 1992 this measure has been set aside in favour of M4. M4 is meant to overcome these objections as it includes all the items included in M2, but also all other sterling deposits at banks and building societies, with no limits on the sum deposited and on the notice time required to withdraw them which, in some cases, could be two years or more.

Official definition of M4

- M2;
- non-retail sterling deposits at banks;
- non-retail sterling deposits at building societies.

Note that M4, like M2, only includes sterling deposits. Money held in Britain in foreign currency deposits, as in the example on financing a house purchase, eludes these calculations, only to form part of other measures of liquidity.

Let's summarize the concepts and exact terminology used in the three definitions of money introduced so far. **Cash** is notes issued by the Bank of England, Scottish and Northern Irish banks, plus the coins made at the Royal Mint and issued by the Bank of England.

Banks' operational deposits at the Bank of England are deposits at the Bank of England held by commercial banks and financial institutions. **Retail deposits** can be classified in three groups:

- non-interest bearing chequeable deposits;
- interest-bearing chequeable deposits;
- interest-bearing, non-chequeable deposits up to £100,000 withdrawable at a penalty under one month's notice.

✍ Activity 6.6

Study Figure 6.1 and explain what M0 and M4 measure.

✓ Answer 6.6

M0 consists of cash held by the public outside the Bank of England, plus bankers' operational deposits with the banking department of the Bank of England. M4 adds in all sterling 'retail' and 'non-retail' deposits at banks and building societies. Retail deposits cover all chequeable deposits, whether interest bearing or not, made by individuals at banks or building societies. **Non-retail or wholesale deposits** are large-scale non-chequeable deposits made by firms at banks and building societies at negotiated interest rates.

Figure 6.1   The M0 and M4 measures of money (£bn)

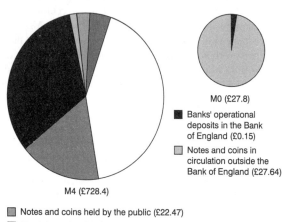

MO (£27.8)

- ■ Banks' operational deposits in the Bank of England (£0.15)
- ☐ Notes and coins in circulation outside the Bank of England (£27.64)

M4 (£728.4)

- ▨ Notes and coins held by the public (£22.47)
- ■ Non-interest bearing bank deposits (£38.93)
- ☐ Other bank retail deposit (£327.96)
- ▨ Building society retail shares and deposits (£95.45)
- ■ Bank wholesale deposits (£229.26)
- ☐ Building society wholesale deposits (£7.17)

Source: HMSO, Financial Statistics, *The Blue Book, 1998*

✍ Activity 6.7

The 1997 (not seasonally adjusted) figures for M0 and M4 are shown in Table 6.1. Compare these with the respective figures for 1993 and comment.

✓ Answer 6.7

	1993	1997	Percentage change over the period
M0	21 729	27 818	28
M4	543 855	720 853	32.5
M0/M4	3.9%	3.8%	–0.1

M0 represented less than 4 per cent of total money supply M4 in 1993 and 1997.

Until 1989, the only definitions of narrow money and broad money officially used were **M1** and **M3** respectively. M1 included:

- notes and coins in circulation with the public but not in banks' tills;
- private sector non-interest bearing, chequeable, sight deposits with banks, but not with building societies.

M3 included:

- M1;
- private sector, interest-bearing, non-chequeable time deposits with banks, excluding building societies.

These measures were dropped in 1989 and replaced by M0, M2 and M4 for the following reasons:

1   Increasingly, sight deposits were paying interest and were often used by firms for short-term, large deposits (non-retail). Sight deposits were becoming

Table 6.1   Monetary aggregates, 1993–7

Annual percentage	M0		M4	
	£ million	Annual percentage change	£ million	Annual percentage change
1993	21 729	5.6	543 855	4.6
1994	23 322	7.3	566 847	4.7
1995	24 539	5.2	623 452	9.9
1996	26 153	6.6	682 963	9.5
1997	27 818	6.4	720 853	11.6

Source: Bank of England, *Monetary and Financial Statistics*, April 1998, vol. 2

quite unrelated to people's requirements of money as a medium of exchange.

2 Various non-retail, non-chequeable time deposits in banks, building societies and national saving banks were increasingly used for expenditure purposes (retail), but were not included in M1.

3 Finally, the distinction between banks and building societies had become increasingly blurred, with building society accounts increasingly chequeable and used as a medium of exchange. Building society accounts were not included, however, in the two measures of liquidity.

M1 and M3 were eventually dropped in 1989 and M0, M2 (subsequently also dropped) and M4 became the official measures of the money supply in Britain. However, M2 and, in particular, M3 remain the official measures of liquidity used by most EU governments.

M3H, which includes M3 (M4 for the UK) plus private-sector and public corporations foreign currency bank deposits (bank and building societies for the UK) is the measure of broad money adopted by the EU for comparisons among members,

MONEY SUPPLY

Economists use the terms money supply or the supply of money to refer to the total amount of money in the economy. They refer to the stock of money. We now understand what we mean by money and we also know the official measures of money in Britain today. We understand that money is notes and coins in circulation, but also certain types of deposits held by the public with financial institutions.

We do not yet know what determines how much money there is in the economy: what determines the money supply. This is what we now want to find out. Money, as we have seen, is two different things: it is notes and coins and also deposits. So we can break our question into two and ask:

- Who or what determines the quantity of notes and coins in circulation?
- Who or what determines the amount of deposits with financial institutions that people have?

The answer to the first question is the **central bank**, in the UK the **Bank of England**. The answer to the second question, which we need to qualify, is the **commercial banks and financial intermediaries**, together with people themselves. So we now know who determines the money supply in an economy: it's the central bank, acting on behalf of the government, and financial intermediaries.

What we still have to explain is how. Ultimately, we want to be able to say how governments can control the money supply in order to influence the interest rate, which in turn affects investment. But one step at a time. Before we explain their part in the process of money creation, let's say something about the role of financial institutions.

Central bank

The Bank of England is the central bank of the UK. All countries have central banks and all central banks fulfil, broadly speaking, the two crucial functions of financial regulator and government's agent. Until the fundamental changes introduced by Gordon Brown in the summer of 1997, discussed in the second part of this chapter, the Bank of England, as the UK central bank, used to fulfil two vital roles:

- **financial regulator:** central banks have the responsibility for the overall management and functioning of the country's monetary system. They ensure that clearing banks and all the other financial institutions operate correctly and efficiently, maintaining adequate liquidity. Since the summer of 1997, the Bank of England is no longer responsible for the detailed supervision of the commercial banking system. This responsibility now rests with the Securities and Investment Board.

- **government's agent:** the Bank of England used to act as the government's agent. In its capacity as the government's banker, it carried out the monetary policy decided upon by the government. For this reason, the Bank of England worked in very close liaison with the Treasury and was obliged to carry out its policies. This is not the case for all central banks. Some, notably the German Bundesbank, have enjoyed, formally at least, considerable independence from their governments. The independence of central banks from their respective governments is now required in the EU as part of stage two, towards monetary integration, laid down by the Maastricht Treaty for the introduction of a single currency in 1999. The changes introduced by the Chancellor in the summer of 1997 are a step in this direction.

The most important functions of the Bank of England include:

1 **banker to the government**: the government banks at the Bank of England where it keeps two major accounts: 'The Exchequer', in which revenues from taxation are collected and from which government spending is financed; the 'National Loan Fund', in which funds from borrowing and lending are collected.

2 **banker to other financial intermediaries:** these include the recognized banks which hold their operational balances at the Bank of England; overseas central banks which may hold sterling deposits there, as part of their official reserves.

3 **lender of last resort:** the Bank of England provides liquidity to banks and other financial institutions which may have become temporarily illiquid, by rediscounting bills (purchasing bills of exchange before they reach maturity) or bond (gilt) repos (buying back government bonds for a short period only, usually two weeks, after which time the bonds are repurchased back by the original borrower), a process known as **repos**.

4 **regulator of the money** supply through:

- control of the monetary base;
- control of commercial banks' reserve requirements;
- open market operations;
- manipulation of interest rates by setting its 'base rate'.

These functions are typical of any central bank. The nature of some of these functions will become clear in the course of the chapter; the changes introduced in 1997 in the UK to comply with the second EU stage will also be discussed at the end of Chapter 7.

Commercial banks

The 1987 Banking Act defined the monetary sector of the economy as consisting of a series of financial institutions supervised by the Bank of England. The largest group of institutions in the monetary sector is the **recognized banks**. To be a recognized bank, institutions have to fulfil certain criteria set out by the Bank of England. If a bank is not recognized it cannot use the word 'bank' next to its name, unless it is a foreign bank operating in the UK that is entitled to use the word bank in its country of origin. The recognized banks include the **clearing banks** as well as the National Girobank, the discount houses and the banking department at the Bank of England.

The clearing banks are the most important recognized banks for the implementation of monetary policy and the functioning of the economy. They include:

- Abbey National;
- Barclays;
- Clydesdale Bank;
- Co-operative Bank;
- Lloyds;
- Midland;
- National Westminster;
- Royal Bank of Scotland;
- Standard Chartered;

- TSB.

The name 'clearing banks' comes from the fact that they operate a clearing system for settling banks' debts with each other on a daily basis through a central clearing house. Being nationwide and computerized, they facilitate the process of transmitting payments. They also facilitate the process of financial intermediation and **credit creation**, or **granting of loans**. It is precisely on this function that their part in the process of **money creation** rests.

Credit creation

Let's now turn to the part played by the commercial banks and the Bank of England in the determination of the **money supply**. It is easy enough to see that the Bank of England is responsible for the money supply in the sense that it decides how much cash, notes and coins, should be printed or made and put into circulation in the economy. But notes and coins are not all the money that there is in an economy. We know that cash only accounts for a small part of the total money supply and that, according to our definition of money as a medium of exchange, money is also various kinds of deposit accounts.

✍ Activity 6.8

If we added up the value of all deposits people have with banks in Britain, do you think that it would be equal to the value of the notes and coins in circulation?

✓ Answer 6.8

The value of all the deposits with the banking system far exceeds the value of notes and coins in circulation or monetary base. The monetary base, M0, represents less than 4 per cent of the broader M4.

But how do these accounts develop? Who controls their quantity and their value? To answer all these important questions we need to understand the **process of credit creation** by commercial banks. Let's consider the functions fulfilled by commercial banks in our economies:

- Commercial banks facilitate the process of **transmitting payments** through their clearing system; this allows us to write cheques to settle our transactions.
- They also facilitate the process of **financial intermediation**; they bring lenders and borrowers together, but they also use money deposited with them to make loans.

Whether depositors are aware of it or not, commercial banks borrow money from them, crediting them with a deposit which earns them interest. The deposit is a lia-bility to the bank, as it is money the bank owes to its depositors. The bank then uses the money deposited with it to make loans to people who want to borrow and charges them interest on the loan. This is the way in which commercial banks make money. They charge more in interest for a loan than they pay in interest for a deposit.

Because banks make money by making loans out of deposits, they are always tempted to make as many loans or as large loans as possible with the money deposited. This is where they can go wrong. When banks make loans out of deposits, they count on the fact that not all depositors will want their money back at the same time. Some will want to withdraw their deposits or part of their deposits, others will open new accounts. There is more likely to be a flow of deposits and withdrawals and is therefore quite safe for the banks to count on this fact and lend out some of the money deposited.

However if all depositors decided to withdraw their deposits on the same day, the banking system would collapse. The banks would not have enough money in the vaults to pay back their depositors; they could only close their doors. But banks count on the fact that this eventuality is unlikely to occur. However, it does some-times happen that runs on banks develop, when more creditors than normal wish to withdraw their funds. On such occasions banks become illiquid; they do not have enough money in their cash tills and vaults as they have lent it out to borrowers, to give back to their depositors. When this happens, to get themselves out of trouble, commercial banks can borrow money from the central bank, in the UK the Bank of England. This is what we mean when we say that the Bank of England acts as a **lender of last resort**. When banks do not know to whom to turn, in order to get money, they look to the Bank of England. Unlike any other bank, the Bank of England can never run out of money as it can simply resort to the printing press and make more.

However, the Bank of England, does not give out money free of charge; it charges interest to the com-mercial banks that might be temporarily illiquid and need to borrow. The interest at which commercial banks borrow from the Bank of England is called the **base rate**. Changes in the base rate are an important indicator of the liquidity of the economy and are watched very carefully by financial operators as they tend to indicate similar changes in the whole compos-ite structure of interest rates. An increase in the base rate by half a point will be followed, for instance, by a similar change in the mortgage rate. An increase in the

base rate will also make commercial banks think twice before they take the risk of becoming illiquid by over-lending: what they gain from making more loans might be wiped out by what they lose in higher interest to the Bank of England, if they are forced to borrow.

To avoid the risk of banks becoming illiquid, in most economies the banking system operates on an imposed or self-imposed **partial reserve basis**. In other words, commercial banks have a legal **reserve requirement** imposed by the central bank, or a self-imposed reserve requirement to hold some fraction of their deposits in the form of liquid cash balances, that is, as money. This is done with a view to preventing banks from becoming illiquid and unable to pay the money to depositors wishing to withdraw their funds.

You should now be a little clearer about the broad function of commercial banks in the economy, so let's return to our main point and explain the role that com-mercial banks play in determining or affecting the **money supply**.

So far, we understand how the Bank of England affects the supply of money: it determines the quantity of notes and coins in circulation. How do commercial banks affect the other component of the money supply, the deposit accounts? We can understand this better with an example. It fully explains the process of money creation by commercial banks, as it develops in the real economy.

Let's start with some assumptions. In our economy:

1 There are only two banks: Bank 1 and Bank 2, and the public. There is also a central bank whose func-tion is to decide the commercial banks' **reserve requirement**. The reserve requirement specifies what percentage of money deposited by the public with the banks should be kept as reserve with the Central Bank and not used to make new loans. The central bank decides the quantity of high-powered money, of notes and coins in the economy.

2 The two banks must hold 10 per cent of their deposits in the form of cash, as a reserve require-ment. What they do with the rest of the money deposited is up to them.

3 The public wishes to hold all its money in the form of deposits and does not wish to hold any currency at all. When people have any money they rush to deposit it in the bank for safe-keeping and, of course, they write cheques against the money deposited to pay for their transactions.

Let us start with a situation where there is no bank-ing system and all the currency in circulation in the economy is £100. Our initial money supply is £100, entirely in the form of cash, notes and coins. Let us see what happens when a banking system is introduced into this economy and our two banks, Bank 1 and Bank 2, open their doors to the public, under our specified assumptions. To monitor how the situation develops and to understand at the same time how these two banks create money, through a process of credit creation, let us look at their balance sheet and at the balance sheet of the third party involved in the process, the public. This is shown in Table 6.2.

The assumptions we have made are:

- reserve requirement = 10% in currency;
- public holds all its money in the form of deposit.

Table 6.2 shows the balance sheet of three groups: Bank 1, Bank 2 and the public. For each group, one column shows the assets and the other the liabilities. If we look at the public's balance sheet first, we see two items under the assets column: the currency held by the public itself (C_P) and the currency the public deposits with the banks (D). The public's liabilities are represented by loans received from banks which need to be paid back at a certain date. They are a liability for the public. The balance sheet of the two banks show, in the assets column, the currency held by the bank itself (C_B) and the loans the bank makes to members of the public. In the liabilities column, we find deposits (D), money deposited with the banks by the public, owned by the public and for which the banks are liable. Table 6.2 needs to be read across from left to right, with each new stage of the process starting on a new row – from (a) to (f). The first column on the left represents the various steps in the process of deposit creation. A plus or minus in front of an item represents an increase and a decrease, respectively, in that particular item.

Step (a) shows the situation of the economy before the introduction of banks. The money people have available for their transactions is represented by £100, all in notes and coins.

Step (b) shows the situation after Bank 1 has opened its doors to the public. The public rushes in and deposits all of its currency (C_P) with Bank 1. The money supply of the economy is still £100 but it is now in the form of deposits, as we had assumed.

This process can be read across row (b) as follows. Let's look at the public's balance sheet first: – 100 under C_P indicates that the public does not hold any currency, but the same amount is deposited (+100 under D) and it is still an asset for the public. Bank 1 receives the money deposited with it (+£100 under C_B), for which it is liable (+£100 under Bank 1's liabilities). Holding £100 is not going to earn Bank 1 any money, so it decides to make a loan to Albert, for which the bank will charge Albert interest. As the bank has to keep 10 per cent of its deposits as currency reserve, to meet this reserve requirement it can only lend £90 as a loan to Albert, while keeping £10 as liquid reserve.

Step (c) describes this new situation. Albert receives a loan from Bank 1, £90 in cash (+£90 under C_P), which is a liability for Albert as eventually he will have to return this money to Bank 1 (+£90 under public's liability). Bank 1's balance sheets also record these changes. The bank loses £90 in cash because it gives it to Albert as a loan and only has £10 left in its vaults as a reserve. At the same time, the bank has £90 worth of loan credited under assets as it is owed £90 by Albert. The total money supply of this economy has increased and is now £190. The public has £100 of deposits and £90 of currency.

✍ Activity 6.9

Can you say what will happen next? Cover up the rest of the table and try to work out for yourself what will happen.

Table 6.2 Creation of money by commercial banks

	Public			Bank 1			Bank 2		
	Assets		Liabilities	Assets		Liabilities	Assets		Liabilities
	C_P	D	Loans	C_B	Loans	D	C_B	Loans	D
(a)	100								
(b)	−100	+100		+100		+100			
(c)	+90		+90	−90	+90				
(d)	−90	+90					+90		+90
(e)	+81		+81				+81	+81	
(f)	−81	+81		+81		+81			
Total	0	1000	900						

Note: C_B = currency held by the banks; D = deposits; C_P = currency held by the public.

✓ Answer 6.9

Step (d) shows what will happen next. Albert now has £90, which he is going to use to pay for the goods and services he wants to buy. He does not like the idea of carrying around all that money in his wallet so he deposits it with Bank 2, where he opens an account. He can still use this money to pay for things; all he has to do is to write cheques against his deposit. So the balance sheet of the public now shows –£90, the cash that Albert no longer has, and +£90 under deposit, as the money deposited with Bank 2 remains an asset for Albert. Bank 2 receives the cash (+£90), for which it is liable (+£90 deposit which is a liability for the bank).

Step (e) describes the stage that follows. Bank 2 does not want to sit on £90 worth of cash without earning anything and decides to make a loan to Beatrice, for which it charges her interest. How much will Bank 2 lend out? It has to retain 10 per cent of its deposit as liquid reserve, that is £9 (10 per cent of £90), so it can make Beatrice a loan of £81. The public, in this case Beatrice, receives £81 worth of extra currency (+£81), which is however, a liability (+£81 under public's liabilities), but an asset (+£81 under loans) for Bank 2, which no longer has £81 worth of cash as it has given it to Beatrice (–£81 under CB for Bank 2).

Beatrice will in turn want to deposit her £81 with a bank, say Bank 1, rather than carrying it around. Step (f) describes this stage, where Beatrice does not have £81 worth of cash any more, but rather £81 worth of deposit with Bank 1; deposit which represents an addition of cash for Bank 1 (+£81 under CB for Bank 1), but also a new liability. And so on and so forth. At each new stage, the people receiving the loan obtained money which they proceeded to use for transactions, having redeposited it.

No one is aware of, or indeed affected by, what the bank does with the money once it is deposited. In fact, only 10 per cent of the money deposited remains in the bank, while the rest is lent out. At stage (f), the money supply is equal to £271 of which £190 is deposits and £81 is currency (Beatrice's). We have assumed that people in this economy do not wish to hold any cash as they would rather have balances at a bank and settle transactions by cheques. So this process will go on until the public has deposited all the cash in circulation and the banks have created the greatest possible amount of loans. With a 10 per cent reserve requirement, this means that the amount of deposits outstanding is equal to £1,000. So, the introduction of the banking system has converted an initial money supply of £100 consisting only of currency into a money supply of £1,000, consisting only of deposits. The final situation is as follows:

	(£)
Total currency in the two banks	100
Total bank loans	900
Total bank deposits	1,000

The money supply has grown, due to the loans granted by the banks on the basis of the money deposited with them, from an initial £100 of currency to a final £1,000, of which £900 is represented by loans and £100 by currency.

Money multiplier

Could we have calculated this outcome in the first place? The answer is yes, using what economists call the **money multiplier**. Let us first see how the money multiplier is calculated. A word of warning! Do not confuse the money multiplier with the spending multipliers we discussed before. They are two completely different concepts.

If we go back to our simple example, we see that we started off with £100 cash, which was entirely deposited, so we had £100 deposit. Cash deposits are also referred to as **reserves** or **reserve assets**. So in our example, the banking system has £100 of reserve assets, that is, currency actually deposited with them. This point is important because it is only on the basis of, and in relation to, the currency actually deposited (not C_P but C_B) and in the hands of the banking system that banks can create loans.

Because we had made the assumption that people did not wish to hold on to any currency in this economy but would rather deposit it all, £100 of initial currency is entirely available to the banking system to make loans. How much credit money will be created by the banking system will depend on the bank's required reserve ratio, in our example, 10 per cent; total deposits were equal to £1,000.

	(£)
Total deposits	1,000
Initial cash	100

$$\text{Money multiplier } \frac{1,000}{100} = 10.$$

The money multiplier is the multiple by which deposits can increase for every pound increase in reserve. This is equal to one divided by the required (or desired) reserve ratio.

In our example, £1 of cash deposited creates £10 of deposit; or £100 of initial cash deposited creates £1,000 worth of final deposit.

If we know the required reserve ratio or reserve requirement of the banking system, we can then calculate the money multiplier:

$$\text{Money multiplier} = \frac{1}{required\ reserve\ ratio}$$

In our example:

$$\frac{1}{0.1} = 10.$$

The money multiplier is 10. If we multiply the initial cash deposited £100 by the money multiplier, 10, we obtain the total money supply of our economy:

$$£100 \times 10 = £1,000.$$

In our example, the final money supply was £1,000. The money multiplier gives the change in the money stock for a £1 change in the quantity of the monetary base. The value of the money multiplier depends on two key ratios:

1 The bank desired ratio of cash reserves to total deposits: the reserve requirement, often also called the **liquidity ratio**.
2 The private sector's desired ratio of cash in circulation to total bank deposits or cash ratio: people's preferences about how much cash they keep in their wallets, outside the bank, and how much they prefer to deposit. Only by making use of the money deposited with them can banks 'create money'.

An increase in either of these two ratios will reduce the money supply and vice versa; a reduction in either of these two ratios will increase the money supply.

Money supply (MS) = monetary base × money multiplier.

We have now seen how the private banking system creates money by making loans. However, private banks are not free to create money at will. Their ability to create money is ultimately controlled by two factors:

- the volume of cash or reserves that the public makes available to the banking system, which in turn depends on the volume of notes and coins, or **monetary base**, injected into the system and controlled by the Bank of England.
- the reserve requirement or liquidity ratio, which can be voluntary and self-imposed by the banks or legally imposed by the Bank of England.

Simplifying somewhat and ignoring the practical difficulties of this task, we can sum up our discussion so far by saying that the Bank of England has, directly or indirectly, the ultimate control over the money supply.

✍ Activity 6.10

Assuming that people hold all their cash in bank deposits as before, if the monetary base (M0) is £21,000 million and the reserve requirement is 4 per cent, calculate the total money supply.

✓ Answer 6.10

The money multiplier is calculated as follows:

$$\frac{1}{0.04} = 25.$$

The total money supply is calculated as follows:

$$M^S = \text{monetary base} \times \text{money multiplier}.$$

So:

$$£21,000 \times 25 = £525,000.$$

M4

Let's summarise the main points so far.

The money supply, M4, comprises currency in circulation in the hands of the public and retail and non-retail deposits at banks and building societies. This measure of the money supply is often referred to as broad measure or 'broad money supply'.

The monetary base (narrow measure or narrow money) is issued by the Bank of England; it is measured by M0 and comprises currency in circulation plus currency held by the banking system. The monetary base is often referred to as 'high-powered' money because part of it, that part which is held by the commercial banking system, is 'multiplied' by the 'money multiplier' as the banking system creates deposits. The monetary base gives a poor indication of the real liquidity of the economy, the money supply, as it excludes the most important source of liquidity, which is represented by bank deposits. 'Credit money or deposit money' represents the larger component of the money supply, as shown in Figure 6.2.

✍ Activity 6.11

The money created by the commercial banking system exceeds the amount of notes and coins in the economy: this must mean that there is too much money in the economy. Do you agree?

✓ Answer 6.11

No, the excess of money supply is measured in relation to the liquidity needs of the economy, which grow as the economy expands. The money supply should only grow in line with the growth rate of the economy, to facilitate its growing number of transactions. A low ratio of cash to deposit money only indicates people's preference to use cheques and debit/credit cards in their transactions,

Figure 6.2 Money supply

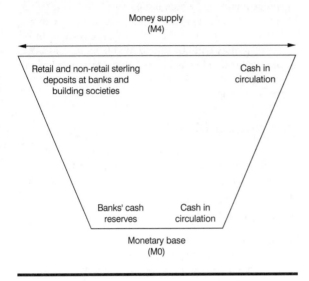

rather than cash. It does not mean that the system is inherently unstable.

✍ Activity 6.12

(a) What is the liquidity ratio?
(b) A bank has £100 million assets of which £10 million are liquid asset (cash), calculate the bank's liquidity ratio.
(c) What is the problem with a too low liquidity ratio?

✓ Answer 6.12

(a) The liquidity ratio is the proportion of a bank's total assets which are held in liquid form.
(b) $\dfrac{10\ million}{100\ million} = 10$ per cent

The bank has a 10 per cent liquidity ratio.
(c) The bank may not be able to meet its customers' demand for withdrawal of funds.

CONTROL OF THE MONEY SUPPLY

As we have seen, the central bank ultimately controls the money supply by:

- controlling the monetary base (currency in circulation): as the monetary base increases, so does the money supply;
- imposing or changing commercial banks' reserve requirement: the higher the reserve requirement, the lower the amount of credit creation;

- changing the base rate at which it lends to commercial banks: the higher the rate, the smaller the amount of credit creation, hence of money;
- selling or buying government bonds to/from the public with **open market operations** (OMO). The selling of government bonds by the Bank of England reduces the money balances held by the public and the banking system, and therefore the process of money creation by the banking system. The purchase of government bonds by the Bank of England has the opposite effect. The normal way in which the Bank of England influences the money supply is through the purchase or sale of government bonds, from or to the public and from or to the government.

The purchase of government bonds by the central bank causes an increase in the money supply.

- *Purchase of government bonds from the government:* the government issues new bonds and sells them to the Bank of England, which pays for them by crediting the government's deposits with an equivalent amount, that is, by giving the government new money. The government can write more cheques against its increased deposits with the Bank of England. By selling the bonds to the Bank of England the government has in effect borrowed from the Bank of England and one day, when the bonds reach their maturity date, that money will have to be repaid. In the meantime, the government has more money, pays out more cheques to people, firms, etc. who in turn deposit it with their banks, who in turn grant more loans to more people and create more money in the process. The way it works in practice is even neater than the one described: the commercial banks hold some of their liquid assets as cash deposited with the Bank of England. People who have received cheques from the government pay them into their commercial bank accounts. The commercial bank presents them to the Bank of England for payment and the Bank of England simply debits (decreases) the government's deposit and credits (increases) the commercial banks' deposits.
- *Purchase of government bonds from the public:* Alternatively, the Bank of England, which used always to act under instruction from the government but now enjoys greater independence, can buy back government bonds from the public. These are referred to as open market operations (OMO). The effect on the money supply is the same as before. This time, instead of the government issuing new bonds and selling them to the Bank of England, people sell old bonds back to the Bank of England.

People sell their bonds, which are pieces of paper promising to pay a fixed yield for a certain period of time, after which the bonds are redeemed, in exchange for a cheque from the Bank of England. They pay the cheques into their accounts with a commercial bank. The number of government bonds held by the public decreases, as they are bought back by the Bank of England and the amount of currency available to the system increases. The same clearing of accounts process takes place: commercial banks present the cheques to the Bank of England for payment and their cash deposits at the Bank of England are increased accordingly.

The sale of government bonds by the central bank reduces the money supply.

■ *Sale of government bonds to the public:* the money supply is reduced as people surrender some of their money (cash in circulation or bank deposits) to pay for the bonds. The Bank of England sells government's promises to pay a fixed yield every year and the whole capital back at a fixed date, in exchange for cash, which as it goes back to the Bank of England gets withdrawn from circulation. Again there is a process of debiting the relevant accounts, rather than cash being physically withdrawn.

■ *Sale of government bonds to the government:* when the government reduces its outstanding debt by buying back from the Bank of England some of its own old bonds, the money supply is reduced as the government's balances at the Bank of England are reduced by an equivalent amount.

Open market operations also affect the interest rate. A purchase of bonds by the central bank reduces interest rates, while a sale of bonds increases it.

✍ Activity 6.13

In the light of what we have said, what causes the money supply to increase?

✓ Answer 6.13

An increase of the money supply is caused by:

■ increase in the monetary base of notes and coins;
■ banks' lower liquidity ratio or reserve requirement, that is, banks hold a lower proportion of their deposits as cash reserve;
■ people lower the desired ratio of cash in circulation to total bank deposits, that is, people hold less cash in their pockets and deposit more with their banks;

■ the Bank of England buys new issue of bonds from the government, which issues new bonds to finance its PSBR – the government will then inject the newly borrowed currency into the economy and more credit money will be created by the banking system;
■ the government sells bonds to overseas purchasers, which also results in injection of extra currency into the economy.

✍ Activity 6.14

If the government sells or buys bonds to/from the general public, rather than to/from the Bank of England or overseas purchasers, what will the effect be on the money supply?

✓ Answer 6.14

The effect on the money supply is zero. No new money, either currency or deposit, is created. Money simply changes hands, from the public to the government.

Money supply and the rate of interest

To sum up our discussions, the money supply is determined by a policy decision taken jointly by the government and the Bank of England. To keep the analysis simple, we assume that the money supply is not influenced by the interest rate, although other more sophisticated models recognize a positive functional relationship between money supply and interest rates. In this rather simpler but still realistic scenario, the money supply is determined by a policy decision taken by the government and the Bank of England; it is 'exogenous'. The money supply can therefore be shown by a vertical line, as in Figure 6.3a. However, if

Figure 6.3 The money supply function: (a) exogenous M^s; (b) endogenous M^s

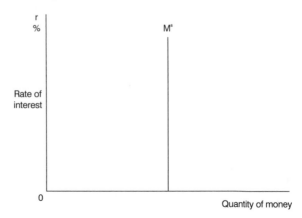

we assume that the money supply is influenced by interest rates and increases as the interest rate increases, then the money supply is 'endogenous', as shown by an upward sloping M^s curve.

The rationale for assuming an endogenous money supply is that the supply of money responds, to a certain extent, to the demand for money. If the demand for credit increases and people want to borrow more, the shortage of credit will drive interest rates up (the cost of credit). Banks will be tempted by the higher interest rates to operate with a lower liquidity ratio and provide extra loans, thus expanding the money supply.

THE DEMAND FOR MONEY

We now understand what is meant by money and we have also seen what determines the supply of money. We can now move on to discuss what determines the demand for money. Always remember that by money we mean cash or deposits, whether they earn interest or not, in other words assets which are liquid enough to be used to settle transactions.

The question we now want to answer is: what determines people's demand for money? A word of warning at this point. By this question we do not mean 'how

much money do people want'. The answer to that would be 'as much as possible, thankyou very much'. The question we are asking is on what basis do people decide how much of their income and wealth they wish to keep in a liquid form as money.

First we need to understand what the alternatives are. In what forms can people hold their wealth? They will need to keep some as cash or deposit ready to hand, but what do they do with the rest? Do they buy a house, a second car, a motorboat, a painting, or shares, government bonds and financial assets? People can choose to hold their wealth in a selection of monetary, near-monetary and non-monetary assets; they can choose, as economists say, a **portfolio of assets**. The options can be listed in order of decreasing liquidity.

Liquidity and assets portfolio

Liquidity, when used in relation to an asset or indeed any form of wealth, refers to the speed and ease with which the asset can be converted into money and used to settle transactions, without loss of value. Liquidity, in a sense, measures the degree to which an asset is convertible into money. Money is obviously fully liquid, while other assets range from being highly liquid, like a current account or high rate account, to far from liquid, like a house or a piece of land (Figure 6.4).

Figure 6.4 Liquidity of assets

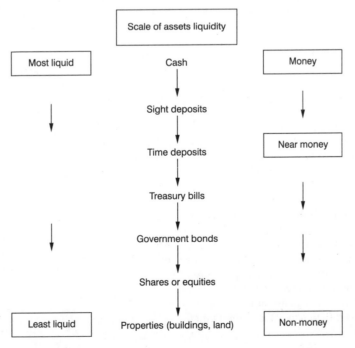

Treasury bills, bonds, shares, capital and properties are non-money forms of holding wealth. We begin to appreciate here – and we will make use of this important concept later on, when we talk more formally about the **demand for money** – that people need money in a liquid or fairly liquid form, cash in their wallets or readily accessible in a bank account, for their daily transactions, as they need to pay for the goods and services they buy.

However, people do not hold all their wealth in that form. They also hold or store part of it, so to speak, in other forms, such as government bonds, shares, or houses, which might be more profitable because they either earn an interest or increase in value. If people fall on hard times they can always sell their shares, bonds or houses. They can **liquidate** these rather more illiquid assets. To do so, however, takes time and may also involve a capital loss. If you are pushed, you might have to sell your assets at a price which is lower than the one you originally paid; the capital loss might be greater than any financial reward you might have earned from holding those assets.

Given this scale of liquidity, people can then choose how to distribute their wealth among the different assets. They choose their assets portfolio or assets mix according to their liquidity preference: cash, current account deposits, time deposits, bonds, shares and real assets.

Cash

People can hold **cash**. Cash is **liquid**, it can be directly used for transactions without loss of time. It is **certain**, there is no risk of making a loss, provided there is no inflation. However, carrying around large amounts of cash may not be very practical.

Current account deposits

People can have **current account deposits**. They are almost as liquid as cash. You can write cheques against the money deposited in current accounts and use them to settle transactions. They pay no or very low interest. In this sense, cash and current accounts do not offer your wealth any protection against inflation.

Time deposits

People can have **time deposits** or **high-rate accounts**. Time deposits are slightly less liquid. They are forms of near-money. You cannot write cheques against money deposited, but need to transfer funds to a current account in order to do so. Transfer, however, can be immediate. They earn interest, which may offer your wealth some protection against inflation, if the interest rate paid on your time deposit is at least equal to the rate of inflation.

Bonds

People can hold **bonds**. Bonds are loans made to the government for a longer period of time than Treasury bills (91 days). The holder of a government bond is entitled to the payment of a fixed sum or yield, for a given period, after which the bond is bought back or redeemed by the government at its face value, not its current market value. Suppose you pay £100 for a government bond which pays you £10 a year for 5 years, after which the government buys it back at £100. What interest rate are you getting? You can calculate the interest rate, r, as follows:

$$r = \frac{Yield}{Price\ of\ bond}$$

In our example, this is:

$$\frac{10}{100} \times 100 = 10\%.$$

Alternatively, you can think of this relationship the other way round. Given that the fixed yield is £10 a year and the interest rate is 10m per cent, what is the price of the bond?

$$0.10 = \frac{£10}{Price(?)} \quad Bond\ price = \frac{10}{0.1} = 100.$$

The yield offered on a new government bond reflects the current market interest rate; in fact, it is usually slightly higher. Market interest rates, however, change in response to changed conditions in the demand and supply of financial assets. You can sell a government bond on the stock market before it reaches its redemption date. When sold on the stock market, the price of the bond is determined by the demand and supply of financial assets and may be lower or higher than the bond's 'face value' or 'redemption value'. To calculate the market price of the bond, you have to divide the fixed yield that the bond holder receives from the government by the market interest rate to obtain the market price. So you can think of the relationship between price of the bond and interest rate the other way round. Given that the fixed yield is £10 a year, if the market interest rate is 10 per cent, what will be the market price of the bond on the stock exchange? If:

$$r = \frac{Yield}{P^B}$$

where r is the market rate of interest and P^B is the price of the bond, then:

$$P^B = \frac{Yield}{r}$$

so:

$$10\% = \frac{£10}{P^B} \quad as\ P^B = \frac{£10}{0.1} = £100.$$

Given that the yield is fixed, the interest rate will change as the price of the bond changes. The interest rate and the price of the bond vary inversely. As:

$$r = \frac{Yield}{P^B}$$

if $P^B \uparrow \rightarrow r \downarrow$ and if $P^B \downarrow \rightarrow r \uparrow$.

If the market price of the bond goes up, the interest rate, given the fixed yield, will go down and vice versa. In symbols:

$$\text{if } P^B \uparrow \rightarrow r \downarrow \text{ and if } P^B \downarrow \rightarrow r \uparrow.$$

If you regret having tied up your money in a bond for five years and want to sell it before it reaches its maturity, you can do so quite easily on the stock exchange. You might discover that the **market price** for bonds has changed, in response to changing supply and demand, so you might have to sell at less than the price you paid for it.

Shares and real assets

Going back to the portfolio of assets people can choose to hold, as an alternative to holding bonds people can hold shares and real assets. As a way of holding wealth, shares and real assets may give you higher returns, but they are also riskier. Shares entitle you to receive a share of the company's profits each year. Dividends can be high, low or negative. There might be no dividends if the company is not doing well. You may lose all your capital if the company goes bankrupt. Selling shares, if liquidity is needed, might also mean you have to sell them at a loss. The same applies to properties. Their returns are not predictable and they are therefore risky. They are also very illiquid, it might take years to sell a house.

🔑 Activity 6.15

You paid £100 for a government bond which pays a yield of £10 a year for five years. You now want to sell it after one year. Suppose you find that on the bond market, where you can buy old bonds as well as newly issued bonds, you can buy an old bond that yields £10 a year for £40. You have no choice but to sell yours at £40.

(a) What is your capital loss?
(b) What is the current rate of interest?
(c) If the government wanted to issue new bonds and was planning to offer £20 a year for a £100 bond, will the government be successful in selling its bonds?

✓ Answer 6.15

(a) Capital loss = face value − market value
= £100 − £40 = £60.

Your capital loss is £60 against which you need to set the yield you have earned while you were holding the bond, to work out your overall gain or loss.

(b) Given that $\frac{r \, 5 \, Yield}{P^B}$, the rate of interest on the old bond is:

$$\frac{10}{40} = 0.25 \text{ or } 25 \text{ per cent.}$$

(c) The government intends to offer new bonds at 20 per cent interest and yield = £10 a year. Given this information we can calculate the price at which the government should offer the new bonds as follows:

$$20\% = \frac{10}{P^B \text{ or } p^B} = \frac{10}{0.2}.$$

Hence:

$$P^B = £50.$$

The price of a bond should be £50. But no one will buy a new bond at £50 which represents a 20 per cent interest rate, when they can get 25 per cent interest on the old ones. The government will have to offer the higher interest rate, which is equivalent to saying it will have to lower the price to £40.

What we now understand is that changes in the price of bonds, caused by changes in the supply and demand for bonds, cause changes in the interest rate. So, although bonds pay a fixed yield and you get your money back at the end of the period, you can also incur a capital loss if you need to sell them at a lower price before they reach their maturity date.

Concluding, how do people choose their portfolio of assets? According to Keynes, the choice people make, when deciding how much money to hold, given their income and wealth, is between money in its liquid form and financial assets. We discuss the reasons for this more fully at the end of this chapter. For the moment let's be clear about one point: when we talk about money and try to determine what affects the demand for money, we are not asking how much money would people like to be paid at the end of the month or how much they earn. We are asking 'in which form, liquid or less liquid, do people want to hold their income and wealth. When making the choice between holding money in a current account or buying government bonds, what factors affect that choice? The question might seem unimportant and undeserving of investigation, but this is not the case. The choice between holding money in liquid form or buying a financial asset like a bond ultimately determines the market interest rate, given the total amount of financial assets available in an economy.

Reasons for holding money

So let's try and understand the reasons for holding money – the demand for money. Let's try and understand the factors affecting the decision of how much of their wealth people want to hold in the form of money, which does not earn interest, and how much they want to hold in the form of interest-bearing securities such as bonds.

✍ Activity 6.16

You (or people you know) may have some money tucked away in a saving account, or you may have bought some company shares or government bonds. What influenced your choice?

✓ Answer 6.16

Whenever you make a choice about where to put your money, whether you are aware of it or not, you are probably asking yourself the following questions: how can I get the maximum return with the minimum risk? How easy and how quick is it to recoup the money and obtain liquidity if I need it?

Of course, everybody always wants the maximum return; but many also want security of capital and/or income. These two aspirations are irreconcilable, at each end of the spectrum. The safest option is to keep your money in some form of saving account. There your capital is quite safe: at worst you will get back in money terms what you put in, although inflation might have reduced the real value in the meantime. 'Granny bonds', guaranteed to keep up with the retail price index, protect the real value of your capital, but do not offer anything much in excess of this. In other words, saving accounts do not give very high returns. At the other end of the spectrum are those who risk their entire savings and perhaps also borrow money in order to pursue a financial venture which offers maximum return but no security. Between these two extremes lies a host of options.

Choosing to hold money in our pockets or in a bank account rather than buying a bond has an opportunity cost: the interest forgone that we could earn if we held bonds instead. If you hold £100 during a year as money in your wallet and the rate of interest is 5 per cent, then the opportunity cost of holding your wealth in the form of £100 cash, rather than in the form of a bond, is £5 a year.

So the choice most people have to make is really how much of their financial assets they should hold in some easily cashable form, as money which does not earn interest, and how much they should hold in interest-bearing securities, such as bonds or shares. It does not

matter which securities specifically; what matters is that they are interest bearing. Because returns on securities are very much in line with one another, with the differences reflecting different degrees of risk and other specific factors, and because of the impact that the government has on the securities market, it makes sense, to simplify the analysis, to refer just to bonds as the only type of interest-bearing asset.

You might be puzzled at this point: we are contrasting holding money, which does not pay interest, with holding bonds, which do have a yield. But even some chequeable accounts, which as you know are money, pay interest nowadays. So holding money can have a positive return. This fact, however, does not really matter for the purpose of our analysis and should not confuse you. Suppose that bonds pay 10 per cent interest and a chequeable account pays 5 per cent.

✍ Activity 6.17

Must chequeable accounts always pay less than bonds?

✓ Answer 6.17

Chequeable deposit accounts must pay less than bonds, otherwise nobody would buy bonds. If the returns on money in deposit or savings account were higher, everybody would hold all their wealth in such accounts. When it comes to choosing whether to hold money in a deposit account or to hold bonds, it is the difference in interest rates that matters. People will look at the extra interest (5 per cent) from holding bonds rather than money. So we can equally legitimately say that the choice is between money, which pays a zero interest, and bonds, which pay 5 per cent. This makes the choice clearer.

✍ Activity 6.18

Calculate the market price for a bond which has a face value of £100 and a yearly yield of £8 when the current market interest rate is 8 per cent, 12 per cent and 6 per cent. What conclusion do you draw from your results?

✓ Answer 6.18

Table 6.3 shows the bond's market price at the various interest rates.

The market price of bonds (P^B) and interest rates (r) are inversely related:

$$\text{if } r \uparrow \rightarrow PB \downarrow \text{ and if } r \downarrow \rightarrow PB \uparrow.$$

So why do people choose to keep some of their income as liquid money and not as interest-yielding bonds?

Table 6.3	Market prices of bonds		
Face value £	Yearly fixed yield	Market interest rate%	Market price
100	8	8	100
100	8	12	66.6
100	8	6	133.3

There are three reasons or motives, according to Keynes, for holding money as opposed to bonds:

- transaction reasons;
- precautionary reasons;
- speculative reasons.

Transaction motive

The transaction motive for holding our wealth, or part of it, in its liquid form as money, rather than buying bonds, arises from the function of money as a medium of exchange. We need money to buy goods and services. There is often a mismatch between the time we are paid and receive our incomes, for example, at the end of the month, and the times we need money to buy goods which are usually spread over the month. For this reason we want to hold money to meet our transaction needs, without first having to undergo the cost and inconvenience of converting some other assets into money. The next question then becomes: what affects the transaction demand for money?

How much money we want to hold for transaction reasons depend on two factors. First, it depends on the volume of transactions we make, which in turn is likely to be related to our income. Note at this point that if the price of the goods and services we buy doubles, we will double the amount of money we wish to hold to meet our transaction needs. In other words, the demand for money measures the demand for real and not nominal money balances. So our real income will affect how much we wish to hold in 'money' form, as cash balances in our pockets or in the bank. The higher our income, the higher our demand for money for the transaction reason, as the amounts of goods and services we want to buy and need cash for will be greater.

The second consideration likely to affect our decision of how much money to hold will be the 'cost' of doing that. The cost of holding money in your wallet is not an obvious one, but it is a real one nonetheless: the interest you could be earning if you had bought a government bond. The opportunity cost of holding money is the interest forgone. What would you do?

If the interest rate were only 3 per cent, it would not be worthwhile to give up much liquidity by holding bonds instead of cash or chequeable money balance in the bank. But if the interest rate were 30 per cent, the opportunity cost of holding money instead of bonds would be quite high. If you had £1,000 to spare and kept it in your current account, at the end of the year you would still have your £1,000. Assuming no inflation, you will be as well off as at the beginning of the year. But if you bought government bonds instead, you will have earned £300 in interest. If you are sensible, you will try and keep as much as possible of your funds in bonds. So we reach an important conclusion here. When interest rates are high, people will want to take advantage of the high return on bonds and will choose to hold very little money. To sum up, the factors affecting the demand for money for transactions reasons are two: income and interest rate.

Income

The higher our real disposable income, the greater the number of transactions, the greater the demand for money balances. Demand for money and income are positively related:

$$\text{as } Y\uparrow \rightarrow M^d \uparrow$$

and vice versa:

$$\text{as } Y\downarrow \rightarrow M^d \downarrow$$

So we can say that the demand for money is positively related to income; in symbols:

$$M^d = f(Y).$$

Interest rate

The higher the interest rate that can be earned holding a bond, the higher the opportunity cost of holding money, the less money people will want to hold. Demand for money for transactions reasons and the interest rate are inversely related:

$$\text{as } r\uparrow \rightarrow M^d \downarrow$$

and vice versa:

$$\text{as } r\downarrow \rightarrow M^d \uparrow.$$

Precautionary motive

This is a slightly vaguer reason for holding money, but possibly just as important. It is useful to take precautions and have money to hand, as a reserve in case things go wrong or something unexpected happens: a sudden illness, an accident, an urgent trip. In many situations in life, we need to be able to have ready access to our money. Say, you are embarking on a long journey abroad; you are likely to feel more comfortable if you know that you can always use your credit card or go to a bank and cash a cheque, if you need to. You have got money in the bank. No great comfort can be derived from the thought that you have £5,000 worth of government bonds redeemable in the year 2005. True, if you get stuck for money, you can always ring up your broker from Australia and ask him to sell them tomorrow. But what if the prices of bonds tomorrow turn out to be low and you only make £2,000 from selling them. This is no way of planning your finances and your liquidity needs. So money is a useful reserve in which to hold wealth and to meet the uncertainties of life. By holding money we can avoid the time, costs and risks involved in converting other assets into money.

The next question then becomes: What affects the demand for money for precautionary reasons? How much money we want to hold for precautionary reasons depends, among other things, on our income and the interest rate. The 'precautionary services' that we derive from holding money are not an inferior good. The better off people are, the more they will want to enjoy the safety of having some money ready to hand in case things go wrong, the more 'precautionary money' they will want to hold. But again this service has a cost; if you hold money, you forgo interest. The interest rate once more measures the cost of holding money. The higher that cost, the more people will squeeze down their money balances for precautionary reasons. We can summarize the demand for money for precautionary reasons as follows:

$$M^d = f(Y, r).$$

Speculative motive

The first two motives explain why the quantity of money people wish to hold increases as income increases, but decreases as interest rates falls (opportunity cost). These reasons are quite intuitive. The speculative motive for holding money focuses only on the relationship between the amount of money people wish to hold and the interest rate. It offers another reason why people wish to hold more money when interest falls and less money when interest rates rise. This reason has to do with people's expectations about the value of the interest rate and the price of bonds and the relationship between interest rates and bond values.

To understand this, you must remember what we have already stated earlier: the market value of bonds, that is, the price at which you can sell them today, is inversely related to the interest rate. We can explain this more easily with an example. Suppose you bought a bond a year ago at the following conditions:

$$P^B = £100$$

$$r = 8\%$$

Fixed yield = £8 a year until the bond reaches maturity in five years time and is redeemed (i.e. you receive your £100 back). You paid £100 for it and it gives you a yield of £8 a year, which represents an interest rate of 8 per cent. Suppose that in the meantime the interest rate has risen because there has been a new issue of government bonds to finance the government deficit, which offers a more attractive 10 per cent in interest.

Suppose you now want to sell your bond as you regret having tied up your money and you would rather spend it on a trip around the world. So you instruct the broker at your bank to sell it for you.

✐ Activity 6.19

Will the broker be able to sell the bond for you at the same price you paid a year ago, that is £100?

✓ Answer 6.19

No, s/he will not. The simple reason is that no one will want to buy it at that price, when they can buy a new bond and earn 10 per cent rather than 8 per cent. The situation in the bond market is now as follows:

(new bond) $P^B = £100$ $r = 10\%$ yield = £10 a year for 5 years.

(old bond) $P^B = £100$ $r = 8\%$ yield = £8 a year for 5 years.

The old bond will not find a buyer. To make your bond attractive and sell it, your broker will have to lower its price.

✐ Activity 6.20

By how much should the price of the old bond be lowered for it to offer the same rate of return as a new bond?

✓ Answer 6.20

The new bonds offer a 10 per cent interest. We know that the yield of the old bond is £8. For that yield to represent an interest rate of 10 per cent, the selling price must be £80. As:

$$r = \frac{Yield}{P^B}$$

hence:

$$10\% = \frac{£8}{P^B(?)} \quad P^B = \frac{8}{0.10}$$

so:

$$P^B = £80.$$

To sell your old bond, the broker will have to lower its price. At a lower price your bond becomes attractive to buyers because the lower price increases the interest rate achieved by the buyer.

✍ Activity 6.21

Suppose your broker sells your bond for £50. What kind of interest rate is the buyer of your bond receiving?

✓ Answer 6.21

The interest rate is the ratio of the yield to the price of the bond. The new price is £50. The yield is fixed and is £8 so the interest rate is 16 per cent. This is calculated as follows:

$$r = \frac{Yield}{P^B} \quad \frac{8}{50} \times 100 = 16\%.$$

When interest rates fall, bond values rise (the price of the bond increases). When interest rates rise, bond values (their price) fall. In symbols:

$$\text{if } r \uparrow \rightarrow P^B \downarrow \text{ and if } r \downarrow \rightarrow P^B \uparrow.$$

✍ Activity 6.22

Suppose you finally sell your bond at £50, after holding it for a year. Did you make a capital gain or a capital loss? And what about the person who buys your bond?

✓ Answer 6.22

Note that a capital gain occurs whenever the value of an asset increases. A capital loss occurs whenever the value of an asset falls.

You have sustained a capital loss. You bought a bond a year ago for £100 and have sold it now for £50. Your capital loss is £50. Your net loss is £42 as the bond yielded you £8 in its first year. As:

$$\text{total return} = \text{capital gain (loss)} + \text{yield}$$

where capital gain is the difference between the price at which you have bought the bond and the price at which you sell it (a capital loss will show as a negative capital gain). So:

$$-£42 = -£50 + 8.$$

Assume now that the person who buys the bond from you at £50 will hold it for four more years, until its maturity date. The owner of the bond will receive £100 for it from the government, its original face value, which is more than its market value. The owner of that bond will make a capital gain of £50 and a total return of £82:

$$\text{Total return} = +50 + (8 \times 4) = £82.$$

So in discussing reasons why people choose to hold money rather than bonds, despite the fact that they forgo the interest if they do so, we can now see that people holding their wealth in the form of bonds are subject to the risk of capital losses if the interest rate rises and capital gains if the interest rate falls. You do not take that risk if you hold your wealth in the form of money.

Summary

When you buy a bond, you exchange your money for a piece of paper which is a promise. Bonds are promises by the government to pay a fixed amount or yield a year for a fixed period, say five years, after which time the bond is repurchased by the government at its face value, the money you originally paid for it. The market price of a bond, if you were to resell it on the bonds market before its redemption date by the government, depends on the fixed yield and the market rate of interest. If a bond promises to pay £50 a year and the market rate of interest is 5 per cent, the price of the bond will be £1,000. If the rate of interest falls to 4 per cent, the price of the bond will rise to £1,250; if the interest rate rises to 8 per cent, the price of the bond will fall to £625.

So if you hold a bond you run the risk of making a capital loss. To avoid this risk you hold money. The price you pay for avoiding this risk is the yield you are forgoing. This is the speculative reason for holding money instead of bonds. The analysis, however, can be taken a step further by bringing in expectations. Remember what we have just proved: that when interest rate falls, the price of bonds rises, and when interest rate rises, the price of bonds falls.

Now suppose that you want to become a 'financial speculator', making money cleverly buying and selling financial assets. Suppose you want to make capital gains, by buying cheap when the price of bonds are low and selling dear, reselling them when prices are high.

You know that interest rates movements affect the price at which bonds are traded, given their fixed yields. You know that:

$$\text{if } r \uparrow \rightarrow P^B \downarrow \text{ and if } r \downarrow \rightarrow P^B \uparrow.$$

For this reason, you have been watching the movement in the interest rates very closely and you think that they are higher than normal and should come down sometime soon. If and when they come down, the price of bonds will go up, which would be a good time to sell bonds. So if you have the expectation that interest rates are high and you expect them to fall, you will buy as many bonds as possible now and hold as little money as possible, with a view to selling the bonds when interest rates come down and the price of bonds is high. So, when interest rates are high, you are speculating that they will fall and you will be able to make a capital gain by selling your bonds.

Similarly, if interest rates are low, prices of bonds high and you expect them to go up in the near future, you will not want to be holding bonds. As interest rates go up as expected, the price of bonds will go down and if you have to sell you will be making a capital loss. So when interest rates are low, you hold on to your money and leave it in your current account, rather than buying bonds and risking a capital loss. So for speculative reasons too, the demand for money, as opposed to bonds, is high when interest rates are low and low when interest rates are high, as people buy bonds.

$$M^d = f(r).$$

The speculative demand for money is negatively related to the interest rate. As the word speculative suggests, holding on to liquid assets (money) for speculative reasons rests on expectations about future interest rates or about future bond prices. There are people who speculate on changes in stock exchange prices and profit on the outcome of their speculations.

Speculators who expect bond and share prices to fall (and interest rates to rise) are often referred to as **bears** in stock market jargon. 'Bears' are those speculators who sell their bonds, expecting to be able to buy them back more cheaply later on. Of course, 'bears' who sell in the expectation that bond prices will go down cause prices to fall or at least prevent them from going up. Bears sell bonds and hold money instead, accumulating albeit temporarily hoards of cash, because of their liquidity preference and the speculative motive of holding money rather than bonds. So as interest rates fall (and government bond prices rise) some speculatively minded people will start getting out of bonds and holding money instead. They anticipate that interest rates will stop falling and will start rising. If interest rates rise (and bond prices fall) they do not want to get caught holding bonds.

However, not everybody holds the same expectations. There are some speculators, referred to as **bulls** on the stock market, who hold the opposite view and expect bond prices to rise (and interest rates to fall). They buy bonds, depleting their portfolios of cash, when bond prices are falling, as they expect them to rise. Their own buying, of course, helps to push bond prices up, in another example of self-fulfilling prophecy.

Demand for money function

From all we've said so far about the reasons for holding money, we can derive a demand for money function which incorporates the assumptions made. For a given level of income, the demand for money balances is shown to be inversely related to the interest rate. This is shown in Figure 6.5.

In Figure 6.5, on the horizontal axis, we measure the quantity of money demanded, and on the vertical axis, the rate of interest. For a given level of income, the quantity of money demanded, that is, the amount of money households and firms wish to hold, is a function of the interest rate. Because the interest rate is the opportunity cost of holding money balances, increases in the interest rate will reduce the quantity of money that firms and households want to hold; decreases in the interest rate will increase the quantity of money that firms and households want to hold.

An increase in the level of output and income Y means that more goods are produced and sold. The level of economic activity and therefore of transactions – people buying goods and services, firms buying capital goods – will be higher. More transactions will require more money. The liquidity needs of the economy increase. People and firms will liquidate and sell some of their bonds to meet their increased liquidity needs. At higher levels of income, more money is demanded.

How do we show this in Figure 6.5? When we draw the money demand function as a negative function of the interest rate we are holding income constant. We are making a 'ceteris paribus' assumption. If income does not change, we can show the demand for money as being affected only by the interest rate. If income

Figure 6.5 Demand for money function

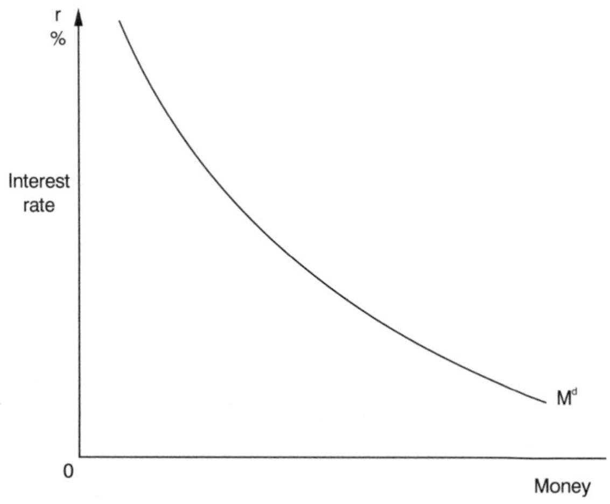

increases, for the same level of interest rate, more money balances will be demanded. We show this with a **shift out** of the demand curve for money. If income falls, less money is needed for transactions as the volume of transactions falls. At the same interest rate as before, we show this as a **shift in** of the demand for money curve.

Figure 6.6 shows a shift out of the money demand curve. As before, we measure interest rate on the vertical axis and money on the horizontal axis. An increase in income (Y) will shift the money demand curve to the right, as there are now more transactions for which money is needed. Both firms and households are likely to sell bonds to increase their holdings of money balances at a given interest rate.

Summing up, changes in the interest rate cause movements along the curve, changes in the quantity of money demanded. Changes in the level of output and income Y or in the price level P cause shifts of the curve out if they increase, or in if they decrease. Changes in Y or P cause a change in the demand for money.

MONEY MARKET EQUILIBRIUM

We are now in a position to bring together the two parts of our analysis, money supply and money demand. The money supply is determined by the monetary authorities. We showed it as a straight line, a given quantity, to indicate that it is independent of the interest rate (Figure 6.7).

Figure 6.6 Shifts of the money demand function

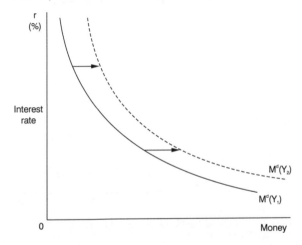

Figure 6.7 The supply of money

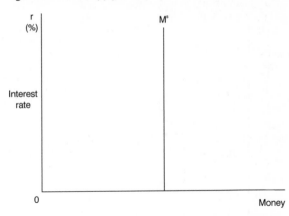

The demand for money balances, at a certain level of income, depends on the level of income and the interest rate. The demand for money, m^d, is simply the horizontal summation of the demand for money for transactions, precaution and speculative reasons. This gives the total demand for money function, sometimes referred to as the liquidity preference schedule. For a given level of income, that is, if income does not change, the demand for money balances will vary inversely with the interest rate. Less money balances are demanded at higher interest rates as the opportunity cost of holding money is greater and people will want to hold more bonds instead.

Now, if we put the two functions together, we obtain the money market, with a supply of money and a demand for money as shown in Figure 6.8. We obtain an important result. The interest rate is determined by the interaction of the supply of money and the demand for money. The equilibrium interest rate is the interest rate at which the money supply is equal to the money demanded.

Equilibrium exists in the money market when the supply of money is equal to the demand for money:

$$M^d = \frac{M^S}{P}.$$

At r_1, the quantity of money supplied exceeds the quantity of money demanded and the interest rate will fall. At r_2, the quantity demanded exceeds the quantity supplied and the interest rate will rise. Only at r^* is equilibrium achieved: point A.

Please note at this point that just as the money supply measures the **stock** of money supplied to the economy, the demand for money also measures the stock of money that firms, households and government desire to hold at a specific point in time, given the current

Figure 6.8 Money market equilibrium

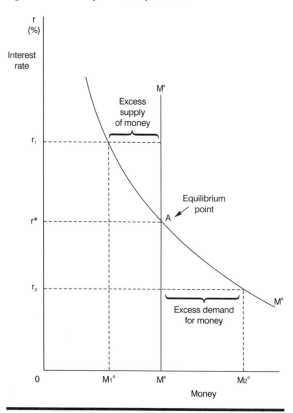

sell some of their bonds and the supply of 'old' bonds to the bond market will increase as a result. They will reduce their bond holding. Vice versa, if they find that they have more money than they need for their transactions, given that holding money has an opportunity cost, that is, the yield they could earn if they held bonds, they will use the excess money balances to buy bonds. The demand for bonds on the bond market will increase as a result.

This process goes on all the time. Bonds are offered for sale on the bonds market when more money is needed so there is an increased supply of bonds; more bonds are demanded on the bond market when less money balances are needed, so there is an increased demand for bonds. But changed demand and supply conditions in the bond market affect bond prices and consequently the market interest rate. An increase in the supply of bonds causes prices to fall and interest rates to rise. An increase in demand for bonds causes prices of bonds to rise and interest rates to fall. Remember what we have said about price of bonds and market rate being inversely related. This situation is summarized in Figures 6.9 and 6.10.

At the same time as people are constantly adjusting their own asset holdings by shifting out of bonds when they need more liquidity and vice versa, the Treasury and business corporations are also active on the bond market. The bond market continuously absorbs new bond issues as well as trading old ones. The Treasury and corporations can attract more people to hold bonds only by offering a higher interest rate than the current one.

So as people are trying to shift out of bonds into money, they will be discouraged from moving by a

interest rate, volume of economic activity and price level.

Equilibrium interest rate

Only at interest rate r^*, the quantity of money in circulation, that is, the money supply is equal to the quantity of money demanded. But what happens when the interest rate is not the equilibrium one? How is the equilibrium interest rate achieved?

To answer these questions we need to go back to the beginning of our discussions about the demand for money. People and firms choose their portfolio of assets. They choose to hold a certain amount of money because of their transactions and precautionary needs and because of the market interest rate; they also choose to hold a certain amount of bonds. Their asset portfolio is likely to contain money in its liquid form as well as bonds. People and firms will be constantly adjusting this balance between assets in the light of their liquidity needs. If they find that as their income increases they need more money balances, they will

Figure 6.9 The bond market: changes in demand

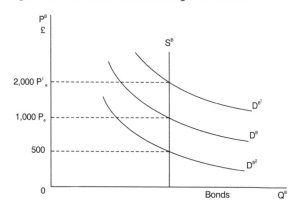

Note: S^B = 'supply of bonds'; D^B = demand for bonds; Q^B = quality of bonds

Figure 6.10   The bond market: changes in supply

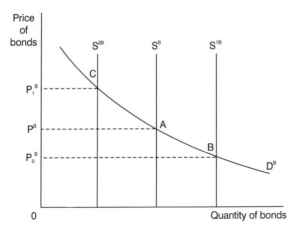

higher interest rate. This process will go on until the equilibrium interest rate is reached. To summarize these points, let's assume the following:

Price of bond   =   £1,000
Fixed yield   =   £100 a year
Interest rate   = $\dfrac{100}{1,000}$ = 10%

$$r = \frac{Yield}{P^B}.$$

So:

■ changes in the price of bonds will determine the interest rate;
■ changes in the prices of bonds are determined by the demand and supply of bonds.

As the demand for bonds increases, the price of bonds will also increase from £1,000 to £2,000, driving the interest rate down, from 10 per cent to 5 per cent, as:

$$r = \frac{100}{2,000} \times 100 = 5\%.$$

Equally holders of bonds will make a capital gain if the interest rate falls, as the price of the bonds they hold will increase. The possibility of a capital gain, if interest rates fall, is tempered by the risk of a capital loss, if interest rates fall.

So, if the demand for bonds falls, so will the price of bonds, causing an increase in the interest rate, given the fixed yields. Assuming that the price of bonds falls to £500, the interest rate will increase from 10 per cent to 20 per cent, given the fixed yield of £100. An increase in the interest rate may cause a capital loss for bond holders wishing to sell.

as P^B = £ 500   then $r = \dfrac{100}{2,000} \times 100 = 20\%$.

Changes in the prices of bonds, and therefore changes in the interest rates, can also be caused by changes in the supply of bonds. The supply of bonds is determined by:

■ government needing to finance a deficit;
■ individuals' private portfolios.

As the supply of bonds to the bonds market increases for the reasons listed above, the price of bonds falls and the interest rate rises; as the supply of bonds to the bond market decreases, the price of bonds rises and the interest rate falls. In symbols:

if $S^B \uparrow \rightarrow P^B \downarrow \rightarrow r \uparrow$ and if $S^B \downarrow \rightarrow P^B \uparrow \rightarrow r \downarrow$

Stock markets and the real economy

We now understand how the price of government bonds and their market return, interest rates, are affected by the economy's liquidity conditions, which in turn are determined by the government, assuming that the expected rate of inflation and the general state of confidence in the economy are unaffected. State of confidence and inflationary expectations are, however, seldom static. Does what we have just learnt about the determination of interest rates and financial asset prices help us to understand what has been happening to the world's stock markets in recent years?

In October 1997 panic about South East Asia's financial crisis sent share prices plunging all around the world. Despite this turmoil and Japan's impending economic recession in the last two years of the 1990s, world stock markets remained buoyant, with annual increases on average greater than 15 per cent. Could these share price rises in Asia and Europe be justified on the basis of economic fundamentals, that is, on the basis of the real growth prospects of world economies? Could American and European firms rightly expect strong earnings growth into the new millennium? The following economic fundamentals would seem to suggest that they could. In Europe:

■ Long-term interest rates have been falling. German ten-year bonds, which set the pace in Europe, yielded less than 5 per cent for the first time in 1998.
■ Oil and commodity prices have been falling, further dampening inflationary expectations.
■ European government borrowing has come down, in preparation for the introduction of the single currency.

- In some European countries, notably Italy, Spain, Ireland and Portugal, short-term interest rates are still considerably higher than in Germany. As a single currency requires a single short-term interest rate, short-term interest rates in those countries are likely to come down, giving a great boost to share and bond prices.
- Europe's economies are beginning to pick up, after years of sluggish growth, also encouraged by the prospects of increased competition and scope for mergers and restructuring brought about by the impending EU.

In the USA high financial asset prices are harder to justify solely on the basis of the economy's growth prospects and interest rates levels. An alternative and quite different explanation has been put forward. This explanation is demographical and often referred to as the 'baby-boomer bull'. As the baby boom generation approaches retirement, it is increasing its savings by buying up government securities. Because they are investing for the long term, these investors do not take much notice of short-term variations in share prices and resist selling. This situation has resulted in an excess demand for bonds, which is pushing up bond prices. This situation is likely to be reversed in eight to ten years time, when this generation will have reached retirement age and will start to live off its savings, taking money out of the market and liquidating their bonds.

However, stock markets are more than just mirrors which reflect the state of economies or telescopes which allow anticipation of them. While high share prices may reflect an economy's good economic performance, they also directly help to boost the economy's performance:

- As higher security prices make consumers wealthier, this in turn increases their spending: the wealth effect.
- Investment is even more sensitive to stock market swings than consumer spending. Higher bond and share prices (lower interest rates) make it cheaper for firms to raise the finance needed for their capital spending.
- Government deficits are reduced, as higher bond and share prices mean higher tax receipts for the government and lower budget deficits.
- Employers who have pension plans for their employees have been able to reduce their contributions and enjoy larger profits, as the rise in share prices has swollen the value of funds assets.

This creates a sort of virtuous circle, whereby strong, low inflationary growth boosts bond and share prices, which boost investment and hence output, income and employment. This helps to sustain growth, sending bond and share prices even higher. The risk remains, however, that an overheated stockmarket creates an overheated economy, pushing up inflation. At this point the government would have to respond by applying the breaks, in the form of higher interest rates.

CASE STUDY: EQUITIES, GILT-EDGED STOCKS AND ECONOMIC FUNDAMENTALS

There are two main types of financial investment quoted on the Stock Exchange:

- shares, or equities as they are often called;
- government securities, or government bonds as economists like to call them, usually known as gilt-edged stock.

Gilt-edged stocks derive their name from the paper on which notes of the most impeccable kind were issued in the early days of stock exchanges. The certificates issued by the Bank of England on behalf of the government are not, nor have they ever been, edged with gold. The name nowadays implies that the government guarantees to pay a fixed sum in interest each year (the fixed yield or bond coupon) and that, in the case of most stocks – with the exception of 2½ per cent consolidated stock or consols which are undated, i.e. they will never be redeemed – it also guarantees to repay the stock on a certain date at 'par' or 'face value', that is £100 repayment for £100 worth of stock originally issued. Some gilt-edged stock is also index linked, i.e. the final capital repayment is adjusted in line with inflation, to maintain its real value.

Clearly, gilt-edged stocks are completely different from shares, where no guarantee of this kind is given by companies to their investors, who might see the value of their shares take a nose-dive. In this sense gilt-

edged stock is technically even more secure than bank deposits, since it is always possible, albeit unlikely, for a commercial bank to go burst, but certainly not for the government.

So are there any risks involved in gilt-edged financial investments? There are two types of risk:

1 *Capital real value reduction due to inflation.* This is the same as the risk people take when they hold any form of fixed interest deposits. If you buy a gilt-edged stock and keep it until its official repayment date, what you get back, your return, is fixed as it is the bond's face value. If inflation has occurred and the gilt-edged stock is not index linked, its capital value may not fully compensate. In fact, for most of the period since World War II gilt-edged stocks were a disastrous investment, because inflation was not recognized as a likely occurrence and not taken into account on government issues. This is no longer the case; in fact, long-term government bond rates are nowadays taken as indicators of the future rate of inflation expected by the government.

2 *Stock market price fluctuations.* The second risk with gilt-edged stock is that, unlike a bank deposit, the stocks are actually quoted in the stock exchange market, where people can buy or sell them at any time and where their market value fluctuates according to trends and

EQUITIES, GILT-EDGED STOCKS AND ECONOMIC FUNDAMENTALS

conditions of the economy and the balance between buyers and sellers. In the short term, therefore, gilt-edged stocks carry the same sort of risk as shares and are affected by similar factors.

As we have seen in this chapter, there are many reasons for the fluctuations in gilt-edged market prices. The most important one is the trend in interest rates generally. Over a medium to long-term period, if inflation is seen or expected to be rising, interest rates will also rise and gilt-edged market prices will tend to fall. The opposite will be true when interest rates are falling. In this sense, since interest rates are affected by inflation expectations, a financial investment in gilt-edged is a sort of bet on inflation coming down further over the long term (together with interest rates, hence causing prices of bonds or gilt-edged stock to rise, resulting in capital gains for stock holders).

Indexed linked gilt-edged stocks, on the other hand, have two guarantees against inflation:

■ The coupon payment, or bond yield, which takes place every six months, increases in line with the retail price index (RPI).
■ The stocks will be repaid at their redemption dates at their issue price, plus or minus the inflation that has taken place in between. There is no absolute guarantee that the value of the bonds will not go down in money terms. If the RPI goes down, so will the redemption price. They are not guaranteed against deflation.

These inflation-linked, gilt-edged stocks are therefore subject to ups and downs in supply and demand on the stock exchange. If inflation falls, the value of the stock will fall as the market will take a lower view of the likely redemption price. If investors start to believe that inflation will continue to decline or that prices might fall, they will not want to buy these gilts at anything like their earlier market price and they will look very unattractive as an investment.

What is interesting to note is that both conventional gilts and index-linked gilts represent differing bets on the future course of inflation over the period of the financial investment. If inflation remains at stable levels, one is likely to get a return from gilts not dissimilar to that from a fixed deposit, no more, no less. In a conventional gilt this will be obtained through the coupon plus the fixed price at redemption; while in indexed gilts from the two inflation linked elements, the coupon and the final payment when the gilts reach their maturity. At any one time however, the market price of the stocks will reflect investors' views on future inflation prospects.

As Figure 6.11 shows, UK long-term interest rates (on ten-year government bonds) fell after Chancellor Gordon Brown announced in May 1997 that the Bank of England was to be given operational responsibility for meeting the government inflation target of 2.5 per cent inflation. This reflects the belief that this new framework puts the conduct of monetary policy on a credible, long-term footing to ensure that price stability is delivered in practice.

If inflation falls further than expected, investors will make some real profit on conventional gilts, but a monetary loss on index linked. If inflation rises more than expected, investors will stand to lose on conventional gilts. So, the best ultimate outcome for conventional gilts would be a world **super slump**, as interest rates would fall and the price of gilts would rise; while for index-linked gilts, it would be **hyperinflation**, as their money value would increase (O'Shea 1994).

'We can now finally make sense of some rather disturbing puzzles we come across in the financial press, such as the one below, blaming good news on the economy for a decline in stock prices:

Exports steer US to robust growth. The US economy grew at a robust annual rate of 3.6 per cent during the second quarter, the US Commerce Department said yesterday, raising its original estimate from 2.2 per cent.

The news helped to unsettle the stock market, with the Dow Jones industrial average falling 92.9 points to close at 7,694.43 ... the Federal Reserve may face further calls to abandon its 'wait and see' stance and consider an interest rate rise when its policy-making board meets at the end of September.' (*Financial Times*, 29 August 1997).

Figure 6.11   UK–German 10-year bond differential

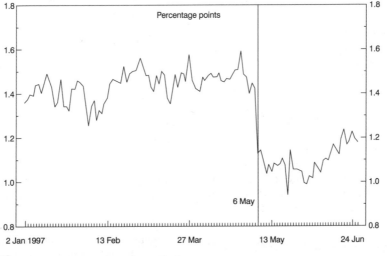

Percentage points

6 May

2 Jan 1997   13 Feb   27 Mar   13 May   24 Jun

Source: HMT, FSBR, 1998

☆ **For revision of this chapter, see the Chapter Summaries at the end of the book, starting on page 411.**

7 Government and monetary policy

Objectives

After studying this chapter, you will be able to understand:

- what is meant by monetary policy;
- the Keynesian view on how monetary policy works;
- the monetarist view on how monetary policy works;
- monetary policy's practical constraints;
- the implications of an independent Bank of England;
- the monetary policy implications of the Maastricht Treaty;
- the pros and cons of the European Single Currency;
- the implications of an independent European Central Bank.

MONETARY POLICY AND INTEREST RATE DETERMINATION

Monetary policy

Monetary policy refers to the government use of monetary tools, such as changes in the money supply and adjustments of interest rates, to control the level of economic activity and inflation. While the focus of monetary policy within the Keynesian model was to manipulate interest rates to achieve the desired output and employment levels and, to a lesser extent, to moderate business cycles, nowadays monetary policy is particularly concerned with controlling the rate of inflation and influencing the foreign exchange value of the currency.

In the preceding chapter we have looked at the tools of monetary policy, we now need to focus on its effects. In the light of what we have just learnt in Chapter 6, it should now be possible to see how changes in the money supply affect the interest rate and how government and central bank can manipulate liquidity conditions in the money market to achieve its target interest rate level.

Effects of changes in the money supply on the interest rate

Suppose the government decides to expand the money supply, as it wishes to lower interest rates to stimulate investment demand, hence output growth and employment. We have learnt that the Bank of England, in consultation with the government, can do so in several ways:

1. It can increase the monetary base.
2. It can reduce the commercial banks' reserve requirement.
3. It can cut the base rate at which it lends to commercial banks.
4. It can buy back government bonds on the open market (OMO).

Any of these methods would cause the money supply to rise. This is shown by a shift out of the money supply curve, which we draw here as a vertical line, as we assume that the Bank of England's money supply decisions are not a positive function of the interest rate (an exogenous money supply function) (Figure 7.1).

The effect of an increase in the supply of money on the interest rate is to lower it. An increase in the supply of money from M^S_0 to M^S_1 lowers the rate of interest from r_0 to r_1. As the money supply increases, some people in the economy will find they are holding more money balances than before. If they were in equilibrium before, and the level of output and income has not changed, they will try and dispose of the excess money balance by buying more bonds on the bond market. This increase in the demand for bonds will push up bond prices, lowering the market interest rate. The

Figure 7.1 Effect of an increase in the money supply

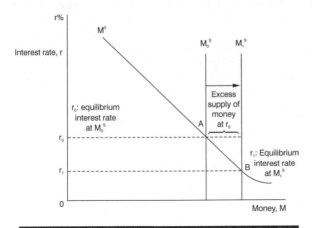

mechanism by which changes in money supply affect interest rates is the same as the one we described before. It depends on people and firms adjusting their money balance by switching in or out of bonds. This affects bond prices, hence interest rates.

✍ Activity 7.1

Briefly describe the effect on interest rates of an expansionary monetary policy.

✓ Answer 7.1

An expansionary monetary policy means that the money supply is increased. As the money supply increases, given that prices and the demand for money have not changed, the demand for bonds increases, which pushes up the price of bonds, causing interest rate to fall. In symbols this can be expressed as follows:

$$\text{as } M^S \!\uparrow \, \rightarrow D^B \!\uparrow \, \rightarrow P^B \!\uparrow \, \rightarrow r \!\downarrow \text{ and vice versa.}$$

An increase in the money supply will cause interest rates to fall.

✍ Activity 7.2

Describe the effect on interest rates of a restrictive monetary policy.

✓ Answer 7.2

A restrictive monetary policy indicates that policies are put in place to reduce the money supply. A reduction of the money supply is shown by a shift to the left of the money supply curve, which will result in an increase of the interest rate. As the money supply is reduced, peo-

ple need more money balances for transactions and precautionary reasons. They switch out of bonds and the demand for bonds falls, exerting a downward pressure on the price of bonds, which also falls. As a result of this, interest rates rise. In symbols, this becomes:

$$M^S \!\downarrow \, \rightarrow D^B \!\downarrow \, \rightarrow P^B \!\downarrow \, \rightarrow r \!\uparrow.$$

A restrictive monetary policy causes the interest rate to rise. This is shown in Figure 7.2.

Effects of changes in income on the interest rate

The interest rate, does not change solely in response to changes in the money supply. Changes in income, which affect the demand for money, also affect the interest rate.

✍ Activity 7.3

Show the effect of an increase of income and output on the interest rate.

✓ Answer 7.3

Changes in the supply of money are not the only factors that affect the interest rate. Shifts in the demand for money can have the same effect. The demand for money increases as the economy's output and volume of transaction increases and people need more liquidity. So an increase in income will cause an increase in the demand for money, which we show with a shift out of the money demand function. The interest rate will increase from r_0 to r_1.

An increase in output and income shifts the money demand curve from $m^d{}_0$ to $m^d{}_1$, which raises the equilibrium interest rate from r_0 to r_1 (Figure 7.3). Why is

Figure 7.2 Effect of a reduction of the money supply

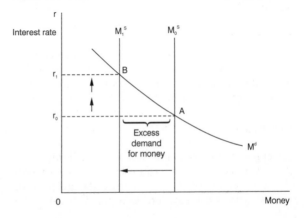

Figure 7.3 Effect of an increase in income on the interest rate

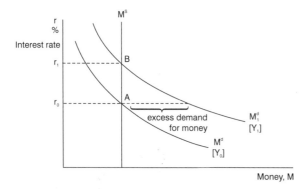

money supply, can bring interest rates back to their desired levels. If income grows faster than anticipated, driving interest rates up via the increased demand for money balances, the central bank can intervene and inject more liquidity, preventing a monetary tightening. Equally, a monetary tightening (higher interest rates) caused by higher than expected inflation can be avoided by an 'accommodating' monetary expansion.

Although quite neat in theory, this manipulation of the interest rate by the central bank has a drawback in practice. To be able to achieve the desired interest rate by increasing or decreasing the money supply by a set, publicly declared amount, the central bank will need to know the exact position and behaviour of the public's liquidity preference. To refer back to our Figure 7.3, you will need to know where the liquidity preference or demand for money function is exactly, to be able to move the money supply curve the correct distance, in order to achieve the desired interest rate. This is more easily said than done, as the demand for money can be volatile and is seldom stable because of its speculative component.

As a result of this practical problem, in recent years the Bank of England has abandoned its policy aimed at set monetary growth targets to stabilize interest rates and inflation at the desired level. Instead it has reversed its strategy and chosen the desired inflation interest rate level, allowing the money supply to vary accordingly in whatever way necessary. This has been a move away from the strict monetarist policy embraced by Mrs Thatcher in the early 1980s – which favoured a clear indication of growth targets for both M0 and M4 and no u-turning – and a return to a monetary practice which prevailed in the 1960s and 1970s. Money supply figures, once regarded as an important measure of government success in controlling monetary growth, have now lost their original importance and indeed significance. They are nowadays regarded as indicators of the demand for credit from the general public, in other words, as a measure of economic activity in the private sector rather than a government monetary target.

that? The reason is as follows: given the new money demand function caused by a higher level of income Y_1, the money market is no longer in equilibrium at the old interest rate r_0. At r_0 money demanded is greater than money supplied, given that more money balances are needed for the new larger amount of transactions. People and firms will switch out of bonds to increase their liquidity. This pushes the price of bonds down, raising the interest rate until a new equilibrium interest rate is reached at r_1. Unless the money supply expands as the economy expands, high interest rates will eventually slow down the growth process.

Effect of inflation on the interest rate

Finally inflation too, by changing the demand for money, affects interest rate levels.

✍ Activity 7.4

Show the effect of an increase in inflation on the interest rate.

✓ Answer 7.4

As all prices increase with inflation, the demand for money will also increase, as more money balances will be needed for transactions. This will shift the money demand curve out, as in Figure 7.3. The process triggered is the same: if the money supply does not change, inflation will cause interest rates to rise and vice versa.

Ultimately, however, interest rates are determined by the government and the central bank's monetary policy. The central bank, by changing the quantity of money in the economy, increasing or decreasing the

Money supply changes and the exchange rate

Changes in the money supply affect not only the real economy, its output and employment via their effect on interest rates and investment; they also affect the economy through their effect on exchange rates. This aspect of monetary policy will be explained in more detail in Chapter 10, but it is worth mentioning here to have a complete picture of how monetary changes affect the level of economic activity. Let's briefly see how this aspect comes into our analysis at this point. If this proves too difficult come back to this point, after you have studied Chapter 10.

The exchange rate expresses the value of the domestic currency in terms of a foreign currency. Say that £1 can be exchanged on the foreign exchange market for DM2. This means that British importers wishing to purchase German goods will first need to buy Deutschmarks at that rate: they will need to surrender £1 to buy DM2. The same applies if British residents wish to buy financial assets denominated in the German currency. The Germans will need to do likewise if they wish to purchase British goods or British financial assets: they will need to convert their currency into sterling at the going market rate.

The exchange rate is determined by the demand and supply of currencies on the foreign exchange market. The demand and supply of currencies is in turn determined by the demand for foreign goods (imports) and foreign assets, which are influenced by the rates of return that can be earned. The value of the pound vis-à-vis, say, the German currency will increase if the demand for sterling by the Germans is greater than demand for Deutschmarks by the British.

Changes in the money supply are likely to affect the exchange rate of the domestic currency in the following way:

- An increase in the money supply increases money balances. These excess money balances are likely to cause not only an increase in the demand for domestic financial assets, such as bonds, but are also likely to cause an increase in the demand for foreign financial assets, which in turn will cause an increase in the demand for foreign currency. As will be explained more fully in Chapter 10, this will cause a depreciation in the value of the domestic currency.
- The increase in the supply of money causes a reduction in the domestic interest rate. This will make domestic financial assets less attractive to domestic residents, compared with foreign financial assets. Domestic asset holders will therefore switch out of domestic financial assets, such as government bonds, and buy foreign financial assets instead. At the same time foreign holders of domestic financial assets will find their returns less attractive and will also switch out of them to buy other, more competitive assets elsewhere. The two combined effects will further depress the value of the domestic currency on foreign exchange markets.
- Foreign exchange speculators will speculate on the likely depreciation of the exchange rate caused by the increase in the domestic money supply. They will

therefore sell sterling in exchange for other stronger foreign currency, wait for sterling to depreciate (i.e. lose its value on foreign exchange market and become cheaper) before buying it back, making a fortune in the process. Their own selling of sterling, of course, will further contribute to sterling depreciation.

Concluding, the overall effect of a change, say an increase, in the money supply can be summarized as follows (a reduction in the money supply will have the opposite effects):

- An increase in the money supply leads to a reduction in interest rate.
- A reduction in interest rate leads to an increase in investment and consumption demand.
- Increased aggregate demand will trigger increased output, income and employment, augmented by the multiplier effect, assuming constant prices and unusual resources.
- An increase in the money supply will cause the exchange rate to depreciate.
- The depreciation of the exchange rate will boost our exports, as they are now cheaper for foreigners to buy. It will also negatively affect our imports.
- Increased export demand will stimulate aggregate supply and generate further growth of output and employment.
- The increased level of economic activity, output, income and employment will be likely to cause an increase in prices and inflation.

THE EFFECTIVENESS OF MONETARY POLICY IN THE KEYNESIAN MODEL

Transmission mechanism

Despite the practical complications discussed above, from a strictly theoretical point of view we have now reached a very important point. In Chapters 3 and 4 we have seen how the level of output in the economy is determined by aggregate expenditure and how the economy is in equilibrium when the goods market, the real sector of the economy, is in equilibrium ($I = S$). We have also learnt that one important component of aggregate demand, that is investment, is affected by the interest rate. The interest rate, however, is determined in what economists call the money market, the financial sector of the economy. What happens in the money market affects the interest rate, which affects investment and the goods market. We have therefore found a link, or **transmission mechanism** between the money market and the goods market, between money and output and employment.

As the interest rate rises – everything else being equal – investment demand falls and so do output and employment. Conversely, as the interest rate falls, investment expenditure increases and so output and employment rise. In symbols, this can be expressed as follows:

$$\text{if } r\uparrow \rightarrow I\downarrow \rightarrow Y\downarrow \text{ and if } r\downarrow \rightarrow I\uparrow \rightarrow Y\uparrow.$$

However, we did not know until now what affected the interest rate. We can add the missing part of this important chain of events and explain the link between the money sector and the output sector, between the money market and the goods market. We now know that changes in the money supply, assuming constant prices, affect the interest rate, hence investment demand and output as follows:

1 $M^S\uparrow \rightarrow D^B\uparrow \rightarrow P^B\uparrow \rightarrow r\downarrow \rightarrow I\uparrow \rightarrow Y\uparrow$

2 $M^S\downarrow \rightarrow D^B\downarrow \rightarrow P^B\downarrow \rightarrow r\uparrow \rightarrow I\downarrow \rightarrow Y\downarrow$

We also know that if the nominal money supply, M^S, does not change, but prices do, then the effect on the economy will be the same as a change in the nominal quantity of money. In other words, what affects the economy is the real money supply.

3 $P\uparrow \rightarrow r\uparrow \rightarrow I\downarrow \rightarrow Y\downarrow$

4 $P\downarrow \rightarrow r\downarrow \rightarrow I\uparrow \rightarrow Y\uparrow.$

However, we now appreciate that there is a link between the two sectors in the opposite direction as well, from the goods market to the money market. Changes in real income affect the demand for money, which in turn affects the interest rate, hence investment and, via it, income and output, as follows:

5 $Y\downarrow \rightarrow m^d\downarrow \rightarrow r\downarrow \rightarrow I\uparrow \rightarrow Y\uparrow$

6 $Y\uparrow \rightarrow m^d\uparrow \rightarrow r\uparrow \rightarrow I\downarrow \rightarrow Y\downarrow.$

✍ Activity 7.5

Explain in words the transmission mechanisms described by points 1 and 6 above.

✓ Answer 7.5

1 As money supply increases, the interest rate falls, because of an increase in the demand for bonds which causes the price of bonds to go up and the interest rate to fall. This stimulates investment expenditure which adds to aggregate demand and causes output to expand, as more capital and consumption goods are produced; income and employment will also rise.

6 As the economy's output and income grow, the number of transactions also grows. Money demand will increase. If money supply does not change, to get

the extra money balances they now need people will switch out of bonds by selling them. This will push the price of bonds down and the interest rate up. Higher interest rates discourage investment expenditure, reduce aggregate demand and ultimately output and employment.

Monetary policy

We can now put all the elements of our analysis together and consider what happens when the government decides to increase the money supply, say by increasing the monetary base. This injects new reserves into the system and expands the money supply. People will find that they are holding more money than they wish; they will adjust their money balances, buy more bonds and the equilibrium interest rate will fall. Planned investment spending will increase and output and employment will expand:

$$M^S\uparrow \rightarrow r\downarrow \rightarrow I\uparrow \rightarrow Y\uparrow.$$

A link is established between the money sector, between monetary factors (M^S and m^d) and the real sector of the economy, its income and output, Y. It must be noted, however, that the power of monetary policy to influence the level of output depends on the existence and effectiveness of two links: between the money supply and the interest rate on the one hand, and between interest rate and investment on the other.

$$M^S\uparrow \rightarrow r\downarrow \text{ and } r\downarrow \rightarrow I\uparrow$$

and vice versa. In the Keynesian model, the effectiveness of monetary policy depends on the responsiveness of interest rates to increases in the money supply and on the responsiveness of investment to interest rates. Keynes argued that both these links could at times be very weak. He described the possibility of a 'liquidity trap' where, at low interest rate levels, the link between M^S and r would not work. He also questioned the responsiveness of investment to lower interest rates. For these reasons, Keynes and the Keynesians considered monetary policy rather ineffective as a tool for government economic management and instead favoured the use of fiscal policies to stimulate and control the level of economic activity.

THE EFFECTIVENESS OF MONETARY POLICY IN THE MONETARIST MODEL

The discussion of the effects of changes in the money supply developed so far reflects Keynes's point of view.

The monetarists disagree. The disagreement centres around two points:

- According to the monetarists, the amount of money in the economy has a major direct effect on aggregate demand.
- Changes in aggregate demand, however, do not affect the level of output and employment, as Keynes believed, but only the level of prices and inflation.

So ultimately according to the monetarists, monetary policy can only be used to control inflation. Inflation is perceived by the monetarists as public enemy number one. The monetarists therefore advocate the setting of target growth rates for the money supply, in line with set inflation targets. Two important points of the monetarists' model need to be clarified:

- The effects of changes in the money supply on aggregate demand.
- The effects of changes in aggregate demand on income, output and employment.

These two points lead us naturally to a discussion of the monetarist supply-side model and of their views on inflation and unemployment, which are developed in Chapters 8 and 9.

Keynes argued that changes in the money supply have an indirect effect on the real economy. Changes in M^S do not affect aggregate demand directly, but indirectly via their effect on the interest rate and the effect that interest rates in turn have on investment. Furthermore, a change in the money supply, M^S, because of the weakness of these two links, does not have a major impact on the economy, which it is not to say that it has no impact at all. Investment does somehow respond to interest rate changes and changes in investment do affect the economy's output, income and employment. So monetary policy, according to Keynes, has an effect on aggregate demand, albeit an indirect effect, a smaller effect than fiscal policies, and not a very predictable one.

In the Keynesian model, changes in aggregate demand have an effect on the level of output and employment as well as some effect on prices and the balance of payments, depending on the slack in the economy. Consequently, monetary policy has an impact, albeit an indirect and not necessarily a strong one, on output and employment. It also has an impact on prices and the balance of payments, as we shall see in Chapter 10.

According to the monetarists, changes in the money supply have a direct impact on aggregate demand, rather than an indirect one. But changes in aggregate demand only affect prices and the balance of payment and not output, income or employment. So monetary policy can only be used to control inflation. It will not work if the aim is to stimulate output and employment. To that effect, Friedman advocates the use of supply-side policies. Now let's go back and explain why according to the monetarists:

- changes in the money supply have a direct effect on aggregate demand;
- changes in aggregate demand only affect prices and the balance of payments, but have no effect on output, income and employment.

Monetarist transmission mechanism

According to the monetarists, changes in the money supply will directly translate into changes in aggregate demand. If the money supply increases, people will find themselves holding more money balances than they wish to. They will buy more of everything as a result: more bonds, but also more goods and services, more durables, more holidays, more cars, etc. An increase in the money supply will increase aggregate demand directly, as follows:

$$M^S \uparrow \rightarrow AD \uparrow$$

and not indirectly, via the effect that changes in the interest rate have on investment demand.

This explanation of how the changes in the M^S affect changes in demand rests on the **portfolio balance approach** discussed earlier. People hold their wealth in a variety of ways; they have a portfolio of assets, real as well as financial. People will have a balanced mix of assets, which will vary in their liquidity and profitability and will reflect people's liquidity preference. As discussed earlier, we can think of assets falling into three categories: money, financial assets and physical goods. Some, like cash, are totally liquid but earn no returns; some, like a house, are totally illiquid since it may or may not appreciate in value and it may take years to sell. The balance people keep between these assets will depend largely on the returns and services they get from them. If the return from one type of asset increases like, say, the interest rate on a financial asset or the capital value of a house, people will switch from one to the other.

This is the main difference between Keynes and the monetarists. According to Keynes, people are mostly concerned with the **returns** from their wealth. They are very responsive to changes in interest rates and therefore switch from money into financial assets which earn a return, as the interest rate rises. For Keynes, money and bonds are close substitutes, just alternative ways of holding wealth. Money is liquid and carries no risk of capital loss, but earns no interest. Bonds earn interest, are riskier and less liquid than money, but still sufficiently liquid to be good substitutes. According to Keynes, as the interest rates go up people hold less of their wealth in the form of money and more in the form of bonds, on the basis of the **liquidity preference**. Using economists' jargon, we say that people, according to Keynes, have an **elastic liquidity curve**. Their demand for liquidity, for money, will be considerably responsive to changes in the interest rate. Keynesians stress the function of money as a **mean of storing wealth**.

The monetarists, on the other hand, stress the function of money as a **medium of exchange**, rather than as a store of wealth. This implies that money, for the monetarists, is not a close substitute for financial assets. On the other hand, real goods can be substitutes for financial assets. If people have more liquid balances than they wish to hold as their cash balances increase, they may not necessarily want to hold more bonds (which is what Keynes's liquidity preference theory assumes); people might prefer to buy another car, another house, etc. They will also buy more goods. An increase in liquid assets (money) will be corrected by an increase in the demand for other illiquid assets as well. The increase in money supply will translate into an increase in aggregate demand. This part of the monetarist theory is known as the **portfolio balance approach**.

The increase in aggregate demand in turn will simply cause prices to rise. This part of the monetarist model is known as the **quantity theory of money**. The quantity theory of money simply states that an increase in the quantity of money leads to an equal percentage increase in the price level. This theory uses **Fisher's equation** as its starting point, which states that the money supply times the velocity of circulation of money must be equal to the number of transactions which take place in a year, times the price at which these transactions take place. In symbols:

$$M^S \times V = P \times T$$

where M^S is the money supply, V is the velocity of circulation of money, P is the price level, and T is the number of transactions. The **velocity of circulation** is the average number of times a pound or currency unit is used annually to finance transactions, i.e. to buy the goods and services produced in the economy. Let's explain this with a simple example.

Suppose there are three people called A, B and C stranded on an island. Suppose the time period is one day, instead of one year. Suppose also that A, B and C

possess one good each, say a packet of cigarettes, a book and a pair of shoes, which they are willing to sell for £1. Suppose that the only money they have, their total money supply, is a £1 coin which A found on the ground. A uses the £1 to buy the book from B; B rushes to use £1 to buy the cigarettes from C. On the same day C buys the shoes from A for £1. Our example corroborates Fisher's equation, as:

M^s = £1 (the £1 coin found on the ground by A)
V = 3 (the £1 coin goes round three times, from A
   to B, from B to C, from C to A)
P = £1 (the three goods cost £1 each)
T = 3 (the number of transactions which take place
   in a day).

So:

$$£1 \times 3 = £1 \times 3 \text{ or } M^s \times V = P \times T$$

However, the quantity theory of money is more commonly expressed as:

$$M^s \times V = P \times Q$$

where Q is the volume of output of the economy. It is quite clear that this 'quantity equation' is true by definition. The money value of national output ($P \times Q$), the economy's GNP, must be equal to the quantity of money necessary to purchase it, total spending on national output, must be equal to the money supply times the velocity at which money circulates in the economy. By saying this, we are not saying that a rise in M^s must be accompanied by a proportional rise in P, which is what the monetarists claim: an increase in the money supply only increases inflation and has no effect on the economy's output. For that to be true, it must be that changes in M^s do not affect V or Q, but only P. This is precisely where the controversy between the monetarists and the Keynesians lies: whether V and Q are affected by changes in M. If they are not, then it follows that changes in M will be reflected by proportional changes in P.

The quantity theory of money therefore rests on two additional propositions:

- velocity of circulation is constant;
- real output of the economy is not affected by the quantity of money.

Both these points are denied by Keynesians. First, they argue that V tends to vary inversely with M: if the money supply increases in the economy, for a given level of output, money will change hands more slowly. The explanation for this is as follows: as liquidity increases, demand for bonds increases, which pushes interest rates down. This increases 'speculative' demand for money which will reduce the velocity of circulation. If interest rates have fallen, they can only rise again; people expecting interest rates to rise and the price of bonds to fall will prefer to hold on to money balances rather then be caught holding bonds when bond prices tumble.

Second, the real output of the economy is affected, via the interest rate–investment–exchange rate–export demand mechanism. As we already said, however, the link between changes in the money supply and output growth is an indirect, weak and unpredictable one. Ultimately, the effect on total spending of an increase in money supply may not be that great; which is not to say, however, that it is not there at all.

Is the velocity of circulation constant?

Monetarists argue instead that V is an institutional constant determined independently of the money supply, by payment practices. An increase in M leaves V unaffected and therefore fully translates itself in an increase in aggregate expenditure ($P \times Q$), for the portfolio balance reasons discussed above:

$$M^s \uparrow \overline{V} = (P \times Q) \uparrow$$

where the bar over V indicates that V is constant. The increased demand for goods and services and financial assets will drive up prices. This will lead to a reduction in the interest rate earned on financial assets and an increase in the price of goods, which will eventually choke off demand.

Does output respond to changes in aggregate demand?

The monetarists maintain that the economy's output does not increase in response to increases in aggregate demand, at least in the long run. This is the cornerstone of the monetarists' model. Monetarists argue that the economy's aggregate supply is totally **inelastic** in the long run. A rather more extreme view is put forward by the new classicists, who argue that the economy's aggregate supply is inelastic even in the short run.

An increase in aggregate demand will tend to drive up prices. Firms will respond to the demand-induced price increases by stepping up production. In turn they will demand more raw materials and partly finished goods, driving up their prices. Their costs of production will start to increase. In the meantime, workers will see that the prices of goods are rising, that demand and production are buoyant, and will demand an increase in wages, to compensate for the increased cost of living which reduces the purchasing power of their wages, and as a reflection of the fact that they

expect demand and prices to go on rising. As firms agree to their workers' higher wage demands, their costs will rise even further.

✍ Activity 7.6

Show with the use of an aggregate demand and supply diagram, the situation described above. What will the long-term outcome be for the economy?

✓ Answer 7.6

As Figure 7.4 (a) shows, the short-run aggregate supply curve is upward sloping. This shows that in the short run, assuming firms' costs and in particular wage costs do not change, firms will produce more at higher price levels, until full capacity is reached. The initial increase in aggregate demand, triggered by the increase in the money supply causing people to adjust their money balances and to demand more, is shown by a shift out of the AD curve from AD^1 to AD^2. Firms respond by increasing their output from Y_1 to Y_2. As intermediate goods producers and raw materials producers increase their prices, in response to the increased demand by firms, firms' costs will start rising. This will shift the AS curve to the left from AS to AS^1. Eventually the cost increases shift the AS curve back by the full amount, pushing the economy back to its initial output level, but at a higher price level: hence the conclusion that in the long run the aggregate supply curve is inelastic (Figure 7.4(b), vertical AS curve). The only permanent effect of an increase in the money supply is to increase the price level by an equal amount, leaving output unaffected. According to the Keynesians (Figure 7.4(c)), aggregate demand stimulates output and employment, despite some inflation, until the full employment level of output is reached (Yf).

Summing up, the monetarists analyse the effect of an increase in the money supply as follows: given that the velocity of circulation is constant, an increase in the quantity of money leads to an increase in aggregate demand. As the aggregate supply of the economy is inelastic, at least in the long run, the increase in aggregate demand will lead only to an increase in prices. As the stock of money determines the price level, the rate of increase in the money supply determines the rate of inflation. Monetary policy can only be effectively used to reduce inflation, and not for the long-term increase of the economy's output.

Empirical evidence

Which of these theories is right? If the Keynesians are right, then so were the governments during the post-war

Figure 7.4 AS response to changes in AD: (a) in the short run; (b) in the long run; (c) according to the Keynesians

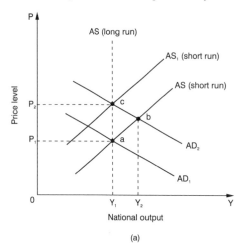

(a)

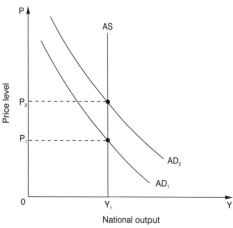

(b)

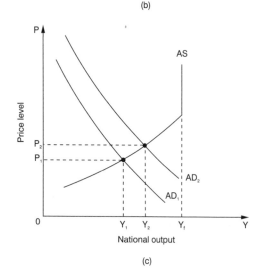

(c)

years and until the 1970s in their the focus on fiscal policy and relative neglect of monetary policy for macro-economic management; would governments have been foolish in embracing the monetarist creed in the 1980s and 1990s. If the monetarists are right, then monetary policy should have been and should still be government's central policy tool. Monetary policy should also be less concerned with influencing interest rates and more with controlling the stock of money itself. In fact, if the relationship between money supply and inflation is as close as the monetarists claim, and if, in consequence, changes in the money supply do not affect the economy's output and income, then the supply of money is indeed the only economic variable that governments need to control.

Can empirical evidence on the velocity of circulation, on changes in the money supply, output and inflation, interest rates and the demand for money help to determine who is right and who is wrong? In principle, both Keynesian and monetarist hypotheses can be tested against empirical data and, in fact, they have been many times over, by many knowledgeable and competent economists. Yet no final, decisive result has emerged, which allows us to resolve the dispute. Many reasons account for this fact:

■ Different studies have produced different results, because of the variety of interpretations of the broad Keynesian and monetarist positions. The definition of what constitutes money, as we have seen, is in itself controversial: narrow or broad, and how broad, if broad. Similar ambiguity exists around interest rates: short-term rates, long-term, expected short-/long-term, nominal, real rates. Which should be the focus? Hence some research has emphasized one feature, some another.

■ It is difficult in a social science such as economics to establish unambiguously the **direction of causality** between variables. If, for example, empirical data were to show that changes in money stock and nominal income are closely related, it would still not follow that changes in the money supply are the cause of changes in income: they could indeed be the effect.

The hypothesis that changes in the money supply are the effect rather than the cause of changes in income is equally plausible. Suppose there is an increase in aggregate demand: households and firms decide to spend more on consumption and investment. They finance their extra spending by reducing their cash holdings, running down their bank deposits, arranging overdrafts with banks and selling their government bonds. These actions will put a strain on liquidity and will cause interest rates to rise and the price of government bonds to fall. At this point, in order to contain the rise in interest rates and/or prevent the price of bonds from falling too much central bank buys up bonds in the open market. This action is taken because the price of bonds and prevailing interest rates determine the terms on which the government can borrow in the future; high interest rates also affect the value of the currency, causing an appreciation which may be damaging for the economy. As the central bank takes this action, it increases the money supply. So we have an increase in the money supply, which results from (is the effect and not the cause of) the increase in spending by households and firms. To relate what we have just said to the equation of exchange, what we have just described is a possible explanation of a reversed causation:

$$PQ \uparrow \rightarrow MV \uparrow$$

as PQ rises, this causes an equal rise in MV. If M does not rise immediately, which is likely, then the rise in PQ will be accommodated by a rise in V. The velocity of circulation will rise, as people try to finance their increased expenditure out of the existing money stock: firms will require payments within shorter periods and people will squeeze down their precautionary balances. A close correlation between M and PQ can be accounted for in Keynesian terms: the rise in income causes the rise in the money supply.

✍ Activity 7.7

Explain how it can be argued that the rise in income causes the rise in the money supply.

✓ Answer 7.7

The close correlation between money supply and national income can be explained as follows: an increase in aggregate demand causes people to increase their liquid balances by switching out of bonds. This drives up the interest rate and the price of bonds down, which prompts the central bank to buy the excess supply of bonds on the open market to prevent interest rates from increasing. Big fluctuations in interest rates are disruptive, affect the balance of payments, and also make future government borrowing more difficult and more expensive. The central bank buys up the bonds on the open market; this increases the money supply. So one could argue that the supply of money rises in proportion to a demand for it. The rise in income is the cause of the change in the money supply and not the effect.

The debate between the monetarists and Keynesians on monetary policy remains open and unresolved. Just as open is the debate on the practical use of monetary policy for macroeconomic management among those who are in charge of it. To this effect, you will find the conclusion of the case study at the end of this chapter very informative and not at all surprising. So, let's now move on to discuss monetary policy in practice.

✍ Activity 7.8

Using the equation of exchange given above, often referred to as the **quantity theory of money equation**, $MV = PQ$, often also written as $MV = PY$ (i.e. GDP), how do you calculate the velocity of circulation of money V?

✓ Answer 7.8

Given the equation of exchange, the velocity of circulation is calculated as follows:

$$V = GDP/M \ or \ 1/V = M/GDP.$$

A rise in the velocity of circulation of money can also be expressed as a fall in the ratio of the money supply to GDP and vice versa.

MONETARY POLICY AND CENTRAL BANK INDEPENDENCE

Economists may still be debating among themselves who is right and who is wrong, whether the Keynesians in their approach to monetary policy, or the monetarists; but life goes on and government decisions on economic policy matters have to be made, albeit within a cloud of doubt.

Monetarism has been and still is, by and large, the dominant economic paradigm which has inspired developed countries' government economic policies in the 1980s and 1990s. The emphasis, at the beginning of the 1980s, was rather crudely on the control of the monetary base, to control the money supply and inflation. That proved more difficult in practice than it was in theory. Nowadays the target variable remains inflation, but the instrument variable to achieve it has become a direct control of the interest rate, rather than the money supply as such. The manipulation of interest rates is once more at the centre of monetary policy. This is not, however, a return to the Keynesian approach to monetary policy, which is to ensure an interest rate level consistent with full employment. Within the monetarist framework, interest rates must be kept at a level which is consistent with the stability of the currency (the target rate of inflation), and not with full employment.

The monetarist creed, with its emphasis on the need to control inflation and government borrowing, its hostility towards 'big government' and the use of fiscal instruments to reduce unemployment, its preference for privatization and supply-side policies, is very much at the base of EU policies. Monetarist ideas imbue the Maastricht Treaty and manifest themselves in the convergence criteria and many other policy prescriptions. The stability of the currency, that is the fight against inflation, is the cornerstone of EU policies; its delivery is at the very heart of the main EU monetary institution, the European Central Bank (ECB), which is responsible for EU monetary policy. To guarantee the independence of the ECB from member governments' political pressures, the Maastricht Treaty requires that EU members' national central banks become independent from their respective national governments.

Central bank independence has therefore, rather understandably, occupied a high place in the debate and the political agenda of most European governments in the second half of the 1990s.

An independent Bank of England

In far-reaching reforms introduced in the summer of 1997, the Chancellor of the Exchequer, Gordon Brown, granted the Bank of England a considerable amount of independence and the right to determine interest rates in order to achieve the government inflation rate target, set at 2.5. Reactions were mixed and predictably polarized. Before we analyse the issues at stake, let's explain the important institutional changes introduced. The new institutional framework works as follows:

- The government sets an inflation target and confirms it in each Budget Statement.
- The Bank of England is required to set short-term interest rates to achieve this target and to support the government's economic policy, including its objectives for growth and employment.
- The government may instruct the Bank of England to set a specific interest rate only in extreme economic circumstances, for reasons of national interest, and for a short time only; and only through legislation approved by Parliament.
- The publication of the Bank's quarterly *Inflation Report* is a statutory requirement. In it the Bank is required to explain its analysis of the economy and how the Bank intends to meet its monetary policy responsibility.
- The Bank's operational decisions on interest rate policy are made by the Monetary Policy Committee (MPC) comprising the Governor, two deputy Governors and six other members, four of

whom are recognized outside experts, appointed by the Chancellor. Each member of the MPC has one vote in decisions on interest rates, while the Governor has the casting vote in the absence of a majority. The Treasury is also represented on the Committee, in a non-voting capacity.

- The MPC meets monthly. Its decisions are made by simple majority vote; they are minuted and announced immediately. The minutes are published within six weeks.
- The Bank is accountable to the House of Commons through regular reports and evidence given to the Treasury Select Committee. The Governor of the Bank of England is required to write an open letter to the Chancellor if inflation strays by more than 1 per cent either side of the set inflation target, explaining why inflation was adrift and how it was planned to bring it back into course.
- The MPC reports to a monthly meeting of the Bank's governing body, called Court, who has the responsibility to review the performance of the Bank as a whole, including the MPC.
- The Bank makes reports and give evidence to the House of Commons through the Treasury Select Committee. (Rodgers 1997)

The new arrangements mean that while the government retains clear responsibility to parliament for defining the goals of monetary policy, the Bank is accountable for their achievement. The well-defined inflation target, publication of the minutes, the Bank's quarterly *Inflation Report* and open letter system provide clear information against which the performance of the Bank in achieving price stability can be judged.

Two other important changes were introduced, regarding the new monetary policy framework:

- The government remains responsible for determining the exchange rate regime, but the Bank has its own separate pool of foreign exchange reserves to use at its discretion to intervene in support of its monetary policy objective. If instructed by the government, the Bank could still act as its agent on the foreign exchange market, buying and selling government's reserves. The Bank of England would also, however, automatically sterilize such interventions (by increasing or decreasing the money supply by an equal amount).
- The Bank's role as the government's agent for debt management, in selling gilts, overseeing the gilts market and in cash management is being transferred to the Treasury.

Without prejudice to the price stability objective, the Bank is still required to support the government's economic policy, including its objectives for growth and employment. However, that is unlikely to represent a conflict in policy objectives, at least at present, as in the March 1998 budget report it is clearly stated that: 'The goal of monetary policy is price stability. Low inflation is central to the Government's economic objectives.'

Economists and observers more Keynesian in their approach to macroeconomic policy regarded these changes as an act of self-mutilation on the part of the government, which seemed to be giving up the control of a tool – the setting of interest rates – so crucial for demand management. One could argue that by giving up the control of interest rates the government is only surrendering the use of a monetary tool and that demand management can be carried out by using fiscal tools of government spending and taxation. Even the use of fiscal stimuli – an expansionary fiscal policy – to stimulate the level of economic activity necessitates, in order to be fully successful, the combined use of monetary tools. Fiscal policy, as you can now appreciate, is not independent from or unaffected by monetary policy, just as the goods sector and the money sector of the economy are not independent from one another. Although in theory we discuss fiscal and monetary policies as two independent sets of tools for the management of the economy, which indeed they are, the manipulation of aggregate demand is in practice achieved by a combination of the two sets of policies.

To understand this, think of a government successfully using fiscal stimuli – reduction in taxation or increase in its own spending – to increase the level of output, income and employment. This fiscal policy impacts on the money market and the economy's monetary conditions in two major ways and requires, for its successful continuation, some monetary policy adjustments:

- First, as income increases, due to the government's successful expansionary fiscal policy, people's demand for money increases, driving up the interest rate. The increase in interest rate – assuming that the money supply does not increase – will choke off investment demand and reduce the expansionary effect of fiscal policy, eventually bringing it to a halt.
- The increase in aggregate demand, caused by the expansionary fiscal policy, will also cause some pressure on prices which, if not accommodated by some increase in the money supply, will also cause

an increase in interest rate and the same effect on investment demand.

- The increase in government spending or tax revenue reduction following a tax cut are also likely to cause an increase in the PSBR, which will need to be financed by a bond issue. This in turn will tend to put pressure on the interest rate, unless the Bank of England finances the deficit by an increase in the money supply (buying up government bonds).

As you can see, fiscal and monetary policies are in practice intertwined: the loss of control over the use of its monetary tools frustrates and fundamentally constrains the use of fiscal tools as well. The government undoubtedly loses its ability to stimulate the level of economic activity through demand management. A move in this direction, the surrender of control over the interest rate, is a step into the grave for Keynesian demand management. It is not surprising that monetarists took the opposite view and applauded the move. One could argue, however, that when, as at present, fiscal policy is no longer used to ensure growth and employment but rather price stability through a reduction of the government PSBR, the surrender of powers to the MPC has already taken place.

The Keynesian view on central bank independence

The main objections which Keynesian economists raise against an independent Bank of England can be summarized as follows:

- loss of freedom in the choice of policy objectives. Government policy objectives are often incompatible: achieving one often means missing out on the other. A case in point is provided by the trade-off between inflation and unemployment. To reduce unemployment a government empowered to decide on its own policy objectives might be prepared to inject a certain amount of inflation into its own economy. Such choice of policy objective might no longer be an easy one to pursue by the government, which now has to negotiate it with the Bank of England.
- loss of freedom in the choice of policy tool mix. The government needs the use of both fiscal and monetary policies to bring about the desired level of economic activity. The government can stimulate the economy by use of fiscal instruments and accommodating monetary conditions. The loss of control over monetary conditions will constrain the government's ability to use fiscal policies effectively.

The monetarist view on central bank independence

According to the monetarists, demand management is ineffective as a tool to reduce unemployment and increase output and income. It is inflationary, it can be destabilizing and, for all these reasons, it should not be pursued.

■ In the eyes of a monetarist, it is therefore no great loss for the government to surrender precisely those tools that it should not be using anyway.

■ The government should focus on specifically targeted supply-side policies; it should abandon any attempt at macro-management of the economy other than ensuring low inflation and price stability through its control over money supply and interest rates.

■ But who could be better placed to ensure price stability and exercise control over monetary variables than the Bank of England itself? If monetary policy is not to be regarded by the government as a discretionary tool to be used to iron out fluctuations in the economy, then the move to grant the Bank of England independence in the setting of interest rates can only be, for the monetarists, a move in the right direction; further proof of the government's serious intention at retaining its fight against inflation as a priority policy objective.

■ Economic adjustment to lower inflation is also likely to be faster and therefore less costly, in terms of unemployment and loss of output, if an independent central bank is entrusted with the task of being the guardian of price stability. Instead governments are subject to political pressure, particularly at election times, and therefore likely to change their set course of action. Suppose the declared objective of a government is to reduce inflation, by reducing the money supply at the expense of unemployment, which will temporarily increase. The increase in unemployment need not be permanent and in fact economic theory predicts that unemployment would start to fall if and when people realize that the rate of inflation is slowing down. Their wage demands should also start to come down, stimulating employment in the process. But if people and trade unions believe that the government, faced by increased unemployment, will relax its fight against inflation and adopt a more lax monetary policy to counteract it, they will not revise their wage demands downward and the unemployment rate will remain high. If, on the other hand, they see an independent central bank responsible for inflation, they are less likely to anticipate a u-turn in policy and will conse-

quently prove more agreeable to a revision of their own wage demands, contributing to a quicker deceleration of inflation and a prompter market recovery.

An eclectic view: a conclusion

The debate on the advantages and disadvantages of an independent Bank of England cast in the terms described above tends to miss several important points and can be quite misleading. First, one needs to recognize that the issue of an independent Bank of England is linked to the wider issue of the European single currency and whether Britain should agree to it. Article 107 of the Maastricht Treaty, which lays down the conditions for European Monetary Union (EMU) states clearly the requirement that national central bank independence is a precondition for the creation of an independent European Central bank and for membership to the EMU:

Neither the European Central Bank, nor a national central bank, nor any member of their decision making bodies shall seek or take instructions from any government or any other body. Community institutions and bodies and governments of member states undertake not to seek to influence the members of decision making bodies of the European Central Bank or of their national central banks in the performance of their tasks.

Britain could not become member of the EMU without the Bank of England becoming 'independent' from the government. Gordon Brown's decision in the summer of 1997 to grant the Bank of England some independence from the government would seem to indicate that the decision to join the EMU, albeit not in the first wave, had already been taken. The institutional monetary reforms of summer 1997 must therefore be seen within the context of the government's European political agenda. The timing of its introduction would then appear to have been chosen on the basis of political expedience. Since the decision on British membership of the EMU was not taken in the summer of 1997, the Chancellor's decision to surrender some of its powers to the Bank of England would not be perceived by the British electorate as a humiliating surrender of government powers to satisfy a European dictat. Taken when it was, in the early summer of 1997, the decision only appeared motivated by strong government resolve to keep up its fight against inflation and to pre-empt the possibility of new rounds of politically embarrassing (for a Labour government), trade-union led, inflationary wage demands. For these reasons, it was applauded. Few commentators were then able to discuss in the open its hidden agenda.

If Britain wants to have a single European currency, it must first have an independent central bank. The debate on the advantages and disadvantages of an independent Bank of England should then broaden to include an analysis of the advantages and disadvantages of an independent European Central Bank and of a single currency: a much more complex analysis than the one provided by the debate referred to above.

Second, we must understand very carefully the extent of the 'independence' granted to the Bank of England. Hence careful consideration of the details of the institutional reforms must be preliminary to any discussion on their consequences. If we do that, we discover that the government might in fact have given very little away in terms of its power to choose its macroeconomic policy mix; although this may not be the case when we come to examine the conditions for EMU membership. This debate also ignores the constraints imposed on domestic macroeconomic policy by the international sector.

This point can be better explained with an example. If the government retains its right to choose its target inflation rate and surrenders to the Bank of England its power to determine interest rates, the government in fact has given away nothing. The right to set one variable – the rate of inflation – is sufficient to constrain the other variable – the rate of interest. Hence, what the government allows the Bank of England to do independently is the mechanical manipulation of monetary instruments, among which are changes in the interest rate and changes in the money supply, to achieve the government target inflation rate. The inflation rate target need not be restrictive, at least in a closed economy scenario. To retain the right to set its target inflation rate in practice means that the government can still choose its preferred trade-off point between unemployment and inflation or between growth and inflation. In other words, even if the Bank of England sets interest rates independently, the government can still choose to stimulate demand to achieve lower unemployment and faster growth. The situation would be quite different if the Bank of England were allowed independently to set the rate of inflation and the interest rate. So the question becomes: in the new institutional reforms, has the government retained its right to set its inflation target?

✍ Activity 7.9

Refer back to the details of the monetary reforms and answer the question mentioned above: has the government retained its right to set its inflation target?

✓ Answer 7.9

The government has retained its power to set inflation targets. The following points also need to be taken into account: how will decisions be reached in the new independent Bank of England? Who sits on the board? Has the government got representatives? How are members of the governing board chosen? Are any elected? Who has majority voting? Which channels of communications are envisaged between the government and the Bank of England? All these questions need to be looked at before we can give the word 'independence' its precise meaning and before we start engaging on debates about whether these institutional changes have meant a surrender of real power on the part of the government to the Bank of England.

A closer examination of the details of the 1997 reforms suggests that the 'surrender of power' has in fact been very limited and that the whole issue has more to do with politics than economics. It also serves to appease the justified fears of those who see the handing over of powers from the government to the central bank as a loss of democratic control. A central bank cannot be independent – it is argued – if it is run by executives who are chosen by the government. But if they are not chosen by the government, those executives have powers to make decisions which impinge upon the lives of millions without being democratically accountable to them. People can vote a government out after five years if they are dissatisfied with its policies, but what about the central bank's governing body? It is obviously possible to conceive ways of making a central bank accountable to its citizens; but the more accountable one makes it, the less 'independent' it becomes as an institution. Summing up, it is more useful to think in terms of 'degrees' of independence, rather than in terms of absolute dependence or independence of the central bank.

The question we should now ask ourselves, at the end of this discussion on central bank independence, is as follows: are there solid economic arguments, other than the political agenda set by the Maastricht Treaty, which prove that countries with independent central banks enjoyed faster growth and lower unemployment as well as lower inflation? The evidence seems to suggest a positive correlation between central bank independence and inflation, but a weak correlation between central bank independence and faster output growth. This would seem to suggest that, despite the monetarist's claim to the contrary, there is a price to be paid for lower inflation in terms of slower growth, lower output and employment. It then becomes a political choice, based on a government's values and priorities, as to whether price stability should come before output and employment.

The analysis developed so far refers to issues of independence of a central bank in a closed economy. We have deliberately ignored the constraints imposed by the international sector, in other words the effect that the interest rate has on the value of currency and the constraints of different exchange rate regimes. However, these cannot be ignored in a discussion of an independent European Central Bank. Because the macroeconomic implications of a European Central Bank can only be appreciated after we have introduced the analysis of an open economy, we will limit ourselves here to a preliminary discussion of some technical and institutional aspects of an independent European Central Bank. We will return to this topic and its wide-ranging implications in the context of a broader discussion of the European Union developed in Chapter 11.

AN INDEPENDENT EUROPEAN CENTRAL BANK

Since the late 1980s European Monetary Union (EMU), the issues of a European single currency, the Euro, and an independent European Central Bank have occupied a place of prominence on the European agenda, where they are likely to remain at least until the end of this century. The EMU has become a major political issue because of its wide economic ramifications, which fundamentally constrain national governments' management of their domestic economies, and because it reaches to the very heart of national sovereignty.

Where did the idea come from?

In the late 1980s the EMU appeared as a logical continuation of the **internal market programme**, which seemed on course for final implementation with:

- freedom of movement of labour and capital;
- abolition of all custom controls with the completion of the single market in 1992.

In the late 1980s the European Monetary System (EMS), based on a system of fixed exchange rates among community members, the exchange rate mechanism (ERM), appeared very stable. A further move towards closer political and economic integration seemed the obvious next step. Monetary union was seen as the final and irrevocable confirmation of a unified and integrated European economy. A common currency – it was argued – would weld national economies together, accelerating the process of political union.

Political changes

There had also been major political changes in Europe in the 1980s:

- the breakdown of old political divisions on the European continent;
- the disintegration of the Soviet Union;
- the collapse of the communist regimes in central and eastern Europe;
- the unification of Germany.

All these events seemed to call for a stronger, more cohesive European Community, strengthened by EMU and capable in particular of providing a stable and secure framework for a larger Germany.

Monetary integration seemed to provide the ideal instrument. As you appreciate now, however, money and the conduct of monetary policy play a crucial role in an economy. According to the Keynesians, it affects the real side of the economy, its income, output and employment. According to the monetarists, it affects the rate of inflation. Any European agreement on money or control over it was likely to be very difficult to achieve and to create huge political problems.

Earlier initiatives in the field of European monetary integration, such as the 'snake' and the ERM of 1979 (discussed in Chapter 10), had been largely motivated by external preoccupations, such as the collapse of the Bretton Woods agreement, the instability of the dollar and more aggressive US stance towards the EC. The initiatives which finally led to the Maastricht Treaty provisions had been dictated by internal reasons:

- the continuation and completion of the single market;
- the need to provide some sort of common monetary framework with the imminence of total capital movement liberalization.

The Delors report

In June 1988 the Committee for the Study of Economic and Monetary Union was set up, under the chairmanship of Jack Delors, to work on a blueprint for European monetary union. The committee included all governors or presidents of EC central banks, an additional member of the Commission, plus a small number of independent experts. Its unanimous report, the Delors Report, was submitted nearly a year later in April 1989.

According to the report, monetary union, which was later to become the Maastricht Treaty, should rest firmly on four pillars:

- complete liberalization of capital movements;
- totally fixed intra-EC exchange rates;
- replacement of national currencies by a single currency;
- centralization of monetary policy.

The Delors Report was explicit about the need for a transfer of powers from national government level to the level of the union and about the need to create a new institution. Not surprisingly, since the committee was made up almost entirely by central bankers, great emphasis was also placed on the independence of the new institution, which would be in charge of monetary policy for the union. This approach also partly reflected the influence of the German Bundesbank, which had provided the committee with a blueprint for the future European central bank. Given the link between fiscal and monetary policies, the Delors Report also called for:

- a system of binding rules governing the size and financing of national budget deficits;
- the need to determine the overall stance of fiscal policy at EC level, with decisions taken on a majority basis.

However, the report did not call for the setting up of a new institution at European level to unify fiscal policy to mirror the monetary one; constraints on national fiscal autonomy were going to be enough. The implementation strategy of monetary unification was conceived as follows:

1 Decision by member countries to enter the process of monetary unification is taken.
2 Major institutional changes are introduced.
3 Real transfer of powers from national to European level takes place.

On the basis of the Delors report a decision was taken:

- to proceed to the first stage of the EMU on 1 July 1990, which coincided with complete liberalization of capital movements in eight members of the community;
- to fix the date for the second stage of EMU for January 1994, which was one year after the expected completion of the internal market;
- to prepare the necessary Treaty provisions for a complete EMU.

In the early 1990s money was firmly at the centre of European high politics, just as energy and agriculture had been in the early 1950s, trade liberalization in the late 1960s and 1970s, and trade protection in the 1980s. During the negotiations and intense preparatory work that followed, the economic and political

desirability of the EMU was not seriously put into question at EC level. The matter seemed settled and despite doubts in the minds of many there was very little public debate on the subject of EMU, with the possible exception of Britain, prior to signing of the Maastricht Treaty. The potential stumbling blocks were represented by four categories of issues:

- the institutional framework of the future EMU;
- the balance between the monetary and fiscal powers of the Union;
- the nature and length of the transitional period, leading up to a complete EMU;
- the criteria for participating in the final stage.

The final document to be signed at Maastricht contained detailed provisions for the final stage of the EMU and very little on the intermediate stages. More importantly, in its final version the Treaty did also seem to enshrine the core of the monetarist ideas.

THE MAASTRICHT TREATY

The Treaty on European Union, generally known as the Maastricht Treaty, signed in February 1992, finally formalized the steps of the transition to a common currency, spelling out its institutional implications and the conditions for participation in a common currency area.

Transition

Transition to European monetary union and a single currency was established in three distinct stages:

Stage 1: 1 July 1990–31 December 1993

- Completion of the internal market, including the abolition of all capital controls.
- Strengthening of existing mechanisms of multilateral surveillance to achieve greater economic and monetary co-ordination.
- Reform of the structural funds.
- Inclusion of all currencies in the narrow band of the ERM.

This stage was meant as a consolidation of the status quo. At the time the ERM seemed very solid and in a position to sustain a further narrowing of bands. Unfortunately, for reasons that we discuss in Chapter 10, the foreign exchange markets did not share Brussels officials' views and the ERM almost reached a breakdown point in 1992, when both sterling and the lira, were forced to leave as a result of intense speculative pressures.

Stage 2: 1 January 1994

■ Establishment of European Monetary Institute (EMI), to strengthen monetary co-ordination among central banks, to oversee the functioning of the EMS, to monitor macroeconomic convergence of member states according to Maastricht criteria and to prepare the organizational and logistical framework for the European Central Bank (ECB).

■ Establishment of the European System of Central Banks (ESCB) based on a federal structure, composed of the European Central Bank (ECB) and the national central banks.

■ During stage two, member states were required to legislate for the independence of their central bank.

The main purpose of the second stage was to secure the economic convergence of member countries in preparation for the complete EMU. Why convergence is a necessary precondition for monetary union and a single currency will become clear in Chapter 10. The temporary institution set up to oversee these transitional tasks was the EMI, based in Frankfurt, which is also the seat of the ECB. It replaces the Committee of Governors of Central Banks (CGCB) and in turn will be replaced by the European Central Bank when it becomes operational at the beginning of the third stage.

The most crucial part of the transitional arrangements relates to the conditions to be fulfilled at the beginning of the third and final stage, when the exchange rates of participant currencies are irrevocably fixed and the single currency, replacing national currencies, is introduced.

Stage 3: 1 January 1999

■ Irrevocable fixing of exchange rates.

■ Introduction of a single currency, the euro.

■ European Central Bank to commence operations, replacing EMI. The ECB issues the Euro, the new European single currency.

■ Member countries' eligibility for EMU to be judged on the basis of five convergence criteria: level of inflation; interest rates; budget deficits to GDP ratio; debt to GDP ratio; exchange rate stability within the ERM.

Needless to say, the most contentious aspect of the third stage is whether countries meet the convergence criteria and qualify for a single currency and membership of the EU. The third stage began on 1 January 1999 irrespective of how many member countries ful-

filled the conditions for admission. Those failing the test were excluded from the new institutional framework, but their position will be reassessed after two years. A voluntary 'opt-out' protocol was subsequently added, specifically to accommodate the UK which refused to commit itself to participating in the final stage of EMU, leaving the final decision to a future parliament.

The new institutions

Monetary policy within the EU is increasingly carried out by the new institutions described above, whose functions centre around the working of the European Central Bank (ECB).

European System of Central Banks

The ESCB is based on a federal structure, composed of the European Central Bank and the national central banks, although their exact relationship remains to be defined. National central banks operate in accordance with the guidelines and instructions issued by the ECB.

The ESCB defines and implements monetary policy for the union as a whole, conducts foreign exchange operations and holds and manages the official foreign reserves of member countries. The Maastricht Treaty allows the Council of Economic and Finance Ministers (ECOFIN), a role in the negotiation of international agreements and the formulation of general orientation on exchange rate matters, leaving exchange rate policy and the division of responsibilities between ECB and ECOFIN rather unclear.

European Central Bank

The ECB is to be governed by a six-member executive board, which includes a president and vice-president, appointed for an eight-year, non-renewable term by the European Council; and by a governing council, consisting of the members of the governing board and the governors of the European central banks. Further to ensure the independence of the European Central Bank, independence of national central banks from their respective governments is also a statutory requirement.

The primary objective of the ECB is to maintain price stability and to be totally independent from political authorities. Arrangements for accountability of the ECB to EU institutions are also in place, but the need for absolute independence of the ECB is firmly stressed. The ECB has the exclusive right to authorize the issue of money. It is not permitted to lend to governments or to bail out indebted governments or other public institutions.

The Maastricht Treaty did not create any new institution for the conduct of fiscal policies, which remain a national responsibility. Indeed, having handed over decision and conduct of monetary policy to the ECB and given the interdependence of fiscal and monetary policies, the creation of a further federal institution for fiscal co-ordination was quite unnecessary.

The fiscal constraints imposed by the Maastricht Treaty as conditions for participation in the EMU and for remaining in it are very tight indeed:

■ a deficit/GDP ratio below 3 per cent, unless declining and close to 3 per cent;
■ a debt/GDP ratio below 60 per cent, or, if above, 'diminishing and approaching the reference value'.

These fiscal constraints are so tight that only one country, Luxembourg, would have qualified for membership in 1999, if they were interpreted to the letter. According to the articles of the treaty, this fiscal policy straitjacket is to be worn at all times by member countries and not just for the EU opening gala in 1999.

Article 104c of the Maastricht Treaty and the attached protocol set out the **excess deficit procedure** to be followed when members of the EU exceed the ceiling of 3 per cent for public deficits and 60 per cent for public debt in terms of GDP. Such measures include:

1 The Commission, which is given the role of fiscal watchdog, will use those public finance ceilings as reference values for the assessment of national budgetary policies of EU members and prepare annual reports on each of them.
2 On the basis of the Commission reports, ECOFIN will decide by qualified majority whether a situation of excessive deficit exists in a member country.
3 On the basis of the ECOFIN decision, the Council will then have a whole range of measures at its disposal to induce the 'offending' member to fall into line and cut its public spending. Such measures include:

   ■ public recommendations;
   ■ recommendation to EIB to reduce or halt lending to offending member;
   ■ requesting the member to make a non-interest bearing deposit with the EU;
   ■ imposition of fines.

Convergence criteria

The convergence criteria for moving to stage three of the EMU, which prospective members needed to achieve before 1 January 1999, include:

■ *price stability* interpreted as consumer price inflation of no more than 1.5 percentage points above that prevailing in 'the three best performing Member States';
■ *sustainability of each government's financial position:*
   — a deficit/GDP ratio below 3 per cent unless declining and close to 3 per cent, or an excess which is 'exceptional and temporary' and remains near 3 per cent;
   — a debt/GDP ratio below 60 per cent or, if above, one which is 'sufficiently diminishing and approaching the reference value at a satisfactory pace'.
■ *exchange rate stability*: the national currency must have remained within the 'normal' fluctuation margins of the ERM for at least two years prior to the decision about the final stage, without any devaluation or severe tension. Since the widening of the bands to + 15 per cent in August 1993, 'normal' is expected to be defined rather loosely as 'the existing margin' of the ERM.
■ *durability of convergence*: measured by nominal interest rate on long-term government bonds not exceeding that of the best performing member states by more than two percentage points.

Although much has been said about the strictness of these criteria, they are in fact more flexible than may at first be apparent. The wording for the national debt/GDP ratio and budget deficit/GDP ratio criteria are quite flexible and can be interpreted in such way as to allow more countries to take part in EMU. 'Satisfactory progress' could allow even Italy to be eligible on this basis. However, relatively rapid declines are expected in the deficits and debt ratios of those countries found to be outside the threshold by the deadline. Decisions on borderline countries are also likely to be influenced by political considerations, as well as by economic facts.

✍ Activity 7.10

Look at the statistics in Table 7.1 and Figures 7.5, 7.6 and 7.7 and state which countries qualify for membership of the EMU according to the Maastricht criteria.

✓ Answer 7.10

If the criteria were to be interpreted to the letter, all countries are eligible for inclusion on the basis of the inflation and interest rates criteria, with the exception of Portugal; but very few are on the basis of the deficit and debt criteria: only Denmark, France, Luxembourg, Finland and very marginally Germany.

Figure 7.5 Reference value and harmonized indices of consumer prices (CPIH) (12-month moving average of annual percentage changes)

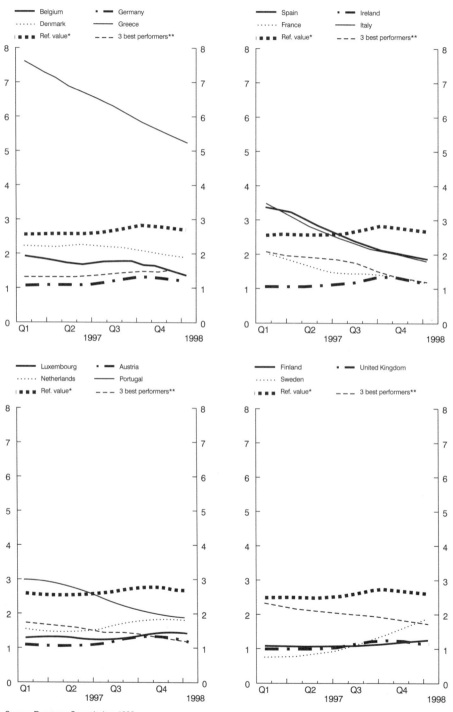

Source: European Commission, 1998

*Unweighted arithmetic average of the three best-performing countries according to the price criterion plus 1.5 percentage points.

**Unweighted arithmetic average of the three best-performing countries according to the price criterion.

Figure 7.6 Reference value and long-term interest rates (12-month moving average in percentages)

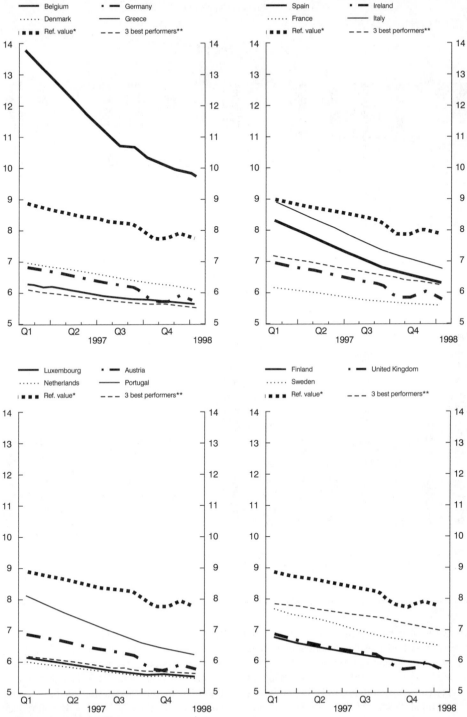

Source: European Commission, 1998
*Unweighted arithmetic average of the long-term interest rates of the three best-performing countries according to the price criterion plus 2.0 percentage points.
*Unweighted arithmetic average of the long-term interest rates of the three best-performing countries according to the price criterion.

Figure 7.7   Performance in relation to Maastricht Treaty fiscal reference values (as a percentage of GDP)

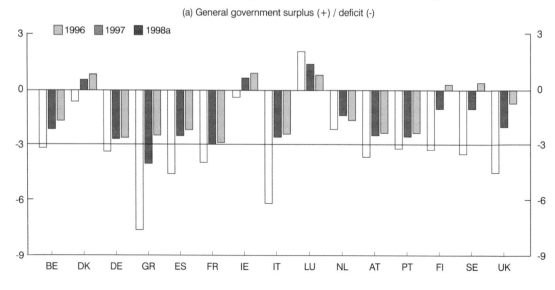

(a) General government surplus (+) / deficit (-)

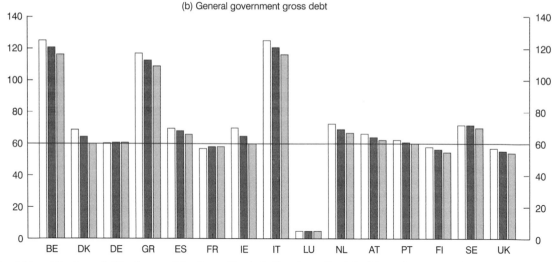

(b) General government gross debt

BE = Belgium, DK = Denmark, DE = Germany, GR = Greece, ES = Spain, FR = France, IE = Ireland, IT = Italy, LU = Luxembourg, NL = Netherlands, AT = Austria, PT = Portugal, FI = Finland, SE = Sweden, UK = United Kingdom

Source: European Commission (Spring 1988 forecasts)

In May 1998 the European Commission announced that eleven countries had met the Maastricht criteria and qualified for membership of the EMU and adoption of the Euro on 1 January 1999: Austria, Belgium, Finland, France, Germany, Ireland, Italy, Luxembourg, Netherlands, Portugal, Spain. Of the countries wishing to join, only Greece did not meet the convergence criteria as its public debt is way outside the limit and its currency has only recently joined the ERM. Italy and Belgium have debts which are more than double the target ratio, but were allowed to join because their governments' debts have been steadily declining and are forecast to continue. The UK would technically have qualified on four accounts, but its currency does not participate in the ERM and it does not wish to join, at least in the first wave of countries. Sweden too remains outside the ERM, hence not meeting one of the admission criteria.

Table 7.1 Maastricht Treaty convergence criteria

Maastricht criteria	Debt as % of GDP		Deficit as % of GDP		Inflation* %		Long-term interest rates†	ERM membership
	1997 60.0	1998 60.0	1997 3.0	1998 3.0	1997 3.2	1998 3.2	7.7	
Austria	66.1	64.7	2.5	2.3	1.1	1.5	5.6	Yes
Belgium	122.2	118.1	2.1	1.7	1.4	1.3	5.7	Yes
Britain	53.4	53.0	1.9	0.6	1.8	2.3	7.0	No
Denmark	65.1	59.5	−0.7	−1.1	1.9	2.1	6.2	Yes
Finland	55.8	53.6	1.1	−0.3	1.3	2.0	5.9	Yes±
France	58.0	58.1	3	2.9	1.2	1.0	5.5	Yes
Germany	61.3	61.2	2.7	2.5	1.4	1.7	5.6	Yes
Greece	108.7	107.7	4.0	2.2	5.2	4.5	9.8	Yes§
Ireland	66.3	59.5	−0.9	−1.1	1.2	3.3	6.2	Yes
Italy	121.6	118.1	2.7	2.5	1.8	2.1	6.7	Yes**
Luxembourg	6.7	7.1	−1.7	−1.0	1.4	1.6	5.6	Yes
Netherlands	72.1	70.0	1.4	1.6	1.8	2.3	5.5	Yes
Portugal	62.0	60.0	2.5	2.2	1.8	2.2	6.2	Yes
Spain	68.8	67.4	2.6	2.2	1.8	2.2	6.3	Yes
Sweden	76.6	74.1	0.8	−0.5	1.9	1.5	6.5	No

*Within 1.5% of average of lowest three †Within 2% of average of inflation's lowest three, Jan 1998 §Since March 1998 ±Since October 1996 **Since November 1996
Source: European Commission 1998

POTENTIAL BENEFITS OF EMU AND A SINGLE CURRENCY

To ask the question whether the Euro will be good for Europe appears pointless now that the future of the euro is certain. It may still be useful, nonetheless, to know where the advantages and disadvantages of the EMU and the single currency originate.

Reduced transaction costs

Savings in currency conversions are seen as the immediate benefit of a monetary union. A single currency will also reduce bank charges, commissions and delays associated with cross-border bank payments. However, these savings are estimated to be rather small (Taylor 1995). The European Commission suggests that elimination of transaction costs of exchanging one EU currency into another could boost the GDP of the countries concerned by an average of 0.4 per cent, roughly Ecu13–19bn a year, for the EU as a whole (European Commission 1990). Transaction costs vary according to the size and openness (ratio of export sector to GDP) of the economy. They are likely to be higher for member states which have small, open economies or weak currencies. They are also likely to be higher for economies with a large number of small

and medium-sized companies, which are more affected by transaction costs than large companies. So the gain is likely to be smaller for countries such as the UK, which have well developed financial markets.

Reduced exchange rate uncertainty

A single currency will reduce the need for expensive hedging, which takes place when firms and institutions dealing with foreign markets reduce the risk of losses associated with exchange rate changes by entering into currencies forward contracts. For example, imagine a British trader is looking forward to a payment in Deutschmarks in six months' time as result of an export to Germany. The trader does not know exactly how much the contract is going to be worth in sterling in six months' time, as that will depend on the rate at which £1 will exchange for Deutschmarks. The uncertainty about the sterling value of the Deutschmarks can be avoided if, immediately after signing the export contract, the British exporter sells the Deutschmark proceeds at the prevailing forward rate on the six-month forward market. Although the actual transaction will not take place until a specific date in six months' time, the six-month forward rate is already known. A forward transaction is always costly, so normally the exporter will pass on the forward market transaction costs in the price of the good or service sold abroad. This will push up the price of the good sold on foreign markets with respect to the price of the same good sold on the domestic market and create a price distortion. The need for such expensive procedures will be eliminated in intra-European transactions by the use of a single European currency, increasing price transparency and competitiveness.

Increased investment

A single currency and the elimination of exchange rate uncertainty is likely to have a positive effect on investment within EMU countries, and hence on output, income and employment growth in those countries. There is no forward market for exchange rate movements over the medium and long term. Investing abroad, either to open up a trade channel or to start production, may require heavy investment with no guarantee for the investor that the venture will be profitable, because of exchange rate uncertainty. At present a good competitive position can be turned into a loss-making export in the future just by exchange rate movements. Economic theory of investment under uncertainty suggests that exchange rate uncertainty can be an important deterrent to investment by firms trading over international borders.

Lower interest rates

Lower interest rates will result from the long-term commitment of EU countries to low inflation. Because such commitment is enshrined into the articles and protocols of the Treaty and because of the independence of the ECB, it will be easier for member countries to control inflation with a lower average level of real interest rates than countries whose commitment to low inflation is less firmly secured. Within a single currency, it is therefore likely that countries with a poor record for inflation control will benefit more from real long-term interest rates lower than those that would otherwise have prevailed than countries with a good record of inflation control. From this point of view, Britain, whose long-term interest rates are higher than other EU countries, would ultimately be a beneficiary.

Economies of scale

While the factors mentioned above provide sources of potential static gains to be achieved by member countries, which will deepen trade and investment integration in Europe, there are also dynamic gains that the

EMU will bring about for businesses operating in the Union, such as financial economies of scale.

Increased price transparency and intra-EMU competition

Evidence suggests that prices for the same goods can still vary considerably across EU countries, despite single market legislation intended to abolish any scope for price discrimination between EU national markets. The need for currency conversions, together with differences in taxation and regulations, may explain why this is so. The use of the same currency, the Euro, should make price differences between countries more obvious and lead to downward pressure on prices in those countries where they are higher.

Increased inward direct investment

Direct investment from the rest of the world is likely to be attracted to a market where 150–200 million people share the same currency. This is one of the strong arguments why Britain should choose to be a member of the EU. Britain is Europe's primary recipient of direct investment from the rest of the world, but this tendency could be reversed if Britain were to find itself outside the new single currency area.

POTENTIAL COSTS OF EU AND A SINGLE CURRENCY

The creation of the EU and introduction of a single currency also present some disadvantages which are the cause of considerable concern among potential EU members.

Loss of sovereignty

The introduction of a single currency would require handing over monetary control from national governments to the ECB, which would then set the interest rate and decide on other financial variables, such as the supply of money, to achieve set monetary objectives for the whole single currency area, rather than for any one country in particular.

Loss of macroeconomic policy autonomy

As we have seen, in order to join the Union and to remain in it, members will surrender to the ECB their control over exchange rates, interest rates, inflation rates and fiscal targets. They will have to surrender, de facto, all the tools necessary for macroeconomic policy management. In particular, EU members will surrender their ability to choose a preferred inflation/unemployment or inflation/growth trade-off. Furthermore, such surrender of monetary and fiscal autonomy will be to an untried institution, the ECB, which many fear unduly restrictive and deflationary.

Inability to react to country-specific economic shocks

Because monetary and, to a large extent, fiscal policy will be determined and administered by the ECB, it is unlikely to react to a country-specific problem unless all other members suffer from it in one way or another. Greater unemployment and slower growth may therefore result in the country which has suffered the shock than would otherwise have been the case. This will be exacerbated by lack of labour market flexibility and geographical mobility, which is prevalent in Europe. However, this scenario is not very realistic as any external shock is likely to affect more than one, if not all, European member countries. Country-specific shocks are also likely to have been initiated by country-specific stop–go policies, which will be ruled out anyway by the monetary and fiscal restrictions that the new economic order will impose upon members. Finally, countries retain some control over the financial tool which could be used to some effect.

Risk of 'real misalignment' within the Union

European countries' economic structure may respond differently to economic shocks or events and cause a divergence rather than convergence over the years, resulting in a real misalignment of currencies. This fact would normally be taken care of by devaluation of the currency of the country in question. This will no longer be possible. The adoption of a single currency may therefore result in higher levels of unemployment and real income decline as the burden of the adjustment would fall entirely on wages and domestic cost flexibility.

Asymmetric policy sensitivity

As Foley (1996) states:

> In the UK a relatively high proportion of borrowing is at floating rates. In Germany, by contrast, much borrowing is at fixed rates. Hence the UK will be more sensitive than Germany, ceteris paribus, to a change in interest rates.

This implies that countries such as the UK could bear a disproportionately large share of the burden of adjustment to monetary policy tightening within a single currency area.

However, it can also be argued, that nothing stops UK borrowers from moving from floating rate borrowing to fixed rate loans. The lower and more stable long-term interest rates that ought to result from the creation of the EMU should encourage a change in this direction.

Conclusion

The EMU became the flagship of the European strategy of both the European Commission, M Delors in particular, and the French government at the end of the 1980s. The Commission saw in the EMU the consolidation of the internal market and further strengthening of European political construction. The move towards a complete EMU would help to secure for France a stronger say in the conduct of European monetary policy and would also provide the instrument for integrating Germany more tightly into the Community system. In many ways, the EMU was a Franco-German pact and a typical Community compromise. The problems and difficulties of the EMU are only beginning to unfold, as the EMU becomes a reality. The adjustment process will undoubtedly continue well into the next century.

SUB-OPTIMAL EUROPE

The EMU started on time at the beginning of 1999, with eleven countries irrevocably fixing their exchange rates and ceding control of monetary policy to the European Central Bank. The eleven EMU countries have made strenuous efforts to meet the Maastricht criteria, so much so that the EMU is rightly often blamed for the poor economic performance and high unemployment suffered by most EU countries in the second half of the 1990s.

Fiscal policy need not be constrained under a single currency

But were those efforts justified and did the Maastricht Treaty set the right sort of targets? It does make sense, for reasons that you will appreciate better after studying Chapter 10, to have converging inflation rates before fixing exchange rates. It is harder to justify the need for the other convergence criteria. Low interest rates would have stemmed automatically from low inflation rates. Membership of the ERM, with a 15 per cent fluctuation band, is no longer a guarantee of exchange rate stability and is a rather meaningless condition. The most controversial measures, however, have been the two public finance criteria imposed by the Maastricht Treaty, constraining the size of the public deficit, which should not exceed 3 per cent of GDP, and of public debt, which should not be more than 60 per cent of GDP. These constraints – many argue – are arbitrary and potentially destabilizing. But have they helped the convergence of the EU countries?

An optimum currency area

For a start, the Maastricht criteria for the EMU and the single currency have failed to bring about real convergence among the eleven countries. Real convergence, as opposed to convergence of arbitrarily chosen indicators, is shown by the existence of a fundamental alignment of member countries' economic structure. Real convergence would make the eleven countries of the EU area an **optimum currency area**.

The concept of optimum currency area was first introduced by the American economist, Robert Mundell, in 1961 to describe the gains to be had from sharing a currency across borders: lower transaction costs, more transparent prices, greater certainty for investors, enhanced competition and price stability. These broad benefits need to be set against the loss of two important policy instruments: an independent monetary policy and the option of changing the exchange rate. This loss is particularly costly for countries within the single currency areas which are structurally different from the rest of the area. Such countries will no longer be able to respond to economic shocks by devaluating their currencies or easing their national monetary policy. The consequences of this loss of national macroeconomic tools are likely to be less severe if the following conditions apply:

- mobility of labour: workers in the affected country are willing and able to move freely to other countries; there should not be linguistic, cultural or legal barriers;
- flexibility of wages and prices: the country must be able to respond to shocks by lowering wages and prices to restore competitiveness;
- single currency area countries should be on similar economic cycles and share similar structures.

If these conditions defining an 'optimum currency area' do not apply, then creating a single currency area is likely to destabilize the participating economies rather than fostering their growth.

Lack of real convergence

Evidence of a lack of real convergence among the eleven EMU countries abounds. Differing unemployment rates in the eleven EMU countries are the first indicator of structural differences.

✍ Activity 7.11

Look at Figure 7.8 and explain what it shows.

Figure 7.8   Unemployment rates in EU

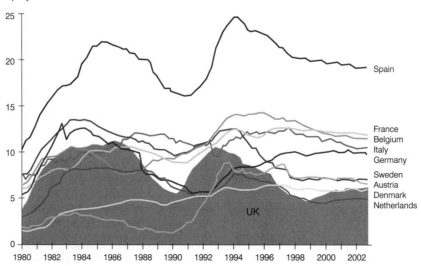

Source: Lloyds Bank Economic Bulletin, 19, 1998

✓ Answer 7.11

Figure 7.8 shows unemployment rates in the EU with forecasts of future unemployment until the year 2002. The countries can be split into three groups: the first group, represented by the Netherlands, Denmark, Austria and Sweden, has and will continue to have relatively low unemployment, similar to the UK, which the chart shows as the darkened area. The second group, including France, Belgium, Italy and Germany, is likely to continue to see unemployment rates near 10 per cent. Spain, on the other hand, is expected to remain at around 20 per cent.

A second indicator of low real convergence is provided by the differing percentage of exports of EMU countries currently going to countries outside the EMU area. As Figure 7.9 shows, this share varies from below 40 per cent for Portugal, Spain and the Netherlands to nearly 60 per cent for Ireland and Germany.

✎ Activity 7.12

Why does a differing percentage of exports to the EMU represent an indication of low real convergence?

✓ Answer 7.12

A differing percentage of exports to the EMU implies that some EU members, those who export more to the EU area such as Ireland and Portugal, have more to gain than others from a single currency. It also implies that some EU members, those with a larger share of their exports to countries outside the Union such as Germany, Italy, France, Austria and Finland, will be less indifferent to the external value of the Euro than others.

Figure 7.9 Share of exports outside EMU area

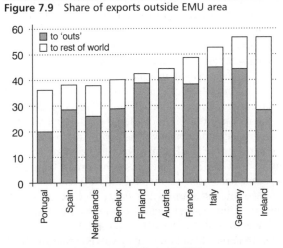

Source: Lloyds Bank Economic Bulletin 19, 1998

Recent IMF research seems also to point at a further indicator of lack of convergence in the different way in which output responds to a monetary policy tightening, for example, a 1 per cent rise in interest rates, in the various EU countries.

✎ Activity 7.13

Look at Figure 7.10 and explain what it shows.

✓ Answer 7.13

European countries seem to fall into two groups. One group, which includes Germany, Netherlands, Belgium, Austria, Finland (and the UK), shows a much larger projected contraction in response to higher interest rates than the other group of countries, which includes France, Italy, Denmark, Sweden, Spain and Portugal. Other studies have also found that the full effect of a rise in rates on output takes twice as long to be felt in the first group of countries than in the second.

These findings point at the possibility that monetary policy changes will have asymmetric effects across the EMU area.

✎ Activity 7.14

How can we explain these results? Why do interest rate changes affect countries' output differently?

✓ Answer 7.14

Higher rates influence economies in three main ways :

- They raise the cost of borrowing and so discourage investment and purchases of consumer durables on credit.
- They have an 'income effect': savers who get a higher interest are better off, while borrowers are worse off.
- They have an exchange rate effect: a raise in interest rates causes an appreciation of the currency and so adversely affects exports.

These effects help us to understand the possible asymmetry in the EU countries' response to interest rate changes:

- The higher the proportion of short-term variable interest borrowing (like in Britain, Italy and Austria), as opposed to long-term fixed interest borrowing (popular in France, Germany and the Netherlands), the greater the 'income effect', the bigger the drop in spending when interest rates rise.
- In some countries, such as Britain, the Netherlands and Spain, short-term bank lending adjusts

Figure 7.10 Output response (per cent) to monetary tightening

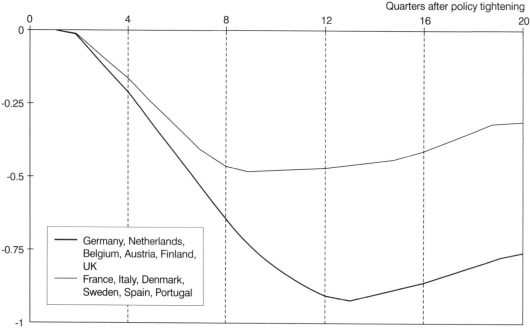

Source: Lloyds Bank Economic Bulletin 19, 1998

promptly (within three months) and fully to changes in base rates (i.e. commercial banks pass on to customers changes in the interest rate they are charged by central banks. In others only slowly (12 months in France, where only three-fifths of the increase is passed on; a similar lag in Germany, where only three-quarters of the increase is passed on).

■ The more open the economy, the bigger the impact on output of an appreciation of the Euro against the dollar or yen, as a result of higher interest rates.

The reasons and the statistics discussed above show that, despite the eleven qualifying countries meeting the Maastricht criteria and the start of the single currency, real convergence among EMU members does not exist. What has been achieved is the forced alignment of some indicators, without countries having undertaken sufficient structural reform. Of course, real convergence takes time to occur – everybody accepts that – and will not happen overnight.

Monetary policy of the European Central Bank

Given the lack of real convergence across the EMU area, the ECB has a delicate balancing act to perform,

particularly in the early stages of EMU. It needs to pursue its objective of monetary stability without upsetting the balance in those EU economies likely to contract more in response to tighter monetary conditions. The ECB also needs to choose its policy targets, both intermediate and final, very carefully. The final target remains without doubt price stability. The intermediate one could be the money supply growth, as for the Bundesbank, or an interest rate target, as for the Bank of England.

To make matters worse, not only are the structural problems of EMU economies different, as shown by the differing unemployment rates and different export markets, but they are also on different economic cycles. Ireland, Spain, Portugal and Finland pulled out of the recession of the second half of the 1990s faster than France and Germany. This is why interest rates at the periphery of the EU area were higher than those at the core in 1998. This suggests that when the single currency becomes a reality and the ECB has to impose a single interest rate on the entire Euro area, it will choose an interest rate which is too low for some and too high for others; one size won't fit all.

On the other hand, one policy variable that the ECB will not need to be too concerned about is the external value of the euro: its policy is likely to become one of 'benign neglect'. This is because, for the EMU area as a whole, international openness is rather limited. This issue will be discussed in greater depth in Chapter 10.

✍ Activity 7.15

What are the likely effects that the single currency will have on Europe's financial centres?

✓ Answer 7.15

The introduction of a single currency in the EU will increase the competition in financial services between London, Frankfurt and Paris. Despite the existing advantage of the City of London over its European rivals, Frankfurt and Paris are in a better shape to compete with London for the new single-currency business, given that the UK has opted to stay out of the single currency area for the time being.

Effect of the single currency on Europe's financial centres

The euro brings both threats and opportunities to Europe's financial centres:

■ Its introduction is likely to cause shrinkage of the foreign exchange market as European currencies disappear. London will suffer most from this as it currently handles most European foreign exchange trading.

■ The euro will become an important international reserve (more on this in Chapter 10). This will encourage extra international borrowing, investment and trading in the euro. Whether London could still handle the bulk of this business, despite being out, is a moot point.

■ The euro will compress a number of financial markets into one: the government bond market, the bond future market, the money market (as a single currency requires a single short-term interest rate across the euro area) and the short-term interest rate futures market (in which to hedge short-term borrowings).

■ Europe's equity markets (buying and selling company shares) will be less affected at first, as stockmarkets will differ because of different local taxes, accounting rules and local stock bought by local investors. However, this will gradually change as fund managers start to invest more money across European borders to build investment portfolios that reflect Europe's economy rather than their domestic one.

■ New financial markets will also be created, such as European corporate bond market, which at present is very small outside Britain.

Which financial centre will benefit most, remains to be seen. Undoubtedly, the City of London will be disadvantaged by sterling being 'out' of the euro, just as Frankfurt 's financial institutions will gain from being at the centre of Euroland, with the ECB on their doorstep.

CASE STUDY: UK BUSINESS AND EUROLAND

The UK has decided not to join the EMU. What will the impact of this decision be on UK business? Before we answer this question, let's look at some statistics. As Figure 7.11 shows, half of UK exports in goods and one-third of UK exports in services go to the EU area countries. Total exports to the region accounted for around 15 per cent of UK GDP in 1997. In the same year, the UK relied on the same bloc for 55 per cent of its goods imports and for 36 per cent of its services imports. The first conclusion that we can derive from this statistics is that the euro/sterling exchange rate and the general performance of the EMU area will have a profound impact on the UK economy.

How independent can UK policy be?

The ECB is likely to follow a policy of benign neglect towards the external value of the euro. This may lead to substantial misalignments against other currencies, including those of the four european 'outs': the UK, Sweden, Denmark and Greece. The 'out' countries face a difficult dilemma (which again will become clearer in Chapter 10). They can either follow an independent monetary policy or try to fix their exchange rates against the euro. They cannot do both at the same time.

The UK, like Sweden and unlike Denmark, has chosen to pursue a domestic inflation target, allowing the exchange rate to stabilize at whatever market value is consistent with the chosen inflation and interest rates. This has meant high interest rates, a strong pound and increased difficulties for the UK manufacturing sector. As a result of this approach, UK businesses will have to cope with periods of misalignment of sterling against its main trading partners which, coupled with interest rates higher than in the EU, will make their prospects of competing successfully all the more difficult.

Impact on UK business

Apart from having to deal with exchange rate fluctuations against its biggest market, UK business will face another difficulty. The formation of a single currency area is likely to cause profound shifts in the structure of european industry, with increasing numbers of cross-border mergers and acquisitions and a redirection of foreign direct investment. These shifts are likely to disadvantage businesses based in an 'out' country.

Let's just reflect on a few figures. The EMU market of the eleven 'in' countries is five times as large as the UK in terms of GDP; capital spending is seven times as high as in the UK. In the EMU there are six times as many cars and five times as many televisions as in the UK (*Lloyds Bank Economic Bulletin*, 1998). The market potential of the EMU area is gen-uinely huge. The main effects on UK business will be: redirection of FDI and business clustering.

Redirection of FDI

One effect of the creation of this market will be a shift in foreign direct investment flows away from the countries that are out and towards those that are in.

✍ Activity 7.16

Look at Figure 7.12 and comment on what it shows.

✓ Answer 7.16

The UK has been a major recipient of foreign direct investment in recent years, with inflows of capital second only to the USA and China.

Business clustering

The second likely effect will be a substantial relocation of european business, as companies take advantage of increasing returns by concentrating production in one area or sector to serve the entire EMU market, forming clusters of activity with similar EMU companies. These external economies of scale stem from: skilled labour market pooling; development of specialized local suppliers; technological spillovers from one firm to others.

Increasing returns to clustering (lower average costs for clustered firms) will imply that whichever region gains an initial cost advantage through this process will be in a better position to sustain and increase that advantage. Only firms located in the EMU area will be able to benefit from the formation of business clusters in europe.The longer UK firms stay out, the greater may become their disadvantage.

✍ Activity 7.17

Look at Tables 7.2 and 7.3 and see how they relate to the concepts introduced in this chapter.

Figure 7.12 Top five world recipients of foreign direct investment (FDI)

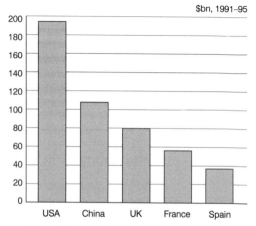

$bn, 1991–95

Source: OECD, 1998

Figure 7.11   UK exports to the EU

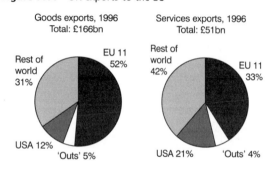

Goods exports, 1996
Total: £166bn

EU 11 52%
Rest of world 31%
USA 12%
'Outs' 5%

Services exports, 1996
Total: £51bn

EU 11 33%
Rest of world 42%
USA 21%
'Outs' 4%

Source: ONS, *Economic Trends*, 1998

Table 7.2 EUR 15[1] main economic indicators, 1961–97

	1961–73	1974–85	1986–90	1991–5	1992	1993	1994	1995	1996	1997
1 Gross domestic product[2]										
At current market prices	10.2	12.08	8.3	5.3	5.5	3.1	5.5	5.4	4.3	4.4
At 1990 market prices	4.8	2.0	3.3	1.5	1.0	–0.4	2.9	2.4	1.6	2.4
2 Gross fixed capital formation at 1990 prices[2]										
Total	5.7	–0.1	5.7	–0.4	–0.9	–6.6	2.4	3.7	1.1	3.0
Construction	—	–1.2	4.8	0.1	0.1	–3.2	1.4	1.6	–0.2	1.4
equipment	—	1.9	7.0	–1.0	–3.4	–11.3	4.1	6.4	2.6	4.8
3 Gross fixed capital formation at current prices (% of GDP)[3]										
Total	23.4	21.3	20.3	19.5	20.1	18.8	18.6	18.9	18.5	18.4
General government	—	3.2	2.8	2.8	2.9	2.8	2.7	2.6	2.4	2.3
Other sectors	—	18.0	17.4	16.7	17.2	16.0	15.9	16.3	16.1	16.2
4 Final national uses including stocks[4]										
At 1990 prices	4.5	1.6	3.6	0.8	0.6	–2.1	2.4	2.1	1.3	2.1
Relative against six other OECD countries	–0.8	–0.9	0.2	–0.9	–0.5	–4.0	–0.8	0.1	–1.4	0.1
5 Inflation[2]										
Prices deflator private consumption	4.7	10.7	4.3	4.1	4.7	4.0	3.3	3.0	2.7	2.2
Prices deflator GDP	5.2	10.6	4.9	3.8	4.5	3.6	2.6	2.9	2.6	1.9
6 Compensation per employee[2]										
Nominal	9.9	12.4	6.2	4.9	7.0	4.1	3.3	3.1	3.5	3.2
Real, deflator private consumption	5.0	1.5	1.9	0.8	2.2	0.1	0.1	0.2	0.8	1.0
Real, deflator GDP	4.5	1.6	1.3	1.1	2.4	0.5	0.8	0.2	0.8	1.3
7 GDP at 1990 market prices per person employed[2]	4.4	2.0	1.9	2.0	2.4	1.5	3.2	1.8	1.5	1.9
8 Real unit labour cost[4]										
1961–73 = 100	100.0	103.6	97.8	96.1	97.7	96.9	94.6	93.5	93.0	92.3
Annual % change	0.2	–0.1	–0.5	–0.8	0.0	–0.8	–2.4	–1.2	–0.5	–0.7
9 Relative unit labour costs in common currency[4] against nine other OECD countries 1961–73 = 100	100.0	101.2	97.4	99.1	108.4	95.3	92.3	95.1	98.2	95.2
Annual % change	1.0	–2.0	5.5	–2.4	4.0	–12.1	–3.2	3.1	3.2	–3.0
10 Employment[2]	0.3	0.0	1.3	–0.6	–1.4	–1.9	–0.4	0.6	0.1	0.5
11 Unemployment rate (% of civilian labour force)[3]	2.3	6.4	8.9	10.1	9.3	10.9	11.3	10.9	11.0	10.6
12 Current balance (% of GDP)[3]	0.3	–0.3	0.1	–0.4	–1.2	0.0	0.0	0.5	0.7	0.9
13 Net lending (+) or net borrowing (–) of general government (% of GDP)[5]	–0.4	–3.7	–3.4	–5.2	–5.1	–6.2	–5.5	–5.0	–4.3	–2.9
14 General government gross debt[3] (end of period % of GDP)	—	53.6	55.3	71.2	60.4	66.1	68.1	571.2	73.2	72.9
15 Interest payment by general government (% of GDP)[1]	—	3.2	4.7	5.3	5.3	5.4	5.3	5.5	5.4	5.2
16 Money supply (end of year)[1,5]	12.6	12.8	10.2	5.1	5.5	6.6	2.4	4.5	5.2	—
17 Long-term interest rate (%)[3]	7.1	11.6	9.8	8.9	9.8	7.8	8.2	8.6	7.3	6.5
18 Profitability (1961–73 = 100)[4]	100.0	72.9	88.2	93.2	90.5	89.2	96.6	99.5	102.6	106.2

Source: European Economy, 1997[1]
[1] Including Federal Republic of Germany, unless otherwise stated.
[2] 1961–91: including West Germany.
[3] 1961–90: including West Germany.
[4] 1961–91: including West Germany.
[5] Broad money supply M2 or M3 according to country (M4 for UK).

continued overleaf

UK BUSINESS AND EUROLAND

Table 7.3   Economic indicators and the Maastricht Treaty convergence criteria (excluding the exchange rate criterion)

		HICP inflation[a]	Long-term interest rate[b]	General government surplus (+) or deficit (–)[c]	General government gross debt[c]
Belgium	1996	1.8	6.5	–3.2	126.9
	1997[d]	1.4	5.7	# –2.1	122.2
	1998[e]	—	—	# –1.7	118.1
Denmark	1996	2.1	7.2	# –0.7	70.6
	1997[d]	1.9	6.2	# 0.7	65.1
	1998[e]	—	—	# 1.1	# 59.5
Germany	1996	1.2	6.2	–3.4	60.4
	1997[d]	1.4	5.6	# –2.7	61.3
	1998[e]	—	—	# –2.5	61.2
Greece	1996	7.9	14.4	–7.5	111.6
	1997[d]	5.2	9.8	–4.0	108.7
	1998[e]	—	—	# –2.2	107.7
Spain	1996	3.6	8.7	–4.6	70.1
	1997[d]	1.8	6.3	# –2.6	68.8
	1998[e]	—	—	# –2.2	67.4
France	1996	2.1	6.3	–4.1	# 55.7
	1997[d]	** 1.2	** 5.5	# –3.0	# 58.0
	1998[e]	—	—	# –2.9	# 58.1
Ireland	1996	2.2	7.3	# –0.4	72.7
	1997[d]	*** 1.2	*** 6.2	# 0.9	66.3
	1998[e]	—	—	# 1.1	# 59.5
Italy	1996	4.0	9.4	–6.7	124.0
	1997[d]	1.8	6.7	# –2.7	121.6
	1998[e]	—	—	# –2.5	118.1
Luxembourg	1996	*** 1.2	*** 6.3	# 2.5	# 6.6
	1997[d]	1.4	5.6	# 1.7	# 6.7
	1998[e]	—	—	# 1.0	# 7.1
Netherlands	1996	1.4	6.2	# –2.3	77.2
	1997[d]	1.8	5.5	# –1.4	72.1
	1998[e]	—	—	# –1.6	70.0
Austria	1996	1.8	6.3	–4.0	69.5
	1997[d]	* 1.1	* 5.6	# –2.5	66.1
	1998[e]	—	—	# –2.3	64.7
Portugal	1996	2.9	8.6	–3.2	65.0
	1997[d]	1.8	6.2	# –2.5	62.0
	1998[e]	—	—	# –2.2	# 60.0
Finland	1996	** 1.1	** 7.1	–3.3	# 57.6
	1997[d]	1.3	5.9	# –0.9	# 55.8
	1998[e]	—	—	# 0.3	# 53.6
Sweden	1996	* 0.8	* 8.0	–3.5	76.7
	1997[d]	1.9	6.5	# –0.8	76.6
	1998[e]	—	—	# 0.5	74.1
UK	1996	2.5	7.9	–4.8	# 54.7
	1997[d]	1.8	7.0	# –1.9	# 53.4
	1998[e]	—	—	# –0.6	# 52.3

Source: european Commission, *Convergence Report*, 1998.
*, **, *** = first, second and third best performer in terms of price stability.
= general government deficit not exceeding 3% of GDP; general government gross debt not exceeding 60% of GDP.
(a) Annual percentage changes.
(b) In percentages.
(c) As a percentage of GDP.
(d) Data for HICP inflation and long-term interest rate refer to the twelve-month period ending January 1998; european Commission (spring 1998 forecasts) for general government surplus or deficit and general government gross debt.
(e) European Commission projections (spring 1998 forecasts) for general government surplus or deficit and general government gross debt.

☆ **For revision of this chapter, see the Chapter Summaries at the end of the book, starting on page 411.**

8 Inflation and unemployment

Objectives

After studying this chapter you will be able to:

- explain what is meant by inflation;
- discuss the costs of inflation;
- explain the causes of inflation;
- explain the relationship between inflation and unemployment;
- discuss possible policies to reduce inflation;
- discuss types and causes of unemployment;
- understand the implications of wage rigidities and inflationary expectations;
- understand the concept of a 'natural rate of unemployment';
- discuss possible measures to reduce unemployment.

WHERE ARE WE NOW?

As we said at the very beginning, macroeconomic theory helps us to find an answer to some fundamental questions related to the economy: what determines the economy's output and employment growth; what determines its rate of inflation and its external balance. But macroeconomic models differ. Keynesians argue that it is the level of aggregate demand that determines the level of output and employment. The monetarists take the opposite view and maintain that the economy's output is determined by supply conditions – the size of the labour force, the amount of capital and machinery, the state of technology – and that changes in demand only affect the price level, at least in the long run. Now that we have looked at money and interest rates, we are in a better position to begin to unravel this debate and to give a more comprehensive explanation of what determines not only the economy's output, but also its inflation and unemployment.

Until now we have ignored price rises. All we said was that, within the Keynesian model, an increase in aggregate demand would cause output and employment to increase, while prices would remain stable. However, this is a rather simplistic assumption which might apply only to a real economy with a great amount of spare capacity, in a situation of deep and prolonged recession.

In normal circumstances, when aggregate demand increases, prices are likely also to increase, in response to the increased demand pressure. When, for example, the demand for consumer durables increases and their supply is the same, their prices will increase and signal the need for some reallocation of resources into consumer durable production. By how much production will increase as a result of the increase in demand will depend on the elasticity of supply. The same applies to the economy as a whole, with the difference that the amount of resources available is given, at least in the short run: the increased demand for the economy's output is likely to cause prices and output to rise. How large and how permanent will the changes in price and output be? This is where opinions differ and disagreements develop. To simplify matters, we can identify four different points of view as to the effect of an increase in aggregate demand: extreme and moderate Keynesian, extreme and moderate monetarist.

- The *extreme Keynesians* argue that an increase in aggregate demand will cause output to grow, but prices will remain stable. Prices will increase only if the economy is already at its full employment level of output and cannot produce more.
- The *moderate Keynesians* argue that an increase in aggregate demand will cause both prices and output to rise.

■ The *moderate monetarists* argue that an increase in aggregate demand will cause prices to rise. Output will rise too, but only in the short run, before going back to its long-run level.

■ The *extreme monetarists* argue that an increase in aggregate demand causes only prices to rise, but has no effect on output whatsoever.

These differing views are summarized below:

Extreme Keynesians:
AD ↑→ $\overline{P}$, ↑, Y ↑ unless economy already at Y_f

Extreme monetarists
AD ↑→   P ↑, $\overline{Y}$ even in the short run

Moderate Keynesians
AD ↑→   P ↑, Y ↑

Moderate monetarists
AD ↑→   P ↑, Y↑ only in the short run

It is therefore time that we relaxed the assumption of price stability to examine what happens to output and employment when prices do change in response to changes in demand. This will lead us to a discussion of inflation and unemployment in these opposing analytical frameworks.

AGGREGATE DEMAND, AGGREGATE SUPPLY AND INFLATION

The Keynesian and monetarist view

The model of the economy put forward in the preceding chapters is also often referred to as 'extreme Keynesian', because it tends to describe relationships in the economy in a very simplified form, in stark contrast to the 'extreme monetarist' view. According to the extreme Keynesian model, as aggregate demand increases, so do output and employment, while prices remain stable, until the point is reached where all the productive resources of the economy are in full use (including full employment of labour) and a full employment level of output is being produced. When the economy has reached its full employment level of output, a further increase in aggregate demand would only cause prices to rise while output remains the same as it has already reached its feasible maximum in the short run. This situation is illustrated in Figure 8.1(a), (b).

The first important point that Figure 8.1 helps us to see is that the price level in the economy is determined by the interaction of **aggregate demand** (AD) and **aggregate supply** (AS), just like the price of any good.

Second, Figure. 8.1 helps us to reflect on the shape of the AD and AS curves.

✍ Activity 8.1

Explain what the aggregate demand (AD) curve shows and account for its shape

✓ Answer 8.1

The aggregate demand relation or AD curve shows the amount of total spending on the economy's output by households, firms, government (and foreigners in an open economy) at the various price levels. The AD curve slopes downwards, indicating that aggregate spending on the economy's output decreases as prices rise. This can be accounted for by the following reasons:

Figure 8.1   The simple Keynesian aggregate demand and aggregate supply model

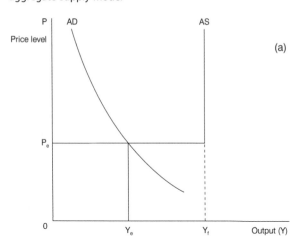

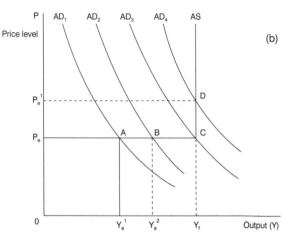

1 As prices rise, assuming that the quantity of money injected into the economy by the central bank and the banking system has not changed, people will need more money for their transactions, as goods and services now cost more. To obtain the extra liquidity people run down their cash balances and sell their bonds. This drives down the price of bonds, pushing up the interest rate. This in turn will discourage investment and consumer spending, reducing aggregate demand.

2 When prices rise, consumption tends to fall as saving rises for the following reason: inflation reduces the real value of people's savings, forcing them to save a higher proportion of their income to compensate for the reduction.

3 In an open economy, where foreign goods and services are available, if the domestic prices of goods increase more than their foreign substitutes, the demand for imports will increase and the demand for the country's exports will fall. The combined effects of increased imports and lower exports will reduce the demand for the economy's output.

For all these reasons, the AD curve slopes downward.

Aggregate supply is the total supply of goods and services in an economy. The aggregate supply curve (AS) shows the relationship between the aggregate quantity of output supplied by all firms in an economy and the overall price level; it shows the level of output which firms are willing to supply at each price level. The shape of the short-run supply curve is a source of great controversy in macroeconomics. Keynes believed that at very low level of aggregate output the AS is fairly flat (due to spare capacity of capital and unemployed labour), while at high levels of aggregate output, when the economy approaches its capacity or maximum output, the AS is vertical or nearly vertical. Anything that affects individual firms' decisions will also shift the AS curve, such as changes in costs, technological conditions or economic policies.

✍ Activity 8.2

Refer to Figure 8.1 again and explain the implications of the shape of the AS curve shown.

✓ Answer 8.2

In the extreme Keynesian model, the aggregate supply curve (AS) is horizontal up to the full employment level of output. In Figure 8.1(b), a rise in aggregate demand from AD_1 to AD_2 will only cause output to grow from Y_e^1 to Y_e^2, while prices remain stable: there is no effect on prices. When full employment is reached, a further increase in aggregate demand from AD_3 to AD_4 will

cause prices to rise to P_e^1. In the extreme Keynesian case we have a situation of demand-pull inflation only when the economy has reached full employment. The difference $P_e^1 - P_e$ measures the excess demand or inflationary gap; it measures by how much aggregate demand exceeds the full employment level of output.

A less extreme and more realistic way of characterizing the supply side of the economy, at least in the short run, is shown in Figure 8.2 where, the aggregate supply curve is upward sloping.

✍ Activity 8.3

How can one account for an upward-sloping supply curve?

✓ Answer 8.3

An upward-sloping supply curve indicates that firms are willing to produce more of all goods and services on aggregate, the higher the prices. This assumes that while product prices rise (the prices at which firms sell their products), firms' costs, in particular wages and intermediate, input product prices remain constant or at least do not rise as fast as final product prices. If this is the case, firms' profitability increases at each level of output if prices rise, which will induce them to produce more. The aggregate supply curve is upward sloping.

When aggregate supply is upward sloping, an increase in aggregate demand will cause output and prices to rise, reflecting the fact that more can be produced, as not all resources are being employed, but at higher prices. At lower levels of output firms will be

Figure 8.2 Moderate Keynesian view: an upward sloping supply curve

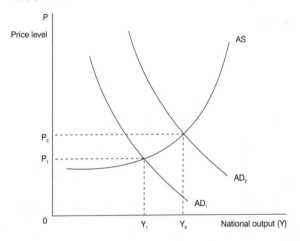

probably operating below capacity, they will typically have large stocks of raw materials and finished goods. They will be able to respond to an increase in demand by supplying more with little or no increase in price. In the short run, the aggregate supply response can be simply seen as the sum of the responses of all the individual firms. If there is generally plenty of spare capacity in the economy, a rise in aggregate demand will have a big effect on output and only a small effect on prices. As the economy approaches full employment of its resources, bottlenecks appear and shortages of labour and raw materials start to develop, which drive prices up. The nearer firms are to full capacity, the more costly it will be for them to expand output, the steeper the economy's aggregate supply curve will be (the higher the price level). Further increases in aggregate demand will have larger effects on prices and smaller effects on output.

According to the moderate monetarists, this situation would only apply to the short run. In the long run the aggregate supply is vertical. If this is the case, an increase in aggregate demand will have no effect on output and employment. It will simply lead to higher prices, that is, to inflation. In this scenario, controlling aggregate demand is indispensable in order to control inflation. Stimulating demand to raise output and employment is on the other hand useless, as it only injects inflation into the system. To stimulate output and employment other policies need to be used: namely supply-side policies, which can increase the productive capacity of the economic system by encouraging a more efficient use of the economy's resources. This is shown by a shift of the aggregate supply curve to the right in

Figure 8.3(a). According to the extreme monetarist position, often referred to as the new classical view (represented by economists such as Edward Prescott), the aggregate supply of the economy is also vertical in the short run. This means that the economy's output is given and cannot be altered in the short run by demand-side policies.

🖎 Activity 8.4

The moderate monetarists accept that an increase in aggregate demand may cause output and prices to increase in the short run (an upward-sloping AS curve), but maintain that in the long run an increase in aggregate demand only affects prices, leaving output unchanged (vertical AS curve). How do you account for their position? Explain your reasoning with the use of a diagram.

✓ Answer 8.4

As Figure 8.4(a) shows, the short-run aggregate supply curve is upward sloping. This shows that in the short run, assuming firms' costs and in particular wages do not change, firms will produce more at higher price levels, until full capacity is reached. The initial increase in aggregate demand is shown by a shift out of the AD curve from AD to AD^1. Firms respond by increasing their output from Y_1 to Y_2 ; this in turn requires an increased amount of inputs of labour, raw materials and intermediate goods. Eventually the prices of the factors of production will start to rise, in response to the increased demand by firms, and firms costs will go up. This will shift the AS curve to the left from AS to AS_1. In particular, trade unions and workers in general will

Figure 8.3 The monetarist model of aggregate demand and aggregate supply

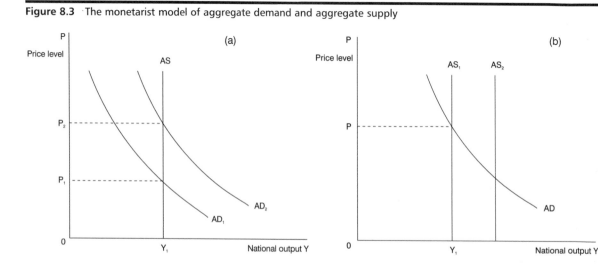

Figure 8.4 AS response to change in AD: (a) in the short run; (b) in the long run

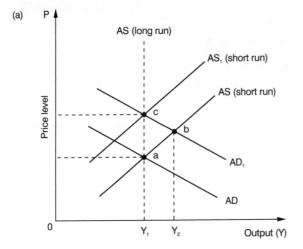

(a)

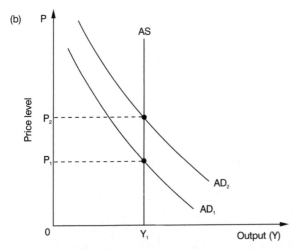

(b)

year period, output is determined by supply factors, by how much the capital stock of the country increases or the labour force expands and technology improves. While in the medium run, both demand and supply factors play a role in the determination of the economy's output.

The debate remains unsettled, but the aggregate demand and aggregate supply analysis developed above provides us with the essential framework to further our discussion of what causes inflation and unemployment. We are now in a position to appreciate that unemployment and inflation depend crucially not only on demand conditions, but also on the behaviour of supply (on the shape of the supply curve). If the aggregate supply (AS) is fairly inelastic (almost vertical), which means that firms' costs of labour and other inputs rise rapidly as a result of demand pressures, an increase in demand will mostly generate inflation. If, on the other hand, the aggregate supply (AS) is fairly elastic (the curve is almost horizontal), indicating the existence of spare capacity and unemployed labour and a slower cost adjustment to price increases, an increase in demand will mostly cause an increase in output and employment. The discussion of inflation and unemployment that follows focuses our analysis on the supply side of the economy, which we have ignored until now. But first we need to be clear about the following:

- the definition of inflation;
- how to measure inflation;
- the economic costs of inflation.

It is only when we come to discuss what causes inflation and, more so, how to cure inflation, that we will need to take into account the debate referred to above.

INFLATION: A DEFINITION

Not all price increases constitute inflation. In any economy prices are continually changing as markets adjust to changing demand and supply conditions. A severe drought may affect crops and push up prices of agricultural products; just as overpumping by oil producers may drive down the price of oil and of its derivative products. These are examples of once-and-for-all changes in the prices of some goods, which do not characterize a situation of inflation.

- **Inflation** is a sustained rise in the general level of prices; a generalized and persistent increase in the **price level**, i.e. in the price of all goods.
- The **rate of inflation** is the percentage change in the overall price level, not the price level itself; i.e.

demand wage increases which at least match the general price level increase, to restore the purchasing power of the nominal wages eroded by inflation. Eventually the cost increases shift the AS curve back by the full amount, pushing the economy towards its initial output level, but at a higher price level. Hence the conclusion that in the long run the aggregate supply curve is inelastic (vertical supply curve shown by Figure 8.4(b). The only permanent effect of an increase in aggregate demand is to increase the price level.

One could argue that both schools of thought are broadly correct, as each applies over a different time horizon. In the short run, from one year to the next, changes in output depend on changes in demand. But over a longer period of time, in the long run, say a ten-the rate at which the price level increases over time, expressed as a percentage.

■ A **negative inflation** is a decrease in the overall price level.

■ A **deflation** is a government policy aimed at reducing aggregate demand to reduce inflation.

■ **Price stability** is achieved when the average price level is stable and does not move up or down.

✍ Activity 8.5

Look at Table 8.1 and Figure 8.5 and explain what they show.

✓ Answer 8.5

The statistics provided in Figure 8.5 and Table 8.1 show that inflation has been a constant feature of post-

Figure 8.5 World inflation, 1964–95

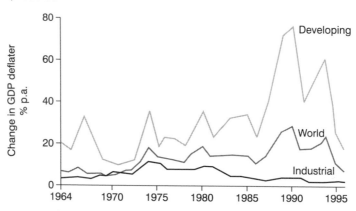

Source: *International Financial Statistics*, 1997

Table 8.1 World inflation rates, 1988–96

	World	Industrial countries	Developing countries	Africa			Asia		
				Kenya	Nigeria	S Africa	China	Singapore	India
1988	17.0	3.5	49.1	11.2	54.5	12.8	187.0	1.5	9.4
1989	14.2	4.6	31.2	12.9	50.5	14.7	18.3	2.3	6.2
1990	29.2	5.2	76.6	15.6	7.4	14.4	3.1	3.5	9.0
1991	18.0	4.4	42.1	19.8	13.0	15.3	3.5	3.4	13.9
1992	18.1	3.1	45.3	29.5	44.6	13.9	6.3	2.3	11.8
1993	19.6	2.8	50.9	45.8	57.2	9.7	14.6	2.3	6.4
1994	23.7	2.3	65.1	29.0	57.0	9.0	24.2	3.1	10.2
1995	11.6	2.5	26.8	0.8	72.8	8.6	16.9	1.7	10.2
1996	7.5	2.3	16.0	8.8	–	7.5	8.3	1.4	–

	Europe			Industrial countries			Western hemisphere		
	Poland	Cyprus	Russia	Greece	Japan	UK	Brazil	USA	Venezuela
1988	58.7	3.4		13.5	0.7	4.9	682.3	4.0	29.5
1989	244.6	3.8		13.7	2.3	7.8	1287.0	4.8	84.5
1990	555.4	4.5		20.4	3.1	9.5	2937.8	5.4	40.7
1991	76.7	5.0		19.5	3.3	5.9	440.9	4.2	34.2
1992	45.3	6.5		15.9	1.7	3.7	1008.7	3.0	31.4
1993	36.9	4.9	874.6	14.4	1.3	1.6	2148.4	3.0	38.1
1994	33.3	4.7	307.4	10.9	0.7	2.5	2668.5	2.6	60.8
1995	26.8	2.6	197.4	9.3	–0.1	3.4	84.4	2.8	59.9
1996	20.0	3.0	47.6	8.5	0.1	2.4	18.2	2.9	99.9

Source: *International Finance Statistics*, 1997

war developed and developing economies. In the industrialized world, the 1950s and 1960s were characterized by rather low rates of inflation (creeping inflation), not perceived as a problem by the governments of the day. It was not until after the accelerating inflation of the 1970s that inflation came to be regarded as a serious problem.

Table 8.1 further shows that while inflation has been brought under control in the industrialized world in the 1990s, with an average inflation rate of 2.3 per cent in 1996, the average inflation rate for the developing countries remains in double-digit figures, at 16 per cent on average in 1996.

Averages often conceal huge differences among countries. This is also the case for inflation, which has been rampant in some countries in recent years. Following the collapse of the communist regimes and the move towards market economies, several of the economies in transition of eastern Europe experienced severe inflation: price increases seemed to get out of hand in Poland, where the inflation rate reached 555 per cent in 1990, only to come down to 20 per cent in 1996. Russia also struggled to bring down its inflation rate from 874 per cent a year in 1993 to 47.6 per cent in 1996. Some Latin American countries are still suffering from **hyper-inflation**: Brazil, whose inflation rate was a staggering 2938 per cent in 1990 and an equally staggering 2669 per cent in 1994, appears to have performed a miracle, bringing the rate down to 18 per cent in 1996. The inflation rate in Argentina between 1985 and 1995 remained in treble figures, at 256 per cent a year on average, and in Peru, at nearly 399 per cent (World Development Report, 1997).

✍ Activity 8.6

Look at the inflation statistics shown in Table 8.2 and comment on what they show.

✓ Answer 8.6

Table 8.2 shows inflation rates in the EU countries from 1961 to 1997. Compared with some of the rates of price increases in Latin America and eastern Europe, the rates of inflation experienced in the EU make you wonder what the fuss is all about and whether inflation should still be regarded – as indeed it is – as a problem at all, let alone as a 'public enemy number one'. If we take a look at the whole period, from 1961, we see that from an annual inflation rate of 4.4 per cent on average experienced in the EU in the decade from 1961 to 1970, after the inflationary 1970s and 1980s, when inflation reached 9.6 per cent and 7.7 per cent on average, inflation in the

EU is now down to an historic low, at 1.9 per cent on average in 1997. However, inflation rates have varied somewhat among EU member countries over the period.

In Britain, prices were fairly stable during the nineteenth century and until World War I, when they rose sharply, to fall back down again after the war. Since the 1930s prices have been rising, but not at a constant rate. As Table 8.2 shows, between 1973 and 1982, partly due to the oil price shocks of 1973 and 1979, the increase was exceptionally high, reaching 26.3 per cent in 1975.

MEASUREMENTS OF INFLATION

The average level of prices is called the price level. The price level is measured by a price index. A price index measures the average level of prices in one period as a percentage of their average level in an earlier period, called the base period. Price indexes are used to measure the overall price level. The most common price indexes are the retail price index (often referred to as the consumer price index) and the GDP deflator.

Retail price index (RPI)

This index measures the average level of prices of the goods and services that a typical household consumes in a year. The RPI represents the average level of consumer goods prices expressed as an index.

How is the RPI calculated?

In the UK, the RPI is calculated by the Office for National Statistics, which publishes it every month. To calculate the RPI, the ONS does the following:

- First it selects a base year, which serves as a benchmark. The base year currently used in the calculation of RPI in the UK is 1987.
- Second, a representative sample of household expenditure is selected, to form an average basket of goods, where each item is given a weight which reflects its share or relative importance in the average family budget. Over 3000 households, 350 products and 200 locations are surveyed to gather the necessary data.
- Once the data have been gathered, the RPI is calculated by valuing the basket of goods and services at the current month's prices.
- That value is then expressed as a percentage of the value of the same basket in the base period.

Table 8.2   EU inflation rates, 1961–97: price deflator GDP at market prices

(national currency: annual percentage change)

Year	B	DK	D¹	EL	E	F	IRL	I	L	NL	Year	A	P	FIN	S	UK	EUR 15¹	US	JP
1961	1.2	4.7	4.7	1.5	1.8	3.4	2.5	2.8	-3.7	2.4	1961	5.4	2.3	5.3	3.0	2.7	3.3	0.9	7.8
1962	1.6	6.6	3.9	4.6	5.7	4.7	4.9	5.8	3.9	3.5	1962	3.8	-0.2	4.0	3.0	4.0	4.4	2.2	4.2
1963	3.0	5.8	3.1	1.4	8.5	6.4	2.7	8.5	3.1	4.7	1963	3.6	2.5	5.1	4.1	2.1	4.7	1.4	5.5
1964	4.6	4.6	3.0	3.7	6.3	4.1	9.7	6.5	5.8	8.7	1964	3.3	1.1	7.2	2.9	3.7	4.5	1.7	5.3
1965	5.2	7.4	3.7	4.0	9.2	2.7	4.5	4.2	2.8	6.1	1965	5.7	3.8	5.0	4.4	5.1	4.6	2.6	5.1
1966	4.2	6.8	3.4	4.9	8.2	2.9	4.4	2.2	3.9	6.0	1966	3.1	5.5	4.7	6.0	4.5	4.1	3.3	5.0
1967	3.1	6.3	1.6	1.7	8.5	3.2	3.2	2.8	0.4	4.2	1967	3.2	3.4	7.4	6.6	2.9	3.3	2.8	5.5
1968	2.7	7.0	2.3	3.4	5.9	4.2	4.2	1.7	5.0	4.2	1968	2.8	1.4	2.1	5.0	4.1	3.5	5.0	4.9
1969	4.0	7.0	4.2	3.9	5.1	6.6	9.1	4.1	5.3	6.4	1969	2.7	6.1	4.2	2.4	5.4	5.0	5.2	4.4
1970	4.6	8.3	7.7	3.1	5.9	5.6	9.7	6.9	15.1	6.1	1970	4.7	3.4	3.8	3.4	7.4	6.6	5.5	6.5
1961–70	3.4	6.4	3.8	3.2	6.5	4.4	5.5	4.5	4.1	5.2	1961–70	3.8	2.9	5.9	4.3	4.2	4.4	3.0	5.4
1971	5.7	7.7	7.7	5.0	7.8	6.3	10.5	6.7	-0.8	8.1	1971	6.2	5.1	7.6	7.1	9.4	7.4	5.6	5.4
1972	6.2	9.2	5.3		8.5	7.0	13.4	6.1	5.8	9.3	1972	7.6	7.8	8.4	7.0	8.1	7.0	5.0	5.1
1973	7.2	10.7	6.4	19.4	11.8	8.5	15.3	13.7	12.2	9.1	1973	8.0	9.4	14.1	7.0	7.6	9.3	6.4	5.6
1974	12.6	13.1	7.1	20.9	16.0	11.8	6.1	20.6	17.0	9.0	1974	9.5	18.9	22.5	9.5	14.6	13.2	8.9	12.7
1975	12.2	12.4	5.7	12.3	16.8	13.0	20.1	16.1	-0.9	10.2	1975	6.5	16.2	13.3	9.5	26.3	14.3	9.8	20.8
1976	7.6	9.1	3.6	15.4	16.5	11.1	21.0	18.3	12.2	8.8	1976	5.6	16.3	13.5	14.5	15.8	11.8	6.4	7.2
1977	7.5	9.4	3.7	13.0	23.4	9.3	13.3	18.4	1.2	6.6	1977	5.1	26.5	9.9	11.9	14.1	11.6	6.7	8.0
1978	4.5	9.9	4.3	12.9	20.6	10.1	10.7	13.8	5.1	5.3	1978	5.7	22.3	8.4	10.5	11.5	10.2	7.7	6.7
1979	4.6	7.6	3.8	18.6	16.9	10.1	13.8	16.1	6.4	4.1	1979	4.1	19.4	8.8	9.5	14.5	10.6	8.8	4.6
1980	3.9	8.2	5.0	17.7	13.4	11.4	14.8	20.9	7.9	5.5	1980	5.2	20.9	9.7	7.9	18.8	12.6	9.4	2.8
1971–80	7.2	9.7	5.2	13.7	15.1	9.8	13.8	15.0	6.5	7.6	1971–80	6.3	16.1	11.5	9.6	13.9	10.8	7.5	7.8
1981	5.5	10.1	4.2	19.8	12.6	11.4	17.5	19.1	7.2	5.4	1981	6.5	17.6	11.1	9.5	11.4	10.9	9.7	4.1
1982	6.9	10.6	4.4	25.1	13.9	11.7	15.2	17.0	10.8	5.4	1982	6.2	20.7	8.9	8.3	7.8	10.3	6.1	1.8
1983	5.9	7.6	3.2	19.1	11.8	9.7	10.8	15.1	6.8	2.1	1983	3.9	24.6	8.6	10.1	5.3	8.5	3.9	1.8
1984	5.2	5.7	2.1	20.3	11.6	7.5	6.4	11.6	4.4	1.4	1984	4.6	24.7	8.9	7.6	4.4	6.9	4.0	2.6
1985	6.1	4.3	2.1	17.7	7.7	5.8	5.3	9.0	3.0	1.8	1985	3.1	21.7	5.3	5.9	5.9	5.9	3.5	2.1
1986	3.6	4.6	3.2	17.5	7.7	5.2	5.8	7.8	2.8	0.1	1986	2.7	20.5	4.6	6.6	3.2	5.5	2.5	1.7
1987	2.2	4.7	1.9	14.3	5.8	3.0	2.2	6.1	0.9	-0.7	1987	2.1	10.1	4.7	6.9	5.0	4.1	3.1	0.1
1988	1.8	3.4	1.5	15.6	5.7	2.8	3.4	6.8	0.7	1.2	1988	1.6	11.8	7.0	4.8	6.1	4.4	3.9	0.7
1989	4.6	4.2	2.4	14.4	7.1	3.0	5.4	6.3	3.5	1.2	1989	2.7	12.2	6.1	6.5	7.1	5.0	4.4	2.0
1990	2.9	2.7	2.8	20.6	7.3	3.1	-0.8	7.6	3.4	2.3	1990	3.5	12.4	5.8	8.8	6.4	5.3	4.2	2.3
1981–90	4.5	5.8	2.9	18.4	6.9	6.3	7.0	10.6	4.3	2.0	1981–90	3.7	17.5	7.1	7.7	6.2	6.7	4.5	1.9
1991	3.1	2.2	3.9	19.9	7.1	3.3	1.8	7.7	1.5	2.7	1991	3.8	12.1	2.5	7.6	6.6	5.5	3.5	2.7
1992	3.6	3.2	4.4	14.5	6.9	2.1	2.1	4.7	4.3	2.3	1992	4.3	10.6	0.7	1.0	4.6	4.3	2.4	1.7
1993	3.8	0.6	3.1	12.7	4.3	2.5	4.3	4.4	0.7	1.9	1993	2.6	6.0	2.4	2.6	3.1	3.4	2.0	0.6
1994	2.5	1.6	2.0	10.1	4.0	1.5	1.1	3.5	5.3	2.0	1994	2.9	5.2	1.3	2.5	1.8	2.5	2.1	0.3
1992	3.6	3.2	5.5	14.5	6.9	2.1	2.1	4.7	4.3	2.3	1992	4.3	10.6	0.7	1.0	4.6	4.5	2.4	1.7
1993	3.8	0.6	3.9	12.7	4.3	2.5	4.3	4.4	0.7	1.9	1993	2.6	6.0	2.4	2.6	3.1	3.6	2.0	0.6
1994	2.5	1.6	2.2	10.1	4.0	1.5	1.1	3.5	5.3	2.0	1994	2.9	5.2	1.3	2.5	1.8	2.6	2.1	0.3
1995	1.4	1.8	2.2	9.3	4.9	1.7	0.5	5.0	1.0	1.4	1995	1.9	5.1	2.2	3.7	2.3	2.9	2.5	-0.5
1996	1.9	1.9	1.0	8.9	4.4	1.6	0.8	5.1	2.6	1.4	1996	1.7	3.3	1.0	0.9	3.1	2.6	1.9	0.2
1997	1.7	2.4	1.2	6.7	1.1	1.4	1.5	2.9	1.2	1.9	1997	1.6	3.1	0.7	2.2	2.7	1.9	1.9	0.9

Source: European Economy, 1997

¹1961–94: WD

¹ 1961–94: including WD; 1992–97: including D.

- The annual change in the RPI index is then used as a measure of the rate of inflation:

Inflation rate $= \dfrac{\text{current year's RPI} - \text{last year's RPI}}{\text{last year's RPI}} \times 100.$

It is easier to understand how the RPI is calculated, if we work through a simplified example, summarized in Table 8.1. Let's assume that the average family only consumes two goods and one service: potatoes, milk and bus rides. The household members consume 10 kg of potatoes and 20 pints of milk in the time period, say a year, and travel by bus 50 times. This is our representative fixed basket of goods. In the **base year** – the year in which we choose to start recording the prices of our basket of goods – potatoes cost £0.50 kg, a pint of milk costs £0.80 and a bus ticket costs £0.50. Let's assume that we choose 1987 as our base year. The total expenditure of the average family on the basket of goods in 1987, the base year, is £46. Let's imagine that we are now in 1999 and that our average family is still consuming 10 kg of potatoes, 20 pints of milk and 50 bus rides. The prices have gone up and potatoes now cost £1 per kg, a pint of milk costs £0.90 and a bus ride costs £0.60. Total expenditure on the same basket of goods is now £58.

It is obvious that the prices have gone up, but by how much? The easiest way to calculate this is to express the value of the basket (total expenditure) in 1999 as a percentage of the base year value of the basket. The RPI is the ratio of the current period's value of the basket to the base period's value of the basket, multiplied by 100. In our example, it is equal to £58 (value of the basket of goods in 1999) divided by £46 (basket value in 1987) multiplied by 100, which is equal to 126. The RPI for the base year is always equal to 100, as in the base year the basket value at current prices (1987 prices) is the same as the basket value at base year prices. We can now compare the RPI in 1999, which is 126, with the RPI in 1987, the base year, which is 100 and can easily calculate that prices have increased by 26 per cent over the twelve-year period.

The RPIX

A new index of average prices, known as the **RPIX**, has been introduced in the UK in recent years. The RPIX does not include mortgage interest repayments in the typical household basket of goods and services because their inclusion distorted figures for the underlying inflation. If mortgage interest repayments were included, an anti-inflationary government policy which raised interest rates would in fact increase inflation. Other indexes, excluding mortgage interest payments and indirect taxes (RPIY) or including all items except housing, are also used. The retail price index commonly used in Britain at present is the RPIX.

✍ Activity 8.7

Using the RPI statistics provided in Table 8.4, calculate the UK rate of inflation over 10 years, since 1987, and the annual rate of inflation in 1997. Repeat the exercise using the RPIX figures below and comment on your results.

✓ Answer 8.7

In 1987, the RPI was 100, so it is easy to see that inflation in 10 years was 57.5 per cent, as the index rose from 100 in 1987 to 157.5 in 1997. The annual rate of inflation (from 1996 to 1997) in 1997 is 3.1 per cent and is calculated using the formula below:

Inflation rate $=$

$\dfrac{\text{current year index} - \text{previous year index}}{\text{previous year index}} \times 100$

Table 8.3 How the RPI is calculated: an example

| Basket chosen in base year | Base Year | | Current Year | |
	Price	Expenditure	Price	Expenditure
10 kg potatoes	£0.50/kg	£5	£1/kg	£10
20 pints of milk	£0.80 each pt	£16	£0.90 pt	£18
50 bus rides	£0.50 each	£25	£0.60 each	£30
Total expenditure		£46		£58
Retail price index (RPI)	$\frac{£46}{£46} \times 100 = 100$		$\frac{£58}{£46} \times 100 = 126$	

Table 8.4   RPI and PRIX in the UK

Years	All items RPI (Jan 1987 = 100)	RPIX (Jan 1987 = 100)
1987	100	100
1989	115.2	
1990	126.1	
1991	133.5	
1992	138.5	
1993	140.7	140.5
1994	144.1	143.8
1995	149.1	147.9
1996	152.7	152.3
1997	157.5	156.5

Source: ONS, *Economic Trends*, 1998

In our example:

$$\text{Inflation rate} = \frac{157.5-152.7}{152.7} \times 100 = 3.1\%$$

Using RPI figures, the rate of inflation over the ten-year period, since 1987, was 57.5 per cent while using RPIX figures it was 56.5 per cent. The percentage change on a year earlier in 1997 was 3.1 per cent using RPI figures and 2.8 per cent using RPIX figures. The use of the RPIX tends to lower inflation statistics.

Harmonized Indices of Consumer Prices (HICPs)

The RPI and the RPIX used in the UK, like many other indices used throughout the European Community, cannot be used within the EU for the purpose of comparison. The Maastricht Treaty set out the criteria for the Economic and Monetary Union (EMU) of the European Union countries. Countries which become members of the EMU are required to have a high degree of economic convergence, as measured by the four criteria discussed in Chapter 7: price stability, limits to the governments' deficit and debt, interest rate convergence and limits to exchange rate fluctuations.

The price stability criterion states that a country must have an average annual rate of inflation which does not exceed by more than one and a half percentage points that of, at most, the three best performing member states. The Maastricht Treaty article also states that price stability should be measured by means of consumer price indices produced on a comparable basis, taking into account differences in national definitions.

HICPs have been developed for the purpose of international comparison of inflation within the EU and to construct an inflation index for the whole of the European Union. The HICPs are used by member states' central banks and by the European Central Bank.

Relationship between HICPs and national CPIs

HICPs are expressly designed for international comparisons of inflation within Europe and are not intended to replace national CPIs. EU member states are likely to continue to produce their existing CPIs for domestic purposes, and this is certainly true for the UK. In the UK, the RPIX remains the main measure of the impact of price changes on consumers and continues to be used for monitoring economic policy, indexation of contracts and social security benefits and wage bargaining.

The first set of HICPs was published by Eurostat in March 1997 and continues to be published on a monthly basis. The figures are for each of the 15 member states, together with those for Norway and Iceland. Indices for the EU and the European economic area (EU plus Norway and Iceland, but not Switzerland) are also calculated.

🖉 Activity 8.8

Look at Figure 8.6 and Tables 8.5 and 8.6 and explain what they show.

Figure 8.6   HICPs for EU countries, December 1997

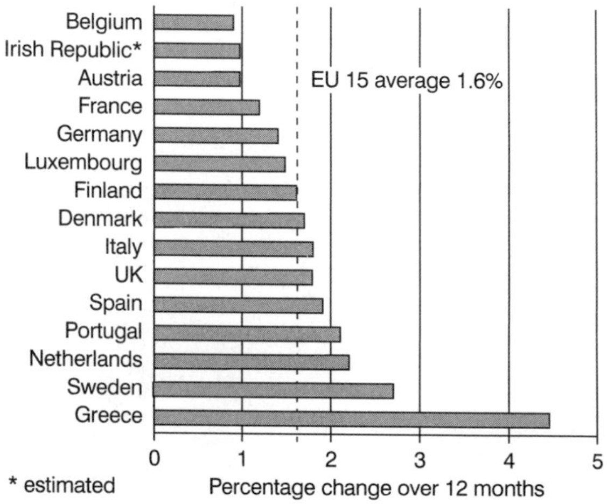

* estimated   Percentage change over 12 months

Source: ONS, *Economic Trends*, 1998

Table 8.5 HICP index levels, 1996 = 100

	UK	Austria	Belgium	Denmark	Finland	France	Germany	Greece	Irish Republic	Italy	Luxembourg	Netherlands	Portugal	Spain	Sweden	EU 15 average
1995	97.6	98.3	98.3	98.1	98.9	96.0	98.8	92.7	97.0	96.2	98.8	98.6	97.2	96.6	99.2	97.7
1996	100.0	100.0	100.0	100.0	100.0	100.0	100.0	100.0	100.0	100.0	100.0	100.0	100.0	100.0	100.0	100.0
1997	101.8	101.2	101.5	102.0	101.2	101.3	101.5	105.4	101.2	101.9	101.4	101.9	101.0	101.9	101.9	101.7

Source: Eurostat, 1998

Table 8.6 HICP percentage change over 12 months

	UK	Austria	Belgium	Denmark	Finland	France	Germany	Greece	Irish Republic	Italy	Luxembourg	Netherlands	Portugal	Spain	Sweden	EU 15 average
1996	2.5	1.8	1.8	1.9	1.1	2.1	1.2	7.9	2.2	4.0	1.2	1.4	2.9	3.6	0.8	2.5
1997	1.8	1.2	1.5	2.0	1.2	1.3	1.5	5.4	1.2	1.9	1.4	1.9	1.9	1.9	1.9	1.7

Source: Eurostat, 1998

Table 8.7 National accounts aggregates, 1993–7

Annual	£ million At current prices		Index numbers (1990 = 100) Implied gross domestic product deflator	
	Gross domestic product at market prices	Gross domestic product at factor cost	At market prices	At factor cost
1993	631 003	547 870	115.0	114.9
1994	669 069	580 135	116.9	116.4
1995	704 156	608 090	119.8	118.8
1996	741 751	642 765	123.3	122.4
1997	787 868	679 081	126.6	125.3

Source: ONS, *Economic Trends*, 1998

✓ Answer 8.8

Figure 8.6 shows the 12-month inflation rates for each EU country at December 1997, while Tables 8.5 and 8.6 show the inflation rates since the start of 1995, which have been derived retrospectively since regulations did not require the production of HICPs prior to 1996. The average inflation rate for the EU at December 1997 was 1.6 per cent

✎ Activity 8.9

Look at Figure 8.7 and comment on what it shows.

✓ Answer 8.9

Figure 8.7 shows a comparison of the UK inflation rate over 12 months in 1997 measured using the two indices, RPIX and HICP. The UK HICP consistently records a lower rate of inflation than the RPIX (which in turn produces inflation statistics which are lower than the RPI). On average, during 1997 the annual rate of inflation for the HICP was 0.9 percentage points lower

GDP deflator index

The GDP deflator measures changes in the level of prices of all the goods and services produced, including capital goods. As such, it is a more comprehensive measure of inflation than the RPI, which only includes some, but not all, prices of consumption goods. The GDP deflators are calculated in a rather different way from the RPI.

As already explained in Chapter 2, if we compare nominal (at current prices) GDP figures for 1997 and 1996 to calculate the rate of change of the economy's output, we cannot say whether the greater value of GDP in 1997 – say approximately an increase of 6 per cent – represents a real 6 per cent growth in the volume of goods and services produced in 1997 or merely an increase in the level of prices by 6 per cent. It is possible that prices rose by, say, 4 per cent and volume rose by 2 per cent, or perhaps prices rose by more than 6 per cent and actual volume fell.

To be able to say by how much the real volume of output has changed, we need to work out what the GDP would be each year using a common set of prices (base year prices). Statisticians do this for us and publish two sets of data, which we looked at in Chapter 2: GDP at current prices (nominal GDP) and GDP at constant or base year prices (real GDP).

Using these two sets of values, GDP at current and at constant prices, it is then easy to work out the GDP deflator index for each year by dividing nominal GDP by real GDP and multiplying the result by 100. The GDP deflator for the base year (1990) is always 100, as for the base year nominal GDP and real GDP are the same (remember, real GDP is GDP at base year prices, but for the base year, base year prices and current prices are the same).

Equally, if we know the nominal value for GDP in a year, say 1997, and the GDP deflator index for that year, we can easily calculate the real GDP by dividing the nominal GDP figure by the GDP deflator and multiplying the result by 100.

✎ Activity 8.10

(a) Use the statistics provided by Table 8.7 to calculate real GDP in 1997.
(b) Compare nominal and real rate of growth of GDP between 1996 and 1997.
(c) Calculate the rate of inflation between 1990 and 1997.
(d) Calculate the annual rate of inflation in 1997.

✓ Answer 8.10

(a) Real GDP is calculated as follows:

$$\text{real GDP} = \frac{\text{nominal GDP}}{\text{GDP deflator}} \times 100.$$

Real GDP in 1997, calculated at market prices using the formula above, is £mn 622,300:

$$\frac{787\,868}{126.6} \times 100 = 622\,300.$$

(b) Nominal rate of growth of GDP between 1996 and 1997 is calculated as follows:

$$\left(\frac{787\,868 - 741\,751}{741\,751}\right) \times 100 = 6.2\%.$$

Figure 8.7   RPIX and HICP inflation rates

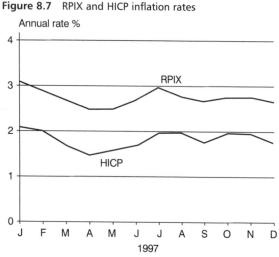

Annual rate %

Source: ONS, *Economic Trends*, 1998

To calculate the rate of growth of real GDP we first need to calculate real GDP in 1996 and 1997. We have already calculated real GDP in our answer (a), so we only need to calculate real GDP in 1996, as follows:

$$\left(\frac{741\ 751}{123.3}\right) \times 100 = \text{£mn } 601\ 500.$$

Real rate of growth of GDP can now be calculated as follows:

$$\left(\frac{622\ 300 - 601\ 500}{601\ 500}\right) \times 100 = 3.4\%.$$

The nominal rate of growth of GDP between 1996 and 1997 was 6.2 per cent, while the real rate of growth was 3.4 per cent. This implies that prices rose by 2.8 per cent. Let's see if this is true by calculating the rate of inflation using GDP deflators (d).

(c) The value of the GDP deflator index was 100 in 1990 and 126.6 in 1997. This implies a rate of inflation of 26.6 per cent over the period.

(d) The rate of inflation between 1996 and 1997 is calculated as follows:

$$\left(\frac{\text{GDP deflator}_{1997} - \text{GDP deflator}_{1996}}{\text{GDP deflator}_{1996}}\right) \times 100.$$

The rate of inflation in 1997 is then calculated as:

$$\left(\frac{126.6 - 123.3}{123.3}\right) \times 100 = 2.7\%.$$

There are other measures of inflation currently in use. These include:

- wholesale price index, which measures changes in prices at factory gates. It is a good indicator of future changes in the retail prices of most goods.
- average earnings or wage rate, expressed as an index, give a measure of changes in income. Used in conjunction with retail price indexes, they give an indication of real income changes for those in employment. For example, a nominal wage rate increase of 6 per cent represents a real increase of only 2 per cent if we know that the inflation rate over the same period, measured by the change in the RPI, was 4 per cent.

EFFECTS OF INFLATION

Inflation statistics show that inflation has come down quite consistently in the industrialized countries throughout the 1980s and 1990s. Yet the fight against inflation remains the main policy objective of most governments.

Is inflation really a problem? Should inflation still be regarded as 'public enemy number one'? What are the costs of inflation?

Activity 8.11

Try and answer these questions before you read on.

✓ Answer 8.11

When asked those questions, most people answer by saying that inflation is a problem because goods cost more and people cannot afford them. This is a good example of a wrong answer which is trying to convey something of value. The idea which this answer is correctly trying to convey is that inflation is a problem because money loses its value. When there is inflation, and prices rise, the same amount of money buys fewer goods, it is like saying that 'money has lost value'. What this answer fails to explain is that this is a problem if the loss of value of money is not anticipated and generalized. If prices increase by 10 per cent, but wages and rents and all sources of income also increase by 10 per cent, people's real income will remain the same. In a situation of **pure inflation** where all prices and wages increase proportionately, inflation would not be such a big problem. People would still need to be aware of inflation in making decisions, but inflation control would not be the major goal of macroeconomic policy.

Inflation is a problem precisely because not all prices and wages go up proportionately during periods of inflation. Inflation affects income distribution. Whether people gain or lose during a period of inflation really depends on whether their incomes rise faster or slower than the prices of the things they buy; whether people were expecting inflation and able to anticipate it fully in their wage or payment claims; or whether people were not expecting it and caught unprepared and unable fully to protect their income by ensuring that it increases proportionately. In other words, what matters is:

- whether inflation is anticipated or unanticipated;
- whether people, having correctly anticipated it, are able fully to protect their incomes from it.

Any discussion of the costs of inflation must therefore distinguish between the costs of anticipated or unanticipated inflation. An example may help to illustrate this point.

Costs of unanticipated inflation

Unanticipated inflation brings about unwanted, unplanned redistribution of income.

Pensioners lose out

People on fixed incomes such as pensioners with pensions which are not index linked, (i.e., do not rise in line with inflation), lose out during inflation. If the money value of their pensions is fixed and prices rise, pensioners will be able to buy fewer goods than before. Many pension plans nowadays are indexed to inflation. The payments they provide rise automatically in line with inflation. If prices rise by 5 per cent, benefits automatically rise by 5 per cent. Social security payments, which are the main source of income for the elderly, are fully indexed. But not all welfare payments are indexed and if the payments do not keep pace with inflation, the poorer section of the population loses out.

Debtors gain and creditors lose out

Suppose you lend me £100 to be paid back in a year with a 10 per cent interest. At the end of the year I pay you £110, which is the money you lent me plus £10, which is 10 per cent interest on the loan.

🖎 Activity 8.12

Suppose that prices suddenly increase by 10 per cent over the year. Who stands to gain?

✓ Answer 8.12

With the £110 you get back, you buy exactly the same amount of goods you could buy with £100 a year ago. In real terms, in terms of what you can actually buy with the money, you have not gained anything, while I have borrowed your money without paying any real interest. I do not have to forego an extra £10 worth of consumption to pay for the interest I owe you, as £110 buys exactly the same amount of goods that £100 bought a year ago.

🖎 Activity 8.13

People learn from inflation. Let's suppose you do too. I borrowed from you last year and I come back to you again, wanting to borrow £100 again this year. You have now learnt to expect a rate of inflation of 10 per cent. What do you do?

✓ Answer 8.13

You are prepared to lend me the money if I agree to pay you £120 at the end of the year. This represents an interest rate of 20 per cent, which is high enough to cover the decrease in value of your money, due to the anticipated inflation of 10 per cent and interest on the loan.

The difference between the interest rate you charge me (20 per cent) and the rate of inflation (10 per cent) is what economists call the real interest rate – in this case 10 per cent. So despite the fact that you are a creditor, you do not suffer from inflation this time because you correctly anticipated it. If, however, inflation turns out to be 25 per cent and not the expected 10 per cent, then again as a creditor you are hurt as the payment of £120 you receive after a year is worth less in real terms than the money you lent in the first place. You got a negative rate of return of 5 per cent. Unanticipated inflation causes an unwanted redistribution of income from creditors to debtors.

Employers gain and employees lose out

Exactly the same applies to employees that agree to work for a given wage over a given period of time, say a year or three years. During that time their wages remain fixed. If during that time the economy experiences inflation and prices increase, the purchasing power of wages falls: workers can buy fewer goods with the same amount of money. They lose out. Employees and trade unions also learn from inflation. When the time comes to renegotiate their contracts, they will take into account the rate of inflation which they expect the economy to suffer during the period of their contract and ask for an increase in wages at least equal to the expected rate of inflation.

🖎 Activity 8.14

If employees expect a rate of inflation of 5 per cent and want a real increase in their wage rate of 4 per cent, which rate of increase should they ask for?

✓ Answer 8.14

They should ask for a 9 per cent increase.

If inflation turns out to be higher than anticipated, wages will have been set too low. There will be a redistribution of income from employees to employers: employers get the higher prices for the products, as their prices go up with inflation, but workers can buy fewer goods with their wages. When nurses in Britain in the early 1990s were resisting a pay increase of 1.5 per cent, at a time when the inflation rate was 3 per cent, they were in fact being asked to take a wage cut of 1.5 per cent. No wonder they were unhappy with the pay offer. If inflation turns out to be lower than expected, wages will have been set higher than intended and firms' profits will be squeezed, as they get lower prices than expected for the products they produce.

Government revenues increase and taxpayers lose out

Inflation leads to distortions, as some prices lag behind others. Taxation may exacerbate such distortions.

Inflation pushes people into higher and higher income brackets as their **nominal incomes** increase, despite the fact that due to inflation their **real incomes**, the purchasing power has decreased. If tax brackets are not **index linked** and automatically adjusted for inflation, inflation leads to what is known as **fiscal drag**.

Costs of anticipated inflation

When inflation is correctly anticipated, it does not cause unwanted redistribution of income, as we have just seen. Inflation still has serious consequences for the individual and the economy as a whole.

Shoe-leather costs

Holding money, whether in your wallet or in a current account which pays no interest, becomes costly when there is inflation. People tend to keep as much money as possible in deposit accounts which earn an interest, without great loss of liquidity.

To have to reduce the amount of money we hold as cash is not easy and it is also inconvenient. We have to make more frequent trips to the bank, more telephone calls to transfer money, put up with greater delays in payments, etc. As a result, people will spend time and wear out their shoes going to and from the bank to minimize their cash holding in order to keep as much money as possible in financial assets that earn an interest.

✍ Activity 8.15

Suppose you have saved £500 and kept it in an envelope under your mattress. Suppose further that the rate of inflation is 10 per cent. How much are your savings worth after a year?

✓ Answer 8.15

They will be worth only £450, as prices have increased by 10 per cent over the period and £500 only buys £450 worth of goods.

✍ Activity 8.16

If the rate of inflation is 5 per cent and the **nominal interest rate** you are given on your deposit account is 6 per cent, what is the real interest rate you receive? What would it be if the interest rate were 4 per cent?

✓ Answer 8.16

The **real interest rate** would be 1 per cent in the first case (6 – 5 per cent) and –1 per cent in the second case (4 – 5 per cent). In the second case, you would be receiving a negative real interest rate, as the nominal interest the bank pays you does not entirely cover the loss of value of money due to inflation.

Menu costs

If prices increase all the time, price lists, price labels and menus have to be constantly changed. This imposes a cost on society. It also creates uncertainty and instability and is unpleasant. We would much prefer stable prices, so that we could make financial plans with greater certainty.

Menu costs and shoe-leather costs are, however, relatively minor compared to the costs that inflation imposes on the economy: on output and employment and, in particular, on the export sector, which comprises domestic firms producing goods for markets abroad.

Changes in relative prices of imports and exports

If the inflation rate in our domestic economy is higher than in other countries with which we trade, and if the value of our currency in terms of other foreign currencies is fixed (we call this a situation of **fixed exchange rates**), we will soon experience a **balance of trade deficit**, as our imports will rise and our exports will fall. With prices rising faster at home than abroad, foreign goods will become more competitively priced and more attractive to us, just as foreigners will find our goods less competitively priced and will buy fewer of them as a result.

✍ Activity 8.17

Bringing forward what we will in fact explain in Chapter 10, see if you can describe what will happen, as a result of this situation.

✓ Answer 8.17

In a regime of flexible exchange rates, domestic inflation will cause a depreciation of our currency. A weaker currency will compensate for the domestic price increase, restoring the competitiveness of domestic goods on foreign markets. A depreciating currency, on the other hand, by making imports of raw materials and partly finished goods more expensive and pushing up firms' costs, might further fuel domestic inflation. In a regime of fixed exchange rates, a balance of trade deficit would cause the Bank of England to intervene on the foreign exchange market, running down its reserves of foreign currency. Because reserves are not unlimited, this situation of trade deficit would have to be redressed by deflationary fiscal and/or monetary policies, which would slow down the economy and increase unemployment.

Changes in relative interest rates

Inflation pushes up the domestic rate of interest, as nominal interest rates will have to be higher than the rate of inflation to ensure positive real rates of interest and attract lenders' funds. Higher rates in turn will attract an inflow of foreign capital, which in a regime of flexible exchange rates will cause an appreciation of the exchange rate. However, a stronger pound will adversely affect the export sector and ultimately have a negative impact on output, the structure of the economy and employment.

Changes in output and employment

Inflation ultimately affects the level of output and employment. In what way exactly and whether the effect is only short lived or long lasting is the subject of intense debate. We shall develop this point further when we discuss the Phillips Curve later in the chapter.

Reviewing the arguments

Let's pause for a moment and reflect on the relative significance of the costs of inflation discussed above. Among the costs of inflation we mentioned: shoe-leather and menu costs, redistribution of income effects, instability and uncertainty which reduce investment, reduction of international competitiveness. In relation to those points, one could argue that:

- Shoe-leather and menu costs may only be significant when inflation reaches very high levels.
- Redistributive effects could be eliminated by adequate and widespread indexation of fixed incomes, like pensions.
- The effect on competitiveness could be compensated by adjustments in the exchange rates. Only in a regime of fixed exchange rates are widely diverging inflation rates a problem.
- It is not at all a proven fact that inflation discourages investment. Investment by firms is in fact affected by many other factors.

So, if the arguments against inflation which point at its costs are not so compelling after all, could one go so far as to argue that inflation is a good thing?

The benefits of inflation

No one would argue that rampant inflation is a good thing. Views on the costs of inflation differ quite fundamentally to the point that some economists, Keynesians among them, stress the benefits of inflation. According to the Keynesians, inflation which accompanies an increase in aggregate demand is not such a bad thing because it stimulates economic activity, increasing the level of output and employment.

Money illusion

The gains in output and employment are due to the fact that not all prices, in particular wages, increase at the same time and in the same proportion as all other prices. Workers in some sense suffer from **money illusion** and are slow to respond to the cut in real wages caused by unanticipated inflation. This paradoxically provides an argument for having a positive rate of inflation.

✎ Activity 8.18

Imagine you have been working for McDonald's for two years. Your wage rate is coming up for review and you are asked either to take a wage cut of 3 per cent or a wage increase of 2 per cent. Which would you choose? The alternative scenarios are summarized below:

	Wage rate(£)	Inflation
Option A	Wage cut of 3%	0%
Option B	Wage increase of 2%	5%

✎ Activity 8.18

Both options lead to the same decrease in real wage, namely to a 3 per cent real wage cut. Which one did you choose? There is some evidence that workers accept a real wage cut more easily in the second case (i.e. they choose option B) than in the first case.

 This evidence – the Keynesians argue – suggests that a situation of inflation allows for a reduction in real wages (a downward real-wage adjustment) more easily than a situation of no inflation. In such cases it is argued that workers suffer from money illusion. They think they are getting a pay increase, while in fact they are taking a pay cut. Lower real wages mean reduced costs for firms, which in turn will take on more people: output, income and employment will all grow as a result.

✎ Activity 8.19

Look at Table 8.8, which shows earnings growth by industry in the UK in 1998. You know that the inflation rate in the UK in 1998 was about 3 per cent. Calculate real earning growth of people working in different industries.

✓ Answer 8.19

People in the agricultural sector have taken a wage cut of 3 per cent, miners' real income has gone down by 2.4 per cent, teachers and nurses have also taken a real

Table 8.8 UK earnings growth by industry, 1998

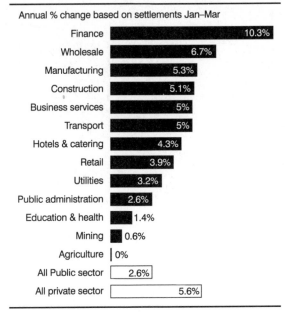

Annual % change based on settlements Jan–Mar

Industry	%
Finance	10.3%
Wholesale	6.7%
Manufacturing	5.3%
Construction	5.1%
Business services	5%
Transport	5%
Hotels & catering	4.3%
Retail	3.9%
Utilities	3.2%
Public administration	2.6%
Education & health	1.4%
Mining	0.6%
Agriculture	0%
All Public sector	2.6%
All private sector	5.6%

Source: TUC, 1998

wage cut of 1.6 per cent, while people in public administration jobs have seen their real income reduced by 0.4 per cent on average in 1998. The categories of people whose real income has seen the largest increases are those in finance (+7.3 per cent), wholesale (+3.7 per cent), and manufacturing(+5.3 per cent). In most industries, productivity per worker has also increased, which coupled with real wage cuts has increased firms' profit margins and/or competitiveness.

Negative real interest rates

While inflation raises **nominal interest rates**, it may cause real interest rates to be negative. Negative real interest rates will boost economic growth. Let's try and understand this important point, which really revolves around the concepts of nominal and real interest rate. The nominal interest rate measures the nominal return which people receive from holding a bond. The nominal interest rate cannot be negative: people will simply not buy bonds and will stuff money under their mattresses instead. The real interest rate is given by the nominal interest rate minus the rate of inflation. If inflation is greater than the nominal interest rate, the real interest rate will be negative. This would in turn boost consumer and investment spending.

This scenario is quite possible when interest rates are very low, as they are at present in some economies. A recent somewhat perverse case in point has been

offered by Japan in 1995, when the Japanese Central Bank, in an attempt to prevent the economy entering recession, lowered nominal short-term interest rates to 0.5 per cent. Expected inflation in 1995 was also negative, i.e. actual prices were expected to fall. In this case, perversely, a reduction in nominal interest rates did not help the economy to recover, as the real interest rate was higher than the nominal interest rate.

✍ Activity 8.20

Can you calculate what the real interest rate would have been in Japan with a nominal interest rate at 0.5 per cent and an expected inflation of 5 per cent?

✓ Answer 8.20

The real interest rate would have been negative, at –4.5 per cent, as:

$$0.5\% - 5\% = -4.5\%.$$

However, expected inflation was negative, say it was –2 per cent. In other words, prices were expected to fall and not to rise, therefore giving a real rate of interest higher than the nominal rate.

$$0.5\% - (-2\%) = +1.5\%.$$

A situation exactly the opposite to the one we have described above: in this case, due to a negative expected inflation, real interest rate is higher than nominal interest rate.

CAUSES OF INFLATION

To find the remedy to an illness, we need to understand its causes. The same applies to inflation. To find a remedy to inflation, we need to understand what causes it. The causes are many and complex and often, in fact, present all at the same time. To simplify matters, however, we can divide the causes of inflation into three groups:

- demand-pull factors, causing **demand-pull inflation**;
- cost-push factors, causing what economists call **cost-push inflation**;
- monetary factors, causing **monetary inflation**.

Because price increases triggered by demand-pull factors may cause wage increases (cost-push inflation) and vice versa, we also talk about a price-wage-price or wage-price-wage **inflation spiral**. Because people learn to anticipate inflation, we also refer to **expectation-augmented** demand-pull *and* cost-push **inflation**.

Whatever its cause, inflation cannot persist without an increase in the money supply. In this sense, it is true what the monetarists say, that inflation is 'always and everywhere a monetary phenomenon', although whether an increase in the money supply causes inflation or whether the existence of inflation causes the money supply to rise remains a moot point.

Demand-pull inflation

Demand-pull inflation is caused by persisting increases in aggregate demand. These may in turn result from:

- government fiscal and/or monetary expansion, such as an increase in government spending, a reduction in taxation, a money supply increase;
- an increase in the demand for exports, in turn caused by higher inflation and/or higher growth in the rest of the world.

In the simple, extreme Keynesian model, a situation of inflation can only develop when the economy is fully employed and has reached its full employment level of output. Recall the distinction introduced earlier between actual output and potential or full employment output. The economy is at its full employment output when it is producing the maximum amount possible, using all its available resources. In the short term, the output of the economy cannot increase further. When the economy has reached this situation, an increase in the demand for goods and services will not lead to more being produced but simply to an increase in prices, as people compete with each other in trying to secure more of the goods they want, bidding prices up in the process. Demand-pull factors will cause inflation, as opposed to once-and-for-all price increases, if they persist over time. This situation of excess demand, measured by what is known as the **inflationary gap** (excess of E over Y in the short run) is shown in Figure 8.8.

Figure 8.8 shows the full employment level of output Y_f which is equal to total desired expenditure at A. A further increase in desired expenditure, shown by a shift of E to E^1, will only cause inflationary pressures, since output cannot rise in the short term given that all productive resources available are already in use.

This can also be shown with an AD–AS model. A shift of aggregate expenditure from E to E^1 corresponds to a shift of the AD curve to AD_1. This causes prices to rise from P_0 to P_1 (Figure 8.9).

In the moderate Keynesian model, characterized by an upward sloping AS curve, the persistence of demand-pull factors will cause prices to increase as output increases, even if the economy's output is well

Figure 8.8 Keynesian inflationary gap

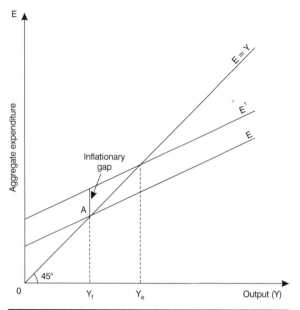

below its full employment level and there is unemployed labour. This situation is shown in Figure 8.10.

As aggregate demand continues to rise, the AD curve shifts to the right from AD to AD^1, driving prices up, from P_0 to P_1. Output also increases, as firms respond to the increase in aggregate demand and higher prices by stepping up production (shown as a movement up along the AS curve). How much output and/or prices increase, in response to an increase in

Figure 8.9 Keynesian inflationary gap shown with AD–AS model

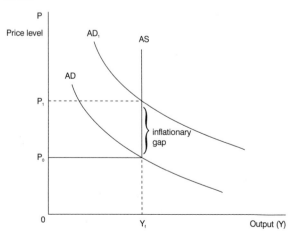

Figure 8.10 Demand-pull inflation

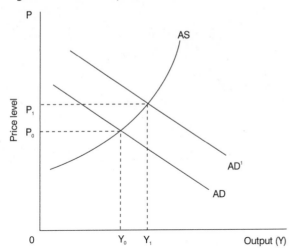

Figure 8.11 Cost-push inflation

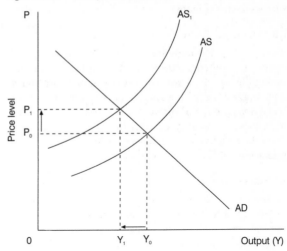

aggregate, depends on how fast firms' costs rise as a result of increased production, which in turn depends on the amount of slack and excess capacity there is in the economy. Demand-pull inflation is typically associated with the expansionary phase of the economic cycle – boom periods – which are followed by recessionary phases, characterized by demand-deficient unemployment.

Cost-push or supply-side inflation

Inflation can also be caused by continuing increases in costs. This type of inflation is referred to as cost-push or supply-side inflation. Cost-push inflation is shown by shifts to the left of the aggregate supply curve, as in Figure 8.11.

Cost-push inflation is triggered by increases in costs of production which occur independently of aggregate demand, i.e. increases in costs which do not reflect a higher utilization of productive resources. To cause inflation, such increases must continue over a number of years and must therefore be distinguished from single, isolated, once-and-for-all increases in costs, which only generate **supply shocks**. Supply shocks cause a sudden, often large increase in the price level, after which the economy reaches a new, stable equilibrium in its price level. Cost push inflation, on the other hand, is caused by persistent increases in cost factors. Such continuing shifts in the economy's aggregate supply curve can be caused by a number of factors: wage increases; import price increases; increased profit margins; increased taxation.

Wage increases

Powerful trade unions pushing for wage increases will also cause an increase in costs, independent of demand conditions. Wage rises achieved by workers in one sector of the economy tend to spread elsewhere, as trade unions emulate each other in their efforts to clinch good wage settlements for members. So wage increases which are justified by demand or productivity gains in one sector of the economy spread to all other sectors, causing cost-push inflation.

Some 2 per cent of the labour force works directly for the government in the UK. Increases in public sector employees' wages, which do not necessarily reflect demand pressures but are simply decided by the government, may also be used by private sectors workers as benchmarks and spread to the rest of the economy. In the UK public sector employees' wage increases have lagged behind the private sector's in recent years.

Import price increases

The two oil price shocks of 1973 and 1979 are typical examples of import price increases. As oil is used directly or indirectly in virtually any type of business, the quadrupling of oil prices created a general increase in costs which caused prices of most products to rise. These price increases spread through the economy, causing a generalized and persistent rise in the average price level.

Import prices can also increase due to depreciation of the domestic currency's exchange rate. Depreciation of the currency increases the costs of firms' imported inputs, particularly raw materials, which in turn trigger cost-push inflation as the initial shocks spread to other sectors of the economy.

Increased profit margins

Supply-side price increases may also be caused by producers in non-competitive markets (oligopolists and monopolists) who wish to increase their profit markups, regardless of demand or cost conditions. Price increases are also often set in relation to price increases imposed by other firms in non-competitive markets. So again cost and price increases spread from one sector of the economy to another.

Increased taxation

Increased taxation causes cost-push inflation. As higher taxes reduce people's disposable income, workers via trade unions will respond by increasing their wage demands to safeguard their real income. Firms, in a similar fashion, push up prices, trying to restore their after-tax level of profits. Tax cuts, rather than tax increases, one could argue, should be part of an anti-inflationary policy.

🖎 Activity 8.21

Does increased taxation reduce inflation or increase it?

✓ Answer 8.21

The answer is both. The problem is that while increased taxation reduces aggregate demand and therefore reduces demand-pull inflation, it also increases cost-push inflation. Taxation, as an anti-inflationary tool, is a double-edged sword.

Cost-push inflation reduces the level of aggregate supply in the economy, for a given level of prices, and this is shown by a shift to the left of the AS curve in Figure 8.11. The supply shift causes the equilibrium price to rise from P_0 to P_1 and aggregate output to fall from Y_0 to Y_1. Cost-push inflation causes output to fall and generates a combination of higher inflation with higher unemployment. If the government were to try and counteract this contraction of output by expansionary fiscal or monetary policies (shift out of AD curve), this would cause prices to rise even further. A cost-push and demand-pull spiral would then develop, as shown in Figure 8.12.

Inflation spiral

This leads us to make an important point: demand-pull and cost-push inflationary pressures can and do occur together. Wage and price rises can be caused by both increases in aggregate demand and independent

Figure 8.12   A wage-price inflation spiral

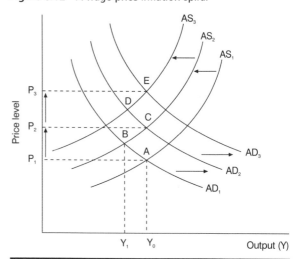

causes pushing up costs. Once the process gets started, it becomes very difficult to separate the two effects, as they cause a spiral of price-wage-price or wage-price-wage increases. The interaction of the two is shown in Figure 8.12.

An increase in prices due to increased demand (demand pull inflation) causes firms' profits to rise and real wages to fall, as nominal wages lag behind the general price increase. Workers eventually catch up with inflation in their wage demands, causing cost-price inflation as firms try to pass on the wage increase into higher prices. A price-wage-price spiral has started. A similar process can be set off by an initial wage increase.

Expectation-augmented demand-pull and cost-push inflation

People learn from inflation. As inflation reduces the purchasing power of their income, they will try to anticipate the expected rate of inflation in their wage demands. The rate of inflation which people and firms expect will affect their price and output decisions. Wrong forecasts of the inflation rate can hurt firms and workers, just like borrowers and lenders. But as people build their expectations of future inflation into their current wage demands or price increases, their expectations become a self-fulfilling prophecy.

🖎 Activity 8.22

Suppose that your union and employer are renegotiating your wages and that both sides expect an inflation rate of 10 per cent. What will be the union's request? What will the employers offer? What do you predict the outcome to be?

✔ Answer 8.22

The unions will press for a nominal wage increase above 10 per cent to secure a real increase in income. The employers' offer will be somewhat below 10 per cent, which would mean a real wage cut for employees and a reduction in firms' costs. In the event, the outcome will be around 10 per cent. The expected rate of inflation becomes the actual rate of inflation.

The crucial role played by expectations of future inflation in the determination of actual inflation has led many economists to investigate more closely how people form their expectations about future inflation.

Adaptive expectations

If prices have been rising and people's expectations of future inflation are adaptive (i.e. if people form their expectations on the basis of past pricing behaviour), then firms may continue raising prices even if demand is slowing or contracting, simply because they expect other firms to raise them as in the past. This would show as a shift of the AS curve for the economy. In this way, inflationary expectations get built into the system and ensure the perpetuation of inflation. Equally, if prices have been rising, by, say, 10 per cent in the past, workers expect the same rate of inflation in the future and build it into their wage claims, ensuring that their inflationary expectations will be fulfilled. In this situation it becomes very difficult for a government to reduce inflation as people's expectations will continue to generate the same rate experienced in the past.

✍ Activity 8.23

Suppose the government wishes to reduce inflation, which for the past few years has been running at an annual rate of 10 per cent. In order to achieve this the government reduces its spending programmes. Assume also that people's expectations of inflation are adaptive. How will this affect the government's deflationary programme? Illustrate your answer with the use of a diagram.

✔ Answer 8.22

Cuts in government expenditure reduce aggregate demand. This is shown by a shift to the left of the aggregate demand curve in Figure 8.13 from AD to AD^1. This in turn causes prices, output and employment to fall to Y_1 and P_1 respectively. As people's expectations of inflation are adaptive, i.e. based on

Figure 8.13 Government deflationary policy with adaptive expectations

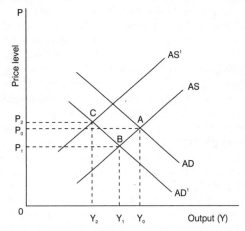

past rates of inflation, they continue to expect the same rate of inflation of 10 per cent experienced in the past and adjust up their wage demand and price increases by 10 per cent accordingly. This will push the AS curve up to the left, from AS to AS^1, causing a further reduction in output and employment to Y_2, coupled with an increase in prices (cost-push inflation), from P_1 to P_2. As a result of this situation, the government deflationary programme will be associated with higher unemployment and higher inflation than it would otherwise have been generated by the reduction in demand. Unemployment which follows the government's deflationary policy will remain above its natural rate by a larger amount and for a longer period if expectations of future inflation are adaptive. The notion of a 'natural rate of unemployment' is explained later in this chapter.

Rational expectations

The assumption that people's expectations are adaptive – and the consequences for governments' deflationary policies – was challenged by two eminent economists from the University of Chicago at the end of the 1970s: Robert Lucas and Thomas Sargent. Their arguments are known as the **Lucas critique**. What Lucas and Sargent rejected was the assumption that people and firms form their expectations of inflation passively, on the basis of past experience, regardless of changes in government policy that may have taken place in the meantime. Instead they argue that people's formation of inflationary expectations changes in response to changes in government policy and other changes.

If the government announced its deflationary measures and such measures were credible, and if wage and price setters could be persuaded that inflation was indeed going to be lower than in the past as a result, then they would decrease their expectations of inflation. This would in turn reduce actual inflation, without necessarily increasing the unemployment rate. Inflation would decrease, with unemployment remaining at its natural rate. The essential ingredient of a successful deflation, they argued, is the credibility of monetary policy.

This situation is illustrated in Figure 8.14. If people's expectations of future inflation are not adaptive, but responsive to policy changes, a deflationary government policy which reduces aggregate demand (shift to the left of AD curve to AD^1) will cause a revision downward of expected inflation (a shift down of the AS curve to AS^1). If this is the case, a deflationary policy does not cause an increase in unemployment. This conclusion was claimed to be supported by empirical data. Sargent, looking at the historical evidence of the cost associated with ending situations of very high inflations, found that the associated increase in unemployment could in fact be small.

Monetary inflation

As we have just seen, the inflationary process can be sparked off by a demand-side shock such as an excessive government budget deficit, private sector's bullish expectations, housing boom and feel-good factors, excessive consumer credit expansion. It can also be triggered by a supply-side shock, such as energy price increases, trade union militancy, sudden shortage of essential raw materials or oligopolistic corporations'

collusive price behaviour. Such initial shocks get transmitted to all sectors of the economy and become firmly embedded through the complex connective tissue represented by institutions' and governments' policies, representative bodies' calculations, individual and group expectations. In this way the initial, isolated shock becomes a generalized phenomenon and its 'temporary' nature is lost, as demand factors react to supply factors and vice versa.

However, in order for the generalized price increases to translate into sustained inflation, the money supply must also increase on a sustained basis. The monetary authorities must accommodate the continuously rising prices with a continuously rising money supply. If they do not, and money supply remains constant in the face of rising inflation, the ensuing shortage of liquidity would cause interest rates to rise and demand to fall, with adverse effects on output and employment. The government may not be prepared to pay such a high price, often for its own political survival. It may choose to validate or accommodate inflation by increasing the money supply, rather than paying the short-term costs in terms of unemployment, social disruption and loss of growth that a reduction would bring.

Monetary expansion must accompany inflationary episodes for inflation to persist through time. This leads the monetarists to conclude that inflation 'is always and everywhere a monetary phenomenon'. The monetarists, however, do not stop there – where all economists would agree – but take this analysis a step further and argue, within the context of the Quantity Theory approach, that the increase in the money supply causes inflation. To sum up their view, which we have already discussed in Chapter 7, monetary expansion does not simply accommodate inflation: it causes it. An increase in money balances caused by an increase in money supply induces people to demand more of everything, causing prices to rise.

More money injected into the economy means more spending. For stable prices, the money supply should increase at a stable rate, commensurate with the economy's output growth. If the money supply exceeds it or the economy's output supply cannot rise accordingly, the excess demand causes inflation. For this conclusion to be true, two conditions must apply:

■ the velocity of circulation of money is constant;
■ the volume of goods and services produced cannot be increased further in the short run.

As we have seen earlier, both assumptions are debatable. How much an increase in demand caused by an increase in the money supply is inflationary depends, in fact, on how firms respond to an increase in demand. Output

Figure 8.14 Government deflationary policy with rational expectations

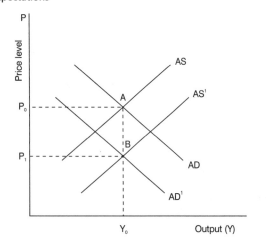

and prices would typically increase. How much firms can increase production as demand rises depends on how fast their costs rise as their output rises. It will depend on the shape of the aggregate supply curve. The curve will be steeper, the closer the economy is to full employment. Keynesian economists do not see such a straightforward and direct link between an increase in the money supply, spending and inflation.

It is undoubtedly true, however, that no inflationary process, whatever its cause, could continue without an increase in the money supply. In a sense we can see why Friedman lays the blame for inflation on governments which are responsible for allowing the growth of the money supply. An increase in prices not accommodated by an increase in the quantity of money in the economy would eventually raise the interest rate and put a brake on demand.

✍ Activity 8.24

How can you explain the fact that similar price shocks such as, say, the oil price increases of the 1970s, may trigger different processes in different countries, leading to a one-off rise followed by a return to price stability in one country and to a never-ending inflationary spiral in another?

✓ Answer 8.24

The capacity of a country to resist inflation depends on many factors, related to demand and supply conditions, which may vary from country to country. It also depends crucially on a country's institutional infrastructure, on the credibility and determination of the country's institutions in restraining inflationary pressures. These institutions include monetary authorities, but also trade unions and government bodies.

✍ Activity 8.25

If inflation cannot persist without monetary expansion, then it must be that the monetarists are right in maintaining that 'inflation is always and everywhere a monetary phenomenon'. Do you agree?

✓ Answer 8.25

To say that inflation cannot persist without monetary expansion is not the same as saying that monetary expansion causes inflation. While it is relatively easy and straightforward to associate inflation with increased liquidity, it is also equally evident that excessive money creation does not take place in a vacuum. The ultimate causes of inflation are much more complex. Nobody maintains anymore that inflation is exclusively associated with excess aggregate demand or that a supply-side shock will inevitably generate a price spiral. Inflation is a complex process which results from the interaction of demand and supply conditions with monetary, institutional and political factors.

THE PHILLIPS CURVE

Implicit in most of the analysis of inflation developed above is the relationship between inflation and unemployment. The **Phillips curve**, developed by Professor Phillips at the London School of Economics in 1958 using data for the British economy, helped to focus on this relationship and showed the existence of a 'trade-off' between inflation and unemployment. Professor Phillips's data showed that higher inflation was associated with lower unemployment and vice versa. Let's see how this could be explained.

Assume that the economy has zero inflation and an 8 per cent unemployment rate and that the government wishes to reduce unemployment using expansionary fiscal and monetary policies. These policies will cause aggregate demand to increase, which in turn will cause output, employment and prices to rise. To start wage demands are based simply on last-year prices and if we begin from a situation of zero inflation people do not expect inflation to occur. Greater demand for labour by firms wishing to expand their output will lead to higher employment, higher output and higher nominal wages. Higher nominal wages lead in turn to higher prices (cost-push inflation), as firms pass the cost increase onto higher prices. Hence, lower unemployment leads to higher prices this year compared with last year, that is, to higher inflation. This was how the trade-off between inflation and unemployment was explained when in 1958 Professor Phillips observed its existence for the British economy. Solow and Samuelson showed that a similar trade-off existed in the USA. This relationship between inflation and unemployment is shown by the Phillips Curve in Figure 8.15.

An increase in aggregate demand causes unemployment to fall at the expense of some inflation. The government chooses to trade off inflation for more employment and move the economy from a situation of zero inflation and 8 per cent unemployment to one characterized by 5 per cent unemployment and 4 per cent inflation.

While it was accepted that any economy would experience at any time some unemployment due to frictional or structural reasons even at zero rate of inflation, the trade-off seemed stable in the years for which data had been collected, suggesting the existence of a trade-off between inflation and unemployment. The government

Figure 8.15 Phillips curve

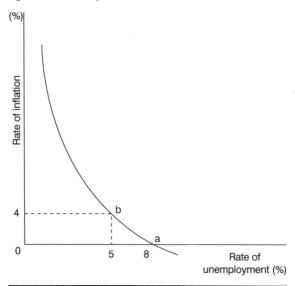

unemployment in a range that appeared consistent with moderate inflation. Throughout the 1960s the negative relationship provided a reliable guide to the relation between unemployment and inflation. In the USA in particular, this relationship seemed to hold particularly well: from 1961 to 1969 the unemployment rate declined steadily from 6.7 per cent to 3.5 per cent, while the inflation rate increased steadily, from 1.0 per cent to 5.4 per cent.

From 1970 on, both in the USA and Europe, this relationship broke down. Subsequent data for unemployment and inflation no longer show a stable, negative relationship. The validity of the relationship shown by the Phillips curve has since been called into question as it did not fit the facts in the 1970s and 1980s, when unemployment and inflation were both rising. The trade-off had vanished and with it a convenient, clear-cut tool for economic policy-making. While the data for unemployment and inflation had shown a clear trade-off between inflation and unemployment in the 1950s and 1960s, those for the 1970s and 1980s did not. The scatter of data, which shows the combinations of inflation and unemployment over this period, seems rather to form loops. Such a scatter of points for the UK economy is shown in Figure 8.16.

What had happened? The monetarists – to be precise, Milton Friedman and Edmund Phelps – came up with an answer which seemed to fit in with the rest of their theory. The explanation rests on the distinction between

using demand management policies, it was argued, was in a position to choose the preferred combination of unemployment and inflation and trade off some inflation for less unemployment (shown by the move from *a* to *b* in Figure 8.15).

In the USA, UK and most European economies in the 1960s, macroeconomic policy was aimed at maintaining

Figure 8.16 From a curve to loops

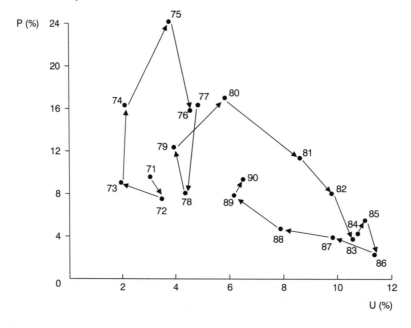

short run and long run, on the response of wage demands to inflation and on the role played by expectation of inflation in the determination of wage demands. For this reason the reinterpretation of the Phillips Curve relationship given in the 1980s is often referred to as the **expectations-augmented Phillips curve**.

The trade-off exists in the short run – the monetarists argue – as people and particularly workers do not expect inflation or do not anticipate the correct rate of inflation. For example, as the government, expands demand to reduce unemployment, more is produced as wage demands do not keep up with inflation, firms have larger profit margins and expand production. This is shown in the Figure 8.17 by a move from point a to point b.

Let's assume that unemployment falls, as a result, from 8 per cent to 5 per cent, while inflation rises from 0 to 4 per cent. So the trade-off exists for a short period of time, between two to five years. As people learn from inflation and now expect the same rate of inflation (adaptive expectations), they will adjust their wage claims accordingly. Firms' profit margins will disappear; they will cut back production and lay off workers. This can be shown by a shift to the right of the original Phillips curve and a movement of the economy to point c, where the original rate of unemployment of 8 per cent is now associated with a rate of inflation of 4 per cent. (actual and expected). The initial government policy of reducing unemployment by stimulating demand proves ineffective, as workers respond to demand-pull inflation by increasing their wage demands by an equal amount (adaptive expectations and cost-push inflation). It has only caused prices to rise, without permanently reducing unemployment.

Firms will not cut back output and employment if they can pass on the increase in nominal wages into higher prices, which will lead to a higher price level. The higher price level leads workers to ask for higher nominal wages next year, prompting yet another increase in prices set by firms, and so on. Inflation has set in. This mechanism, which we referred to earlier as a price-wage-price spiral, well describes the basic forces at work. If the government insists on its policy of stimulating aggregate demand to reduce unemployment, the same will happen once more; this time, however, inflation will accelerate further. In the short run, people who had wrongly anticipated the rate of inflation will be caught unprepared by the higher inflation; they will suffer from money illusion and accept real wages lower than before. So unemployment will temporarily fall. As people, adjust their wage claims to the new higher rate, unemployment will rise again and return to its original level. The Phillips curve will have shifted out once more.

In the long run, the Phillips curve will be vertical, at the rate of unemployment where there is no excess demand. This is the rate that the monetarists call the **natural rate of unemployment** or **U^n**, sometimes also referred to as the **non-accelerating inflation rate of unemployment (NAIRU)**. The concept of a

Figure 8.17 The expectations-augmented Phillips curve: (a) short-run, (b) long-run

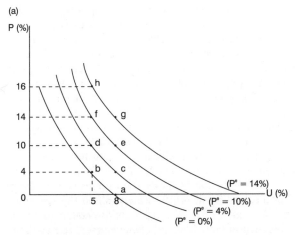

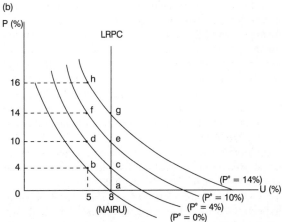

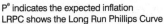

P^e indicates the expected inflation
LRPC shows the Long Run Phillips Curve

natural rate of unemployment is also related to the analysis of the Phillips curve. The major implication of the original Phillips curve was that there was no natural rate of unemployment. If the government was willing to tolerate a higher inflation rate, it could maintain full or lower unemployment forever, provided it continued to sustain demand.

The monetarists' long-run vertical Phillips curve shows that the trade-off ultimately disappears and that the unemployment rate cannot be sustained below a certain 'natural rate' by the use of aggregate demand policies. Summing up, two new factors were at work in the 1970s and 1980s, which explain why the Phillips relationship broke down. First, there were two very severe supply-side, non-wage shocks, caused by the OPEC oil price increases. The effect of these increases in costs was to force firms to increase their prices, for the same wage costs. So, for a given rate of unemployment and demand in the 1970s, there were additional, significant unpredictable sources of inflation.

Second, in response to increased inflation, firms and workers changed the way in which they formed their expectations of inflation, which in turn affected their prices and wage demands respectively. This change came from an alteration in the actual process of inflation. From being close to zero in the late 1950s, inflation had been steadily creeping up and rather than going from positive to negative, as it had done at the turn of the century and in the inter-war period, it had become steadily and consistently positive.

When inflation is consistently positive, expecting that prices this year will be the same as last year becomes systematically wrong. People tend to learn from their mistakes. As inflation became more persistent and consistently positive, people started to adjust their expectations to incorporate this fact. The change in the way in which expectations of inflation were formed altered the nature of the relationship between unemployment and inflation. As long as inflation was low and not persistent, it was reasonable for firms and workers to ignore past inflation and to assume that this year's price level would be roughly equal to the previous year. In this scenario, an increase in aggregate demand would cause a reduction in unemployment and the Phillips curve holds.

As inflation became more persistent, firms and workers started assuming that if inflation had been high last year, it was also likely to be high this year. By the 1970s, empirical evidence shows that people formed expectations by anticipating that this year's inflation rate would be the same as last year's. When this is the case, the Phillips curve starts shifting, as the inflation rate depends not only on the unemployment rate but

also on last year's inflation rate. Hence, the unemployment rate affects not the inflation rate itself but rather the change in the inflation rate: lower unemployment leads to accelerating inflation, higher unemployment leads to decelerating inflation.

The relationship that fits the data in the 1990s is no longer the original Phillips curve, between the rate of inflation and unemployment, but rather the expectation-augmented Phillips curve, which shows a relationship between unemployment and the rate of change of inflation. If we plot the change in inflation rate versus the unemployment rate for each year since 1970, we still obtain a clear negative relation between unemployment and the change in inflation. The estimated relationship for major industrialized economies seems to indicate that an increase in the unemployment rate of 1 per cent in a year leads to a decrease of 1.15 per cent in inflation.

The implications of the process described above and of a vertical Phillips curve for government policy purposes are quite important: government policies aimed at reducing unemployment by stimulating aggregate demand only work in the short run. They are totally ineffective in the long run and only inject inflation into the system. For this reason, the monetarists recommend supply-side policies to reduce the natural rate of unemployment, rather than demand-side policies.

✍ Activity 8.26

Does the fact that the Phillips curve broke down during the 1970s and 1980s mean that there is no trade-off between inflation and unemployment ?

✓ Answer 8.26

Not at all. It simply means that there are other things that affect inflation, apart from unemployment; in particular cost factors, other than wages, expectations and government policies. Take a standard demand curve for a good: it shows the relationship between quantity demanded and price (the lower the price, the greater the quantity demanded), other things being equal. If any of the 'other' factors affecting demand (income, price of substitutes, etc.) change, the demand curve shifts: the quantity demanded also changes irrespective of prices. Similarly, the relationship between unemployment and inflation changes (and the curve shifts) when other factors change. The high unemployment and high inflation of the 1970s were caused partly by an increase in oil prices, which shifted the aggregate supply curve of most industrialized economies to the left (causing inflation and unemployment to rise at the same time); partly by expectations of continued inflation, which kept prices rising despite the high levels of unemployment (again, causing inflation and unemployment to rise at the same time); partly by contractionary monetary policies adopted by most governments in response to this situation, which shifted the aggregate demand (AD) curve to the left and caused even higher unemployment. The persistence of governments' contractionary policies throughout the 1980s, particularly in Europe, eventually succeeded in reducing inflationary expectations and bringing down inflation, but at the price of very high unemployment.

POLICIES TO ELIMINATE INFLATION

Just as we have identified demand-side and supply-side causes of inflation, similarly we can talk of demand-side and supply-side policies to reduce inflation. Policies aimed at reducing inflation are referred to as deflationary policies. *On the demand side*, the government can use deflationary fiscal and monetary policies. **Deflationary fiscal policies** aim at reducing the level of aggregate demand by either reducing government spending or increasing taxation or a combination of the two. **Deflationary monetary policies** aim at reducing the level of aggregate demand by reducing the liquidity of the system: altering the money supply and making less money available or increasing the rate of interest, which makes borrowing more expensive, reduces investment and consumption expenditure.

On the supply side, the government can introduce policies aimed at containing supply-side inflationary pressures, whether they come from trade unions or monopolistic and oligopolistic firms. The government can therefore encourage more flexibility and competitiveness in the labour market, by limiting and restraining the activities of trade unions. The government can also contain the power which large firms have on prices, preventing mergers and takeovers and monitoring and controlling their pricing policies.

The government can introduce policies aimed at increasing supply-side productivity. The more firms are able to expand output, in response to an increase in demand, the less inflationary that increase in demand will be. Such policies include:

- *tax incentives* to reduce firms' costs;
- *government-financed labour training schemes*, as the productivity of a more skilled labour force is greater;
- *relocation grants* to encourage labour mobility;
- *research and development grants* to encourage technological development and *investment grants* to firms, to encourage them to modernize.

UNEMPLOYMENT

As we have seen, the issues of inflation and unemployment are closely linked and a discussion of one inevitably leads to a discussion of the other. The debate on inflation and unemployment centres around the role of aggregate demand policies and the shape of the economy's aggregate supply curve.

Within the simple Keynesian model put forward in the first chapters, unemployment is caused by lack of demand. That model tells us that if people, firms, government and foreigners all demand more goods and services, more will be produced by firms and more jobs will be created in the process. This analysis does not take into account what happens to prices when demand increases, and assumes that prices do not rise. If prices increase as a result of demand pressures, then firms will want to produce more only if wages remain stable and do not increase by as much or as fast as product prices. It must be that workers suffer from money illusion. But if workers don't suffer from money illusion – as the monetarists maintain – and wages are flexible and adjust promptly to price changes, then trying to stimulate demand to reduce unemployment will not work. Product price increases will be matched (or anticipated) by equal wage price increases and firms will not expand their output (a vertical AS curve in the long run, if not in the short run). These are the terms of the debate.

Who is right and who is wrong? To form a view on these issues, we need to understand how the labour market operates and how the existence of unemployment can be explained by factors other than a lack of demand. Ultimately the controversy is whether the labour market works efficiently and is flexible enough to bring about full employment (i.e. equality between the quantity of labour demanded and supplied) or whether wages are sticky in the downward direction and workers suffer from money illusion.

According to the monetarists, workers do not suffer from money illusion and the labour market does work efficiently, or at least it can be helped to work efficiently. From this it follows that unemployment arises mainly from frictions and rigidities in the labour markets and from the fact that it takes time in real life for adjustments to be made to changed demand conditions and for labour to be reallocated to different sectors of the economy. According to this view, the unemployment we experience in our economies is therefore only frictional, temporary and voluntary.

According to Keynes and the Keynesians, workers suffer from a certain degree of money illusion.

Furthermore, wages are not flexible, particularly downwards, and do not adjust quickly enough to ensure full employment. If the demand for labour falls in the economy during a recession, as firms cut back their production to adjust to reduced demand conditions, wages will not fall and unemployment will rise. The policy Keynes advocates, however, is not one of wage cuts, which would further reduce demand and worsen the situation, but rather one of stimulating demand, which would lead to increased employment.

Like many other areas of the Keynesians versus monetarists controversy, this one too remains largely unsettled. All we can do at this stage is to understand more clearly what the real bones of the contentions are and what indications can be derived from this debate for the conduct of governments' macroeconomic policy. To do this, we need to focus on the supply side of the economy, in order to understand how labour markets operate. The rest of this chapter will provide:

- a definition of unemployment;
- an assessment of the current size of the unemployment problem, through an analysis of relevant statistics;
- a discussion of different explanations for the existence of unemployment;
- a discussion of possible policy measures to reduce unemployment;
- a final reassessment of the debate on inflation and unemployment.

Definitions and data

A clear understanding of the definitions of labour force, participation rate and unemployment rate is very important to avoid confusion in the discussion that follows. The first problem we need to solve is how to measure unemployment. When we talk about unemployment, we refer to it as a percentage; for example, we say that the unemployment rate in Britain is currently 5.6 per cent, but of what? To define unemployment we need to distinguish between the following concepts:

- the **population**, which comprises all the individuals living in a country;
- the **population of working age**, which excludes children and retired people;
- the **labour force**, which comprises all the people of working age holding a job or looking for a job and able to work;
- the **participation rate**, which is the percentage of the population of working age who is in the labour force:

$$\text{Participation rate} = \frac{\text{labour force}}{\text{population of working age}} \times 100$$

- the **unemployment rate,** which is the percentage of the labour force that is out of work, but is willing and able to work and looking for a job. Expressed in symbols, if L = labour force and U = unemployed people, the unemployment rate is defined as:

$$\text{Unemployment rate} = \frac{U}{L} \times 100.$$

A graphical representation of the way these concepts relate to one another is shown in Figure 8.18.

Although the definitions given above seem straightforward, the measurement of unemployment has been highly contentious, particularly in Britain. Since the early 1980s there have been several changes made to the definition of unemployment in the UK. The aims of such redefinitions, the critics argue, was to massage the unemployment figures and to produce statistics which showed the unemployment rates as falling.

The **standard international definition** used by the International Labour Organization for international comparison defines unemployment as: the number of people of working age who, in a specified period, are without work and are both available for, and have taken specific steps to find, work. Slight differences in the interpretation of the definition and in compilation procedures lead to national statistics which are often different from the international ones.

The **UK government official definition** of unemployment is much narrower than the ILO definition,

Figure 8.18 Measuring the unemployment rate

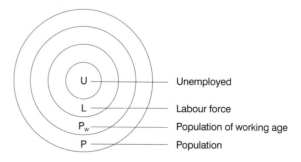

The activity rate is the ratio of $\dfrac{L}{P_w} \times 100$

The unemployment rate is $\dfrac{U}{L} \times 100$

counting in its official statistics as 'unemployed' only those who are receiving unemployment benefits (now called job-seeker's allowance) and who are available to do any suitable work. This measure excludes school leavers under 18, who are found places on government training schemes (YTS) if they cannot find employment, and men over 60 who, although are not entitled to a state pension until they are 65, can receive benefits without having to register as unemployed. The UK definition leads to some understatement of unemployment when compared with the standardized international measure.

 Activity 8.27

The workforce in Britain in 1997 was 28,122,000 and the unemployed claimants were 1,582,800. Calculate the unemployment rate.

✓ Answer 8.27

Using the formula above, the unemployment rate was

$$\left(\frac{1,582,800}{28,122,000}\right) \times 100 = 5.6\%.$$

Both measures of unemployment are not comprehensive. They do not take into account:

- the number of part-time workers who would rather have a full-time job, but cannot find one. These involuntary part-timers count as fully employed people. This leads to lower unemployment statistics.
- the 'discouraged worker' effect: people who lose hope of ever finding a suitable job and give up looking for a job do not show up in unemployment statistics. This effect may not even show up in the participation rate statistics. The discouraged workers will often be middle-aged men, whose reduced participation rate could be obscured in official statistics by the increased participation rates in part-time employment, particularly of women, and by early retirement. Because of the discouraged worker effect, the official unemployment statistics tend to underestimate the extent of the unemployment problem.
- the fact that people who register as unemployed or looking for a job are often employed in the underground economy. Unemployment rates in Spain and Italy, for example, are deemed to be much lower than the official statistics would lead us to believe.

The net impact of these conflicting influences is hard to quantify. There are also other factors such as geographical distribution, composition and duration which characterize unemployment beyond its mere size.

Geographical distribution of unemployment

 Activity 8.28

Look at Figure 8.19 and Table 8.9 and comment on what they show us.

Figure 8.19 UK unemployment rates, 1930–97

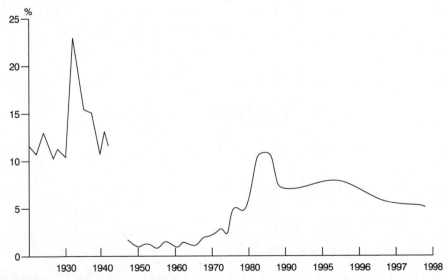

Source: HMT, FSBR, 1998

Table 8.9   EU unemployment rates (percentage of civilian labour force)

	B	DK	D¹	EL	E	F	IRL	I	L	NL	A	P	FIN	S	UK	EUR 15¹	US	JP
1960	2.8	1.5	1.0	6.1	2.4	1.4	5.8	5.7	0.0	0.7	2.6	1.7	1.5	1.7	1.4	2.3	5.5	1.7
1961	3.0	1.3	0.7	5.9	2.4	1.3	5.3	5.1	0.0	0.5	2.0	2.0	1.2	1.5	1.2	2.1	6.7	1.4
1962	2.5	1.3	0.6	5.1	1.6	1.4	5.2	4.4	0.0	0.5	2.0	2.3	1.3	1.5	1.7	2.0	5.5	1.3
1963	1.9	1.7	0.6	5.0	2.0	1.6	5.4	3.6	0.0	0.5	2.2	2.4	1.5	1.7	2.0	2.0	5.7	1.3
1964	1.4	1.2	0.5	4.6	2.8	1.2	5.2	4.0	0.0	0.5	2.1	2.5	1.5	1.6	1.4	1.9	5.2	1.1
1965	1.6	0.9	0.4	4.8	2.6	1.5	5.0	5.0	0.0	0.6	2.1	2.5	1.4	1.2	1.2	2.0	4.5	1.2
1966	1.7	1.1	0.5	5.0	2.2	1.6	5.1	5.4	0.0	0.8	1.9	2.5	1.5	1.6	1.1	2.0	3.8	1.3
1967	2.4	1.0	1.4	5.4	3.0	2.1	5.5	5.0	0.0	1.7	2.0	2.6	2.9	2.1	2.0	2.6	3.8	1.3
1968	2.8	1.0	1.0	5.6	3.0	2.6	5.8	5.3	0.0	1.5	2.2	2.6	3.9	2.2	2.1	2.7	3.6	1.2
1969	2.2	0.9	0.6	5.2	2.5	2.3	5.5	5.1	0.0	1.1	1.9	2.6	2.8	1.9	2.0	2.4	3.5	1.1
1970	1.8	0.6	0.5	4.2	2.6	2.4	6.3	5.1	0.0	1.0	1.6	2.5	1.9	1.5	2.2	2.3	4.9	1.1
1961–70	2.1	1.1	0.7	5.1	2.5	1.8	5.4	4.8	0.0	0.9	2.0	2.5	2.0	1.7	1.7	2.2	4.7	1.2
1971	1.7	0.9	0.6	3.1	3.4	2.7	6.0	5.1	0.0	1.3	1.3	2.5	2.3	2.5	2.7	2.6	5.9	1.4
1972	2.2	0.8	0.8	2.1	2.9	2.8	6.7	6.0	0.0	2.3	1.1	2.6	2.5	2.7	3.1	2.8	5.6	1.3
1973	2.2	0.7	0.8	2.0	2.6	2.7	6.2	5.9	0.0	2.4	1.0	2.5	2.3	2.5	2.2	2.6	4.9	1.4
1974	2.3	2.8	1.8	2.1	3.1	2.8	5.8	5.0	0.0	2.9	1.2	1.7	1.8	2.0	2.0	2.7	5.6	1.9
1975	4.2	3.9	3.3	2.3	4.5	4.0	7.9	5.5	0.0	5.5	1.7	4.4	2.4	1.6	3.2	3.9	8.5	2.0
1976	5.5	5.1	3.3	1.9	4.9	4.4	9.8	6.2	0.0	5.8	1.8	6.2	4.2	1.6	4.8	4.6	7.7	2.0
1977	6.3	5.9	3.2	1.7	5.3	4.9	9.7	6.7	0.0	5.6	1.6	7.3	6.3	1.8	5.1	4.9	7.1	2.2
1978	6.8	6.7	3.1	1.8	7.1	5.1	9.0	6.7	1.2	5.6	2.1	7.9	7.7	2.2	5.0	5.2	6.1	2.1
1979	7.0	4.8	3.1	1.9	8.8	5.8	7.8	7.2	2.4	5.7	2.1	7.9	6.5	2.2	4.6	5.3	5.8	2.0
1980	7.4	5.2	2.7	2.7	11.6	6.2	8.0	7.1	2.4	6.4	1.9	7.6	5.3	2.2	5.6	5.8	7.1	2.0
1971–80	4.6	3.7	2.2	2.2	5.4	4.1	7.7	6.1	0.6	4.4	1.6	5.1	4.1	2.1	3.8	4.0	6.4	1.8
1981	9.5	8.3	3.9	4.0	14.4	7.3	10.8	7.4	2.4	8.9	2.5	7.3	5.7	2.8	8.9	7.4	7.6	2.2
1982	11.2	8.9	5.6	5.8	16.3	8.0	12.5	8.0	2.4	11.9	3.5	7.2	6.3	3.5	10.3	8.7	9.7	2.4
1983	11.1	9.0	6.9	7.1	17.5	8.1	14.0	7.7	3.5	9.7	4.1	7.8	6.4	3.9	11.1	9.1	9.6	2.6
1984	11.1	8.5	7.1	7.2	20.3	9.7	15.5	8.1	3.1	9.3	3.8	8.5	6.3	3.4	11.1	9.7	7.5	2.7
1985	10.3	7.1	7.2	7.0	21.6	10.1	16.9	8.5	2.9	8.3	3.6	8.7	6.3	3.0	11.5	10.0	7.2	2.6
1986	10.3	5.4	6.5	6.6	21.2	10.2	16.8	9.2	2.6	8.3	3.1	8.4	6.8	2.8	11.5	9.9	7.0	2.8
1987	10.0	5.4	6.3	6.7	20.5	10.4	16.6	9.9	2.5	8.0	3.8	6.9	5.2	2.3	10.6	9.1	6.2	2.8
1988	8.9	6.1	6.2	6.8	19.5	9.8	16.1	10.0	2.0	7.5	3.6	5.5	4.6	1.9	8.7	8.3	5.5	2.5
1989	7.5	7.4	5.6	6.7	17.2	9.3	14.7	10.0	1.8	6.9	3.1	4.9	3.5	1.6	7.3	7.7	5.3	2.3
1990	6.7	7.7	4.8	6.4	16.2	8.9	13.4	9.1	1.7	6.2	3.2	4.6	3.5	1.8	7.0	7.0	5.6	2.1
1981–90	9.7	7.4	6.0	6.4	18.5	9.2	14.7	8.8	2.5	8.5	3.4	7.0	5.5	2.7	9.8	9.0	7.1	2.5
1991	6.6	8.4	4.2	7.0	16.4	9.5	14.8	8.8	1.7	5.8	3.5	4.0	7.6	3.3	8.8	8.1	6.8	2.1
1992	7.3	9.2	4.5	7.9	18.5	10.4	15.4	9.0	2.1	5.6	3.6	4.2	13.0	5.8	10.1	9.1	7.5	2.2
1993	8.9	10.1	6.0	8.6	22.8	11.7	15.6	10.3	2.7	6.6	4.3	5.7	17.5	9.5	10.4	10.6	6.9	2.5
1994	10.0	8.2	6.7	8.9	24.1	12.3	14.3	11.4	3.2	7.1	3.7	7.0	17.9	9.8	9.6	11.1	6.1	2.9
1991	6.6	8.4	5.6	7.0	16.4	9.5	14.8	8.8	1.7	5.8	3.5	4.0	7.6	3.3	8.8	8.3	6.8	2.1
1992	7.3	9.2	6.6	7.9	18.5	10.4	15.4	9.0	2.1	5.6	3.6	4.2	13.0	5.8	10.1	9.3	7.5	2.2
1993	8.9	10.1	7.9	8.6	22.8	11.7	15.6	10.3	2.7	6.6	4.3	5.7	17.5	9.5	10.4	10.9	6.9	2.5
1994	10.0	8.2	8.4	8.9	24.1	12.3	14.3	11.4	3.2	7.1	3.7	7.0	17.9	9.8	9.6	11.3	6.1	2.9
1995	9.9	7.1	8.2	9.1	22.9	11.6	12.4	11.9	2.9	7.0	3.8	7.3	16.6	9.2	8.8	10.9	5.6	3.1
1996	9.8	6.0	9.0	9.0	22.2	12.3	12.3	12.0	3.1	6.6	4.1	7.3	15.7	10.0	8.2	11.0	5.4	3.4
1997	9.5	5.1	9.7	8.9	21.3	12.5	11.7	12.0	3.3	6.0	4.2	7.0	14.0	9.9	6.8	10.6	5.4	3.4

¹ 1960–94: WD

¹ 1960–94: WD; 1991–97: including D.

Source: European Economy, 1997

✓ Answer 8.28

The data for UK unemployment since the mid-1930s are shown in Figure 8.19. We can clearly see how severe the unemployment problem was in the 1930s and mid-1940s, reaching a peak of 23 per cent over this period. After the war, together with most governments of industrialized countries, Britain undertook to regulate the economy by the use of fiscal and monetary policies in order to guarantee full employment. Unemployment went down to unprecedented low levels, around 1.5 to 2 per cent of the labour force. It started its dramatic ascent in the mid-1970s and remains at a high level of about 5.6 per cent of the labour force (approximately 1.5 million people were unemployed in the UK in 1997).

Table 8.9 shows the unemployment rates for the EU from 1960 to 1997, revealing a similar picture of generally high rates of unemployment in the EU, where the average has increased from a rather low 2.3 per cent unemployment rate in 1960 to 4 per cent in the 1970s, 9 per cent in the 1980s, to reach 10.6 per cent in 1997.

Unemployment can also be unevenly distributed within countries, causing what is known as a **regional problem**. In the UK unemployment is much higher in the north of the country than it is in the south, while the opposite is true for France and Italy. Germany too has major regional differences in unemployment, not only between east and west, but also within Western Germany where there is high unemployment in northern regions compared with much wealthier southern regions, such as Bavaria.

✍ Activity 8.29

Look at Table 8.10 and explain what it shows.

✓ Answer 8.29

Table 8.10 shows the regional distribution of unemployment in the UK, measured using the UK definition of unemployment and the ILO definition. Tables 8.10(a) and (b) both show that unemployment is higher than the national average in some areas. According to the UK definition (a), unemployment is highest in the Merseyside region, where the rate is 13.1 per cent, compared with a national average of 7.5 per cent in 1996. Northern Ireland and the North East also have above average unemployment rates of 10.9 per cent and 10.6 per cent respectively, while the South East and the South West have below average rates of unemployment (5.4 per cent and 6.2 per cent respectively). This pattern is confirmed using the ILO measure. The rates of unemployment in 1996 are higher when measured using the ILO definition.

Composition of unemployment

Some groups of people within the economy tend to experience higher than average unemployment:

■ *Young people*, between the ages of 16 and 25, experience great difficulty entering the labour market as they leave school.
■ *Women* tend to experience higher unemployment than men in some European countries, although the opposite is true in countries such as Japan, the USA and UK. Severe unemployment spells also tend to discourage women more than men from staying in or entering the labour market.
■ *Older workers* may have been made redundant due to restructuring or downsizing, after years of employment in an industry.
■ *Unskilled workers* also suffer higher than average unemployment rates, together with foreign nationals, racial minorities and lone parents.

Duration of unemployment

People take up new jobs or lose jobs all the time. This movement of people in and out of the pool of unemployed labour affects the unemployment rate in two ways: with respect to the size of the flow (in and out of unemployment); with respect to the duration of the unemployment period.

The rate of unemployment is determined by two factors: the proportion of the labour force which becomes unemployed within the time period and the average length of the unemployment period. So the same unemployment rate can be consistent with a large number of people becoming unemployed, but staying unemployed only for a short period of time, or with a lower inflow into unemployment of people who remain unemployed for longer. This distinction is very important, particularly its implications for policymaking and for an analysis of the possible causes of unemployment.

People who have been unemployed continuously for over a year are referred to as **long-term unemployed**. Long-term unemployment is particularly high in Europe where, according to OECD (1997) statistics, over 40 per cent of the unemployment is long term, compared with 12 per cent in the USA and 17 per cent in Japan. Once out of the labour market for over a year, it becomes increasingly difficult for the long-term unemployed to get back into a job, as employers often positively discriminate against them. A vicious circle of isolation and discrimination begins, which results in the marginalization of the long-term unemployed 'outside' the labour market.

Table 8.10   UK regional unemployment: UK and ILO measures

(a) Claimant unemployment rates (percentages)

	Seasonally adjusted annual averages				
	1992	1993	1994	1995	1996
United Kingdom	9.7	10.3	9.3	8.2	7.5
North East	12.1	12.9	12.4	11.6	10.6
North West and Merseyside	10.5	10.6	9.9	6.7	8.0
North West	9.4	9.5	8.7	7.6	6.9
Merseyside	15.0	15.1	14.9	13.7	13.1
Yorkshire and the Humber	9.9	10.2	9.6	8.7	8.0
East Midlands	9.0	9.5	8.7	7.6	6.8
West Midlands	10.3	10.8	9.9	8.3	7.4
Eastern	8.7	9.4	8.1	6.9	6.1
London	10.5	11.6	10.7	9.7	8.9
South East	8.0	8.6	7.3	6.2	5.4
South West	9.2	9.5	8.1	7.0	6.2
England	9.6	10.2	9.2	8.1	7.3
Wales	10.0	10.3	9.3	8.7	8.2
Scotland	9.4	9.7	9.3	8.1	7.9
Northern Ireland	13.8	13.7	12.6	11.4	10.9

(b)   ILO unemployment rates (percentages)

	Spring quarter of each year				
	1992	1993	1994	1995	1996
United Kingdom	9.7	10.3	9.6	8.6	8.2
North East	11.8	12.0	12.5	11.4	10.8
North West and Merseyside	10.1	10.8	10.3	9.0	8.4
North West	9.1	9.8	9.5	8.3	7.3
Merseyside	14.0	15.4	13.6	11.7	13.3
Yorkshire and the Humber	10.1	10.0	9.9	8.7	8.1
East Midlands	8.8	9.1	8.3	7.5	7.4
West Midlands	10.7	11.8	10.0	9.0	9.2
Eastern	7.7	9.2	8.2	7.5	6.2
London	12.0	13.2	13.7	11.5	11.3
South East	7.8	8.0	7.1	6.4	6.0
South West	9.1	9.0	7.5	7.8	6.3
England	9.7	10.3	9.5	8.6	8.1
Wales	8.9	9.6	9.3	6.8	8.3
Scotland	9.5	10.0	10.0	8.3	8.7
Northern Ireland	12.3	7.5	11.7	11.0	9.7

Source: ONS, Regional Trends, 1997

The labour market in the USA is rather deregulated; employers can hire and fire with greater ease. As a result people may lose their jobs but also find new ones more easily. Compared with the USA, the labour market in Europe is more regulated and constrained by legislation aimed at protecting the rights of people in employment. Hiring and firing is more difficult and more costly in Europe than it is in the USA. As a result, those who are in employment in Europe, the insiders of the labour market, enjoy greater job security, while those who lose their jobs find it harder to get back into employment. So, in the USA, unemployment is characterized by a higher rate of people becoming unemployed over the time period, but staying unemployed for a shorter period of time; while in Europe unemployment is characterized by a lower rate of new entrants into the pool of unemployment who stay unemployed for a longer period. The fact that the long-term unemployed become 'outsiders' in the labour market and find it harder to be offered employment, coupled with the fact that a large proportion of unemployment in Europe is long term, helps to explain why the unemployment rate is so much higher in Europe than the USA.

WHAT CAUSES UNEMPLOYMENT?

The working of the labour market is of crucial importance to the economy as a whole and to the conduct of macroeconomic policy. Because labour is an **input** in the production of the economy's **output**, the way in which the labour market works determines what the economy can produce. The labour market affects the behaviour of the supply side of the economy; in other words, it affects the shape of the aggregate supply curve. The persistence of unemployment – a situation of excess supply of labour – could be taken as an indication of malfunctioning of the labour market that needs to be explained. Unlike other markets – Keynes argued in the unemployment-ridden 1930s – the market for labour will not necessarily clear out of its own accord. If this is the case, only government intervention, in the form of expansionary policies, will bring about full employment. The classical economists in the 1930s and the neo-classical economists of the 1990s disagree. We are now going to focus on this debate.

Types of unemployment

Although all unemployed people are equally unemployed, the reasons why they are unable to find a job may vary considerably. The traditional classification of the causes of unemployment distinguishes between different types of unemployment:

- frictional;
- structural;
- demand-deficient or cyclical (Keynesian);
- classical.

The debate nowadays tends however to focus more on the issue of whether unemployment is voluntary or involuntary. From this point of view, Keynesians would argue that, with the exception of frictional unemployment, most unemployment is caused by a lack of demand in the economy and that demand-deficient or cyclical unemployment is involuntary, while the classical economists would maintain that all the types of unemployment listed above can be deemed to be voluntary.

We shall discuss these causes of unemployment in reverse order, starting with the classical explanation of the labour market and the argument that unemployment is always voluntary, followed by Keynes' counter-argument that unemployment is involuntary and caused by a lack of demand. We then move on to explain what is meant by structural unemployment and what causes frictional unemployment.

The classical analysis of unemployment is developed using a standard demand and supply model of the labour market, which is also useful to illustrate the points where Keynes's explanation differs. We shall therefore start with the classical supply-side explanation of unemployment, which is endorsed by the monetarist camp.

Classical view of labour market: monetarist approach

The term labour market refers to a broadly defined market, where households and firms interact: households provide the pool of labour available to firms as they supply their labour services to the firms(S^L); the firms, on the other hand, as an aggregate, represent the economy's demand for labour (D^L).

The labour supply (S^L)

When choosing whether and how much to supply of their labour services to firms, household members look at the going market wage rate and compare it with the value they place on their own leisure time, including the value of staying at home to bring up the family or to grow vegetables in the back garden. If a household member of working age and capable of work is not in the labour force, i.e. is not looking for outside employment by firms, it is because that person values free time more than the value firms place on it, expressed by the wage rate they offer for that person's services. If the going wage rate is very low, many people will choose to stay at home and will drop out of the labour force altogether. So the labour supply measures the amount of hours of work or units of labour people are willing to work at given wage rates. The higher the wage, the greater the amount of people willing to work and joining the labour force. The labour supply curve is upward sloping.

Demand for labour (D^L)

Each point on the labour demand curve represents the amount of labour that firms want to employ at that particular wage. Each firm decides how much labour to employ in the light of its profit-maximizing considerations. Firms make profit by selling their output to households. The firms' profits are affected by the prices they sell at and by the costs of production, including the cost of labour. A firm will employ an extra person if the value of that extra person's output is at least equal to the wage the firm has to pay. Hence the employment decision by firms is determined by how productive labour is in relation to its cost and by the value of the product (i.e. the price at which the product sells). The demand for labour is downward sloping: everything else being equal, in particular the price of the product sold, technology and other costs, the lower the wage rate, the higher the demand for labour. (See Figure 8.20)

Full employment at equilibrium wage rate

According to the classical economists, the way the labour market works is no different from the working of any other market, say the market for shoes or potatoes. If people want more goods than are currently being produced, aggregate demand will increase. This drives up the prices of goods and services, the demand for labour by firms increases (shown by a shift to the right of the D^L curve). This in turn pushes up wages, which attract more people into the labour force and more labour becomes available (movement up along the S^L curve). A new labour market equilibrium is reached, at a new higher equilibrium wage rate W_e, at which all those who want to work are in employment and the labour market clears. At the equilibrium wage rate W_e, the people who are not working are those who have chosen not to work at that going wage rate. The labour market will always clear: there will always be full employment, in the sense that all who want employment at the market wage rate find a job. It is important to understand that the concept of full employment in this context does not mean that all who would like a job can find one at the wage they want, but rather that all who would like a job at the going equilibrium wage can find a job.

✍ Activity 8.30

What if at the going market wage more people want jobs than there are jobs available?

Can it be really true that all those who want jobs at that wage will be able to find one?

✔ Answer 8.30

If at the market wage rate there are more people wanting jobs than there are jobs, in other words, at the going wage rate there is an excess supply of labour, then that particular wage rate is not the 'right' one; it is not the equilibrium wage rate at which labour supply equals labour demand. If there is an excess supply of labour – i.e. unemployment – it must be that the wage rate is too high (W_0). Some of those who are unemployed, when wages are W_0, will be willing to accept a lower wage and wages will fall as a result. Others, who are willing to work at a wage of W_0 but cannot find a job, will be unwilling to work for less and will drop out of the labour market when wages fall below W_0. As wages fall, fewer and fewer people will be willing to work and they will drop out of the labour market. In the end, the labour market will reach a point where the number of people willing to work at the lower going wage is just equal to the number of people that firms are willing to take on. At that **equilibrium wage**, the labour market will clear and there will be full employment.

However, it must be appreciated that the concept of full employment in this context is a relative one; it does not mean that all the able-bodied people of working age will find a job which fully utilizes their human resource potential at a wage which is a true reflection of their skills and qualifications. All it means is that wages have reached a level which is sufficiently low for firms to be taking on all those willing to work at that wage. The equilibrium wage may be regarded as too low by many people, who therefore do not offer their labour services to the market.

The labour market, like any other market, will eventually clear and full employment will be reached at the 'right' equilibrium wage. In this explanation of the labour market, the people who are not working are those who have chosen not to work at the market wage rate. Unemployment is always voluntary – people unwilling to work at the going market wage – and temporary, while wages adjust downward to the level which will eventually clear the market. As wages adjust downward, some people will drop out of the labour market and will not be referred to as unemployed any longer, as they will not be looking for a job or willing to work at the lower market wage rate. They will belong to that section of the population which is called inactive, despite being of working age. This is precisely what the participation rate quantifies indirectly, as it measures the percentage of people of working age who are in the labour market. (See Figure 8.20.)

Figure 8.20 The labour market

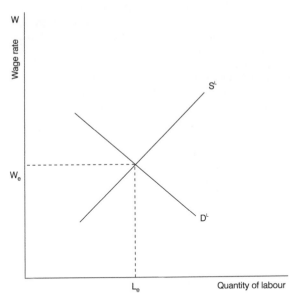

Figure 8.21 Equilibrium wage in the classical labour market

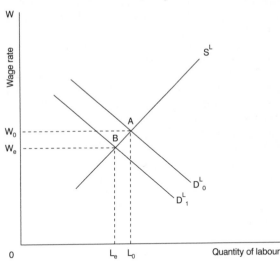

This is how classical economic theory describes the functioning of the labour market. The analysis of the market for labour treats workers as if they were potatoes or shoes, in no way different from any other good or service you can buy. If there is an excess supply of potatoes on the market, it must mean that the price of potatoes is too high. The excess supply will push the price of potatoes down, until the market will clear as less will be supplied at the lower price and more will be demanded. If there is unemployment – an excess supply of labour – it must mean that the price of labour, the going wage rate, is too high. Unemployment will push wages down, until the market clears as fewer people supply their services at the lower wage and firms demand more. Classical economists believe that the labour market always cleared. If the demand for labour shifts from D^L_0 to D^L_1, equilibrium wage falls from W_0 to W_e. Every person who wants a job at W_e will find one (Figure 8.21).

✍ Activity 8.31

The classical and neo-classical economists claim that the labour market works well and always clears to ensure full employment. If their claim is correct, how can we account for the high and persistent rates of unemployment experienced by most economies? If millions of people are looking for a job at the prevailing wage rates, can it still be maintained that unemployment is voluntary?

✓ Answer 8.31

The neo-classical economists argue that the existence of unemployment is not a proof that the labour market is not working well. First, it may take some time for the labour market to adjust to changes in demand, particularly to structural changes which cause a mismatch of skills, as people need to review their expectations, both in terms of wages and new jobs available, which may not match their skills and expertise. Second, the existence of unemployment points to **labour market rigidities**, which prevent the market from functioning properly, bringing about the full employment outcome predicted by the model. If labour market flexibility is increased and its rigidities removed, then the economy will always be at full employment and unemployment will always be only voluntary.

Summing up, classical or voluntary unemployment is the unemployment that monetarists, like the classical economists, attribute to rigidities within the labour market. Powerful trade unions and/or minimum wage legislation prevent wages from falling and employment from adjusting to their new equilibrium level.

Classical view of labour market and absence of money illusion

A vertical AS curve

We can now add the missing link and relate the classical view of the labour market to the theory that what the economy can produce with its given amount of capital and existing technology is fixed and cannot be increased by the use of aggregate demand policies. If the economy's aggregate supply is fixed, the AS curve is vertical.

The classical view that wages adjust to clear the labour market is consistent with the view that wages respond quickly to price changes. As Figure 8.4 shows, if AD exceeds what the economy is currently producing in the short run, at Y_1, then prices will rise. If wages also rise, in response to the general price rise, the AS curve shifts to the left and pushes Y back to its original level Y_1. If, on the other hand, aggregate demand contracts and the AD curve shifts to the left, then all prices, including wages will fall, shifting the AS curve to the right and pushing the economy's output back to its original level. In other words, flexibility of prices and wages in both directions, up and down, ensures that the economy remains at full employment and produces the maximum amount of output compatible with its existing stock of capital and technology. Workers do not suffer from money illusion and are prepared to take lower real wages when the demand for the economy's output falls, hence ensuring that output and employment do not fall as a result.

Classical economists and neo-classical economists believe that the wage rate adjusts quickly to clear the labour market. In consequence they also believe that the AS curve is vertical (or almost vertical) and that monetary and fiscal policies have no effect on output and employment.

Demand-deficient or cyclical unemployment

The Keynesian approach

The classical analysis of the labour market identified the cause of unemployment as too high wages and the persistence of workers' reluctance to accept lower wages. As we said before, this analysis treats labour like any other commodity and the policy prescription – a price (wage) reduction – is the same as for any market situation of excess demand. The classical analysis stops there – precisely where Keynes's 'analysis refuses to stop – and does not question the effect that lower wages have on the economy and society.

Workers, unlike potatoes, are active economic agents who are an integral part of the economic system. Lower wages, Keynes pointed out, will mean lower consumption, which will reduce aggregate demand and cause further contractions of the economy's output and employment, therefore frustrating the prime objective of the wage cut, which was to increase employ-

ment; to say nothing of the social cost of a policy of wage reductions, in terms of poverty, destitution and crime. How low can a wage rate be? What if wages are already at a mere subsistence level and still unemployment persists (which happened in the 1930s); can wages be pushed down any further?

Keynes turned the classical economists' analysis of the labour market on its head. He pointed out that the equilibrium wage which clears the market also depends on the level of demand. The lower the level of aggregate demand, the lower the demand for labour, the lower the equilibrium wage, for a given supply of labour. If aggregate demand were higher, the equilibrium wage would also be higher, as Figure 8.22 shows.

Given the demand for labour, D^L, and the supply of labour S^L, at the market wage rate of W_0, above the equilibrium wage rate W_e, there is excess supply of labour, measured by $L_2 - L_0$, while the number of people in employment is measured by L_0. The classical economists' prescription to bring about full employment is a policy of wage cuts, which by reducing wage rates from W_0 to W_e would increase employment from L_0 to L_1. That increase in employment would never materialize – argued Keynes. Even assuming that a policy of wage cuts could be accepted by workers and trade unions, lower wages would reduce income and consumption demand by workers. This would translate into a reduction of the demand for firms' products: firms would cut down on production and consequently on their demand for labour, shifting the demand for labour to the left. A policy of wage cuts would make

Figure 8.22 Keynes's analysis of the labour market with 'sticky' wages

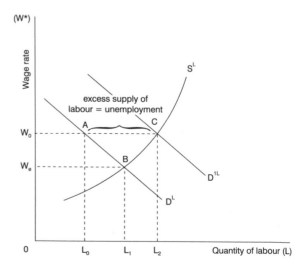

unemployment worse rather than reducing it. The labour market would not clear as a result and the economy would be caught in a spiral of falling prices, falling wages, falling output and rising unemployment.

The Keynesian prescription to restore full employment is a policy of stimulating aggregate demand, through the use of appropriate government fiscal and monetary policies. As the demand for the economy's output increases, so does the demand for labour by firms, shown by a shift of the D^L curve out from D^L to D^{1L}. For the same wage rate W_0, employment increases from L_0 to L_2: a movement from A to C.

Keynesian view of labour market and existence of money illusion

An upward sloping AS curve

As a result of the increase in aggregate demand, employment will increase from L_0 to L_2 and the economy's output will increase. What will happen to output prices? They will have increased too, as a result of increased demand, and yet the increase in employment from L_0 to L_2 takes place at the same wage rate W_0: workers suffer from money illusion, as they do not realize that working for the same nominal wage rate, when the prices of goods and services increase, is like taking a real wage cut. Hence, the result that the classical economists were trying to achieve through a painful and divisive policy of wage cuts can be more easily achieved through an expansionary government policy, which by injecting some inflation into the system and causing prices to rise brings down the real cost of labour and leads firms' output to grow. The Keynesian aggregate supply is upward sloping (Figure 8.23).

Let's assume that the economy is producing the output Y_0 at the price level P_0; this is associated in the labour market to an employment level of L_0 at the wage rate W_0. To reduce unemployment, the government stimulates aggregate demand, which shifts from AD to AD^1, causing prices to rise to P_1 and output and employment to grow to Y_1 and L_2 respectively. To reach full employment, aggregate demand will need to increase further to AD^2, where the full employment level of output will be produced (Y_f).

To sum up, according to Keynes, unemployment is due to a lack of aggregate demand; hence the term 'demand deficient unemployment' often used to describe the Keynesian type of unemployment. This type of unemployment is also associated with the recognition that, in the short run at least, wages are sticky in the downward direction and do not adjust quickly enough to restore equilibrium in the labour market. Wage cuts, on the other hand, depress demand

Figure 8.23 A Keynesian upward sloping aggregate supply curve

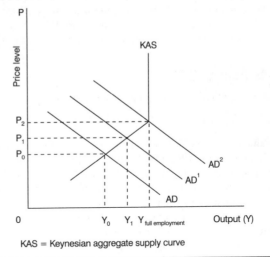

KAS = Keynesian aggregate supply curve

and would be counterproductive. Keynesians regard this type of unemployment as **involuntary**, as workers are willing but unable to find a job at the going wage rate.

Structural unemployment

Structural unemployment is caused by the changing pattern of demand. As people's tastes and technology change over time, the economy's supply needs to adjust. The demand for record players has gone down in Britain in the last ten years, but the demand for CD players has gone up. As income increases over time, goods with a relatively low income elasticity of demand, such as food, tend to become less important and account for a smaller share of total expenditure, while there is an increase in the demand for goods with a high income elasticity. International patterns of comparative advantage also change, causing the decline of some industries in some countries. In Britain, for instance, the shipbuilding and textile industries have dramatically declined in the last 30 years or so.

As these changes occur, the economy needs to adjust, changing the pattern of both output and employment. At any moment in time, some sectors in the economy will decline and some will expand. The sharp decline of the manufacturing sector in Britain in recent years has been counterbalanced by an equally rapid increase in the service sector. But the expanding service sector does not require the same skills as the contracting manufacturing sector. Firms may be reluctant to sustain the cost of retraining older workers made redundant by contracting sectors. Structural unemployment is associated and exacerbated by what economists call workers' **occupational immobility**: a skills/jobs mismatch, often compounded by lack of proper training, closed shop and qualification barriers.

✍ Activity 8.32

Study Table 8.11 and explain what it shows.

✓ Answer 8.32

Table 8.11 shows how the structure of employment has changed in the UK since 1978. The aggregate number of people in employment has declined by about 2.6 per cent over the period, but the structure of employment by sector has changed radically. If we look at the data for manufacturing industry, and calculate the decline in employment that has taken place there, we see that employment in manufacturing has fallen from over 7 million in 1978, which represented 32 per cent of total employment, to about 4 million in 1996, equivalent to 18 per cent of total employment. Employment in banking and financial services, on the other hand, has more than doubled in 18 years, having gone up by 140 per cent, from 7 per cent to 17 per cent of total employment. Employment in agriculture, on the other hand, has fallen by nearly a third, from 1.7 per cent of total employment in 1978 to 1.2 per cent in 1996.

These changes have further repercussions on the *pattern* of unemployment. Manufacturing activity has traditionally employed a high proportion of male workers and has been concentrated in certain parts of the country. Employment in services, on the other hand, tends to absorb a much higher proportion of female workers and does not follow the same pattern of geographical location.

Under the general umbrella of structural unemployment, economists also tend to group unemployment due to the **geographical immobility** of labour. The classical theory predicted that, as a result of disinvestment of capital in one geographical area, labour will move to other areas where there is plenty of capital investment and where employment can be found more easily; just as capital will move to those areas where plenty of unemployed labour can be found. In real life the labour market does not work that smoothly, as unemployed workers do not necessarily move from high unemployment areas to those where jobs are easier to find. Labour, in other words, far from being totally mobile, is characterized instead by geographical immobility, due to people's social and family ties, housing and relocation problems, schooling problems, etc.

Frictional unemployment

Frictional unemployment is the minimum level of unemployment to be found in any modern economy.

Table 8.11 Analysis of UK employees by industry, 1978–96 (in thousands)

Year	Agriculture, forestry and fishing	Coal, oil and natural gas extraction and processing	Electricity, gas, other energy and water supply	Manufacturing	Construction	Banking, finance, insurance etc.	Public administration and defence	Education and health services	Other* services	Total
1978	395	358	359	7281	1199	1569	1728	2834	7066	22 789
1979	380	354	368	7253	129	1647	1719	2893	7320	23 173
1980	373	355	371	6937	1243	1695	1667	2900	7449	22 990
1981	363	344	366	6222	1130	1739	1623	2908	7197	21 892
1982	358	328	352	5863	1067	1798	1594	2902	7153	21 415
1983	350	311	338	5525	1044	1875	1606	2886	7133	21 068
1984	340	288	328	5409	1037	1969	1602	2900	7355	21 238
1985	357	289	270	4988	1055	2754	1478	3664	6568	21 423
1986	345	246	262	4868	1027	2841	1473	3777	6548	21 387
1987	337	211	257	4799	1049	2958	1492	3924	6557	21584
1988	329	188	257	4839	1091	3163	1477	4121	6793	22 258
1989	316	174	252	4828	1129	3333	1401	4155	7073	22 661
1990	314	162	241	4709	1143	3480	1442	4200	7229	22 920
1991	306	149	230	4299	1053	3419	1462	4244	7108	22 270
1992	309	126	216	4084	951	3396	1464	4288	7097	21 931
1993	326	92	205	3906	865	3445	1460	4284	7030	21 613
1994	299	70	192	3923	864	3465	1441	4322	7125	21 700
1995	272	67	170	4021	838	3633	1404	4375	7245	22 028
1996	267	65	130	4016	825	3774	1383	4380	7355	22 195

Source: ONS, *Blue Book*, 1997

* Other services includes wholesale and retail trade; repairs, hotels and restaurants, transport and storage, post and telecommunications.

Even if the economy is running at full capacity, the unemployment rate will never be zero. In a dynamic economy, there will always be people who are unemployed because they are in-between jobs: people change careers or directions in their lives. They resign from their jobs in the hope of finding something better. Some businesses go bankrupt and close down, while new ones develop. Some firms will be hiring people, others will be firing them. Frictional unemployment is typically short term.

Natural rate of unemployment and labour market rigidities

The concept of the existence of a natural rate of unemployment has gained increasing currency in recent years, partly as a spin-off of the classical analysis of the labour market and the monetarist approach to the problem of unemployment, and partly as an attempt to explain the persistence of large rates of unemployment in most industrialized economies.

Natural rate of unemployment is the amount of unemployment caused by the institutional and economic rigidities described above, which would therefore persist even if and when the labour market cleared. It measures the amount of people in the labour force not prepared to accept job offers at the going equilibrium wage rate, for whatever reason: trade union pressure, occupational immobility, geographical immobility, hope for a better position. It includes structural, frictional and classical unemployment. The natural rate of unemployment, according to this analysis, is entirely voluntary. In Figure 8.24 if union power succeeds in maintaining the wage W_1 in the long run, the labour market will be at A and the natural rate of unemployment AC would show the amount of unemployment indirectly chosen by the labour force by allowing trade unions to enforce the wage W_1.

The schedules D^L, S^L, and S^{AW} show, respectively, labour demand, the supply of labour and the number of workers willing to take job offers at any real wage. S^{AW} lies to the left of S^L because some labour force members are either between jobs or are hoping for a better job offer. When the labour market clears at E, EF measures the natural rate of unemployment, the number of people in the labour force not prepared to take job offers at the equilibrium wage W^*.

✐ Activity 8.33

Try to identify the main features of a flexible labour market.

✓ Answer 8.33

In response to rapid changes in technology and unstable demand conditions, firms have fundamentally changed the way in which they make use of their labour force. The emerging feature is one of increased flexibility: people are no longer, it seems, appointed on a permanent basis to specific jobs. Firms want to have the flexibility to tailor their response to demand conditions: if demand falls, they want to be able rapidly to get rid of people, without having to pay huge redundancy costs. If demand rises, they want to be able to take on people equally quickly. To accommodate changes in technology, firms nowadays want the flexibility of shifting people around, changing their job specifications. They want to be able to take on people in some areas and shed them in others, frequently reassessing the situation. To accommodate this new brand of 'flexible firms', which in turn are a product of uneven demand and volatile capital, labour markets have become more flexible.

It seems that firms increasingly demand different types of flexibility. They demand **financial flexibility**, by increasingly rewarding individual productivity rather than paying a given rate for a given job. This is reflected in a tendency for local contracts to replace national ones, with wage differentials both within the same industry and across regions growing wider. Firms increasingly demand **size flexibility**, by adjusting the

Figure 8.24 The natural rate of unemployment

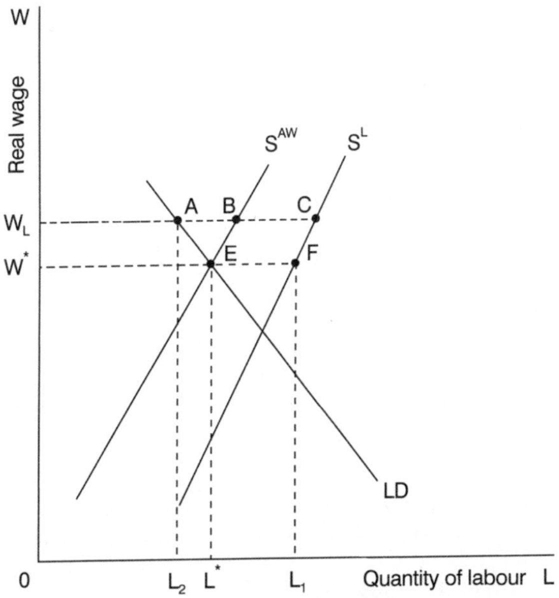

size and composition of their labour force to changing demand conditions. This is reflected in employment being increasingly offered on a part-time, sub-contractual or even casual basis, rather than on a full-time basis; this in turn is responsible for a change in the gender/race balance of employment and unemployment. Firms increasingly demand **task flexibility**, whereby workers are frequently reassigned to different tasks, unlike the 'old days' when people were employed to do a specific job. This behaviour on the part of firms is reflected in a move away from specialisms towards an increasing demand for people with transferable skills.

You may have observed some of these tendencies taking place around you: in firms or organizations you know, job specifications you have come across, friends or members of your family in employment, your own direct work experience, your knowledge of the labour market from job centres and employment agencies. Concluding labour market flexibility results from many factors, such as: pay flexibility, flexibility in hours worked, flexibility in conditions of employment, functional flexibility, labour redeployment within the firm, ease of hiring and firing and contracting out.

Equally, labour market rigidities stem from different sources. Among these are: sticky wages; minimum wage laws; efficiency wages; imperfect information; hysteresis. Let's briefly look at these different sources of labour market rigidities.

Sticky wages

One explanation for the persistence of unemployment, which goes beyond frictional and structural unemployment, is that wages are 'sticky' in the downward direction, as workers and trade-unions resist cuts in real wages. Wage stickiness results in a higher level of unemployment than would otherwise be the case (Figure 8.25).

If the demand for labour falls and wages are prevented from adjusting downward to a new lower equilibrium level W_e, then unemployment will emerge and persist as long as aggregate demand does not recover. The problem with wage stickiness as an explanation for unemployment is that it rather begs the question why wages are not flexible downward, if indeed they are not; what causes their rigidity? Several explanations for this have been put forward in recent years, none of which seems totally convincing:

- the **implicit contract theory,** according to which firms enter an implicit social contract with their employees not to cut wages. Only exceptional events this century have resulted in nominal wage

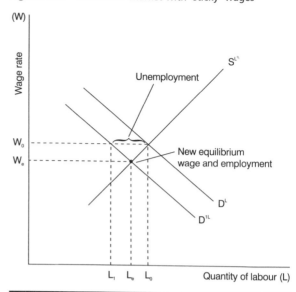

Figure 8.25 The labour market with 'sticky' wages

cuts. It is precisely because of this recognized resistance to nominal wage cuts that Keynes advocated a policy of reflation, rather than deflation, to achieve the same result of cutting real wages, without causing social conflict.

- the **explicit contract theory**, which points at the fact that many categories of workers, in particular unionized ones, only renegotiate their contracts at three- or four-year intervals. Once wages are fixed, the occurrence of unforeseen events will have no effect on them. Wages may turn out to be either too high or too low.

- the **relative-wage explanation** of unemployment, according to which workers are more concerned with the level of their wages relative to that of other workers and would resist any wage cut which makes them worse off with respect to other groups of workers.

Minimum wage laws

The existence or introduction of minimum wage laws goes some way towards explaining the persistence of unemployment. Government legislation fixes a minimum hourly rate for any kind of job, which provides a floor for wage rates.

✍ Activity 8.34

With the use of a demand and supply diagram, show the effect of the introduction of minimum wage legislation. Where do you draw the minimum wage : above or below the equilibrium wage rate? Carefully explain your answer.

✓ Answer 8.34

As Figure 8.26 shows, the effect of minimum wage legislation on competitive labour markets is to create unemployment, by preventing wages from falling to their equilibrium level. In the case of minimum wage legislation, it must also be noted that it tends to hurt young school-leavers the most, as they try to enter the labour market with little or no job experience. The Labour government in Britain avoided this problem in 1997 as it exempted people under the age of 21 from its newly introduced minimum wage legislation.

The effect of minimum wage legislation on non-competitive markets, such as those characterized by monopsonistic demand for labour (where there is a single employer either in a geographical area or an employment sector), is instead to increase both wages and employment.

Efficiency wage

The efficiency wage theory maintains that the productivity of workers increases, the higher their wage rate. Empirical studies have indicated that firms which pay their workers wages above the market equilibrium wage experience lower turnover, better morale and greater productivity. If this is the case, firms may have an incentive to pay their workers a wage above the market-

clearing rate, which is referred to as the **efficiency wage**. If all employers behave in a similar way, then the general level of wages will tend to rise over time. However, at the higher efficiency wage, firms' demand for labour will be the same as before (a firm will continue to hire workers up to the point where the value of the marginal product of the last person employed is at least equal to the wage rate paid) but the supply of labour will be greater, causing unemployment.

The efficiency wage theory, although certainly applicable in some cases – Ford is a case in point – cannot convincingly be used to justify the large-scale unemployment experienced by most industrialized economies in the 1980s and 1990s.

Imperfect information

This explanation for the existence of unemployment points at the fact that firms do not behave in the way described by textbooks. For a start, individual firms may not know which is the correct equilibrium wage rate when they offer employment contracts to their employees. If they offer wages which are too high, this will result in attracting too many applicants to the firms, and some will have to be turned down. If the process is widespread enough, this will ultimately cause some unemployment. Furthermore, this unemployment will tend to persist, because of the lags and imperfect information which characterizes real-life situations. It takes a long time for firms and individuals to recognize the existence of disequilibria and to identify and respond to its causes.

Hysteresis

As well as persisting through time, the natural rate of unemployment also tends to grow over time. This fact too needs to be explained. Recent research seems to suggest that prolonged periods of high unemployment tend to cause an increase in the natural rate of unemployment. This phenomenon is called **hysteresis**. Hysteresis, which is a term used in physics, is said to occur when a variable which has been temporarily subjected to an external force, does not return to its original value even after the external force is removed. The terms suggests that the natural unemployment rate may rise and remain at a higher level, as a result of some temporary shock which has caused the unemployment rate to rise. Applied to unemployment, hysteresis can be explained as follows: trade unions represent the interests of their members who are in employment. To pursue their interest, they will tend to bargain for wages which are above the equilibrium wage, provided their

Figure 8.26 The effect of minimum wage laws on competitive labour markets

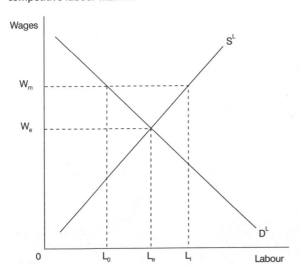

own members stay in employment, 'inside' the firm. Higher wages will hurt those who are 'outside' and not in employment; they will find it harder to find employment and will remain stuck in unemployment.

However, the boundary between insiders and outsiders tends to change according to the pattern of actual unemployment. If unemployment persists over time, the chances that insiders will get fired increases. Insiders who lose their jobs become outsiders. The trade unions, however, continue to represent the interests of those who remain insiders, raising wage demands further and perpetuating the process; temporary increases in unemployment may become permanent. As a result, the natural rate of unemployment is seen to increase over time. The importance of this effect for actual movements in the natural rate of unemployment remains open to debate. Empirical measures of the natural rate of unemployment have proved as elusive as its definition and the explanations of its determinants (see Table 8.12).

POLICIES TO REDUCE UNEMPLOYMENT

Policies to reduce unemployment can be divided into two main categories: demand-side policies associated with Keynes and the Keynesians, and supply-side policies, favoured by Friedman and the monetarists. While the Keynesians refute the ability of the economy and of market forces to bring about full employment, monetarists believe in the market mechanism and consider unemployment beyond the 'natural rate' as only temporary, caused by incorrect expectations or imperfect information.

The Keynesians argue instead that wages in real life are determined by collective bargaining and by administrative decisions in internal labour markets and in the public sector. These decisions bear no relationship with the marginal revenue product of labour and the equilibrium wage of the classical economists.

Keynesian policies

Keynesian policy prescriptions to reduce unemployment are based on demand management:

- increased government spending, particularly on investment and infrastructure;
- reduction in taxation, to increase disposable income and spending, both direct and indirect.

However, these policies, could be inflationary and counter-productive. The moderate Keynesians therefore advocate their implementation in conjunction with some other policy, such as:

Table 8.12 Unemployment rates in OECD countries, 1950–96*

	1950s	1960s	1970s	1980s	1990	1996
North America						
Canada	3.8	4.7	6.6	9.3	8.1	9.2
USA	4.4	4.7	6.1	7.2	5.4	5.7
Japan	2.1	1.3	1.7	2.5	2.1	3.4
Europe						
France	1.5	1.7	3.8	9.0	8.9	11.3
Germany	4.9	0.6	1.9	5.7	4.9	9.3
Italy	7.2	3.8	4.7	7.5	8.2	11.6
Netherlands	1.5	0.9	4.0	9.6	7.5	6.9
Spain	2.1	2.3	4.2	17.5	15.9	21.9
UK	1.7	2.0	4.4	10.1	6.9	8.2
Austria	4.3	2.1	1.6	3.3	3.2	4.6
Finland	1.6	2.1	3.7	4.9	3.4	16.1
Norway	1.7	1.7	1.6	2.8	5.2	4.6
Sweden	1.7	1.5	1.8	2.2	1.7	7.3
Switzerland	0.3	0.1	1.2	1.5	1.1	3.9
Australia	1.5	2.0	3.9	7.5	7.0	8.1
New Zealand	0.9	0.9	1.5	4.1	7.7	6.4
OECD	3.5	2.8	4.3	7.0	6.0	7.7

Source: OECD, *Economic Outlook* (various issues)
*The figures are averages total labour force unemployed over the period.

- Price and income policies, often used in the 1950s and 1960s, to freeze prices and incomes to prevent them from rising, causing inflation.
- The Cambridge school of Keynesian economists in particular recognizes the fact that stimulating demand to reduce unemployment may cause balance of payments problems, as imports would exceed exports and low interest rates would cause an outflow of capital, with an impact on the exchange rate. In response they advocate import controls, which are not politically acceptable nowadays, at least on a large scale, and are likely to cause problems within the EC and the WTO.
- The trade-off between inflation and unemployment is still accepted by most Keynesians, who reject the vertical Phillips curve analysis. In their view, therefore, some inflation must be accepted as a price for reducing unemployment.

Monetarist policies

Monetarists policies focus on supply-side economics, which uses microeconomic incentives to alter the level of full-employment, of potential output and the natural rate of unemployment. Supply-side policies are analysed in the next chapter. The monetarist strategy is aimed at improving the labour market mechanism, making it more flexible and responsive to market forces. They recommend:

- making work more attractive by cutting unemployment benefits, which would reduce voluntary unemployment, and by reducing direct taxes, which would give people a greater incentive to work;
- improving the competitiveness and profitability of industry, which would in turn create more jobs. This could be achieved through lower inflation, which helps exporting firms, lower interest rates to stimulate investment, lower taxes on companies, which would increase incentives, and less controls imposed by the government on industry.

General policies

All economists, would agree on the following set of measures to improve the functioning of the labour market and increase employment:

- more and better information on vacancies;
- better career guidance and manpower planning;
- more retraining of the workforce, in particular youth training schemes;
- incentives to encourage greater flexibility and mobility of the labour force;
- regional specific measures to solve local structural problems, such as regional development grants, enterprise zones, relocation allowances, subsidies, improvement in the infrastructure, particularly the road networks.

Some, however, would argue that these measures are sufficient on their own to tackle unemployment on the scale experienced by the industrialized economies in recent years.

CASE STUDY: DOWNSIZING THE POUND

How the value of cash has declined and how purchasing priorities have changed

In the second part of the 1990s the UK achieved its best inflation performance for nearly 40 years (Figure 8.27). The framework for UK monetary policy has become increasingly open through a series of steps which have included giving the Bank of England independence in the setting of interest rates to achieve the government inflation target and publication of its Inflation Report and the minutes of Monetary Policy Committee (MPC) meetings.

This openness has also exposed the declared uncertainty and 'ignorance' of real economic fundamentals within which monetary decisions are made by the MPC. Monetary policy influences inflation only with a lag, so interest rate decisions are based on an assessment of the prospects for inflation up to two years ahead. Interest rate decisions are not based solely on any one indicator, such as the RPI, but on an assessment of all the relevant information concerning the prospects for inflation:

- **monetary and financial indicators**, including narrow and broad money, exchange rates, asset prices and expectations about future inflation;

- **indicators of activity**, including measures of the level of demand, such as measures of spare capacity, retail sales growth and the state of the labour market;
- **fiscal policy**'s overall stance is also taken into account;
- **indicators of costs**, in particular wage costs and material input prices.

The published minutes of MPC monthly meetings reveal the inherent difficulty for monetary policy decisions related to the achievement of the target rate of inflation. Opinions are still divided over whether measuring inflation is useful for the conduct of monetary policy. Germany's central bank, the Bundesbank, uses a broad measure of money supply as its target instead.

Recent studies in the USA have also argued that conventional measures of inflation such as the retail price index (RPI), can overstate the rate of inflation, as it cannot easily measure changes in productivity and quality. The price of computers, for example, has hardly changed in recent years, but their capacity has greatly increased.

Despite these criticisms and doubts as to whether the RPI should be used as a target measure for setting interest rates, it remains the most

continued overleaf

DOWNSIZING THE POUND

Figure 8.27   UK inflation rates, 1949–2000

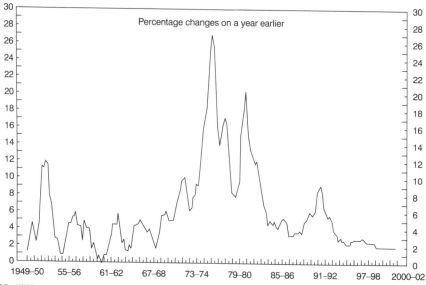

Source: HMT, FSBR, 1998

important measure of inflation in the UK and the government target measure for monetary policy. The Bank of England's task remains to keep RPI inflation to 2.5 per cent and City of London analysts continue to focus on the behaviour of this index.

The index provides us with much more than a crude measure of inflation. It also shows how spending patterns have shifted over the years, as a result of increasing wealth and changed lifestyles. The study of RPI statistics offers a fascinating portrait of changes in fashion and tastes (Figure 8.28).

Figure 8.28   Purchasing priorities across decades

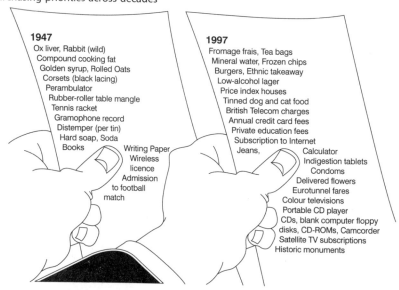

The way we were: lard and mangles in 1947, fromage frais and CD-ROMS in 1997

Source: Observer, August, 1997

DOWNSIZING THE POUND

The RPI was introduced by the Labour government in 1947, to replace the Cost of Living Index for the Working Classes, a crude attempt to measure the price of 14 essential items established in 1914. It was compiled on the basis of a wide survey which aimed at estimating the costs of running a typical household. The focus of the survey in 1947 was still provided by the working-class family, defined then as a household earning £250 a year or less. This benchmark definition did not change until 1956.

A comparison of what enters the average household basket of goods in 1997 provides an interesting insight into social changes. In 1947 over a third of working-class household incomes was spent on food, while only 8 per cent was spent on services. Drink and tobacco accounted for a substantial 22 per cent of household expenditure and those categories only included beer, whisky, cigarettes and pipe tobacco.

The average household of the 1990s smokes and drinks much less, only 11 per cent of total expenditure, partly due to the fact that prices of drinks and tobacco have increased the most. A pint of beer cost 7p in 1947 compared with an average of £1.65 in 1997. Food only accounts for 14 per cent of the average household's expenditure, while a generous 33 per cent is spent on services (Figure 8.29).

The value of cash has also decline dramatically since 1947, as Figure 8.30 shows.

Figure 8.29 Where the money goes: 1947–97

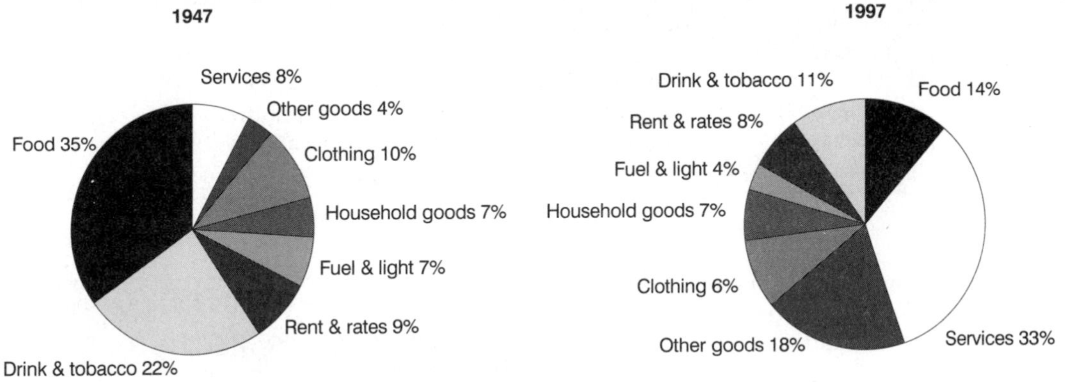
1947
Services 8%
Other goods 4%
Food 35%
Clothing 10%
Household goods 7%
Fuel & light 7%
Rent & rates 9%
Drink & tobacco 22%
1997
Drink & tobacco 11%
Food 14%
Rent & rates 8%
Fuel & light 4%
Household goods 7%
Clothing 6%
Other goods 18%
Services 33%

Source: R. Adams, *Observer*, August, 1997

Figure 8.30 Downsizing the pound. How the value of cash has declined

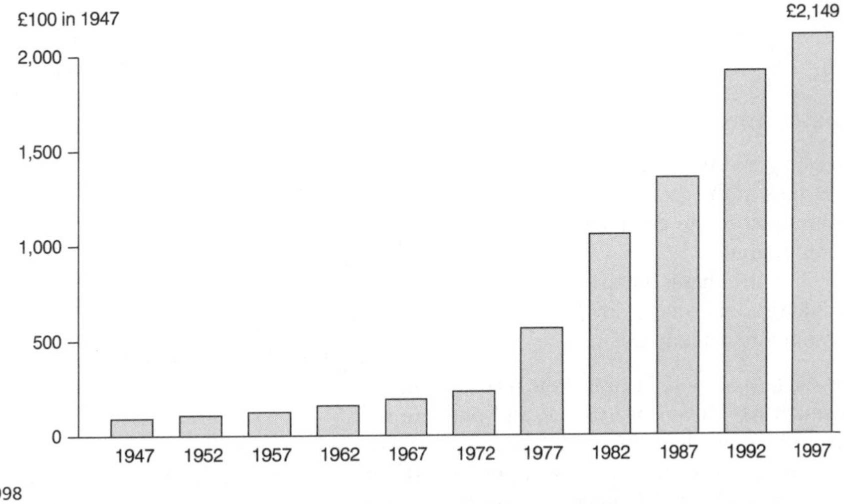
£100 in 1947
£2,149
2,000
1,500
1,000
500
0
1947
1952
1957
1962
1967
1972
1977
1982
1987
1992
1997

Source: ONS, 1998

☆ **For revision of this chapter, see the Chapter Summaries at the end of the book, starting on page 411.**

9 Supply-side economics: The monetarist model

Objectives

After studying this chapter you will be able to:

- understand the terms of the debate between Keynesians and monetarists;
- explain the implications of price and wage flexibility in the monetarist model;
- explain the implications of wage rigidity in the Keynesian model;
- understand what supply-side policies are;
- understand the implications of supply-side policies for business;
- explain what determines the rate of growth of potential output;
- understand the relationship between economic growth and the business cycle;
- understand what determines output growth in the short run and long run.

There have been many occasions throughout the book where the disagreement between Keynesians and monetarists has surfaced in relation to some specific topic.

✍ Activity 9.1

Try and make a list of areas of disagreement between the two schools of thought already mentioned.

✓ Answer 9.1

We mentioned their differing views about:

- the role of monetary and fiscal policies;
- the effect of changes in the quantity of money;
- the role of government in the economy;
- the exchange rate regimes;
- the desirability of central bank independence;
- the causes of inflation and unemployment and the policies better suited to remedy them.

Now that all the main sectors of the domestic macro-economic environment have been introduced and put together in the preceding chapters, the time has come to take a more systematic approach to the analysis of the two opposed Keynesian and monetarist models, and to focus on supply-side policies.

THE RISE OF MONETARISM: AN HISTORICAL PERSPECTIVE

The monetarist counter-revolution began to emerge in the early 1960s as an alternative explanation for the operation of the economy to Keynes's demand management. Keynes's *General Theory of Employment, Interest and Money*, published in 1936, had proved to be one of the most influential books this century. Its assumptions, as we have seen, essentially argue that demand is the economy's engine, that government policies aimed at controlling it are its steering wheel and that the economy, left to its own devices, will not necessarily bring about full employment. If the government wants the economy and employment to grow faster and stay on track, it should create a virtuous circle of expansion, by investing directly into the economy, by giving people more money to spend, by running budget deficits and printing more money, if necessary: more goods and services will be produced to satisfy this increased demand.

Demand creates its own supply. The acceptance of the Keynesian paradigm by most governments in the industrialized west in the post-war period led to the widespread use of demand side macroeconomic policies. Hence the subsequent polarization of the debate in terms of demand-side versus supply-side economics.

Supply creates its own demand

Keynes's views had been deemed revolutionary in the 1930s because they contradicted the classical economic thinking which had prevailed since the publication of Adam Smith's *Wealth of Nations* in 1779. A distillation of such thinking was provided in the 1830s by the French economist, Jean Baptist Say, who encapsulated it in his famous law, **Say's Law**, which states that **supply creates its own demand**. It could be argued that Say was a forerunner of modern **supply-side economics** as he explicitly argued against the use of demand policies to stimulate the economy:

> The encouragement of mere consumption is of no benefit to commerce; for the difficulty lies in supplying the means, not in stimulating the desire of consumption; and we have seen that production alone, furnishes those means. Thus, it is the aim of good government to stimulate production, of bad government to encourage consumption. (Say 1821)

According to Say's Law, supply creates its own demand: the production of goods creates the real wealth, which can then be spent to purchase the goods produced by the economy.

Writing in the depth of the Great Depression of the 1930s, it was easy for Keynes to point at the glut of unsold goods and idle factories as a counter-example to Say's Law: plenty of goods, but no money to buy them. Economies, argued Keynes, could find themselves locked into a depression, stuck in a situation of equilibrium at less than full employment, in other words, in a situation of fundamental disequilibrium: only government demand management could come to the rescue. Just as the experience of the Great Depression provided the historical counter-example which eventually lead to the demise of the classical paradigm and the triumph of Keynesianism, the stagflation of the 1970s, characterized by high inflation and high unemployment, led to the demise of Keynesianism and the rise of monetarism. Keynes had advocated the use of expansionary, though inflationary, policies as a remedy to unemployment. The persistence of high rates of unemployment, despite rampant inflation, in most industrialized countries seemed to disprove the core of his theory and led to its abandonment.

Supply-side economics, as we know it today, developed as an explicit repudiation of Keynes's demand-side principles. Led by Milton Friedman it developed almost as a by-product of the work which Friedman and a group of economists of the Chicago School had done on the effect of changes in the money stock on the economy. The name **monetarism**, given to this school of thought, stems from the central role that their theory attributes to the supply of money in the economy. This view is often summed up in the statement that for the monetarists 'money is all that matters for changes in nominal income and for short-run changes in real income'; a statement partly endorsed by Friedman, who regards it as an exaggeration of his views, but one which 'gives the right flavour' of his conclusion.

The monetarists' best-known claim is that there is a direct, though lagged, causal relationship between changes in the money supply and inflation: 'Inflation is always and everywhere a monetary phenomenon.' The governments of the inflation-ridden 1980s fought their battles against inflation waving sharp, monetarist swords. But where is the link between this monetarist claim and supply-side economics? If it is true that changes in the money supply only affect prices but not output, then the use of demand side-policies, such as an expansionary fiscal or monetary policy to stimulate output growth, is ruled out. An expansionary fiscal policy which is not accompanied by an increase in liquidity will cause interest rates to rise and cannot be successful in the long run; while increases in the money supply only cause prices to rise, as wages also rise by the same amount of inflation (vertical AS curve). In this kind of scenario, only supply-side policies work to stimulate output growth.

THE CORE OF THE DEBATE

Let's remind ourselves once more of why this is so: why can't demand-side policies work and why should supply-side policies succeed where demand-side policies fail? Just as it takes two to tango, it takes a demand and a supply together to determine an equilibrium market price and quantity, not simply one or the other in isolation. The first thing you need to be aware of is that in order to favour either demand-side or supply-side policies you must be making some assumptions about the other 'missing' side of the market. So the first step towards understanding the demand-versus-supply debate is to understand those hidden assumptions.

As Figure 9.1 shows, the interaction of demand and supply conditions determines the price of a product and the quantity produced; just as changes in those conditions cause prices to change. Price changes act as a signal, transmitting the information that market conditions have altered, to which economic agents respond, buyers and sellers alike, by revising their actions. Their revised decisions about how much to

Figure 9.1 Market equilibrium: an increase in demand

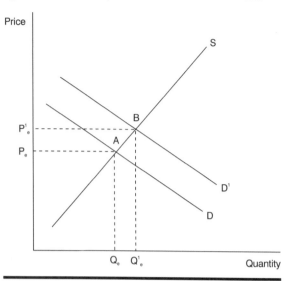

demand or supply of a certain product at the new price will eventually restore a new equilibrium, at a different price/quantity relationship. These general principles hold whether we look at one individual market in isolation or at the economy as a whole.

✍ Activity 9.2

Given unchanged supply conditions, what will be the effect on the equilibrium price of an increase in the demand for a product?

✓ Answer 9.2

Given a certain supply, an increase in demand for a product will cause the product price to rise, as shown in Figure 9.1.

✍ Activity 9.3

Can you think of a situation where prices would not rise as a result of an increase in demand?

✓ Answer 9.3

Prices would not rise if there were an unlimited amount of productive resources, which could be used to produce more when demand increases. Prices would not rise only in the case of an infinitely elastic supply.

The price rise signals the fact that people want more. Producers and sellers respond to this information, conveyed by the price rise, by producing and supplying more, assuming that their costs of produc-

tion and distribution are unchanged. This is shown by a shift out of the demand curve from D to D^1 which will lead to a new, greater, equilibrium quantity Q_1 at the higher equilibrium price P_1 (a movement along the upward-sloping supply curve). If firms' wages and input prices rise as a result of the generalized price increases, supply will shift back, causing a new equilibrium position to be reached at a higher price than before, but not necessarily at a higher quantity. Whether the quantity supplied will increase at all will depend on the responsiveness of factor prices to output price increases. The greater their responsiveness, the smaller the quantity increase as a result of an increase in demand. This is shown by Figures 9.2 and 9.3 which compare the response to a change in demand conditions of two supply situations with differing price elasticities.

This point has several important implications, particularly when it is explored from a supply-side or labour market angle, assuming a reduction in the demand for output takes place. If the demand for potatoes decreases, there will be a temporary glut of potatoes that nobody wants on the market. As a result of this, the price of potatoes will fall, thereby inducing an increase in demand, as more is demanded at a lower price, and at the same time a reduction in supply, as less is supplied at a lower price. The combined effect of these two opposing forces brings the market back to a new equilibrium position, where both equilibrium price and equilibrium quantity are lower than before. The fall in the price of potatoes restores equilibrium.

Figure 9.2 An extreme case: a perfectly inelastic aggregate supply

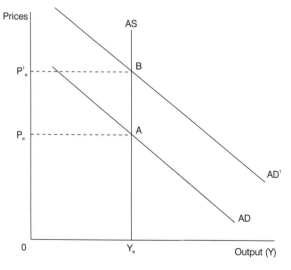

Figure 9.3 An extreme case: a perfectly elastic aggregate supply

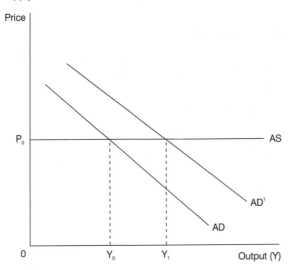

Figure 9.4 Effect of a reduction in the demand for labour, assuming flexible nominal wage rates

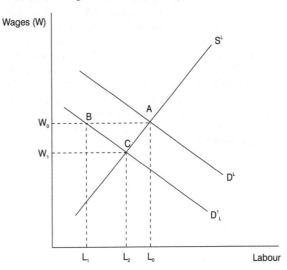

Are wages flexible?

The same mechanism should apply to the market for labour: when output demand falls short of its current level and goods prices fall, firms will want to produce less and save on costs. They will demand less labour. As a result, there will be an excess supply of people willing to work at the going nominal market wage with respect to demand for it. This is what we call unemployment: an excess supply of labour at the going market wage. The unemployment will fall, but not by the full amount of the cut in demand, if nominal wages fall. This situation is shown in Figure 9.4 as $(L_0–L_2)$.

If nominal wages are flexible in the downward direction and workers are willing to take a cut in their real wage, then a reduction in the demand for labour will cause a fall in wages and a new labour market equilibrium at a lower nominal and real wage and lower level of people in full employment. If nominal wages are fixed, then the burden of the adjustment to the new situation will fall entirely on the quality of labour, as the resulting unemployment will be greater, as Figure 9.5 shows.

If nominal wages are rigid and inflexible in the downward direction, a way of achieving real wage reduction, avoiding ensuing large unemployment, would be for the government to inject some inflation into the economy by pursuing expansionary fiscal and monetary policies. If prices rise but nominal wages remain the same, real wages fall (defined as nominal wages/price level, the amount of goods one can buy with one's wages). As Keynes (1936) put it in the *General Theory*:

Whilst workers will usually resist a reduction of money-wages, it is not their practice to withdraw their labour whenever there is a rise in the price of wage goods. It is sometimes said that it would be illogical for labour to resist a reduction of money wages, but not to resist a reduction of real wages … but whether logical or illogical, experience shows that this is how labour in fact behaves.

Inflationary policies should be used in a situation of wage rigidity, to minimize the effect of a contraction in

Figure 9.5 Effect of a reduction in the demand for labour, assuming sticky nominal wage rates

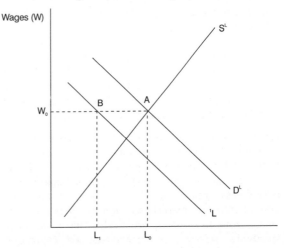

demand on unemployment. Keynes therefore agreed with the classical economists on one very important point that: real wage rate reductions would reduce unemployment – but disagreed with the classical economists on the best way of achieving this. Given workers' and trade union resistance to cuts in their nominal wages (the take-home pay), the inflationary cure for unemployment is far less painful, Keynes would argue, than the orthodox approach, of trying to achieve the same result by forcing workers and trade unions to accept a lower nominal wage rate. The same result of reducing real wages could be achieved by injecting inflation, assuming, however, that nominal wage claims stay the same.

Keynes's approach was a combination of monetary and employment policy, the effect of which was later captured by Phillips in his famous relationship between inflation and unemployment. Monetary policy and employment policy could no longer be regarded as independent from one another.

But this is not where the story ends, retorts Friedman. Workers learn from inflation the monetarists say – and adjust their wage demand accordingly. Inflation, far from reducing unemployment, would contribute to its growth, by causing a self-perpetuating spiral of price-wage-price increases. So what would the monetarists suggest instead?

THE MONETARIST MODEL

At the core of the monetarist model are the beliefs that:

■ If prices are flexible, markets will clear, i.e. markets are stable and will reach equilibrium; this would apply in particular to the market for labour.
■ If markets are competitive, then market equilibrium is reached at the largest possible quantity for the lowest possible price;
■ Workers do not suffer from money illusion. An increase in the general price level will lead them to press for higher nominal wages, to safeguard their real wages. An increase in demand which causes prices to rise will not be followed by an increase in supply which is sustainable in the long run.

From these beliefs it follows that the government's main aim should be to encourage price flexibility and foster market competition, eliminating as far as possible those factors, such as government taxation and benefits, minimum wage legislation and trade-union power that distort markets and prevent the price mechanism from functioning efficiently. The government should also refrain from demand-side policies, as they

are ineffective as a means of increasing output and employment in the long run.

✍ Activity 9.4

Try and justify, once more, the monetarist view that demand-side policies are ineffective to stimulate output and employment, at least in the long run.

✓ Answer 9.4

The monetarist view is better explained with the use of a diagram.

Figure 9.6 shows an economy where AD and AS conditions determine equilibrium output Y_0 and price level P_0. The level of output Y_0 is associated to a labour market situation such that, with price level P_0 and nominal wage W_0, employment is L_0 and unemployment is measured by L_1–L_0, as shown in Figure 9.7.

As, say, the government increases AD to reduce the amount of unemployment by injecting inflation, the demand for labour will temporarily increase as real wages fall due to inflation (shift of D^L to D^{IL}. Employment increases from L_0 to L_1). As nominal wages are renegotiated to take inflation into account (shift of S^L to S^{IL}), the level of employment and aggregate supply will go back to the original level; only prices will change in the long run as a result of this policy.

Rolling back state frontiers and reducing government intervention makes sense only if you believe that markets are competitive and that, left to regulate themselves, they will bring about the best possible outcome: full employment of the economy's resources, that is the largest possible output at the lowest possible price.

Figure 9.6 The response of supply to demand changes (where $W_1 > W_0$)

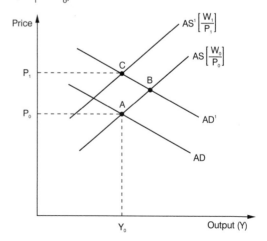

Figure 9.7 The labour market with no money illusion

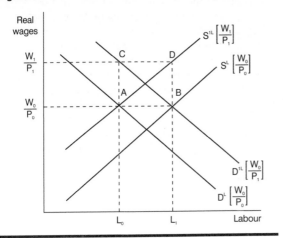

These are 'strong' beliefs, whose realism raises doubts in the minds of many. Yet in the last three decades of this century, the governments of major economies, such as the USA or the Commission of the European Union (which originates policies in the EU), have tried to implement monetarist policy prescriptions. They have focused on the conclusion of the monetarist syllogism, markets should be left to regulate themselves, without questioning the realism of its premises: markets are competitive and competitive markets bring about the best possible outcome.

For the outcome of 'full employment of all resources and largest possible output at the lowest possible price' to be achieved, prices would need to be flexible; in particular the following three crucial prices:

- the price of money, i.e. the interest rate;
- the price of foreign currency, i.e. the exchange rate;
- the price of labour, i.e. wages and salaries.

Interest rate flexibility

Given the demand for money, the cost of borrowing money, i.e. the interest rate, will vary according to the quantity of money injected into the economy by the monetary authorities: it will fall as the money supply increases and increase as the supply of money falls. The interest rate will settle at whatever level is compatible with the state of the economy, given a certain demand and supply of money. According to the monetarists, the government should set its monetary targets and allow the interest rate to find its own free market level; this would ensure that the money market is always in equilibrium.

At the heart of the monetarist approach towards interest rates is the analysis of what affects the demand for money. In the Keynesian model, as we have seen in Chapter 6, the demand for money is determined by the level of national income (transactions and precautionary motives) and the interest rate (speculative motive). But given the level of national income, the demand for money is determined by the interest rate (to be precise, by the difference between actual and expected rates). In the monetarist model, on the other hand, the interest rate has a very limited influence on the demand for money. It is only affected by the level of income, as people are used to holding a certain amount of money in relation to their money income. According to the monetarists, it is this fixed relationship between the amount of money people wish to hold and the level of their money income which determines the economy's demand for money.

Whether the interest rate plays an important part in determining the demand for money, as Keynes thought, or whether it is of little consequence, as the monetarists believe, has important implications for the whole model of how the economy works. The monetarist view leads to the conclusion that changes in the supply of money directly affect national income, and may in fact be the only thing that affects national income. The Keynesian view, on the other hand, leads to the conclusion that changes in the supply of money affect national income only indirectly (via its effect on interest rates, hence investment and possibly consumption), but in some cases, it may not affect it at all (liquidity trap situation, irresponsiveness of investment to interest rates).

Let's pause here for a moment and review these points, which we introduced in earlier chapters, so that we can see them in their broader context.

✍ Activity 9.5

Try and explain once more what happens, according to each school of thought, when the central bank increases the quantity of money by, say, buying government securities in the open market (open market operations).

✓ Answer 9.5

According to the Keynesians, money and other financial assets are a good substitute for each other. Quite a small rise in the price of government bonds, caused by the Bank of England entering the market for bonds and buying them, will lead people to sell bonds and hold money instead. This will lead to a new overall equilibrium, where people will hold more money and fewer bonds than they did before. Interest rates will also be lower and this will possibly lead to an increase in investment and consumption expenditure, although the induced increase in expenditure may not be very large.

The monetarists, on the other hand, believe that the money is a good substitute not only for financial assets, but for all assets. The end result of people selling their bonds to the Bank of England in exchange for money (and they do so because, given the increased demand for bonds, the price of bonds has increased) will not just be that they hold on to more money in its liquid form. Rather it will be that people will hold more of other assets as well, such as houses, durable goods, etc. A change in the supply of money causes people to change not only the structure of their financial assets, by shifting between government securities and money, but also the structure of their overall portfolio of assets, which includes money, government securities, houses, durables goods, etc.

Contrary to what Keynes thought, money and other financial assets are not very good substitutes for one another. If the central bank wishes to increase the money supply by buying back bonds from the public, it will only be able to induce people to part with their securities in exchange for money by bidding up the price of securities substantially. This in turn will mean a substantial fall in interest rates, a fall, in other words, in the yield on government bonds and other securities. At the same time, however, the yield in terms of consumer satisfaction that people get from owning other assets, such as a house, car or refrigerator, have not changed. In an attempt to maximize the overall yield they receive on their assets as a whole, people will therefore sell (or not buy) government securities and buy durables and other consumer goods instead.

The same reasoning, only in reverse, applies if the central bank wishes to reduce the supply of money by selling government bonds. According to Keynes, people will end up holding less money and more bonds, which will have an effect on income mainly thorough the higher interest rates (causing a reduction in investment). According to the monetarists, a reduction in the money supply, caused by people buying bonds in exchange for money, will create a reduction in people's money holdings with respect to their income, to which they will respond by selling assets to restore their money balances, but also by reducing their consumption.

This leads the monetarists to the view that there is an empirically observed, stable relationship between the demand for money and the level of income (a stable velocity of circulation). This piece of monetarist doctrine is often referred to as the theory of a 'stable money demand function'. The amount of money people wish to hold, in cash or bank deposits, is related in a stable, predictable way to their income. If the central bank increases the money supply by buying back government securities held by the public, those who have sold back the securities in exchange for money will find that their money holdings have risen in relation to their income. To restore their conventional money balances, they will spend the excess money, instead of just holding it as extra liquidity or for buying other financial assets, as Keynes thought. On what will they spend it? On anything – is the monetarists' answer – and not just financial assets. They will buy other financial assets, but also other goods and services; in so doing they reduce their money balances and add to the demand for goods and services.

✍ Activity 9.6

Can you summarize what the upshot of this analysis is?

✓ Answer 9.6

The main conclusions which can be derived from this analysis are:

■ for the Keynesian theory, the relatively twisted way in which monetary policy affects output and income, as it does so only indirectly if at all, via the effect of interest rates on investment. The control of interest rates, in this scenario, is of paramount importance as they affect the level of investment and provide the only meaningful link between monetary policy and the rest of the economy. The interest rate becomes an important control variable for management of the economy. Efforts should be made to keep interest rates low, to stimulate investment, hence demand, output and employment.

■ for the monetarist theory, the importance of monetary policy, which directly affects aggregate demand and the price level. Attention should be focused, for the monetarists, not on influencing interest rates but on controlling the money supply itself, as the money supply affects aggregate demand directly.

But will an increase in aggregate demand raise output, income and employment? Not in the long run is the monetarists' answer, as wages will adjust to rising prices and real wages will remained unchanged. We are back to the 'vertical aggregate supply' arguments discussed earlier. If the monetarist model holds, then the supply of money is really the only macroeconomic variable which the government needs to control in order to control inflation and the price level. To affect output, the government needs to implement a series of sector-specific, supply-side policies instead.

Exchange rate flexibility

What about the external balance of the domestic economy? What about ensuring that the balance of payments of the domestic economy with the rest of the world stays in balance, that the outflows of domestic money in payment for imports of goods and investments abroad are balanced by equal inflows of foreign money in payment for exports and foreign investments? Should not the government pursue an active policy to ensure these factors? The monetarists argue that a system of flexible exchange rates (for reasons that will become clear in the next chapter) would ensure that the balance of payments is in equilibrium, without the need for further intervention.

The demand for import and exports depends, among other factors, on the relative price levels of the countries concerned. Suppose that inflation which is higher in Britain than in the USA causes the demand for US imports to increase and the demand for UK exports to the USA to fall. This will result in a change of demand for the respective currencies. The pound will depreciate vis-à-vis the dollar, making British goods cheaper for Americans to buy and therefore restoring the competitiveness lost because of the higher rate of inflation. The same would apply to the demand and supply of foreign currency associated with movements of capital. What is more, the flexibility of exchange rates ensures monetary policy independence of the country in question. For all these reasons, the monetarists favour a system of flexible exchange rates.

✍ Activity 9.7

The monetarists tend, however, to support the introduction of a single currency in Europe. Is there a contradiction in this?

✓ Answer 9.7

As we have seen, the introduction of the single currency prevents national governments from pursuing demand management policies, as budget deficits and inflation rates are capped. Furthermore, centrally controlled monetary growth would be geared to the achievement of set inflation targets. The single European currency would also be free to float vis-à-vis other currencies. All these aspects of EMU do fit in with the monetarist approach.

Wage flexibility

We have already dealt with this aspect of the monetarist model. According to the monetarists, the excess supply of labour at the going nominal wage – people looking for jobs but unable to find them – is an indication that the price of labour is too high. If wages were to come down, more people would be offered employment. If wages do not come down in the face of unemployment, then the unemployment is voluntary: no one would want a job at a lower wage. People choose to be unemployed rather than accepting a lower wage: they are not involuntarily unemployed.

MONETARISTS VERSUS KEYNESIANS

To sum up, the debate between the monetarists and the Keynesians centres around three main issues:

- the effectiveness of monetary versus fiscal policy;
- the Phillips curve;
- supply-side policies versus demand-side policies.

Monetary versus fiscal policy

This is the aspect of the debate which we have explored more fully, and repeatedly, in the course of the preceding chapters. Keynes stressed the importance of fiscal rather than monetary policy, particularly to fight recessions. Investment is rather irresponsive to changes in the interest rate, the Keynesians argue; hence changes in the interest rates have little effect on demand and output. This explains why monetary policy is not considered a very effective tool. Fiscal policy, on the other hand, by acting directly on demand, can affect output and employment more quickly and reliably.

Friedman challenged this conclusion, particularly in *A Monetary History of the United States 1867–1960*, written in collaboration with Anna Schwartz, where he reviewed the relationship between quantity of money and output in the USA over a century. Friedman and Schwartz concluded that the evidence proved that changes in the quantity of money could explain most of the fluctuations in output over the period, in particular the Great Depression, which was caused in their view by a sudden and sharp contraction of the money supply (due to a string of bank failures which the Federal Bank failed to counteract with an increase of the monetary base). Monetary policy, they concluded, was a powerful instrument for the control of economic activity. However, governments should refrain from the use of even monetary policy to produce fine adjustments in economic activity: 'There are serious limitations to the possibility of a discretionary monetary policy and much danger that such a policy may make matters worse rather than better,' (Friedman, 1958).

A consensus of opinion has been reached, after the intense research which has followed the debate, on the respective effects of monetary and fiscal policies. Economists nowadays broadly agree that if the government wishes to affect the composition of the economy's output and take into account the openness of the economy, then the best policy is a mix of fiscal and monetary policy. They also broadly agree on the need to combine demand and supply-side policies and on a preference for less interventionist governments.

The Phillips curve

The Phillips curve was not originally part of the Keynesian model, as it was developed so much later by Professor Phillips. It seemed, however, to explain the movements of wages and prices in a way that fitted perfectly Keynesian theory in a way which was empirically reliable. For this reason it became associated with the Keynesian model (or rather with the later rationalization of it, provided by the neo-classical synthesis). Keynesians in the 1960s believed that there was a stable trade-off between unemployment and inflation, even in the long run.

Friedman and Edmund Phelps disagreed and argued that such trade-off would exist only in the short run and would quickly vanish even if government persistently tried to exploit it by injecting inflation to reduce unemployment. Workers would learn from past experience of inflation, would start to expect inflation and, in order not to lose from it, would anticipate it in their wage claims. As we saw when we looked at the empirical data for inflation and unemployment, Friedman and Phelps were right to deny the existence of a trade-off in the 1970s and 1980s. UK unemployment and inflation data in the 1990s seem to indicate the reappearance of a trade-off. Rather then representing a counter-argument, this could simply reflect a combination of factors, such as a reduction of inflationary expectations coupled with weaker trade unions and large unemployment. These factors have made people possibly less able and less willing to protect the level of their real wages in the 1990s.

The outcome of the debate on the Phillips curve also reflects on the more general discussion of which policy or set of policies should governments follow to ensure full employment and faster output growth.

SUPPLY-SIDE POLICIES AND GROWTH

Keynes focused on the use of demand-side policies to stimulate growth. He argued that a strong aggregate demand for more goods and services would give firms the incentive to invest in order to produce more, adding to their capital stock and ultimately increasing the economy's ability to produce more, its potential growth.

Potential growth is defined as the percentage annual increase in the economy's output capacity (the rate of growth of potential output), as opposed to **actual growth**, which is the percentage annual increase in national output (the rate of growth of actual output).

✍ Activity 9.8

It is often maintained that Keynesian demand-side policies are short-run policies aimed at ensuring that actual output is kept as close as possible to potential output, which do not, however, address the long-run issue of what determines the rate of potential economic growth. Do you agree?

✓ Answer 9.8

An increase in the demand for goods and services (an increase in consumption demand, ΔC) gives firms an incentive to invest. An increase in investment has a double function in the economic system: on the one hand it represents a further addition to aggregate demand (ΔI), as firms demand more capital goods to expand their productive capacity. Capital goods industries respond to the increase in demand for capital goods by expanding their production of such goods (and the employment in their sector) to the point of full utilization of their firms' capacity. This is the *short-run demand-side effect*, where an increase in aggregate demand ensures the full utilization of the economy's existing productive capacity. However, the addition to capital, which is the result of the additional investment by firms, adds to their output capacity, hence to the economy's potential growth. This is the *long run supply-side effect* on the capacity of the economy to produce more, triggered nonetheless by an initial increase in aggregate demand.

The monetarists, as we have seen, deny that increases in aggregate demand provide businesses with an incentive to invest, as increases in aggregate demand cause prices to rise, leading to proportionate wage and cost increases which rapidly erode the greater profitability margins generated by a strong demand. Hence, growth in potential output can only be achieved by the use of supply-side policies which increase the ability of the economy to produce more regardless of demand conditions.

✍ Activity 9.9

What are the main determinants of the economy's growth potential?

✓ Answer 9.9

There are two main determinants of the growth of the economy's output capacity or potential output and they are:

- the growth in the amount of productive resources available, in particular capital and labour (assuming that land reclamation possibilities have been exhausted, that the rate of exploitation of raw materials is at its maximum and ruling out invasion of neighbouring countries, the amount of land and raw materials available in an economy is fixed);
- the growth in the productivity of those resources.

Growth in the amount of productive resources

Growth of labour

The growth of the economy's output is determined by the growth of labour and by an increase in the productivity of labour. The growth of labour is determined by an increase in the size of the working population, which is determined in turn by two factors:

- the rate of population growth;
- the activity rate, i.e. percentage of the population of working age who join the labour market.

For an increase in the amount of labour employed to generate a sustained increase in the economy's output, it must also be that the amount of capital used also increases, to avoid the setting in of diminishing returns. Alternatively, diminishing returns can be avoided by increasing the productivity of labour. Labour productivity is increased by better education and training; hence the importance attributed to schemes aimed at retraining the labour force, in particular unemployed people.

Growth of capital

The economy's output also depends on the stock of capital (K). Consequently, the growth of the economy's output depends on the growth of its stock of capital (ΔK) and on the productivity of capital.

The growth in the stock of capital depends on the proportion of national income that is invested (i):

$$i = \Delta I / \Delta Y.$$

The productivity of capital is measured by the marginal capital/output ratio (k). The **marginal capital/output ratio** is the amount of extra capital ΔK divided by the extra annual output it produces:

$$k = \Delta K \, / \, \Delta Y.$$

Ultimately, growth (g) will be determined by:

$$g = i/k$$

or assuming that all saving is invested:

$$g = s/k.$$

✍ Activity 9.10

Assume that 20 per cent of the economy's income is spent on investment and that every £1 spent on new investment generates an extra 20p worth of output a year. Calculate the rate of growth of this economy.

✓ Answer 9.10

If i = 20 per cent (i.e. $\Delta I/\Delta Y$ = 20 per cent) and k = 5 (i.e. $\Delta K/\Delta Y$ = 1/0.20) then the rate of growth would be 4 per cent as:

$$g = 20\%/\,5 = 4\%.$$

The next crucial question then becomes: what determines the rate of investment? We answered this question in Chapter 4.

✍ Activity 9.11

See whether you remember our discussion of what affects investment and list its main determinants.

✓ Answer 9.11

Investment is determined by:

- the rate of interest, as higher interest rates increase the costs of investment and reduce the value of future income streams;
- business profitability, which in turn is affected by the tax system and the behaviour of the labour market;
- demand conditions, as they affect business expectations and confidence about future demand conditions. In order to invest in an expansion of their output capacity, business must believe that there is going to be a sustained increase in the demand for their products. Firms may need first to experience an increase in the current demand for their products. Hence, it can be argued that growth in potential output is affected by growth in actual output, in turn determined by demand conditions.

Supply-side policies

Specific supply-side policies, rather than macroeconomic policies, should be used to increase the competitiveness and productivity of the economy, its actual output. Supply-side policies, such as measures to encourage technological innovation and training and tax incentives to encourage investment and employment, should also be used to increase the economy's potential output. On the whole, supply-side policies aim at enhancing the economy's productivity by increasing the efficiency, competitiveness and flexibility of markets through the following.

Increased wage flexibility

This is achieved through weakening the power of the trade unions. Important legislation with far-reaching effects was introduced in Britain in the 1980s to limit the activities of trade unions and reduce their collective strength in the process of wage bargaining. As part of such legislation, secondary picketing (picketing by workers not directly affected by a trade-union dispute, but in solidarity with other workers) was outlawed, together with the practice of closed shop (trade-union membership as a precondition for employment by a firm).

Reduction in unemployment benefits and income support

Unemployment benefits, it is argued, have a disincentive effect on workers, who prefer to stay idle and live on state benefits; they become choosier as to which jobs to accept and more hard nosed about wages. A reduction in benefits will increase the labour supply and exert a downward pressure on wage demands.

One significant, recent change in this respect, has been the replacement of the unemployment benefit with the **jobseeker allowance**, qualification for which is more difficult to obtain. The change, however, does not address the disincentive to work caused by the **poverty trap**, into which many people fall at the bottom of the income scale. A previously unemployed person who takes a job and earns an income may end up being poorer than before since entitlement to family benefits, housing benefit, etc. is greatly reduced or lost.

Increasing the mobility of labour

Labour mobility can be interpreted and assisted in different ways. Labour mobility between jobs can be increased by providing unemployed people with more information about job vacancies and equipping them with the relevant skills through training schemes. Geographical mobility of labour, to encourage people to move from depressed regions with low employment opportunities, can be helped by relocation grants, etc.

Increasing the mobility of firms

Firms can be encouraged to establish their businesses in depressed, high unemployment areas, via tax incentives and capital investment rebates.

Tax rate cuts

Tax rate cuts would lead people and firms to work harder and produce more. The resulting increase in activity would lead to an increase and not a decrease in tax revenues.

Privatization and deregulation

Private ownership of productive assets, it is argued, leads to greater productivity and efficiency. Areas of economic activity previously managed and owned by the state were opened to market forces and privatized in many industrialized economies. A huge wave of privatizations, initiated by Mrs Thatcher's Conservative government, swept Britain in the 1980s and 1990s, as Table 9.1 shows. The expected gains in terms of efficiency and productivity remain hard to detect, while greater unemployment has resulted from ensuing rationalizations.

SUPPLY-SIDE POLICIES IN THE UK

Monetarism, in its broad interpretation, has influenced economic policy in the UK in recent years. It is quite useful, therefore, to analyse the government policies in some detail as they help to understand the practical implications of the supply-side approach.

Table 9.1 Major UK privatizations since 1979

Year	Company	Revenue (£m)
1979	BP (part)	276
1981	BP (part)	200
1981	Cable and Wireless (part)	182
1982	Britoil (part)	627
1983	BP (part)	543
1983	Cable and Wireless (part)	263
1984	BT (part)	3916
1984	Jaguar	297
1985	Britoil (part)	449
1985	Cable and Wireless (part)	900
1986	British Gas	5600
1987	British Airways	900
1987	Rolls-Royce	1100
1987	BAA	600
1987	BP (part)	7200
1988	British Steel	2400
1989	Water Companies	3500
1990	Electricity Distribution Companies	5200
1991	Electricity Generators (part)	3200
1991	BT (part)	1100
1994	British Coal	800
1995	Electricity Generators (part)	1800
1996	Railtrack	1900
1996	Nuclear Power	2500

Source: ONS, Economic Trends, 1997

The scope for policies aimed at stimulating growth and employment in the UK is highlighted by the extent to which the UK is currently lagging behind other major industrial countries.

✍ Activity 9.12

Look at Figure 9.8 and explain what it shows.

✓ Answer 9.12

Figure 9.8 shows that output per head of population is about 50 per cent higher in the USA and 20 per cent higher in Japan than in the UK. The output per head gap reflects a number of factors, including:

- *low employment rate:* according to the statistics discussed in Chapter 8, around one in four of the working-age population are either unemployed or economically inactive. Around one in five working-age households have no one in work, which is double the level in 1979 and higher than most other developed economies.
- *capital stock per employee* is also lower: in other leading economies, such as Japan, Germany and the USA, capital stock per employee is at least 50 per cent higher than in the UK.
- *research and development (R&D)* has fallen in the UK relative to almost every other major country between 1981 and 1995.

As structural weaknesses have deepened, **income inequality** has grown in the UK. By the mid-1990s together with the USA, the UK had the unenviable record among the major industrialized countries of the widest disparity between high and low incomes. The income share of the bottom 20 per cent of household (lowest quintile) fell from 9.6 per cent in 1979 to 6.3 per cent in 1995. By contrast, the income share of the top 20 per cent of the households increased from 35 per cent to 43 per cent.

We have looked at the rationale, from a theory point of view, for supply-side policies. We are aware of the problems faced by the British economy. Let's now look at the supply-side policies introduced by the UK government in recent years, in order to tackle these problems. The government supply-side measures can be grouped under three headings:

- policies aimed at promoting enterprise and stimulate long term investment, through incentives and reduced taxation;
- policies aimed at improving the flexibility of the labour market, through reforms of the welfare system, training initiatives and trade-union reforms;
- policies aimed at increasing market competitiveness, through privatizations and deregulation.

Policies to promote enterprise and stimulate long-term investment

To reduce unemployment and increase output growth potential, the UK government is set to improve the performance and competitiveness of British business. Its recent policies are aimed at creating and sustaining a more dynamic and innovative business environment, removing the barriers which have traditionally held back investment in the UK, in particular a tax system which has discouraged enterprise.

As we have seen in Chapter 4, since at least 1960 the UK has consistently invested less as a share of GDP than the OECD countries on average. The UK share has averaged around 18 per cent, compared to the OECD average of almost 21 per cent. The UK has also invested out of a lower level of GDP per head. This has translated into a lower level of investment per worker. As a result of lower investment per worker, the UK has a lower level of capital stock per worker, as Figure 9.9 illustrates.

✍ Activity 9.13

Look at Figure 9.9 and explain more precisely what it shows.

✓ Answer 9.13

Figure 9.9 shows that, compared with the UK, the amount of capital per worker is almost twice as high in Japan and Germany, while in the USA and France it is more than 50 per cent greater.

Figure 9.8 GDP per head selected countries, 1997

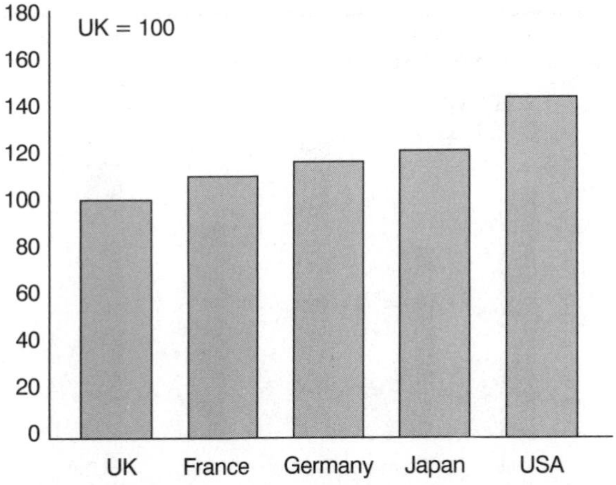

Source: Adapted from *OECD Economic Outlook* June 1998: 63. Copyright OECD 1998

Figure 9.9 Capital stock per worker, 1994: selected countries

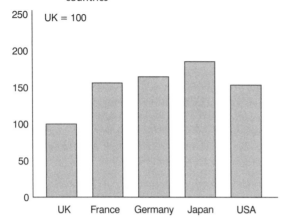

Source: HMT, FSBR, 1998
Note: Data in capital stock are extremely unreliable and are difficult to estimate. Different countries are using different accounting procedures and different depreciation rates. Therefore these data should be seen as illustrative.

The fact that the UK has a lower level of capital stock per worker helps to explain why UK productivity is nearly 40 per cent lower than among major competitors, which results in lower GDP per head. To improve its relative position, the UK needs to invest more than other countries as a proportion of GDP, while improving the quality of its investments.

For these reasons, one of the government's declared objectives is to create an improved climate for long-term investment. To achieve this objective the British government introduced the following tax measures in 1998:

- *a reduction in the main corporation tax rate* from 33 to 31 per cent, which did benefit some 50,000 companies;
- *a reduction in small companies' rate* of corporation tax, from 23 to 21 per cent, which again benefited some 400,000 companies;
- *temporary doubling of capital allowances for small and medium enterprises' plant and machinery:* expenditure on plant and machinery by small and medium-sized enterprises qualified for about 50 per cent of write-down allowance.

Policies to promote innovation and research and development

Investment is not just about building up a physical capital stock. Investment in research and development (R&D) is also an important element in fostering growth

and employment. In this respect too, however, UK investment lags behind its major competitors.

✍ Activity 9.14

Look at Figure 9.10 and explain what it shows.

✓ Answer 9.14

Figure 9.10 shows two worrying features of R&D expenditure as a proportion of GDP in the UK:

- It is lower than all UK main competitors.
- While almost all UK major competitors have increased R&D's share of GDP in the past decade, the UK's share has actually fallen.

The reforms to capital gain tax, corporation tax and other investment incentives outlined above are intended to have a positive spill-over effect and create a more favourable environment for investment in the UK, which will also include research and development.

To encourage better exploitation of ideas generated by its scientists and universities, the government has set up a University Challenge Fund, to bridge the funding gap which has traditionally prevented universities from transforming good research into good business through innovation.

Policies to increase the flexibility of the labour market

Policies to increase employment

To stimulate employment, in 1998 the British government introduced a Welfare to Work programme aimed at attacking youth and long-term unemployment and

Figure 9.10 Research and development expenditure as proportion of GDP: selected countries

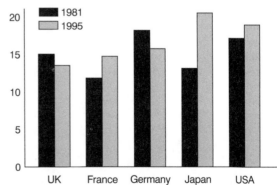

Source: Adapted from *OECD Economic Outlook*, December 1996: 60
Note: Germany 1995 figure distorted by unification

the low levels of employment among lone parents. The programme, financed by a one-off tax on the excess profits of privatised utilities, planned a £5.2bn expenditure to be spent over a six-year period.

New Deal for the young unemployed

This programme started nationally in April 1998 and for each young unemployed it initially envisages:

- a **gateway period** of careers advice and intensive help with looking for work and training in the skills required by the job market;
- an **employer option** to help young people move straight into a job. To encourage employers to play their part in the scheme, the British government offers a £60 a week subsidy for the first six months to firms offering employment to young people, coupled with £750 allowance per person to finance training towards accredited qualifications.
- a **full-time education** for some young unemployed people, either as on-the-job training in vocational skills or as a course at a local college.
- a **job with the voluntary sector** which would provide young people with the work experience and skills that will help their employability. Voluntary sector placements are envisaged to provide 50,000 new trained childcarers to support other aspects of the Welfare to Work programme.
- a **job with the environmental task force** in projects of benefit to the whole community, in particular projects for heat conservation and efficiency.

New Deal for the long-term unemployed

This programme was introduced in June 1998. The British government pays a subsidy of £75 a week for six months to firms offering employment to people who have been unemployed for two years or more. The money is intended to cover the initial costs sustained by firms in retraining the long-term unemployed back into work. New measures within the scheme are envisaged to help in particular unemployed people over 50 to move back into work. People over 50 have suffered most from the failure of the UK labour market to extend employment opportunity to all, as the proportion of working-age men over 50 out of work has doubled during the last 20 years. Women over 50, on the other hand, have equally failed to share in the increasing rate of female labour market participation in recent years.

New Deal for lone parents

The programme was introduced in October 1998. It is voluntary and aimed at offering help with job search, training and, if necessary, childcare to lone parents whose youngest child is in the second term of full-time education.

New Deal for partners of the unemployed

This programme is to be introduced in 1999–2000. Partners of the unemployed are disproportionately likely to be without work themselves, contributing to the 3.5 million working-age households in the UK with no one in a job. There are nearly 300,000 partners of people receiving income-related jobseeker's allowance, who will benefit from the £60 million set aside by the government scheme to help them find a job.

New Deal for disabled people

The programme was introduced in 1999 to restore the opportunity to work for many disabled people. This part of the government's New Deal is surrounded by a great deal of controversy in Britain, as the 'new deal' initiative to help the disabled into work was accompanied by a reduction of their disabled allowance, which left some disabled people worse off than before.

Activity 9.15

Look at Table 9.2 and explain what it shows.

✓ Answer 9.15

Table 9.2 shows how the funding for the Welfare to Work programme provided by a windfall tax on public utilities' profits is going to be distributed. The table shows illustrative levels of spending based on the current levels of unemployment. The total proceeds from the windfall tax of £5,200 million are going to be spent on the Welfare to Work programme over a period of six years.

Policies aimed at reducing the disincentive to work

It is often argued that a too generous unemployment benefit system, coupled with a system of national insurance contributions which bears disproportionately on the low paid, exacerbates the unemployment problem. High **replacement ratios** (the ratio of income received out of work to income received in work) discourage many people who can and want to work from doing so. The lack of incentive to find work and the financial difficulties faced by people in the lowest income bracket, when they start work or increase their earnings, tend to keep people in two different, but connected traps:

- the **unemployment trap**, where the income people can make from working is little or no higher than the income they receive if they did not take a job. This discourages people from taking up low paid jobs and traps them in unemployment.

Table 9.2   Funding Welfare to Work (£ million)

	1997–8	1998–9	1999–00	2000–01	2001–02	1997–2002
Spending by programmer						
A New Deal for the young unemployed	100	580	650	640	640	2620
A New Deal for the long-term unemployed	0	120	160	90	80	450
A New Deal for lone parents	0	50	50	50	50	190
A New Deal for the sick and disabled	0	10	20	80	80	200
A New Deal for partners of the unemployed	0	0	20	20	20	60
A New Deal for schools	100	300	300	300	300	1300
Childcare	0	40	0	0	0	40
University for Industry	0	5	0	0	0	5
Total expenditure	200	1090	1200	1170	1170	4850
Unallocated						350
Windfall tax	2600	2600				5200

Source: HMT, FSBR, 1988

■ the **poverty trap**, where due to the structure of the national insurance contributions (NICs) and lower entitlement to benefits for people with jobs, there is little encouragement for someone who is in work to work more in order to increase their earnings.

It is difficult in practice to assess the extent to which unemployment benefits create inflexibility in the labour market, causing an unemployment trap. The claim that the payments are overgenerous is difficult to substantiate; calculations recently carried out by the Department of Health and Social Security (DHSS) seem to indicate that only a very small percentage (less than 3 per cent) of the unemployed was better off out of work than in work. Clearly, the 'high replacement ratio' explanation cannot convincingly account on its own for current high levels of unemployment.

Tax reforms

In addition to reforming welfare payments, the UK government has attempted to increase labour market flexibility by reducing the burden of taxation, to make work effort more worthwhile. Major tax changes were introduced by the government between 1979 and 1996:

■ The marginal rate of income tax on the top income bracket was reduced to a uniform rate of 40 per cent from its previous high level of 83 per cent on earned income and 93 per cent on interest and dividends (unearned income).
■ The basic rate of income tax, which is the rate paid by about 90 per cent of income tax payers, was reduced from 33 per cent to 24 per cent, while a lower rate of 20 per cent applies to the first £3,900 worth of income.

■ Corporation tax on company profits was reduced from 52 per cent and 40 per cent, depending on profits declared, to 33 per cent and 24 per cent respectively.
■ Income tax thresholds, income values beyond which income tax becomes payable, were increased, freeing many people in low income brackets from the burden of taxation, reducing the extent of fiscal drag.
■ Reductions in capital gain tax and other tax exemptions for investment in plant and buildings or new companies were also offered.

It is difficult to assess the impact of these tax reductions on the labour supply and investment on the basis of empirical data. If anything, recent studies seem to suggest that changes in the number of hours worked in the UK were by and large the effect of changes in demand constraints, rather than the effect of changes in taxation: that is, tax cuts have a greater impact on aggregate demand than on aggregate supply, as indeed Keynesians would have argued.

Nevertheless, in 1998 the new Labour government began a reform of its tax and benefits system to improve work incentives and eliminate the ensuing distortions to the labour market.

National insurance contributions: the old system

The current structure of national insurance contributions (NICs) in the UK bears particularly hard on the low paid and discourages job creation at the lower end of the earning distribution. The structure of NICs is provided by 'steps', whereby a one-penny increase in pay can trigger an increase in NICs of up to £6.30 a week. This distorts the labour market as it discourages progression up the earnings ladder. These distortions are greatest at the lower earning limit, where a rise in earnings from £63.99 to £64 a week triggers a NIC charge or 'entry fee' from employees of £1.28 and for employers of £1.92 a week. This explains why some people become worse off when they earn more.

✍ Activity 9.16

Look at Figure 9.11 and explain what it shows.

✓ Answer 9.16

Figure 9.11 shows how the old NICs measures imposed an 'entry fee' for employers and employees with additional steps in employers' contributions at £110, £155 and £210 a week. From April 1999, the threshold for employer national insurance contributions was aligned with the personal allowance for income tax at £81 a week.

National insurance contributions: the new system

From April 1999, employees pay no NICs on their first £64 a week of earnings, and 10 per cent thereafter up to the upper earnings limit of £485 a week. Employers pay no NICs in respect of their employees' first £81 of earnings a week and then pay a single rate of 12.2 per cent thereafter.

These reforms represent a reduction in the burden of national insurance contributions which aims to reduce the unemployment and poverty traps.

✍ Activity 9.17

Look at Table 9.3 and explain what it means.

✓ Answer 9.17

The NIC reform introduced by the British government in 1998 represents a reduction of £1.28 a week in the contribution paid by the employee earning £64 a week and a reduction of £1.92 a week in the contribution paid by the employer. This represents an overall reduction of £3.20 a week. For an employee earning £220 a week, which is half the male average weekly earning, the employee NIC reduction is the same, but the saving for the employer is much larger, at £4.90 a week, which gives a total reduction of £6.18 a week.

Policies aimed at improving labour market flexibility

Monetarists argue that one of the main factors which contributes to the high level of unemployment is trade-union power. Powerful trade unions affect the labour market by increasing wage rigidity in the downward direction and by being responsible for the process of hysteresis described in Chapter 8.

Table 9.3 Reduction in burden of national insurance contributions

	(£ per week) Employee	Employer	Total
£64 a week	1.28	1.92	3.20
£220 (half male average earnings)	1.28	4.90	6.18

Source: HMT, FSBR, 1998

Figure 9.11 Employer and employee NICs

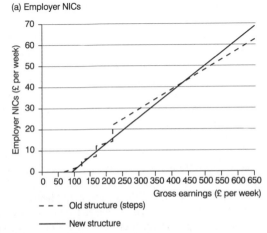

Source: HMT, FSBR, 1998

This view was deeply shared by the successive Conservative governments that governed in Britain from 1979 to 1997. They passed some very significant legislation in the 1980s and early 1990s aimed at curbing the power of trade unions, namely the Employment Act (1980 and 1982), Trade Union Act (1984), Employment Act (1988 and 1989), Employment Bill (1990) and the Trade Union Reform and Employment Rights Act (1993). As a result of such legislation the ability of trade unions to organize mass pickets was severely curtailed, as all forms of industrial action now have to be balloted. Secondary picketing in solidarity with other industries' workers and closed shops (i.e. trade-union membership as a condition for employment in an industry) were made illegal.

The Employment Act of 1980, which restricted secondary industrial action, also limited employees' unfair dismissal rights, while the Employment Act of 1989 repealed specific laws regulating the work of young people and removed the legal requirement for small firms to provide written statements relating to disciplinary procedures. These measures, aimed at 'taming the unions' and increasing the flexibility of the labour market, resulted in a British labour force which was for many years in the 1990s among the cheapest in Western Europe, as Table 9.4 shows.

A move away from this direction seemed to have been taken by the Labour government in 1998 with the reintroduction of a national minimum wage. The case study at the end of this chapter is devoted to a discussion of the implications of this policy measure on the UK labour market and on the prospects for growth of the British economy.

SUPPLY-SIDE POLICIES IN THE EU

Securing a high level of employment seems to be once more among the agenda items of EU policy. Article 125 on the new Title VIII on Employment, of the Amsterdam Treaty signed in 1997 states that: 'Member States and the Community shall work towards developing a co-ordinated strategy for employment and particularly for promoting a skilled, trained and adaptable workforce and labour markets responsive to economic change.'

Article 127 states that: 'The objective of a high level of employment shall be taken into consideration in the formulation and implementation of Community policies and activities.' Article 128 requests each member state to provide the European Council and the Commission with an annual report on the principal measures taken to implement its employment policy in the light of those guidelines.

Therefore, let us now look at the main labour market reforms introduced in EU countries in recent years, together with other supply-side policies. Such policies and reforms need to be seen within the 1996 EU macroeconomic policy guidelines, aimed at the improvement and consolidation of governments budgetary position (i.e. aimed at a reduction of EU governments' budget deficits) which were:

1   Restraining expenditure increases, particularly on pensions, healthcare and subsidies.
2   Redirecting government spending towards productive activities, such as infrastructure, human capital and other active labour market measures.
3   Improving the efficiency of public services, in some cases through privatization and the introduction of user fees.
4   Reducing the overall tax burden, without jeopardizing the overall aim of a reduction of the budget deficit.

Policies aimed at fostering employment and labour market reforms

Wage developments

The EU 1996 guidelines on wages recommended that real wage increases should be smaller than increases in productivity, in order to increase firms' profit margins and stimulate employment creating investment.

🖉 Activity 9.18

Look at Table 9.5 and comment on what it shows.

✓ Answer 9.18

Table 9.5 shows that wage trends in the Community have been in line with the objective of reducing inflation and increasing investment profitability. For the Community as a whole, real wage costs, measured by nominal compensation per employee deflated by the GDP deflator, increased by less than 1 per cent for the fourth consecutive year in 1996. This was sufficiently behind both trend and actual growth in labour productivity – at around 2 per cent and 1.5 per cent respectively – to provide businesses with higher remuneration and strengthen the return on investment in the Community.

The condition that real wage costs should increase at a slower rate than labour productivity was respected in nearly all member states. Percentage changes of real unit labour costs in 1996, shown by the last column in Table 9.5, show negative increases for almost all member states, with the exception of Greece, Portugal, Finland and Sweden where increases in real unit labour

Table 9.4 Competitive positions: relative unit labour costs

	1980	1981	1982	1983	1984	1985	1986	1987	1988	1989	1990	1991	1992	1993	1994	1995	1996	Estimates and projections 1997	1998	1999
USA	125	130	142	147	152	157	134	114	104	105	102	100	97	97	94	94	98	104	104	104
Japan	81	87	76	85	87	85	114	118	122	108	95	100	105	129	140	141	119	110	110	108
Germany	91	83	87	88	86	85	94	104	103	101	103	100	107	115	116	125	121	111	109	109
France	110	108	104	104	105	108	110	108	102	98	101	100	101	103	100	100	99	94	94	94
Italy	87	87	89	94	92	90	91	91	90	94	98	100	95	79	75	67	76	80	81	81
UK	116	120	113	103	99	101	95	96	100	97	98	100	94	84	86	84	88	106	111	113
Canada	82	86	94	96	89	86	81	86	94	98	97	100	90	83	76	76	80	82	81	82
Australia	104	118	125	118	124	103	86	84	94	104	103	100	90	83	86	86	96	100	97	99
Austria	112	112	112	111	108	107	112	113	106	103	103	100	100	100	96	97	94	91	90	89
Belgium–Luxembourg	133	121	101	92	92	93	99	101	98	95	101	100	102	101	103	112	108	104	104	104
Denmark	88	82	81	82	83	86	94	104	101	97	105	100	101	98	99	103	102	103	105	107
Finland	91	95	99	96	99	99	95	93	95	100	104	100	77	62	68	77	74	72	72	73
Korea	66	60	65	66	63	66	56	61	74	102	101	100	95	91	96	97	99	96	90	90
Mexico	140	170	126	65	83	80	61	62	73	81	86	100	115	132	134	85	83	94	99	106
Netherlands	123	111	115	112	101	99	106	111	108	101	102	100	103	105	101	104	101	97	98	98
New Zealand	123	120	117	114	96	94	94	104	113	104	102	100	89	92	97	104	114	121	117	117
Norway	92	97	99	100	98	98	97	98	103	104	100	100	97	96	99	104	104	106	109	110
Portugal	75	82	81	76	75	75	77	74	78	82	89	100	111	107	110	116	117	118	118	119
Spain	99	91	89	77	79	78	77	77	82	89	98	100	102	93	85	82	85	84	86	87
Sweden	100	102	88	80	82	86	86	86	90	94	96	100	98	72	68	68	77	73	74	74
Switzerland	72	72	78	87	86	84	91	95	96	91	99	100	98	99	108	116	114	107	109	108
Chinese Taipei	71	77	78	75	88	84	75	83	94	109	104	100	107	103	104	98	99	104	94	93
Hong Kong	80	110	109	96	95	109	85	75	78	89	94	100	101	114	125	123	128	137	138	137
Singapore	76	82	96	109	116	122	89	80	82	90	94	100	107	105	107	108	114	117	111	111

Source: OECD, *Economic Outlook*, December 1997: 62
Note: Indices are expressed in a common currency and concern the manufacturing sector. The relative unit labour cost indices take into account both export and import competitiveness.

Table 9.5 EU growth, employment, productivity and labour costs, 1990–96

	Real GDP growth (% change pa)			Employment (% change pa)			Labour productivity (% change pa)			Real wage costs per employee (% change pa) GDP deflator			Real unit labour cost (% change pa)		
	1990–92	1993–6	1996	1990–92	1993–6	1996	1990–92	1993–6	1996	1990–92	1993–6	1996	1990–92	1993–6	1996
B	2.3	1.1	1.4	0.5	-0.4	0.0	1.9	1.4	1.3	3.6	0.7	-0.1	1.7	-0.7	-1.4
DK	1.0	2.7	2.4	0.0	-0.4	1.0	2.1	2.4	1.5	1.5	1.5	1.2	-0.6	-0.8	-0.3
D	4.2	1.2	1.4	1.8	-1.0	-1.2	2.0	2.2	2.5	1.6	1.1	1.4	-0.4	-1.1	-1.1
EL	1.2	1.8	2.6	0.1	1.2	1.0	0.9	0.6	1.5	-2.0	0.8	2.6	-2.8	0.2	1.1
E	2.2	1.5	2.2	0.3	0.1	2.9	1.2	1.6	0.8	2.5	-0.5	0.2	1.3	-2.0	-0.6
F	1.5	1.2	1.3	0.2	0.0	-0.1	1.3	1.3	1.5	1.6	0.6	1.0	0.3	-0.6	-0.4
IRL	5.0	7.5	8.4	1.8	3.1	3.8	3.3	4.4	4.5	4.2	1.5	1.9	0.9	-2.8	-2.5
I	1.3	1.1	0.7	0.7	-1.5	0.4	1.1	2.3	0.5	1.6	-0.2	0.4	0.6	-2.4	-0.1
L	4.2	5.0	3.6	3.6	2.3	2.4	0.6	2.7	1.2	2.6	0.8	-1.0	1.9	-1.9	-2.2
NL	2.8	2.3	2.8	2.1	1.1	1.9	1.2	1.3	1.0	1.6	0.5	-0.2	0.4	-0.8	-1.1
A	3.1	1.3	1.0	2.0	1.1	-0.7	1.7	1.7	1.7	1.9	1.0	0.2	0.2	-0.6	-1.5
P	2.9	1.6	3.0	0.9	-0.5	0.7	2.0	2.4	2.4	5.5	1.5	3.1	3.4	-0.9	0.7
FIN	-3.6	2.8	3.3	-4.2	-0.9	1.4	0.7	4.0	1.9	2.5	1.2	2.1	1.8	-2.7	0.3
S	-0.4	1.4	1.1	-2.1	-1.4	-0.6	1.3	2.8	1.7	1.4	2.4	6.4	0.1	-0.5	4.6
UK	-0.7	2.7	2.1	-1.5	0.2	0.7	0.6	2.4	1.4	1.6	0.9	0.5	0.9	-1.5	-0.9
EUR	1.7	1.6	1.6	0.3	-0.4	0.3	1.4	2.0	1.5	1.7	0.6	0.8	0.3	-1.4	-0.7
USA	1.1	3.0	2.4	0.3	1.7	1.4	1.2	0.8	1.0	1.7	1.0	1.8	0.5	0.2	0.8
JAP	3.4	1.3	3.6	1.6	0.2	0.6	1.8	1.0	2.9	1.5	0.8	0.5	-0.3	-0.1	-2.3

Source: European Economy, 1997

costs outpaced labour productivity, while remaining rather modest on the whole.

Real wage moderation, however, did not seem to have a great positive impact either on employment growth or on output growth in 1996, although its effect is likely to be lagged.

Labour market reforms

EU 1996 guidelines encourage member states to intensify their actions to reform labour markets, targeting in particular the following areas:

- occupational and regional mobility;
- provision of employment services;
- improvement of education systems;
- active labour market policies, particularly for the long-term unemployed;
- incentives for the employment of low-skilled labour.

The commitment to reduce unemployment as the main aim of economic policy has become part of the EU-wide strategy for employment, initiated by the Essen European Council in 1994. Since then the policy recommendations have been refined and made more precise. A close process of monitoring their implementation has also been developed in co-operation with member states.

On the demand side of the labour market, attention has generally focused on wage moderation, on measures aimed at reducing non-wage labour costs, on the promotion of flexible types of work arrangements, and on the reduction of hiring and firing costs. On the supply-side of the labour market, work incentives and employability have been fostered through reforms of social protection systems, i.e. unemployment benefits, active labour market policies and better training facilities.

Some general patterns of labour market reform have emerged in recent years and can be identified across the EU:

Revision of unemployment benefits systems

Countries characterized by a traditionally high degree of social protection have started to curb their support levels, mainly through tightening of eligibility rules, controls on active job search by recipients and a revision of benefit duration.

Greater working time flexibility

A reduction of income support measures for the unemployed have been coupled with policies aimed at increasing the flexibility of working time, particularly in the Netherlands, and on greater emphasis on training and other active labour-market policies. These latter measures, however, have proved expensive for public finances, at least in the short run.

Labour markets deregulation

Measures to deregulate the labour market have been implemented in high employment countries. Spain, in particular, in an attempt to tackle its 21.3 per cent unemployment rate, relaxed statutory employment protection for permanent employees in 1997. This represented a move away from previous policies of deregulation 'at the margin', through spreading of temporary contracts, which had deepened segmentation of the labour market.

Poverty trap avoidance measures

Countries such as the UK and Ireland that rely on a system of in-work benefits to top up income from work, have introduced measures to reduce the high marginal effective rates, which may give rise to poverty trap situations.

Non-wage labour costs reduction

A large number of countries have introduced reductions in non-wage labour costs, either through cuts in social security contributions – as in Spain, Portugal, Finland, UK and the Netherlands – or via reductions of contributions on low wages, to stimulate demand for low skilled labour, as in France, Belgium and the Netherlands.

Wage moderation

As discussed earlier, a generalized tendency towards wage moderation has prevailed in recent years across EU member countries.

Structural reforms such as these are not immediately effective in creating new employment opportunities and it is somewhat early to assess their impact. For the moment, the rate of unemployment in the EU, at 10.6 per cent in 1997, remains unacceptably high; it has been in double figures since 1993 and shows no signs of any improvement. What can be said at present is simply that structural reforms across the EU appear to be comprehensive, as opposed to limited or occasional, and to address in a coherent manner the complex issue of incentives in creating and taking up work. Structural reforms aimed at the promotion of employment within the EU take place within the broader commitment to a stable macroeconomic framework, in line with the Maastricht criteria, aimed at ensuring sustained convergence of member countries' economic performance.

EU policies to increase market competitiveness

Reinforcement of competition policies and reduction of state aids have been a common pattern followed by EU member governments in recent years. A variety of measures has been taken, both at Community and national level, to boost the competitiveness and efficiency of the European economies. Most importantly, great effort has gone into the transposition of Community single market measures into national law and into the effective enforcement of Community legislation.

As a result of these forces, the markets for goods and services in the Community have become more integrated and globalized. However, for goods and services subject to public procurement or nationally distinct regulations, such as pharmaceuticals, integration has been limited. Integration seems greater in the manufacturing sector, where domestic demand for manufacturing products has increasingly been satisfied by imports from other member states, reflecting an increase in intra-EU competition and firms' reductions in price-cost margins. Convergence in prices of identical products around the Community also suggests that further integration is taking place, although markets in services have remained significantly less integrated than goods markets.

Varying levels and forms of state aids, national taxes and domestic regulations continue to fragment many EU markets. The uneven enforcement of EU legislation is a further barrier to trade and fair competition.

Competition policies

Within this scenario, the chief policy target of supply-side policies at Community level has been to foster greater internal competition:

- in the **telecommunications field**, competition has been opened up in mobile telephones and monopoly rights still retained by some governments in this sector have been removed.

- in the **energy sector**, common rules have been introduced in the Community for the internal market in electricity, requiring the gradual opening to competition over a period of six years; similar rules will apply to the gas industry in the near future.
- in the **transport sector**, competition for the provision of ground services at airports has now been introduced.

EU policies have also been directed towards harmonizing legislation concerning intellectual property rights and the diffusion of innovation.

To give new impetus to the promotion of small and medium enterprises (SMEs), the European Council in 1996 adopted its third SME multi-annual programme; while in the area of environment and taxation, proposals were put forward to restructure the system of excise duties to extend the scope of taxation to all energy products that damage the environment.

In 1997, at the national level, besides the UK government's measures discussed earlier:

- The German government put forward a comprehensive programme to promote SMEs (reducing taxation on new businesses, offering credit subsidies and mobilizing risk and venture capital) and innovation, through financing applied R&D and reduced patenting costs for SMEs. Shopping hours have also been liberalized and numerous other measures to improve the functioning of the economy are planned.
- The Spanish government put forward a package of structural measures, which include a reduction of state aid to public enterprises coupled with a reduction of taxation of SMEs, to increase market competitiveness.
- In Finland several measures were introduced to favour SMEs, such as easier financing conditions and better training opportunities.
- In Austria, increased financial and institutional support has been given to innovation and R&D projects.
- In Denmark, new competition laws were put forward to strengthen anti-trust rules and bring the national framework more in line with other member countries.
- Similar policies to those described above were introduced by the French government.

SUPPLY-SIDE POLICIES AND BUSINESS CYCLES

One of the strongest arguments used by Keynes to support his claim of the need for active government intervention in the economy was the existence of business cycles. Economies do not grow smoothly. They go through what are known as **business cycles** as they move from periods of expansion, the **booms**, when everything grows – demand, output, employment, but also prices and balance of trade deficits – to periods of contractions, the **recessions**, when almost everything falls – demand, output, employment, etc. The resulting uncertainty discourages investment, exacerbates the problem of unemployment and reduces growth potential. Hence the need for government counter-cyclical policies to smooth out this pattern and keep the economy's actual output in line with its potential output.

To understand whether supply-side policies could be at all effective to reduce business cycles, we need first of all to understand what causes them. Several economic theories to explain such causes have been developed over the years: the underconsumption theory, put forward by the British economist, John Hobson; the innovation theory, developed by the Austrian economist, Schumpeter; the over-investment theory, sustained by the Austrian-born economists Friedrich von Hayek and Ludwig von Mises, and the monetary theory.

The accelerator theory of the business cycle

Common to all the theories of business cycle fluctuations mentioned above is the relationship between investment and consumption described by the **accelerator theory**. This theory rests on the multiplier effect of new investment.

The fact that all theories of business cycles need to explain is why, after a period of sustained expansion – when investment, consumption, output and employment are all rising – does the expansionary process come to an end. The basic explanation provided for the flattening out of the upswing and the subsequent onset of contractionary forces is that during the upswing of the cycle capital goods industries expand faster than consumption goods industries.

✍ Activity 9.19

Redefine the concepts of capital goods industry and consumption goods industry introduced earlier.

✓ Answer 9.19

Consumer goods are the goods bought in shops by consumers.

Consumption goods industries are industries producing consumer goods, destined for final consumption by consumers.

Capital goods are machinery and equipment bought by firms and used by them in the process of production of other goods.

Capital goods industries are industries producing capital goods, destined to be used by other firms.

As a result of the overexpansion of the capital goods industry, the distribution of resources between the two sectors becomes unbalanced: too many resources, in terms of labour and capital, end up being employed in the capital goods sector, making steel and heavy machinery, and too few in the consumption goods sector, making prams and sofas. The demand for capital goods falls, people are made redundant and cannot be absorbed quickly enough or easily enough by the consumer goods sector. The unemployed people's consumption falls and causes a further contraction in the demand for capital goods, as investment demand also falls. In this way the downturn gathers momentum.

But why do capital goods industries over-expand during booms? This is where the accelerator principle comes in. The **accelerator principle** states that a small change in the demand for consumption goods results in a much bigger – accelerated – change in the demand for capital goods needed to make the consumption goods. Why this should be the case can be better explained with a numerical example.

Let's assume that a firm produces 10,000 video-cassettes a year and sells them at £5 each. Let's also assume that in order to make these video-cassettes, the firm needs capital equipment worth £200,000, which means that it takes £20 worth of machinery to make one video-cassette. Capital equipment wears out with use and needs to be replaced. If this firm's capital depreciation is 10 per cent a year, i.e. 10 per cent of its machinery wears out every year and needs to be replaced, this firm has to buy £20,000 worth of new machinery every year, as capital replacement, to carry on producing the same amount of video-cassettes. Suppose that this is a stable situation, in which the firm has been for a number of years: it sells £50,000 worth of video-cassettes and buys £20,000 worth of capital equipment every year.

Let's assume now that there is a 5 per cent increase in the demand for this firm's video-cassettes, which means that the firm can now sell 10,500 video-cassettes a year. To produce 500 extra video-cassettes, the firm needs to buy an extra £10,000 worth of capital, as it needs £20 worth of capital to produce one video-cassette. To meet the increased demand, this firms buys £30,000 worth of capital equipment, instead of its usual £20,000, which was this firm's normal capital replacement expenditure.

In other words, to meet a 5 per cent increase in the demand for its product, this firm increases its demand for capital goods by 50 per cent (from £20,000 to £30,000). At this point, the firm producing capital equipment for the video-cassette producer finds that its orders suddenly increase by 50 per cent; to be able to meet a 50 per cent increase in demand, the capital goods producer may have to increase its own capacity by 50 per cent, which in turn might mean that its own purchases of raw materials and further machinery will increase exponentially. So we can see how a modest increase in the demand for and output of a consumption good can lead to a much bigger increase in demand and output of capital goods. But this is not the end of the story. We still have not explained how things go into reverse after a while, although at this point we can begin to guess.

✍ Activity 9.20

Can you carry on with this story ?

✔ Answer 9.20

A 5 per cent increase in the demand for video-cassettes led to a 50 per cent increase in the demand for the machinery needed to make them. Now suppose that the following year the demand for video-cassettes is back to what it was and the firm's output is back to 10,000 video-cassettes, the demand for capital equipment will fall from £30,000 to £10,000. The firm will in fact have £210,000 worth of machinery, but will only need £200,000 for its current production. If £20,000 worth of capital wears out as usual, it will only need to buy £10,000 worth of capital goods. So a fall of 5 per cent in the demand for consumption goods leads to a fall of two-thirds in the demand for capital goods.

In reality, the economy is even more volatile than this example, as a simple slowing down in the rate of increase in the demand for consumer goods – and not necessarily an actual fall in demand back to its previous level – can trigger a snowballing effect on the demand for capital goods, similar to the one described. If the demand for video-cassettes had continued to rise in the second year, instead of falling back to its previous level, but had only risen by 4 per cent instead of 5 per cent, then the firm's purchases of capital equipment in the second year would still have fallen. In other words, it only takes a slowing down in the rate of increase of consumer goods production to cause an actual fall in the output of the capital goods industry.

Now we can put all the pieces of the puzzle together. As the economy expands during the upswing of a cycle and approaches full employment, the rate of increase of consumer goods production is bound to slow down, due to shortages of labour and/or wage costs increases. Due to the accelerator principle, this slowing down will result in an actual fall in output (and consequently in employment) of capital goods industries, and this fall will eventually snowball the economy into a recession.

Regulating the cycle

While the classical economists who preceded Keynes took an almost fatalistic view of business cycles, favouring a standback approach and letting events take their course, Keynes advocates government intervention, through the use of counter-cyclical fiscal policies, to ease the severity of contractions and to reduce over-expansions.

The existence of automatic fiscal stabilizers built into most developed economies reduces the extremes of business cycles nowadays, even without the use of governments' discretionary monetary or fiscal policies. Fear of fuelling government deficits makes major government spending programmes to fight recessions a thing of the past; while increases in interest rates or taxation to moderate overheating during upswings are still tools very much used by governments, as part of their anti-inflationary pledge. There is a distinct deflationary bias built into governments' discretionary policies, as economies enter the new millennium. It is quite clear, however, from our discussion of the accelerator principle and the causes of business cycles, that supply-side policies are not a suitable instrument for counter-cyclical intervention.

Who is right?

At the end of this analysis of the debate between the Keynesians and the monetarists and of the monetarists' policy prescriptions, can we now reach a conclusion and say who is right and who is wrong? Can we say whether supply-side policies, rather than demand-side, are most suited to stimulate growth and employment and to reduce the extent of business cycles? Unfortunately, the answer is no.

In principle, both Keynesian and monetarist claims can be tested with the use of empirical data, and indeed they have been tested repeatedly by different people. Economics, however, is a social science and not an empirical science such as chemistry or physics. Experiments cannot be conducted under controlled conditions in order, once and for all, to test a hypothesis. Empirical data are affected by many variables changing at the same time and cannot be used like data in a laboratory testing.

Empirical testing of the two approaches to macroeconomic analysis has proved inconclusive:

- *Variety of tests:* one reason for this is that many different studies have been conducted, in different circumstances. Comparisons of results are therefore difficult.
- *Testable hypothesis:* it is difficult to translate abstract theory into testable hypothesis.
- *Different interpretations:* broad Keynesian and monetarist positions are all susceptible to different interpretations. Some researchers think one feature is more important than another, and consequently devise different tests. Some use narrow money as a basis for testing; some use broad money; some consider short time lags more important for macro policy; some disagree and take the opposite view; some test short-term interest rates; some test long-term rates; some nominal, some real, some expected, etc. With such huge amounts of different relationships being examined, it is not surprising that inconclusive results should emerge.
- *Direction of causality:* in social sciences a main difficulty often arises in determining the direction of causality. If data show that changes in the money supply and national income are closely related, it does not necessarily follow that changes in the money supply are the cause of changes in national income; they could equally be the effect.

The only conclusion one can reach is that extreme positions on each side, like the ones taken in the 1960s or 1970s, have become more difficult to sustain. Few people would still wish to argue nowadays that the money supply is totally irrelevant or that it is the only thing that matters. Positions are far less polarized, but between the extreme positions there is a wide field still left for debate.

CASE STUDY: UK STATUTORY MINIMUM WAGE – PROGRESS WITH PRUDENCE

In June 1998, with trepidation and amid great controversy, the Labour government passed legislation which sanctioned the introduction of a statutory national minimum wage in the UK. This decision was taken following a unanimous recommendation from the Low Pay Commission, chaired by George Bain, but it seemed at odds with the general guiding principles of the supply-side policies approach followed by the government. A statutory minimum wage arguably reintroduces in the UK labour market precisely that downward rigidity in wages which successive governments had been trying to remove for the last 20 years or so. What effect is this policy measure likely to have on UK unemployment and the economy?

To answer this question, we first review some labour market statistics related to the people in employment who are likely to be directly affected by the government's new measures. We then move on to discuss how economic theory analyses the effect of a statutory minimum wage, before we attempt a conclusion.

A look at the statistics

The Low Pay Commission Report, published by the government on 18 June 1998, recommended unanimously the introduction of a statutory national minimum wage for over 20 year olds of £3.60 an hour from April 1999, rising to £3.70 an hour in June 2000. Young workers were not to be covered by a minimum wage, while 18 to 20 year olds would receive £3.20 an hour next April and £3.30 an hour from June 2000.

Minimum wage: who benefits

The report highlights the hospitality, retailing and private security sectors as those – across all regions – with the lowest pay, particularly for employees of small enterprises. According to the report's estimates:

■ Nearly 2 million workers will benefit from this measure, with average pay rises of 30 per cent.

■ Of the beneficiaries from this measure 80 per cent are women, representing 9 per cent of the labour force. They include women in low-paid sectors, such as cleaning and healthcare and young people working in the catering business, hotels and restaurants.

■ People from ethnic minorities, disabled workers, part-time employees, lone parents, homeworkers and seasonal workers will also benefit from this measure.

■ As many as 440,000 employees in London and the South East earned less than £3.50 an hour in 1998.

■ Only 5 per cent of public sector employees earn less than £3.50 an hour, compared with 14 per cent in the private sector. (See Figures 9.12 and 9.13.)

Minimum wage: how to calculate it

The definition of **low pay** used by the Commission is based on calculations of actual working time averaged over a worker's normal pay reference period: say someone gets £140 a week, working from Monday to Friday. If the total number of hours actually worked is 40, the pay rate is £3.50 an hour, but if the number of hours actually worked is 45, the hourly rate is down to £3.11. Furthermore:

■ *shift premiums* (say, if you work at night or on Sundays) and *overtime pay* are not counted as *standard pay* within the minimum wage figure. This is important to ensure some degree of pay flexibility.

■ *piecework payment* is to be included in the minimum wage, whatever the piece rate set and output achieved, so that it is no less than the average for the pay reference period.

continued overleaf

Figure 9.12   Characteristics of the lowest paid

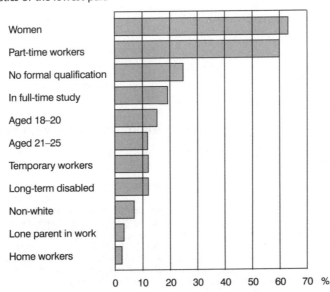

Source: Low Pay Commission, OECD, 1998

UK STATUTORY MINIMUM WAGE – PROGRESS WITH PRUDENCE

Figure 9.13 Incidence of low pay by age

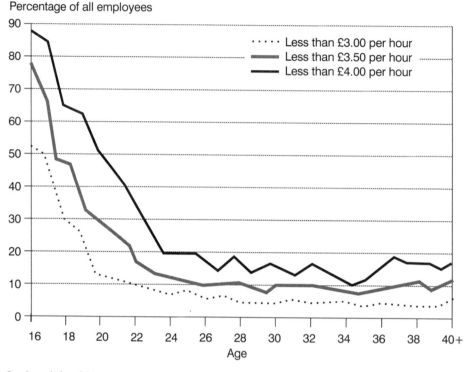

Percentage of all employees

Legend:
- ····· Less than £3.00 per hour
- — Less than £3.50 per hour
- — Less than £4.00 per hour

Age

Source: Low Pay Commission, OECD, 1998

■ *payment by output* rather than time worked must be at least equivalent to the minimum wage on average for the pay reference period. Say a window-cleaning firm used to pay a windowcleaner £10 to 'do a house with ten windows'. If it took the cleaner three hours to do a ten-window house, the wage paid would now be below the statutory minimum wage of £3.60, as in fact it would amount to a wage rate of £3.33 an hour.

■ all *fringe benefits* except *accommodation* are to be excluded from the minimum wage calculation,

■ *service charges* or a 'centrally organised system of distributing tips and gratuities, where workers get their share through the payroll' should be included in the minimum wage figure. Cash tips paid directly to staff by customers should be excluded.

The UK government, while broadly agreeing with Commission recommendations, was obviously concerned not to damage its Welfare to Work programme for the long-term jobless under 25 years old. Hence, it ultimately decided that:

■ the adult rate should be £3.60 an hour from April 1999, but with no commitment to its uprating in the year 2000;

■ apprentices aged between 16 and 17 should be excluded from the minimum wage;

■ the rate recommended by the Commission for young people should be

reduced from £3.20 to £3.00 an hour and should be extended to 21 year olds.

The changes made by the government to the Commission's recommendations for young workers meant a fall of 91,000 in those covered to 224,000 (15 per cent compared with 21 per cent) and a 1.1 per cent point drop in the overall wage bill for the 18 to 21 year olds, which is now going to increase by 2.4 per cent. (See Table 9.6 and Figure 9.14.)

Minimum wage: who pays for it

The Commission estimates that the minimum wage will add 0.6 per cent to the UK wage bill. More specifically, the report calculates that:

■ wage bills in the *cleaning industry* will go up by *3 per cent;*
■ wage bills in the *security services* will go up by *2.4 per cent;*
■ wage bills in the *hospitality industry* will go up by *1.7 per cent;*
■ wage bills in the *footwear and clothing industry* will go up by *0.8 per cent;*
■ wage bills in the *retail industry* will go up by *0.5 per cent;*
■ wage bills in *public services* will go up by *0.2 per cent;*
■ *small companies* employing less than ten people will see their wage bill increase on average by 0.9 per cent.

UK STATUTORY MINIMUM WAGE – PROGRESS WITH PRUDENCE

Table 9.6 National minimum wage: estimated coverage and cost

	Numbers affected (000s)	Proportion of group affected (000s)	Increase in wage bill (%)	Average increase for those affected (%)
All 18+	1960	9	0.6	30
18–21	225	15	2.4	*30
22+	1735	8	0.6	30
Male full-time	295	3	0.3	—
Male part-time	230	25	3.0	—
Female full-time	320	5	0.7	—
Female part-time	1120	21	2.7	—

Source: Low Pay Commission, OECD, 1998
*Approximate

Minimum wage: its impact on employment

The Commission believes that the introduction of a statutory minimum wage will not increase unemployment; on the contrary, it will 'create opportunities for unemployed people to take up work and for those in work to develop their skills'.

The employers' view is divided: some predict job losses as a result of the £3.60 national minimum wage; some predict an uneven distribution of the impact of higher wages within industries, likely to be felt more by small and medium-size businesses; some predict that the measure will have no effect at all; finally, some predict an increase in employment, as higher wages will attract better recruits to industries.

In the **sports and leisure industry**, for example, some executives estimate that the new rate will add £400mn to the industry's wage bill and

continued overleaf

Figure 9.14 Minimum wage as a percentage of median earnings

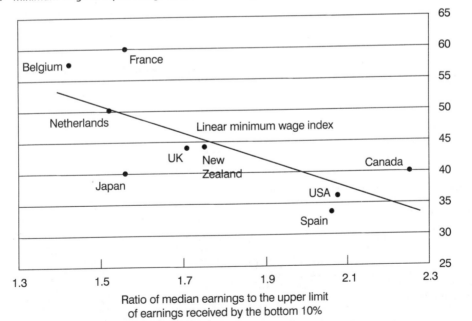

Source: Low Pay Commission, OECD, 1998

UK STATUTORY MINIMUM WAGE – PROGRESS WITH PRUDENCE

lead to 38,000 people losing their jobs out of the 2.5 million people working in the industry. The industry group of the 80 largest companies instead anticipates that the minimum wage will not affect employment in their group and that job losses will be among small and medium companies which operate on very small profitability margins. The deputy chief executive of the British Hospitality Association believes that shaking off the low pay image of the hospitality industry will ease the problem of finding suitable recruits.

Similar diverging views were expressed by the **retailing industry**: the British Retail Consortium, the umbrella trade association for retailers, welcomed the government move and warned about the risk of overstating the impact of the policy measure, as many of the lowest paid shopworkers are under 21 year olds, for whom the lower rate of £3 an hour would apply. Tesco, Britain's largest food retailer, admitted to be unaffected by the government's measure as more than 80 per cent of its staff were already paid more than £4 an hour. Fears were expressed about the inflationary effect of the minimum wage in the retailing sector. In order to preserve differentials, wages will go up at all levels as a result of the minimum wage and not just at the bottom end of the scale. Retailers will also suffer higher costs as a result of the minimum wage knock-on effect on distribution and manufacturing costs, and in areas such as security and cleaning. Ultimately, retailers will pass on wage and cost inflation into higher goods prices.

The **security industry** anticipates that the minimum wage will have no substantial effect, at least among the larger groups employing about 90,000 people, as the average hourly rate is £4.50; a modest impact is foreseen only in the north, where wages are relatively low and long hours are worked.

The response of the **textiles industry** to the new legislation has been more critical. The sector's largest employers' organization, the British Apparel and Textiles Confederation, estimates that the minimum wage will set a climate for pay increases of more than 5.5 per cent in the clothing industry and between 7 and 8 per cent in footwear and knitwear (*Financial Times*, 19 June 1998).

Minimum wage: what the theory says

Simple demand and supply analysis applied to the labour market predicts that a statutory minimum wage set above the market equilibrium rate will cause unemployment to rise, as Figure 9.15 below shows.

✍ Activity 9.21

Look at the Figure 9.15 and explain what it shows.

✓ Answer 9.21

Figure 9.15 shows a competitive labour market where the quantity of labour demanded (D^L) is equal to the quantity of labour supplied (S^L) at the equilibrium wage rate W_e. The introduction of a statutory wage rate above the equilibrium level will cause the demand for labour to fall to L_0 and the supply of labour to increase to L_1, causing an increase in unemployment measured by L_1-L_0 and a fall in employment measured by L_e-L_0.

The effect of a statutory minimum wage is not always likely to cause unemployment. The introduction of a minimum wage can also have no effect on wages and employment, or can cause both wages and employment to increase. Let's examine these two important cases.

If a minimum wage rate is set at or below the equilibrium market rate, the statutory rate will have no effect on wages or employment, as Figure 9.16 shows.

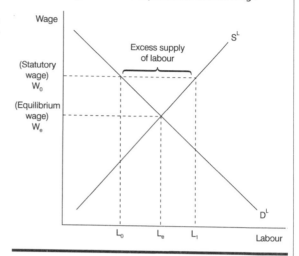

Figure 9.15   The labour market: effect of a statutory minimum wage set above equilibrium market wage

✍ Activity 9.22

Look at Figure 9.16 and explain what it shows.

✓ Answer 9.22

The introduction of a statutory wage rate below the market equilibrium rate has no effect, either on the equilibrium level of employment or on the equilibrium market rate. This is explained as follows : at the lower statutory rate W_0, there will be an excess demand for labour measured by

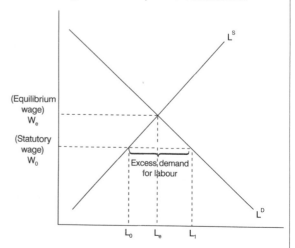

Figure 9.16   The labour market: effect of a statutory minimum wage set below equilibrium market rate

UK STATUTORY MINIMUM WAGE – PROGRESS WITH PRUDENCE

L_1-L_0. Employers will be willing to employ more people at the lower wage rate(L_1), but fewer people will be willing to work at that rate (L_0). The shortage of labour will drive wages up until equilibrium is reached at W_e, above the statutory rate. A statutory rate set at the prevailing market rate or below it, will have no effect on wages or employment. Referring back to the UK statistics discussed in the previous section, the situation described by Figure 9.16 seems to be the situation prevailing in the UK economy, where the market rate is already above the statutory rate introduced by the government case, in most industries. Even in those industries characterized by low wages, the statutory wage is likely to affect only those fringe sections, where rates are below the statutory level.

In those industry subsectors where current wage rates are below the statutory level, the introduction of a minimum wage is likely to increase employment, rather than reduce it. This statement clearly goes against what Figure 9.16 shows. How can we justify it?

If employers in an industry are in a position of using their market power over their employees, then the labour market situation is no longer characterized by competition, like the one described by Figure 9.16. The 'classical ' labour market situation described by Figure 9.16 assumes, in fact, that it is characterized by competition. This implies that if wages offered in an industry are lower than the market wage, workers will not be attracted to it and will go elsewhere. To retain their workforce, firms in competition with each other will be forced to offer higher wages. This process will go on until the equilibrium market wage is reached.

Figure 9.17 Wage determination in a monopsonistic labour market

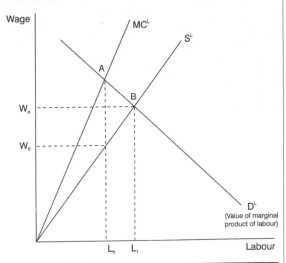

A monopsonistic labour market

However, if workers have no one else to whom they can offer their services – either because their skills are industry-specific, like nurses and teachers, or because they have no specific skills, which makes them suitable only for industries requiring unskilled labour, or because they are not prepared to move to other parts of the country, which makes them subject to local employers' conditions – then employers will enjoy control over their labour market. This situation is referred to as a **monopsonistic labour market**. A monopsonist, like the **monopolist**, characterizes an industry in an unique position. The **monopolist** is the **sole seller** or producer of a good, who can exploit its market dominance position by restricting the quantity produced to drive up its price. The **monopsonist**, on the other hand, is the **sole buyer** of a good, who can exploit this unique market position by restricting the quantity demanded of a good, in order to keep its price down.

To understand how this situation can apply to the labour market, let's think of the situation in which nurses working in the National Health Service find themselves. Do they have an alternative employer? Those who can work in private hospitals or clinics do, but the number who can be offered employment by the private sector is very limited, although wages are predictably higher. All the others have no choice but to accept the low wages offered by the only employer they can find.

Of course, for this analysis to apply in real life, we need not assume that there is one sole buyer of a specific labour. The sole purchaser in the labour market can be represented by few purchasers forming an employers' association and acting as a single decision-taking unit in the labour market.

The sole purchaser of labour quickly realizes that s/he can offer any wage rate and that workers have only one choice: either they work for that wage or literally they get on their bikes. They can change occupation or move location. To show this situation with a diagram (Figure 9.17) is rather tricky, as it involves the use of a marginal cost concept.

The labour supply curve S^L shows the amount of labour supplied at each wage rate. This represents the average cost of labour for the monopsonist. However, the monopsonist, as the sole purchaser of this labour, knows that hiring more labour drives up its wage; hence, for the monop-

sonist, the marginal cost of employing extra units of labour exceeds average cost. If, for example, 100 workers are employed at £3 an hour, then the total cost per hour is £300 and the average cost per worker per hour is £3. If 101 workers are employed and the hourly wage rate is pushed up to £3.10 an hour as a result, the total cost becomes £313.10, the average cost per worker per hour is £3.10, but the total cost has increased by £13.10 as a result of hiring one more worker. The marginal cost of obtaining an extra hour of work from an extra worker exceeds the hourly wage paid (£3.10), because the increased hourly wage rate necessary to attract the worker must also be paid to all the workers already employed. This is shown in Figure 9.17 by a marginal cost curve for labour which lies above the average cost curve (the labour supply curve, S^L).

The profit-maximizing monopsonist will continue to hire labour until the last unit of labour employed increases total costs by as much as it increases total revenue (at point A). For that amount of labour L_0, the monopsonist will pay a wage W_0, which is lower than the equilibrium wage W_e. Thus in equilibrium, the monopsonist equates the marginal cost of labour and not its average cost, with the marginal revenue product of labour, the labour demand curve (which are equal at B). It also follows that, since the supply curve of labour is upward sloping, the volume of employment will be less, in a monopsonistic labour market, than it would be if the labour market were competitive.

We can therefore conclude that a monopsonistic labour market will result in a lower level of employment and a lower wage rate than that prevailing in a competitive labour market.

The effect of a minimum wage on a monopsonistic labour market

Let's now reconsider the effect of a minimum wage, this time assuming a monopsonistic labour market. We can see that this time a statutory

continued overleaf

UK STATUTORY MINIMUM WAGE – PROGRESS WITH PRUDENCE

minimum wage can raise both wages and employment This situation is shown in Figure 9.18.

This result is explained by the fact that before the introduction of the statutory minimum wage, employment was held down by the monopsonistic employer, who was aware that increasing employment would drive up wages. The introduction of a statutory minimum wage faces the monopsonistic employer with a perfectly elastic supply curve: there is no longer any point in holding employment down for fear of driving up the wage rate that must be paid to everyone. At the statutory wage rate employment increases to L_1.

Now even if you have found it difficult to follow this analysis, you should still be able to see intuitively that employers' associations can exploit their monopsony power on the people employed by their industry and behave like a single monopsonist. Economic theory predicts that, by restricting employment, they will 'force' wages down. Those who are offered employment have no choice but to accept the lower wage as they have no alternative employer. In this situation, which is in fact more common in real life than we tend to think, the introduction of a statutory minimum wage will both increase wages and employment.

Minimum wage: its impact on inflation and the economy

The introduction of a minimum wage, assuming that the minimum wage is higher than the prevailing market wage, at least for some groups of workers, is likely to have repercussions on the whole economy which are wider than the effect on the individual industry's employment. We now turn to the macroeconomic effects of a statutory minimum wage.

With UK inflation already edging upwards in 1998 (RPI in May 1998 up by 4.2 per cent on a year earlier, its biggest rise in six years), many economists anticipate that the introduction of a national minimum wage will add to rising prices. It will lead directly to higher pay for between 2 to 3 million people, who are currently below the threshold. It will lead indirectly to generalized pay increases, as employers will have to adjust wage rates to maintain differentials among employees higher up the earnings ladder.

Higher inflation in turn will prompt the Bank of England into raising interest rates further, making monetary conditions even tighter. The increase in interest rates will have several, important consequences:

■ reduce disposable income of people with mortgages, hence reduce consumption;
■ reduce investment, particularly in the manufacturing sector, which is in greater need of funding;
■ cause an appreciation of the exchange rate, which will make UK goods less competitive on foreign markets and discourage exports;
■ a stronger pound will in turn make imports cheaper, strengthening the hold of foreign competition on domestic markets.

The final effect of these combined forces will be to slow down economic growth and increase unemployment.

According to Professor Minford of Liverpool University and former Treasury adviser, the new wage could push up average earnings by 2 per cent, adding about £10bn to the UK employers' wage bill and causing retail price inflation of a similar amount; 250,000 people will lose their jobs as a result. However, other economists regard these estimates as too extreme and anticipate the overall impact of the minimum wage on average earnings to be limited to a modest increase of 0.75 per cent.

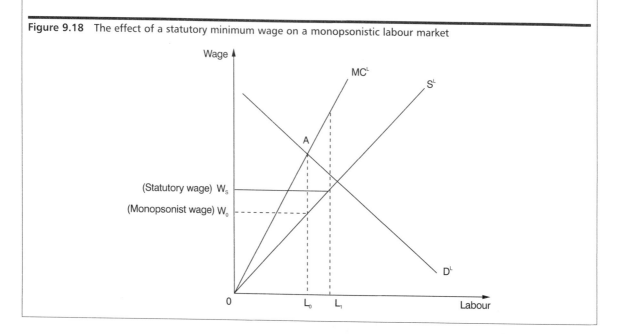

Figure 9.18 The effect of a statutory minimum wage on a monopsonistic labour market

☆ **For revision of this chapter, see the Chapter Summaries at the end of the book, starting on page 411.**

10 The domestic economy in an international context

Objectives

After studying this chapter you will be able to:

■ explain what is meant by exchange rate;
■ explain how the exchange rate is determined;
■ explain what determines the demand for imports and exports;
■ explain what affects capital flows between countries;
■ distinguish between the two main exchange rate regimes;
■ discuss the advantages and disadvantages of the two regimes;
■ explain the difference between the current account and the capital account of the balance of payments;
■ explain how balance of payments imbalances can be corrected.

THE INTERNATIONAL SCENARIO

Until now we have focused on the domestic economy in isolation from the rest of the world. This has allowed us to keep the explanation of the forces at play in the economic system fairly simple. In the next four chapters, however, we are going to move forward and explain how international economic relations affect the domestic economy. Chapter 10 explains the depreciation of the exchange rates and the factors affecting the balance of payments. Chapter 11 deals with international flows of money and the monetary arrangements which have regulated them since World War II, including the recent development of the Economic and Monetary Union (EMU) in the European Community. Chapter 12 deals with international trade: it examines the arguments in favour of free trade, contrasting them with the arguments for protectionism, before assessing the case for a Customs Union, such as the European Union. Chapter 13 deals with the institutional arrangements which have regulated trade in the post-war period and discusses the problems and imbalances of the global economy, which are likely to persist into the new millennium.

The study of international trade and international money is a controversial part of economics. Through increasing volumes of international trade in goods and services and even larger international flows of money, the economies of different countries are more closely linked to one another than ever before. At the same time, however, the world's economy is more unbalanced and, in many respects, more unstable than it has been in many decades. Understanding this shifting and complex international environment has become the central concern of both business strategy and national economic policy.

The open economy

Since World War II economies have become more open, markets increasingly interdependent, production and distribution more and more globalized. Recent statistics on international trade and capital flows are discussed in the next chapters. Even without looking at the data, however, it is not difficult to persuade ourselves of the increased globalization of production and distribution; it is enough to check the country of origin of the goods we buy on a daily basis at our local shops or in larger department stores: strawberries from the USA, oranges from Israel, teatowels from Bulgaria, glass vases from Poland, pencils from China, blouses from Taiwan.

✍ Activity 10.1

Look at Figure 10.1 and Table 10.1 and comment on what they show.

✓ Answer 10.1

Figure 10.1 shows how economic interdependence has increased over the years, as measured by the more rapid growth of world trade over world production from 1984 to 1995. Table 10.1 confirms the continuation of this trend to the end of this century. While real GDP of the major seven countries is expected to grow by 2 per cent in real terms in 1998, trade in manufacture is expected to grow by 7 per cent, down from the 11 per cent growth recorded in 1997. The recent reduction in the rate of growth of world trade is a reflection of Asia's financial difficulties. The growth rate of world trade is expected to remain robust by historical standards. UK export market growth is likely to be less affected and is expected to average about 8 per cent by the year 2000.

Figure 10.1 Growth of world productivity and trade, 1984–95; annual percentage changes

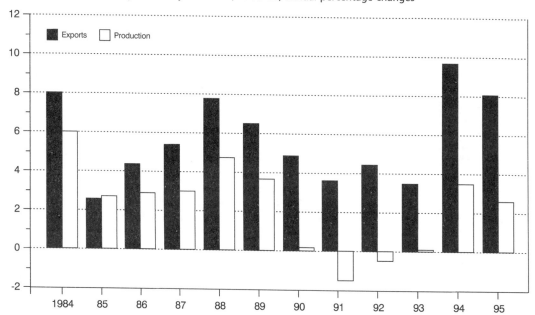

Source: World Trade Organization, *GATT Activities*, 1996

Table 10.1 The world economy, 1997–2000

	Percentage changes on a year earlier forecast			
	1997	1998	1999	2000
Major seven countries[1]				
Real GDP	3	2	2	2
Consumer price inflation[2]	2	2	2	2
World trade in manufactures	11	7	7	8
UK export markets[3]	10	8	8	8

Source: HMT, FSBR, 1998
[1] 7: USA, Japan, Germany, France, Italy, UK and Canada.
[2] For UK, RPI excluding mortgage interest payments – rounded up figures.
[3] Other countries' imports of manufactures weighted according to their importance in UK exports.

While the importance of international trade continues to increase, its composition varies from country to country and it varies also over time.

✍ Activity 10.2

Look at Tables 10.2 and 10.3 and comment on the changes in the structure of UK exports between 1958 and 1994.

✓ Answer 10.2

UK trade with continental Europe has increased in importance in recent years, with the percentage of UK exports to the EU[12] growing from 21.7 per cent in 1958 to 54.1 per cent in 1994 (and imports from EC countries up from 22 per cent to 50 per cent) while trade with North America has remained relatively constant (although trade with Canada has decreased from 5.8 per cent to 1.4 per cent, while trade with the USA has increased from 8.8 to 12 per cent). At the same time, the share of UK trade with Australia has fallen, with exports to Australia down from 7.2 per cent in 1958 to 1.4 per cent in 1994 and imports from Australia down from 5.4 per cent to 0.7 per cent.

But how do international trade and the international movements of capital fit into the model of the domestic economy developed so far? How are trade flows and capital flows between countries generated and what is their impact on the domestic economy? These are the questions to which we now need to turn.

The open economy and the Keynesian model

According to Keynes, the level of aggregate expenditure or aggregate demand determines the economy's output, its aggregate supply. A strong demand will justify the production of an ever-increasing quantity of goods and services, which in turn will create a greater number of jobs and reduce unemployment. Within Keynes's framework of analysis, a sustained and vigorous demand is the key to economic growth and employment. The various components of aggregate demand were then examined to identify the factors affecting them. We looked at:

■ the demand for consumption goods (consumption demand or consumption expenditure) by households, which is determined by people's disposable income;

■ the demand for investment goods (investment demand or investment expenditure) which is determined, among other factors, by the interest rate.

The interest rate, in turn, is determined by the money supply decided by the government, given certain demand for money conditions;

■ the demand for consumption and investment goods by the government (government expenditure), which is determined by government policy decision and constrained by the need to finance it.

The last source of expenditure that we need to examine is the expenditure on domestic goods and services by foreigners – what we call **export expenditure** – net of the amount that British people, firms and government spend on foreign goods, which we call **import expenditure**. In other words, we need to look at what determines **net export**.

The components of aggregate demand examined so far and just listed above were all determined within the domestic economy; consumption demand by British households, investment demand by firms operating in Britain, expenditure on domestically produced goods by the government. However, real world economies do not exist in isolation. Countries trade with one another; British people and British firms buy products made by countries abroad, use services provided by firms abroad or invest abroad, just as people living in other countries buy British-made goods, use services provided by British firms, buy shares in British companies or set up business in Britain.

✍ Activity 10.3

Look at Tables 10.4 and 10.5 and Figure 10.2 and explain what they show.

✓ Answer 10.3

Net export is a component of aggregate demand, which adds to the demand for domestically produced goods by domestic consumers, firms and the government, and, in the Keynesian model, stimulates output and employment. Table 10.4 shows the contribution of net export ($X - M$) to the demand for domestically produced goods, with data for the UK aggregate demand from 1993 to 2000 (forecast). Values are at 1990 prices, hence they show the real contribution of net export to total demand. The rising trend of imports and exports confirms once more the increasing economic interdependence. Figure 10.2 shows the shares of expenditure at current market prices, in 1996. Export expenditure by foreigners represented 22.5 per cent of total final expenditure in 1996, the second largest category of total expenditure after domestic consumers' expenditure, which was 49.2 per cent.

Table 10.2 Structure of EC exports by country and region, 1958 and 1994 (percentage of total exports)

Export from → / to ↓	B/L 1958	B/L 1994	DK 1958	DK 1994	D 1958	D 1994	EL 1958	EL 1994	E 1958	E 1994	F 1958	F 1994	IRL 1958	IRL 1994	I 1958	I 1994	N 1958	N 1994	P 1958	P 1994	UK 1958	UK 1994	EUR 12 1958	EUR 12 1994
B/L	—	—	1.2	1.9	6.6	6.7	1.0	1.6	2.1	2.8	6.3	8.5	0.8	3.9	2.2	3.0	15.0	13.9	3.7	3.7	1.9	5.5	4.8	6.0
DK	1.6	0.9	—	—	3.0	1.8	0.2	0.8	1.7	0.6	0.7	0.9	0.1	1.1	0.8	0.8	2.5	1.6	1.2	2.3	2.4	1.4	2.0	1.3
D	11.6	20.8	20.0	23.0	—	—	20.5	21.1	10.2	13.4	10.4	17.7	2.2	14.1	14.1	19.0	19.0	28.6	7.7	18.7	4.2	12.9	7.6	13.6
EL	0.8	0.5	0.3	0.7	1.3	0.8	—	—	0.1	0.9	0.6	0.7	0.4	0.3	2.0	1.8	0.6	1.0	0.3	0.5	0.7	0.7	0.8	0.9
E	0.7	2.9	0.8	1.8	1.2	3.2	0.1	2.2	—	—	1.6	6.9	0.8	2.3	0.5	4.6	3.2	3.6	2.5	14.3	0.9	3.8	1.0	3.8
F	10.6	19.3	3.0	5.6	7.6	12.0	12.8	5.4	10.1	19.0	—	—	0.8	9.2	5.3	13.1	2.0	4.5	6.6	14.7	2.4	10.2	4.7	10.6
IRL	0.3	0.4	0.3	0.5	0.3	0.5	0.4	0.3	0.3	0.4	0.2	0.6	—	—	0.1	3.9	0.4	0.6	0.1	0.4	3.5	5.4	1.1	1.1
I	2.3	5.2	5.3	4.0	5.0	7.6	6.0	13.9	2.7	8.7	3.4	9.8	0.1	3.9	—	—	2.0	2.9	2.5	5.2	6.8	6.5	3.1	6.1
N	20.7	13.0	2.2	4.3	8.1	7.5	2.0	2.5	3.2	3.6	2.0	4.5	0.4	5.5	2.0	2.9	—	—	2.7	3.5	3.2	7.1	5.3	5.7
P	1.1	0.8	0.3	0.5	0.9	0.9	0.3	0.4	0.4	7.4	0.8	1.4	0.1	0.4	0.7	1.3	0.4	0.8	—	—	0.4	1.0	0.8	1.3
UK	5.7	8.3	25.9	8.8	3.9	8.0	7.6	5.9	15.9	7.6	4.9	9.8	76.8	27.5	6.8	6.5	11.9	9.6	11.3	11.7	—	—	5.9	7.7
Total Intra-EC trade	55.4	72.1	59.3	51.2	37.9	48.9	50.9	54.2	46.8	64.5	30.9	60.7	82.4	70.0	34.5	53.4	58.3	74.7	38.9	75.1	21.7	54.1	37.2	58.4
Other European OECD countries	8.7	5.8	16.6	22.2	22.7	16.9	10.3	8.1	12.4	5.8	9.0	7.8	0.9	6.9	18.9	11.3	11.9	6.7	5.1	8.1	9.1	8.2	13.7	10.7
USA	9.4	4.9	9.3	5.5	7.3	7.9	13.6	4.8	10.1	4.6	5.9	7.0	5.7	8.1	9.9	7.8	5.6	4.0	8.3	5.3	8.8	12.0	7.9	7.3
Canada	1.1	0.4	0.7	0.5	1.2	0.6	0.3	0.5	1.3	0.5	0.8	0.7	0.7	0.9	1.2	0.9	0.8	0.4	1.1	0.7	5.8	1.4	2.3	0.7
Japan	0.6	1.3	0.2	4.0	0.9	2.6	1.4	1.0	1.7	1.1	0.3	1.9	0.0	3.1	0.3	2.1	0.4	1.0	0.5	0.8	0.6	2.3	0.6	2.1
Australia	0.5	0.3	0.3	0.6	1.0	0.7	0.1	0.4	0.3	0.4	0.5	0.4	0.1	0.6	0.8	0.7	0.7	0.4	0.6	0.3	7.2	1.4	2.4	0.7
Developing countries	18.0	11.3	9.3	10.9	20.9	12.7	18.4	17.2	18.4	20.7	46.9	18.0	1.6	6.7	26.2	17.1	17.6	8.3	42.3	7.9	33.6	16.4	27.4	14.2
of which: OPEC	3.3	1.7	2.3	1.8	4.8	2.6	2.6	4.0	2.6	3.0	21.3	3.7	0.2	1.4	7.5	3.8	4.5	1.8	2.0	0.8	7.0	3.6	7.6	2.9
Other developing countries	14.7	9.6	7.0	9.1	16.1	10.1	15.8	13.2	15.8	17.7	25.6	14.3	1.4	5.3	18.7	13.3	13.1	6.5	40.3	7.1	26.6	12.8	19.8	11.3
Rest of the world and unspecified	6.3	3.9	4.3	5.1	8.1	9.7	5.0	13.8	9.0	2.4	5.7	3.5	8.6	3.7	8.2	6.7	4.7	4.5	3.2	1.8	13.2	4.2	8.5	5.9
World (excluding EC)	44.6	27.9	40.7	48.8	62.1	51.1	49.1	45.8	53.2	35.5	69.1	39.3	17.6	30.0	65.5	46.6	41.7	25.3	61.1	24.9	78.3	45.9	62.8	41.6
World (including EC)	100	100	100	100	100	100	100	100	100	100	100	100	100	100	100	100	100	100	100	100	100	100	100	100

Source: European Economy, 1997
D: 1958: West Germany; 1994: unified Germany

Table 10.3 Structure of EC imports by country and region, 1958 and 1994 (percentage of total imports)

Import from / to	B/L 1958	B/L 1994	DK 1958	DK 1994	D 1958	D 1994	EL 1958	EL 1994	E 1958	E 1994	F 1958	F 1994	IRL 1958	IRL 1994	I 1958	I 1994	N 1958	N 1994	P 1958	P 1994	UK 1958	UK 1994	EUR 12 1958	EUR 12 1994
B/L	—	—	3.8	3.7	4.5	7.1	3.3	3.8	1.8	3.9	5.4	10.3	1.8	1.6	2.0	4.7	17.8	10.7	7.3	3.5	1.6	4.6	4.4	6.2
DK	0.5	0.6	—	—	3.4	1.9	0.7	1.5	1.3	0.8	0.6	1.0	0.7	0.7	2.2	1.0	0.7	1.1	0.8	0.8	3.1	1.4	2.0	1.2
D	17.2	18.9	19.9	21.8	—	—	20.3	16.4	8.7	15.3	11.6	20.4	4.0	7.0	12.0	19.2	19.5	20.9	17.6	14.0	3.5	14.2	8.7	13.4
EL	0.1	0.1	0.0	0.2	0.7	0.5	—	—	0.2	0.3	0.6	0.2	0.2	0.1	0.4	0.8	0.2	0.1	0.1	0.1	0.2	0.2	0.4	0.3
E	0.5	1.6	0.7	1.2	1.6	2.8	0.1	3.1	—	—	1.2	6.0	0.4	0.9	0.4	3.8	0.4	1.6	0.4	19.8	1.0	2.4	0.9	3.2
F	11.6	15.2	3.4	5.4	7.6	11.3	5.4	8.1	6.8	18.0	—	—	1.6	3.4	4.8	13.6	2.8	6.9	7.7	12.7	2.7	9.8	4.4	9.5
IRL	0.1	1.0	0.0	0.8	0.1	1.1	0.0	0.9	0.6	0.9	0.0	1.3	—	—	0.0	0.9	0.0	1.1	0.1	0.7	2.9	4.7	0.9	1.5
I	2.1	4.1	1.7	4.2	5.5	8.4	8.8	16.7	1.8	8.9	2.4	9.9	0.8	2.0	—	—	1.8	3.4	3.7	8.5	2.1	4.9	2.7	6.2
NL	15.7	17.0	7.3	6.9	8.1	10.5	4.8	7.5	2.6	4.5	2.5	6.5	2.9	3.3	2.6	5.7	—	—	2.9	4.4	4.2	6.5	5.2	7.5
P	0.4	0.5	0.3	1.3	0.4	0.9	0.3	0.4	0.3	2.8	0.4	1.1	0.2	0.3	0.4	0.8	0.2	0.5	—	—	0.4	0.8	0.3	0.9
UK	7.4	9.1	22.8	6.7	4.3	6.3	9.9	6.2	7.8	8.0	3.5	8.2	56.3	41.2	5.5	6.1	7.4	8.5	12.9	6.7	—	—	5.4	6.8
Total Intra-EC trade	55.5	68.1	60.0	52.1	36.3	50.7	53.7	64.4	31.8	63.5	28.3	65.0	68.9	63.3	30.2	56.2	50.7	54.8	53.4	71.4	21.8	49.9	35.2	57.0
Other European OECD countries	7.7	6.8	18.6	25.5	15.2	16.5	11.5	6.6	8.4	5.5	6.7	7.6	3.4	4.8	13.1	11.6	7.2	9.0	8.6	6.0	8.7	10.8	10.1	11.1
USA	9.9	5.9	9.1	4.3	13.6	5.9	13.7	3.2	21.6	6.2	10.0	7.3	7.0	16.9	16.4	4.6	11.3	8.7	7.0	3.6	9.4	12.8	11.4	7.4
Canada	1.4	0.7	0.1	0.4	3.1	0.6	0.8	0.3	0.5	0.4	1.0	0.6	3.0	0.6	1.5	0.9	1.4	0.7	0.5	0.3	8.2	1.2	3.6	0.7
Japan	0.6	2.7	1.5	3.1	0.6	4.8	2.0	3.8	0.7	2.8	0.2	2.5	1.1	4.3	0.4	2.4	0.8	4.4	0.0	2.8	0.9	5.9	0.7	3.9
Australia	1.7	0.3	0.0	0.2	1.2	0.2	0.3	0.0	0.8	0.3	2.4	0.3	1.2	0.1	3.0	0.5	0.2	0.4	0.9	0.1	5.4	0.7	2.6	0.4
Developing countries	19.2	10.0	5.9	8.3	23.9	11.0	9.6	13.6	32.0	17.0	45.6	12.6	9.3	7.3	29.4	14.2	24.4	17.3	27.6	13.3	34.7	13.2	29.5	12.8
of which: OPEC	5.7	1.4	0.3	0.7	6.7	2.1	1.7	5.3	17.7	6.1	19.7	3.8	0.7	0.3	13.9	5.3	11.5	5.3	6.3	5.8	11.3	2.4	10.8	3.2
Other developing countries	13.5	8.6	5.6	7.6	17.2	8.9	7.9	8.3	14.3	10.9	25.9	8.8	8.6	7.0	15.5	8.9	12.9	12.0	21.3	7.5	23.4	10.8	18.7	9.6
Rest of the world and unspecified	4.0	5.5	4.7	6.1	6.1	10.3	8.4	8.1	4.2	4.3	5.8	4.1	6.1	2.7	6.0	9.6	4.0	4.7	2.0	2.5	10.9	5.5	6.9	6.7
World (excluding EC)	44.5	31.9	40.0	47.9	63.7	49.3	46.3	35.6	68.2	36.5	71.7	35.0	31.1	36.7	69.8	43.8	49.3	45.2	46.6	28.6	78.2	50.1	64.8	43.0
World (including EC)	100	100	100	100	100	100	100	100	100	100	100	100	100	100	100	100	100	100	100	100	100	100	100	100

Source: European Economy, 1997
D: 1958: West Germany; 1994: unified Germany

Table 10.4   UK GDP and its components, 1993–2000 (£ billion at 1990 prices)

	Consumers' expenditure	General government consumption	Total fixed investment	Stock-building	Domestic demand	Exports of goods and services	Total final expenditure	Less imports of goods and services	Less adjustment to factor cost	Plus statistical discrepancy	GDP at factor cost
1993	348.1	115	96.5	0.3	561	143	703	154	72	–	476
1994	357.8	118	100.7	2.8	578	156	736	163	74	–	498
1995	364	119.5	102.2	4.1	589	168	758	170	76	–	511
1996	377	121.9	104.1	2.6	606	180	785	184	74	1	525
1997	394.5	120.5	108.7	2.2	626	194	820	201.6	79.8	2.1	540.5
1998	410	122.0	114.0	1.3	646.7	200	846.8	216.8	80.5	2.3	551.9
1999	418	124.6	118	2.5	665.7	209	869.9	228.6	81.9	2.3	561.7
2000	427	127.0	120.0	3	686.5	221	897.2	241.2	83.8	2.4	574.6

Source: Derived from HMT, FSBR, 1998; ONS, UK Economic Accounts, 1997.
Figures have been rounded up.

Table 10.5   UK GDP and shares of income and expenditure, 1994–7

	Gross domestic product at current factor cost	Total final expenditure (current market prices) (£mn)	Percentage share of total final expenditure					
			Consumers' expenditure	General government consumption	Gross fixed investment			Exports
					General government	Public corporations	Private sector	
Annual								
1994	580 135	852 024	50.2	16.9	1.5	0.6	9.8	20.8
1995	608 090	908 536	49.1	16.4	1.4	0.6	10.0	22.0
1996	642 765	963 660	49.2	16.1	1.1	0.4	10.4	22.5
1997	679 081	–	–	–	–	–	–	–

Source: ONS, Economic Trends, 1998.

Figure 10.2 UK shares of income and expenditure, 1996

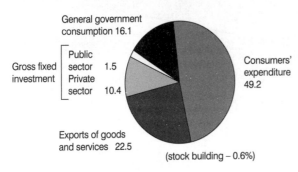

Total final expenditure

Share at current market prices 1996

General government
consumption 16.1

Gross fixed investment
Public sector   1.5
Private sector   10.4

Consumers' expenditure
49.2

Exports of goods
and services 22.5

(stock building – 0.6%)

Source: ONS, *Economic Trends*, 1998

✍ Activity 10.4

As Table 10.4 shows, in 1997 British exports at 1990 prices were £193.9bn, while British imports were £201.6bn. Given that GDP at factor cost was £540.5 that year, what percentage of GDP were exports and imports respectively? What was the trade balance?

✓ Answer 10.4

According to these data, British imports in 1997

accounted for 37.2 per cent of real GDP, while British exports accounted for 35.8 per cent of GDP. The balance of trade was in deficit at –£7.7bn.

The study of international economics or open economy macroeconomics focuses on the effects that international transactions have on the domestic economy. International considerations play a major role in the formulation of domestic economic policies. Exchange rate depreciations or appreciations, balance of trade deficits or surpluses, runs on currencies and currency speculation and financial capital international movement regulation are all examples of issues which are high on the agenda of government officials and domestic policymakers. This is true for all countries.

Degree of openness

The constraints that international economy considerations impose on domestic policymaking will depend on the relative size of the foreign sector, which includes all international transactions of a country, with respect to the size of GDP. For countries like Britain, France, Italy or Germany, where the foreign sector represents about 30 per cent of GDP, international considerations are very important and effectively constrain, in ways that this chapter will clarify, domestic policymaking. The export sector is likely to affect the domestic economy less in countries where it represents a smaller percentage of GDP, as in the USA or Japan, where it is just over

Figure 10.3 UK trade dependency ratio, 1950–90

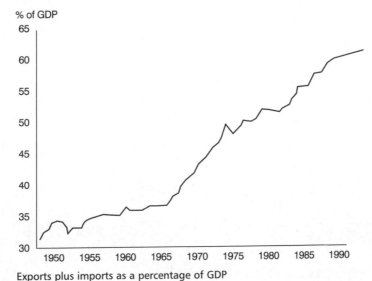

Exports plus imports as a percentage of GDP

Source: *Economic Review,* 1997

Table 10.6   EU exports of goods and services at current prices, 1960–97

	(Percentage of gross domestic product at market price)															(Percentage of gross domestic product)		
	B	DK	D[1]	EL	E	F	IRL	I	L	NL	A	P	FIN	S	UK	EUR 15[2]	USA	JP
1960	38.3	32.2	19.0	7.1	8.9	14.5	30.2	13.1	85.6	45.7	23.6	16.0	22.5	22.7	20.9	19.7	5.2	10.7
1961	39.6	29.9	18.0	7.2	8.6	14.0	32.9	13.4	85.9	43.6	23.3	15.0	21.2	22.0	20.6	19.2	5.1	9.3
1962	41.2	28.5	17.4	7.6	8.8	12.9	30.6	13.2	78.9	43.0	24.2	17.2	21.3	21.6	20.1	18.6	5.0	9.4
1963	42.3	30.3	17.8	7.8	8.2	12.7	31.9	12.7	76.7	43.1	24.4	17.5	20.3	21.6	20.0	18.5	5.1	9.0
1964	43.1	29.7	18.1	7.1	9.4	12.7	31.7	13.4	77.8	41.7	24.2	23.5	20.2	22.0	19.4	18.6	5.3	9.5
1965	42.6	29.2	18.0	7.0	8.7	13.3	33.1	14.9	79.7	41.1	24.5	24.6	20.2	21.5	19.2	18.8	5.2	10.5
1966	44.2	29.2	19.2	8.8	9.5	13.4	35.4	15.4	76.3	40.0	24.4	24.8	19.9	21.1	19.4	19.2	5.3	10.6
1967	43.3	27.2	20.4	8.3	9.1	13.2	36.0	15.0	77.5	38.9	25.0	25.0	19.7	20.8	19.1	19.2	5.3	9.6
1968	45.5	27.5	21.4	7.5	11.3	13.3	36.9	15.9	79.5	39.3	25.0	23.0	22.7	21.2	21.4	20.2	5.3	10.1
1969	49.4	27.4	21.7	7.6	12.1	14.1	35.5	16.6	83.2	40.8	27.6	22.4	24.2	22.5	22.3	21.1	5.3	10.5
1970	51.8	27.9	21.2	7.8	13.2	15.8	35.1	16.5	87.8	43.1	30.3	22.4	25.7	23.8	23.1	21.9	5.8	10.8
1961–70	44.3	28.6	19.3	7.7	9.9	13.5	33.9	14.7	80.3	41.5	25.2	21.5	21.5	21.8	20.5	19.5	5.3	9.9
1971	50.4	27.6	20.8	8.0	14.2	16.4	34.3	17.0	87.0	43.5	29.9	23.0	25.3	24.1	23.2	22.0	5.7	11.7
1972	50.9	27.1	20.6	9.1	14.5	16.7	32.8	17.8	81.8	43.3	29.8	23.9	25.5	23.9	21.7	22.0	5.8	10.6
1973	55.4	28.5	21.8	11.1	14.4	17.6	36.1	17.4	88.2	45.4	29.7	24.5	25.4	27.1	23.7	23.3	6.9	10.0
1974	61.1	31.8	26.4	12.5	14.4	20.7	40.4	20.2	101.3	51.9	32.2	24.6	27.5	31.8	28.0	25.1	8.6	13.6
1975	53.5	30.1	24.7	13.1	13.5	19.1	40.6	20.6	91.3	47.9	31.0	18.7	24.0	27.8	25.9	26.3	8.6	12.8
1976	56.9	28.8	25.7	13.7	13.7	19.6	44.0	22.1	87.0	49.3	31.8	16.0	25.3	27.3	28.5	26.3	8.3	13.6
1977	56.3	28.8	25.5	13.1	14.5	20.5	47.0	23.4	85.8	45.2	31.4	16.9	28.8	27.1	30.1	26.8	8.0	13.1
1978	54.8	27.8	24.8	13.7	15.2	20.4	47.4	23.7	82.7	43.9	32.5	18.4	30.2	27.9	28.5	26.4	8.3	11.1
1979	60.1	29.2	25.1	13.6	15.0	21.2	47.2	24.4	89.8	47.9	34.8	24.8	31.7	30.1	28.0	27.1	9.1	11.6
1980	62.4	32.7	26.4	16.3	15.7	21.5	47.0	21.9	87.4	51.1	35.9	25.1	33.2	29.5	27.3	27.5	10.2	13.7
1971–80	56.2	29.2	24.2	12.4	14.5	19.4	41.7	20.9	88.2	47.0	31.9	21.7	27.6	27.7	26.5	25.4	8.0	12.2
1981	67.6	36.5	28.7	16.0	17.8	22.6	46.0	23.3	85.6	56.6	37.3	23.8	33.4	29.9	26.7	28.8	9.9	14.7
1982	71.2	36.4	28.7	14.3	18.4	21.8	45.6	22.9	87.9	55.9	37.1	24.7	31.1	32.2	26.3	28.8	8.9	14.6
1983	74.0	36.4	29.9	15.4	20.7	22.5	49.7	22.0	89.1	55.4	36.5	28.7	30.5	35.6	26.5	29.0	8.0	13.9
1984	78.4	36.7	30.6	16.9	23.0	24.1	56.4	22.7	99.8	59.8	38.4	34.2	30.9	36.3	28.4	30.8	7.9	15.0
1985	76.2	36.7	32.5	16.5	22.7	23.9	57.1	22.8	107.2	60.8	40.2	34.2	29.6	35.3	28.8	31.2	7.4	14.5
1986	70.0	32.0	30.2	17.4	19.9	21.2	52.1	20.2	98.6	50.7	36.5	32.0	25.9	32.8	25.6	28.0	7.4	11.4
1987	68.7	31.4	29.0	19.1	19.4	20.6	55.6	19.4	96.5	49.7	35.5	30.4	25.0	32.5	25.3	27.3	7.9	10.4
1988	71.8	32.6	29.6	18.5	18.9	21.3	59.3	19.0	99.2	52.5	38.3	32.5	25.0	32.3	23.0	27.3	9.0	10.0
1989	76.3	34.5	31.5	18.2	18.1	22.9	62.8	20.0	97.9	55.2	40.6	34.6	24.0	32.0	23.8	28.5	9.6	10.6
1990	73.1	35.5	32.1	16.8	17.1	22.6	58.6	20.0	97.9	54.2	40.8	34.3	23.1	29.9	24.4	28.4	10.0	10.7
1981–90	72.7	34.9	30.3	16.9	19.6	22.3	54.3	21.2	96.2	55.1	38.1	30.9	28.0	29.9	25.9	28.8	8.6	12.6
1991	71.6	37.0	33.6	16.1	17.1	22.7	58.9	19.0	96.8	54.0	40.4	30.8	22.3	27.9	23.5	28.3	10.5	10.2
1992	69.7	36.1	33.4	16.7	17.6	22.7	61.4	19.7	94.6	52.1	39.1	28.1	26.9	27.9	23.9	28.5	10.6	10.0
1993	68.5	34.3	32.4	16.2	19.4	22.0	66.2	22.9	93.0	50.4	37.6	27.9	32.7	32.7	25.6	29.5	10.3	9.3
1994	71.5	35.4	33.8	16.8	22.3	22.8	69.7	24.4	93.8	51.2	40.4	30.8	35.7	36.4	26.6	31.0	10.6	9.3
1991	71.6	37.0	25.5	16.1	17.1	22.7	58.9	19.7	96.8	54.0	39.1	28.1	22.3	27.9	23.9	26.1	10.5	10.2
1992	69.7	36.1	23.8	16.7	17.6	22.7	61.4	19.7	94.6	52.1	37.6	27.9	26.9	27.9	23.9	26.7	10.6	10.0
1993	68.5	34.3	22.1	16.2	19.4	22.0	66.2	22.9	93.0	50.4	38.1	30.8	33.1	32.7	25.6	28.0	10.3	9.3
1994	71.5	35.4	22.8	16.8	22.3	22.8	69.7	24.4	93.8	51.2	39.1	28.1	35.7	36.4	26.6	29.6	10.6	9.3
1995	72.6	34.1	23.6	16.5	23.7	23.5	74.6	27.6	91.8	53.5	39.6	33.2	38.0	40.9	28.5	30.0	11.4	9.4
1996	74.8	33.8	24.3	15.8	25.2	23.9	74.7	26.5	90.4	53.8	41.0	33.0	38.1	40.0	29.2	30.8	11.6	10.0
1997	77.5	34.3	25.8	15.8	27.3	24.9	74.7	27.3	93.1	55.2	42.6	34.0	38.6	41.1	27.4	30.8	11.7	11.1

Source: European Economy, 1997

[1] 1960–94: WD

[2] 1960–94: including WD; 1991–97: including D

1960–94: WD

1991–97: including D

Table 10.7 EU imports of goods and services at current prices, 1960–97

							(Percentage of gross domestic product at market price)										(Percentage of gross domestic product)	
	B	DK	D¹	EL	E	F	IRL	I	L	NL	A	P	FIN	S	UK	EUR 15²	USA	JP
1960	39.2	33.4	16.5	14.2	7.4	12.4	35.4	13.5	72.4	44.2	24.4	21.3	23.2	23.3	22.3	19.3	4.4	10.2
1961	40.6	31.5	15.8	14.0	9.3	12.2	37.7	13.5	78.7	43.7	23.1	25.0	22.3	21.6	20.9	18.7	4.3	10.9
1962	41.4	31.6	16.1	14.4	11.1	12.0	36.9	13.9	77.8	42.9	22.8	21.1	22.3	21.3	20.3	18.5	4.4	9.3
1963	43.5	30.0	16.3	15.3	11.8	12.3	38.7	15.1	76.1	44.0	23.4	21.9	20.2	21.4	20.4	18.8	4.3	9.8
1964	43.7	31.8	16.5	16.2	12.1	12.9	38.9	13.4	77.3	44.0	24.1	26.9	22.1	21.7	21.1	19.1	4.3	9.7
1965	42.8	30.7	17.8	17.3	14.0	12.4	41.6	12.7	78.4	42.0	25.0	28.3	21.9	21.8	20.0	19.1	4.3	9.7
1966	45.1	30.0	17.5	16.0	14.4	13.1	41.0	13.7	73.7	41.6	25.8	28.0	21.5	21.8	19.5	19.2	4.8	9.7
1967	43.0	29.2	16.8	15.4	12.6	13.0	38.8	14.2	69.3	39.9	25.1	26.6	20.6	20.8	20.2	18.8	4.9	9.0
1968	45.2	28.9	17.7	15.6	13.4	13.3	42.9	13.9	69.1	39.6	25.2	26.8	21.1	21.4	22.2	19.6	5.2	9.4
1969	48.5	29.6	18.9	15.9	14.0	14.6	44.0	15.3	68.4	41.2	26.4	25.8	23.2	22.9	21.8	20.6	5.3	9.0
1970	49.3	30.9	19.1	15.7	14.2	15.3	42.7	16.3	74.3	45.0	29.3	27.8	26.9	24.4	22.2	21.5	5.5	8.9
1961–70	44.3	30.4	17.3	15.6	12.7	13.1	40.3	14.2	74.3	42.4	25.0	25.8	22.2	22.0	20.9	19.4	4.7	9.5
1971	48.2	29.4	19.0	15.7	13.4	15.3	41.2	16.2	82.8	43.7	29.1	28.9	26.1	22.9	21.7	21.2	5.7	9.0
1972	47.5	26.5	18.6	17.1	14.4	15.7	37.9	17.0	75.3	40.7	29.2	28.8	25.2	22.4	21.8	21.1	6.1	8.3
1973	53.3	30.4	18.9	21.5	15.3	16.7	42.6	19.3	75.1	42.3	29.3	30.4	26.1	24.4	26.1	22.9	6.8	10.0
1974	60.5	34.7	22.0	21.8	19.2	21.7	54.3	24.3	79.9	49.2	32.5	38.0	31.2	32.6	33.0	27.9	8.7	14.3
1975	53.1	31.0	21.8	22.9	17.3	17.9	46.3	20.7	86.4	44.7	30.4	29.5	30.0	28.0	27.6	24.9	7.7	12.8
1976	56.4	33.5	23.4	22.0	18.2	20.3	51.5	23.3	80.7	46.0	33.2	27.8	27.3	29.0	29.6	26.8	8.5	12.8
1977	57.0	32.5	23.1	21.5	16.5	20.4	55.6	22.4	81.2	45.0	34.0	30.1	27.0	28.7	29.3	26.5	9.2	11.5
1978	55.6	29.9	22.3	21.0	14.4	19.1	56.8	21.4	80.8	43.9	32.4	29.3	26.3	26.9	27.1	25.2	9.5	9.4
1979	62.0	32.1	24.4	21.5	14.7	20.6	62.7	23.3	85.2	48.4	35.1	34.1	30.2	31.1	27.7	27.1	10.2	12.5
1980	64.9	33.8	26.9	22.3	18.1	22.7	59.7	24.8	87.5	51.6	37.7	37.9	34.0	31.4	25.0	28.5	10.9	14.6
1971–80	55.8	31.4	22.0	20.7	16.1	19.0	50.8	21.3	81.5	45.5	32.3	31.5	28.3	27.7	26.9	25.2	8.3	11.5
1981	69.2	35.8	27.9	23.1	19.9	23.5	59.4	25.5	87.8	53.0	38.6	40.7	32.0	30.1	23.8	29.0	10.5	13.9
1982	72.2	35.9	27.5	24.4	20.3	23.7	52.5	24.2	88.9	51.5	35.4	40.5	30.3	32.7	24.5	28.8	9.6	13.8
1983	72.2	34.4	26.7	25.6	21.6	22.6	52.3	21.5	88.3	51.5	35.2	39.7	30.0	33.4	25.6	28.2	9.7	12.2
1984	76.6	35.5	28.2	25.5	20.9	23.5	56.6	23.1	97.5	54.6	38.3	40.7	28.3	32.7	28.6	29.7	10.8	12.3
1985	73.7	36.3	29.0	27.9	20.8	23.2	55.3	23.3	101.4	56.0	40.0	37.3	28.5	33.6	27.8	29.8	10.4	11.1
1986	66.1	32.5	25.0	26.3	17.7	20.2	49.8	18.8	92.8	46.9	35.6	32.4	25.3	29.7	26.4	26.0	10.7	7.4
1987	65.7	29.6	23.9	27.0	19.2	20.5	50.1	18.9	94.5	47.1	35.2	37.2	25.3	30.6	26.6	26.0	11.3	7.2
1988	68.2	29.4	24.3	25.7	20.0	21.2	51.8	18.9	96.2	48.6	37.8	41.1	25.3	30.6	26.7	26.5	11.4	7.8
1989	73.2	31.1	26.1	27.5	21.4	22.8	55.8	20.2	95.1	51.3	39.6	41.2	25.9	31.5	27.9	28.0	11.3	9.2
1990	70.4	30.1	26.3	28.1	20.4	22.6	51.7	20.0	96.4	49.5	39.5	41.9	24.6	29.5	27.1	27.5	11.4	10.5
1981–90	70.8	33.1	26.5	26.1	20.2	22.4	53.6	21.4	93.9	51.0	37.5	39.3	27.5	31.5	26.5	27.0	10.7	8.4
1991	68.7	30.9	27.8	27.0	20.3	22.3	52.4	19.0	98.6	49.3	39.6	39.5	22.9	26.4	24.7	27.0	11.0	7.7
1992	66.0	29.3	26.6	27.0	20.4	21.3	51.8	19.7	89.2	47.5	38.1	37.0	25.6	26.2	25.3	26.7	11.3	7.0
1993	63.9	27.3	24.7	26.3	20.0	19.8	53.1	19.5	85.0	44.3	37.0	35.4	27.7	29.1	26.9	26.2	11.6	7.2
1994	66.5	29.4	25.9	26.4	22.2	20.6	56.9	20.7	82.3	45.0	38.3	37.8	29.4	32.2	27.5	27.5	12.3	8.4
1991	68.7	30.9	25.6	27.0	20.3	22.3	52.4	19.0	98.6	49.3	39.6	39.5	22.9	26.4	24.7	26.5	11.0	7.7
1992	66.0	29.3	23.8	27.0	20.4	21.3	51.8	19.7	89.2	47.5	38.1	37.0	25.6	26.2	25.3	26.0	11.3	7.0
1993	63.9	27.3	21.6	26.3	20.0	19.8	53.1	19.5	85.0	44.3	37.0	35.4	27.7	29.1	26.9	25.3	11.6	7.2
1994	66.5	29.4	22.2	26.4	22.2	20.6	56.9	20.7	82.3	45.0	38.3	37.8	29.4	32.2	27.5	26.4	12.3	8.4
1995	67.8	30.0	22.8	26.9	23.3	21.1	59.5	23.3	80.5	46.9	40.4	37.8	29.5	34.6	29.3	27.7	12.3	7.9
1996	70.0	29.5	23.0	26.5	24.0	21.2	59.7	21.1	77.8	47.8	41.9	39.0	30.2	33.3	30.1	27.7	13.0	9.4
1997	72.5	29.8	24.0	26.4	25.6	22.0	59.1	21.5	79.3	49.7	43.0	40.8	31.1	33.8	28.6	28.3	13.4	10.2

Source: European Economy, 1997
¹ 1960–94: WD
² 1960–94: including WD; 1991–97: including D

11 per cent, than it does in countries like Luxembourg, where the export sector in 1997 represented 93.1 per cent of GDP. The size of the export sector relative to the size of GDP measures the degree of **openness** of the economy. So we say that the British economy, where the share of export to GDP in 1997 was 27.4 per cent, is more open than the Japanese or US economy, where the ratios were 11.1 per cent and 11.7 per cent respectively.

✍ Activity 10.5

Looking at the data in Table 10.6 spanning almost thirty years, from 1961 to 1997, what can you say about the openness of EU countries and of the US and Japan? Have they all become more open? Which country was most open and which least open in 1997?

✓ Answer 10.5

All countries have become more open. The most open in 1997 was Luxembourg, the least open was Japan.

The world economies have in fact become increasingly **interdependent** over the last three decades. International trade plays a major part in today's world economies. Britain is no exception. Billions of pounds of imports and exports are exchanged between Britain and the rest of the world each year, while billions of pound also flow through the international capital market each day. A measure of the importance of trade for a country can be obtained by calculating the **trade dependency ratio**, which is measured by the ratio of exports plus imports to GDP.

✍ Activity 10.6

Using the statistics provided by Tables 10.6 and 10.7, calculate the trade dependency ratio of the UK economy at ten-year intervals and show your results with a graph.

✓ Answer 10.6

You should have obtained a graph that looks approximately like Figure 10.3.

We now turn our attention to this category of transactions, international transactions, in order to understand what affects them and what impact they have on our domestic economy.

EXCHANGE RATE DETERMINATION

Countries trade with one another to obtain goods and services for a number of reasons:

1 They cannot produce the goods themselves, for example, minerals and raw materials can only be found in some parts of the world.
2 They cannot produce them as cheaply or as well as other countries. A country will export those products for which it has the greatest **comparative advantage** in production (or distribution) and will import those products for which it has the greatest **comparative disadvantage**.
3 By selling to foreign markets, firms enjoy economies of scale (can produce each unit of product more cheaply as more of it is produced); hence they become more competitive and more able to sell abroad.

✍ Activity 10.7

What do you think other countries supply the UK with? What does the UK supply to other countries? Think only in very general terms.

✓ Answer 10.7

Foreign countries supply the UK with:

- **goods and services**, like French cheese and holidays on the Italian Riviera;
- **labour**, like immigrants, remitting their wages to their country of origin in order to support their relatives there;
- **capital**, both in the form of direct investment, as in the case of a Japanese car manufacturer buying a factory and capital equipment and setting up car production in the UK; or portfolio investment, which takes place when foreigners buy financial assets like British government bonds or shares in British companies.

The UK, on the other hand, equally supplies other countries with:

- **goods and services**, like Amstrad computers or Lloyds insurance services;
- **labour**, in the form of large numbers of expatriates working as high-ranking consultants, managers, administrators in Hong Kong, India, China, etc.;
- **capital**, like direct investments in the Far East and many other world countries.

✍ Activity 10.8

In what way does international trade differ from domestic or national transactions?

✓ Answer 10.8

International trade differs from domestic or national transactions only in one fundamental respect: as different countries use different national currencies, in order to buy a foreign good or service the importing country (its firms and individuals) needs first to acquire the appropriate currency.

Foreign currencies are bought on the foreign exchange market, the international market in which one national currency can be exchanged for another.

Let's say you are planning to go to Italy on holiday at Easter. Holidays abroad are a form of imports: while you are abroad you spend income earned in Britain on goods and services produced in another economy. If you are a well-organized person, before you leave you go to your local bank and order a certain amount of Italian lira – this is to make sure the bank actually has all the foreign currency you require, particularly if it is a large amount – which you then buy using British pounds. You use your domestic currency to buy some foreign currency: that is what you are doing. In fact, prior to that, the international department of the bank with whom you have lodged your request for lira will have bought foreign currencies in exchange for pounds on the foreign exchange market, to be able to satisfy the foreign currency needs of its customers, whether private individuals or firms. With your lira, the bank clerk also hands over a slip which tells you the rate at which your money has been exchanged for foreign money: the **exchange rate**. The exchange rate tells you how many units of a foreign currency you can buy with £1. The exchange rate measures the international value of sterling: the rate at which £1 exchanges for Italian lira on the foreign exchange market.

✍ Activity 10.9

Suppose you hand over £100 to be changed into the Italian currency and you are given L240,000. What is the exchange rate between sterling and lira?

✓ Answer 10.9

The rate at which you have exchanged your British currency for the Italian currency was £1 = L2,400 or L240,000/100.

If you are not a prudent and well-organized person and go to Italy with only British money in your pocket, you will soon discover, once you are there, that you cannot buy anything, as the Italians won't accept your pound notes. And not just the Italians in fact: generally, with some exceptions, notably some developing countries or countries in transition, like the ex-Eastern bloc countries where hard currencies like dollars would be acceptable to settle some transactions, traders in every country only accept their own currency for payments. Faced with impending problems, you then decide to go

to a local bank in Italy and change some of your pounds into Italian lira. You hand over £100 and you are given L220,000.

✍ Activity 10.10

Is that a mistake? What exchange rate have you been given? Can you explain why? Has this to do with the fact that you changed your money with an Italian bank in Italy, rather than with a British bank in Britain?

✓ Answer 10.10

No, it is not a mistake. The exchange rate between pound sterling and Italian lira has changed. It is now £1 = L2,200. The pound has lost some of its value expressed in lire: it has depreciated. Before you left, only a few days ago, £1 was worth L2,400, now it is worth L2,200. One unit of your domestic currency buys fewer units of the foreign currency.

This has nothing to do with the fact that you have changed your money in Italy rather than in Britain. Exchange rates are the same worldwide, regardless of where, in which country or at which bank the currency exchanges take place. When foreign currency exchange kiosks at street corners, inside hotels, railway stations or airports give you 'rip-off rates' that are worse than the official foreign exchange rates (which, incidentally, vary constantly as they adjust to market conditions) they are extracting a 'monopolist' price. They are exploiting the fact that you cannot go somewhere else to change your money because you need it there and then. This has nothing to do with exchange rate determination in exchange rate markets. The change in the exchange rate is caused by changed demand and/or supply conditions on the foreign exchange market. Let's try and explain what we mean by this.

The foreign exchange market

On the foreign exchange market individuals, firms and banks buy and sell any tradeable foreign currency: US dollars, French francs, Swiss francs, Japanese yen, German marks, Brazilian real, Polish zlotys, Italian lira, Spanish pesetas, British pounds, and so on.

The foreign exchange market is not limited to a place or defined geographically: rather it is composed of all the locations in the world where any currency is bought and sold for other currencies. It is a 24-hour market, given the time differences between Tokyo, Frankfurt, Paris, London and New York, just to mention a few international financial centres. Dealings are clinched and cleared instantly through the international computer networks of banks and financial centres. Since the banks buy and sell foreign currencies on behalf of their individual and corporate clients, the foreign exchange market is an inter-bank market.

The function of foreign exchange markets is to allow the transfer of funds from one currency into another. The exchange rate between any two countries is kept the same in different monetary centres by **arbitrage operations**. By arbitrage operations we mean the purchase of currency in the monetary centre where it is cheaper for immediate resale in the monetary centre where it is more expensive. This process increases the demand for the currency in the monetary centre where it is cheaper, driving up its price marginally. As it is immediately offered for sale in the monetary centres where it is more expensive, it increases its supply there, marginally lowering its price. If dollars, say, could be bought more cheaply in exchange for pounds on the New York foreign exchange market than in London, currency dealers would quickly respond and start buying dollars on the New York market, selling them on the London market. This process adds to the demand for dollars on the New York market, driving up the price of dollars, and lowers the price of dollars on the London market, where they are resold, bringing the exchange rate between the two currencies in line with the one prevailing the world over. This process of arbitrage continues until the exchange rate between the two currencies is the same in all centres. In fact it is the existence of this process that prevents exchange rates from diverging in different monetary centres.

For any specific country, the expression **foreign exchange** or **foreign currency** simply refers to all currencies other than the domestic one: in the case of Britain, all currencies other than the sterling count as foreign currency.

The rate at which one unit of domestic currency exchanges for foreign currency, the exchange rate, is determined by the demand and supply of foreign currency on the foreign exchange market. The exchange rate can also be calculated in terms of the number of units of domestic currency bought by one unit of foreign currency. The two definitions are equivalent.

Demand for foreign currency

The demand for foreign currency arises because British households and British firms want to buy goods and services or financial assets from other countries, whose prices are therefore quoted in foreign currencies. The demand for **imports** of goods and services and the existence of **capital outflows**, in the form of either direct investment or portfolio investment (when British people or British financial institutions want to start up businesses in other countries or to buy foreign bonds or shares in foreign companies, which have a foreign currency denomination) determines the **demand for foreign currency**. Domestic residents 'offer' their domestic currency in exchange for foreign currency. Hence the demand for foreign currency translates itself into a supply of domestic currency, offered in exchange. The demand for foreign currency reflects the need by British people, firms and institutions to get hold of the appropriate foreign currency for their transactions. So on the foreign exchange market, British residents will offer pounds in exchange for much-needed foreign currency. Hence the supply of domestic currency on foreign exchange markets, in exchange for foreign currency, is provided by domestic residents for the following reasons:

$$\text{Supply } S^{dc} = \text{function of } (X, DI, PI)$$

where X represents export demand, and DI and PI the demand for direct investment and portfolio investment respectively.

Supply of foreign currency

Who is supplying foreign currency to the foreign exchange market in exchange for pounds? Foreign firms, foreign people and foreign governments wanting to buy British goods and services or British financial assets, like government bonds or companies' shares, which have a sterling denomination (their prices are quoted in pounds). In order to buy them, foreign residents must first convert their currencies into pounds. As in any market, the **equilibrium price** depends on demand and supply. The **exchange rate**, which is the price of one unit of domestic currency expressed in terms of units of foreign currency, also depends on the demand and supply of foreign currency.

Exchange rates always refer to the exchange of one currency for another, in other words, they refer to two currencies at a time. There is a £–$ exchange rate, a £–French franc exchange rate, a £–Deutschmark exchange rate, a £–yen exchange rate, etc.

✍ Activity 10.11

Look at Table 10.8 and comment on the changes of the sterling exchange rate against the major currencies since 1993.

✓ Answer 10.11

Table 10.8 shows the exchange rate of sterling vis-à-vis the yen, the US dollar, the Swiss franc, the French

Table 10.8 Sterling exchange rates and UK official reserves, 1993–7

	Sterling exchange rate against major currencies								UK official reserves at end of period ($ million)	Sterling exchange rate index 1990 = 100
	Japanese yen	US dollar	Swiss franc	European currency unit (Ecu)	French franc	Italian lira	Deutsch-mark	Spanish peseta		
Annual										
1993	166.73	1.5015	2.218	1.2845	8.5073	2360	2.483	191.33	42 926	88.9
1994	156.40	1.5329	2.090	1.2924	8.4852	2467	2.481	204.83	43 898	89.2
1995	148.37	1.5783	1.865	1.2211	7.8730	2571	2.260	196.71	46 986	84.8
1996	170.00	1.5617	1.931	1.2467	7.9890	2408	2.350	197.82	46 300	86.3
1997	198.12	1.6382	2.376	1.4499	9.5606	2789	2.840	239.87	38 418	100.6

Source: ONS, *Economic Trends,* 1998

franc, the Italian lira, the Deutschmark, the Spanish peseta and the Ecu. The sterling exchange rate has appreciated vis-à-vis all currency since 1993, for reasons which will be shown further along this chapter. From 1993 to 1997 the sterling exchange rate index appreciated by about 12 per cent.

Once the exchange rate between each pair of currencies with respect to a third one, say the US dollar, is established, the exchange rate between the two currencies themselves or **cross rates** can be determined. So if, for example, £1 = $2, and DM1 = $0.5 then the cross rate is calculated as follows:

$$\frac{\$ \text{ value of } \pounds}{\$ \text{ value of } DM} = \frac{2}{0.5} = 4.$$

So the cross rate is £1 = DM4. These are, of course, only hypothetical values chosen for ease of calculation. Sterling exchange rate values prevailing in 1997 are shown in the Table 10.8.

✍ Activity 10.12

Using the sterling exchange rates shown in Table 10.8, can you calculate the cross rate between the Italian lira and the Deutschmark?

✓ Answer 10.12

The cross rate between the lira and the Deutschmark is L982 to the Deutschmark. The result is obtained by dividing the respective exchange rates of lira and Deutschmark with sterling as follows:

$$2789/2.840 = 982.$$

Hence, DM1 = L982.

In order to assess the overall change in the value of a currency, a weighted average of movements in the exchange rates between the domestic currency and the currencies of the country's most important trade partners is often used, with weights reflecting the relative importance of these other currencies, from a trade point of view. The overall value of the currency so calculated, expressed as an index, is referred to as the **effective exchange rate index**.

✍ Activity 10.13

Look at Table 10.9 and compare the strength of the pound in 1985, 1990, 1995 and 1999.

✓ Answer 10.13

The exchange rate started depreciating in the second part of the 1980s and continued to depreciate in the first part of the 1990s. This trend is, however, reversed in the latter part of the 1990s when the sterling appreciated quite dramatically, particularly between August 1996 and July 1997.

The appreciation of about 20 per cent between 1995 and 1997 severely affected UK exports, particularly of manufactures. Let's now go back to our discussion of how exchange rates are determined, by looking at a two-country situation. We use Britain and Italy as an example to see how the exchange rate between pounds and Italian lira is determined. As we said before, the exchange rate is a **price**, the price of one unit of domestic currency expressed in a foreign currency, and as such it is determined by demand and supply: the demand for pounds in exchange for lira and the supply of pounds in exchange for lira, as shown in Figure 10.4.

✍ Activity 10.14

Who demands pounds in exchange for Italian lira on the foreign exchange market? Who supplies pounds in

Table 10.9   Effective exchange rates, 1985–99 (indices 1991 = 100, average of daily rates)

	Monetary unit	1985	1986	1987	1988	1989	1990	1991	1992	1993	1994	1995	1996	Estimates and assumptions[a] 1997	1998	1999
USA	Dollar	130.6	113.9	105.2	100.0	102.8	101.0	100.0	98.6	100.7	100.1	101.0	107.6	115.3	117.8	117.9
Japan	Yen	68.3	89.9	97.5	106.5	99.9	91.8	100.0	105.4	126.6	136.3	143.9	125.5	120.5	121.7	121.8
Germany	Deutschemark	81.2	89.8	96.0	95.8	95.1	100.4	100.0	103.8	107.9	109.7	116.8	115.0	110.5	111.0	111.8
France	Franc	96.4	99.6	99.8	98.1	97.0	101.6	100.0	103.3	106.6	108.0	111.8	112.3	108.9	109.4	109.7
Italy	Lira	98.2	100.8	100.9	98.1	99.1	101.1	100.0	97.4	82.1	79.1	72.1	79.3	80.1	80.6	80.9
United Kingdom	Pound	107.4	99.5	97.9	103.8	100.6	99.1	100.0	96.5	88.4	89.2	85.4	87.3	101.6	105.0	105.3
Canada	Dollar	91.8	86.0	87.5	93.0	97.9	98.2	100.0	94.1	88.8	83.5	83.1	84.8	85.2	84.1	84.1
Australia	Dollar	125.1	100.8	94.9	100.5	105.5	101.3	100.0	92.3	86.3	90.1	86.6	95.6	97.3	93.9	93.9
Austria	Schilling	90.4	94.9	98.0	97.9	97.4	100.3	100.0	102.5	105.2	106.5	111.5	110.8	108.7	109.5	110.1
Belgium–Luxembourg	Franc	85.7	91.8	96.1	95.3	94.5	99.9	100.0	102.7	103.9	106.3	11.8	109.9	105.3	105.5	105.7
Czech Republic	Koruna	—	—	—	—	—	—	100.0	103.4	111.0	114.7	117.9	121.3	118.4	115.5	117.5
Denmark	Krone	90.0	95.4	98.9	97.2	94.9	101.3	100.0	102.7	106.3	106.9	112.1	111.3	108.2	108.4	108.7
Finland	Markka	98.6	96.5	97.2	98.6	102.1	103.8	100.0	87.6	76.8	93.8	93.3	91.0	89.1	89.0	89.4
Greece	Drachma	211.9	162.0	144.0	133.6	123.8	112.6	100.0	92.5	84.9	79.7	77.9	76.8	75.4	75.9	76.2
Hungary	Forint	—	—	—	—	—	—	100.0	91.8	85.7	74.6	8.0	49.1	44.9	40.1	37.0
Iceland	Krona	213.4	173.9	161.7	140.8	112.6	99.3	100.0	99.4	93.2	88.6	88.5	88.1	90.1	90.0	90.2
Ireland	Pound	92.6	98.9	97.8	95.9	94.9	101.5	100.0	103.6	98.0	98.3	99.2	101.9	102.6	100.9	101.1
Korea	Won	101.3	90.1	90.6	99.4	112.1	104.1	100.0	92.4	90.6	88.8	89.3	89.8	84.8	79.4	79.5
Mexico	Peso	1,119.1	529.3	232.3	132.9	123.2	106.5	100.0	96.8	97.3	89.5	46.6	39.5	38.7	37.4	37.4
Netherlands	Guilder	84.3	92.2	97.4	97.1	96.2	100.6	100.0	102.9	106.2	107.4	113.0	111.2	105.9	105.9	106.2
New Zealand	Dollar	16.5	105.7	109.1	113.0	106.0	103.9	100.0	92.4	96.0	101.4	108.2	115.6	118.4	114.7	114.8
Norway	Krone	113.0	106.3	102.1	102.0	101.9	101.7	100.0	101.6	100.0	99.2	102.2	102.4	103.1	103.3	103.6
Poland	Zloty	—	—	—	—	—	—	100.0	95.5	61.5	48.5	42.0	39.3	35.9	31.8	29.3
Portugal	Escudo	130.9	120.2	110.2	104.5	101.4	99.1	100.0	103.6	97.9	94.2	96.5	96.1	94.4	93.3	93.4
Spain	Peseta	91.5	89.4	88.8	91.8	96.0	99.7	100.0	97.9	86.6	81.0	80.9	81.7	78.3	78.4	78.5
Sweden	Krona	103.7	102.0	100.8	101.1	101.7	100.0	100.0	101.6	82.7	82.0	81.7	90.0	87.1	88.3	88.5
Switzerland	Franc	88.5	96.6	101.4	100.8	95.6	101.3	100.0	98.6	101.7	109.1	117.2	115.8	109.6	112.8	113.2
Turkey	Lira	1,189.9	747.1	513.2	303.2	210.7	154.8	100.0	58.5	39.6	15.5	8.7	5.1	3.0	1.7	1.1
Chinese Taipei	Dollar	83.3	77.5	85.9	92.7	104.8	100.1	100.0	104.0	100.4	98.2	93.9	94.6	96.8	89.3	89.4
Hong Kong	Dollar	129.7	113.3	104.0	99.9	103.7	99.4	100.0	98.8	103.1	102.3	98.5	103.1	110.6	112.6	113.3
Singapore	Dollar	100.7	89.4	85.3	86.1	91.6	95.3	100.0	103.9	107.6	111.9	115.7	121.1	123.2	118.5	118.7

Source: OECD, Economic Outlook, 1998
[a] On the technical assumption that exchange rates remain at their levels of 3 November 1997, except for Hungary, Poland and Turkey where exchange rates vary according to official exchange rate policy.

Figure 10.4 Foreign exchange market: exchange rate determination, sterling vis-à-vis Italian lira

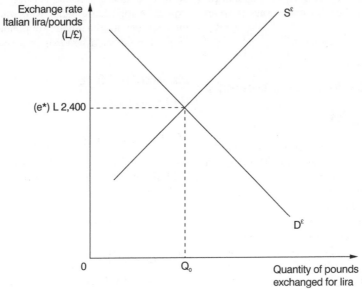

Note:
e* represents the equilibrium exchange rate at which the demand for £ (in exchange for Italian lira) is just equal to the supply of pounds (in exchange for lira).

exchange for Italian lira to the foreign exchange market?

✓ Answer 10.14

It's the Italians, wishing to buy British goods and services like Scotch whisky, Lloyds insurance policies or British assets (shares in Alan Sugar's Amstrad Company, UK government bonds or Treasury bills). They demand pounds in exchange for Italian lire. The British, on the other hand, bring a supply of pounds to the foreign exchange market in exchange for lira, as they wish to buy Italian wine, holiday on the Italian Riviera, buy shares in Gianni Agnelli's car company Fiat, buy Italian government bonds (which incidentally, in the light of returns prevailing in June 1998, would not be a good idea, as the highest returns were from British government bonds with a yield of 7.25 per cent and American corporate shares with a yield of 6.62 per cent, and not from Italian government bonds which had a yield of 5.05 per cent or corporate shares, with an average yield of 5.57 per cent).

In Figure 10.4 the price of £1 expressed in so many units of Italian lira, the various possible exchange rates in other words, is measured on the vertical axis, while the horizontal axis shows the total quantity of pounds, exchanged for lira at the various exchange rates. The demand curve for pounds is downward sloping. This

simply indicates that when the price which Italians have to pay for £1 is high, for example, when £1 exchanges for 3,500 Italian lira (the sterling in that case is said to be **strong**), Italians demand fewer pounds in exchange for lira. When, on the other hand, the price which Italians have to pay for £1 is low, say £1 exchanges for 2,000 Italian lira (the sterling in that case is said to be **weak**) the quantity of pounds they demand in exchange for lira increases. This is to do with the fact that the exchange rate, the rate at which £1 exchanges for lira in this case, affects the price that Italians have to pay to buy the British goods, services or assets they are after. Say, they want to buy a bottle of whisky that sells in Britain for £10. Remember that to be able to buy the bottle of whisky, the Italians need first to buy £10 worth of British currency. When the exchange rate is £1= L2,000, to buy the bottle of whisky will cost the Italians L20,000. When the exchange rate is higher and £1= L3,500 (sterling is said to have appreciated), the bottle will cost the Italians 35,000 Italian lire. The price of a bottle of whisky has not changed in the UK for British people, but it has changed for the Italians, simply because the cost of acquiring the relevant foreign currency, in this case sterling, has changed. As the exchange rate **appreciates** the cost of British goods, services and assets increases for the Italians; fewer goods are required and, as a result, less British currency is needed and demanded on the foreign exchange market by the Italians, as the number of transactions between the two countries falls.

✍ Activity 10.15

How would you show this demand for pounds with a diagram?

✓ Answer 10.15

As shown in Figure 10.5, a larger quantity of pounds is demanded at a lower L/£ exchange rate. The demand for pounds curve is downward sloping.

The same applies, but in reverse, to British people and firms wishing to buy Italian goods and services and needing Italian lira for their transactions. The supply schedule for pounds, $S^£$, depends on the quantity of Italian lira which UK residents require to pay for UK imports from Italy or purchases of Italian financial or capital assets. Their supply of pounds to the foreign exchange market in exchange for Italian lira is shown as an upward-sloping curve. This simply indicates that when the exchange rate is high and the pound strong, when in our example £1 = L3,500, Italian goods and services are relatively cheap, more of them are demanded, more Italian lira are needed and more pounds are offered on the foreign exchange market by UK residents in exchange. If the pound **depreciates**,

losing value in the exchange with lira, the opposite will be true: Italian goods and services will become more expensive for UK residents, who will demand fewer of them and reduce the quantity of pounds which they offer on the foreign exchange market in exchange for lira.

✍ Activity 10.16

How would you show this supply of pounds with a diagram?

✓ Answer 10.16

As shown in Figure 10.6, at a lower exchange rate, the UK will import fewer goods from Italy: the lower the exchange rate, the smaller the quantity of pounds supplied to the foreign exchange market. The supply of pounds curve is upward sloping.

✍ Activity 10.17

Suppose a week in a three-star hotel on the Italian Riviera costs L1,000,000. Consider the effect of a change in the exchange rate between sterling and lira from L3,500/£ to L2,000/£.

✓ Answer 10.17

When the exchange rate is L3,500/£ the holiday costs a UK resident £285.7. When the exchange rate is L2,000/£ the holiday costs a UK resident £500.

Figure 10.5 The demand for pounds on the foreign exchange market

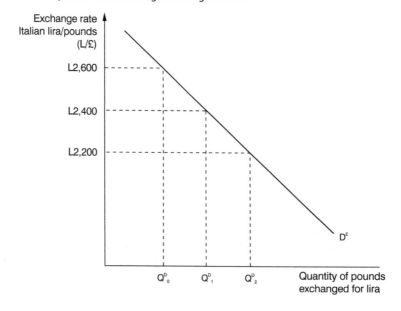

Figure 10.6 The supply of pounds on the foreign exchange market

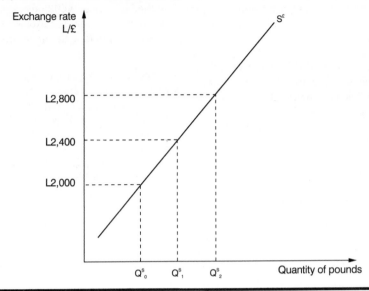

In Figure 10.4 the equilibrium exchange rate is e*. At e*, the quantity of pounds supplied in exchange for lira is just equal to the quantity of pounds demanded in exchange for lira. What would change this equilibrium exchange rate? Changed demand for the respective imports and exports and capital or financial assets between the two countries. If, at each sterling price, the demand by the Italians for British goods, services or assets increases, the demand schedule for pounds will shift to the right, increasing the equilibrium lira–sterling exchange rate from L2,400 to L2,600. This is shown by a shift out of the $D^{\pounds}$ curve from A to B in Figure 10.7.

In the same way, if the demand by British residents for Italian goods, services or assets is reduced, for whatever reason, at each sterling price, the supply schedule for pounds shifts to the left, again increasing the equilibrium

Figure 10.7 Foreign exchange market: an increase in the demand for pounds in exchange for Italian lira

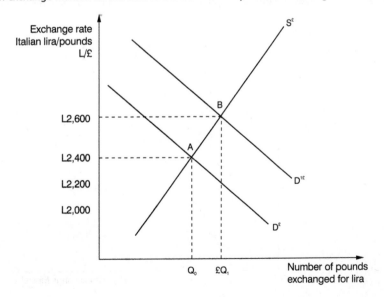

lira–sterling exchange rate. This is shown by a shift to the left of the $S^£$ curve from A to B in Figure 10.8.

✍ Activity 10.18

What do you think determines the British demand for imports of goods and services from Italy, or indeed from any country? What determines the demand for Italian capital or financial assets? What determines the demand for any foreign capital or financial asset?

✓ Answer 10.18

The *demand for imports*, and therefore the demand for the foreign currency needed to purchase those imports, is determined by two factors:

■ *aggregate income*: as income rises people consume more of everything, including imported goods. They eat more French cheese, drink more Italian wine, go on holiday to Portugal more often, etc. As income and output rise, more is produced. Firms need to import more raw materials, parts and equipment needed for production.

■ *the relative price of the foreign good*: if the foreign good is cheaper to buy than a similar, domestically produced good. As prices of foreign goods increase, the demand will decrease and imports will fall. The price of imports, however, is affected not only by the production price of the good in its country of origin, but also by the exchange rate. In our earlier example, a week on the Italian Riviera which

costs L1,000,000 can cost the UK holidaymaker either £285.7 or £500, according to the prevailing exchange rate. So the exchange rate as well as the domestic price of the good affects the demand for imports.

The demand for imports is therefore determined by the level of income, the relative rates of inflation in trading countries and the exchange rates.

The *demand for capital and financial assets* is determined by the relative yields that assets abroad can offer, compared with what is attainable at home. For a given exchange rate, an increase in interest rates on financial assets abroad will cause an increased demand for them on the part of UK residents, who will therefore supply pounds to the foreign exchange market to acquire the foreign currency needed to purchase the foreign financial asset.

To sum up, the supply of pounds on the foreign exchange market is determined by the UK demand for imports and by the UK demand for foreign financial and capital assets. These combined demands are in turn affected by the level of income and the value of the exchange rate, inflation rate and interest rate in the domestic economy.

✍ Activity 10.19

What do you think determines the demand for UK exports of goods and services and the demand for UK capital or sterling denominated financial assets?

Figure 10.8 Foreign exchange market: a reduction in the demand for pounds in exchange for Italian lira

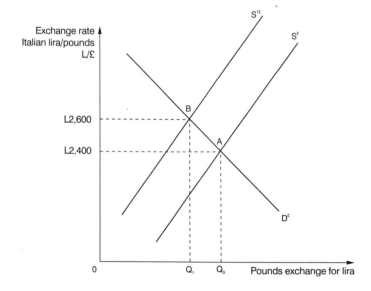

✓ Answer 10.19

The *demand for UK exports* will be influenced by two factors:

- the level of income of trading foreign countries: the higher the level of income in the rest of the world, the higher will be the demand for UK exports by world countries.
- the relative price of goods, for a given exchange rate: the cheaper the British products in relation to similar products on world markets, the greater the demand for them. Again the price of British goods on world markets will be affected not only by their production prices and how much it costs to produce them in Britain, but also by the exchange rate: how much one unit of British currency costs to the foreigners buying British goods.

The *demand for UK capital and financial assets* will be influenced by the relative yields that assets in the UK can offer compared with what is attainable elsewhere in the world.

To sum up, the demand for pounds on the foreign exchange market is determined by the foreign demand for UK exports and by foreign demand for UK capital and financial assets. These combined demands are in turn affected by the level of income, inflation and interest rates prevailing in the rest of the world, as well as by the exchange rate.

International competitiveness

From what we have said, it follows that international competitiveness is determined by the relative prices of goods traded and the exchange rate. International competitiveness is measured by the **real exchange rate**, as follows:

$$\text{real exchange rate} = \frac{\text{UK price index}}{\text{foreign currency price index}} \times \text{nominal exchange rate}$$

The real exchange rate, in other words, is the nominal exchange rate adjusted for changes in aggregate prices in the two trading countries. The price of a British good on a foreign market depends upon two things: the production price of the good and the exchange rate. We express this in symbols as follows:

$$e \cdot P = Pw$$

where e is the nominal exchange rate, P is the domestic price of the good and Pw is the price of the good on world markets, expressed in the relevant foreign currency.

✍ Activity 10.20

Suppose a British Amstrad computer costs £1,000 to make. Calculate how much it costs the Italians to buy

the computer, depending on the exchange rate. First assume that L/£ = 2,000; then assume that the exchange rate goes up to L3,000.

✓ Answer 10.20

If e = 2,000 it will cost 2,000 × £1,000 = L2,000,000
If e = 3,000 it will cost 3,000 × £1,000 = L3,000,000.

At a lower exchange rate, the computer is cheaper and Britain will be able to export more of them. Lower exchange rates favour exports. On the other hand, however, at a lower exchange rate foreign goods become more expensive for UK residents and fewer will be demanded. A lower exchange rate reduces imports, as they become more expensive.

The domestic price of a foreign good is determined by the foreign price of the good divided by the exchange rate:

$$P = \frac{Pw}{e}.$$

✍ Activity 10.21

Assume that a small BMW costs DM30,000 in Germany. Calculate how much the BMW would cost in Britain at three different exchange rates: when the exchange rate DM/£ = 2, DM/£ = 3 and DM/£ = 4.

✓ Answer 10.21

DM30,000/2 = £15,000
DM30,000/3 = £10,000
DM30,000/4 = £7,500

The stronger the sterling exchange rates, i.e. the more units of foreign currency are bought by one unit of the domestic currency, the cheaper the foreign good, the greater the amount of its import. In symbols this can be summarized as follows:

$$e\uparrow \underset{\searrow X\downarrow}{\overset{M\uparrow}{<}} \qquad e\downarrow \underset{\searrow X\uparrow}{\overset{M\downarrow}{<}}.$$

On the other hand, as we pointed out earlier:

$$M\uparrow \rightarrow e\downarrow \underset{X\uparrow}{\overset{M\downarrow}{<}} \Big\rangle e\uparrow \text{ and } X\uparrow \rightarrow e\uparrow \underset{X\downarrow}{\overset{M\uparrow}{<}} \Big\rangle e\downarrow$$

until a new equilibrium exchange rate is found, at which the demand for imports by domestic residents is just equal to the demand for exports by foreigners. It can be said, therefore, that an exchange rate which is allowed to find its market value can automatically correct an external imbalance. An excess demand for a country's export will push up the value of its currency, which will make exports more expensive and imports into the country cheaper, therefore reversing the trend. We will see later on in the chapter that this result may not always necessarily apply, at least in the short run, as it takes time for consumption and investment patterns to change in response to changes in the relative prices of internationally traded commodities.

✍ Activity 10.22

Look at Table 10.10 and comment on what it shows.

✓ Answer 10.22

Table 10.10 shows some measures of UK competitiveness in trade in manufactures from 1993 to 1996. Such measures are given by the behaviour of relative export prices and relative import price competitiveness of UK manufactures over the period. The statistics show clearly a deterioration in the competitive position of UK manufactures on world markets. UK manufactures relative export prices increased by 4.3 per cent in four years, while the price competitiveness of foreign imports, with respect to domestically produced goods, increased by about 3 per cent. The export price of UK manufactures increased by 15 per cent in four years,

compared with a 3 per cent increase in the price of US exports, a 7 per cent increase in Japanese, a 12 per cent in French and an 8.6 per cent increase in the price of German exports of manufactures. As we shall see later on, when we look at the changes in exchange rates over these years, the sterling exchange rates appreciated over this period. At the same time, the UK price level and the cost of labour also rose in 1996, further worsening the UK manufacturers position.

✍ Activity 10.23

Use the statistics of Table 10.11 and calculate the rate of change of wholesale prices and unit labour costs between 1993 and 1996 for the countries shown. What do these statistics help us to explain?

✓ Answer 10.23

Table 10.11 further explains the worsening of the UK competitive position between 1993 and 1996. While wholesale prices remained stable in Japan and increased only moderately in the USA (7 per cent), they rose by nearly 12 per cent in Germany, and by 14.2 per cent in France and the UK. At the same time, unit labour costs

Table 10.10 Measures of UK competitiveness in trade in manufactures, 1993–6 (1990 = 100)

	Summary measures					Export unit value index				
	Relative export prices	Relative wholesale prices	Unit labour costs	Import price competitiveness	Relative profitability of exports	UK	USA	Japan	France	Germany
1993	102.0	96.1	88.0	95.3	105.1	97.8	102.3	124.4	92.5	92.1
1994	104.1	97.6	90.5	94.2	105.2	102.5	103.1	134.3	96.0	93.1
1995	103.9	94.1	87.9	89.9	105.2	113.1	106.3	144.8	107.2	107.6
1996	106.4	98.3	92.1	92.5	101.8	112.2	105.6	133.6	103.7	100.1

Source: ONS, *Economic Trends*, 1998

Table 10.11 Wholesale prices and labour costs, selected countries, 1993–6

	Wholesale price index					Unit labour costs index				
	UK	USA	Japan	France	Germany	UK	USA	Japan	France	Germany
1993	95.0	100.8	124.4	96.1	101.5	91.8	103.8	142.7	105.7	114.3
1994	99.4	102.2	132.6	98.8	104.0	93.7	104.0	156.4	101.9	114.6
1995	106.7	105.1	143.0	111.7	119.8	98.3	104.3	163.1	110.7	132.0
1996	108.4	107.6	124.1	107.8	113.4	101.1	103.9	137.1	108.1	126.8

Source: ONS, *Economic Trends*, 1998

actually fell in Japan (– 4 per cent), remained stable in the USA, increased only moderately in France (+2.2 per cent), and increased by 10 per cent in the UK and by 11 per cent in Germany.

✍ Activity 10.24

Look at the statistics of Table 10.12 and comment on the competitive position of the USA, Japan, Germany and the UK in 1996 compared with 1980.

✓ Answer 10.24

The competitive position of the USA has improved, Japan's and Germany's have deteriorated, while the UK's improved in the first half of the 1990s but is projected to deteriorate.

Purchasing power parity (PPP) theory

For the reasons just explained, countries experiencing high rates of inflation will tend to have depreciating exchange rates. This was the case of the Italian economy for most of the post-war period. The opposite tends to apply in countries with a low rate of inflation: their currencies appreciate. This situation applied to the German economy over the same period. The empirical observation of this inverse relationship between inflation and the value of the exchange rate has led economists to formulate what is known as the **purchasing power theory** of the determination of exchange rates. The theory explains exchange rate changes in terms of the relative purchasing power of the domestic currencies in their respective countries.

So, for example, if £1 buys a Big Mac in London and Yn8 buy a Big Mac in Beijing, the equilibrium exchange rate between sterling and the Chinese yuan should be £1 = Yn8. In other words, the two currencies' nominal exchange rate should be such as to make the cost of an identical good the same, ignoring transport costs and the like. If the official, nominal exchange rate is different from the PPP exchange rate, then some economists would argue that the nominal exchange rate is out of line with the real value of the currency and predict that it will soon change. If, say, the official exchange rate between the pound and the yuan is £1 = Yn10, a comparison with the PPP exchange rate would indicate that the pound is overvalued. At the official rate, £1 would buy more fast food in China than in Britain. Does it matter?

'Yes it does!', is the answer. An overvalued pound would make Chinese goods cheaper to import and British goods more expensive to exports. Imports into Britain will increase and exports will fall; in a flexible exchange rate regime, this will cause the value of the

pound to fall on the foreign exchange market, until the nominal exchange rate is in line with the real PPP rate.

If the exchange rate reflects the *relative purchasing power* of two currencies, than it must be that any changes in the purchasing power caused by differing rates of inflation will also be reflected in changes to the exchange rate. To go back to our earlier example, let's assume that there is no inflation in Britain and that £1 still buys one Big Mac in London; while China has experienced some inflation and one Big Mac now costs Yn20. The PPP exchange rate has changed too, to reflect the changed purchasing power of the yuan, which has fallen. The PPP exchange rate, which was £1 = Yn8, is now £1 = Yn20. If we calculate the exchange rate in terms of the domestic currency equivalent of one unit of the foreign currency, while before Yn1 = 12.5p, now Yn1 = 5p.

The PPP theory of the exchange rate predicts that exchange rate changes will reflect differences in the rates of inflation between countries. In the light of empirical data, this theory has not proved very successful in predicting exchange rate changes in the short run. The PPP theory of exchange rate determination has proved more successful in the prediction of long-term movements of exchange rates. Countries that experience relatively high rates of inflation over a period of years also experience a depreciation in the value of their currencies on the foreign exchange market, if the rates are allowed to float.

EXCHANGE RATE REGIMES

What we have described so far is an exchange rate which is freely determined by the demand and supply of the currency in question on the foreign exchange market. This situation is known as a freely floating or **flexible exchange rate regime**.

The word regime is used to describe the type of exchange rate policy being pursued by the government. Economists distinguish between two main types of exchange rate policies which governments can choose: fixed exchange rate policies and flexible or free-floating exchange rate policies. In reality there are several other different kinds of regimes between these two extremes, that governments can choose to adopt:

■ the **crawling peg**, where the government allows a gradual adjustment of the exchange rate by small amounts;
■ the **adjustable peg**, where exchange rates are fixed for a period of time, but may be revalued or devalued if the deficit in the balance of payments becomes substantial;

Table 10.12   Competitive positions: relative export prices, 1980–99 (1991 = 100)

	1980	1981	1982	1983	1984	1985	1986	1987	1988	1989	1990	1991	1992	1993	1994	1995	1996	Estimates and projections 1997	1998	1999
USA	118	131	139	143	144	142	123	110	105	105	101	100	97	97	94	86	85	85	84	83
Japan	82	87	82	83	84	86	95	96	98	96	92	100	106	120	128	131	126	128	128	128
Germany	96	88	89	90	88	89	98	102	99	97	101	100	104	106	106	110	108	102	103	104
France	102	99	96	96	97	99	103	104	103	100	103	100	100	99	101	101	101	98	99	100
Italy	87	90	90	88	89	90	92	92	89	95	99	100	99	88	86	87	93	95	96	96
UK	105	104	99	97	94	97	93	94	98	97	98	100	98	98	99	98	101	110	110	110
Canada	95	94	93	97	97	96	93	96	100	102	100	100	96	94	93	96	101	105	106	107
Australia	121	117	109	112	116	103	96	102	115	116	107	100	93	90	90	90	94	96	94	95
Austria	111	108	109	108	106	105	109	111	114	104	106	100	99	100	97	98	97	95	96	96
Belgium-Luxembourg	105	98	94	95	94	94	98	99	98	100	103	100	101	100	100	103	103	103	104	104
Denmark	91	87	87	89	88	90	97	102	98	96	102	100	102	101	103	104	104	103	105	106
Finland	83	88	91	88	89	91	91	93	96	102	101	100	92	82	87	102	101	96	96	97
Korea	87	90	88	87	91	90	89	92	96	109	101	100	91	89	89	93	81	75	71	71
Mexico	88	84	90	63	71	65	82	91	97	96	102	100	102	111	110	105	109	121	127	133
Netherlands	108	104	106	105	100	97	97	104	104	100	102	100	100	100	102	107	105	103	104	104
New Zealand	100	103	104	105	103	100	94	100	113	112	107	100	97	100	107	111	114	112	110	111
Norway	104	104	101	99	104	100	95	96	112	116	106	100	95	91	90	100	97	94	94	94
Portugal	111	112	107	104	107	108	105	103	103	98	99	100	102	97	96	97	93	91	90	89
Spain	84	77	78	74	77	79	86	88	91	91	96	100	102	95	89	87	90	88	89	89
Sweden	98	98	91	88	90	92	94	95	97	98	99	100	99	86	87	87	93	90	91	91
Switzerland	76	77	82	86	84	82	92	96	96	91	98	100	99	101	107	108	108	105	108	109
Chinese Taipei	86	88	87	85	90	88	84	91	98	105	100	100	99	99	96	104	104	109	99	98
Hong Kong	117	116	115	107	116	118	108	104	100	102	98	100	99	102	101	97	101	108	109	109
Singapore	116	126	128	133	130	126	99	98	95	97	101	100	98	97	97	97	101	104	99	98

Source: OECD, Economic Outlook, 1998
Note: Indices are expressed in a common currency and concern manufactured goods. The relative export price indices take into account both export and import competitiveness.

- the **exchange rate band**, where a currency is allowed to float between an upper and a lower value but is not allowed beyond;
- **dirty floating**, where the government intervenes in the foreign exchange market to prevent excessive exchange rate fluctuations.

However, an understanding of the two extreme cases of flexible and fixed exchange rate regimes will allow you also to understand how the intermediate regimes work.

Flexible exchange rate regime

A flexible exchange rate regime is the one we have described in the preceding pages. In a flexible or freely floating exchange rate regime, the exchange rate is allowed to reach its equilibrium level on the foreign exchange market. In this case, movements in the value of the exchange rate are caused by changing demand and supply for foreign currency, which in turn reflect changes in the demand for imports and exports, and changes in the demand for capital and financial assets. Changes in the values of the exchange rate in turn affect the demand for imports and exports: a depreciation increases the demand for exports and reduces the demand for imports and vice versa. The exchange rate will eventually find a market value at which the demand and supply of foreign currency are in equilibrium.

✍ Activity 10.25

With the use of a diagram, show the effect on the sterling exchange rate of changes in the demand for imports and exports and in the demand for capital and financial assets.

✓ Answer 10.25

- An increased demand for imports causes a depreciation of the exchange rate. This is shown by a shift out to the right of the supply curve for pounds on the foreign exchange market (from A to D in Figure 10.9).
- A reduced demand for imports causes an appreciation of the exchange rate. This is shown by a shift in to the left of the supply curve for pounds on the foreign exchange market (from A to E in Figure 10.9).
- An increased demand for exports causes an appreciation of the exchange rate. This is shown by a shift out to the right of the demand curve for pounds on the foreign exchange market (from A to B in Figure 10.9).
- A reduced demand for exports causes a depreciation of the exchange rate. This is shown by a shift to the left of the demand curve for pounds on the foreign exchange market (from A to C in Figure 10.9).

An increase/decrease in the demand for foreign capital and financial assets will have the same effect on the exchange rate as an increase/decrease in imports. An increase/decrease in the demand for domestic capital or financial assets by foreigners will have the same effect on the exchange rate as an increase/decrease in the demand for exports.

So, a flexible exchange rate is one whose value is determined by market forces, in the absence of any central bank intervention. In practice, however, all exchange rates are influenced by some degree of central bank intervention (*dirty floating*). Central banks affect the market value of exchange rates by buying or selling currencies on the foreign exchange market.

Advantages and disadvantages of flexible exchange rates

A flexible exchange rate regime has advantages and disadvantages. The advantages are:

- automatic correction of balance of payments disequilibria, without the need for government intervention or the risk of using up reserves. So, there is no international liquidity problem;
- insulation of the domestic economy from shocks and pressures coming from other economies, such as having to maintain similar rates of inflation or of economic growth. Inflation rates of trading countries can differ. Inflation-ridden countries have

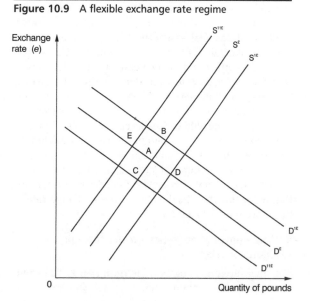

Figure 10.9 A flexible exchange rate regime

weaker currencies. Faster growing countries will also tend to have depreciating currencies.

■ governments' greater freedom to pursue their independent domestic policy objectives, like faster growth and lower unemployment.

The disadvantages are:

■ exchange rate instability and volatility, at least in the short run;

■ increased scope for currency speculation;

■ greater uncertainty for international traders. The uncertainty surrounding the value of market determined exchange rates discourages international trade and investment, as exporting or importing firms may find themselves making losses or facing prohibitive costs due to changes in the exchange rate.

Fixed exchange rate regime

A fixed exchange rate regime exists when governments commit to maintaining a 'par' value (usually plus or minus a small percentage variation) between the domestic currency and foreign currencies. A fixed exchange rate is one whose value is pegged by the country's central bank, acting for the government. The central bank 'fixes' the value of the exchange rate of the domestic currency vis-à-vis foreign currencies by buying or selling domestic currency on the foreign exchange market.

Buying domestic currency on the foreign exchange market

This measure is taken to prevent its value from falling. The value of the domestic currency tends to fall (the exchange rate depreciates) when imports are greater than exports and UK residents are buying more foreign capital and financial assets than foreigners are buying domestic capital and financial assets in the UK (which causes an outflow of financial capital). In order to prevent the exchange rate from depreciating, the central bank uses up its reserves of foreign currency, making them available on the foreign exchange market in exchange for surplus domestic currency. The Bank of England holds a certain amount of **foreign exchange reserves**. These represent the stock of foreign currency held by the domestic central bank. Central banks do not have unlimited reserves. Central bank intervention to sustain the 'fixed' value of the exchange rate is therefore only feasible for a limited period.

Selling domestic currency on the foreign exchange market

This measure prevents its value from rising. The value of the domestic currency tends to rise (the exchange

rate appreciates) when exports are greater then imports and foreign residents are buying more British capital and financial assets than UK residents are buying foreign assets (this causes an inflow of capital). In order to prevent the exchange rate from appreciating, the central bank intervenes on the exchange rate market by making more domestic currency available in exchange for surplus foreign currency. When this happens, central bank's reserves of foreign currencies increase. This situation, which reflects a balance of payments surplus, does not require urgent redress by the government as central banks are usually more comfortable with accumulating rather than depleting foreign reserves. However, this situation causes the domestic money supply to rise, as more domestic currency is made available on the foreign exchange market by the central bank to foreigners wanting to buy British exports and UK financial assets. So balance of payments surpluses, when exchange rates are fixed, may be inflationary and need to be rectified with the use of **sterilization operations**. These consist of reducing the money supply by an amount equal to the currency inflow created by the trade and capital account surpluses. The same process can be applied to deficits, which would otherwise reduce the domestic money supply: their effect on the money supply can also be sterilized.

✍ Activity 10.26

With the use of a diagram, show the effect of a substantial increase in UK consumption of Italian wine, assuming a fixed exchange rate of L2, 200/£, assuming in other words that £1 exchanges for L2,200 and that both governments have agreed to maintain that parity fixed (as indeed they did in 1992, when both countries were members of the EC Exchange Rate Mechanism).

✓ Answer 10.26

As Figure 10.10(a) shows, the increased demand for imports of Italian wine causes an increase in the supply of pounds to the foreign exchange market, in exchange for lira (a shift out of the $S^£$ curve). As a result, the exchange rate will tend to fall from A to B. To prevent the exchange rate from falling, the Bank of England intervenes on the foreign exchange market, demanding pounds in exchange for lira (or, which is the same, offering lira in exchange for pounds) thereby reducing the excess supply of pounds which exerts downward pressure on the exchange rate. This is shown by a shift out of the $D^£_{CB}$ curve, which denotes the demand for pounds by the central bank. This will restore the exchange rate to its par value (movement from B to C).

Figure 10.10   Central bank intervention in a fixed exchange rate regime

(a)

Exchange rate (L/£)

$S^£$

$S^{1£}$

e appreciates

L2,200 $\bar{e}$

e depreciates

A   C

B

Fixed exchange rate value

$D^£_{CB}$

$D^£$

Quantity of £ exchanged for lira

(b)

Exchange rate (L/£)

$S^£$

$S^£_{CB}$

e appreciates

L2,200 $\bar{e}$

e depreciates

B

A   C

Fixed exchange rate value

$D^£$

$D^£$

Quantity of £ exchanged for lira

Note, however, that in order to intervene in this way the Bank of England must have sufficient reserves of Italian lira and that, as a result of this situation, its reserves of this particular foreign currency become depleted. For this reason, the central bank will not be able to sustain the parity in this way indefinitely.

✍ Activity 10.27

With the use of a diagram, show the effect on the foreign exchange market of an increase in the demand for UK financial assets by the Italians, assuming a fixed exchange rate of L2,200/£.

✓ Answer 10.27

As Figure 10.10(b) shows, an increase in the demand for sterling denominated financial assets by the Italians causes an increase in the demand for pounds on the foreign exchange market, which is shown by a shift to the right of the $D^£$ curve. This causes an appreciation of the pound above the fixed exchange rate. £1 will buy more than L2,200 (change from A to B). To prevent the appreciation of the pound, the Bank of England will intervene on the foreign exchange market and offer pounds in exchange for lira. This is shown by a shift out of the $S^£$ curve, which will bring the exchange rate back to its par value (from B to C). Note that the result of this situation is also, on one hand, to increase central bank reserves of lira and, on the other, to

increase the domestic money supply. By making pounds available to the Italians in exchange for their currency, the Bank of England increases the amount of money in circulation in the domestic economy; at the same time, its foreign currency reserves increase.

Advantages and disadvantages of fixed exchange rates

A fixed exchange rate regime has advantages and disadvantages. The advantages are:

- *reduced uncertainty*: traders are certain of future exchange rates. International trade and investment become less risky.
- *encourages international trade* and foreign investment.

The disadvantages are:

- *inability to absorb shocks*: caused by unforeseen economic events, like the oil price increases of the 1970s. When fundamental balance of payments imbalances develop, there might not be a sufficient amount of foreign reserves to maintain the par value.
- *encourages speculation*: countries with fixed exchange rates experiencing large deficits are easy targets for currency speculators. If speculators believe that the deficit is not likely to be reversed and that the currency is likely to be devalued, they will sell the domestic currency on the foreign

exchange market and temporarily move into a safe foreign currency. Their huge selling of domestic currency forces the central bank to abandon the parity, out of lack of sufficient foreign currency to ride off the speculative attack. The devalued domestic currency will then be bought back by speculators using the foreign currency in which they have 'parked' their capital. But because the domestic currency has been devalued, more of it will now be obtained in the exchange.

Let's illustrate this point with an example. Say a speculator expecting a devaluation of the pound sells £100m on the foreign exchange market and buys US dollars at the exchange rate $2 = £1. The speculator is now holding $200m. If this is a shared expectation and other speculators do the same, the pound will have to be devalued against the dollar, say it falls to $1.80 = £1. The $200m which the speculator is holding can now repurchase £111m, more than the initial £100m: the speculator has made a handsome £11m profit, ignoring trading commissions and taxes.

Bretton Woods system, ERM and EMU

For most of the post-World War II period, international economies operated a system of fixed exchange rates agreed upon at a world conference on monetary order which took place at Bretton Woods, New Hampshire, USA, in 1944. That system came to be known as the **Bretton Woods system**. It is generally maintained that this system served the international economies rather well until 1973, when it finally collapsed because of a combination of internal difficulties and international events. Since then most international economies have either allowed their rates to float freely or have reintroduced fixed exchange rates, but on a regional basis.

In 1979, the European Monetary System (EMS) was created by the members of the European Community. The system rested on the introduction of fixed exchange rates among its members, the exchange rate mechanism (ERM). Although Britain was a member of the EMS, it did not wish to join the rest of the EC countries, which were keeping their exchange rates fixed vis-à-vis each other, while allowing them to float vis-à-vis other currencies, like the dollar or the yen. The UK eventually joined the ERM in 1990, but had to leave it again in 1992 because of persistent balance of payments problems and severe speculative attacks against the pound by currency speculators. Eleven EC countries have sinced moved further down the path of monetary integration and agreed to the introduction of

a single currency, the euro, which can be seen as an extreme case of fixed exchange rates. Both the Bretton Woods system, the ERM and the single currency are discussed in some detail further on in this chapter.

The debate among economists as to which regime, fixed or flexible, should be favoured is still open and views differ. Monetarists tend to oppose fixed exchange rates because they make monetary policy rather ineffective and favour allowing the free forces of the market to set the exchange rates. Keynesians tend to favour fixed exchange rates because they make fiscal policy more effective and monetary policy ineffective. Provided they are not set too high, business people tend to favour relatively fixed, if not absolutely fixed, exchange rates, as they allow businesses to predict both revenues and costs stemming from international transactions.

✐ Activity 10.28

Suppose that you have £100 to spare which you wish to invest in some financial asset for a year. Let's assume that in Britain the current market rate of interest is 12 per cent. You could, however, buy financial assets in the USA, where the current rate of interest is, say, 9 per cent (these are not historical rates). Let's further assume that the present nominal exchange rate is $1.70/£.

(a) What additional piece of information would you require to be able to decide whether to buy financial assets in the UK or USA?
(b) Suppose that you expect the exchange rate at the end of the year to be $1.50/£, where will you invest?
(c) Where would you buy financial assets if you expected the exchange rate to fall only to $1.65/£?
(d) Given that you expect the exchange rate to fall to $1.65/£, where would you invest if the US interest rate was 8 per cent?
(e) Would you suppose expectations about future exchange rates to be stable or volatile? Does it matter?

✓ Answer 10.28

(a) You would need to know the end of year exchange rate needed to convert dollars back into sterling.
(b) If the funds are invested in the UK, at the end of the year you will have £112 as at a 12 per cent interest rate, £100 × 1.12 = £112. If the funds are invested in the USA, then at the $1.70/£ exchange rate, you will have $170 with which to buy financial assets.

At 9 per cent interest rate, the end of year return in $ is $170 × 1.09 = $185.3.

Converting this back at the expected exchange rate of $1.50/£, the yield in £ of the investment in US assets will be:

$$185.3/1.5 = £123.5.$$

The depreciation of sterling over the year, from $1.70/£ to $1.65/£, more than compensates for the interest rate differential. You invest in the USA.

(c) 185.3/1.65 = £112, hence you will be indifferent.
(d) 170 × 1.08 = £183.6; 183.6/1.65 = £111. You will invest in the UK, where the return will be £112.
(e) Expectations about future exchange rates can be volatile. They depend on how you view the current rate compared with its long-term equilibrium rate. Expectations about exchange rates will vary with different perceptions of factors affecting the economy. Expectations about exchange rate values matter because there are large quantities of footloose capital being invested internationally which, by moving in and out of currencies, can affect the value of exchange rates quite dramatically.

THE BALANCE OF PAYMENTS

The balance of payments is a record of all the transactions in goods, services and assets that a country has with the rest of the world. In fact, to be more precise, we should say that the balance of payments account records all the monetary transactions between UK residents and the rest of the world involving the purchase or sale of domestic currency in a given period. Whenever there is a foreign currency transaction, there is a corresponding payment or receipt in the balance of payments account.

The balance of payments account is divided into two main accounts, each recording specific types of transactions: current account and capital account. Each account is in turn divided in sub-accounts. These divisions and subdivisions are useful because different kinds of transactions have different causes and shed further light on the functioning of the UK economy.

The current account

The current account is divided into two separate accounts: visible trade account; invisible trade account.

Visible trade account

The visible trade account records the imports and exports of goods such as cars and computers, but also carrots and potatoes. Please note that we are referring here only to **physical goods** and not services, which are recorded in the invisible trade account. To be more precise, the visible trade account records the currency transactions needed to finance the actual buying and selling of goods. In the accounts, any transaction that earns foreign exchange for the UK is entered as credits and show up as a plus in the balance of payments accounts. Any transaction that uses up foreign exchange is regarded as debits and entered with a minus sign in the balance of payments accounts. So, in the visible trade account, exports are entered as credit items, as they result in an inflow of foreign exchange, while imports are entered as debit items, as they result in an outflow of foreign exchange. The **balance of trade** or **visible balance** is the balance between these two items, exports and imports of physical goods. We talk about a **balance of trade deficit** when imports are greater than exports (a negative balance of trade), and a **balance of trade surplus** when exports are greater than imports (a positive balance of trade).

Invisible trade account

The invisible trade account records:

■ **expenditure on services**, like banking, insurance, tourism and transport, by UK residents buying such services from countries abroad and by foreigners buying such services from the UK. For example, in shipping cars to England the Italian car manufacturer Fiat might purchase shipping insurance from Lloyds of London. In this case, the UK is exporting insurance services and earning foreign exchange, as Fiat will have to exchange lira for pounds on the foreign exchange to purchase the insurance policy from Lloyds. UK holidaymakers choosing a package holiday in Rimini, on the Italian Adriatic coast, are importing tourist services from tourist industry operators in Italy. Although they are quoted prices in pounds for their holiday and pay the British tour-operator in pounds, the British tour operator will exchange some of the money paid (part of it will be their 'cut') in lira to cover for the British holidaymakers' accommodation and entertainment in Italy.

■ **property income payments** or investment income, such as interests and dividends to overseas countries and receipts from overseas. UK residents may hold foreign assets like buildings and factories, shares and government bonds abroad. These assets earn them an income represented by rents, interests and profits. As this income is earned abroad, it will be denominated in foreign currency which will then have to be exchanged back into pounds on the foreign exchange market. Conversely, when foreigners earn dividends, interests and profits on assets held in the UK, foreign exchange is used up as the property income which is earned in Britain in pounds is converted into the relevant foreign exchange. Here again the inflows of property income are credit items, while the outflows are debit items.

■ **transfer payments**, transactions which involve payments but no purchase of products, assets or rewards between countries or people living in different countries, like Britain's contribution to the EC budget, foreign aid, maintaining military bases abroad or monetary gifts that people might give or receive (your aunt from Australia sending you a big cheque for your birthday).

The **invisible balance** is the balance of these three items taken together. The **current account balance** is the overall balance comprising visible and invisible items. In other words, if we add together the balance of trade, net export of services, net property income and net transfer payments we obtain the current account balance. 'Net' here refers to the difference between payments from the UK to foreigners and payments from foreigners to the UK.

The current account of the balance of payments of the UK economy between 1993 and 1997 is shown in Table 10.13 and Figure 10.11.

The capital account

The second major account of the balance of payments is the **capital account**. The capital account records a country's capital inflows and outflows. People, firms and governments around the world exchange real assets, like houses or factories, and financial assets, such as shares and bonds, across international boundaries. The capital account of the balance of payments records such transactions. Capital account transactions (transactions in external assets and liabilities) include:

■ **direct investment** transactions, involving the purchase of real assets such as land, houses, office buildings, factories;
■ **portfolio investment** transactions, involving the purchase of companies' shares and government bonds, or simply the placing of money in foreign banks.

The item **transactions in external assets** of the capital account records the total value of foreign investment by UK residents. The item **transactions in external liabilities** records the amount of investment by foreigners in the UK.

Balancing item

The balance of payments account also contains a balancing item, which is a statistical adjustment, that would be zero if all the items of the balance of payments have been correctly recorded. But not all transactions enter the official statistics. The sum of the current account, capital account and balancing item gives us the balance of payments account.

The balance of payments shows the net inflow of money to the country. It is in **surplus** when there is a net inflow of money into the country; it is in **deficit** when there is a net outflow of money.

The final item in the balance of payments accounts is **official financing**. Governments, via their central banks, hold foreign assets in the form of foreign reserves. Governments use their foreign reserves to

Table 10.13 UK balance of payments, current account, 1993–7   £ million

	Export of goods	Imports of goods	Balance on trade in goods	Exports of service	Imports of services	Service balance	Investment income balance	Transfers balance	Current balance
			Trade in goods and services						
Annual									
1993	121 398	134 858	–13 460	39 066	33 550	5516	2595	–4946	–10 295
1994	134 664	145 793	–11 129	41 938	37 162	4776	9667	–4969	–1655
1995	153 077	164 659	–11 582	46 598	39 721	6877	7920	–6889	–3672
1996	166 921	179 578	–12 657	50 156	43 186	6970	8546	–4725	–1866
1997	170 145	183 124	–12 979	53 132	43 652	9480	–	–	–

Source: ONS, Economic Trends, 1998

Figure 10.11   UK balance of payments, current account, 1993–7

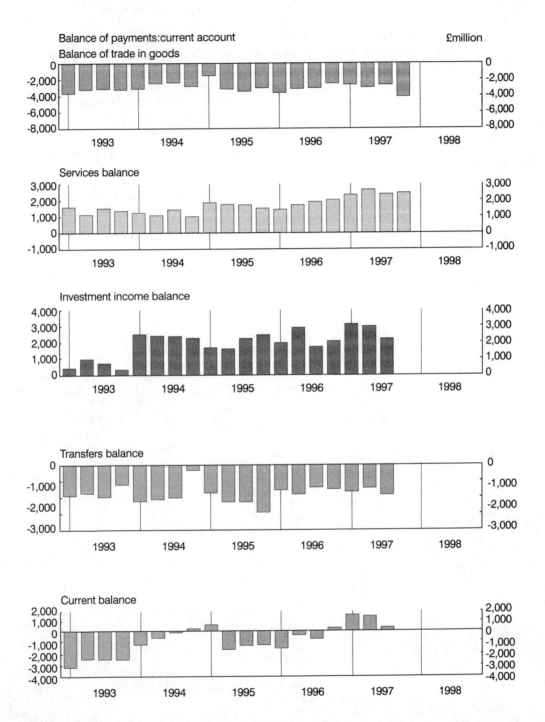

Source: ONS, *Economic Trends*, 1998

balance out all the other transactions shown in the balance of payments account. This is always equal in size and opposite in sign to the balance of payments total shown in the line immediately above it in the official accounts, so that the sum total of all entries of the balance of payments account is always zero.

Activity 10.29

Summarize in a table the items included in the balance of payments accounts.

✓ Answer 10.29

(i)   Visible Trade
   + exports of goods
   — imports of goods

   VISIBLE BALANCE

(ii)   Invisible Trade
   + earnings from services
   — payments for services

   + net dividends/interest/profits
   + net current transfers

   INVISIBLE BALANCE

(iii)   CURRENT ACCOUNT (A)

(iv)   Capital Account
   + inflow of direct and portfolio capital
   – outflow of direct and portfolio capital
   + inflow to banks
   – outflow to banks

   UNCORRECTED CAPITAL FLOW (B)

   BALANCING ITEM (C)

   BALANCE FOR OFFICIAL FINANCING
   (A+B+C) = NET CURRENCY FLOW

Under Fixed e: Financed by additions to reserves (–)
   Withdraws from reserves (+)

Under Flexible e: No official financing needed, Bp is always equal to zero.

Table 10.14   UK balance of payments, 1971–95

Year	Exports (fob)	Imports (fob)	Visible balance	Invisible balance	Current balance	Net transactions in UK assets and liabilities	Other recorded transactions	Balancing item
1971	9030	8820	210	904	1114	–1504	125	265
1972	9412	10 154	–742	945	203	448	124	–775
1973	11 881	14 449	–2568	1570	–998	924	59	133
1974	16 282	21 513	–5231	2047	–3184	3119	75	140
1975	19 185	22 440	–3255	1731	–1524	1528		–4
1976	25 080	29 041	–3961	3189	–772	356		416
1977	31 683	34 005	–2322	2375	53	–3892		3839
1978	34 981	36 573	–1592	2715	1123	–2871		1748
1979	40 471	43 814	–3343	2890	–453	–742	195	1000
1980	47 149	45 792	1357	1487	2844	–3940	180	916
1981	50 668	47 416	3252	3496	6748	–7436	158	530
1982	55 331	53 421	1910	2741	4651	–2519		–2132
1983	60 700	62 237	–1537	5066	3529	–4562		1033
1984	70 265	75 601	–5336	6817	1481	–8534		7053
1985	77 991	81 336	–3345	5583	2238	–3720		1482
1986	72 627	82 186	–9559	8688	–871	–3115		3986
1987	79 153	90 735	–11 582	6599	–4983	6710		–1727
1988	80 346	101 826	–21 480	5005	–16 475	10 847		5628
1989	92 154	116 837	–24 683	2285	–22 398	19 605		2793
1990	101 718	120 527	–18 809	–484	–19 293	18 121		1172
1991	103 413	113 697	–10 284	1751	–8533	8527		6
1992	107 343	120 447	–13 104	3636	–9468	5059		4409
1993	121 409	134 787	–13 378	2336	–11 042	13 512		–2470
1994	134 666	145 497	–10 831	8751	–2080	–2216		4296
1995	152 671	164 221	–11 550	4880	–6670	4798		1872

Source: ETAS, UKEA: 13, 1995
Note: Series for visible and current balances and the balancing item are calculated from other items in the tables, so there may be minor differences with other published data.

✍ Activity 10.30

Now compare your summary with the UK balance of payment statistics in Table 10.14. First, check that all items that should be there are indeed present. Second, make sure you understand the meaning of each item. If you are in doubt, go back and re-read the preceding section. Then answer the following questions:

(a) In which years, since 1971, was the UK visible balance and current account balance in surplus?
(b) In which years, since 1971, was the UK capital account in surplus?
(c) What does the balancing item indicate?

✓ Answer 10.30

(a) The balance of payments is the set of accounts that itemizes the transactions between UK residents and the rest of the world. It comprises a current account and a capital account.The visible balance of the current account was in surplus in 1971 and 1980–82. It was in deficit every year from 1983 to 1997 (–£12,979mn in 1997, not shown in Table 10.14). The current account was in surplus in 1971, 1972, 1977, 1978, 1980–85; it was in deficit consecutively from 1986–95.

(b) The capital account was in surplus in 1972–6, 1987–93 and in 1995. Transactions in UK assets and liabilities make up the capital account. These transactions include both private and official, i.e. government, transactions. Thus intervention in support of the exchange rate that involves changes in the official reserves will be reflected in these figures.

(c) The balancing item ensures that the overall accounts always sum to zero and reflects the fact that full recording of transactions is not possible. This situation is shown clearly in Figure 10.12.

Further ask yourself:

■ What is the relationship between current balance and GDP?
■ Does the size and persistence of a current account deficit matter?
■ To what extent should the authorities be concerned about the size of the capital account surplus that has existed, since 1987, during the same period of current account deficits?

No government intervention or depletion of foreign reserves are required, however, in a flexible exchange rate regime. When exchange rates are allowed to change in response to changes in the demand for imports, exports and capital expenditure, a disequilibrium in the current account or the capital account will

Figure 10.12   UK balance of payments, 1980–95

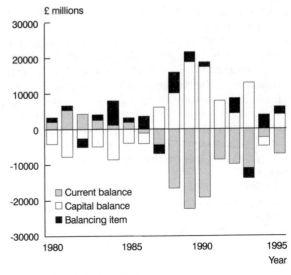

Source: *Economic Review,* 1997

simply cause the exchange rate to change, and depreciate or appreciate until equilibrium is once more restored. When exchange rates are flexible, the quantities of pounds supplied and demanded are equal and official financing is zero. When exchange rates are fixed, the balance of payments may not be zero; in which case official financing is required.

✍ Activity 10.31

What will be the consequences of a balance of payments surplus?

✓ Answer 10.31

If there is a balance of payments surplus in the current account or capital account, or both, this simply means that the government has adopted a fixed exchange rate policy and that the central bank is accumulating foreign reserves in exchange for the domestic currency it makes available on the foreign exchange market. As a result both reserves of foreign currency and domestic money supply increase. The increase in the money supply forced on the domestic economy by its international scenario may be inflationary.

✍ Activity 10.32

What will be the consequences of a balance of payments deficit?

✓ Answer 10.32

If there is a balance of payments deficit the situation is rather more serious. A balance of payments deficit means that total outflows of currency in exchange for foreign currency are greater than total inflows on the combined current and capital accounts. This in turn means that on the foreign exchange market the supply of pounds in exchange for foreign currency (reflecting UK residents' desire to import goods and services and/or to buy assets) is greater than the demand for pounds (reflecting the desire on the part of foreigners to buy British goods and services and/or capital assets).

In order to maintain the fixed exchange rate, the central bank has to offset this excess supply of domestic currency by demanding an equivalent amount of pounds on the foreign exchange market, in exchange for foreign currency. In so doing the central bank runs down its reserves of foreign currency. This shows up in the balance of payments accounts as official financing. As reserves of foreign currency are not unlimited, under a fixed exchange rate regime any prolonged imbalance in the accounts requiring official financing must be redressed and steps to affect the domestic economy in that direction must be taken.

To conclude this part of our analysis, the demand for net exports, which adds to aggregate demand for domestic output, increases when British goods are competitively priced and the exchange rate is not set too high (as the value of the exchange rate determines, together with the domestic price of the good, the price at which British goods are sold on foreign markets). To maintain competitiveness on foreign markets and sustain export demand, it is therefore important that inflation is kept under control and exchange rates are not too high.

POLICIES TO CORRECT BALANCE OF PAYMENTS DISEQUILIBRIA

The balance of payments, as we have just explained, refers to the current and capital accounts taken together. A deficit on the balance of payments is then taken to mean a situation in which total debits, i.e. transactions which add to the supply of sterling on the foreign exchange market, exceed total credits, i.e. transactions which add to the demand for sterling. In a regime of flexible exchange rates, this disequilibrium will cause the value of sterling to fall on foreign exchange markets, until equilibrium is restored. In a regime of fixed exchange rates, the monetary authori-

ties will have to intervene on the foreign exchange markets to maintain the parity and to ensure that sterling continues to be traded as a currency on the foreign exchange markets. This intervention shows up as official financing in the balance of payments accounts.

Either situations are not ideal. Although depreciation of the domestic currency increases the competitiveness of the country's exports, it makes imports more expensive and can be inflationary. It further affects the structure and industrial base of the economy. It is also politically unacceptable and destabilizing.

Exchange rate changes and external equilibrium

In practice depreciations of the domestic currency may take some time to work through the economy to correct balance of payments imbalances: hence we can see deficits persisting for sometime after a depreciation. This is due to several reasons. It takes time for people to adjust their consumption habits or investment plans: current import expenditure patterns may continue even after a fall in sterling's value has pushed up import prices. Likewise, it takes time for foreigners to adjust their pattern of consumption in response to a change in the exchange rate. Hence, they may not respond immediately to a fall in the value of sterling, placing orders for British goods.

This situation of low initial responsiveness of demand for both imports and exports to a depreciation indicates a low, albeit temporary, price elasticity of demand. Hence the conclusion, often known as the **Marshall-Lerner condition**, that a depreciation will lead to an improvement in the current account situation only if the sum of the price elasticities of demand for exports and imports exceeds unity. Elasticity is simply a measure of the responsiveness of demand to price changes. If the price elasticity of demand for exports plus the price elasticity of demand for imports exceeds unity, then the increased cost of imports is outweighed by the value of the growth of exports. Hence, the country's trade position improves.

If the Marshall-Lerner condition is not satisfied, then as the value of the currency of the deficit country falls, the result may be a worsening of the balance of payments, as the import bill will be higher, while export revenue will stay the same (at least in the short run). Hence, as a result of a depreciation or devaluation, the current account can deteriorate, as shown in Figure 10.13.

As the J-curve suggests, however, the balance of payments of a deficit country is likely to improve over time, as the demand for cheaper exports starts to grow

Figure 10.13 The J-curve

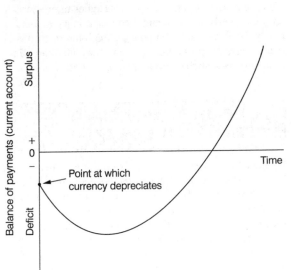

Figure 10.14 Inverted J-curve effect

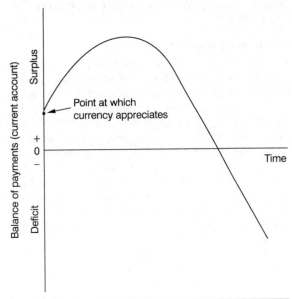

and the demand for more expensive imports falls. Empirical data for the UK seem to show that it may take on average about 18 months for the UK balance of payments to start showing signs of improvement after a depreciation.

The opposite situation applies to surplus countries whose currency is appreciating. In the short term, if demand does not respond promptly to price changes, an appreciation is likely to increase the surplus, at least temporarily. With time, the demand for imports and exports will respond to the price changes and the position of the balance of payments will show an inverted J-curve effect, as shown in Figure 10.14.

For all these reasons, even in a regime of flexible exchange rates, central banks will want to intervene on the foreign exchange markets to affect the rate (dirty floating) and governments will want to redress this situation using fiscal and monetary policies. On the other hand, intervention is inevitable if the exchange rate is fixed. This means using up reserves of foreign currency to sustain the parity, which also cannot continue indefinitely.

What can the government do to correct balance of payments disequilibria? Remember that the balance of payments comprises two accounts: the current account and the capital account. So the policy tools used for the achievement of overall equilibrium will depend on where the source of disequilibrium is: whether it is in the current account or in the capital account of the balance of payments. Overall equilib-

rium can also been achieved by compensating a current account deficit with a capital account surplus or vice versa.

Current account deficits

Current account deficits occur when imports of goods and services are greater than exports, and/or the inflow of property income and transfer payments from abroad are smaller than their respective outflows. In this situation the government can use several weapons to try and reduce the deficit, but each has some drawbacks.

First, the government can reduce the demand for goods and services at home, using deflationary policies. Deflationary policies can be achieved by the use of fiscal measures (deflationary fiscal policies) or monetary measures (deflationary monetary policies).

Deflationary fiscal measures

These imply reducing government spending and/or increasing taxation. As a result of these policies, the demand of goods and services by the government is reduced (less government spending) and the demand of consumption goods and services by households and firms is also reduced. Higher taxes, whether expenditure taxes or income and corporation taxes, reduce people's disposable income and firms' revenues, so less is demanded. There will be fewer imported goods and the current account deficit will gradually disappear. However, the drawback of this policy is that the demand for domestically produced goods is also reduced, causing a reduction in the level of output and employment.

Deflationary monetary measures

These imply reducing the money supply and raising interest rates and have the effect of reducing demand in the economy, by reducing consumption and investment demand, which in turn result in fewer imports into the country. Demand for domestic goods also falls as a result, as does employment. These measures, while reducing the deficit of the current account, also have a positive impact on the capital account. Higher interest rates attract an inflow of foreign portfolio investment into Britain, since sterling denominated securities now yield a higher return. This inflow of capital adds to the demand for sterling on the foreign exchange market and shows as a credit on the capital account of the balance of payments. This results in a capital account surplus which might overcompensate for the current account deficit.

Second, the government can place restrictions on convertibility, such as restricting the amount of currency that can be taken out of a country by tourists travelling abroad or firms wishing to import goods. These measures were used in the 1950s and 1960s, but are increasingly politically unacceptable nowadays for industrialized economies, particularly for EC members.

Third, the government can impose tariffs or quotas on imports. A tariff is a tax on imports. The effect of the tax is to raise the price of the import relative to the price of a similar substitute good produced domestically. Consumers therefore buy less of the now more expensive foreign good in favour of the domestically produced substitute. A quota is a limit imposed on the physical quantity of a good that can be imported into a country (so many cars from Japan, so many from the USA, etc.). These measures also restrict the spending on imports by reducing the availability of imported goods to consumers. The imposition of tariffs and quotas is nowadays strictly regulated by the World Trade Organisation (WTO), and by the EC, which is also member of WTO. For this reason and because the imposition of tariffs and quotas creates retaliation by the affected countries, such policy measures are very irksome to use in practice to correct current account disequilibria.

Capital account disequilibria

Capital account disequilibria occur when the outflow of portfolio investment from one country is greater than the inflow into the country. Such disequilibria can be corrected by increasing interest rates, which have the effect of attracting foreign capital. Higher interest rates are obtained by introducing a contractionary monetary policy. The drawback of a policy of high interest rates is that it affects investment demand, which falls, thus reducing domestic output and employment.

THE DOMESTIC ECONOMY IN AN INTERNATIONAL CONTEXT

We have finally reached the end of our long journey. We have now got all the pieces of the economic puzzle, which we can try and reassemble to obtain a comprehensive model of the economy that takes into account the interplay of both domestic and international factors. This helps us to see more clearly the new links and constraints that the interaction of the domestic economy with other economies, what we have called the **international sector**, brings into our previous model of a closed economy.

The overall summary presented here assumes that wages are not flexible; in other words, we are assuming, alongside Keynes, that in the short to medium term wages do not adjust rapidly or perfectly to price and demand changes but are characterized by a substantial degree of stickiness. This summary, however, could be also adapted to incorporate the assumption of wage flexibility. Let's first divide the economy into four sectors:

- the **money sector**, where the *interest rate* is determined;
- the **goods sector**, where the level of *output demanded* is determined;
- the **employment sector**, which determines the level of *output supplied*: the interaction of aggregate demand (level of output demanded) and aggregate supply (level of output supplied) determines the *price level*;
- the **international sector**, or **balance of payments sector**, which determines the *exchange rate*.

✍ Activity 10.33

Spend a little time studying Figure 10.15 before you read on. The arrows connecting the variables represent the links which transmit changes within and between the sectors of the economy. See in particular if these arrows make sense to you, in the light of what you have learnt about the domestic economy and its relationships with the international economy.

Figure 10.15 The domestic economy in an international context: internal and external equilibrium

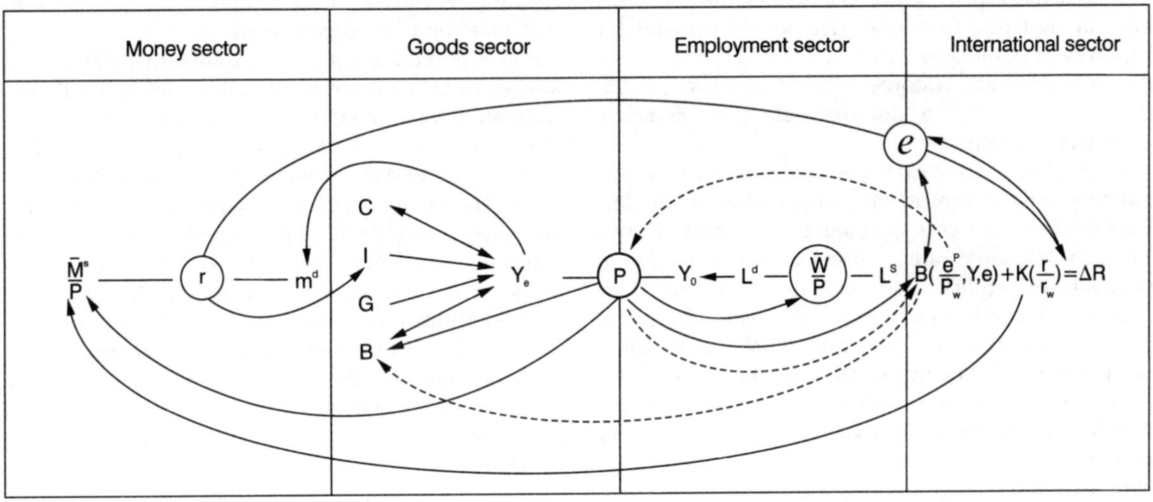

✓ Answer 10.33

The existence of an international sector adds some new constraints to the money and goods sectors of the domestic economy, but no new links between them: more precisely, changes to the money sector.

Changes to the money sector

There is now a link between the money sector and the balance of payments sector via the effect of the rate of interest on capital flows. A domestic interest rate which is higher than interest rates prevailing internationally will now cause an inflow of foreign capital. This inflow of capital has two different effects, according to whether the exchange rate is flexible or fixed.

If the exchange rate is flexible the capital inflow causes an appreciation of the exchange rate, which in turn affects the real side of the economy, reducing the demand for domestic output, as domestically produced export goods are more expensive and less competitive and imported goods are cheaper.

If the exchange rate is fixed, and in the absence of central bank's sterilization, the inflow of foreign capital causes an increase in the money supply, which in turn leads to a lower level of domestic interest rates, bringing them in line with those prevailing internationally. The existence of the international economy, coupled with a fixed exchange rate regime, constrains domestic monetary policy as it causes a convergence of interest rates via changes in the domestic money supply. Interest rates in turn, as Figure 10.5 shows, affect the level of domestic demand and ultimately output. Under these con-straints an economy cannot use monetary tools to deflate or reflate its economy in isolation from the rest of the world. This is a powerful conclusion.

Changes to the goods sector

The introduction of the international sector introduces two new links within the goods sector. There is now a new link between the real balance of trade (B) and aggregate demand or desired expenditure (Y_e), which in turn determines the level of output Y_o. This is a two-way link, because we have assumed that the demand for imports, one of the two elements of the balance of trade, is determined by the level of income (as well as by relative prices). So as domestic income rises, so does the demand for imports. It is because of this two-way link that the open economy multiplier is smaller than the domestic economy multiplier, as it incorporates in the denominator the further leakage of the marginal propensity to import. So, in the open economy, changes in the level of income affect both domestic consumption (positively: $Y\uparrow \rightarrow C\uparrow$) and the balance of trade (negatively: $Y\uparrow \rightarrow M\uparrow \rightarrow B_T < 0$).

The more important and analytically complex new link introduced by the international economy is that between the price level and the balance of trade. This link arises from the fact that both exports and imports depend on the domestic price level relative to that of the rest of the world. So, for example, a domestic inflation rate higher than the inflation rate prevailing in the rest of the world has a different effect on the domestic economy according to whether exchange rates are fixed or flexible.

In a regime of flexible exchange rates, higher inflation at home causes a depreciation of the exchange rate, in turn due to a reduction in the demand for exports and an increase in imports. The depreciation of the exchange rate restores balance of trade equilibrium, but also has a different effect on domestic exporters and importers.

In a regime of fixed exchange rates, higher domestic inflation requires central bank intervention on the foreign exchange markets to counteract downward pressures on exchange rates, caused by the reduction in demand for exports and increase in demand for imports. Central bank's reserve of foreign currency is depleted as a result. This situation of imbalance cannot be sustained indefinitely and the government will have to introduce policies to reduce the level of domestic inflation, which are at the root of it all. This is a very important point, which shows that a domestic economy with a fixed exchange rate regime, operating internationally, cannot allow its rate of inflation to differ substantially from the rate of inflation prevailing internationally. Once more domestic policymaking is constrained by the international scenario. Here, however, we come across an interesting asymmetry: a country with fixed exchange rates can deflate in isolation from the rest of the world (assuming sterilization by the central bank) but cannot reflate in isolation.

If it reflates in isolation, its demand for imports will increase faster than the world's demand for exports, thus causing a balance of trade deficit, which reduces reserves and must be redressed. If it deflates in isolation, interest rates will go up and demand will fall, causing a surplus on the current and capital account. If the effect of this movement on the domestic money supply is sterilized, the only other consequence is an accumulation of foreign reserves.

It is important to notice at this point that a change in foreign currency reserves (ΔR) does not by itself generate an automatic effect on any other domestic variable, if we assume sterilization. There is no direct link between changes in currency reserves and other variables. The changes will be brought about by government and central bank policy aimed at redressing the imbalance to maintain the exchange rate parity.

The important general conclusion that we have reached at this point is that not all of the relevant variables which affect the performance of the domestic economy are under the direct control of domestic economic policy. While the domestic price level, the exchange rate and disposable income can all be changed by the use of monetary and fiscal policy, the price level and the interest rate level prevailing in other countries abroad are not under the control of domestic policymakers.

What we can also see very clearly at this point is that the achievement of equilibrium on the balance of payments (external balance) does affect and constrain the achievement of equilibrium in the domestic economy (internal balance). An increase in the level of domestic income and employment, or the reduction of interest rates to stimulate domestic investment, may be legitimate goals of a government's domestic economic policy, irrespective of the balance of payments situation. They will nonetheless have balance of payments implications which will in turn impact back on them. There are conflicts, in other words, between the achievement of internal and external balance.

CASE STUDY: ECONOMIC GROWTH AND THE BALANCE OF PAYMENTS

The UK balance of payments has been seen as one of the main hindrances to fast growth in Britain. Can the British economy achieve high rates of growth without triggering a balance of payments crisis? Can economic theory help us to calculate a rate of growth for the British economy which is consistent with balance of payments equilibrium? To answer those questions, it is necessary first of all to review the economic data for the British economy introduced in this chapter. It is then necessary to derive the growth rate which is consistent with balance of payments equilibrium and finally to assess whether that growth rate is feasible, using the world trade elasticity of demand for exports and the income elasticity of demand for imports concepts (Turner 1998).

The UK balance of trade

Because of the importance of trade in goods and services for the growth of output and employment of an economy, we focus on the current account of the balance of payments and, in particular, on the difference between exports and imports, which we have called net exports.

The statistics for the British economy discussed in this chapter have shown that over the long term exports and imports of goods and services have tended to move together, but that in the short run there have been substantial differences between the two. We have also seen that the UK balance of trade has been mostly in deficit over the last 30 years.

Growth and the balance of payments

To answer the question of whether the balance of payments places any constraints on the growth rate of the economy, we need to recall the determinants of imports and exports discussed in this chapter and to establish the extent to which they are linked to the overall growth rate of the economy.

As Figure 10.2 showed, the demand for exports accounted for over 22 per cent of GDP in 1997, while the trade dependency ratio had reached about 60 per cent of GDP. The UK, however, is a small open economy, that is, it is in no position to affect the overall volume of world trade significantly. Hence, the UK is not in a position to affect the demand for its

ECONOMIC GROWTH AND THE BALANCE OF PAYMENTS

exports, which will depend on two factors, as we have explained in the course of this chapter:

■ the growth rate of overall world trade, in turn affected by world output growth;
■ the relative competitiveness of UK goods.

The data on the relative competitiveness of UK goods examined earlier show that although UK competitiveness has changed quite substantially in the short run due to changes in the exchange rate, over the long run it has remained quite stable. We can therefore estimate the growth potential of UK exports by measuring the responsiveness of UK export demand to world trade growth. To do that we use the concept of the **world trade elasticity of export demand**. This elasticity defines the percentage response of exports to a 1 per cent change in world trade. To calculate this elasticity, we need to know the percentage change in world trade and the percentage change in UK exports. Once we know the elasticity of demand for UK exports, we can then use it to predict the growth in demand for UK exports from the expected growth rate of world trade. For example, if the value for the elasticity of export demand is 0.5 and world trade is expected to expand by 4 per cent, then the demand for UK exports will rise by 2 per cent.

Similarly, we need to calculate the elasticity of demand for imports. To do that, we need to recall the main determinants of import demand. As explained earlier in this chapter, the main determinants of import demand are:

■ the rate of growth of domestic output and income, i.e. the percentage change of GDP;
■ the relative competitiveness of UK goods vis-à-vis substitute foreign imports.

The **income elasticity of import demand** measures the responsiveness of demand for imports to changes in income as the percentage response of imports to a 1 per cent rise in GDP. To calculate the income elasticity of import demand we need to know the percentage change in import demand and the percentage change in GDP. Once we know the income elasticity of import demand, we can then use it to predict the increase in import demand given a forecasted value of GDP growth. For example, if the value for the income elasticity of import demand is 2 and GDP is expected to rise by 3 per cent, then the demand for imports will rise by 6 per cent.

Domestic growth and external equilibrium

Clearly, once we have calculated the income elasticity of import demand and the world trade elasticity of export demand, we need to put them together to see whether, on the basis of the expected rate of growth of world trade (which is outside UK government control), given the world trade elasticity of demand for exports, and the expected rate of growth of UK GDP (which can be affected by government policy), given the income elasticity of demand for imports, the balance of trade is going to be in equilibrium. For the balance of payments to be in a stable, long-run equilibrium it must be that the rate of growth of both imports and exports is the same. This condition can be expressed with an equation as follows:

$$E^w_x \times g_w = E^y_m \times g_y$$

where E^w_x is the world trade elasticity of exports, g_w is the growth rate of world trade, E^y_m is the income elasticity of imports and g_y is the growth rate of GDP.

If we now divide both sides of this equation by the income elasticity of demand for imports, we obtain that the growth rate of GDP which is consistent with long-run balance of payments equilibrium is determined by

the growth rate of world trade multiplied by the ratio of the world trade elasticity of exports and the income elasticity of imports, as shown below:

$$g_y = (E^w_x / E^y_m) \times g_w.$$

Domestic growth and balance of payments equilibrium in practice

How do we use this analysis in practice? What kind of data do we need? What we are trying to find out is the rate at which the domestic economy should grow if the government wants to maintain a balance of payments equilibrium. The government cannot affect external constraints, such as the rate of growth of world trade or the world trade elasticity of demand for UK exports, nor can it affect the income elasticity of demand for imports. What the government can control, albeit indirectly, is the rate of growth of the domestic economy.

The formula we have just derived above tells us how to calculate which rate of growth of the domestic economy is consistent with a balance of payments equilibrium. What we need to know in practice is the rate of growth of world trade and world trade elasticity of demand for UK exports and the income elasticity of demand for imports.

First we need some data. We could start by collecting data on the annual percentage change of UK imports, exports, GDP and world trade (defined as the sum of exports of manufactured goods by the G7 economies). They are shown in Table 10.15.

A closer analysis of these data reveals, however, that it is quite difficult to infer directly from them some systematic relationships between, say, the rate of growth of imports and GDP or between export growth and world trade.

To find out whether there is a consistent relationship between two variables and to measure the degree of closeness, a better approach is given by the use of scatter diagrams, which plot the scatter of points we obtain when we measure the values of one variable (say rate of growth of imports) on the

Table 10.15 Annual percentage changes in exports, imports, world trade and UK GDP, 1985–95

	Exports	Imports	World trade	UK GDP
1985	5.96	2.59	4.70	4.02
1986	4.47	6.89	1.48	4.01
1987	5.75	7.79	5.06	4.62
1988	0.49	12.59	9.55	4.94
1989	4.65	7.40	9.48	2.25
1990	4.99	0.45	5.39	0.56
1991	−0.69	−5.18	3.31	−2.08
1992	4.11	6.62	4.31	−0.52
1993	3.46	3.01	2.09	2.21
1994	9.21	5.39	7.52	3.98
1995	8.03	4.37	10.75	2.49

Sources: Exports, imports and GDP figures are taken from *Economic Trends Annual Supplement*, 1997. World trade is defined as the sum of exports of manufactured goods by the G7 economies and is taken from the CUSUM model database: Turner, 1998.

continued overleaf

ECONOMIC GROWTH AND THE BALANCE OF PAYMENTS

vertical axis and the values of the other variable (say the rate of growth of GDP) on the horizontal axis. If there is a close (linear) relationship between the two variables, then the scatter of points we obtain should turn out to be grouped around a straight line on our graph. Once we have got our scatter of points on the graph, we can then derive the 'best fit' line by choosing the straight line which generates the minimum sum of squared deviations of the observations from the values predicted by our hypothetical relationship. This rather complicated technique is called the **least squares curve fitting** and is widely used in economics and the social sciences. The scatter diagram for the growth in UK exports against the growth of world trade between 1971 and 1995 is shown in Figure 10.16, while Figure 10.17 shows the scatter diagram for the growth of imports against the rate of growth of GDP. Figures 10.16 and 10.17 both show that there is a positive relationship between growth of exports and world trade on one hand and between growth of imports and growth of domestic output on the other.

In Figure 10.16 the slope of the best fit line measures by what percentage UK exports will increase if there is a 1 per cent rise in world trade, which is the world trade elasticity of demand for UK exports. This elasticity is estimated to be 0.57, that is UK exports can be expected to grow at just over half the rate of growth of world trade.

In Figure 10.17 the slope of the best fit line measures by what percentage UK imports will increase if there is a 1 per cent rise in UK GDP, which is precisely the income elasticity of demand for imports. This elasticity is estimated to be equal to 1.64, which means that the demand for imports can be expected to grow at a rate just over one and a half times the overall growth rate of GDP. This is clearly a problem for the UK economy: these figures predict that attempts by the government to stimulate growth to reduce unemployment would result in a rapid growth of imports and a balance of payments problem.

What is the equilibrium rate of growth for the UK economy?

Given these constraints, more specifically the fact that a 1 per cent rise in world trade causes the demand for UK exports to rise by about half a percentage point, while a 1 per cent rise in UK GDP causes import demand to rise by over 1.5 per cent, the rate at which the UK economy should grow, to maintain a balance of payments equilibrium, is just over a third (0.35) of the growth rate of world trade. As:

$$g_y = (0.57/1.64) \times g_w = 0.35\, g_w.$$

As world trade grew on average by 5.84 per cent over the period 1971–95, the equilibrium growth for the UK economy can be calculated to be 2.04 per cent.

$$g_y = 0.35 \times 5.84 \text{ per cent} = 2.04 \text{ per cent.}$$

Any actual growth rate above that would (and did) cause balance of payments disequilibria. This analysis by Turner (1998) gives strong support to the idea that the growth rate which the UK economy can achieve is constrained by its balance of payments.

Figure 10.16 Growth of exports and world trade, 1971–95

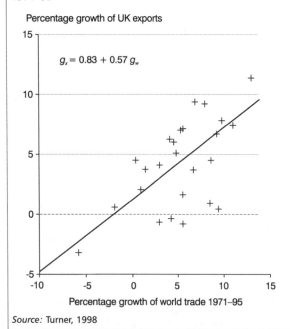

Percentage growth of UK exports

$g_x = 0.83 + 0.57\, g_w$

Percentage growth of world trade 1971–95

Source: Turner, 1998

Figure 10.17 Growth of imports and gross domestic product, 1971–95

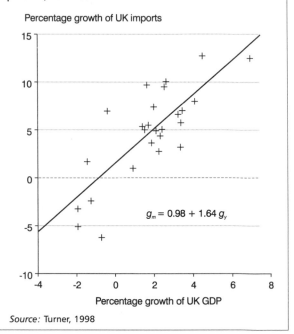

Percentage growth of UK imports

$g_m = 0.98 + 1.64\, g_y$

Percentage growth of UK GDP

Source: Turner, 1998

☆ **For revision of this chapter, see the Chapter Summaries at the end of the book, starting on page 411.**

II Part II

The International Scenario

11 International monetary systems and institutions

Objectives

After studying this chapter you will be able to:

- understand the need for international monetary institutions;
- explain the principles underpinning the gold standard system;
- explain the principles of the gold exchange standard system;
- discuss the main features of the Bretton Woods system;
- explain the function of the International Monetary Fund (IMF);
- explain the main features of the European Monetary System (EMS);
- understand the problems of the EC exchange rate mechanism (ERM);
- understand the current debate in Europe on the single currency and EMU.

Now we are finally in a position to appreciate the effect that international liquidity and exchange rates have on the domestic economy. But who controls how much money there is in the world economy as a whole? By which institutions and how is world liquidity managed?

The world does not possess a central government with coercive powers which can regulate the supply of money or change financial institutions in the interest of maximizing world welfare. Yet, the existence of a well-functioning financial system is as important for the international economy as it is for national economies. Just as savings in the form of notes stuffed under people's mattresses and not rechannelled through financial institutions to borrowers act as a brake on the domestic economy, depriving it of much needed liquidity, persistent trade surpluses not rechannelled by surplus countries back into the world economy in the form of loan capital do much to destabilize global economic relations.

Therefore we now need to turn to a discussion of the specific international arrangements which have regulated currency and capital flows among countries since the end of World War II. We look in particular at the Bretton Woods Agreement signed in 1944, at the role of the International Monetary Fund (IMF), also set up

in that year, and at the more recent European Monetary Union (EMU). We will compare and contrast them with alternative forms of international monetary order, such as the gold standard and the gold exchange standard, and discuss their alleged advantages and disadvantages. In Chapter 12 we look at international trade theory and institutions and at the development of the European Union.

INTERNATIONAL MONETARY SYSTEMS

In a sense it is true to say that history repeats itself. If we look at the international monetary system and the way it has evolved, it is certainly true to say that there is a common, consistent pattern which runs through it. So, to understand what prompted economies in Europe to expand the exchange rate mechanism (ERM) of 1979 into a fully fledged European Monetary Union (EMU) we need to retrace the history of the Bretton Woods system, which regulated international monetary flows from 1944 to 1973. To understand why the 40 signatory members of the 1944 Bretton Woods

Agreement validated a complex system of fixed exchange rates, we need to look into the gold exchange standard which was in place in the inter-war period. To understand why countries like Britain endured severe unemployment and deflation to introduce such a standard, we need to refer to the gold standard which had prevailed during the latter part of last century, from about 1870 until the outbreak of World War I in 1914.

In a sense, all the attempts of this century to reform the international monetary system on the basis of fixed exchange rates (gold exchange standard, Bretton Woods, EMU) can be viewed as efforts to build on the perceived strengths of the gold standard, while avoiding its weaknesses. We need, therefore to start our account of the international monetary system by examining, albeit briefly, how well the gold standard functioned in practice before World War I and how well it enabled countries to achieve the goals of internal and external balance.

THE GOLD STANDARD, 1870–1914

The gold standard is an international and domestic payment system based on the use of gold coins as medium of exchange, store of value and measure of value. Although the use of gold coins dates back to ancient times, the gold standard became a legal institution in Britain with the Resumption Act of 1819, which lifted restrictions on the export of gold coins and bullion from Britain introduced during the Napoleonic war. Germany, Japan and other countries also adopted the gold standard later in the nineteenth century, while the USA officially linked the value of the dollar to gold in 1900. Because of Britain's economic strength, its large share of the international markets and the development of its financial institutions, London was the centre of the international monetary system built on the gold standard.

Under the gold standard, currencies are valued in terms of a gold equivalent and paper notes are fully convertible, on demand, into gold. Over the gold standard period, one ounce of gold was worth $20.67. When each currency is defined in terms of its gold value, the value of all currencies vis-à-vis each other is also fixed, in what amounts to a system of fixed exchange rates. For instance, if currency A is worth 0.10 ounces of gold and currency B is worth 0.20 ounces of gold, then one unit of currency B is worth twice as much as A; hence an exchange rate of 1B = 2A between the two currencies is also established. So currencies on a gold standard were also, de facto, choosing a fixed exchange rate regime vis-à-vis one another.

Under the gold standard the primary responsibility of the central bank was to preserve the official parity between its currency and gold. Currencies were fully backed by gold and gold was accepted in payment for international transactions. To maintain the gold parity of their currencies, central banks needed to have adequate stock of gold reserves; a country on the gold standard allowed its residents to ship gold abroad to finance a payment deficit, while banks stood ready to buy or sell gold in exchange for its currency. This situation could be maintained if countries were neither gaining too much gold from abroad nor, more importantly, were losing it to foreigners.

The gold standard system rested on certain automatic adjustment processes. Governments' implicit obligations were not to tamper with those processes: a loss of gold meant an obligation to accept a monetary contraction (and the consequent temporary loss of output and employment), while a gain of gold implied an obligation to allow the monetary base to expand (and to have inflation as a consequence).

However, the gold standard system seemed to provide an automatic adjustment mechanism for balance of trade imbalances, described by the economist and philosopher David Hume (1752) as a **specie flow mechanism**. To explain how this mechanism was supposed to work, let's use a simple example.

Suppose there are two countries trading with each other, country A and country B. Suppose that at the beginning, the two countries are in an equilibrium situation, where their balance of trade is in equilibrium and prices are stable. Now let's assume that country A discovers a new gold mine and has more gold than before. As a result of more gold being in circulation, more goods will be demanded than can actually be produced in the domestic economy. This will drive up prices in country A, making country B's goods more attractive. If country A now buys more goods from country B and imports more than it exports, it would lose some of its gold to country B. Gold will flow out of A and be shipped out in payment for goods to country B.

This would reduce the quantity of money in circulation (gold) in country A, demand would fall, output and employment would fall and prices would also fall. The surplus country B, on the other hand, which receives the gold in payment for its exports, would see its gold supply increase. As the quantity of money (gold) in circulation in country B increases, demand would rise in excess of what the domestic economy can produce and prices in B would rise as a result (Figure 11.1).

At this point a perfectly symmetric international trade flow and gold flow reversal takes place. Country A, whose prices had fallen because of the trade imbalance

Figure 11.1 The specie-flow mechanism

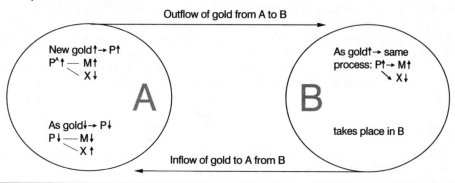

and consequent loss of gold, would see some of the gold flowing back to it and so the process would start all over again. Progressively smaller balance of trade imbalances would continue to alternate between countries A and B until a new external equilibrium, at a higher price level, is reached. This is a powerful mechanism and two main policy implications stem from it:

1 Governments are encouraged to take a laissez-faire attitude towards both external and internal balance. Both balance of trade deficits and periods of unemployment or inflation would work themselves out automatically over time.
2 Fully linking paper money to gold meant restricting the supply of money to the supply of gold. Given that gold was a commodity with relatively fixed supply, this would provide a safeguard against central banks over-issuing paper money and would ensure price stability.

In the inter-war years, and even after World War II, people used to look back to the years of the gold standard with nostalgia, as the golden era of price stability and sustained economic growth. Bankers and government officials strove to bring the gold standard back, after World War I. The gold standard was undoubtedly still in the minds of the many negotiators at the Bretton Woods conference. But did it really work well when it was in use?

The gold standard in practice

Several reasons may be given to account for the survival of the gold standard fixed rate regime over a period of 35 years:

1 First, the world economy was relatively stable. There had been no major wars; governments ran relatively small budget deficits and monetary and fiscal conditions tended to be rather stable. Output growth was also rather steady.
2 The economic cycles of the countries on the gold standard were synchronized, avoiding the emergence of large disequilibria.
3 Substantial differences in cost competitiveness and prices were not allowed to surface because participating countries took pre-emptive monetary policy measures. An outflow (inflow) of gold tended to be promptly associated with an increase (decrease) in the central bank discount rate which triggered a counterbalancing gold flow. For the UK, in particular, the bank rate mechanism worked very quickly and effectively.
4 As a result, the system did not have to rely on changes in relative prices and on long periods of unemployment to bring back balance of trade equilibrium, as envisaged by the theory. Evidence suggests that movements in interest rates and not in price levels worked in fact as the adjustment mechanism.
5 Sterling played a dominant role at the centre of the world financial scene and this facilitated the workings of the gold standard system. Britain ran a current account surplus for almost every year in the 35 years of the gold standard. This inflow of gold on the trade account was, however, matched by a consistent outflow of gold on the capital account, as Britain tailored its lending overseas to the small fluctuations in its current account. This process kept a stable flow of funds circulating through the world economy.
6 The world supplies of gold were adequate to meet the world economy liquidity needs and allow the smooth functioning of the international payment system. Gold supplies increased steadily over the period, as trade and payments flows expanded, so that the system was never permanently braked by sharply rising interest rates due to a shortage of cash. Despite its international role, Britain had rather meagre gold reserves;

despite the fact that Britain's sterling liabilities to foreigners exceeded its gold holdings (the Bank of England would have not been able to maintain the convertibility of its paper notes to gold, had all the foreigners holding sterling requested their conversion into gold), and were in fact twice as much in 1913. Sterling however was never under speculative attack in those years.

✍ Activity 11.1

Explain the adjustment mechanism to balance of payments disequilibria under the classical gold exchange standard, both in theory and in practice.

✓ Answer 11.1

In theory the adjustment should have taken place through changes in relative prices, periods of temporary output and employment contractions and temporary balance of trade deficits without government intervention. In practice, however, equilibrium was maintained by governments intervening to manipulate short-term interest rates, to attract capital inflows and prevent the loss of gold. So short-term capital movements, rather than price changes, worked in the end as the equilibrating factor.

THE GOLD EXCHANGE STANDARD, 1925–31

At the outbreak of World War I gold convertibility was suspended, because of the impracticality of gold shipments in war time and because of inflationary financing of their massive war efforts on the part of most countries. Countries, however, assumed that the gold standard would be reintroduced once hostilities were over. The war had a major effect on the balance of the world economy. Europe emerged from the war in shambles, much weakened economically and financially. It had lost a considerable part of its productive capacity and its dominant position on world markets. The USA, which had instead gained economically and financially from World War I, emerged almost by default as the new world power.

Several countries in Europe experienced runaway inflation as governments tried to finance the reconstruction of their economies through public expenditure financed by printing money. The most famous episode of inter-war inflation is the German hyperinflation: Germany's price index rose from 262 in January 1919 to 126,160,000,000,000,000 in December 1923, a factor of 481.5 billion.

The restoration of monetary stability was regarded as a matter of some urgency after World War I. In the absence of a clearly defined alternative to the gold standard and in view of its apparent success, it was considered highly desirable that each nation should return to a fixed gold parity as soon as possible. But the stabilization process proved to be a long drawn-out affair, which lasted most of the decade and ended in failure.

The USA returned to gold in 1919. Other countries strived to do the same. At the Genoa conference held in Italy in 1922 the major industrialized countries, including Britain, France, Italy and Japan agreed to return to the gold standard and to co-operate among themselves to operate the international system to achieve common external and internal balance. Because of the uneven distribution of world gold reserves after World War I (now mostly with the USA), the Genoa conference sanctioned the return to a partial gold exchange standard, where smaller countries could hold as reserve assets the currencies of several large countries, whose own international reserves would consist entirely of gold. This was, in other words, a watered down version of the old gold standard:

- Some countries, such as the USA, were on a full gold standard (or gold coin standard).
- Some countries, such as Britain, Denmark and Norway, were on the gold bullion standard, whereby notes could not readily be converted into gold on demand except for export purposes and in large minimum amounts.
- The majority of countries opted for a gold exchange standard, whereby the monetary authority of a country tied its currency to gold indirectly, by maintaining a fixed exchange rate with a foreign currency that was either on a gold coin or gold bullion standard.

In other words, the central bank had the obligation to maintain the value of a national currency at par with other gold currency countries by buying or selling foreign exchange at the gold parity. Britain, despite a considerable loss of the value of sterling vis-à-vis the dollar, returned to convertibility with gold in 1925 at the pre-war parity. This implied a revaluation of the pound against other foreign currencies, which shifted world demand away from British products even more and contributed much to the severe depression that the economy suffered throughout the 1930s.

The gold exchange standard system did not work. In the wake of the deep international recession that followed the Great Depression of 1929–32, most countries renounced their gold standard obligations and allowed their currencies to float on the foreign exchange market. Some countries temporarily suspended convertibility, while allowing their currency to devalue, like the USA which left the gold standard in 1933 but returned to it in 1934, having raised the dollar price of gold from $20.67 to $35 per ounce. Other competitive devaluations followed in Europe, as countries tried to retain their gold reserves by steering world demand towards their output. These 'beggar-my-neighbour' exchange rate policies, coupled with measures aimed at restricting trade such as tariffs and quotas on foreign imports, as they were practised by almost all countries at the same time, only succeeded in increasing the instability of the international economy, further reducing world output and employment.

Difficulties of the gold exchange standard

The reasons for the system's disintegration are many:

■ Britain's position had changed in the world ranking of economic and financial powers. Sterling was overvalued at its pre-war parity rate when Britain returned to gold convertibility in 1925. Furthermore, the war had transformed Britain's trade account from surplus to deficit and Britain from a lender to a borrower nation.

■ Sterling had ceased to be the international currency and the City of London had ceased to be the heart of world financial institutions. There were now other financial centres, notably New York, all competing with London.

■ The adjustment mechanism could not work in a satisfactory manner during the restored gold exchange standard because of the maldistribution of gold reserves. The USA and France had excessive gold holdings, while Britain's gold stocks were inadequate. What is more, both the USA and France, intent on strengthening the convertibility of their currencies, actually hoarded their gold reserves, starving the rest of the world of much needed liquidity. At the same time, Britain pursued the opposite policy and continued to expand credit, despite its small and declining gold stocks.

■ Because of severe domestic economic problems, high unemployment and lower outputs, governments in the post-war period were more concerned with the state of their domestic economies than with issues of external balance of payments. Consequently, their priorities had shifted away from the external equilibrium target towards achievement of domestic targets.

■ The political and economic environment had become generally less conducive towards the efficient func-

tioning of the gold standard. Individual economies cycles were less synchronized. The structure of external payments had changed fundamentally, with countries suspending their currencies' convertibility and resorting to bilateral barter agreements.

■ The weakened position of London as the financial centre of the industrialized world, now competing with New York and to a lesser extent Paris, the heightened competition between countries and the uneven distribution of gold reserves exposed reserve currencies, such as the dollar and sterling, to the risks of speculative attacks. It also exposed the system to more 'hot money' flows between centres.

■ Partly due to isolationism, political immaturity, hostility to the idea of investment abroad and inadequacy of its central banking structure, still too decentralized and complex, the USA seemed ill-equipped to assume the dominant role that Britain had played in the management of the international financial system.

■ Finally, all these difficulties associated with the restored gold exchange standard were vastly exasperated by the onset of the Great Depression of 1929–31. The immediate reasons for the collapse of the gold standard and Britain's withdrawal were a succession of banking and financial crises triggered by the sudden collapse of the powerful Austrian Credit-Anstalt Bank in May 1931. Withdrawals from further Austrian banks intensified and a run on German banks ensued. This caused difficulties for Britain, which had been liberal in its advances to German banks and industry. When the collapse occurred in Germany and the Berlin banks closed, Britain's German assets were frozen. There was consequently a huge run on sterling which the Bank of England could not sustain. The abandonment of convertibility was announced in September 1931. The years that followed were marked by rising protectionism and a succession of competitive exchange rate adjustments. The USA left the gold standard in 1933; France withdrew in 1936.

✍ Activity 11.2

How would you describe the functioning of the international monetary system in the inter-war period?

✓ Answer 11.2

The monetary system officially in use in the inter-war period was the gold exchange standard. Generally chaotic conditions prevailed, however, in international trade and payments over the period and the system never worked adequately.

THE BRETTON WOODS SYSTEM, 1944–73

Determined to avoid the monetary chaos of the 1930s, the USA and Britain started negotiations on the future international monetary institutions even before World War II was over, in 1941. The intention of creating a new international economic order was clear on both parts. This liberal, multilateral economic order would express itself through the workings of a triad of new, international economic institutions: the International Trade Organization (ITO), discussed in Chapter 12, the International Monetary Fund (IMF) and the World Bank or Bank for Reconstruction and Development, which we discuss in the rest of this chapter.

The British and American negotiators, Keynes as adviser to the Treasury for Britain and Harry Dexter White from the US treasury, found some common ground on the following:

■ They were both opposed to a system of freely fluctuating exchange rates, which they felt had adversely affected world economies in the immediate aftermath of World War I and again in the latter part of the 1930s.
■ Because of the failure of the gold exchange standard, they were also opposed to a system of absolutely fixed exchange rates.

There were also, however, profound differences in the attitudes of the two negotiating parties:

■ Keynes's emphasis was on the need to preserve countries' ability to change the exchange rate to suit the achievement of domestic goals, such as full employment. The USA, on the other hand, wanted to limit countries' ability to change the exchange rates only to situations of fundamental disequilibrium, which would occur infrequently.
■ Britain's view was that both surplus and deficit countries should be required to correct their balance of payments disequilibria. The USA took the view that the burden of adjustment should fall largely on the deficit countries.
■ Britain wanted to retain some role for sterling as a reserve currency, while the USA did not envisage a major reserve currency role for the dollar.
■ Britain, as a potentially large debtor country after the war, wanted an institution which would provide relatively generous credit to member countries. The USA, as a potential creditor, envisaged the new institution as providing only modest international financing, on a sound conservative basis.

■ Britain was quite adamant on the need for countries to retain the right to exercise control over their capital movements, while the USA wanted full liberalization of capital movements, with individual countries retaining the right to limit such movements only with respect to disequilibrating short-term speculative capital, but not with respect to productive capital.
■ Britain was particularly concerned with the risk of unemployment, while the USA was rather more concerned with the possible risks of inflation.
■ Britain was anxious to avoid political interference by the international body on domestic economic policy matters, while the USA appeared to have far fewer reservations about this.

Not surprisingly, given US economic and political pre-eminence after World War II, the White Plan in the end won the day. Having achieved a substantial measure of bilateral agreement on the main issues, Britain and the USA called an international conference of all the wartime allies at Bretton Woods, in New Hampshire, to draft the Articles of Agreement of the International Monetary Fund (IMF) and the World Bank. The draft articles of the IMF were released in April 1944 and became finally operative in 1946.

THE INTERNATIONAL MONETARY FUND (IMF)

The principal provisions of the IMF fall conveniently into three categories:

■ exchange rate regime;
■ reserve regime and supply of credit to member countries;
■ adjustment mechanism to correct balance of payment disequilibria.

The principal controversies surrounding the IMF design and provisions can also be discussed under the same headings.

Exchange rate regime

The exchange rate regime established at Bretton Woods as the basis of the IMF was one of managed flexibility:

■ Exchange rates were normally to be fixed within a margin of ±1 per cent. The par values of all exchange rates were to be expressed in terms of gold or US dollars.

- The US dollar was priced in terms of gold, at $35 per fine ounce of gold.
- Changes in the par values were possible only in cases of fundamental disequilibrium, such as persistent balance of payments deficits or surpluses.
- Changes in par values of less than 10 per cent only needed to be notified to the IMF; greater changes needed approval. Changes, however, were expected to be infrequent as countries had an obligation 'to promote exchange stability, to maintain orderly arrangements with other members'.
- Since members were required to maintain their par value within a small margin, they would need to intervene regularly in foreign exchange markets as their currencies approached the upper or lower limit. Intervention required the availability of international reserves, which the IMF would make available under specific conditions.

Drawing rights and pool of international credit

The greater the inflexibility of the exchange rate system, the greater the need for reserves of foreign currency. The IMF therefore provided a pool of currency available to members experiencing balance of payments difficulties, according to the following set of criteria:

- The borrowing rights of a member were determined by its quota or contributions to the fund, itself depending on the economic and political importance of members.
- Of a country's quota 25 per cent had to be contributed in gold or US dollars, the remaining 75 per cent in the domestic currency of the member.
- As a member drew foreign currency from the IMF, it had to deposit a corresponding amount of its own currency.
- Members drawing rights were limited to 25 per cent of its quota plus 'such total amount as will increase the Fund's holdings of its currency to not more than 200 per cent of its quota'.
- Once the Fund held 200 per cent of quota in the member's domestic currency, the member's drawing rights were exhausted until: (a) a member repurchases its own currency, paying in a currency acceptable to the fund (the Fund holds less than 75 per cent of that currency's quota); (b) another member draws that specific currency, reducing the Fund's holding below 200 per cent. It should be noted at this point that repayments, until 1963, were normally in dollars.

Adjustment mechanism

The IMF articles did not spell out very explicitly how countries were supposed to adjust in a case of disequilibrium. The general principles which had inspired the agreement seemed to imply that:

- a high priority should be given to the preservation of internal balance;
- temporary imbalances should be financed by borrowing from the Fund, rather than by adjusting the exchange rate;
- modest but persistent imbalances should be corrected by slight adjustment of fiscal and monetary policies, provided they did not fundamentally upset a country's internal balance;
- large and persistent imbalances could be met by exchange rate changes;
- destabilizing speculative capital movements could be eliminated by exchange controls.

✍ Activity 11.3

With respect to the Bretton Woods system, explain the following:

1 What type of exchange rate system was established?
2 How were countries supposed to finance payment deficits?

✓ Answer 11.3

1 The Bretton Woods system was a sort of dollar–gold exchange standard. Each member country was required to fix the value of its currency in terms of gold or dollars and then actively intervene on the foreign exchange market to keep the exchange rate within a narrow band of plus or minus 1 per cent of the agreed parity.
2 Countries were supposed to finance temporary deficits in their balance of payments out of their international reserves and by borrowing from the IMF, without devaluations (which would have led to similar competitive devaluations by other members), or import restrictions (which would have also led to retaliation). Borrowing from the IMF was intended to be for short periods only (three to five years), not to tie up the Fund's resources into long-term loans.

For long-term development finance, the International Bank for Reconstruction and Development (generally known as the World Bank) was created at the same time as the IMF, together with the International Finance Corporation and the Agency for International Development. Changes in par values were to be considered only in cases of fundamental disequilibrium.

✍ Activity 11.4

With what did the Bretton Woods system provide its members?

✓ Answer 11.4

It provided them with:

- a code of rules for the conduct of international trade and finance;
- borrowing facilities for countries in temporary balance of payments difficulties.

The IMF in operation

The Fund accomplished little in its first decade. This was mostly due to the fact that quotas were far too small to provide the liquidity, particularly dollars, needed to sustain the European payment deficit caused by the reconstruction of war-torn Europe. Those much needed dollars were finally made available by the USA to the European economies through Marshall Aid, a programme of dollar grants from the USA to the European countries. In the four years of the Marshall Aid programme, from mid-1948 to mid-1952, the USA gave out some $11.6bn in grants and another $1.8bn in loans to countries in Europe. There is no doubt that these huge hand-outs put the USA in a position of considerable political and economic strength, from which it could exercise substantial leverage over the countries it assisted. It was agreed at the time that countries receiving Marshall Aid would not also borrow from the Fund.

The Fund began to be called into action only in 1956, when Britain and France needed bailing out from the financial consequences of the Suez crisis. Two years later, however, the dollar shortage started to turn into a dollar glut, just as European currencies finally became convertible. What had happened?

US trade deficits

In the early post-war years, particularly from 1946 to 1949, the US balance of payment was very strong, recording an average trade surplus of about $8bn dollars a year. The US trade position vis-à-vis Europe was so strong that the USA was in fact encouraging European discrimination against its imports. In 1949, encouraged by the USA, sterling was devalued about 30 per cent against the dollar, followed by some 30 other countries. This massive realignment, together with the first signs of European recovery and the debit financing of the Korean war by the American government, brought about a major change in the US balance of payments, which went into deficit for the first time in 1950.

These deficits continued and grew larger throughout the 1950s, as US military expenditures abroad increased, together with US net foreign investment. The deficits were financed by a large increase in US liabilities to foreigners (the USA was issuing more and more dollars) and by a huge drain on its gold reserves.

Almost by default, in the absence of any other mechanism for reserve creation, given that IMF quotas were too small, the dollar began to assume a dominant role as the world reserve currency. This process was not viewed with any alarm at the time, if anything it was welcomed by the world economies, which saw the growth in world reserves of dollars, originating in continuing US deficits, as much needed to allow the rest of the world to build up its reserves and to keep up with the rapid growth of international trade and output.

Not surprisingly, until 1956, borrowing from the IMF was very slight and the IMF role in the international scenario remained largely passive. The IMF began to find its feet and assume an increasing role just as the role of the USA was slowly diminishing, in the second half of the 1950s and the 1960s. The problems with this system then began to surface.

✍ Activity 11.5

How did the Bretton Woods system operate with respect to adjustments to fundamental disequilibria?

✓ Answer 11.5

Under the Bretton Woods system, countries were reluctant to devalue or revalue even when in fundamental disequilibrium. Devaluations were regarded as a sign of weakness. Revaluations were equally resisted, as countries preferred to carry on accumulating reserves.

The system's contradictions

The sources of problems and contradictions within the Bretton Woods system were many. For a start, the quotas were too small to allow member countries' governments real macroeconomic policy flexibility, which would compensate for the straitjacket imposed by fixed exchange rates. In the early negotiations, Keynes had called for a reserve fund of $35bn. In the event, as constituted, the IMF overall quota amounted to a meagre $8bn. Only half the value of the total Fund quota could be borrowed at any one time ($4bn), as for any deficit recorded by one member there had to be an equivalent surplus gained by another member; and only 25 per cent of that could be borrowed in one year. So the total borrowable fund in any one year by all member countries was $1bn.

Second, quotas were fixed once and for all, failing to take into account changes in the economic importance of members. This proved particularly constraining for Germany and Italy which both recorded extremely high rates of growth in the post-war period.

So, what we see taking place throughout this time are periodic, ad hoc revisions of members' quotas. In June 1960 the quotas of most members were raised by 50 per cent, while Germany's quota increased by 140 per cent. As new members joined the IMF, its size was increased to $15bn dollars by 1960, while the USA retained the right to sell new amounts of dollars for foreign exchange or gold, to restore the Fund's holding of dollars to the original 75 per cent of its quota. The General Agreement to Borrow (GAB), signed in Vienna in 1961 by 10 member countries, increased the Fund's pool of reserves by another $6bn. The Special Drawing Rights (SDR) agreement signed in 1969 provided additional instalments of credit totalling $9.5bn, this time in the form of SDRs, or artificial reserve assets, to be accredited to members in proportion to their quotas. However, SDRs were 'too little, too late', as the system was already showing signs of great strain and was soon to collapse. Table 11.1. offers an idea of the size of the successive quota adjustments.

✍ Activity 11.6

If quotas were too small and fixed once and for all, how did world trade manage to grow?

✓ Answer 11.6

World liquidity necessary for the growth of world trade and output was provided outside the IMF system by the US balance of payment deficits financed by printing more dollars, thereby increasing the world supply of dollars.

This meant that the provision of world liquidity was left to the unregulated discretion of one individual country, the USA, operating outside the international monetary constraints set out at Bretton Woods for the provision and management of world liquidity.

The major principle of monetary management at the basis of the Bretton Woods agreement was the requirement that members' exchange rates be fixed to the dollar, which in turn was tied to gold. If a central bank other than the Federal Reserve pursued a policy of excessive monetary expansion, this would eventually lead to a balance of trade deficit which would put strain on the currency's dollar parity and would have to be redressed. The Federal Reserve's excessive monetary expansion, on the other hand, would be constrained by its obligation to redeem any amount of dollars into gold. Fixed exchange rates were viewed in this context as an effective way of imposing monetary discipline on the system. While this monetary discipline worked for

Table 11.1 IMF quotas				$ millions
	30 June 1947 $	30 June 1960 $	Credit agreement 1961 $	Ration of 1961 agreement to 1960 quota (per cent)
Belgium	225.0	337.5	150	44.4
Canada	300.0	550.0	200	36.4
France	525.0	787.5	550	70.0
Germany	(330.0)*	787.5	1 000	127.0
Italy	180.0	270.0	550	203.7
Japan	(250.0)*	500.0	250	50.0
Netherlands	275.0	412.5	200	48.5
Sweden	(100.0)*	150.0	100	66.7
UK	1 300.0	1 950.0	1 000	51.3
USA	2 750.0	4 125.0	2 000	48.5
All other	2 166.5	4 509.2	0	0
Total	7 721.5	14 379.2	6 000	60.8†

Source: International Monetary Fund, International Financial Statistics
* These countries joined after 1947, Sweden in 1951 and Japan and Germany in 1952. The figures are the original quotas.
† For the ten countries.

all other member countries, it did not apply to the USA, which was allowed to print more dollars to paper over its fundamental trade imbalances.

✍ Activity 11.7

Look at Table 11.2 and comment on US gold reserves from 1949 to 1958.

✔ Answer to 11.7

US gold reserves in relation to its external liquid liabilities deteriorated throughout the period. Despite this, the USA still had more than enough gold by the end of 1958 to meet any demand for convertibility. By 1958, the ratio of total liquid liabilities to its gold reserves had risen from nearly 0.3 in 1949 to over 0.8 in 1958. In 1958 the real US position was, however, stronger than suggested by this ratio. Although all liquid liabilities were potentially convertible into gold, only official liabilities, which were much smaller, were legally convertible.

As a result of large and persistent US deficits and the continuing decline in US gold stock, foreign holdings became equal to US gold reserves in 1959 and

became much larger every year. Eventually it became quite clear that the USA would not be able to maintain convertibility of dollars with gold at $35 per ounce. This turned the dollar shortage into a dollar glut, as countries became increasingly unwilling to hold dollars.

This situation was beginning to expose a fundamental contradiction of the Bretton Woods gold–dollar standard system. The system's contradiction, summed up as 'either gold dollar convertibility or world growth', is often referred to as the Triffin dilemma, from the name of the influential Yale economist, Robert Triffin, who in 1960, when the US gold stocks were still in excess of US official liabilities, clearly envisaged what would happen and in fact did happen in 1971: the collapse of the Bretton Woods system.

Triffin's reasoning exposed the **confidence problem** at the root of the system. Throughout the 1950s foreign central banks had been happy to accumulate dollars because dollars were 'as good as gold', given the gold–dollar convertibility. They also needed fast-growing international reserves to finance the world's expanding trade. As central banks' international reserve needs grew over time, their holdings of dollars

Table 11.2 US gold reserves and external liabilities, 1949–71 (billions of US dollars)

Year	Gold reserves (1)	External liquid liabilities (2)	Official liabilities (3)	Ratio (2):(1) (4)	Ratio (3):(1) (5)
1949	24.56	6.94	3.36	0.28	0.14
1950	22.82	8.89	4.89	0.39	0.21
1951	22.87	8.85	4.16	0.39	0.18'
1952	23.25	10.43	5.56	0.45	0.24
1953	22.09	11.36	6.47	0.51	0.29
1954	21.79	12.45	7.52	0.57	0.35
1955	21.75	13.52	8.26	0.62	0.38
1956	22.06	15.29	9.15	0.69	0.41
1957	22.86	15.83	9.14	0.69	0.40
1958	20.58	16.85	9.65	0.82	0.47
1959	19.51	19.43	10.12	1.0	0.5
1960	17.80	21.03	11.09	1.2	0.6
1961	16.95	22.94	11.83	1.4	0.7
1962	16.06	24.27	12.91	1.5	0.8
1963	15.60	26.39	14.43	1.7	0.9
1964	15.47	29.36	15.78	1.9	1.0
1965	14.07	29.57	15.82	2.1	1.1
1966	13.24	31.02	14.89	2.3	1.1
1967	12.07	35.67	18.19	3.0	1.5
1968	10.89	38.47	17.34	3.5	1.6
1969	11.86	45.91	15.99	3.9	1.4
1970	11.07	46.95	23.77	4.2	2.1
1971	11.08	67.81	50.64	6.1	4.6

Source: International Monetary Fund, *International Financial Statistics*

also grew. The time would come eventually Triffin argued when these dollar holdings would exceed the US gold stock. The US, which was obliged under the Bretton Woods agreement to redeem these dollars at $35 an ounce, would no longer be able to meet its obligations, should all dollar holders simultaneously try to convert their holdings into gold. Dollars would cease to be 'as good as gold'; bankers would be unwilling to hold them and might try to cash the dollars in, bringing down the system.

This is exactly what happened in 1931, when official holders of pounds, aware of Britain's meagre reserves of gold, tried to redeem their pound holdings for gold and forced Britain off the gold standard. The same happened again at the end of the 1960s, and for exactly the same reasons.

Another difficulty that increasingly characterized the working of the Bretton Woods system was associated with the fixed exchange rate mechanism, its lack of clear adjustment procedures and the constraint it imposed on the achievement of countries' internal balance. The restoration of currencies' convertibility in 1958 and the increased movement of funds across borders particularly helped to expose this other serious difficulty of the system.

As we noted before, monetary policy is not an effective policy tool under fixed exchange rates. This is because any attempt by the central bank to alter the money supply causes an offsetting change in foreign reserves, leaving the domestic money supply unchanged. The level of output and employment cannot be affected using monetary tools when exchange rates are fixed.

A government can also use fiscal policy or exchange rate changes to affect the level of output and employment to achieve internal balance, i.e. a full employment level of output. Fiscal policy is often referred to as **expenditure-changing policy**, because it alters the level of the economy's total demand for goods and services. A tax cut or increased government spending will stimulate demand and, under certain conditions, output, income and employment. Fiscal expansion will also cause a balance of trade deficit. For this reason, it needs to be accompanied by an appropriate exchange rate adjustment (a devaluation). The exchange rate adjustment is called an **expenditure-switching policy** because, by changing the relative price of imports and exports, it changes the direction of demand (away from foreign goods and towards domestically produced goods in the case of a depreciation).

Under the Bretton Woods system, expenditure switching policies (exchange rate changes) were supposed to be infrequent. As a result of this exchange rate inflexibility, policymakers often found themselves faced by a dilemma. If they expanded their economies to reduce unemployment, they would cause a balance of payments crisis, which would prompt speculators' activity. Suspicion of an impending devaluation could, in turn, exacerbate a balance of payments crisis.

Anyone holding, say, pounds during a devaluation would suffer a loss as the foreign currency value of pound-denominated assets would decrease by the amount of the exchange rate change. People would then tend to switch their wealth out of sterling denominated assets in an attempt to beat devaluation, and by so doing bringing it about. To maintain sterling parity with the dollar, the Bank of England would have to buy the unwanted sterling in exchange for dollars or whichever currency the market may wish to hold, thereby depleting its reserves of foreign currency. If the central bank is left without sufficient reserves to sustain the parity, it might be forced to devalue.

Similarly, countries with large current account surpluses would be viewed by speculators as candidates for revaluation. In this case, central banks would find themselves swamped with official reserves as they try to prevent an appreciation of the exchange rate by making more domestic currency available on the foreign exchange markets. A country in this position would lose control over its money supply, which would grow uncontrollably under the influence of external demand. This unwanted increase in liquidity in turn may cause inflation in the domestic economy.

For these reasons, during the Bretton Woods period, countries experiencing balance of payments difficulties were like sitting ducks and easy targets for speculators. A combination of all these factors contributed in the end to the demise of the Bretton Woods system. Runs on currencies, particularly on the dollar, finally brought the system down. The USA abandoned convertibility in 1971 and exchange rates were allowed to float freely.

The demise of the Bretton Woods system

The events which unfolded in the 1960s and led to the demise of the system must be read in the light of its underlying fundamental contradictions. Summing up, the chronology of events of this momentous decade was as follows:

■ Six major European economies sign the Treaty of Rome in 1957, creating the European Community. Europe starts to provide contravailing power to the USA.

■ In 1958 currency convertibility is restored in Europe.

■ After falling sharply in 1959, the US current account moves into deficit for the first time since the war in 1960. This year marked the end of the dollar shortage and the beginning of the 'dollar glut', as foreign central banks converted nearly $2bn into gold that year, having converted approximately $5bn in 1958 and 1959.

- US economic and political supremacy begins to be challenged. Confidence crisis in the dollar (1959–60), runs on the Deutschmark in 1961 and on sterling in 1964 and 1967 force the German currency to revalue and the British currency to devalue.
- Throughout this period, the German, French, Italian and Japanese economies grow in strength, while the US and British economies become gradually weaker.
- Due to the persistence of US balance of trade deficits, plus the deficit financing of the Vietnam War and deepening military involvement, the ratio of gold reserves to external official liabilities worsens further, as shown in Table 11.2. Speculation against the dollar intensified, as asset holders switched from dollars to DM in anticipation of a revaluation of the DM against the dollar. On 4 May 1971 the German central bank, the Bundesbank, had to buy $1bn to maintain DM parity with the dollar and prevent its appreciation, while on the morning of 5 May it had to purchase the same amount of dollars in the first hour of trading on the foreign exchange market! (Krugman and Obstfeld 1994). At that point the Bundesbank allowed its currency to float and de facto abandoned the system. Renewed speculation forced President Nixon to suspend convertibility on 15 August 1971. After repeated attempts at propping up the dollar on the part of the major central bank, on 19 March 1973 most European currencies, together with the Japanese yen, started floating against the dollar and the system was finally abandoned. This marked the beginning of a turbulent period in international monetary relations.

THE NON-SYSTEM, 1973–85

The collapse of the Bretton Woods system, coupled with Triffin's early explanation of the built-in contradiction which was dooming it, led to an intense and wide-ranging debate in the 1970s on possible reforms of the international monetary system. Five distinct plans emerged during this debate:

1 *Triffin plan: a World Bank*: the idea at the basis of this plan was that, like the domestic economy, the world economy needs adequate liquidity. The world reserve stock provides a monetary base which needs to grow at the appropriate rate: if it

grows too fast, with respect to the world's output growth rate, world inflation rates rise; if reserves grow too slowly or fall in absolute terms, worldwide deflation follows. World output growth will be stunted, unemployment will rise and trade will fall as countries introduce protectionist measures in an attempt to safeguard their domestic economies. As a solution to the problem of world liquidity, Triffin suggested the expansion of the IMF into a proper world bank, i.e. a deposit bank for central banks. Each central bank would hold a certain proportion of a new reserve asset as deposits at the IMF, while the Fund would have control of its total supply. This view was supported in the 1960s by US official circles.

2 *Non-system – floating exchange rates*: this school of thought favoured fully flexible exchange rates, 'leaving it to the markets' to find the equilibrium exchange rates which would automatically bring about balance of payments equilibria.

3 *A gold standard*: this school of thought, strongly favoured by the French economist Jacques Reuff and President de Gaulle, wanted a return to the full gold standard. As a compromise, this school also advocated revitalizing the Bretton Woods agreement by increasing the dollar price of gold.

4 *A dollar standard*: this school favoured a system based on the dollar as reserve asset, which would not be convertible with anything else. Other countries would simply peg the value of their currencies to the dollar, adjusting the parity until a value consistent with internal balance could be found. The USA would not intervene on its balance of payments, allowing it to be determined as a 'residual' of the global system. This school was favoured by US academics and, in some measure, by the Nixon administration.

5 *Triffin model with a crawling peg*: this school advocated the adoption of Triffin's proposal, combined, however, with a certain amount of exchange rate flexibility.

The Triffin view had some currency in the 1960s when it led to the creation of the special drawing rights (SDR) at a meeting of the IMF in Rio de Janeiro in 1967. The SDR system, however, was a typical example of 'too little, too late' and did not provide a real solution to the need for world monetary order.

After the collapse of the Bretton Woods agreement, exchange rates were allowed to float freely in what became to be known as the non-system. The non-system was officialized at the IMF meeting in Jamaica in January 1976. The non-system of the **Jamaica Accords** derives its name from its guiding principle that there is no guiding principle on exchange rate matters.

The IMF articles were then modified to allow countries to float or peg. Countries can peg the values of their currencies to anything except gold. Currencies' values can be pegged to another currency, like the dollar, to a basket of currencies, or to each other's currencies as a group. The Jamaica Accords formally allowed countries the choice of the exchange rate regime they wanted, provided their actions did not prove disruptive to established trade patterns and the world economy generally.

THE EUROPEAN MONETARY SYSTEM (EMS)

Despite the demise of the Bretton Woods system in 1973 and in the midst of a heated debate about the desirability of fixed versus flexible exchange rates, in March 1979 the nine-member EC expressed a strong preference for exchange rate stability and set up the European Monetary System (EMS), as part of its aim towards greater monetary integration. The decision to readopt, albeit on a regional basis, a system of relatively fixed exchange rates, can be explained on the basis of the following considerations:

- EC countries saw the collapse of the Bretton Woods system as caused by the dollar problem, which it was felt would not apply to the EMS.
- Reducing exchange rate volatility would be beneficial for the EC as a group, given the large amount of **inter-regional trade**, i.e. the amount of trade conducted by EC countries with the rest of the world.
- The EC was also characterized by a large amount of **intra-regional trade**, i.e. trade of EC countries with one another and with the European Free Trade Association (EFTA) countries. It was strongly felt at the time that cost uncertainty and hedging caused by exchange rate volatility created a barrier to trade which was as damaging and pervasive as tariffs. Exchange rate changes complicate accurate costing for assembly and intermediate products and therefore discourage intra-EC direct investment.
- The EC had already successfully applied 'green exchange rates' to manage its intervention in the agricultural sector as part of the Common Agricultural Policy (CAP). This proved that a system of fixed exchange rates could be successfully managed by the Community.

These arguments taken together led to the view that the EC needed a joint float, if not a single currency.

The establishment of the EMS involved the following measures:

- the introduction of the **European Currency Unit**, the Ecu (not to be confused with the single currency, the Euro, adopted by eleven EU members in place of their domestic currencies from January 1999). The Ecu was the weighted average of the currencies of the member nations, where the weights reflected their relative economic importance.
- the adoption of a **system of relatively fixed exchange rates**. The currency of each member was allowed a fluctuation band of $\pm$ 2.25 per cent around its central rate or par value (6 per cent for the escudo, sterling and the peseta). The mechanism to establish the system was as follows: each central banker would announce a par rate for each national currency in terms of the Ecu. Once individual currencies' parity with the Ecu are decided, cross-rates for all European currencies can be calculated. Once calculated they can be formed into a grid of central rates, where floor and ceiling values requiring central bank intervention can also be determined. Intervention at the limit is mandatory. This was a fixed but adjustable exchange rate system, where the currencies of EMS countries jointly floated against the dollar and other currencies;
- the establishment of the **European Monetary Cooperation Fund (EMCF)** to help members with short and medium-term balance of payment problems.

The exchange rate mechanism

The first step in setting up the ERM was the creation of the Ecu, as a weighted average of EU currencies, with weights reviewed every five years.

✍ Activity 11.8

Look at Figure 11.2 and comment on the relative weights assigned to the various EU currencies in the determination of the value of the Ecu.

✓ Answer 11.8

Figure 11.2 shows that half of the Ecu's value is accounted for by the Deutschmark and the French franc; all the EU currencies are included, however, in the determination of its value. To calculate the value of the ECU vis-à-vis an external currency, say the dollar,

Figure 11.2   Composition of the Ecu

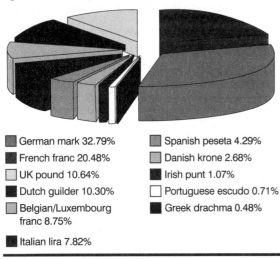

- German mark 32.79%
- French franc 20.48%
- UK pound 10.64%
- Dutch guilder 10.30%
- Belgian/Luxembourg franc 8.75%
- Italian lira 7.82%
- Spanish peseta 4.29%
- Danish krone 2.68%
- Irish punt 1.07%
- Portuguese escudo 0.71%
- Greek drachma 0.48%

one would need to add up the weighted values of the exchange rates of the individual EU currencies, vis-à-vis the dollar. On 25 October 1997, the Ecu was buying $1.11 and the pound was buying $1.64, so the Ecu was worth about 67p in sterling terms. (See Table 11.3.)

The exchange rate stability around currencies' par values was further safeguarded by the existence, within the EMS, of a divergence indicator, which reflects a currency's performance relative to the Ecu and is expressed as a percentage of the total possible movement against the Ecu given the ERM limits on cross-rates. When this indicator reaches plus or minus 75 per cent, a 'threshold of divergence' is reached and the central bank is expected to intervene to bring the currency back within safer values. If the exchange rate does reach the upper/lower limit of its range, the central bank is expected to intervene on the foreign exchange market by selling or buying domestic currency.

The role of the European Monetary Cooperation Fund (EMCF) was envisaged to be similar to that of the IMF pool of foreign currencies. Each member is given a quota into the EMCF, 20 per cent of which is to be paid in gold and the remainder in dollars, in exchange for Ecus. Over the years Ecus have become an important reserve asset and intervention currency. The total reserve pool of the EMCF was over $50bn in 1994.

Compared with the Bretton Woods system, the EMS was based on a system which allowed exchange rates some flexibility and where realignments were not discouraged. The system was not based on a key currency, which would provide an anchor, like the dollar had been for Bretton Woods because of its convertibility

with gold. No neutral European monetary authority was created to manage the system, as the IMF had been for Bretton Woods.

Performance of the EMS

After a period of frequent realignments in the early 1980s, the economic convergence of ERM members improved and realignments became less frequent. In June 1989 the then president of the European Commission, Jaques Delors, put forward a three-stage plan for the achievement of complete monetary union, with a single currency and a European Central Bank (ECB) by 1999. The plan was agreed by the EU members at Maastricht, Netherlands, in December 1991 and became known as the **Maastricht Treaty**. A discussion of the plan and its implication has been provided in Chapter 7.

After a period of relative stability in the 1980s, the exchange rate mechanism (ERM) suffered a severe blow in 1992 when in the wake of financial turmoil – partly caused by the abolition of capital controls in 1992, high German interest rates to contain inflationary pressures resulting from the cost of restructuring East Germany and a recession in Europe – the system came under the attack of speculation and the UK and Italy had to abandon the ERM. This allowed Italy and the UK to lower their interest rates and stimulate growth in their unemployment ridden economies. Within the next eight months, the Spanish peseta, the Irish pound and the Portuguese escudo all devalued.

The entire exchange rate mechanism finally collapsed on 2 August 1993, triggered by the Bundesbank's refusal to agree to a much needed (by the rest of the EU) and speculated about reduction in its discount rate. The markets responded with a huge sale of all the other EU currencies against the Deutschmark. No amount of intervention could stem the tide of speculation. It is estimated that about $100bn was spent on market intervention by all the EU central banks in an attempt to prop up the ERM; small change compared with the $1 trillion exchanged on a daily basis on foreign exchange markets (Salvatore 1995). The allowed band of exchange rate fluctuation for ERM members was subsequently broadened to ±15 per cent in August 1993, raising the question of whether the ERM can still be regarded as a system of 'fixed' exchange rates. (See Table 11.4.)

What went wrong? Was it wise, given these difficulties, to proceed further down the path of tighter monetary union with the introduction of a single currency and the EMU? To answer these questions, we need to discuss the following: the issues in the ERM controversy; the transition to EMU; the pros and cons of EMU.

Table 11.3   Central rates against the Ecu

National currency units per ECU

	BEF/LUF	DKK	DEM	GRD[1]	ESP	FRF	IEP	ITL[2]	NLG	ATS	PTE[3]	FIM[4]	GBP[4]
13.3.1979[5]	39.4582	7.08592	2.51064	–	–	5.79831	0.662638	1 148.18	2.72077	–	–	–	(0.663247)
24.9.1979	39.8456	7.36594	2.48557	–	–	5.85522	0.669141	1 159.42	2.74748	–	–	–	(0.649821)
30.11.1979	39.7897	7.72336	2.48208	–	–	5.84700	0.668201	1 157.79	2.74362	–	–	–	(0.648910)
23.3.1981	40.7985	7.91917	2.54502	–	–	5.99526	0.685145	1 262.92	2.81318	–	–	–	(0.542122)
5.10.1981	40.7572	7.91117	2.40989	–	–	6.17443	0.684452	1 300.67	2.66382	–	–	–	(0.601048)
22.2.1982	44.6963	8.18382	2.41815	–	–	6.19564	0.686799	1 305.13	2.67296	–	–	–	(0.557037)
14.6.1982	44.9704	8.23400	2.33379	–	–	6.61387	0.691011	1 350.27	2.57971	–	–	–	(0.560453)
21.3.1983	44.3662	8.04412	2.21515	–	–	6.79271	0.717050	1 386.78	2.49587	–	–	–	(0.629848)
18.5.1983	44.9008	8.14104	2.24184	–	–	6.87456	0.725690	1 403.49	2.52595	–	–	–	(0.587087)
17.9.1984[6]	44.9008	8.14104	2.24184	(87.4813)	–	6.87456	0.725690	1 403.49	2.52595	–	–	–	(0.585992)
22.7.1985	44.8320	8.12857	2.23840	(100.7190)	–	6.86402	0.724578	1 520.60	2.52208	–	–	–	(0.555312)
7.4.1986	43.6761	7.91896	2.13834	(135.6590)	–	6.96280	0.712956	1 496.21	2.40935	–	–	–	(0.630317)
4.8.1986	43.1139	7.81701	2.11083	(137.0490)	–	6.87316	0.764976	1 476.95	2.37833	–	–	–	(0.679256)
12.1.1987	42.4582	7.85212	2.05853	(150.7920)	–	6.90403	0.768411	1 483.58	2.31943	–	–	–	(0.739615)
19.6.1989[7]	42.4582	7.85212	2.05853	(150.7920)	133.804	6.90403	0.768411	1 483.58	2.31943	–	–	–	(0.739615)
21.9.1989[7]	42.4582	7.85212	2.05853	(150.7920)	133.804	6.90403	0.768411	1 483.58	2.31943	–	(172.085)	–	(0.728627)
8.1.1990[8]	42.1679	7.79845	2.04446	(187.9340)	132.889	6.85684	0.763159	1 529.70	2.30358	–	(177.743)	–	(0.728615)
8.10.1990[9]	42.4032	7.84195	2.05586	(205.3110)	133.631	6.89509	0.767417	1 538.24	2.31643	–	(178.735)	–	0.696904
14.9.1992	42.0639	7.77921	2.03942	(251.2020)	132.562	6.83992	0.761276	1 636.61	2.29789	–	177.305	–	0.691328
17.9.1992[10]	41.9547	7.75901	2.03412	(250.5500)	139.176	6.82216	0.759300	(1 632.36)	2.29193	–	176.844	–	(0.689533)
23.11.1992	40.6304	7.51410	1.96992	(254.2540)	143.386	6.60683	0.735334	(1 690.76)	2.21958	–	182.194	–	(0.805748)
1.2.1993	40.2802	7.44934	1.95294	(259.3060)	142.150	6.54988	0.809996	(1 796.22)	2.20045	–	180.624	–	(0.808431)
14.5.1993	40.2123	7.43679	1.94964	(264.5130)	154.250	6.53883	0.808628	(1 793.19)	2.19672	–	192.854	–	(0.786749)
9.1.1995	40.2123	7.43679	1.94964	(264.5130)	154.250	6.53883	0.808628	(1 793.19)	2.19672	13.7167	192.854	–	(0.786749)
6.3.1995	39.3960	7.28580	1.91007	(292.8670)	162.493	6.40608	0.792214	(2 106.15)	2.15214	13.4383	195.792	–	(0.786652)
14.10.1996	39.3960	7.28580	1.91007	(292.8670)	162.493	6.40608	0.792214	(2 106.15)	2.15214	13.4383	195.792	5.80661	(0.786652)
25/11/1996	39.7191	7.34555	1.92573	(295.2690)	163.826	6.45863	0.798709	1 906.48	2.16979	13.5485	197.398	5.85424	(0.793103)

Source: The European Economy 1997

1 Notional central rates.
2 Temporary notional central rates from 17 September 1992.
3 Notional central rates until escudo entry into the exchange rate mechanism (ERM) on 6 April 1992.
4 Notional central rates until 8 October 1990 (sterling entry into ERM) and as from 17 September 1992 (suspension of sterling participation in the ERM).
5 Initial parities at the start of the European Monetary System (EMS).
6 Revised composition of the Ecu and inclusion of the drachma.
7 Revised composition of the Ecu and inclusion of the peseta and the escudo. The central rate of the peseta was fixed on 19 June 1989 when it entered the ERM.
8 Accompanied by a narrowing of the Italian lira fluctuation band from 6 to 2.25%.
9 Sterling entry into the ERM with a fluctuation margin of 6%.
10 Accompanied by a suspension of their participation in the ERM by sterling and the Italian lira.

Table 11.4 Bilateral central rates and intervention limits in force since 25 November 1996

	Percentage margin	100 BEF/LUX	100 DKK	100 DEM	100 ESP	100 FRF	1 IEP	1 000 ITL	100 NLG	100 ATS	100 PTE	100 FIM
Brussels	+16.1187	100	627.8800	2 395.2000	8.152500	714.0300	57.74450	24.192000	2 125.6000	340.42000	23.364500	787.8300
in BEF	Central rate	100	540.7230	2 062.5500	24.244700	614.9770	49.72890	20.833700	1 830.5400	293.16300	20.121400	678.4680
	−13.8813	100	465.6650	1 776.2000	20.879500	529.6600	42.82600	17.941700	1 576.4500	252.47000	17.328500	584.2900
Copenhagen	+16.1187	21.47470	100	442.9680	5.206400	132.0660	10.67920	4.474000	393.1050	62.95610	4.321000	145.6990
in DKK	Central rate	18.49380	100	381.4430	4.483760	113.7320	9.19676	3.852940	338.5370	54.21700	3.721190	125.4740
	−13.8813	15.92660	10	328.4510	4.861400	97.9430	7.92014	3.318100	291.5440	46.59100	3.204600	108.0570
Frankfurt	+16.1187	5.63000	30.4450	100	1.365000	34.6250	2.80000	1.172900	103.0580	16.50500	1.132800	38.1970
in DEM	Central rate*	4.84837	26.2162	100	1.175480	29.8164	2.41105	1.010100	88.7526	14.21360	0.975560	32.8948
	−13.8813	4.17500	22.5750	100	1.012300	25.6750	2.07600	0.869900	76.4326	12.24100	0.840100	28.3280
Madrid	+16.1187	478.94400	2 589.8800	9 878.5000	100	2 945.4000	238.17500	99.78000	8 767.3000	1 404.10000	96.367000	3 249.5000
in ESP	Central rate	412.46100	2 230.2700	8 507.1800	100	2 536.5400	205.11300	85.931100	7 550.3000	1 209.18000	82.992700	2 798.4100
	−13.8813	355.20600	1 920.7000	7 326.0000	100	2 184.4000	176.64100	74.000000	6 502.2000	1 041.3000	71.469000	2 410.0000
Paris	+16.1187	18.88000	102.10000	389.4800	4.577800	100	9.38950	3.933790	345.6500	55.35450	3.799200	128.1070
in FRF	Central rate	16.26080	87.92570	335.3860	3.942370	100	8.08631	3.387730	297.6610	47.67060	3.271880	110.3240
	−13.8813	14.00500	75.72000	288.8100	3.395100	100	6.96400	2.917500	256.3500	41.05330	2.817700	95.0096
Dublin	+16.1187	2.33503	12.62610	48.1696	0.566120	14.3599	1	0.486472	42.7439	6.84544	0.469841	15.8424
in IEP	Central rate	2.01090	10.87340	41.4757	0.487537	12.3666	1	0.418944	36.8105	5.89521	0.404620	13.6433
	−13.8813	1.73176	9.36403	35.7143	0.419859	10.6500	1	0.360789	31.7007	5.07688	0.348453	11.7494
Rome	+16.1187	5 573.60000	30 138.00000	1 14 956.0000	1 351.000000	34 276.0000	2 771.70000	1 000	102 027.0000	16 339.00000	1 121.500000	37 816.0000
in ITL	Central rate	4 799.91000	25 954.20000	99 000.4000	1 163.720000	29 518.3000	2 386.95000	1000	87 864.7000	14 071.50000	965.805000	32 565.8000
	−13.8813	4 133.60000	25 351.00000	85 259.0000	1 002.200000	25 421.0000	2 055.61000	1000	75 668.0000	12 118.00000	831.700000	28 045.0000
Amsterdam	+16.1187	6.34340	34.30020	130.8340	1.537930	39.0091	3.15450	1.321560	100	18.59630	1.276370	43.0378
in NLG	Central rate	5.46286	29.53890	112.6730	1.324450	33.5953	2.71662	1.138110	100	16.01490	1.099200	37.0636
	−13.8813	4.70454	25.43850	97.0325	1.140600	28.9381	2.33952	0.980132	100	13.79180	0.946611	31.9187
Vienna	+16.1187	39.60890	214.17400	816.9270	9.603380	243.5860	19.69710	8.252190	725.0650	100	7.970000	268.7350
in ATS	Central rate	34.11070	184.44400	703.5500	8.270080	209.7730	16.96290	7.106550	624.4170	100	6.863560	231.4310
	−13.8813	29.37570	158.84100	605.8770	7.122000	180.6540	14.60820	6.120320	537.740	100	5.910860	199.3050
Lisbon	+16.1187	577.09000	3 120.50000	11 903.3000	139.920000	3 549.0000	286.98300	120.240000	10 564.0000	1 691.80000	100	3 915.4000
In PTE	Central rate	496.98400	2 687.31000	10 250.5000	120.493000	3 056.3500	247.14500	103.541000	9 097.5500	1 456.97000	100	3 371.8000
	−13.8813	428.00000	2 314.30000	8 827.7000	103.770000	2 632.1000	212.83800	89.170000	7 834.7000	1 254.70000	100	2 903.8000
Helsinki	+16.1187	17.11480	92.54380	353.0080	4.149380	105.2530	8.511070	3.56570	313.2950	50.17440	3.443760	100
in FIM	Central rate	14.73910	79.69760	304.0000	3.573450	90.6422	7.329600	3.07071	269.8060	43.20940	2.965700	100
	−13.8813	12.69310	68.63470	261.8010	3.077400	78.0597	6.312170	2.64438	232.3530	37.21140	2.554020	100

Source: European Economy. 1997

Note: The Greek drachma (Dr) and the Swedish krona (Skr) do not participate in the exchange rate mechanism (ERM). Italian lira (ITL) intervention limits temporarily not applicable and sterling participation (GBP) in the ERM suspended, as from 17 September 1992. Their notional central rates are Dr 292.867, L2 106.15 and GBP 0.786652 respectively for Ecu1.

Reasons for the ERM crisis

Four main reasons can be put forward to explain the ERM crisis of 1992–3:

1 The existence of divergent political and economic needs. High interest rates were needed in Germany to reduce inflationary pressures. Low interest rates were needed in the UK and Italy to counteract the onsetting of recessionary forces, causing the need for realignment of the pound and the lira. This was nothing more than a periodic realignment of currencies, some argue, caused by changing economic circumstances, and not a major failing of the system.

2 The existence of a fundamental deficiency in the rules for adjustment within EMS, once *convergence* became a criteria for joining the EMU after the Maastricht Treaty was signed. While previously central banks could decide to realign their currencies to adjust for different inflation rates and economic conditions, after 1991 they lost that freedom. Because of the Maastricht convergence criteria, the binding inflation rate was Germany's. But why Germany's? In this new situation, created by the signing of the Maastricht Treaty and the endorsement of convergence, there was a clear transfer of monetary independence away from individual EMU members toward Frankfurt. This proved unacceptable to some members, notably the UK.

3 The lifting of capital controls in 1992 and the total liberalization of capital movements within the EU. The evidence to support this thesis, however, is rather mixed as the 'crisis' situation was mostly determined by the actions of the central banks. Undoubtedly the increased size of hot money flows has reduced the monetary authorities' control over markets, but this could not be held responsible for economic and political divergence among members.

4 Poor macroeconomic performance of the EU economies, in particular the high rate of unemployment. This can be taken as an indication of the existence of an unhealthy deflationary bias within the EU.

Some of these failures were operational. The EMS failed to eliminate currency fluctuations. After a period of relative stability in the 1980s, the grid of exchange rate parities suddenly exploded. The EMS also failed, however, as a method of international cooperation, intended to bring about faster growth, lower inflation and lower unemployment.

If we compare the performance of these economic indicators (growth, inflation and unemployment) during the 1980s and in 1992, before the virtual collapse of the system, with those of the USA and Japan, we see that the EU does not fare well. In 1992, as during the preceding decade, the EU inflation rate of 4.8 per cent was on average higher that of the USA (2.5) or Japan (2.2). During the 1980s, real GDP growth had been lower (2.2 per cent compared with 2.6 per cent in the USA and 4.1 per cent in Japan). Finally, unemployment had been higher in the 1980s and remained higher in 1992 (9.8 per cent), compared with 7.6 per cent in the USA and 2.3 per cent in Japan.

This is a poor record of performance. The optimists argue that closer monetary integration will improve the performance of the EU economies. The sceptics point at the EMU deflationary bias, caused in their view by the dominant role of the DM, which has left the German Bundesbank setting interest rates for the whole union largely on German domestic criteria.

Transition to EMU

The issues in the ERM controversy point to one fundamental weakness of the EMS – the attempt to keep exchange rates within narrowly defined limits without constraining members' ability to pursue independent monetary and fiscal policies. In this light, the EMU, which denies members the use of monetary tools altogether and indirectly constrains the use of fiscal tools as well, seems to be the logical step forward. The EMU appears to be a step in the right direction if genuine monetary union is the EU's main goal. But should it be? This is what we finally need to discuss.

Pros and cons of EMU

EMU is partly a response to the flaws of the earlier EMS, which sought monetary stability and exchange rate convergence through autonomous and discretionary cooperation between central banks. The EMU removes the discretionary elements and fundamentally binds monetary policy. It involves pooled, as opposed to independent, monetary policy. This helps to explain why the EMU is still on the agenda, despite the ERM crisis. Arguments in favour of the EMU can be identified as follows:

- ease of transactions across the EU, which are cost effective, saving money and time;
- simplified cash management for business;
- the EMU totally eliminates the possibility of exchange rate variation within the euro zone, which could also be seen as a cost, as exchange rate changes help to achieve internal balance;
- control of inflation through the European Central Bank which will be of greater benefit to inflation prone countries like Italy, the UK, Portugal and Spain;
- lower inflation will also mean lower interest rates and higher growth;

- greater control of government borrowing, imposed by the convergence criteria.

Arguments against the EMU include:

- loss of monetary policy as an independent tool for dealing with economic cycles;
- reduced ability to respond to asymmetric economic shocks;
- loss of fiscal policy tool;
- lack of political accountability.

Summing up, the EMU is intended to eliminate exchange rate uncertainty and bring low inflation and economic stability to its members. However, the institutional framework of EMU shows serious weaknesses that could lead to more instability than before. Furthermore, while greater certainty in exchange rates may be achieved within the Euro zone, this could be at the expense of more uncertainty vis-à-vis other currencies such as the yen and the dollar.

THE PRESENT SYSTEM

Since the collapse of the Bretton Woods system in March 1973, the world has had a **managed floating exchange rate system**. Under this system, governments' monetary authorities are expected to intervene in foreign exchange markets to smooth out temporary fluctuations in exchange rates, without attempting to affect long-run trends.

By 1994, more than half of the 178 IMF members had adopted some form of exchange rate flexibility, including all the major industrial nations and many large developing nations. About four-fifths of total world trade is now moved between nations which manage their exchange rates, either independently or as a group, such as the EU. Most of the remaining 76 nations have pegged their currencies to the US dollar (20 countries), the French franc (14 countries), the Russian rouble (5 countries) or other currency composite (IMF 1994).

Under the present managed float, countries still need to hold international reserves in order to intervene in foreign exchange markets to smooth out temporary fluctuations in the exchange rates. At present, as Table 11.5 shows, such interventions are made mostly in dollars, followed by the Deutschmark, the yen and sterling.

✍ Activity 11.9

Study Table 11.5 and explain what it shows.

✓ Answer 11.9

Table 11.5 gives the total volume of foreign exchange transactions per currency in 1989 and 1992, in absolute terms and in percentages. The table shows that the dollar has remained by far the most important currency for foreign exchange transactions. If we compare the 1992 figures with those for 1989 we see, however, that the importance of the dollar as international currency has declined by 7 per cent over the period, while the share of the Deutschmark has increased by 11 per cent over the same period. The Deutschmark has now become the second most important currency, at the expense of the dollar and, to a lesser extent, the yen.

Since 1974 the IMF has measured all reserves and other official transactions in terms of SDRs instead of US dollars. When SDRs were first introduced in 1970, one SDR was valued at $1. One SDR is now worth

Table 11.5 Gross daily turnover on foreign exchange markets in a number of selected currencies ($bn %)

| Currency | April 1989 | | April 1992 | | Change |
	Daily volume	Share %	Daily volume	Share %	
US dollar	838	90	1114	83	−7
Deutschmark	247	27	544	38	11
Yen	253	27	313	24	−3
Sterling	138	15	185	14	−1
Swiss franc	n/a	n/a	116	9	n/a
French franc	n/a	n/a	51	4	n/a
Canadian dollar	n/a	n/a	44	3	n/a
Ecu	8	1	40	3	2
Australian dollar	n/a	n/a	32	2	n/a
Remainder	380	40	269	19	−21
Total	1864	200	2707	200	0

Source: Bank for International Settlements, 1993

$1.3736. To stabilize the value of the SDR, as a result of successive devaluations of the dollar, the value of one SDR has been made equal to the weighted average of a basket of five major currencies, as follows:

- 40 per cent of the value of the dollar;
- 21 per cent of the value of the Deutschmark;
- 17 per cent of the value of the Japanese yen;
- 5.5 per cent of the value of British sterling;
- 5.5 per cent of the value of the French franc.

The IMF is still in operation, having undergone substantial changes:

Quotas of member countries have been increased several times. The Fund resources totalled $205bn in 1994. Member countries can now borrow from the fund up to 150 per cent of their individual quota in any single year and 450 per cent in the next three years, with an overall limit of 600 per cent of the original quota.

- Borrowing facilities have been extended and made more flexible. In 1993 the **Systemic Transformation Facility (STF)** was set up to grant financial assistance to Russia, former soviet republics and other eastern European economies in transition.
- IMF loans are now specified in terms of SDRs.

The Fund has recently added to its main monitoring function of world monetary conditions the responsibility of providing members with financial help to overcome their structural problems.

Total fund credit outstanding was about $11bn in 1980 and is now about $40mn. During the second part of the 1980s in particular, due to the growing international debt problems of many developing countries, particularly some large countries in Latin America, the IMF has been involved in rescue operations and debt rescheduling. It became the target of intense criticism, particularly from developing countries, for the social insensitivity of its monetary management. The fund often attached the implementation of severe fiscal austerity programmes by the governments of developing countries as a qualifying condition for a loan. The stringency of such requests relaxed slightly in the latter part of the 1990s.

A heated debate still continues on the advantages or disadvantages of the current system of managed floating. The evidence from a selection of world economies and comparisons of performance over time remains fundamentally inconclusive.

CASE STUDY: THE UK AND THE EMU – TO JOIN OR NOT TO JOIN

Given the existence of a deflationary bias in the working of the international economy, arising from the fact that the world financial community tends to validate deflationary policies and discourage expansionary ones, does de-linking or indeed coordinating macroeconomic policies really make a difference to a country's economic performance? Should the UK join the EMU or not? Would it make a real difference if it did?

To answer this question we examine the UK economic outlook in 1998 and 1999 in the light of the fact that the UK is not joining in 1999, and reflect on possible implications of future membership (On this, see in particular, Foley and Williams, 1997).

The outlook of the UK economy 1999–2000

The UK remained outside the initial EMU group of 11 countries comprising Germany, France, Italy, Netherlands, Luxembourg, Belgium, Austria, Ireland, Finland, Spain and Portugal. By staying outside, the UK economy is possibly less influenced by international events than if it were to enter. It is still, however, affected by the changes in European interest rates, which may result from the EMU or by the upsurge in continental European business investment, which again may follow decisions on membership.

As a result of tighter monetary policies and higher interest rates in 1997, the pound became stronger in 1997. This fed through into slower export and manufacturing growth. Overall growth in 1997 showed signs of a slow-down which became more evident in 1998, as the windfall gain effect on consumption, caused by building societies converting to plc status shares offers, waned. Consumption growth fell to 2.8 per cent in 1998. Given that consumer spending accounts for roughly 70 per cent of GDP, this resulted in a fall in GDP growth of over 1.5 per cent between 1997 and 1998. GDP growth rate fell from 3.5 in 1997 to 2.25 in 1998; it is forecasted to fall further to between 1 and 1.5 per cent in 1999, to pick up slightly in the year 2000 (between 1.8–2.5 per cent).

The continuing impact of recessions in Asia and sluggishness of European growth caused a disappointing growth in export volumes of 2.75 per cent in 1998, which is forecasted to fall to between 0.25 and 0.75 in 1999, only to pick up again in the year 2000 (4.5–5 per cent). The deficit of the current account of the balance of payments, £2.25 billion in 1998, is forecasted to grow bigger in 1999 (–£10bn) and 2000 (–£10.5bn). Inflationary pressures on the other hand remain modest, around 2.5 per cent and unemployment seems to have stabilized around 5 per cent. Slower growth rate and a steady inflation rate are likely to point towards lower interest rates. Current and forecast values of the main indicators for the UK economy are shown in Table 11.6. The analysis of these data suggest that the UK economy's cyclical position, hedging on the verge of recession in 1999, is now more synchronized with the rest of the EU economies

Should the UK enter the EMU?

Financial markets have left the government in no doubt as to its answer to this question. In September 1997 rumours of a possible early entry after the 1999 launch prompted a strong, positive reaction: sterling dropped four pfennigs to DM2.83, the equity market jumped 161 points and the spread between UK and German ten-year bonds fell below 1 per cent. Later suggestions that entry is unlikely prompted a strong reaction in the opposite direction. Financial markets think that a move to join the EMU would cause:

- long-term interest rate convergence;
- an entry rate lower than the current exchange rate, perhaps around DM2.50–2.60;
- a more favourable business environment for UK plcs.

continued overleaf

THE UK AND THE EMU – TO JOIN OR NOT TO JOIN

Table 11.6 Outlook for the UK economy, 1999–2000

Percentage change	1998	Forecast for 1999	Treasury forecast for 2000	Independent forecast for 2000
Economic growth (Gross Domestic Product)	2.25	1 to 1.5	2.25 to 2.75	1.8
Spending by consumers	2.75	2 to 2.5	2.5 to 3	1.9
Govt and Local Authority spending	1.5	3	2.25	2.4
Investment (public and private)	8	2 to 2.5	2.75 to 3.25	1.3
Stockbuilding (% of GDP)	0.25	–0.25	–0.25 to 0	1.2
Exports	2.75	0.25 to 0.75	4.5 to 5	3.7
Imports	7.75	3.75 to 4.25	4.5 to 5	3.7
Balance of Payments (current account, £bn)	–2.25	–10	–10.5	–6.8
RPI (4th quarter, excluding mortgage interest)	2.5	2.5	2.5	2.1
Money GDP (total value of economy, £bn)	848	880 to 885	925 to 936	–
PSBN (excess of spending over revenue, £bn)	9.1	3	3	9.1

Source: HMSO, FSBR, March 1999

In 1998 analysts argued the real obstacles to entry were not the meeting of the convergence criteria, which can be attained, but rather:

■ the lack of convergence of the UK business cycle with the rest of the EU. The advanced state of the UK recovery compared with the rest of Europe would make entry disastrous. The reduction in UK short-term interest rates which would result from aligning with German rates would be incompatible with the monetary tightness necessary in Britain to control domestic spending and inflation.
■ lack of evidence of EU policy moves designed to create a more flexible labour market;
■ lack of evidence of EU policy moves designed to solve the impending public pension crises.

In response to the economic cycle argument, however, one can point to the fact that:

■ according to the UK economy forecast discussed above, the UK econ-omy is now bordering on a recession and is no longer in an advanced state of recovery; interest rates have been coming down in line with European rates, to avoid a damaging appreciation of the exchange rate, despite the fact that Britain is 'out';
■ euro rates will be determined by the European Central Bank (ECB) with reference to the economic situation of all participating countries and not just Germany;
■ European recovery will require higher rates in the majority of those countries.

This situation is illustrated in Figure 11.3, where the shaded area represents the range of rates of the initial EMU members in recent years, and forecasts up to the end of 2001.

In conclusion, recent research suggests that the cyclical imbalance between the UK and Germany or other EU members has narrowed and is not an impediment to entry. With other economic arguments supporting entry, the decision on balance becomes largely a political one.

Figure 11.3 European short-term interest rates

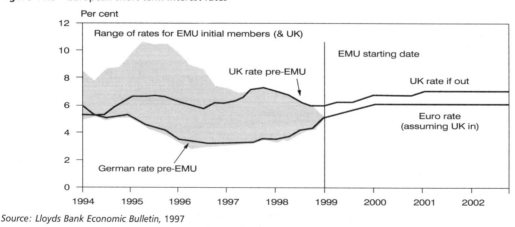

Source: Lloyds Bank Economic Bulletin, 1997

☆ **For revision of this chapter, see the Chapter Summaries at the end of the book, starting on page 411.**

12 International trade, protectionism and the European Union

Objectives

After studying this chapter you will be able to explain:
- the economic basis for international trade;
- the concepts of absolute and comparative advantage;
- what determines a country's comparative advantage;
- the case for free trade and protectionism;
- contemporary theories of trade;
- the effect of trade barriers such as tariffs, quotas and export subsidies;
- the trade effects of customs unions;
- the origin and operation of the European Union.

Since the war, world trade has grown faster than world output and both have grown at sustained rates until the 1990s. How does economic theory explain this? If the argument used to justify this process is that trade is beneficial to the world economy, why then do countries still protect their markets from the influence of external trade through various forms of trade barriers? These are the questions we now set out to answer. What we need to explain is:

- how it can be argued that international trade is potentially beneficial to all participating countries;
- what are the arguments in favour of trade liberalization;
- what are the arguments in favour of trade protectionism;
- which economic arguments can be made in favour of partial forms of free trade such as the European Union.

REASONS FOR TRADE

Countries engage in international trade fundamentally for three reasons:

1 To obtain from other countries those goods that they cannot produce at all or as efficiently as other countries.
2 To expand into larger markets in order to achieve economies of scale in production.
3 To affect other economies' markets, with a view to removing international competition in order to expand production further.

The current pattern of international trade, which we analyse in Chapter 13, reflects the interaction of all these motives.

Specialization

One of the most obvious reasons for international trade is provided by the fact that countries cannot produce all the goods they need, or cannot produce them as efficiently as other countries. Hence, it pays a country to specialize in the production of some goods only. Specialization is undoubtedly one of the bases for trade: countries specialize in the production of certain goods, producing more than they need and exporting the surplus product which is not domestically consumed. Revenues earned from exports are then used to import goods which are not produced at home, or not produced in sufficient amounts.

When a country exports more than it imports, it has a **trade surplus**. When the opposite is the case and the country imports more than it exports, it has a **trade deficit**. In which goods should a country specialize in?

The theory of comparative advantage

David Ricardo, the nineteenth-century economist who laid the foundations of modern trade theory in his famous work *Principles of Political Economy and Taxation*, published in 1818, answered that question with his **theory of comparative advantage**. According to Ricardo, countries gain from specialization by producing those goods in which they have a **comparative advantage**. The subtlety of Ricardo's theory rests in his proof that specialization and free trade can potentially benefit all trading partners, even those who may be absolutely less efficient than others at producing a good.

To explain Ricardo's law of comparative advantage we need to introduce two important concepts: the concept of absolute advantage and the concept of comparative advantage.

To produce any good, firms need to use the economy's resources, its factors of production. The main **factors of production** are : land, labour and capital. Countries have different **endowments** of factors of production, as they differ in:

■ population density;
■ labour skills;
■ climatic conditions;
■ land fertility;
■ availability of raw materials;
■ availability of capital.

These differences in the endowments of factors of production are likely to persist over time as long as factors of production are relatively immobile. For these reasons, the relative costs of producing goods will vary from country to country.

A country is said to have an **absolute advantage** over another in the production of a good, if it can produce it with less resources. Suppose there are two countries, A and B, both producing wheat and cloth. Suppose that the weather conditions in country A are more suitable for growing wheat than in country B, and suppose also that A's labour force is more productive than B's in cloth making. In this situation we say that country A has an advantage, with respect to country B, in the production of both goods. It can produce more of both with the same amount of resources as B.

A country is said to have a **comparative advantage** over another country in the production of a good if it

can produce it at a lower opportunity cost, that is, if it has to forgo less of the other goods in order to produce it.

The **opportunity cost** of a good is the value of the forgone alternative. Given one's limited budget, the opportunity cost of a packet of biscuits is the box of chocolates which could have been bought instead (**opportunity cost in consumption**). Given the economy's limited resources of steel, for example, the opportunity cost of producing guns is the amount of washing machines and cars which could have been produced instead (**opportunity cost in production**).

Let's assume once more that there are two countries, A and B, both producing wheat and cloth. Let's further suppose that A has an absolute advantage in the production of both goods. Should country A not trade at all and simply produce everything domestically? Ricardo's answer was 'no': even countries which have an absolute advantage can benefit from trade, provided the **exchange ratios** at which the two goods are exchanged for one another in the two countries are different. Exchange ratios will reflect the opportunity costs of the two goods in the two countries. Suppose country A has to give up two units of wheat in order to be able to produce one extra unit of cloth, while country B has to give up two units of cloth to produce one unit of wheat. In this case the opportunity cost of producing wheat at the expense of corn is different in the two countries. Their exchange ratios will differ too. According to Ricardo's law of comparative advantage, both could gain from specializing in the production of the good in which they have a comparative advantage.

The concepts of opportunity cost and of absolute and comparative advantage can be better understood with reference to the concept of a **production possibility frontier** or production possibility curve.

Let's go back to the example of two countries, A and B, each producing wheat and cloth. As we have said before, the production of any good requires the combined use of three factors of production: land, labour and capital, the quantity of which is fixed in an economy, at least in the short run. Let's assume that people in both countries have similar preferences with respect to food and cloth, and that the two populations wish to consume both goods. Let's also assume that, for equal amounts of capital and land used, the yield per unit of labour is different in the two countries. One unit of labour yields 2 kg of wheat and 1 kg of cotton for clothing in country A; while one acre of land yields 8 kg of wheat and 16 kg of cotton for country B, as shown in Table 12.1.

Table 12.1   Yield per acre of wheat and cotton

	Country A	Country B
Wheat	2	8
Cotton	1	16

As we can see, country B has an absolute advantage in the production of both goods, as it can produce both with less resources per unit of output than country A. Should country B trade at all with country A? Would country B gain at all? Ricardo's theory of comparative advantage shows that even in this case it is advantageous for country B to specialize in the production of the good in which it has a comparative advantage and trade the surplus amount, which is not consumed domestically. To prove this we need to show two points:

- that the opportunity cost of producing the two goods differs in the two countries;
- that each country can gain from specializing in the production of the good in which it has comparative advantage and trading its surplus amount, assuming certain trade conditions apply.

From Table 12.1 we can see that the opportunity costs for the production of wheat and cotton in the two countries are different. If country A wanted to produce more cotton, it would have to forgo two units of wheat to produce one extra unit of cotton. If country B wanted to do the same, it would have to give up half a unit of wheat to produce one extra unit of cotton. The opportunity cost ratios in the two countries are 2:1 in country A and 1:2 in country B. Country B has a comparative advantage in the production of cotton with respect to country A. The opportunity cost of producing one extra unit of cotton in country B is half a unit of wheat, while it is two units of wheat in country A. The opportunity cost of producing one extra unit of cotton in country A is four times the opportunity cost of producing one extra unit in country B.

✍ Activity 12.1

Compare the opportunity cost of producing one extra unit of wheat in the two countries.

Table 12.2   Opportunity cost ratios

	Country A	Country B
Wheat	2	1
Cotton	1	2

✔ Answer 12.1

The opportunity cost of producing one extra unit of wheat is four times greater in country B than in country A. Country A has to give up half a unit of cotton to produce one extra unit of wheat, while country B has to give up two units of cotton to produce one extra unit of wheat. Country A has a comparative advantage in the production of wheat.

Under the assumption of **constant opportunity costs,** that is, if we assume that the opportunity cost of producing the two goods remain constant, regardless of how much of one good relative to the other one country produces, then we can show the production possibilities frontiers for the two countries A and B. The **production possibility frontier** shows the combined quantities of the two goods each country can produce, given its factors of production and the opportunity cost of the two goods.

Let's look at the production possibility frontier for country A first. Given its factors of production, country A could produce a maximum of 200 units of wheat, if all its resources were used entirely for the production of wheat. In this case, however, the production of cotton would be zero and people in country A would have to go without clothes. Alternatively country A could use all its resources for the production of cotton: in that case it could produce 100 units of cotton, but zero wheat. People in country A would be clothed, but would die of starvation. Alternatively country A, allocating resources to the production of both goods, could produce alternative combinations of the two goods. Let's assume that country A chooses to produce 100 units of wheat and 50 units of cotton, at point *a* of the production possibility frontier for country A, shown in Figure 12.1.

We can now apply the same reasoning to country B. If country B were to use all its resources for the production of wheat, it would produce 800 units of wheat but zero cotton (hence no clothes). If it were to use all its resources for the production of cotton, it would produce 1600 units of cotton, but no wheat. Alternatively, it could choose to allocate its resources to the production of both goods and the production possibility frontier shows us all the possible outcomes in terms of production, given that country B's opportunity cost of cotton in terms of wheat is 1:2. Let's assume that country B chooses to produce 400 units of wheat and 800 units of cotton and is at point *b* on its production possibility frontier, as shown in Figure 12.2.

So far we have not introduced trade between the two countries. Each country produces a combination of the two goods and consumes what is produced

Figure 12.1 Country A's production possibility frontier

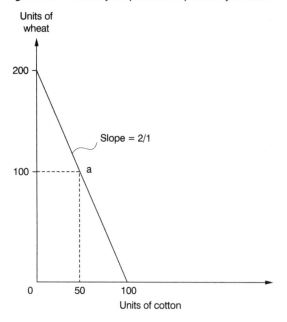

Note: The slope of the production possibility frontier (PPF) is given by the relative opportunity costs of the two goods (ratio of 2:1). The PPF is shown as a straight line as we have assumed that opportunity costs are constant.

Figure 12.2 Country B's production possibility frontier

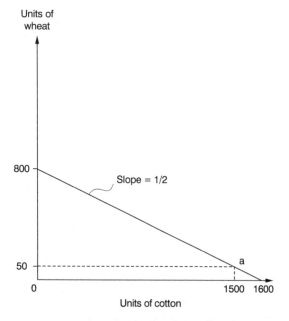

Note: The slope of the production possibility frontier (PPF) is given by the relative opportunity costs of the two goods (ratio of 1:2). The PPF is shown as a straight line as we have assumed that opportunity costs are constant.

domestically. At this point we have to make some assumptions about the prices at which the two goods exchange for one another in the two respective domestic markets. We shall assume that the price ratios of the two goods reflect the opportunity costs of producing them.

So let's assume that in country A the price of one unit of wheat is half the price of one unit of cotton, and vice versa, the price of one unit of cotton is twice the price of wheat. The price ratio of the two goods in country A is 1:2, which is the reciprocal of the exchange ratio. In country B the price of one unit of wheat is twice the price of one unit of cotton, and vice versa, the price of one unit of cotton is half the price of wheat. The price ratio of the two goods in country B is 2:1, which is the reciprocal of exchange ratio.

🖾 Activity 12.2

What can you say about the relative prices of the two goods in country A and country B, before the two countries open up to trade with one another?

✓ Answer 12.2

The relative prices of the two goods in the two countries are different. While one unit of wheat costs half as much as one unit of cotton in country A, it costs twice as much in country B. Wheat is more expensive in country B than in country A. Equally, one unit of cotton in country A costs twice as much as one unit of wheat, while in country B it costs half as much as one unit of wheat. So cotton is more expensive in country A than in country B.

This reflection allows us to draw the following conclusion: provided the international trade prices at which country A and country B trade the two goods with one another are somewhere in the region of the domestic price ratios for the two goods, which were 1:2 for country A and 2:1 for country B, then both countries would gain from specializing in the production of the good in which they have a comparative advantage in production, selling the surplus production to the other country.

If we assume that the international trade price ratio is 1:1, that is one unit of wheat exchanges for one unit of cotton, then specialization will allow greater consumption of goods for both countries. Both countries will be better off as a result of specialization and international trade.

Country A's production possibility frontier is shown in Figure 12.3. Country A's pre-trade position is at *a*, where 100 units of wheat and 50 units of cotton are produced. It must be noted that, in the absence of

Figure 12.3 Country A's production and consumption possibility frontiers after trade

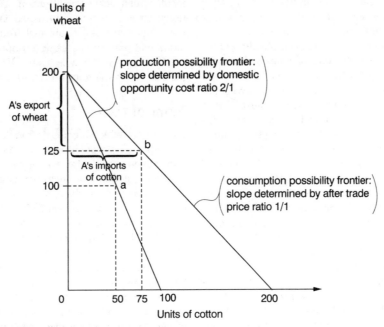

Note: Before Country A opens up to trade, people can only consume what is produced domestically. The consumption possibility frontier is the same as the production possibility frontier. Point *a* shows the combination of the two goods the country produces and consumes (100 units of wheat and 50 units of cotton). After A starts trading with B, the consumption possibility frontier is different from the production possibility frontier. A only produces wheat, in excess of what is domestically consumed. The surplus is exported to B in exchange for cotton. Despite the fact that only wheat is produced in A after trade has started, people in A can consume both goods in greater amounts than before. Point *b* shows a combination of goods which could be consumed after trade has started: 125 units of wheat and 75 units of cotton.

international trade, a country's consumption possibility frontier (that is what the people in that country can consume) coincides with the country's production possibility frontier, that is what the country can produce. So, point *a* also shows the consumption combination possibility chosen by country A. Before trade with country B opens up, country A produces and consumes at *a*, 100 units of wheat and 50 units of cotton. One unit of wheat costs half the price of one unit of cotton. So, in country A, before trade begins, one unit of cotton costs, say £1, while one unit of wheat is 50p.

Now trade with country B opens up, as country A can specialize in the production of wheat, in which it has a comparative advantage, and sell it to country B at a higher price, as we have assumed that the international wheat and cotton price ratio is 1:1. So one unit of wheat would exchange internationally for one unit of cotton. If country A were to specialize in the production of wheat and produce no cotton, it could exchange 200 units of wheat for 200 units of cotton. Its consumption possibility frontier would be different from

its production possibility frontier, allowing country A to consume more of both goods than before. Let's assume country A chooses to consume at point *b*, 125 units of wheat and 75 units of cotton: that is 25 units of wheat more than before and 25 units of cotton more than before. How can country A achieve that? It can achieve it through specialization and trade.

If country A specializes in the production of wheat, it can produce 200 units. It can keep 125 units for the domestic market and sell the remaining 75 units to country B in exchange for 75 units of cotton (remember wheat and cotton trade internationally 1:1). In this way, country A exports 75 units of wheat and imports 75 units of cotton and can consume, as a result, more wheat and cotton than before. This situation is shown in Figure 12.3.

The same analysis can be applied to country B, which chooses to specialize in the production of cotton in which it has a comparative advantage. Again, for country B, before trade commences, domestic consumption is constrained by domestic production. 'Let's assume that people in country B produce and consume at *a*, 400 units of wheat and 800 units of cotton. After trade is opened and wheat and cotton are exchanged at 1:1, B could specialize in the production of cotton (1600 units), consume 1000 units domestically, export 600 units and import 600 units of wheat, shown by point *b* of Fig. 12.4(a). After trade, people in B can consume more of both goods. However, in a two country case, for trade equilibrium to exist, it must be that what one country exports is equal to what the other country imports. If country A wishes to export 75 units of wheat, for equilibrium to exist, country B must import 75 units of wheat in exchange for 75 units of cotton, as shown by point *b* of Fig. 12.4(b).' A appears to 'gain more' from trade because of the relative size of the two economies: A is small with respect to B and exports a larger proportion of its domestic product (37.5 per cent as opposed to 4.6 per cent). *Both* countries nonetheless gain from trade, as they both consume more than they did before trade.

'World' production and consumption have increased as a result of trade. Before trade, world production (in a two country world, the combined production of A and B) was 150 units of wheat and 1550 units of cotton. After trade, A and B combined production is 200 units

of wheat and 1600 units of cotton. This is a powerful result which needs qualification. To say that international trade is *potentially* beneficial to *all* participating countries is not equivalent to say that all participants will gain in the same proportion, or that there may not be losers. The gains will be determined by the ratio at which the goods are traded internationally.

Terms of trade

The ratio at which a country trades domestic products for imported products is called the **terms of trade**. The existence of a difference in the opportunity cost of producing goods is a necessary condition for international trade to take place, but it is not a sufficient condition for a country to benefit from trade. How much a country benefits from trade is determined by its terms of trade. These determine how the gains from trade are distributed between trading partners. In our example, we assumed that the agreed upon terms of trade between the two countries were 1:1, that is one unit of wheat exchanged internationally for one unit of cotton. In this case both countries gained from international exchange. But if wheat exchanged internationally on a ratio of 1.99:1, country A would still trade as it would

Figure 12.4 Country B's production and consumption possibility frontiers after trade

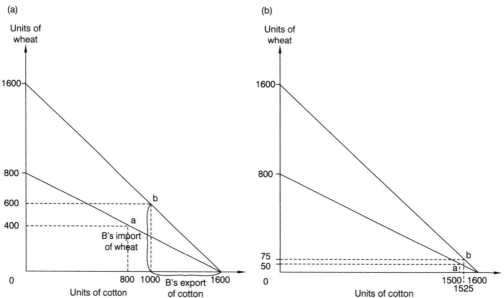

Note: Before Country B opens up to trade, people in B can only consume what is produced domestically. Point *a* shows the pre-trade combination of the two goods Country B produces and consumes, 50 units of wheat and 1500 units of cotton. After trade with A has started, people in Country B consume 75 units of wheat and 1525 units of cotton: more of both goods. Country B could enjoy different combinations of the two goods, such as *c*, if there were other countries prepared to sell wheat at the same price ratio. If not, B can only import the amount of wheat A is willing to export at that price, which is 75 units.

Figure 12.5 Determination of the equilibrium price of an internationally traded commodity: a two-country case

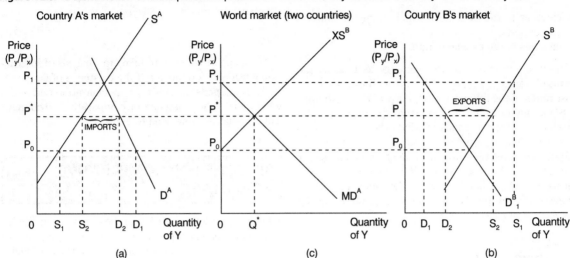

Note: Country A is a high-cost producer of good Y, while Country B is a low-cost producer. Before trade, in Country A the equilibrium price, at which domestic demand is equal to domestic supply, is P_1, as shown in (a). In Country B the domestic, pre-trade equilibrium price is at P_0, lower than P_1 as shown in (b). Country A is willing to import good Y at any price below P_1. Country B is willing to export good Y at any price above P_0. The world or international trade equilibrium price is $P*$. At that price, the quantity of good Y that Country A is willing to import is just equal to the quantity of good Y that Country B is willing to export.

have a small marginal advantage (1p per unit exchanged) from trading internationally, but country B would gain most. The same would apply to country B if cotton were exchanged internationally on a ratio of 1.99:1, as opposed to the 1:1 which we have assumed. It is the economic strength of a country vis-à-vis another, together with the elasticity of demand and supply of the product traded, which greatly affects a country's ability to gain from international trade (Figure 12.5).

For countries trading many goods, the terms of trade are defined as

$$\frac{\text{average price of exports}}{\text{average price of imports}} \times 100 \quad \text{or} \quad \frac{P_X}{P_M} \times 100$$

expressed as an index, where the price changes are measured against a base year, in which the terms of trade are assumed to be 100.

The terms of trade are said to have improved when the price of exports rises relative to the price of imports. The terms of trade are said to have worsened when the opposite is true and the price of exports falls relative to the price of imports. As we have just seen in Chapter 10, before a country can buy goods from another, an exchange of currencies must also take place. The relative price of goods traded internation-

ally will also be affected by the exchange rates, i.e. the rate at which one unit of domestic currency exchanges for a foreign currency.

So, for any pair of countries there is a range of exchange rates which will lead to both countries gaining from specialization and trade. Within that range, the exchange rate will determine which country gains the most from trade. In other words, exchange rates determine the terms of trade, given the relative prices of imports and exports. We can also say, therefore, that the trade flows are determined by the values of the exchange rates.

✍ Activity 12.3

If the exchange rate of sterling for French francs changes from £1 = FFr10 to £1 = FFr2.50, assuming that nothing else changes, have the terms of trade improved or deteriorated?

✓ Answer 12.3

They have deteriorated. The sterling exchange rate has depreciated, as one unit of domestic currency buys fewer units of foreign currency. Therefore it must be that less imports can be purchased for a given quantity of exports, that is P_X/P_M has fallen. This is a deterioration in the terms of trade.

So, changes in the terms of trade are caused by:

- changes in the demand for and supply of imports and exports;
- changes in the exchange rate.

Trade is advantageous to a country as long as the terms of trade P_X/P_M are different from the opportunity cost ratios of the two goods. $(P_X/P_M > MC_X/MC_M)$.

Summing up, countries gain from specializing in the production of those goods in which they have a comparative advantage (not necessarily an absolute advantage), exporting the surplus product in exchange for imports. The size of the gain will be determined by the terms of trade, which in turn are determined by world demand and supply for the goods in question and by the exchange rates.

✍ Activity 12.4

Study Figure 12.6 which shows the demand and supply of leather goods in two countries, A and B. State:

1. Which country will export the good.
2. What the equilibrium price will be.
3. The quantity of leather goods consumed in B.
4. The quantity of leather goods traded between the two countries.

✔ Answer 12.4

1. A will, as the cost and hence the price at which leather goods are produced in A is lower. A will export to B for any price between P_1, its own domestic equilibrium price, and B's equilibrium price P_4.
2. P_2 as this is the price at which the quantity A wishes

to export is just equal to the quantity of the good B wishes to import.

3. Q_6.
4. $Q_6 - Q_2$.

At this point we need to take our analysis of international trade a step further. If the existence of comparative advantage is the basis for specialization and trade, what causes the existence of comparative advantage? This is what we now need to explain.

REASONS FOR COMPARATIVE ADVANTAGE

What we have seen so far is that the difference in relative commodity prices between two nations is evidence of their comparative advantage and forms the basis of mutually beneficial trade. We now want to go one step further and explain the reason for the difference in relative commodity prices. This question, left unanswered by Ricardo, was settled by two Swedish economists, Heckscher and Ohlin, in a theory which is named after them. The **Heckscher–Ohlin** theory not only explains the reason for comparative advantage, but also provides an explanation of the effect that trade has on how much factors of production, such as labour, earn in trading nations.

The factor proportions model

A detail explanation of the Heckscher–Ohlin theory goes well beyond the scope of this book and will not be attempted here. What we can achieve, nonetheless, is an understanding of the main concepts used by

Figure 12.6 Demand and supply of leather goods in countries A and B

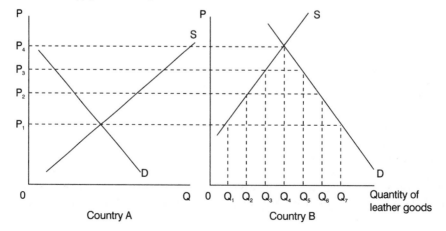

Heckscher–Ohlin to explain comparative advantage and international trade.

Stated very simply, and subject to many limiting assumptions, the Heckscher–Ohlin theory maintains that countries have a comparative advantage in the production of those goods whose production is intensive in their abundant factor.

There are two important concepts here, which need to be clearly defined: one is **factor abundance**, and the other is **factor intensity in production**. Country A is said to be **capital abundant** if the ratio of the total amount of capital to the total amount of labour (TK/TL) available in country A is greater than in country B. The same definition applies to the other two factors, labour and land. Assuming two commodities (x and y) and two factors (capital K and labour, L), commodity y is **capital intensive** if the capital/labour ratio (K/L) used in its production is greater than the K/L ratio used in the production of x.

For example, Canada, with an abundance of fertile land, will have a comparative advantage in the production of grain, because grain production is land intensive. The fact that grain production is land intensive means that grain requires relatively more land than capital or labour for its production. Southeast Asia, with an abundance of low-wage labour, will have a comparative advantage in the production of clothing, whose production is more labour intensive. Japan, the USA and Europe, with an abundance of capital, will have a comparative advantage in the production of manufactured goods, which are capital intensive.

The Heckscher–Ohlin theory provides a basis on which to explain countries' comparative advantage: countries have a comparative advantage in the production of those goods whose production is intensive in the factor which is abundant in the country.

The theory also allows us to analyse the effect that trade has on factor earnings in the two economies. The theory predicts that owners of a country's abundant factors will gain from trade, while owners of a country's scarce factor will lose, but that trade will lead to equalization of factor prices over time.

✍ Activity 12.5

Can you explain why factor prices should become the same worldwide, as a result of this theory?

✓ Answer 12.5

The theory maintains that countries gain by specializing in the production of a good whose production is intensive in the factor which is abundant in the country. A factor which is abundant commands a low price. For example, labour is abundant in India, with respect to capital, which is relatively scarce. As a result of this factor's abundance, wages are low. Hence, the production of labour-intensive textiles in India will have a cost advantage with respect to a country such as Germany, say, where labour costs are high. The more India specializes in textiles, the more labour will be demanded for textile production. The increased demand for labour will eventually drive up its price. A similar process will take place all over the world, as a result of specialization and trade. In the long run, the returns to factors will be equal. For this result to hold, however, a number of other constraining assumptions, such as perfect competition and immobility of factors between countries, need to be made.

✍ Activity 12.6

Look at the data for relative resource endowment of major industrial countries provided in Table 12.3. Explain what it shows and comment on the US endowment of resources.

Table 12.3 Factor endowments of major industrial countries, 1994 as a percentage of world total

Country	Physical capital %	R&D scientists %	Skilled labour %	Semi skilled labour %	Unskilled labour %	Arable land %	All resources (world GDP) per cent
USA	33.6	50.7	27.7	19.1	0.19	29.3	28.6
Japan	15.5	23.0	8.7	11.5	0.25	0.8	11.2
W. Germany	7.7	10.0	6.9	5.5	0.08	1.1	7.2
France	7.5	6.0	6.0	3.9	0.06	2.6	6.0
UK	4.5	8.5	5.1	4.9	0.09	1.0	5.1
Canada	3.9	1.8	2.9	2.1	0.03	6.1	2.6
Rest of world	27.3	0.0	42.7	53.0	99.30	59.1	39.3
Total	100.0	100.0	100.0	100.0	100.0	100.0	100.0

Source: World Development Report, 1994

✓ Answer 12.6

Table 12.1 shows the share of the world's resource endowments of six of the world major industrial countries. The USA has approximately 34 per cent of the physical capital, 50 per cent of research and development scientists, 28 per cent of skilled labour and 29 per cent of arable land of world total. On the basis of these data, given that the USA has the greater relative share of the world resources of capital, R&D scientists and arable land, we would expect the USA to have a comparative advantage in capital and technology intensive goods, as well as in agricultural production.

Empirical tests conducted on the basis of the Heckscher–Ohlin theory, however, have failed to support the predictions of the theory. The first of such tests was conducted by Wassily Leontieff in 1951 using data for the US economy, spanning 25 years. Given that the USA has relative abundance of capital and technology, the Heckscher–Ohlin theory would predict that the USA should specialize in the production and export of capital and technology intensive goods. The result of Leontieff's empirical test is known as the **Leontieff paradox**, as the empirical data he collected indicated instead that the USA was exporting labour intensive goods and importing capital intensive manufactures.

The theory was further tested in 1987 by Bowen, Leamer and Sveikauskas, who used a sample of 27 countries: again actual data on international trade flows did not fully support the predictions of the theory. If anything, their findings seemed to suggest that the pattern of trade is driven by international differences in technology, rather than in resources. It is quite clear that the Hecksher–Ohlin theory leaves a great deal of today's international trade unexplained and contemporary trade theory has had to put forward different explanations to justify current trade flows.

The inability of the Heckscher–Ohlin theory to predict actual trade flows accurately seems to suggest that there are other factors, other than factor endowment and factor intensity, that need to be taken into account. The main criticisms levied against the Heckscher–Ohlin factor endowment theory of comparative advantage centre on the following points:

■ There are limits to the extent to which a country can specialize in the production of one product or group of products.

■ There are other sources of comparative advantage, apart from different factor endowments, which can explain international trade, in particular the existence of internal and external economies of scale; imperfect competition, differences among countries and over time in the development and spread of new technologies and, finally, the existence of different demand conditions.

Limits to specialization and trade

Will countries really specialize in the production of a small range of goods and import everything else? This is not what we observe around us. What we see is that most countries produce most goods. Take, for instance, the case of Germany. One could argue that Germany has a comparative advantage in the production of capital intensive goods, given its relative abundance of capital with respect to, say, a developing country. Indeed Germany is a net exporter of manufactured goods. From this it does not follow, however, that Germany should turn the use of its fertile agricultural land or should cut down its extensive forests to specialize only in the production of manufactures. Germany does produce agricultural products and does use its forests for timber production. Does this contradict the theory of comparative advantage as a basis for specialization, trade, growth of output and consumption? It does not contradict the theory as such; it simply reflects the fact that there are factors which limit specialisation and therefore trade in real life.

Increasing opportunity costs from specialization

The theory developed so far needs to be made more realistic, by dropping the assumption introduced earlier that the opportunity cost of producing more of one good at the expense of the other is constant. It was this assumption which led us to draw the production possibility frontiers as straight lines.

In real life, however, the opportunity cost of producing more of one good at the expense of the other is not constant, but increasing. To produce more of one good you need to give up increasing quantities of the other good and not constant quantities, as said earlier. In other words, one extra unit of cotton will cost more and more in terms of forgone wheat, the more you specialize in the production of cotton. This is explained by the fact that as you increasingly specialize in the production of one good only, you will be using resources which are increasingly less suitable for cotton production and hence less productive. The increasing cost of specialization will eventually outweigh the country's comparative advantage; the country will cease to specialize and trade further. Increasing costs give rise to a concave production possibility frontier, as opposed to the straight line shown before (Figure 12.7).

Existence of transport costs

Transport costs may also represent a limit to specialization. A country may have a comparative advantage

Figure 12.7   Country A's and B's production possibility frontier with increasing opportunity costs

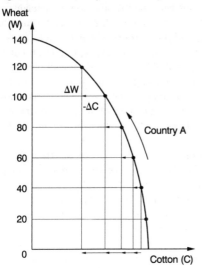

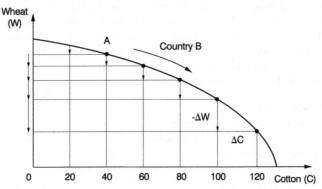

Note: In Country B the opportunity cost of cotton in terms of wheat increases as more and more cotton is produced. The amount of wheat that needs to be given up to produce one more unit of cotton increases. This is shown by downward arrows of increasing length. Similarly Country A incurs increasing opportunity costs in the production of wheat.

in the production of bricks, but the cost of transporting them over long distances may outweigh any comparative advantage it might have in their production.

Movements of factors of production

Country B might have a comparative advantage in the production of say, textiles, which are labour intensive, because of the abundance of cheap labour. But if this cheap labour migrates to another country, country B will lose its source of comparative advantage and the recipient of the migration flow will gain. Increasingly, it is factors of production, rather than goods, that move among countries nowadays. So cheap labour tends to move away from poor underdeveloped countries to those which have a greater endowment of capital, but not sufficient labour. On the other hand, capital in the form of direct investment flows from the rich industrialized countries to developing ones where capital is the relatively scarce factor. These processes limit the possibility of explaining trade flows only on the basis of specialization and factor endowment.

Existence of factor reversals

A fundamental weakness of the Hecksher–Ohlin model is its assumption that sectors can be arranged in order of capital or labour intensity, which is assumed to be the same for all countries and over time. For example, agricultural goods are assumed to be labour intensive anywhere in the world. This assumption is too simplistic. In reality what is known as **factor reversal** may occur. The agricultural sector, which is typically labour intensive in developing countries, often has above average capital

intensity in industrialized countries, such as Canada or the USA. This may result in a capital intensive country such as the USA exporting agricultural products.

The main implication of this analysis is that there is no clear-cut dividing line between goods which are capital intensive and those which are labour or land intensive. But this was precisely the core assumption of the Heckscher–Ohlin model of international trade. If this assumption no longer holds, then it also follows that countries do not have a comparative cost advantage by nature, so to speak, because of natural resources and country-specific conditions of production, which can be identified universally and once and for all.

Countries can then develop or acquire a comparative advantage, because of specific measures that a government might take to foster certain industries, because of a technological breakthrough, or other reasons. From this it follows that it may be difficult to detect a systematic pattern in countries' specialization processes and consequently in the patterns of trade.

Government restrictions

Governments may also limit the extent of product specialization for political or social reasons, to avoid trade dependence from other countries.

Other sources of comparative advantage and trade

As we have just seen, the Heckscher–Ohlin theory focuses on the combination of factor endowments and factor intensity as the basis for specialization and trade.

Not all international trade, however, can be explained on that basis. Intra-industry trade, for example, i.e. trade in the same type of goods, could not be explained. There are therefore other important reasons that need to be taken into consideration in order to account for the current pattern of international trade. Contemporary trade theories identify the following:

Differences in demand

Differences in demand are in turn sustained by differences in tastes and income. This is one of the reasons which explains, for instance, intra-industry trade. One of the reasons why Germany, say, exports its cars abroad, but also imports cars from Japan, Italy or France, is that consumers' tastes differ and market opportunities can be exploited more fully by offering more choice on more markets. Intra-industry trade can also be explained with reference to economies of scale which can be achieved through specialization. It is more cost effective to produce just a few different car models than it is to try and supply a whole range of them.

External economies of scale

A byproduct of expansion into wider markets is that companies can enjoy economies of scale. Firms experience **external economies of scale** when their average cost of production falls as the industry's output expands. External economies of scale arise because a larger and geographically concentrated industry is likely to provide more specialized labour and related services, hence higher productivity and lower costs for all the firms in the industry. External economies of scale depend on the expansion of the number of firms in the industry, rather than on the size of the individual firm, and are therefore perfectly consistent with conditions of perfect competition. With external economies, firms enjoy lower average costs of production because the industry, rather than the firm, is large. External economies affect the pattern of international trade. The country where the industry is large is likely to have lower average costs of production. Once established, an industry is likely to gain even greater cost advantages over time.

Internal economies of scale

The situation described above must be distinguished from internal economies of scale or increasing returns to scale, which refer to a firm's average cost of production as the firm's output expands. In other words, output grows proportionately more than the increase in the inputs of factors of production. If all inputs are doubled, output more than doubles. Increasing returns to scale may occur because at a larger scale of operation a greater and more productive specialization of production is possible, together with the introduction of specialized and more productive machinery. When this is the case, it pays firms to expand their production as much as possible, as this will lead to lower average production costs and hence the possibility of a cost advantage over competitors. With increasing returns to scale, mutually beneficial trade can take place even when the two economies are identical in respect of factor endowments. This is a type of trade that the Hecksher–Ohlin model could not explain.

It is also important to note that when trade takes place on the basis of internal economies of scale which firms in a specific industry may be able to enjoy, it is a matter of indifference which nations specialize in what. This in fact may be the result of historical accident. If economies of scale can be enjoyed in a particular industry, it is also likely that one or few national firms will capture the entire market for a given product. This will lead to the establishment of a domestic **monopoly** – a single producer of a good for which there is no substitute – or **oligopoly** – a few producers of a homogeneous or partially differentiated product. Trade and expansion into foreign markets of a domestic monopoly or oligopoly can affect the market structure of the importing country and may lead to counteractive protective measures.

Product differentiation

As we have just pointed out, a large amount of trade takes place nowadays in goods produced by the same industry. Italy exports cars and imports cars, albeit of different makes. This type of trade originates from the fact that a large proportion of the output of modern economies involves differentiated products. A Volvo is not identical to a BMW, a Fiat or a Renault. A great deal of international trade involves the exchange of **differentiated products** of the same industry. In other words, a great deal of international trade is **intra-industry trade** in differentiated products, rather than trade in completely different products.

How do we explain this? Firms in the industry try to take advantage of economies of scale and it pays them to specialize in the production of one particular make, rather than try to produce several. International competition forces producers in a country to specialize in the production of one or few varieties of styles. In this way costs can be kept down. With fewer varieties more specialized machinery can be used, etc. A country then imports other varieties and types of the same product from other countries. Intra-industry trade benefits consumers by offering greater choice of products at lower prices.

Multinationals

The activities of **multinational corporations** and their dominance of international markets further challenges the traditional theory of locational advantage. The competitive advantage that multinationals enjoy is the result of company specific factors which may include some locational advantage, but cannot be easily captured by the simple factor endowment theory.

Summing up, the picture that emerges from studying the pattern of international trade seems to suggest that a comparative advantage in the production of a good may emerge from a combination of factors, such as internal and external economies of scale and diversity of demand. The factors are often the result of firms having expanded abroad and not a precondition of their expansion to foreign markets.

This concept that comparative advantage can develop as a result of trade, rather than as a precondition for international trade is at the centre of another popular, contemporary trade theory, often referred to as **strategic trade theory**.

✍ Activity 12.7

1 How do economies of scale arise?
2 How does each nation determine the export commodity to specialize in?
3 What happens within each nation if economies of scale persist over a sufficiently long period of time or over a large range of outputs?

✓ Answer 12.7

Economies of scale arise because division of labour and specialization become possible when the scale of operation is sufficiently great. Each worker can specialize in performing a limited amount of simple tasks, with a resulting increase in productivity. More specialized and productive machinery can be introduced for a larger scale of operation.

If economies of scale persist over a sufficiently long period of time or range of output then a single firm or few firms will capture the entire market for the commodity, leading to a monopoly or oligopoly situation.

✍ Activity 12.8

How does trade theory account for the fact that countries or a group of countries such as the USA or EU both import and export similar types of goods, such as cars, cigarettes, chemicals and many other industrial products?

✓ Answer 12.8

There is a substantial amount of international trade which is not explained by the factor endowment theory.

Countries with similar factor endowments exchange similar goods. This type of trade is referred to as intra-industry trade in differentiated products. Differentiated products are similar, but not identical products. A BMW and a Volvo are both types of cars, but they are not identical. Intra-industry trade arises in some cases as producers, to keep down costs, cater for the 'majority' tastes within their nation, leaving 'minority' tastes to be satisfied by imports. The increase of intra-industry trade is also due to increased trade in parts and components, as multinational corporations produce parts and assemble them in different nations in order to minimize production costs.

CONTEMPORARY TRADE THEORIES

So how do trade theorists explain contemporary international trade flows? Do economists still labour over demonstrations of the advantages of specialization and free trade? Do governments advocate liberal trading systems and the removal of trade restrictions?

Economists increasingly recognize that the assumption of perfectly competitive markets on which traditional trade theory rests, no longer comfortably fit the data of economies in the 1990s. Huge conglomerates, which enjoy economies of scale, increasingly dominate all spheres of production and distribution; new strategic sectors have emerged. Long-established patterns of comparative advantage have disappeared in response to an ever-faster world and increased capital mobility. All these factors have led to the demise of traditional, comparative advantage theories and free trade policies in favour of more sophisticated and less general analysis.

The famous **Porter diamond analysis** (Figure 12.8) owes its name to the economist who propounded it and to his diagram, in the shape of a diamond. Porter uses it to summarize the factors affecting international competitiveness which are a combination of production location and business organization.

Porter studied a sample of the most successful industries of ten major industrial countries over a 15-year period, from 1970 to 1985, in order to identify the sources of their success. The result of his analysis was that the international competitiveness of those industries depended mostly on their innovation and modernization of production facilities, as well as on country-specific location advantages.

It is also increasingly recognized that international trade can be based on **dynamic technological differences**. This strand of analysis dates back to Posner who, in 1961, pointed out that new products give innovative firms and nations a temporary monopoly power, often

Figure 12.8 The Porter diamond

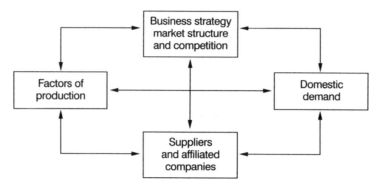

based on the exploitation of copyrights. On similar lines, Vernon put forward what is often referred to as the **product cycle** explanation of the pattern of international trade. According to his theory, a new product requires highly skilled labour in the initial stages of its introduction. Countries with plenty of highly skilled labour and large R&D budgets would typically lead and exploit their advantage when trading internationally. As the product matures, however, it becomes more standardized and can be mass produced with techniques that no longer require highly skilled labour. Hence, the comparative advantage shifts at this point to countries such as newly industrialized countries (NICs) or less developed countries (LDCs), where labour is cheaper and mass production more cost effective.

Summing up, contemporary trade theory recognizes that international trade can be based on different factors: on factor endowments, on increasing returns to scale, on differentiated products, on innovation, location and organization, as well as on dynamic technological differences. While differences in factor endowments may still be appropriate to explain most trade taking place between developed countries (DCs) and less developed countries (LDCs), as such trade is by and large inter-industry, large amounts of trade between DCs is intra-industry and mostly based on economies of scale enjoyed in the production of differentiated products.

GAINS FROM TRADE

International trade can bring mutual gains to trading countries, regardless of the reasons underpinning their trade flows. Such gains are brought about by:

- *increased productivity*: through specialization and economies of scale. Trade can be thought of as

an indirect method of production, which allows countries to specialize in the production of those goods in which they have a comparative advantage, buying in the goods they do not produce.

- *increased consumption possibilities*: in the absence of trade, consumption possibilities are the same as production possibilities, which may be very restricted, at least for some countries. Once trade is allowed, each economy can consume a choice of goods which is much wider than the one afforded on the basis of domestic production only.

- *increased domestic market efficiency*: international trade has other positive, albeit less direct, effects on the domestic market. Assuming fairly competitive markets, the presence of foreign competition on domestic markets will stimulate greater efficiency of domestic firms, forcing prices down. This in turn will provide domestic firms with an incentive to introduce new cost saving or quality enhancing technology in order to restore their competitive edge. Import competition will also provide a greater variety of products for domestic consumers, as domestic firms will respond by refining and diversifying their products.

- *export-led growth*: expansion into foreign markets may be a driving force for the growth of the whole economy through the multiplier effect. Growing employment and income in the export sector, that is, firms producing mostly for foreign markets, will spill over to other sectors of the economy, causing a positive multiplier effect. Export-led growth was experienced by the Italian economy and partly also by Germany in the 1950s and early 1960s.

- *non-economic advantages*: there are advantages to be gained from international trade which cannot be monetized, but are nonetheless very important. International trade increases international political stability, as economic interdependence strengthens cultural and social links. Both the USA and European countries saw a way towards greater political co-operation and stability in the liberalization of trade which took place in the post-war period. Both GATT and the EC, which we discuss later, were conceived after World War II with this broader objective in mind.

✍ Activity 12.9

Say which of the following factors that account for gains from trade apply to the examples below: increased competition, decreasing costs, differences in demand, non-economic factors.

1 A country may become increasingly skilled and more efficient in the production of a good simply by specializing in its production.
2 People in country A like to use cars more than people in country B.
3 Competition from Japan has made European businesses more efficient.
4 EU trade with central and eastern Europe will encourage political stability in Europe

✓ Answer 12.9

1 Decreasing costs and economies of scale.
2 Differences in demand due to different tastes.
3 Increased competition increases efficiency and growth.
4 Trade can be beneficial for non-economic reasons.

ARGUMENTS FOR PROTECTIONISM

If trade is beneficial to participating countries why do so many governments intervene by imposing protectionist measures aimed at restricting international trade? To understand this point, let's go back to Figure 12.5, which shows the determination of the terms of trade which takes place when two countries start trading with one another.

After international trade is established, the exporting country will experience an increase in the price of the exported good, while the importing country will experience an overall decrease in the price of the imported good. Now you must remember that there are domestic producers as well as consumers of the goods which are imported and exported. Cases of absolute specialization, where countries produce only one good or very few goods and import all the rest, are just not realistic. How are domestic producers and consumers going to react to the price changes brought about by the opening up to trade?

Changes in the domestic economy caused by exporting a good

As the price of the exported good is likely to increase from its pre-trade level:

■ domestic producers will gain, as they now receive a higher price for their product. They will make larger profits and also try to expand further. Expansion of domestic production will have a positive effect on domestic employment in the export sector.
■ domestic consumers will lose, as they will have to pay a higher price for the domestic product which is now also exported. Typically, however, consumers are in no position to make their voices heard or exert any influence on policy decisions.

Changes in the foreign economy caused by importing the good

As prices of the imported goods are likely to be lower than the domestic prices, the result of opening up to trade and allowing in foreign goods will be to lower the prices of the goods which can now be offered by foreign competition. As a result:

■ domestic producers will suffer as they will now have to sell at a lower price and some will simply go out of business as a result. Those who stay in the industry will have lower profit margins. Less will be produced domestically on the whole. Some people employed in the import sector will lose their jobs and their income. This will have a negative multiplier effect on the rest of the economy. Lobbying from domestic producers faced by price-cutting competition and the increased unemployment in the import sector, which represents an increased cost for the government in social security benefits, is likely to have an impact on governments. They may be tempted to introduce measures aimed at protecting the domestic industry.
■ domestic consumers will gain, as they will now consume more at a lower price than before.

Gainers and losers

The theory of international trade helps us to see that each country has both an import and an export sector: while the import sector loses out as a result of trade, the export sector gains. This provides the market with an incentive to reallocate its resources away from the import sectors where firms have a comparative disadvantage, into the export sectors where firms can exploit their comparative advantage. So, ultimately trying to protect the domestic market from the effects of competition prevents the domestic economy from reallocating resources efficiently. Also, protection always leads to retaliation and what you do to other countries, they will do to you.

However, adjustment to changes in comparative advantage that lead to changes in international trade patterns can take a long time. The increase in car imports suffered by Britain in recent years has severely affected domestic car producers and employment in the British car industry, but has not been compensated by equal expansions in emerging export sectors. The displaced workers have not been able to find equally good jobs in other industries. Real life is just not what textbooks of economics make it out to be. It takes time for adjustments to take place and change is always painful. So, although in the long run everyone may potentially gain from international specialization and trade, in the short run adjustment costs can be very large and relatively prolonged. They are also unevenly distributed, as they are borne only by some sectors of the working population, namely those which have lost their comparative advantage.

Partly because of the costs of adjustment to changing international trade patterns described above, but partly also for other reasons, governments intervene in international trade, either restricting or affecting its volume. It is to these other reasons for trade restrictions which we now turn. The reasons for trade protectionism can be broadly grouped into three categories:

■ to stimulate the growth of domestic industry;
■ to protect domestic markets from the distorting effects of foreign monopolies or oligopolies;
■ for social, political or ecological reasons.

Infant industry argument

The most common argument brought forward for trade protectionism is the so-called **infant industry** argument. Young industries, particularly in developing countries, may have difficulties in competing with established industries in other countries. In order to develop, such industries need trade protection. This argument for protection is often advocated by developing countries, in order to allow their domestic industry with potential comparative advantage to develop the know-how and size necessary to compete with established foreign firms. While enjoying temporary protection from competition, firms can acquire dynamic comparative advantage which arises from learning by doing. It is a historic fact that both the USA and Japan at the early stages of their industrial development protected their infant industries from the full blow of competition from the already industrialized countries, particularly Britain.

The counter-arguments to this powerful infant industry argument for trade protection are many.

■ Once a protective tariff is established, it is always very difficult to decide when to remove it. The protected industry will always put forward reasons for its continuation.
■ Protection that shields the infant industry from competition may encourage inefficient firms to survive, while consumers lose out as they are forced to buy products which are inferior and more expensive than those offered by the competition.
■ If protection is needed, it should be granted in the form of subsidy to the infant industry, rather than a tariff. The subsidy would help the industry to survive, despite its small operating scale or higher costs, still exposing it to the sobering experience of foreign competition, which would also ensure lower prices for consumers. In the end the subsidy would come from taxes paid by consumers who would enjoy the lower price for the product. Subsidization of the domestic industry may also have growth and employment spillover effects which would compensate for the tax.

Senile industry argument

Similar types of arguments and counter-arguments to the ones put forward for the protection of infant industries are used for the protection of a senile industry. Some industries, it is argued, still have potential comparative advantage, but are not in a position to exploit it because they have been allowed to deteriorate. Without protection and/or injection of government funds, these potentially competitive industries would not be able to raise the capital necessary to finance the investment that would lead to their regeneration. This argument has often been used for the protection of the US car and steel industry.

Anti-dumping argument

Protection is often justified to prevent **dumping** from other countries. Dumping takes place when a foreign firm, which receives export subsidies from its government, sells its exports at a price that is below costs on foreign markets. The result of selling at an artificially low price is to force producers in the importing country out of business, as they cannot compete with the artificially low prices of subsidized products. Once domestic competition has been disposed off in this way, the foreign firm is in a position to establish a monopoly on the foreign market and raise its prices.

Anti-dumping is an accepted reason for protectionism, which often results in the levying of tariffs on the dumped product. The less developed countries have often accused the EU of dumping its subsidized agricultural products on their markets, forcing domestic farmers out of business. The counter-argument against anti-dumping is that dumping is rather difficult to prove, as it is virtually impossible to know a foreign firm's costs. As a result, the practical way to prove that dumping takes place is if a firm's export price for a good is lower than its domestic price. This again is a debatable argument, as a firm could be justified in charging two different prices if the elasticities of demand for its product abroad and at home are different.

Environmental arguments

Environmental arguments for restrictions are becoming increasingly popular. Many countries, particularly developing countries, have laxer environmental standards; hence they can produce at lower costs and also pollute the global environment. Penalizing measures are then advocated to counteract such actions.

These arguments for trade protection are rather weak. If a lack of economic development is causing the lax attitude of developing countries on environmental matters, increasing their poverty by discriminating in trade with them is likely to exacerbate the problem rather than solve it. More trade with these countries might encourage their development and hence a more responsible attitude towards such matters.

The arguments in favour of trade restrictions discussed above have a general validity, despite their debatable strength. There are arguments for protection, however, which apply only selectively to specific areas or group of countries and have no general validity. There follow a number of examples of such protectionist arguments.

Restrictions to improve the terms of trade

Trade restrictions are often imposed by countries which are trying to change the terms of trade in their favour. This situation arises when a country has a monopoly supply of an export. The Organisation of Petroleum Exporting Countries (OPEC) cartel took this action in the 1970s. In order to raise the price of oil, the OPEC countries restricted its supply by imposing an export levy, which reduced the price received by the exporting country, thereby reducing its incentive to export more. Foreigners still paid a higher price for oil, but part of that price was a government levy which did not accrue to the producer. By reducing the price received by each cartel member producer, the cartel succeeded in keeping oil production down, which in turn caused the international price of oil to go sky high.

A country with a monopsony power in the demand for imports, like a large industrialized country providing the sole export market to a small developing country, may also restrict its own demand for the imported good by use of a tariff, in order to maximize its gain from trade. By reducing the amount of the imported good, the monopsonist buyer will succeed in keeping its price down.

Non-economic arguments for protectionism

There are also social and political, non-economic arguments often advocated for the introduction of protectionist measures. Governments may grant subsidies to firms for **strategic or national security reasons**. Many governments support their agricultural sectors, despite the fact that it would be cheaper to import the food, for reasons of national security. Governments often aid declining industries, such as shipbuilding in Britain, for social reasons to prevent undue hardship to large sections of the population, often concentrated in the specific geographical areas.

To explain why trade is still so often restricted, despite all its alleged benefits, we must remember that, although it is potentially beneficial to the trading parties, the gains from trade are not necessarily evenly distributed within a country and between countries. Just as it is not practically possible for a government to compensate those who lose from trade out of the gains of those who win, equally it is not possible on a global scale to induce countries that benefit from international trade to compensate those who lose.

WHERE ARE WE NOW?

The theoretical pendulum seems to have swung away from unrestricted liberalism, as the gains from trade of the classical theory are unlikely to follow as predicted, in a world increasingly characterized by the dominance of economic giants on the international scenario. Economists no longer labour over demonstrations of the advantages of free trade and governments no longer advocate totally liberal trading systems. Rather, many theorists of international trade nowadays favour **strategic trade theory** and many governments follow **strategic trade policy**. Others take an eclectic approach and look at each specific trade situation in isolation.

Strategic trade theory

Production on today's world markets is often characterized by a small number of giant firms earning excess profits that are able to affect their countries' terms of trade. These companies will do so by restricting the amount of the good they bring onto world markets, in order to drive up its price. A country which removes its trade barriers in this situation will undoubtedly expose its domestic market to the full blow of these giants' competition. However, the nature of this competition may be such that the benefits from greater trade would not accrue to the importing country, but to the foreign oligopolists. In this situation, it is argued, trade intervention, rather than simply protection, on the part of the importing country's government is needed to help raise domestic welfare. An interventionist government policy will allow domestic firms a greater share of the profits of the industry on a global scale, at the expense of foreign rivals. This is the theoretical standpoint of strategic trade policy. It rests firmly on the uncompetitive nature of many international markets.

Strategic trade policy

Strategic trade policy advocates domestic government intervention to counteract uncompetitive foreign dominance of domestic markets. It derives its name from the fact that, under these circumstances, government intervention can change the nature of the strategic game between rival firms in different countries, in favour of the domestic economy. National governments represent the interests of their domestic monopolists or cartelized oligopolists and fight with each other over sharing the global market.

How do governments compete with each other in such a situation? Just as there is no fixed rule to suggest how firms compete in an oligopolistic situation, equally there is no fixed rule or policy prescription which forms the basis for government intervention. Policy prescriptions for governments' strategic trade policy decisions are typically very thin.

Together with Brander and Spencer (1985), one of the strongest advocates for strategic trade policy is Lester Thurow of the Massachusetts Institute of Technology. According to these economists, a nation can create its comparative advantage, by granting

some of its industries temporary trade protection, subsidies or tax benefits. Governments need to do two things:

- First, they need to identify sectors of strategic importance for the domestic and global economy.
- Second, they need to encourage their development in an active and selective way.

Semiconductors, computers and telecommunications have proved to be crucial sectors on a world scale, with high growth potential. There are several examples of **strategic sectors**: steel was the strategic commodity in Europe in the 1950s; semiconductors were crucial in the establishment of Japan's industrial supremacy in the 1970s and 1980s; the European Airbus consortium successfully challenged McDonnell Douglas's second position, after Boeing, in the world ranking of aircraft carriers and was of strategic importance to European industrial growth in the 1970s and 1980s. In all these cases, supremacy in the field was established through substantial and extended financial support and strategic trade policies from the respective governments.

High technology industries are subject to high risks and require large-scale production to achieve economies of scale; they also give rise to substantial external economies when successful. Governments should therefore encourage their development to enable the domestic economies to enjoy the substantial benefits that these industries bring in terms of growth. Japan, it is argued, is an example of how strategic industrial and trade policies can bring about fast economic growth.

In oligopolistic markets, subject to extensive external economies, strategic trade theory can increase a country's growth and welfare. The difficulties with this approach, however, rest with its implementation:

- How can a government choose which area of possible future strategic importance to support? Which industries will provide large external economies in the future?
- If I stand on tiptoe at a football match to get a better view, the person behind me will do the same. We will all end up standing on tiptoe, but no one will get a better view. Strategic trade policy will trigger retaliation. It is questionable whether great benefits can be achieved by any country from strategic trade policies, if all countries independently pursue similar policies. If a country is successful, through the use of strategic trade policy, this can only be at the expense of its trading partners, which are likely in turn to retaliate and start a vicious circle of beggar-my-neighbour policies.

These considerations have lead the majority of economists to the conclusion that trade liberalization may still be the most sensible, if not optimal, policy option after all. The theoretical pendulum has not fully swung away from liberalism.

FORMS OF TRADE RESTRICTION

However, countries do restrict or affect trade flows with one another for the reasons discussed above. How do they achieve that? Which tools can governments use to restrict trade? More importantly, what are the effects of trade restriction measures on the domestic economy, on foreign trading partners and on the global trading system as a whole? These are the questions which we are now going to address.

Protectionism is the term used with reference to measures which restrict trade in order to shield a sector of the economy from foreign competition. The most common forms of trade restriction are the use of tariffs, quotas and export subsidies.

Increasingly common forms of trade restrictions are also **non-tariff barriers** such as: exchange controls, technical or administrative barriers, import licences and voluntary exports restraints (VERs). Embargoes, which are temporary trade suspensions with a country or group of countries for political or security reasons, are not a commonly used form of restriction.

Tariffs

Tariffs can be imposed on imports or exports. **Import tariffs** are the most common and most important form of trade restriction. A discussion of international attempts at controlling the use of tariffs is given in Chapter 13. Export tariffs are not used very frequently. They are imposed on the exported good, in order to raise its price and improve the country's terms of trade.

An import tariff is a tax on imports. Most imported goods have tariffs, albeit small ones in most cases. Tariffs can be *ad valorem*, when they are applied as a percentage of the price of the imported good. They can also be in the form of a *lump sum*, a fixed amount which is added to the price. There are also *compound tariffs*, which comprise a fixed levy with a percentage of the price of the good. In all cases, the effect of a tariff is to increase the price of the imported good, which in turn causes a reduction of imports. Figure 12.9 shows the effect of a tariff on the importing country's market for the good.

Figure 12.9(a) shows a country's domestic demand and supply curve D_d and S_d for a good which is produced domestically; let's assume it is cars. Equilibrium in the domestic market is reached at price P^*, where quantity Q^* is produced and sold on the domestic market.

Figure 12.9(b) shows how the situation changes when imports of foreign cars are allowed into the country. The country is in no position to influence the world price for the imported product (the country is a *price taker*). For this reason the world supply of cars is shown as a horizontal line, S_w at the price prevailing in the rest of the world P_w. The quantity of cars demanded by the domestic market at the price P_w increases from Q^* to Q_4, but of that only Q_1 is now produced by domestic producers, the rest (Q_4-Q_1) is imported. Domestic car production falls from Q^* to Q_1 as a result of the influx of imports, as many of the domestic producers cannot compete with the much lower world price P_w. Domestic production is cut as a result.

Figure 12.9 Economic effect of a tariff

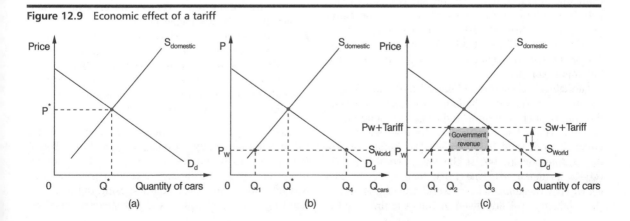

Figure 12.9(c) shows how this situation is affected by the introduction of a tariff on imports of cars. The tariff raises the price of imported cars by the amount of the tariff, which is shown by the vertical difference between S_w and S_{w+t}. The effect of the tariff is:

■ to reduce domestic consumption of cars, which falls from Q_4 to Q_3. (**consumption effect**);
■ to increase the domestic production of cars, from Q_1 to Q_2 (**production effect**);
■ to reduce the amount of car imports, from $(Q_4 - Q_1)$ to $(Q_3 - Q_2)$ (**import effect**);
■ to provide the government with revenue, in the form of the tariff collected $(Q_3 - Q_2) \times (P_{w+t} - P_w)$ (**revenue effect**).

As a result of the impositions of a tariffs, consumers lose, as they pay a higher price for cars and consume less of them; but domestic producers gain, as they can now produce more. Government's gain is really a transfer of resources from consumers. So the net loss of the tariff is the reduction in consumption which results from the higher prices, together with the fact that cars which are now produced domestically, could have been produced more cheaply and efficiently, albeit by foreign firms.

Subsidies

There are two main types of subsidy which governments can give to domestic firms: an export subsidy to increase exports or a production subsidy to reduce imports.

Production subsidy

Production subsidies are payments given by governments to domestic producers faced by the threat of low priced import goods coming into the domestic market. If, say, American wheat can be sold in Britain for £100 a tonne, while wheat in Britain costs £110 a tonne and cannot be produced more cheaply, the government can help British farmers to survive the competition either by imposing a tariff of £10 on American wheat or giving the farmers a £10 subsidy. The subsidy will enable British farmers to sell at £100 a tonne, hence eliminating import competition.

This situation is shown in Figure 12.10. The effect of the subsidy is to reduce the industry's costs, increasing its supply and therefore reducing the amount of imports. The subsidy shifts out the domestic supply curve S_d to S^1 until the amount Q^* as before is produced domestically, but at the lower world price P_w ($Q_4 - Q^*$ is imported). The price that domestic consumers pay remains the lower world price P_w. However, the production subsidy given to domestic firms by the

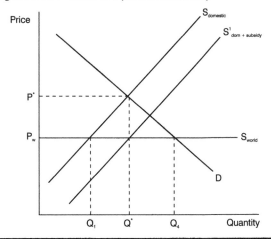

Figure 12.10   Effect of a production subsidy

government will ultimately have to be paid for by consumers and producers in the form of higher taxes.

Export subsidy

An export subsidy is a payment to a firm to encourage it to export its product abroad. Like a tariff, an export subsidy can be either specific, a fixed sum per unit, or ad valorem, a proportion of the value exported. The effect of an export subsidy on the price of the good is the exact reverse of that of a tariff (Figure 12.11).

■ The price increases in the exporting country as a result of an export subsidy. If producers export the good, rather than selling it to the domestic market, they will get the subsidy on top of the domestic market price. Hence, producers will now offer the good to the domestic market at the same price (price + subsidy) which they receive when they sell abroad. In the exporting country the price goes up and consumers are hurt, as they pay more and consume less of the good, while producers gain as they produce more at a higher price.
■ The price falls in the importing country as more of the good is now available. Hence, consumers gain as they consume more at a lower price, but producers lose in the importing country, as some will be unable to compete with lower prices and will have to cut down on production.

This situation applies to the export subsidy that the European Community's Common Agricultural Policy (CAP) pays to producers to dispose of their surplus products. As we explain later in this chapter, the CAP was introduced not as an export subsidy, but as a system to guarantee high prices to European farmers. To

Figure 12.11 Effect of an export subsidy on the exporting country's market

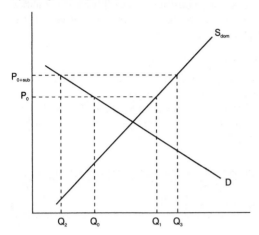

Note: At the marked price P_0, which is higher than the equilibrium price, consumers are demanding quantity Q_0 but producers are producing Q_1. Let's assume that the government decides to pay producers an export subsidy to encourage them to export their surplus production abroad. At the new price (P_0 plus subsidy) domestic consumers will demand Q_2 and producers will produce Q_3; the surplus actually increases. As a result export production increases but domestic consumption falls, as the price of the product goes up.

guarantee high prices, the EC would buy up agricultural products from farmers whenever the prices fell below specified target levels. This policy was further backed by the introduction of external tariffs, to prevent foreign imports of agricultural commodities from coming into the community, undercutting the target price.

These support prices were set too high, well above the EC internal market equilibrium level. As a result, there was overproduction of EC agricultural goods, which the EC market would not absorb. Under this scheme, the EC was obliged to buy up the unsold quantities in order to prevent prices from falling below the support threshold. Hence butter mountains and wine lakes had to be stored at great expense to the EC budget. To reduce this huge amount of surplus production, the EC now pays an export subsidy to farmers. When subsidized EC exports reach world markets, they increase world supply and cause world prices of agricultural commodities to fall, further distorting world markets. As consumers, EC households pay a price for their food which is higher than the world price; as taxpayers, they pay for the export subsidies which lower the price of agricultural commodities bought by the rest of the world.

Quotas

A quota is a direct restriction on the quantity of a good which may be imported into the country. The restriction is enforced by issuing licences to specific importers which are allocated the right to import a maximum amount. Sometimes the 'right to sell' is given directly to the governments of the exporting countries.

While tariffs directly affect the price of imports, quotas are aimed at controlling their quantity. However, the quantity restriction imposed on the imports has the effect of driving up the price of the good. So, ultimately, the economic effect of a quota is the same as that of a tariff. The quantity of imports is restricted. This drives up the domestic price of the good, which reduces consumption and increases domestic production, as shown in Figure 12.12.

Figure 12.12 Economic effect of a quota: (a) The domestic market equilibrium. (b) Effect of cheaper imports from abroad. Domestic production falls from Q^* to Q_1 and imports rise by $Q_4 - Q_1$. (c) The quantity of imports allowed into the country is restricted to $Q_3 - Q_1$. This drives the price up to P_0. Domestic production increases from Q_1 to Q_2.

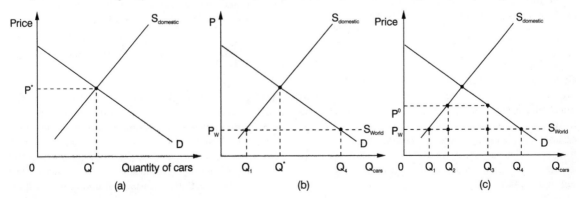

The main difference between this form of protection and a tariff is that, while the government gains extra revenue from the tariff, with quota restrictions the benefit of the higher price from the restricted supply goes to the seller of the good. The government receives no revenue. The quota 'rent' is received by whoever has the import licence. When the 'right to sell' is given to the governments of exporting countries, the transfer of rent abroad makes the cost of a quota higher than the equivalent tariff.

Non-tariff barriers

Import licences

Import licences are issued by governments to foreign firms for the import of their goods into the domestic economy. Import licences are a way of implementing quota restrictions, which in fact eliminates the problem of lost government revenue, associated with the use quotas to restrict imports. To achieve this, the government can auction import licences so that the highest bidder pays for the licence to sell the volume of goods required. Alternatively, licences may simply be sold by the government to overseas suppliers on the basis of established trade links.

Voluntary export restraints (VERs)

Voluntary export restraints (VERs) are a self-imposed restrictions on the part of the exporting country. The economic effect of VERs is the same as that of a quota, as VERs are in fact self-imposed quotas. Chapter 13 discusses causes and consequences of VERs in great detail.

Technical and administrative barriers

Technical and administrative barriers are very common ways of flaunting free trade agreements. Governments can impose technical specifications, health standards or administrative procedures which deliberately exclude foreign goods or make it more difficult or more costly for them to penetrate the domestic markets.

Exchange controls

Governments can limit import penetration by restricting the amount of foreign exchange available for their purchase. It was common in the past for government to restrict the amount of currency available to domestic residents wishing to take a holiday abroad. These forms of restriction are less common nowadays in industrialized countries, but are still used by developing countries.

🖎 Activity 12.10

Say whether the imposition of a tariff by a small nation increases or decreases the relative price of the imported good for producers and consumers.

✓ Answer 12.10

The imposition of a tariff raises the price of the imported commodity. Domestic producers of the good gain, as they can increase production. Domestic consumers lose, as they consume less of the good and pay a higher price.

FREE TRADE AREAS AND CUSTOMS UNIONS

The dominance of world markets by large conglomerates, coupled with countries' quest for world market dominance, has increasingly led countries to aggregate into ever larger, more powerful regional areas of economic integration. The nature and degree of integration can vary, as Table 12.4 shows.

Free trade areas

Countries can form free trade areas, where member countries abolish trade restrictions on trade between themselves, but each member pursues independent external trade policies with the rest of the world. The North Atlantic Free Trade Area (NAFTA), between the USA, Canada and Mexico, is one of the largest.

Customs unions

Countries can also form customs unions where:

- all tariffs on imports from member countries are eliminated;
- a common external tariff (CET) is adopted on imports from the rest of the world;
- customs revenue is divided among the member states according to an agreed formula.

This form of economic association combines a move towards free trade among members with the retention, and in some cases the increase, of barriers to trade against non-members. It represents a case of **discriminating trade liberalization** and as such it has both positive and negative repercussions on union members, non-union members and the world as a whole.

The establishment of a customs union is likely to alter the relative prices of goods in the domestic markets of the member countries, which in turn causes changes in trade flows, production and consumption.

Table 12.4 Forms of regional economic association

Requirements	FTA	CU	CM	EMU
(a) No tariffs or quotas	*	*	*	*
(b) Common external tariff and quota system		*	*	*
(c) Uniform harmonized legal framework for market			*	*
(d Uniform/harmonized indirect tax system, common policies on state aids and public procurement			*	*
(e) Fixed or harmonized exchange rates (in extreme single currency)			*	*
(f) Common or harmonized monetary policies				*
(g) Common or harmonized fiscal policy				*

(a), (b)	Fully attained by EC	FTA	= Free Trade Area
(c)	Partially attained by EC	CU	= Customs Union
(e)	Partially attained by ERM	CM	= Common Market
(d), (f), (g)	Partially attained by EMU	EMU	= Economic and Monetary Union

Although economic theory cannot accurately predict the overall effect of the formation of a customs union, it can nonetheless help us to analyse its short-run trade and welfare effects. The results of this analysis also apply to closer forms of economic co-operation based on the principle of internal liberalization and external protection.

Common markets

Common markets behave like customs unions, where members operate as a **single market**, and have:

- a common system of taxation;
- a common system of laws and regulations, particularly competition policies;
- free movement of capital and labour;
- a common procurement policy;
- fixed or harmonized exchange rates.

Economic and monetary union (EMU)

An economic and monetary union behaves like a common market, with the difference that integration is tighter and members have a common monetary and fiscal policy.

Economic effects of a customs union

The patterns of trade change as a result of a customs union. The formation of a customs' union has three main measurable effects: trade creation effect, trade diversion effect, welfare effect.

Trade creation occurs when some domestic production of a member country is replaced by lower cost imports from another member. The trade creation effect increases the welfare of members because it

leads to greater specialization in production, based on comparative advantage.

Trade diversion occurs when lower cost imports from non-members are replaced by higher cost imports from union members. Trade diversion reduces welfare as it shifts production away from more efficient producers outside the union to less efficient producers inside the union. In other words, trade diversion shifts production away from comparative advantage.

Both effects are present, when customs unions are formed. Hence customs unions can increase or reduce the **welfare** of union members, depending on the relative strength of the two forces.

These effects can be better seen with the use of Figure 12.13 which shows the markets for a commodity in two countries, country A and country B, before the two countries form a customs union. As Figure 12.13 shows, country A has a comparative disadvantage in the production of this good, as it is a high cost producer (equilibrium price in A higher than in B); while B has a comparative advantage (low cost producer, lower domestic equilibrium price).

D^a and S^a denote domestic demand and supply in country A, while D^b and S^b denote domestic demand and supply in country B. The upward-sloping supply curves indicate that both countries face increasing production costs. However, market equilibrium for the good in country A is at a higher price than the equilibrium price prevailing in country B.

Let's also assume that this particular good can be produced in the rest of the world at a price P_w. The world supply of the good is infinitely elastic at price P^w and is shown here by the horizontal line S^w. This indicates that, given the small size of the markets of countries A and B relative to the world market for this good, the world supply and price for the good are unlikely to be affected by

Figure 12.13 Effects of a customs union: (a) before countries A and B form a customs union; (b) after countries A and B have formed a customs union

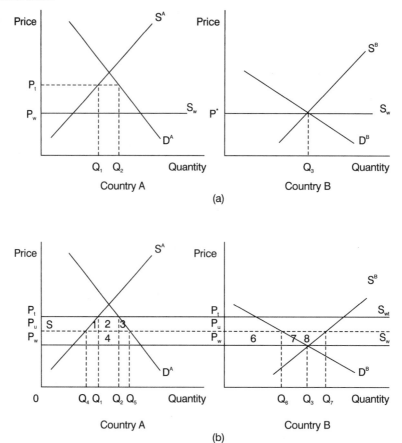

(a)

(b)

Note: Before countries A and B form a customs union, and after the imposition of an import tariff, country A imports quantity $Q_2 - Q_1$ from the rest of the world at the price $P_{w+tariff}$. After the customs union is formed between A and B, A has to remove tariffs on products coming from B, while retaining them on products coming from the rest of the world. Country B can now export to A at the price P_u, at which the demand for imports is just equal to the supply of exports.

how much countries A and B consume. Countries A and B can import any quantity they wish of this good, without affecting the world price, which is given at P_w.

Country B's equilibrium price is the same as the price prevailing in the rest of the world for this good, so country B is not affected by world competition and does not import any quantity of this good from abroad. Country A, on the contrary, is affected by lower priced competition, as its domestic equilibrium price for the good is higher than the world price. As a result, country A needs to protect its market by imposing a tariff. The tariff raises the domestic price of the good to P_t and reduces the quantity imported.

After the imposition of the tariff in country A, the final situation in the two countries is as follows: in

country A, at price P_t, Q_1 is produced domestically and $Q_2 - Q_1$ is imported from the rest of the world. In country B, at price P^w which is lower than P^t, domestic producers produce the equilibrium quantity Q_3 and no amount of good X is imported.

Now, let us suppose that the two countries A and B form a customs union, retaining B's tariff as the common external tariff. Let's see now how the creation of a customs union affects exports and imports of the two countries and the rest of the world.

While imports of good X into country A are reduced by the tariff, imports from country B, which is a member of the union, are unrestricted. The price differential for the good in countries A and B will cause them to trade. While world competition is kept at bay by the common external tariff, producers in country B, now faced only by competition from the less efficient producers of country A, will be able to export good X to country A, where it will sell at a higher price than at home. An equilibrium price within the customs union (countries A and B) will eventually emerge at P_u, at which B's exports are equal to A's imports.

Let's now look at the final oucome. In country A, at price P_u, Q_4 is now produced domestically, $Q_5 - Q_4$ is imported from B, and Q_5 is the quantity consumed domestically. The total of A's imports now comes from B and is due to three effects:

■ substitution of imports from country B for imports from the world, $Q_2 - Q_1$;
■ substitution of imports from B for domestic output, $Q_1 - Q_4$;
■ increase in domestic demand $(Q_5 - Q_2)$, resulting from a lower price P_u.

As a result of the customs union, the imports of country A have undergone an expansion and a change of origin. The import expansion is positive and beneficial, because it was caused by a reduction of high-cost domestic production and an increase in demand, shown by areas 1 and 3. In customs union theory this area is called **trade creation**.

However, the change in the origin of imports involved substituting low priced world imports for higher cost imports from country B. This redirection of trade is detrimental to country A, as it causes a negative welfare effect, shown by area 4. This area shows the **trade diversion** effect.

Area 2, which before was part of the government's tariff revenue, and area 5, which was a transfer from consumers to producers, now remains with the consumers.

From the point of view of country B, the export sector expands and therefore gains, because of the higher price of X, but consumers in B lose out as they now consume less, Q_6, at a higher price than before (P_u). B's producers gain areas $6 + 7 + 8$, while the consumers lose the area $(6 + 7)$. While area 6 is a transfer within country B from consumers to producers, area 7 is an outright loss for the consumers. B's producers gain areas 7 and 8.

To sum up, the **welfare effect** of a customs union arising from internal trade liberalization and external tariffs is equal to areas $(1+3+8-4)$ and is distributed as follows:

Country A	Trade creation	$1 + 3$
	Trade diversion	$- 4$
	Net welfare effect	$1 + 3 - 4$
Country B	Trade creation	8
	Trade diversion	none
	Net welfare effect	8

If you consider that there are 15 member countries in the EU and that each trades millions of different products, with different tariff structures and degrees of protection, you begin to understand the complexity of EU trade issues. In the end, it is difficult to predict whether each individual country will gain or lose. That will in great part depend on the economic structure of the countries participating in the customs union. The analysis above only takes into account short-term, static effects of a customs union and not its possible long-term, dynamic effects. However, the dynamic effects cannot be accurately estimated or predicted.

Estimates of the trade creation and trade diversion effect of the customs union show that they are typically very small. The **dynamic effects** which derive from the creation of a customs union are therefore all the more important. Among them are:

■ intensification of competition within the EU area;
■ external economies of scale that firms can enjoy as a result of larger market;
■ more rapid spread of technology;
■ greater stimulus to investment.

✍ Activity 12.11

'Trade creation is defined as a situation where production shifts from a higher cost producer to a lower cost producer.' Is this statement correct?

✔ Answer 12.11

Yes, it is correct. Trade creation takes place when the removal of trade barriers allows greater specialization according to comparative advantage.

Closer regional agreements, such as the Economic and Monetary Union, require increasingly tighter harmonization of policies. This process, and its domestic policy implications, can be usefully described with reference to the European Union. Given the importance of the European Union, both for the future of the individual country members and the rest of Europe and given also its role within the global economy, it becomes very important to understand the EU structures and policies.

The aspects of the EU at the centre of our analysis will be:

■ EU integration process;
■ EU main policies.

THE EUROPEAN UNION

With a total population of 373 million, as against 265 million for the USA and 125 million for Japan, the EU is the largest economic union in the world. The combined GDP of its fifteen members (Austria, Belgium, Denmark, Finland, France, Germany, Greece, Ireland, Italy, Luxembourg, the Netherlands, Portugal, Spain, Sweden and the UK) in 1996 was Ecu 6742 bn, roughly 1.17 times that of the USA and almost twice that of Japan. The EU, USA and Japan form the three largest trade blocs in the world.

Although significant progress toward European integration has been made since the signing of the **Treaty of Rome** in 1957, with an internal market now in place and economic and monetary union since 1999, the process of economic and political integration in Europe is far from complete. Substantial differences still exist between countries in terms of national institutions and policies, population sizes and per capita incomes.

The process of European integration

The reconstruction period following World War II was marked by a constructive attempt to foster international economic co-operation and rebuild the European economy. Economic and political considerations were conveying a great sense of urgency. After the war, the European economies were in shambles and a huge reconstruction effort was required. The threat of a Soviet invasion of Europe had become very real, after the Soviet-inspired Communist takeovers in Romania in 1945, Bulgaria in 1946, Hungary in 1947 and Czechoslovakia in 1948. There was an urgent need to integrate the newly established Federal Republic of Germany as tightly as possible to the other European countries. A strong Europe, both economically and politically, was thought to be essential.

As far as the immediate task of European reconstruction was concerned, the most important contribution came from US aid, administered through the **Marshall Plan**, for three years from 1948. The US aid, intended to speed up the process of economic reconstruction in Europe, was distributed through an international organization specially created for the purpose of co-ordinating the relief and aid operation: the **Organization for European Economic Co-operation (OEEC)**. At the end of the Marshall Plan, the OEEC was not dismantled, but continued instead to promote economic integration and co-operation among the European economies and the industrialized world. In 1961 it became the **Organization for Economic Co-operation and Development (OECD)**.

Economic co-operation was sought initially with the creation of the **European Coal and Steel Community (ECSC)** in 1951 between France, the Federal Republic of Germany, Italy and the Benelux countries, to which the **European Atomic Energy Commission** and the **European Economic Community (EEC)** were added with the Treaty of Rome in 1957. The three communities were later amalgamated to form the **European Community** in 1965.

One of the aims of the six signatories of the Treaty of Rome was the achievement, within 12 years, of a common market characterized by the following:

- free trade among members;
- common external tariff;
- free mobility of factors of production (labour and capital).

The realization of an economic union, which would require further harmonization of economic policies, was not set as a task of the EEC when the Treaty of Rome was signed in 1957.

The realization of a common market proved difficult enough in the years that followed. By 1970, only the first two aspect of the common market had been achieved, while it took another 20 years before free mobility of labour and capital was allowed with the single market in 1992. Impediments to the speedy realization of the common market had been the existence of contrasting national interests, further exacerbated by successive enlargements of the community. The UK, Ireland and Denmark joined in 1973, Greece in 1981 and Spain and Portugal in 1986. While British membership opened up the thorny question of the contributions of individual members to the EC budget, the membership of Greece, Spain and Portugal added a Mediterranean dimension to the problem of economic harmonization. The recessionary decades of the 1970s and 1980s provided little inducement towards economic concessions and trade liberalization, as national governments resorted to protectionist measures in an attempt to help domestic industries and employment.

The movement toward closer European integration regained momentum in 1979, with the creation of the **European Monetary System (EMS)** and the fixing of currencies in the exchange rate mechanism (**ERM**). It was further strengthened in 1985, with the signing of the **Single European Act**. In particular the Single Act set the European Community on course for a more united Europe:

- It replaced the unanimity rule, for matters concerning the internal market, with the qualified majority voting rule.
- It set 1992 as the completion date for the internal market without frontiers.

- It amended the original Treaty of Rome with the introduction of policies aimed at economic integration, social cohesion, environment protection and monetary and political co-operation.

Deepening of the Union

The Single Act was a major step towards the ultimate goal of an economically united Europe, which involved the establishment of an **Economic and Monetary Union (EMU)**. The EMU would in turn, as discussed in Chapter 10, involve tight co-ordination of monetary and fiscal policies among members.

In the Delors Plan of 1990, the broad outlines of a treaty on EMU were set. According to this plan, EMU should be reached in three stages, at the end of which monetary policy would be transferred from national authorities to an independent European system of central banks, led by a European Central Bank (ECB), and national currencies would be replaced by a common currency. In the field of fiscal policy, national governments would retain formal autonomy, which would be constrained, in practice, by common policies and restrictions.

The **Treaty on European Union**, as outlined by the Delors plan, was finally ratified in 1991 and became known as the **Maastricht Treaty**. According to the Treaty, economic and monetary union were to be established within the EU by 1999. They were to be preceded by **economic convergence programmes**, aiming to bring about convergence of main macroeconomic variables which directly affect the stability of exchange rates, such as inflation and interest rates and budget deficits. EMU was to be instituted on 1 January 1999, but would be confined to those countries meeting the convergence criteria.

The Treaty attached great importance to the achievement of real economic convergence (measured by standard of living and unemployment) and social cohesion. To this effect, a special cohesion fund was set up to give financial support to environmental and transport projects in member states with per capita income which is less than 90 per cent of the EU average (Greece, Ireland, Portugal and Spain) between 1993 and 1999.

The Maastricht Treaty also contained provisions on political and social issues, such as the introduction of a union citizenship, freedom of movement, right of free residence, right to vote and to be eligible for elections at municipal and European level. Provisions for a common foreign and security policy and a social charter for the consolidation of workers' basic rights throughout the EU were also included. Britain opted out the signing of the social charter.

Finally, the Treaty contained provisions aimed at ensuring that decisions would be made at the Union level only if they could not be made by individual members. These provisions are written into the subsidiarity principle (Art. 3b), which is intended to avoid excessive centralization of power and reduce the **democratic deficit**, i.e. the limited input that elected representatives at Euro level have on the decision-making process. The Maastricht Treaty has now given the European Parliament the power of veto over a large number of EU rules.

The Maastricht Treaty represents a huge step forward toward a federal Europe, although the EU remains, for the moment at least, a community of nation states. It was finally approved by the twelve EU members. In 1996, three new countries, Sweden, Finland and Austria, joined the EU.

✐ Activity 12.12

Which of the following preferential trading arrangements best describes the European Union at the beginning of the 1980s: a customs union, a common market, a free trade area or an economic and monetary union?

✓ Answer 12.12

A customs union, as tariffs and quotas had been removed from trade between members and a system of common external tariffs was imposed on trade with the rest of the world.

EU POLICIES

There are many important EU common policies aimed at fostering economic, social and political harmonization of member countries.

Competition policy

This is aimed at creating a more competitive environment, by forbidding firms' restrictive practices, the abuse of a dominant position and national governments' subsidies to businesses. These restrictions apply to firms or businesses only insofar as they affect the trade between member states. National cartels operating only in their own domestic economy are not affected by these restrictions, unless they are outlawed by national legislation.

Taxation policy

This policy aims at minimizing the indirect effects of one member's tax system on the others, without pressing for absolute equalization of tax bases or tax rates. The idea is that differences in individual tax systems should not affect the international free movement of goods, people and capital. In other words, the EU decided not to aim at full harmonization of indirect taxes, but only at an approximation. In line with this principle, it was decided in 1993 that the minimum standard VAT rate throughout the Union should be 15 per cent, and 5 per cent for optional necessities. Zero rates could be maintained for a very limited number of products and for a transitional period only. A common VAT system, with equal structure and equal rates is not foreseen in the near future. Direct taxes and other matters of fiscal policy are accepted to be a matter of national sovereignty.

Social policy

This has received very little attention in the EU. In the first few decades or so, some progress has been made only in the fields of equal treatment for men and women, health and safety measures and workers' freedom of movement. Social policy gathered momentum with the adoption of the Social Charter in 1989. The Social Charter covers the improvement of living and working conditions, social protection, such as a minimum wage and guaranteed unemployment benefit, health protection, etc. However, the **Social Charter** is simply a set of principles which still needs to be transformed into regulations by means of a social action programme.

Transport policy

This policy aims at harmonization of transport costs as a way of ensuring equality of cost conditions to firms across the EU. Transport costs form a substantial part of production costs. In many countries, large parts of the transport sector are subsidized by respective governments, in an effort to encourage greater use of energy efficient, and environmentally friendly public transport. Without an appropriate policy at EU level, this situation would result in widely different transport costs for different firms in different member states, with grave damage to the EU economies. The completion of the internal market in 1992 has led to a number of new directives which should open up national transport markets to EU competitors. The EU has also come up with a series of proposals for the development of **Trans-European Networks (TENs)**.

Environmental policies

Policies for the protection of the environment were not included in the Treaty of Rome. They were launched in 1973 in the **Environmental Action programmes (EAPs)**. These programmes rely on the use of taxes or tradeable permits for the reduction of pollutant activities. The last environmental programme to be launched was proposed in 1992, under the title *Towards Sustainability*. The programme stresses the concept of sustainable growth, which will take the needs of future generations into account. By comparison with the environmental programmes of other countries, the EU standards are generally set at only minimal levels.

Regional policy

This policy is intended to support poorer or disadvantaged regions of the Union. Such regions comprise:

- poorer areas lagging behind in development;
- areas which have suffered industrial decline;
- high long-term unemployment regions;
- underdeveloped rural areas;
- areas with low population density.

As these policies suggest, they were introduced because of the wide variation in per-capita income across the EU. On this basis, Portugal, Greece, Spain and Ireland have per-capita incomes far below the EU average. The poorest regions – Alentego in Portugal, Macedonia and some islands in Greece, and East Germany, have per capita incomes which are between 40 and 50 per cent of the EU average. Among the wealthier countries, internal regional disparities can still be found. The southern region of Italy, the *mezzogiorno*, records incomes which are only two-thirds of the EU average.

The problem with regional disparities is that they are large and also likely to remain so and not to disappear. This is because the more prosperous areas tend to enjoy considerable external economies of scale, due to the availability of a developed infrastructure and skilled labour. EU policies are aimed at counteracting these imbalances, drawing from the EU **Structural Fund**, which includes the **European Regional Development Fund (ERDF)**, the **European Social Fund (ESF)**, the **European Investment Bank** and the **European Cohesion Fund**. The funds available through these sources have not been substantial and, as a consequence, the impact of these policies, has also been rather limited.

Monetary policy

EU monetary policy aims at the creation of a monetary union by 1999. This policy is discussed at length in Chapter 10.

Common agricultural policy (CAP)

The Common Agricultural Policy (CAP) is by far the most important common policy of the Union so far. For this reason it deserves a fuller analysis. First, before we discuss CAP, let's be aware of the fact that governments intervene in the agricultural sector almost everywhere in the world. The EU is not unique in this respect. Table 12.5 gives us an idea of the extent of protection.

The Common Agricultural Policy formed the core of EEC policies in 1957. Its main objectives, as stated in Art. 39 of the Treaty of Rome, were:

■ to increase agricultural productivity by promoting technical progress and ensuring rational development of agricultural production and the optimum utilization of the factors of production, in particular labour;

■ to ensure a fair standard of living for the agricultural community;

■ to stabilize markets;

■ to assure availability of supplies;

■ to ensure that supplies would reach consumers at reasonable prices.

Agricultural incomes were on the whole low at the time. They tended to fluctuate widely and their rate of growth lagged behind the national average. It was also feared that, in the absence of an active government policy, the process of economic growth would make this gap wider. When the six original signatories decided to tackle the agricultural problem together by establishing a common agricultural programme, they embarked on a huge task of immense economic and social implications.

The working of CAP rests on three principles:

1 **Single market**: the free movement of agricultural products within the community, which required the elimination of any national support or protection scheme for agricultural products.

2 **Community preference**: common external tariff and protection from competitive imports or price fluctuations on world markets.

3 **Financial solidarity**: sharing of the costs of the CAP through the administration of a common fund, the **European Agricultural Guidance and Guarantee Fund (EAGGF)**.

CAP intervention mechanism

CAP is essentially a comprehensive system of subsidies for agriculture, which operates through the price mechanism. It covers all the quantitatively important agricultural products of the EU. The CAP intervention mechanism is described by Figure 12.14.

Every year the EU Council of Ministers for Agriculture fixes the EU **target price** (P^t) for each individual agricultural product. The target price represents the maximum price or upper limit for a standard quality of product. The target price, which is set well above the **world price** (P^w) and the domestic **equilibrium market price** (P^e), in the 'zone of greatest deficit' between production and demand, causes both **excess domestic supply** and **competition from world imports**. Therefore both these problems need to be dealt with by CAP.

The lower limit of acceptable market price fluctuations, known as the **intervention price** (P^i), is also set. When the market price reaches this floor value,

Table 12.5 Agricultural subsidies and producer subsidy equivalents in industrial countries, 1993–5

Country	Billions of US $			Subsidy as a percentage of agricultural output		
	1993	1994	1995	1993	1994	1995
USA	23.2	21.6	14.5	23	20	15
EU	78.2	81.6	96.9	49	49	49
Japan	30.0	39.1	37.7	72	74	77
Australia	1.0	1.2	1.2	9	10	9
Austria	3.1	3.4	—	59	61	—
Canada	4.8	4.0	4.7	31	26	27
Finland	2.6	3.1	—	64	69	—
New Zealand	0.1	0.1	0.2	3	3	4
Norway	2.2	2.0	2.0	75	74	74
Sweden	2.0	1.8	—	54	57	—
Switzerland	4.4	4.6	4.7	80	81	81
All industrial countries	141.7	149.9	139.6	42	42	41

Sources: OECD, *Agricultural Policies, Markets and Trade in OECD Countries*, 1996

Figure 12.14   CAP intervention mechanism

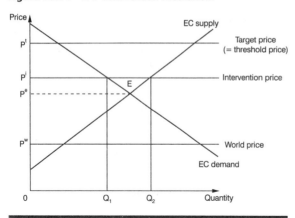

caused by the downward pressure on price of excess supply, the EU has to intervene to stop the price fall by buying up the excess supply. So farmers in the EU have absolute certainty that the lowest price they can expect to receive for selling their output is the intervention price.

The minimum **import price**, at which a product may be imported from any non-member country, is the **target price** (P^t), which is achieved by imposing the appropriate **levy** $(P^t - P^w)$. The levies are calculated daily and then applied equally to all imports. Thus the levy is variable and operates as an equalizing tariff, calculated as the difference between the current world price and the EU internal target price. If, on the other hand, EU prices were to exceed the target price, then imports at the target price become competitive and, by entering the market at the target price, keep EU domestic prices steady at the target level.

Surpluses created by EU prices being set above domestic equilibrium prices and mopped up by EU compulsory 'intervention buying' are used as **buffer stock** for maintaining the market price within the permissible limits of variations. The storage of these surpluses, the infamous 'butter mountains' and 'wine lakes', has scarred the EU's image in recent years. Bad publicity and international trade rows have also been caused by the EU often **dumping** (selling abroad at below cost prices) part of these excess stocks of food on world markets at or often below world market prices.

An intervention system similar to the one described above covers approximately 70 per cent of the EEC agricultural production (dairy products, meat, sugar, fruits, table wine, etc.). Another 25 per cent of agricultural production (eggs, poultry, etc.) is covered by a

looser scheme, which sets external tariffs only without support measures for the internal market.

As well as the **prices policy** and the **trading policy** just examined, the EU also has a **structural policy** aimed at restructuring the agricultural sector to reduce the impact of the structural diversity of European agriculture. Structural policies are aimed at encouraging: the implementation of more advanced technical forms of production; modernization of farms; rationalization of production; improved processing of agricultural products.

EU agriculture under the CAP

The outcome of the Common Agricultural Policy has been a mixed bag of successes and failures. CAP has undoubtedly achieved the following:

- Farmers' incomes and agricultural products prices have been stabilized. However, the amount of protection granted by CAP has largely favoured the products of northern countries, to the detriment of the Mediterranean countries whose products have not enjoyed an equally favourable treatment. This has exacerbated regional inequalities within the EU. Prices have been stabilized, albeit at high levels.
- Self-sufficiency in food production has been created. Europe is now a substantial exporter of food, while before CAP it was a net importer.
- Agricultural productivity has increased enormously, thanks to intensive farming and better technologies.

On the downside, we must list the following:

- EU consumers pay for CAP twice. They pay for CAP through the very high prices of their food, higher than world prices. They also pay for CAP via the EU budget, about 70 per cent of which is used up to support CAP.
- CAP has arguably contributed to Europe's ecological degradation by encouraging the use of growth-enhancing chemicals to maximize the amounts of surplus production.
- CAP redistribution procedures have also been arguably regressive, granting larger rewards to the wealthier northern members.

Reforms of CAP and Agenda 2000

There have been attempts at reforming the CAP, which have proved largely unsuccessful. The first attempt at reform was by the **Mansholt Plan** in 1968, which proposed a radical restructuring of the CAP, a reduction of agricultural employment by 50 per cent and trade liberalization in agricultural products. The plan aroused strong political opposition and was never accepted.

A second attempt was made in 1981, with a proposal by the EU Commission, the **Guidelines for European Agriculture**. The plan aimed at reducing the huge surpluses by reducing prices, with a view to bringing EU prices in line with world prices in the long run. As a result of these proposals, price support was restricted to pre-specified levels of production, with various slightly punitive measures to be applied if pre-agreed quotas were exceeded. These reforms did not resolve the problem of overproduction, with EU production continuing to be three or four times higher than EU consumption.

A crisis point was reached in 1984 when, due to chronic overproduction, the budgetary funds were exhausted and CAP was threatened with financial collapse. Emergency measures were subsequently adopted to contain the size of surpluses, without fundamentally resolving the problem. In 1987, the EU agricultural ministers failed to freeze farm prices and implement policy reforms. CAP reached crisis point once more.

The problems of CAP have become more complicated after the last Mediterranean enlargement, with Portugal and Spain joining the Union. After their accession the share of Mediterranean products has increased, while CAP expenditure is still heavily biased in support of producers of the northern member countries. Dairy products, cereals and meat, which are typically northern products, absorb about 70 per cent of the total CAP budget.

Attempts to shift from protection and guaranteed prices to restructuring and output restriction have further intensified in recent years, through the **MacSharry Plan** and the Uruguay Round of GATT negotiations (discussed in Chapter 13).

The MacSharry reforms, named after the Commissioner MacSharry, were implemented in three stages, from 1993 to 1995. The reforms were successful in bringing production under control and reducing surpluses, but they did not result in a reduction of EU agricultural spending because of built-in income compensations given to farmers to induce them to reduce production. EU farmers were in fact paid not to produce.

Further pressure to reduce farm subsidies came from the **Uruguay Round** of GATT negotiations. An agreement by the EU to reduce average tariffs and subsidies on agricultural products by about one-third was reached at the end of the Uruguay Round in 1993. A more detailed discussion of that outcome is provided in Chapter 13.

Finally, the need to fundamentally reconsider CAP is coming from the enlargement of the EU to Hungary, Poland, Estonia, Czech Republic and Slovenia, as well as Cyprus. The accession of these countries by the year 2003 will have a profound effect on the EU agricultural budget. The economic impact of **Agenda 2000**, the document published on 16 July 1997 in which the European Commission outlines the broad perspectives for enlargement and its financial implications, is discussed in the case study at the end of this chapter.

The fundamental problem at the root of CAP still remains the fact that millions of consumers pay heavily to protect the interests of a minority of large farmers. Other industries, equally needy of funds and equally crucial to domestic economies such as steel or coalmining, have not enjoyed such preferential treatment and have been fully exposed to the cold winds of world competition.

Rationale of European integration

The European integration process was designed to realize a large, free, internal market characterized by strong and fair competition. This approach was very much in line with the aspirations of greater economic integration and trade liberalization which were common to the USA and Europe in the immediate post-war period.

During the years of the Cold War, the emphasis shifted towards the need to provide a strong counterforce to the Communist threat coming from central and eastern Europe, in defence of freedom and democracy. The countervailing power, however, was to be economic rather than political, based on a large and free market, as envisaged by the Treaty of Rome in 1957.

The Single Market of 1992 can be seen as an attempt by Europe to keep up with the USA and Japan, which enjoyed large, competitive home markets. The Maastricht Treaty on European Union was the final step towards an economically united Europe, still based on free market principles. The bringing into line of national and EU interests and policies, particularly in the light of imminent further enlargement of the EU to central and eastern Europe, represents a huge challenge that European countries will have to face in the coming years.

CASE STUDY: AGENDA 2000

The European Commission presented its communication 'Agenda 2000' on 16 July 1997. The document offers an insightful vision of the European Union as it enters the twenty-first century. It also assesses the impact of enlargement to ten prospective new members from central and eastern Europe, with particular reference to the financial framework of the Union, and recommends that accession negotiations start with Hungary, Poland, Estonia, the Czech Republic and Slovenia. It is a document of great importance as it sets out a possible blueprint for EU development in the years to come.

This case study focuses on the economic impact of the new proposed enlargement to include Hungary, Poland, Romania, the Slovak Republic, Latvia, Estonia, Lithuania, Bulgaria, the Czech Republic and Slovenia as new EU members, as assessed in Agenda 2000. Enlargement is not an issue. Agenda 2000 sees the enlargement process as irreversible, as it reflects fundamental European interests, and assesses the costs of its non-implementation as even higher. The question which Agenda 2000 addresses is not the 'if', but only the 'when' and 'how' of the proposed enlargement.

A look at the statistics

As Table 12.5 shows, the external dimension of the proposed enlargement is considerable. The area of the new applicants taken together represents 33 per cent of the whole EU15; its population 28 per cent; but the combined GDP is only 9 per cent of EU15 GDP; their average per capita income only 32 per cent of the EU15. The agricultural sector, on the other hand, has a far greater importance for the economies of the ten prospective members than it has for the EU, providing on average 22 per cent of total employment (but as high as 34 per cent in Romania and 26 per cent in Poland), compared with the 5 per cent represented by agricultural employment in the EU15.

Figure 12.15 further illustrates the income gap between the current EU15 members – where the poorest, in Greece, have an income per capita of ECU11,320 (66 per cent of average EU per capita income) and the better off in Denmark enjoy on average ECU19,960 (116 per cent of EU average) – and prospective members, where a Latvian on average has a meagre ECU3160, which represents only 18 per cent of the EU average income per head.

Potential economic benefits

The Commission's study estimates that the economic effects of enlargement will be beneficial for the Union in the longer run. Enlargement will mean the creation of a larger economic area, with up to 500 million consumers, compared with the current 370 million. Liberalized factor and goods markets, common competition policies and, eventually, a common currency will allow for a better allocation of resources and greater economies of scale. This in turn could trigger a high growth with low inflation scenario for the whole area and improve the EU's competitive position in the world.

In particular, enlargement will create new output and employment opportunities, by providing new markets where existing EU countries could expand. These markets would also need a large amount of investment, particularly in infrastructure, which again existing EU members could help to provide. The new member countries would also provide a large pool of labour, ensuring greater non-inflationary growth, as well as new competitive supplies of goods and raw materials. Further growth by new members will also mean greater import demand from other EU members.

However, these benefits will not be achievable immediately, nor will they be evenly spread. Enlargement is likely to create the need for prolonged, painful sectoral adjustments throughout the Union, causing economic, social and political tensions. It is argued, however, that the EU would need to undergo fundamental changes, regardless of enlargement, if it wishes to improve its competitive position vis-à-vis Southeast Asia and on world markets generally.

Problem areas and risks

This enlargement is different from the previous ones because the prospective members are all rather poor countries still trying to catch up. The major challenges related to their accession are therefore:

■ their low per capita income;
■ the heavy bias of most of their economies toward agriculture;
■ the inadequacy of their transport, telecommunication and energy infrastructures and networks;
■ their weak administrations.

Figure 12.15   GDP per capita (at Purchasing Power Standards): enlarged EU, 1995

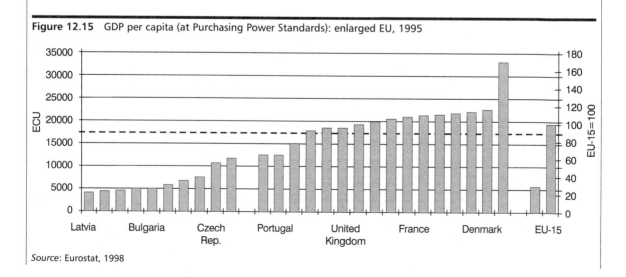

Source: Eurostat, 1998

Table 12.6 Basic statistics of the proposed EU enlargement, 1995

	Area (1000 km²)	Population		GDP at current market prices			GDP at purchasing power standards			Agriculture	
		(millions)	density (inh./km²)	(billion ECU)	(in Ecu per head)	(in Ecu per head as % of EU average)	(billion Ecu at PPP rates)	(in Ecu per head at PPP rates)	(in Ecu per head as % of EU average)	(% of total gross value added)	(% employment)
	1	2	3	4	5	6	7	8	9	10	11
Hungary	93	10.2	110	33.4	3340	19	64.6	6310	37	6.2	8.0
Poland	313	38.6	123	90.2	2360	14	203.3	5320	31	7.6	26.0
Romania	238	22.7	95	27.3	1200	7	94.3	4060	23	20.5	34.0
Slovak Rep.	49	5.4	110	13.3	2470	14	38.0	7120	41	6.3	9.0
Latvia	65	2.5	38	3.4	1370	8	7.9	3160	18	9.9	18.0
Estonia	45	1.5	33	2.8	1850	11	5.9	3920	23	8.1	13.0
Lithuania	65	3.7	57	3.5	930	5	15.3	4130	24	9.3	23.0
Bulgaria	111	8.4	76	9.9	1180	7	35.4	4210	24	13.9	23.0
Czech Rep.	79	10.3	130	36.1	3490	20	97.2	9410	55	5.2	6.0
Slovenia	20	2.0	100	14.2	7240	42	20.1	10110	59	5.0	7.0
CE-10	1078	105.3	98	234	2220	13	582.0	5530	32	8.6	22.0
in % of EU-15	33	28	85	4	13		9	32		358	42
Belgium	31	10.1	332	205.9	20310	118	196.0	19340	112	1.7 *	2.0
Denmark	43	5.2	121	132.1	25260	146	104.4	19960	116	3.7 *	4.0
Germany	357	81.5	228	1845.2	22600	131	1556.8	19070	110	1.0 *	3.0
Greece	132	10.4	79	87.4	8360	48	118.4	11320	66	14.7 *	20.0
Spain	506	39.2	77	428.1	10920	63	518.8	13230	77	3.7 *	9.0
France	544	58.0	107	1174.3	20200	117	1076.5	18520	107	2.5 *	4.0
Ireland	70	3.6	51	49.2	13740	80	57.4	16020	93	7.5 *	1.0
Italy	301	57.3	190	831.4	14250	83	1036.8	17770	103	2.9 *	7.0
Luxembourg	3	0.4	157	13.3	32370	187	11.9	29140	169	1.5 *	3.0
Netherlands	42	15.4	371	302.5	19570	113	284.3	18390	107	3.6 *	3.0
Austria	84	8.0	96	178.4	22180	128	155.5	19320	112	2.4 *	7.0
Portugal	92	9.9	108	77.1	7770	45	115.2	11620	67	5.1 *	11.0
Finland	338	5.1	15	95.6	18720	108	84.5	16550	96	5.2 *	7.0
Sweden	450	8.8	20	176.3	19970	116	153.5	17390	101	2.1 *	3.0
UK	244	58.5	240	844.8	14410	83	971.7	16580	96	1.6 *	2.0
EU15	3236	371.6	115	6441.5	17260	100	6441.5	17260	100	2.4 *	5.0

Source: CEECs, Statistical Institutes, 1998

continued overleaf

AGENDA 2000

This situation is likely to persist through time. Implementing change will be particularly difficult because of the high levels of unemployment throughout the EU. People losing their jobs because of the regional restructuring brought about by EU enlargement would find it very difficult to find other jobs elsewhere in the EU. In this climate, any adjustment that leads to a substantial loss of jobs will be politically difficult.

Adjustment will be very painful in regions or industries already suffering from excess supply of labour or excess capacity. It will be easier in sectors such as **telecommunications**, **energy supply**, **financial services** or **tourism**, where no existing industries need to be displaced.

Sectoral adjustments

Sectoral adjustment in the enlarged Union is likely to be most marked in **agriculture**, **coal**, **mining** and traditional industries such as **textiles**. Greater expansion is likely to be enjoyed by sectors such as **food processing** and **clothing**.

Structural change and adjustment will be substantial, particularly in agriculture. Enlargement will greatly increase the agricultural potential of the Union, while the market for European primary products and processed food will increase by more than 100 million consumers.

However, extension of the Common Agricultural policy (CAP) in its present form to the acceding countries would create difficulties. Given the existing price gap between the new members and much higher CAP prices, even a gradual introduction of CAP prices would tend to stimulate **surplus production**, in particular in the livestock sector, thus adding to existing surpluses.

The constraints of the World Trade Organization (WTO) on subsidized exports would prevent the enlarged Union from selling its surpluses on world markets. Extension of the CAP would also entail a substantial budgetary extra charge, estimated at around Ecu11bn per year, two-thirds of which would be represented by direct payment to farmers. These budgetary implications of enlargement make the reform of CAP all the more urgent.

☆ **For revision of this chapter, see the Chapter Summaries at the end of the book, starting on page 411.**

13 Trade organizations and trade flows

Objectives

After studying this chapter you will be able to discuss:

- the main global economic issues of the 1990s;
- the origin and function of the General Agreement on Tariffs and Trade (GATT) and World Trade Organization (WTO);
- the relationship between GATT, the EU and less developed countries (LDCs);
- the causes and consequences of new protectionism;
- the volume and pattern of global trade flows;
- the challenges and opportunities of the new global age.

GLOBAL ECONOMIC ISSUES

In this final chapter we are going to take a broad view of the world economy, focusing on main global economic issues. The increased internationalization of economic activities has had widespread repercussions on many aspects of businesses. Globalization affects the 'real world' of commodity markets (the trade in goods and services) and factor markets (the international buying and selling of labour, capital or technological know-how). Globalization also affects the 'financial world' of currency and capital markets. An understanding of global issues is therefore essential for both those interested and involved in the management of businesses and those with a broader interest in world economic issues and development.

✍ Activity 13.1

Make a list of current global economic issues of which you are aware.

✓ Answer 13.1

The following issues have been at the forefront of the political agenda since the beginning of the 1960s:

- slower growth and increased regionalization of world trade;
- new protectionism;

- widening inequalities in world income distribution
- world debt problems;
- globalization of capital markets and exchange rate volatility;
- internationalization of production and the control of multinational corporations;
- global use of non-renewable energy sources;
- control and management of world environmental dangers.

A full discussion of these issues goes well beyond the scope of this text. In what follows we will mostly focus on international trade institutions and the changing global scenario of current international trade relations.

COUNTRY GROUPINGS

Before we examine these issues in greater detail, we need to identify the main global players. World trade and economic activity are polarized among groups of countries or **trade blocs**. Data and statistics are often collected and discussed separately for each group. These groupings have altered over the years in response to changing economic circumstances of some of their individual member countries.

Until the collapse of the Communist regimes at the beginning of the 1980s, four main country groupings were used in most data analyses of the global economy:

- industrial countries;
- centrally planned economies;
- oil exporters or OPEC countries;
- developing countries or less developed countries (LDCs).

The end of the old Communist regimes and the beginning of economic liberalization in eastern Europe, which started with the collapse of the Berlin Wall in 1989 and the disintegration of the former USSR, coincided with the emergence on the world scene of new dynamic markets in Southeast Asia. Hence, the country groupings most currently in use have become the following:

- industrialized or developed countries (DCs);
- European economies in transition and the Russian Federation;
- dynamic Asian economies (DAEs) and China;
- less developed countries (LDCs).

The names given to these groups and the boundaries between them can vary, depending on the analytical purposes pursued. Groupings may also be further disaggregated: EU countries, for example, can be seen as a subgroup of the industrialized countries.

The **industrialized countries** include: Australia, Austria, Belgium, Canada, Finland, France, Germany, Ireland, Italy, Japan, Netherlands, New Zealand, Norway, Spain, Sweden, Switzerland, UK, USA. The group may be further subdivided into USA, Japan, Germany and the EU, or major four European countries (Germany, France, Italy, UK), the Group of Seven countries or G7 (USA, Canada, Japan, Germany, France, UK, Italy), the Group of Five countries or G5 (USA, Japan, Germany, France, UK).

The **European economies in transition** include: Bulgaria, Romania, Russia, Slovak Republic, Slovenia, Ukraine and the Baltic states (Estonia, Latvia, Lithuania).

The **dynamic Asian economies (DAEs)** include Chinese Taipei, Hong Kong, Malaysia, the Philippines, Singapore, Thailand and China. The European economies in transition and the dynamic Asian economies are also sometimes referred to as the **emerging markets**.

The **less developed countries (LDCs)** are further subdivided into middle-income and low-income countries. LDCs are eligible for aid and loans on more favourable terms than richer developing countries.

✍ Activity 13.2

Look at the statistics shown in Tables 13.1, 13.2 and 13.3 and Figure 13.,1 and discuss what they show.

✓ Answer 13.2

The statistics presented in Tables 13.1, 13.2 and 13.3 and Figure 13.1 show a greatly diversified world economy, with huge differences in income per head, great inequalities between rich and poor countries and among poor countries themselves.

The total population of low-income LDCs is over 3.1 billion people, with an average annual per capita income of about $400 in 1997. Projections of distribution of GDP per capita into the year 2020 reflect a global distribution of income still profoundly uneven. Considerable improvements in absolute, but not relative terms, is predicted for some emerging economies of Southeast Asia. The opening up of some LDCs' large new markets, as explained at the end of this chapter, is likely to benefit most the DCs.

Many factors have contributed to this situation. The study of world trade organizations and their development in the post-war period, together with international capital movements and financial flows, partly helps us to explain the persistence of an uneven distribution of world income and current trade and investment flows.

INTERNATIONAL TRADE ORGANIZATIONS AND PATTERN OF INTERNATIONAL TRADE

The Great Depression that hit the American economy in 1929–31 spread with unprecedented speed and devastating virulence to the whole of Europe, with the exception of Russia and lingered on for over ten years. This episode provided a painful example of the dangers of economic interdependence, often summed up by the expression 'when America sneezes, Europe catches pneumonia'. A recession in the USA could cause deep depression and have magnified effects in Europe. In the wake of the depression, and for a whole decade, international trade collapsed and protectionism ruled.

The lesson of the 1930s was not lost on the governments of major industrialized countries after the war. Even before the war was over, government officials, bankers and bureaucrats were busily forging the international institutions which were to regulate international trade and liquidity after the war. These institutions, such as the World Bank, International Monetary Fund (IMF) and the General Agreement on Tariffs and Trade (GATT), now known as the World Trade Organization (WTO), have shaped

Table 13.1 Low-income economies: basic indicators

		GNP per capita		PPP estimates of GNP per capita		Poverty % of people living on less than $1 a day (PPP) 1981–95	Life expectancy at birth (years) 1995	Adult illiteracy % 1995
	Population (millions) mid-1995	Dollars 1995	Avg. ann. growth (%) 1985–95	US = 100 1987	1995			
Low-income economies	3179.9	430 w	3.8				63	34
Excluding China and India	1050.3	290 w	−1.4				56	46
1 Mozambique	16.2	80	3.6	2.5	3.0	—	47	60
2 Ethiopa	56.4	100	−0.3	2.0	1.7	33.8	49	65
3 Tanzania	29.6	120	1.0	2.6	2.4	16.4	51	32
4 Burundi	6.3	160	−1.3	3.2	2.3	—	49	65
5 Malawi	9.8	170	−0.7	3.1	2.8	—	43	44
6 Chad	6.4	180	0.6	2.5	2.6	—	48	52
7 Rwanda	6.4	180	−5.4	3.8	2.0	45.7	46	40
8 Sierra Leone	4.2	180	−3.6	3.2	2.2	—	40	—
9 Nepal	21.5	200	2.4	4.0	4.3	53.1	55	73
10 Niger	9.0	220	—	3.6	2.8	61.5	47	86
11 Burkina Faso	10.4	230	−0.2	3.3	2.9	—	49	81
12 Madagascar	13.7	230	−2.2	3.1	2.4	72.3	52	—
13 Bangladesh	119.8	240	2.1	4.8	5.1	—	58	62
14 Uganda	19.2	240	2.7	4.7	5.5	50.0	42	38
15 Vietnam	73.5	240	—	—	—	—	68	6
16 Guinea-Bissau	1.1	250	−2.0	2.8	2.9	87.0	38	45
17 Haiti	7.2	250	−5.2	5.8	3.4	—	57	55
18 Mali	9.8	250	0.8	2.3	2.0	—	50	69
19 Nigeria	111.3	260	1.2	4.4	4.5	28.9	53	43
20 Yemen, Rep.	15.3	260	—	—	—	—	53	—
21 Cambodia	10.0	270	—	—	—	—	53	35
22 Kenya	26.7	280	0.1	5.7	5.1	50.2	58	22
23 Mongolia	2.5	310	−3.8	10.6	7.2	—	65	—
24 Togo	4.1	310	−2.7	5.5	4.2	—	56	48
25 Gambia, The	1.1	320	—	4.5	3.5	—	46	61
26 Central African Republic	3.3	340	−2.4	5.0	4.0	—	48	40
27 India	929.4	340	3.2^c	4.4	5.2	52.5	62	48
28 Lao PDR	4.9	350	2.7	—	—	—	52	43
29 Benin	5.5	370	−0.3	6.9	6.5	—	50	63
30 Nicaragua	4.4	380	−5.4	11.8	7.4	43.8	68	34
31 Ghana	17.1	390	1.4	7.4	7.4	—	59	—
32 Zambia	9.0	400	−0.8	4.2	3.5	84.6	46	22
33 Angola	10.8	410	−6.1	8.9	4.9	—	47	—
34 Georgia	5.4	440	−17.0	28.1	5.5	—	73	—
35 Pakistan	129.9	460	1.2	8.4	8.3	11.6	60	62
36 Mauritania	2.3	460	0.5	6.0	5.7	31.4	51	—
37 Azerbaijan	7.5	480	−16.3	21.8	5.4	—	70	—
38 Zimbabwe	11.0	540	−0.6	8.6	7.5	41.0	57	15
39 Guinea	6.6	550	1.4	—	—	26.3	44	—
40 Honduras	5.9	600	0.1	7.9	7.0	46.0	67	27
41 Senegal	8.5	600	—	7.3	6.6	54.0	50	67
42 China	1200.2	620	—	6.3	10.8	29.4	69	19
43 Cameroon	13.3	650	8.3	15.1	7.8	—	57	37
44 Côte d'Ivoire	14.0	660	−6.6	8.2	5.9	17.7	55	60
45 Albania	3.3	670	—	—	—	—	73	—
46 Congo	2.6	680	−3.2	11.5	7.6	—	51	25
47 Kyrgyz Republic	4.5	700	−6.9	13.6	6.7	68	—	—
48 Sri Lanka	18.1	700	2.6	10.6	12.1	4.0	72	10
49 Armenia	3.8	730	−15.1	25.4	8.4	—	71	—

Source: World Development Report, 1997

Table 13.2   Middle-income economies: basic indicators

	Population (millions) mid-1995	GNP per capita Dollars 1995	GNP per capita Avg. ann. growth (%) 1985–95	PPP estimates of GNP per capita US = 100 1987	PPP estimates of GNP per capita US = 100 1995	Poverty % of people living on less than $1 a day (PPP) 1981–95	Life expectancy at birth (years) 1995	Adult illiteracy % 1995
Middle-income economies	1590.9	2390	–0.7				68	18
Lower-middle income	1152.6	1670 w	–1.3				67	—
50 Lesotho	2.0	770	1.2	6.1	6.6	50.4	61	29
51 Egypt, Arab Rep.	57.8	790	1.1	14.3	14.2	7.6	63	49
52 Bolivia	7.4	800	1.8	9.1	9.4	7.1	60	17
53 Macedonia, FYR	2.1	860	—	—	—		73	—
54 Moldova	4.3	920	—	—	—	6.8	69	—
55 Uzbekistan	22.8	970	–3.9	12.6	8.8	—	70	—
56 Indonesia	193.3	980	6.0	9.8	14.1	14.5	64	16
57 Philippines	68.6	1050	1.5	10.3	10.6	27.5	66	5
58 Morocco	26.6	1110	0.9	13.2	12.4	1.1	65	56
59 Syrian Arab Republic	14.1	1120	0.9	18.5	19.7	—	68	—
60 Papua New Guinea	4.3	1160	2.3	8.5	9.0	—	57	28
61 Bulgaria	8.4	1330	–2.6	23.4	16.6	2.6	71	—
62 Kazakstan	16.6	1330	–8.6	24.2	11.2	—	69	—
63 Guatemala	10.6	1340	0.3	13.2	12.4	53.3	66	44
64 Ecuador	11.5	1390	0.8	15.8	15.6	30.4	69	10
65 Dominican Republic	7.8	1460	2.1	13.7	14.	19.9	71	18
66 Romania	22.7	1480	–3.8	22.2	16.	17.7	70	—
67 Jamaica	2.5	1510	3.6	11.3	13.	4.7	74	15
68 Jordan	4.2	1510	–4.5	23.8	15.	2.5	70	13
69 Algeria	28.0	1600	–2.4	26.5	19.	1.6	70	38
70 El Salvador	5.6	1610	2.8	8.2	9.	—	67	29
71 Ukraine	51.6	1630	–9.2	20.7	8.	—	69	—
72 Paraguay	4.8	1690	1.2	13.3	13.	—	68	8
73 Tunisia	9.0	1820	1.9	18.3	18.	3.9	69	33
74 Lithuania	3.7	1900	–11.7	25.2	15.	2.1	70	—
75 Colombia	36.8	1910	2.6	20.7	22.	7.4	59	9
76 Namibia	1.5	2000	2.9	15.8	15.	—	70	—
77 Belarus	10.3	2070	–5.2	26.3	15.	—	65	—
78 Russian Federation	48.2	2240	–5.1	30.9	16.	1.1	69	—
79 Latvia	2.5	2270	–6.6	24.5	12.	—	66	—
80 Perti	23.8	2310	–1.6	17.9	14.	49.4	77	11
81 Costa Rica	3.4	2610	2.8	19.8	21.	18.9	68	5
82 Lebanon	4.0	2660	—	—		—	69	8
83 Thailand	58.2	2740	8.4	16.2	28.	0.1	73	6
84 Panama	2.6	2750	–0.4	26.1	22.	25.6	67	9
85 Turkey	61.1	2780	2.2	20.4	20.	—	70	18
86 Poland	38.6	2790	1.2	21.5	20.	6.8	70	—
87 Estonia	1.5	2860	–4.3	25.5	15.	6.0	72	—
88 Slovak Republic	5.4	2950	–2.8	17.6	13.	12.8	68	—
89 Botswana	1.5	3020	6.1	15.3	20	34.7	71	30
90 Venezuela	21.7	3020	0.5	33.0	29.	11.8		9
Upper-middle income	438.3 t	4260 w	0.2 w					14 w
91 South Africa	41.5	3160	–1.1	22.4	18.	23.7	64	18
92 Croatia	4.8	3250	—	—		—	74	—
93 Mexico	91.8	3320	0.1	27.8	23.	14.9	72	10
94 Mitirititis	1.1	3380	5.4	39.0	49.	—	71	17
95 Gabon	1.1	3490	–8.2	—		—	55	37
96 Brazil	159.2	3640	–0.8	24.2	20.	28.7	67	17
97 Trinidad and Tobago	1.3	3770	–1.7	38.1	31.	—	72	2
98 Czech Republic	10.3	3870	–1.8	44.9	36.	3.1	73	—
99 Malaysia	20.1	3890	5.7	22.9	33.	5.6	71	17
100 Hungary	10.2	4120	–1.0	28.9	23.	0.7	70	—
101 Chile	14.2	4160	6.1	24.6	35.	15.0	72	5
102 Oman	2.2	4820	0.3	33.2	30.	—	70	—
103 Uruguay	3.2	5170	3.1	23.6	24.	—	73	3
104 Saudi Arabia	19.0	7040	–1.9	43.0		—	70	37
105 Argentina	34.7	8030	1.8	31.6	30.	—	73	4
106 Slovenia	2.0	8200	—	—		—	74	—
107 Greece	10.5	8210	1.3	44.2	43.	—	78	—

Source: World Development Report, 1997

Table 13.3 High-income economies: basic indicators

	Population (millions) mid-1995	GNP per capita Dollars 1995	GNP per capita Avg. ann. growth (%) 1985–95	PPP estimates of GNP per capita US = 100 1987	PPP estimates of GNP per capita US = 100 1995	Poverty % of people living on less than $1 a day (PPP) 1981–95	Life expectancy at birth (years) 1995	Adult illiteracy % 1995
Low and middle income	4770.8		0.4				65	30
Sub-Saharan Africa	583.3	1090	–1.1				52	43
East Asia and Pacific	1706.4	490	7.2				68	17
South Asia	1243.0	800	2.9				61	51
Europe and Central Asia	487.6	350	–3.5				68	—
Middle East and N. Africa	272.4	2220	–0.3				66	39
Latin America and Caribbean	477.9	3320	0.3				69	13
High-income economies	902.2	24930	1.9				77	—
108 Korea Rep.	44.9	9700	7.7	27.3	42.4	—	72	h
109 Portugal	9.9	9740	3.6	41.6	47.0	—	75	—
110 Spain	39.2	13580	2.6	50.5	53.8	—	77	—
111 New Zealand	3.6	14340	0.8	63.3	60.6	—	76	h
112 Ireland	3.6	14710	5.2	44.2	58.1	—	77	h
113 †Israel	5.5	15920	2.5	56.3	61.1	—	77	—
114 †Kuwait	1.7	17390	1.1	86.3	88.2	—	76	21
115 †United Arab Emirates	2.5	17400	–2.8	84.4	61.1	—	75	21
116 United Kingdom	58.5	18700	1.4	72.0	71.4	—	77	h
117 Australia	18.1	18720	1.4	70.1	70.2	—	77	h
118 Italy	57.2	19020	1.8	72.5	73.7	—	78	h
119 Canada	29.6	19380	0.4	84.6	78.3	—	78	h
120 Finland	5.1	20580	–0.2	72.9	65.8	—	76	8
121 †Hong Kong	6.2	22990⁹	4.8	70.7	85.1	—	79	h
122 Sweden	8.8	23750	–0.1	77.7	68.7	—	79	h
123 Netherlands	15.5	24000	1.9	70.5	73.9	—	78	h
124 Belgium	10.1	24710	2.2	76.3	80.3	—	77	h
125 France	58.1	24990	1.5	77.6	78.0	—	78	9
126 †Singapore	3.0	26730	6.2	56.1	84.4	—	76	h
127 Austria	8.1	26890	1.9	75.0	78.8	—	77	h
128 United States	263.1	26980	1.3	100.0	100.0	—	77	h
129 Germany	81.9	27510	—	—	74.4	—	76	h
130 Denmark	5.2	29890	1.5	78.7	78.7	—	75	h
131 Norway	4.4	31250	1.7	78.6	81.3	—	78	h
132 Japan	125.2	39640	2.9	75.3	82.0	—	80	h
133 Switzerland	7.0	40630	0.2	105.4	95.9	—	78	h
World	5673.0	4880	0.8				67	—

Source: World Development Report, 1997
† Economies classified by the United Nations or otherwise regarded by their authorities as developing.
h. According to UNESCO illiteracy is less than 5 per cent.

the world economic order of the last 50 years or so. This world order has seen the gap between developed and developing countries grow bigger rather than smaller. The uneven distribution of world income remains one of the most difficult and intractable problems at a global level.

✎ **Activity 13.3**

Look at Figure 13.2 and comment on what it shows.

✓ **Answer 13.3**

According to the findings of the UN Conference on Trade and Development (UNCTAD), inequality between industrial and developing countries is rising rather than falling. Figure 13.2 divides countries into five income groups, each representing 20 per cent of the world population. The share of world income owned by the richest quintile has increased by 14 per cent since 1965, to reach 83 per cent of world GDP in 1990.

Figure 13.1 GDP per capita: world, 1970–2020. In Purchasing Power Parities.

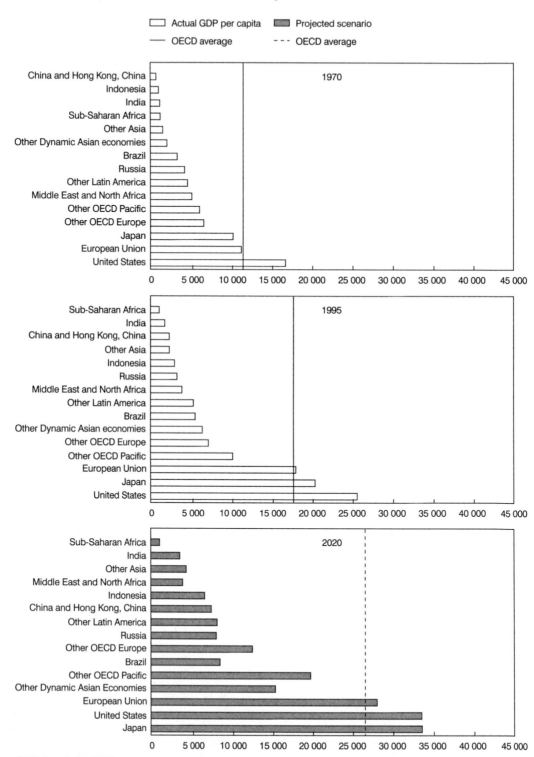

Source: OECD Secretariat, 1997

Figure 13.2 World GDP share of total, 1965–90, %

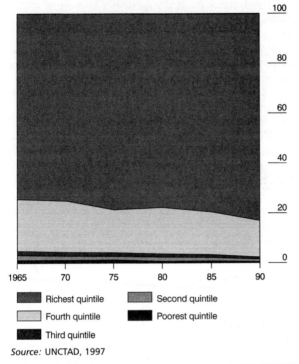

Richest quintile   Second quintile

Fourth quintile   Poorest quintile

Third quintile

Source: UNCTAD, 1997

Figure 13.3 Percentage change in real earnings of urban labour, Latin America, 1990–94

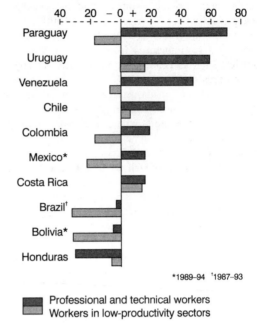

*1989–94 '1987–93

Professional and technical workers

Workers in low-productivity sectors

Source: UNCTAD, 1997

According to UNCTAD's report, in 1965 the average income per head in the richest quintile was 31 times the income of the poorest quintile; in 1990 it was 60 times.

✍ Activity 13.4

Look at Figure 13.3 and comment on what it shows.

✓ Answer 13.4

According to the UNCTAD report, the earnings gap within developing countries has also widened. As a result, inequality has increased as the wages of skilled workers have tended to rise faster than those of the less skilled. As Figure 13.3 shows, this has been particularly true of Latin America. With the exception of Chile, Costa Rica and Uruguay, real earnings of unskilled workers actually fell between 1990 and 1994. The decline in real wages was as much as 30 per cent in Bolivia and Brazil, and 20 per cent in Colombia and Mexico.

Of the main global issues, the one that strikes most is undoubtedly the uneven distribution of world income. While millions of people are dying of hunger in Africa, the EU Common Agricultural Policy creates food mountains and wine lakes in Europe. While millions of people in Latin American countries daily walk huge distances or travel for hours in crammed buses to reach their destinations for ill-paid jobs, the average North American family has two cars, often used for the shortest of journeys. While the average family in Australia enjoys the use of at least two bathrooms in their flats or houses, one outdoor toilet often serves several blocks of flats in China. While the average Japanese can expect to live for 78 years, you are lucky to reach your mid-forties if you live in an African country.

According to the LDCs, the uneven distribution of world GDP is a consequence of the international 'economic order' brought about by the international organizations which were set up after World War II. So let's first of all discuss these institutions and their international role, before we move on to examine the policies and issues that emanated from them.

The liberal international economic order

Before World War I, 43 per cent of world trade was still in the hands of Britain, USA and Germany. However, the UK share had declined from 20 per cent in 1870 to

15 per cent, while Germany and the USA had 14 per cent each, France 8 per cent and the Netherlands 7 per cent. Of the developing countries, only India had a significant share, about 5 per cent (Luard 1983: 64).

International trade consisted primarily of the exchange of manufactures from the most developed countries, such as Britain, the USA and Germany, for raw materials and food, mainly from the white-settled countries such as Canada, Australia, New Zealand and Argentina. While these countries imported almost all their manufactures and exported almost exclusively primary products, most industrialized countries did the reverse. Only the USA and France were exporters of agricultural produce as well as manufactures, as they are now.

The relationship between primary produce and manufactures in world trade remained stable, with primary produce representing over 60 per cent of all trade. As time went on, the proportion of food in world trade declined as that of manufactures increased. Throughout this period the total volume of trade increased rapidly, especially in the last 15 years before World War I, at an annual rate of 3.4 per cent.

Depression and protectionism in the 1930s

The distribution of world trade changed significantly after World War I. The liberal and fairly stable order that had prevailed before the war was shattered. The war imposed a severe check to European income and output growth, but most importantly caused the beginning of the decline of Europe in the world economy. Many European countries became dependent on external sources of supply and finance, while some were forced to sell both domestic and foreign assets.

In a global context, the USA had become the major world player. Its economy had been little affected by World War I and flourished during the subsequent ten years. This was reflected in the growth of US exports, especially of manufactures, but also of agricultural produce, to war-stricken Europe and to the markets previously supplied by European countries. World War I also made Europe financially dependent on the USA.

Most countries in Europe suffered a reversal in their levels of economic activity. Given the run-down condition of most capital assets and machinery together with the dislocation following the war, levels of economic activity in 1919 and 1920 were still below those of 1913. The extent of the shortfall varied from country to country.

Britain was not only more severely affected than other countries, but also adopted a deliberate policy of overvaluation of the pound in order to reintroduce the gold standard for sterling, which had been suspended during the war. This not only crippled Britain's export competitiveness, causing a decline in its share of world trade, but also kept the economy in deep depression for most of the 1920s and 1930s.

Germany had been more damaged by the war, but enjoyed a period of rapid recovery. By 1929, when the industrialized world was about to experience its worst and longest depression, Britain's share of world exports had declined to 11 per cent, Germany's was 10 per cent, France's still only 6 per cent, while the US share had risen sharply to 17 per cent.

The Great Depression of 1929–32 and the prolonged and widespread recession that followed changed this pattern once more. An idea of the magnitude of the depression is illustrated in Table 13.4, which shows the fall in industrial production and GDP between 1929 and 1932 for all European countries for which data are available.

✍ Activity 13.5

Look at Table 13.4 and comment on what it shows.

✓ Answer 13.5

Virtually all countries suffered substantial declines in industrial production and domestic output, the major exception being Russia which, under Stalin's first Five Year Plan, was insulated from the rest of the capitalist countries. Outside the USA, the most severe declines in economic activity occurred in Austria, Germany, France, Italy, Luxembourg, Czechoslovakia and Poland. Denmark and Bulgaria were something of an exception, as they managed to record a rise in domestic output over the course of the depression.

Other indicators of economic activity tell a similar story: commodity prices, share prices, exports and imports fell sharply, while unemployment rose to alarming levels. For Europe as a whole it has been estimated that unemployment totalled 15 million. Many firms, banks and financial institutions went out of business. In 1931 alone, about 17,000 enterprises closed down in Germany (Aldcroft 1978:82).

The main consequence of the depression in world trade was that the total volume dropped dramatically. Between 1929 and 1932 world trade in manufactures dropped by 40 per cent and in raw materials by 25 per cent. The distribution between regions also changed. The US share declined to 14 per cent, Britain to 9 per cent, on a par with Germany, while France fell to 3.6 per cent. The value of European trade declined from $58bn in 1928 to $20.8bn in 1935. Primary producers were hit hardest, both by the reduction in the volume of their trade as well as by the disastrous fall in prices.

Table 13.4 Percentage changes in industrial production and output (GDP): selected countries 1929–38

Country	1929–32 Industrial production	GDP	1932/3–37/8 Industrial production	GDP	1929–37/8 Industrial production	GDP
Austria	−34.3	−22.5	53.8	18.6	1.0	−4.8
Belgium	−27.1	−7.1	42.3	9.8	3.7	2.0
Denmark	−5.6	4.0	47.1	15.1	38.9	19.7
Finland	−20.0	−5.9	96.2	48.7	56.9	39.9
France	−25.6	−11.0	20.0	7.9	−11.8	−4.0
Germany	−40.8	−15.7	122.2	67.5	31.6	41.1
Italy	−22.7	−6.1	48.5	20.8	14.8	13.5
Luxembourg	−32.0	na	40.2	na	4.7	na
Netherlands	−9.8	−8.2	35.1	12.2	22.0	3.1
Norway	−7.9	−0.9	40.8	29.2	29.9	28.0
Spain	−11.6	−8.0	3.0[1]	9.0[1]	−13.1[2]	0.4[3]
Sweden	−11.8	−8.9	72.4	38.3	53.8	26.0
UK	−11.4	−5.8	52.9	25.7	35.4	18.4
Bulgaria	na	26.8	na	17.7	na	49.2
Czechoslovakia	−26.5	−18.2[3]	51.5	20.3[4]	−3.9	−1.6
Hungary	−19.2	−11.5	58.7	24.5	29.9	10.2
Poland	−37.0	na	86.2	na	17.4	na
Romania	−11.8	na	49.3	na	31.6	na
Yugoslavia	na	−11.9	na	28.0	na	12.8
USSR	66.7	6.9	146.7	59.3	311.1	70.2
USA	−44.7	−28.0	86.8	46.6	3.3	5.6

[1]1933–5 [2]1929–35 [3]1929–35 [4]1935–7
Source: Aldcroft, 1978

The depression caused governments to take actions which contracted trade even further. In a desperate attempt to protect their domestic markets from competition and imports, while trying to sell in foreign markets to sustain domestic production, governments raised tariffs on imported goods, while devaluing their currencies in order to sell more competitively on foreign markets. Quantitative restrictions, in the form of quotas, were widely introduced; exchange controls were imposed and bilateral trade arrangements proliferated. Governments everywhere were mainly concerned with restoring employment at home and they believed that this could be best achieved by excluding those imports which were competing with domestic goods.

The US Congress Tariff Act of 1930, better known as the Smoot-Hawley Act, amended upwards specific tariff schedules for over 20,000 items, establishing the highest general tariff rate structure that the USA had ever experienced, with taxes on imports reaching about 60 per cent of their value.

Needless to say, competitive devaluations and 'beggar-my-neighbour' policies only served to depress international trade even further, as each country responded to the imposition of tariffs by raising domestic tariffs in retaliation. High tariffs became the rule rather than the exception, while world trade stagnated. The Great Depression, already well under way in 1930, deepened and became truly global. World War II followed less than a decade later. It is against this background that we need to look at the setting up of the General Agreement on Tariffs and Trade (GATT).

A return to economic liberalism

When World War II came to an end there was a general desire among the developed countries to abandon the competitive restrictions of the inter-war period and return to a more liberal trading system. This was inevitably favoured by the country with the strongest economy, which was likely to benefit from the establishment of free trading. Just as Britain, the strongest industrial power at the time, pressed hardest for free trade in the mid-nineteenth century, during the 1940s the USA played a leading part in promoting trade liberalization (Luard 1983: 73).

World War II was still being fought in Europe when American and British experts were meeting in

Washington DC to discuss the international institutions that were to regulate and structure economic relations once the war was over. The idea was to steer the international economies away from the protectionism which had plagued them in the 1930s and to favour lasting conditions for economic co-operation. In this context the **International Trade Organization (ITO)** was to be the third leg in a triad of post-World War II economic organizations, along with the International Monetary Fund (IMF) and the International Bank for Reconstruction and Development (IBRD).

After the war, the discussions for the ITO became multilateral. A Preparatory Committee was appointed to draft the ITO charter. Members of the Committee, who were to become the GATT founding fathers, considered the idea of holding tariff-cutting negotiations among themselves in advance of the ITO. To do this they drew on the commercial provisions of the draft ITO charter. This governing instrument was to become the General Agreement. In the spring of 1947 the committee reassembled in Geneva and completed 123 negotiations on tariff reductions in seven months. The resulting 20 schedules containing some 45 000 reductions and covering about $10bn in trade became an integral part of the GATT. In November 1947 delegations from 56 countries met in Havana, Cuba, to consider the ITO draft. Disagreements emerged, triggered by conflicting trade interests, and the ITO plan eventually floundered but GATT remained.

GATT AND WTO

The General Agreement on Tariffs and Trade (GATT), signed by 23 nations in 1947, developed almost by default into a multilateral treaty for the regulation of international trade. However, GATT proved remarkably robust and grew into an organization with a permanent secretariat in Geneva and a substantially increased number of members. GATT, which has now become the World Trade Organization (WTO), remains the main vehicle for negotiating multilateral reductions of trade barriers and for constraining further trade restrictions. International trading relationships have changed dramatically over the post-war period. The aim of what follows is to trace those changes and explain their commercial implications.

The main purpose of GATT throughout the post-war period remained to provide a framework of rules for the orderly conduct of world trade and at the same time to supply a vehicle for the negotiated reductions of tariff barriers. These rules continue to provide the broad agreed framework under which trade between market economies is conducted, although GATT, despite its considerable contractual influence, cannot impose demands upon sovereign governments. The GATT Treaty is set out in 38 Articles of Agreement, whose aims are as follows:

- to provide an orderly framework for the conduct of international trade;
- to steer the conduct of individual trading nations away from trade impeding, unilateral actions, encouraging multilateralism and trade liberalization. When disputes do arise, GATT provides a forum for negotiation.
- to foster trade liberalization through the reduction of customs tariffs and the general elimination of quantitative restrictions and other non-tariff barriers to trade. Although it recognizes that free trade cannot be achieved overnight, it regards tariffs which affect trade indirectly by their effects on prices as the only acceptable instrument of trade restriction. This is because tariffs are 'transparent', i.e. they provide a clear indication of the extent of protectionism; they work within the market mechanism through their effect on prices and they are amenable to across-the-board reductions. Quotas, on the contrary, tend to be applied by governments in an arbitrary way outside the market mechanism. GATT therefore legitimized protection by tariffs only. The agreement itself consisted of two main parts: a set of rules for the conduct of international trade; a list of national tariffs, fixed through international negotiations.

GATT rules

GATT's main rules are the 'Rule of Non-discrimination' and the 'Reciprocity Rule'.

Rule of Non-discrimination

Non-discrimination is by far the most important feature of GATT and is enshrined in Article 1 of the Treaty. Simply stated, it requires that 'any advantage, favour, privilege or immunity affecting customs duties or other trade charges which is granted to trade with another contracting party (GATT member) must be accorded immediately and unconditionally to like products traded with any other contracting party'. In other words, each GATT member must receive the most-favoured nation (MFN) treatment. For each product category under negotiation a country must establish a single rate of tariff which applies to imports from all other member countries. This requirement is intended to prevent countries from discriminating between trading partners.

Reciprocity Rule

This rule states that if one GATT member grants a tariff concession to another, that partner is obliged to reciprocate; conversely, if one GATT member increases a tariff on a product, other GATT trading partners affected by that measure can retaliate and increase their tariffs by an equal amount on products traded with the first country.

Rounds of negotiations

Once negotiated, tariff rates are fixed without time limits. GATT signatories are encouraged to engage in tariff reductions by participating in GATT's periodic rounds on trade negotiations. Since the beginning of GATT there have been eight rounds of trade negotiations.

Many observers would agree that GATT's achievements in liberalizing trade look impressive when examined with reference to the actual tariff reductions that have occurred during its existence. To give an idea of the size of the gains, at the end of World War II the average tariff on imported goods was over 50 per cent in the USA and over 30 per cent in the UK. By the end of the Tokyo Round in 1979, the average tariff for all industrial products was estimated to be around 5 per cent.

Table 13.5   GATT negotiation rounds

Date	Negotiation round
1947	Geneva Round: 23 countries sign the GATT
1947–1948	Havana Conference: ITO Charter
1949	Annecy Round
1950–51	Torquay Round: 30 GATT signatories, accounting for 80 per cent of world trade
1956	Geneva Round
1960–62	Dillon Round
1964–67	Kennedy Round
1971	Generalized System of Preferences introduced as a derogation from GATT
1974	First Multi-Fibre Arrangement (MFA)
1973–79	Tokyo Round
1986–94	Uruguay Round
1995	GATT replaced by the World Trade Organization

✍ Activity 13.6

Identify from the list below the 'most favoured nation' (MFN) clause of the GATT agreement:

(a) If a country offers more favourable trade terms to one country, it must then offer them to all other signatories.

(b) If one country imposes a lower tariff than other countries on a particular product, the other country must follow suit.

(c) A country is forbidden from taking retaliatory action against other countries suspected of unfair practice.

(d) Underdeveloped countries are permitted a greater use of protection than developed countries.

✓ Answer 13.6

The correct answer is (a).

GATT and LDCs

When the original ITO charter was being discussed at the Havana Conference in 1947, the objections raised by the participants to the original US proposal were so many and so profound that the amended draft was never presented to the Congress for ratification. Objections to the ITO came from many European countries which wanted to include employment protection as a justification for trade barriers. Objections to ITO also came from many LDCs, particularly Latin American countries, but also India and Lebanon, which wanted the ITO charter to include the right to use trade barriers for development purposes.

However, this proved unacceptable to the US and West European delegates. As a result, few LDCs signed the GATT, preferring instead to pursue their independent trade policies without multilateral external constraints. Staying out of GATT did not help LDCs in the long run. Apart from the obvious self-inflicted harm that stems from protective trade policies, a further negative consequence of their refusal to accept GATT rules was that subsequent GATT negotiations paid little attention to LDCs interests. So throughout the first 20 years of its existence GATT was dominated by high-income economies, primarily concerned with their own interests.

Without a place at the negotiating table, LDCs had little influence on which trade barriers were reduced by the major trading nations. Predictably, tariff reductions on items of special interest to LDCs such as food and primary products tended to be small. More importantly, exemptions from the application of normal GATT rules were granted for the application of non-tariff barriers on LDC exports, notably textiles and clothing.

Textile and clothing trade agreements were gradually taken out of the normal GATT framework and placed under special regimes negotiated in the Multi-Fibre Arrangements.

At the Havana Conference the LDCs had put forward two further requests, which were not accepted by the other delegates but nonetheless remained part of the recurring demands raised in international fora in the years that followed.

■ LDCs wanted special arrangements for the trade in primary products, whose prices were subject to large fluctuations.

■ LDCs wanted to be granted favoured access to developed countries' markets and to be exempt from GATT's MFN principle, on the grounds that equal treatment for unequally competitive countries was not equal.

Summing up, the LDCs had little interest in accepting the liberal economic order during the 1950s and 1960s, since most were trying to reach self-sufficiency by pursuing import-substitution strategies which were contrary to GATT principles. The LDCs continued to exert pressure internationally during this period for a reform of international markets. As more LDCs gained independence, they started working as a group within the UN. There the one country, one vote principle gave them a majority which they could have never enjoyed in the other major international institutions of the postwar period, where weighted voting reflected economic power (Pomfret 1977: 122).

UNCTAD

In 1964 the LDCs finally managed to secure the establishment of another organization more responsive to their needs: the United Nations Conference on Trade and Development (UNCTAD). With a permanent secretariat in Geneva, UNCTAD held regular conferences over the period and became the prime forum for the discussion of LDC demands. UNCTAD, however, was not a separate agency but part of the UN. As a political body with no executive power, its main function was limited to the organization of highly publicized conferences every three or four years to discuss controversial trade issues between rich and poor countries. UNCTAD's main but not unqualified success, came on 1 May 1974 when the UN General Assembly passed a programme of action for a **New International Economic Order (NIEO)**.

However, the NIEO existed largely only on paper in the years that followed.

UNCTAD was therefore above all an instrument through which the underdeveloped south of the world could make its demand for change to the developed north. These demands were generally ignored, as in the case of their demand for debt relief, but sometimes they produced partial results. This was the case for:

■ the demand for a generalized system of preferences for poor countries (GSP);
■ the demand for a 'common fund' to finance commodity stocks.

Generalized system of preferences (GSP)

The first request put forward through UNCTAD conferences was for the introduction of a generalized system of preferences (GSP) under which all exports from LDCs would be granted free entry into the markets of developed countries. The GSP proposal was initially rejected by the USA and Sweden at the first UNCTAD conference, but eventually endorsed. GATT was amended in 1971 to allow the introduction of the GSP scheme as an exception to the MFN principle.

The GSP was to prove more of a victory on paper than in practice and showed the inadequacy of the UN as an instrument for reform of the international economic system. LDCs could use their voting power within UN to have the GSP adopted, but without offering anything in return, they had to accept whatever GSP scheme the individual trading partner presented. They had no bargaining counters. As a result, the very slow and ad hoc implementation of the principle of GSP resulted in much less than the hoped for 'free access for all LDC exports'. At the end of the 1990s, still less than 20 per cent of LDC exports (excluding oil) entered DC markets on preferential terms under the GSP. A large part of this meagre proportion has also been taken up by a small number of successful NICs. The main restrictions imposed on the practical implementation of the GSP scheme have been as follows:

■ *discretionality*: the donor countries decide which products are included in their GSP scheme. The pattern of product exclusion is very detailed and can be unilaterally changed by the donor country. Agricultural and fishery products, as well as textiles, where most LDCs have a comparative advantage, are almost totally excluded. Goods which the LDCs could export more competitively tend to be the most restricted.

- *ceilings*: a system of ceilings was introduced as part of the GSP scheme which placed quantitative limits on the imports of an individual good or on the imports from one individual country. Once the ceiling is reached, the country in question becomes subject to the imposition of the MFN tariff and not the GSP tariff. This quantitative limit has had the effect of capping LDC investment in the export sector, severely crippling their chances of development.
- *no free access*: few GSP schemes actually grant tariff-free access to imports from LDCs. Tariffs tend to be lower than the MFN level, but always greater than zero.
- *administrative barriers*: 'rules of origin' further complicate the application of the GSP scheme. While rules of origin are clearly needed to ensure that goods coming from a non-beneficiary country do not gain preferential access by simply being rerouted through the beneficiary country, they did become instruments of further discrimination; for example, the importing country can specify how much of the imported good's value added should have been produced in the LDC. The requirement of a high local value added prevents LDCs from specializing in assembling operations in which, given their abundance of cheap labour, they have a comparative advantage.
- *differences in definition*: donor countries differed in their definition of LDC. While Japan and New Zealand excluded Hong Kong from their GSP scheme, the European Community excluded Taiwan, while the USA included it. The USA excluded many other LDCs from their GSP scheme on social or political grounds. Most GSP benefits in the 1980s have arguably gone to Hong Kong, Taiwan and South Korea.
- *principle of graduation*: in 1989 the USA introduced the principle of 'graduation'. Countries that have developed considerably, such as Hong Kong, Taiwan, South Korea and Singapore, are no longer considered 'less developed' and as such cease to qualify for GSP treatment.
- *preferential access*: the EU's preferential trade agreements with the Mediterranean countries and the signatories of the Lomé agreement, give preferential access to 70 LDCs.

LDCs continued to exert international pressure in order to obtain not only the GSP but also a programme of debt relief and the establishment of a Common Fund to create a commodity stock. Why LDCs were pressing for a Common Fund and what came of it are now briefly explained.

Integrated programme for commodities and international commodity agreements

Let's first understand why LDCs were pressing for **commodity agreements**. LDCs' main exports tend to be primary products. The price of primary products, unlike the price of manufactured goods, fluctuates considerably due to unpredictable changes in demand and supply. The LDCs' request was for the creation of a fund which could prevent such fluctuations.

While the market for agricultural products such as coffee or cocoa is subject to supply shocks (large, unpredictable changes in supply), the market for metals such as copper or tin is subject to demand shocks. The buffer stock mechanism could work in either situation to stabilize prices around their long-term trend.

In 1976 UNCTAD approved an integrated programme for commodities with a common fund of $6bn. The purpose of the fund was to build up buffer stocks, aimed at stabilizing the price of ten core commodities, and to intervene in the market for eight others. The products included in such scheme are listed in Table 13.6.

Activity 13.7

With the use of a diagram, show how the creation of a buffer stock would help to stabilize prices. Assume a supply shock such as a particularly good harvest of coffee.

Answer 13.7

Figure 13.4 shows that the buffer stock intervention agency would buy up the excess supply of coffee, $Q_1 - Q_0$, at the current market price, p_e, preventing it from falling, and would make the commodity available to the market (i.e. selling it back) when there is a shortage to prevent its price from rising.

The mechanism would apply to a demand shock, which is shown by a shift in or out of the demand

Table 13.6 Integrated programme for commodities

Buffer stocks	Some intervention
Cocoa	Bananas
Coffee	Bauxite
Copper	Iron ore
Cotton	Manganese
Jute	Meat
Rubber	Phosphates
Sisal	Tropical timber
Sugar	Vegetable oil
Tea	
Tin	

Figure 13.4   Buffer stock

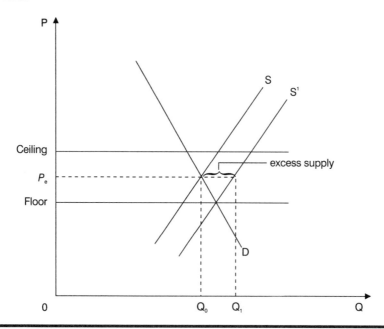

curve. Say, a world recession caused the demand for tin to fall (shift to the left of the demand curve). This would prompt intervention buying by the agency to prevent the price of tin from falling.

The impact of this programme has been very limited, particularly given the paucity of money made available by the developed economies which were never whole-heartedly in favour of the scheme. Typically, the intervention agency has either run out of commodity stock, at which point the price has shot above the ceiling, or has run out of money, at which point the price has dropped through the floor. The potential instability of primary product prices and the tendency for a deterioration of their terms of trade has led many LDCs to promote the export of manufactures.

✍ Activity 13.8

Why is a buffer stock agency not needed for manufactured goods?

✓ Answer 13.8

The relative stability of the price of manufactured goods is achieved through stocking and de-stocking by firms and sellers. Rather than immediately changing prices, producers and sellers respond to changes in demand by building up or running down their inventories of the good. Equally, consumers respond to a reduction in price caused by excess supply by buying more and by delaying their purchases, therefore buying less, when prices increase. Clearly this is not possible, to a large extent, for agricultural goods, which cannot be easily stocked by producers, when the product to be stocked is bulky, or for metals when the fluctuations in demand may be very large and unpredictable.

GATT AND EU: AN EXCEPTION TO MULTILATERALISM

The rules of non-discrimination and reciprocity which form the cornerstone of GATT's trade liberalizing efforts were allowed many exceptions. Following mounting international pressure, in 1971 GATT had to accommodate LDC demands. Article 36 of Part IV of the GATT Charter, which deals with economic development, waived the principle of reciprocity in favour of LDCs, allowing them to benefit from tariff reductions without having to reciprocate.

An earlier exception to GATT's multilateral approach was allowed when trade preferences already in existence between countries before the formation of the GATT were excluded from MFN treatment.

While the articles of the GATT outlawed in principle the use of quantitative restraints on imports, quotas were allowed under certain circumstances. Under Article 12 of the GATT, a country can introduce temporary quotas to alleviate a balance of payment crisis or if a sudden increase in imports causes 'serious injury' to a competing domestic industry. An unequivocal definition of what constitutes 'serious injury' was not provided in the articles of agreement. Attempts have been made to give a clear, empirical estimate of the increase in protectionism by counting the number of escape clauses invoked before the GATT in recent years.

The most drastic departure from the principle of free trade and multilateralism is allowed by Article 24 of the GATT, which permits member countries of a customs union, like the European Community (now European Union), a free trade area like the North Atlantic Free Trade Association (NAFTA), or countries entering interim agreements leading to economic integration, to give preferential treatment to imports from other member countries or future member countries.

A number of conditions were specified under Article 24 to ensure that the formation of customs unions and free trade areas did not harm the trade interests of other GATT members and that they would not be used simply as a device to avoid the non-discrimination rule:

- The tariffs of the customs union must not be higher than those of the member countries prior to union.
- The arrangements must cover 'substantially all trade between the parties'.
- The customs union or free trade area must be completed 'within a reasonable length of time', i.e. within a relatively short period.

There were lengthy discussions in 1957 over the compatibility of the proposed EEC and the rules of GATT. Many GATT members objected to its creation but political pragmatism prevailed in the end; mostly because the USA did not challenge the EEC creation, in view of the political advantages of a more united western Europe against the communist threat represented by the Soviet Union.

The use of Article 24 to legitimize the formation of the EEC set a precedent which the EEC has repeatedly exploited in the elaboration of its trade relations with third countries. As a result the EC has been able 'to spin a world-wide web of preferential trade agreements, whilst claiming to adhere to the rules of the GATT' (Hine 1985: 42–5). There is little doubt, however, that Article 24 conflicts with the general principle of non-discrimination, since the abolition of tariff barriers between countries forming a customs union is necessarily regional and preferential and does not extend to all of GATT's contracting parties.

NON-TARIFF BARRIERS AND NEW PROTECTIONISM

What matters is not so much the individual conformity of particular EC agreements with the GATT rules but the effect that the proliferation of these discriminatory trade arrangements has had on the GATT system as a whole. While the clash between GATT principles and EC practice is most obvious in the EC preferential trade agreements, the EC is also guilty, along with the USA and Japan, of undermining other aspects of GATT in its increasing use of non-tariff barriers.

Toward the end of the 1960s the USA and EC started to impose quantitative restrictions on the imports of certain goods from Japan and other developing countries. Textiles and clothing were initially the target of restrictions, followed by some manufactured goods. The use of voluntary quotas became widespread in the 1970s and 1980s and is by far the most important form of non-tariff barrier exploited in the last twenty-five years or so. These forms of restraints are called **voluntary export restraints (VERs)**. Imports into the EC and the USA of textiles from the developing countries are regulated by the Multi-fibre Arrangement, which is an example of a VER.

The main characteristic of a voluntary quota, or voluntary export restraints, is that the exporting country voluntarily limits its exports. The export restraint is not voluntary in the normal sense of the word, but is often preferred by exporting countries to other forms of trade barrier, such as quotas, tariffs or technical barriers, that the importing country threatens to use. At present VER agreements limit the following sectors:

- LDC export of clothing to the EU and North America;
- Japanese exports of passenger cars to Belgium, France, Germany, Italy, UK and USA;
- exports of EU and Japanese steel to USA;
- exports of NICs steel to EU;
- exports of consumer electronics from Japan, Korea and Taiwan to the EU and USA;
- export to the EU of a few agricultural commodities.

Economic impact of VERs

Newly industrialized countries are particularly hard hit by VERs and other quantitative restrictions.

✍ Activity 13.9

What will be the effect of a VER on the export of a product, for the exporting and the importing countries?

✓ Answer 13.9

When a country agrees to apply a VER on a particular product, it normally reduces the quantities exported. This drives up the price of the product in the importing country, allowing the less competitive domestic industry to survive. The effect of VERs on the final price and quantity of the product in question is the same as in the case of a tariff. The 'protectionist impact' of a VER can therefore be measured in terms of its 'import tariff equivalent'.

✍ Activity 13.10

Show the effect of a VER on the importing country with the use of a diagram. Hint: there is more than one way to do so. You may wish to show two separate supply curves, one for the domestic supply of the good and the other for the world supply of the good, assuming that the good is allowed unrestricted access to the domestic market.

✓ Answer 13.10

This is shown in Figure 13.5.

The diagram shows the market for one product in the importing country: Dd shows the domestic demand curve, Sd the domestic supply curve, while Sw shows the world supply curve of that particular product, which includes the domestic supply.

Before restrictions are imposed, equilibrium is reached at quantity Q_0 and price P_0. Of the quantity Q_0, only OQ_1 is produced by the domestic industry, while the remaining quantity Q_0Q_1 is imported. Suppose a VER is now introduced which limits the volume of imports allowed into the country to $Q_3 - Q_2$, which is smaller than $Q_0 - Q_2$. As the quantity of the product available is reduced, its price goes up from P_0 to P_1, while the supply price of the world producers is P_2. As a result of this, domestic production increases from Q_1 to Q_2, which is precisely why VERs are favoured instruments by the governments of importing countries.

The Multi-Fibre Arrangements

Textiles and clothing in particular have been subject to extensive VER regulation through successive negotiations of international agreements. Restrictions on imports of such items from Japan, eastern Europe and developing countries were already being introduced during the 1950s. The USA initially put pressure on Japan in 1955 to agree to a voluntary five-year restraint on cotton textile exports to the USA. However, the USA did not succeed in getting a similar restraint agreement with Hong Kong, while Britain succeeded in negotiating VERs on cotton fabrics with Hong Kong, Pakistan and India in 1959. This led, among other things, to pressures from the USA to seek a global solution.

Figure 13.5 The effects of a VER on the importing country

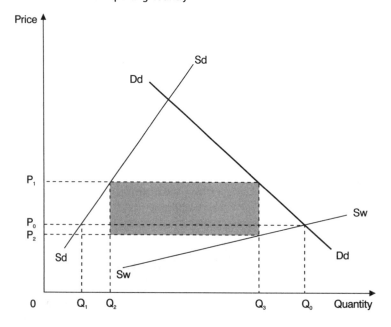

Use of GATT market disruption clause

In November 1959 the USA filed a complaint of *market disruption* due to sudden large increases of imports from low-wage countries with GATT. A GATT working party was set up in 1960 and a definition of market disruption was adopted that allowed a new textile and clothing regime to exist, under the auspices of GATT, which was against many of its rules. Against this background a **Long-Term Arrangement Regarding International Trade in Cotton Textiles (LTA)** was reached in February 1962, for a period of five years. This was subsequently extended until 1974 when it became included in the first broader and more restrictive **Multi-Fibre Arrangement (MFA)**.

LTA (1962–7, 1968–74)

Under LTA quantitative restrictions were permitted only when the importing country was experiencing market disruption from unrestrained imports of such products. These restrictions could be enforced with or without the agreement of the exporting country. Article 4 of the LTA contained provisions which permitted bilateral arrangements 'on other terms', thereby allowing other countries to impose restrictions even when they were not threatened with market disruption.

LTA was against the spirit of GATT since it was obviously against the main principle of non-discrimination and by-passed Article 19, which entitled exporting countries affected by restraints to claim compensation. Despite this, LTA was negotiated under GATT auspices and became regarded as a lesser evil than what otherwise might have occurred.

MFA I (1974–7)

LTA soon proved too narrow as it only regulated cotton textile exports, while Asian countries increasingly used synthetic fibres, particularly polyester and acrylic. With high and rising unemployment rates, the USA once more took the initiative in GATT to start discussions for a broader agreement that would regulate and restrict the import of all textiles and clothing of cotton, manmade fibres and wool from LDCs. The new arrangement was reached at the end of 1973 and is commonly referred to as the first Multi-Fibre Arrangement (MFA I). It lasted until the end of 1977 and was signed by almost all countries which export textiles and clothing, 42 countries in all, with the EEC counting as one participant.

MFA II (1977–81)

The MFA provisions dealt with base-level quotas, their annual growth rate and flexibility. Annual growth in quotas was not to be less than 6 per cent, although exceptions were to be tolerated. The successive renegotiation of the original MFA in 1977, for a further four years (MFA II), considerably tightened the protection of developed countries from imports from developing countries, with greater emphasis put on clothing, rather than textiles. The 6 per cent growth provision was not maintained and the real rates of growth of imports allowed into the USA and EC were in fact much lower, even zero in some particular products.

MFA III (1981–6) and MFA IV (1986–91)

The 1981 renewal of MFA II meant even tighter European protection of domestic markets. The world economy in 1981 was still trying to recover from the post-1979 recession and EC textile and clothing industries were at levels of production and employment below those of 1973. Tight monetary policies were used to control inflation. MFA III, in effect from 1981 to July 1986, further cut back existing VER quotas of major developing countries. The restrictions were kept in place without any relaxation for the period from 1986 to 1991 (MFA IV). Subsequently they became the object of renewed negotiations during the Uruguay Round of GATT, discussed later in this chapter.

✍ Activity 13.11

Why do you think exporting countries agree to voluntarily limit their exports?

✓ Answer 13.11

They agree partly because they cannot do anything about it and fear other forms of restriction, like higher tariffs, even more; partly also because the rent that stems from the VER situation goes to the exporting country which administers VERs.

Let's look at this point more closely. Producers of the exporting country now subject to VER are willing to produce quantity Q_3 at the price P_2. In fact the demand price for Q_3 is P_1, which is greater than P_2. The difference between the two prices multiplied by the quantity exported $Q_3 - Q_2$ is the rent element of the VER that accrues to the exporting country. So someone gains from this form of restriction, namely the producers of the restricted exporting country and the producers of the protected domestic market. The consumers of the importing country lose out and the developing countries or a group of producers who are left out altogether by this quota system also lose out.

🖎 Activity 13.12

Why have VER agreements proliferated in recent years?

✔ Answer 13.12

As we have seen, GATT rules explicitly forbid increases of tariffs above negotiated values without a just cause and even then tariff increases have to be agreed upon and compensated for by GATT members.

In this context:

- VERs prove a much more flexible instrument of protection as they can be negotiated in private between the governments of the countries involved, without the interference of international bodies.
- VERs favour importing countries' domestic industries, which normally form very powerful and vociferous lobbies capable of putting considerable pressure on their governments.
- VERs are also seen to offer something to the exporting country (the rent element of the VER), which is therefore willing to accept them.
- Those who suffer from the imposition of VERs, the consumers who end up paying a higher price, are precisely those who have no say in the handling of the whole process.

EU AND US TRADE RELATIONS

Increased protectionism by means of a combination of tariffs, quotas and other forms of NTBs has increasingly characterized trade between the EU and the USA, as well as trade between industrialized and developing countries. Trade relations between the EU (formerly EC) and the USA worsened in the late 1970s and throughout the 1980s due to the economic difficulties experienced by the economies on both sides of the Atlantic. The strain on trade relations has worsened in recent years, together with protectionist pressures in the USA, caused by record budget deficits, a stronger dollar and a deep crisis in farming.

In a sense it can be said that the trade issue between the USA and EU was born simultaneously with the establishment of the EC in 1957. Quite apart from the political aspects of the creation of the EC, then favourably perceived by the USA as a way of strengthening the Atlantic partnership, the USA–EC trade relationship soon proved very difficult. The co-existence of different sets of rules for regulation often threatened to turn US–EC relations into a form of continuous cross-national litigation.

Signs of strain often emerged over agricultural products because of the extensive protection granted to the sector by the major trading partners: CAP for the EC, price support schemes and income transfers in the USA, high tariffs and import quotas in Japan. The agricultural sector, it must be stressed, was never included in GATT's negotiations, although it was an item on the agenda of the Kennedy and Tokyo Rounds. It was once more at the centre of the Uruguay Round which ended in 1994. Some progress was made this time in bringing the agricultural sector under the general umbrella of GATT rules, as we discuss later in this chapter.

There are many reasons for conflict. Different countries have interests in different commodities. Thus the USA complains bitterly that CAP denies access to the European market for US grain producers, while the EC claims that US policies deny access to their market for European dairy produce, etc. Protection often results in overproduction by all concerned and their subsidized surpluses are often dumped on third world markets at prices well below production costs. This adds a third party to the squabble, as many LDCs rightly claim that dumping further disrupts their markets and causes bankruptcy among domestic producers.

As well as CAP-subsidized exports competing with US production at home and with US exports to third countries, the other major source of conflicts with the USA are the EU bilateral agreements of preferential trading with third countries. Disagreements between the EU and USA have multiplied in recent years regarding both imports and exports of agricultural and industrial products and have usually been resolved by recourse to GATT dispute settlement procedures and various forms of retaliation. Retaliation by the USA often takes the form of protective taxes on US imports from the EU and/or underbidding EU export prices by increasing the subsidies to American exporters.

In retaliation to CAP and EU protectionist policies, the USA set up the Domestic International Sales Corporation (DISC) and Bonus Incentive Commodity Export Programme (BICEPS), which provided subsidies to US exporters to help them compete with EU goods. What has GATT's position been when called in on these transatlantic trade disputes? Generally GATT has preferred to be non-committal and has rejected calls for further action from the USA.

The 'pasta war' that broke out in the second half of the 1980s provides a useful example of the intricate issues and mechanics of trade disputes between the

USA and EU. The pasta dispute broke out in 1985–6 between the USA and EU (then EC) over EU-subsidized pasta exports, only months after another long dispute over EU steel imports into the USA had been resolved. The conflict over pasta products had existed for several years and started in June 1985 when the USA imposed high duties on EU pasta in retaliation for the EU Mediterranean preferential trade agreements. Brussels pays refunds to pasta exporters to compensate them for the price they pay for EU wheat, which is higher than the world price due to CAP. The USA disputed the legality of this export refund for EU pasta products, believing that pasta constituted a processed product and that refunds were therefore contrary to international trade rules, even though no condemnation of the refunds had been obtained from GATT. In retaliation, in June 1985, the USA raised customs duties on imports of pasta products from the EU by up to 40 per cent. The EU then hit back with countermeasures that sharply increased duties on exports of US lemons and walnuts. After difficult negotiations, the two parties eventually reached an agreement in 1986, which did not, however, challenge the principle of the EU refunds.

EU AND LDC TRADE RELATIONS

There is no unifying EU policy towards developing countries but there are important isolated considerations which have inspired EU trade policies and agreements towards LDCs. Such considerations and objectives have often proved to be inconsistent with one another and not generally shared by all EU governments, whose individual positions have often differed from those taken by the European Commission. Generally speaking, the **guiding principles** which have directed EU policies towards LDCs have been as follows:

- *protection from import competition*: protection of EU domestic industries from import LDCs competition, in particular in agriculture, sensitive labour-intensive manufacturing industries such as textiles and some high technology industries;
- *export promotion*: to promote EU's exports to LDCs;
- *political influence*: to maintain EU political and economic influence in regions and LDCs traditionally linked to it or to some of its members;
- *enlargement*: to extend EU influence to less developed regions or countries perceived to be of growing importance to the Union;

- *promotion*: to facilitate or be perceived to facilitate economic development in developing countries.

Summing up, the EU policies towards LDCs have developed as follows:

- The have evolved within the context of GATT, culminating in the Uruguay Round of trade negotiations.
- They have been conditioned by EU internal market arrangements.
- They reflect historical trading relationships between members of the Union and former colonies.
- They have also often been dictated by economic and political expediency (Brenton, Scott and Sinclair 1997: 318).

Statistics of EU trade with LDCs show a sharp downward trend and a parallel increase in EU intra-regional trade.

✍ Activity 13.13

Look at Tables 13.7 and 13.8 and comment on the changes in the structure of EU trade between 1958 and 1994.

✓ Answer 13.13

The volume of trade between the EU and LDCs reflects the world downward trend and provides further evidence of the reduced participation of LDCs in international trade. Imports from developing countries to the EU have fallen sharply, from about 30 per cent of total EU imports in 1958 to about 13 per cent in 1994. This is a considerable decline, which does not apply uniformly to all developing countries. There is a considerable decline in the share of the OPEC countries, despite their rise in the 1970s, from about 11 per cent to 3.2 per cent, and a continuous decline in the share of the African, Caribbean and Pacific (ACP) countries, despite the preferential trade agreements discussed above. There is an increase in the share of the Association of South East Asian Nations (ASEAN) countries, despite EU policies being generally hostile to imports from them.

The volume of exports from the EU to LDCs has also declined, from 27.4 per cent in 1958 to 14.2 per cent in 1994, reflecting the general decline of extra-EC trade. While the structure of EU exports to LDCs has not changed, remaining firmly in manufactures, there has been considerable change in the structure of EU imports from LDCs (Brenton, Scott and Sinclair 1997: 318). In the early 1960s the 12 EU member were essentially exporters of manufactured goods and

Table 13.7 Structure of EC imports by country and region, 1958–94 (percentage of total imports)

Import from to	B/L 1958	B/L 1994	DK 1958	DK 1994	D 1958	D 1994	EL 1958	EL 1994	E 1958	E 1994	F 1958	F 1994	IRL 1958	IRL 1994	I 1958	I 1994	N 1958	N 1994	P 1958	P 1994	UK 1958	UK 1994	EUR12 1958	EUR12 1994
Total intra-EC trade	55.5	68.1	60.0	52.1	36.3	50.7	53.7	64.4	31.8	63.5	28.3	65.0	68.9	63.3	30.2	56.2	50.7	54.8	53.4	71.4	21.8	49.9	35.2	57.0
Other European OECD countries	7.7	6.8	18.6	25.5	15.2	16.5	11.5	6.6	8.4	5.5	6.7	7.6	3.4	4.8	13.1	11.6	7.2	9.0	8.6	6.0	8.7	10.8	10.1	11.1
USA	9.9	5.9	9.1	4.3	13.6	5.9	13.7	3.2	21.6	6.2	10.0	7.3	7.0	16.9	16.4	4.6	11.3	8.7	7.0	3.6	9.4	12.8	11.4	7.4
Canada	1.4	0.7	0.1	0.4	3.1	0.6	0.8	0.3	0.5	0.4	1.0	0.6	3.0	0.4	1.5	0.9	1.4	0.7	0.5	0.3	8.2	1.2	3.6	0.7
Japan	0.6	2.7	1.5	3.1	0.6	4.8	2.0	3.8	0.7	2.8	0.2	2.5	1.1	4.3	0.4	2.4	0.8	4.4	0.0	2.8	0.9	5.9	0.7	3.9
Australia	1.7	0.3	0.0	0.2	1.2	0.2	0.3	0.0	0.8	0.3	2.4	0.3	1.2	0.1	3.0	0.5	0.2	0.4	0.9	0.1	5.4	0.7	2.6	0.4
Developing countries	19.2	10.0	5.9	8.3	23.9	11.0	9.6	13.6	32.0	17.0	45.6	12.6	9.3	7.3	29.4	14.2	24.4	17.3	27.6	13.3	34.7	13.2	29.5	12.8
of which OPEC	5.7	1.4	0.3	0.7	6.7	2.1	1.7	5.3	17.7	6.1	19.7	3.8	0.7	0.3	13.9	5.3	11.5	5.3	6.3	5.8	11.3	2.4	10.8	3.2
Other developing countries	13.5	8.6	5.6	7.6	17.2	8.9	7.9	8.3	14.3	10.9	25.9	8.8	8.6	7.0	15.5	8.9	12.9	12.0	21.3	7.5	23.4	10.8	18.7	9.6
Rest of the world and unspecified	4.0	5.5	4.7	6.1	6.1	10.3	8.4	8.1	4.2	4.3	5.8	4.1	6.1	2.7	6.0	9.6	4.0	4.7	2.0	2.5	10.9	5.5	6.9	6.7
World (excluding EC)	44.5	31.9	40.0	47.9	63.7	49.3	46.3	35.6	68.2	36.5	71.7	35.0	31.1	36.7	69.8	43.8	49.3	45.2	46.6	28.6	78.2	50.1	64.8	43.0
World (including EC)	100	100	100	100	100	100	100	100	100	100	100	100	100	100	100	100	100	100	100	100	100	100	100	100

Source: European Economy, 1997
D: 1958: West Germany; 1994 unified Germany

Table 13.8 Structure of EC exports by country and region, 1958–94 (percentage of total exports)

Export from to	B/L 1958	B/L 1994	DK 1958	DK 1994	D 1958	D 1994	EL 1958	EL 1994	E 1958	E 1994	F 1958	F 1994	IRL 1958	IRL 1994	I 1958	I 1994	N 1958	N 1994	P 1958	P 1994	UK 1958	UK 1994	EUR12 1958	EUR12 1994
Total intra-EC trade	55.4	72.1	59.3	51.2	37.9	48.9	50.9	54.2	46.8	64.5	30.9	60.7	82.4	70.0	34.5	53.4	58.3	74.7	38.9	75.1	21.7	54.1	37.2	58.4
Other European OECD countries	8.7	5.8	16.6	22.2	22.7	16.9	10.3	8.1	12.4	5.8	9.0	7.8	0.9	6.9	18.9	11.3	11.9	6.7	5.1	8.1	9.1	8.2	13.7	10.7
USA	9.4	4.9	9.3	5.5	7.3	7.9	13.6	4.8	10.1	4.6	5.9	7.0	5.7	8.1	9.9	7.8	5.6	4.0	8.3	5.3	8.8	12.0	7.9	7.3
Canada	1.1	0.4	0.7	0.5	1.2	0.6	0.3	0.5	1.3	0.5	0.8	0.7	0.7	0.9	1.2	0.9	0.8	0.4	1.1	0.7	5.8	1.4	2.3	0.7
Japan	0.6	1.3	0.2	4.0	0.9	2.6	1.4	1.0	1.7	1.1	0.3	1.9	0.0	3.1	0.3	2.1	0.4	1.0	0.5	0.8	0.6	2.3	0.6	2.1
Australia	0.5	0.3	0.3	0.6	1.0	0.7	0.1	0.4	0.3	0.4	0.5	0.4	0.1	0.6	0.8	0.7	0.7	0.4	0.6	0.3	7.2	1.4	2.4	0.7
Developing countries	18.0	11.3	9.3	10.9	20.9	12.7	7.2	17.2	18.4	20.7	46.9	18.0	1.6	6.7	26.2	17.1	17.6	8.3	42.3	7.9	33.6	16.4	27.4	14.2
of which OPEC	3.3	1.7	2.3	1.8	4.8	2.6	0.9	4.0	2.6	3.0	21.3	3.7	0.2	1.4	7.5	3.8	4.5	1.8	2.0	0.8	7.0	3.6	7.6	2.9
Other developing countries	14.7	9.6	7.0	9.1	16.1	10.1	6.3	13.2	15.8	17.7	25.6	14.3	1.4	5.3	18.7	13.3	13.1	6.5	40.3	7.1	26.6	12.8	19.8	11.3
Rest of the world and unspecified	6.3	3.9	4.3	5.1	8.1	9.7	16.2	13.8	9.0	2.4	5.7	3.5	8.6	3.7	8.2	6.7	4.7	4.5	3.2	1.8	13.2	4.2	8.5	5.9
World (excluding EC)	44.6	27.9	40.7	48.8	62.1	51.1	49.1	45.8	53.2	35.5	69.1	39.3	17.6	30.0	65.5	46.6	41.7	25.3	61.1	24.9	78.3	45.9	62.8	41.6
World (including EC)	100	100	100	100	100	100	100	100	100	100	100	100	100	100	100	100	100	100	100	100	100	100	100	100

Source: European Economy, 1997
D: 1958: West Germany; 1994 unified Germany

importers of primary products. The 15 EU members are now essentially importing manufactures (manufactures share is up from 30 per cent to 70 per cent over the period), while the import share of agricultural products has declined. This is partly explained by the protective EU agricultural policy, but also by the low income elasticity of demand for primary products. As EU income has increased, the demand for food products has increased less than proportionately, causing the diminishing role of developing countries in European trade. On the other hand, the Southeast Asian countries that have been able to develop their manufacturing base have expanded their share of the EU market, despite strong protectionist measures.

Uruguay Round

The eighth round of trade negotiations under GATT auspices, the Uruguay Round, was signed in Marrakech, Morocco, on 15 April 1994. This round of negotiations, which lasted seven years, was successful in bringing under GATT rules the sectors previously excluded, namely agriculture and textiles and clothing. New issues were also included, such as trade in services, intellectual property and investment distorting trade polices. Let's look more closely at the progress made in these areas.

Agriculture

This sector is now subject to the discipline of GATT, while previously it was subject to special treatment which allowed for the use of import quotas and export subsidies.

As a direct result of the Uruguay Round, domestic subsidies to agriculture, defined by the Aggregate Measure of Support (AMS) must be reduced by 20 per cent over six years. Certain types of subsidy involving direct payments to farmers are excluded from the AMS, such as the deficiency payment system applied in the USA and the compensation payments to EU farmers allowed by the CAP reform of 1992. So some loopholes still exist.

All non-tariff barriers must be converted into equivalent tariffs. Tariffs must then be reduced by an average of 36 per cent, with a minimum of 15 per cent reduction for each product over a six-year period from the end of the Round. These reductions are likely to have little practical significance, given the very high initial tariffs. The tariff equivalent of the EU variable import tax on some dairy products, shown in Table 13.9, gives an idea of the extent of the existing protection.

Table 13.9 CAP tariff-equivalent protection, selected products.

Product	Tariff equivalent (%)
Butter	314
Skimmed milk powder	267
White sugar	267
Beef carcasses	181
Barley	171

Source: Ingersent, Rayner and Hine, 1995.

Export subsidies remain legal, contrary to general GATT rules, but are capped both in terms of level of expenditure and volume of subsidized exports prevailing in the base period (given by the average over the years 1986–90). Expenditure on export subsidies is to be reduced by 36 per cent and the volume of subsidized exports is also to come down by 21 per cent over the six-year period.

Many areas of the agreement remain undefined and leave room for manoeuvre. Implementation of the agreement allows for a great deal of flexibility. It is unlikely that the Uruguay Round commitments in agriculture will have a major impact on world food markets or the CAP in the near future. The agreement is nonetheless a step towards greater transparency and less protection in agriculture and is subject to revision in 1999.

Textiles and clothing

The Uruguay Round seeks to bring textiles and clothing back under GATT rules. As we have just seen, trade restrictions were first introduced under the short-term agreement to allow industrialized countries to adjust to new market conditions and competition; but thirty years later, the Multi-Fibre Arrangement (MFA) still allows for an extremely complex set of bilateral arrangements restricting trade in textiles and clothing

Under the new agreement reached at the end of the Uruguay Round, the bilateral quotas of the MFA will have to be phased out over a ten-year period from the creation of the World Trade Organization (WTO) and the volume of imports of textiles and clothing of each member gradually brought within GATT rules.

Remaining restrictions will also have to be relaxed. In the first three years of the agreement, the yearly growth rate of quotas carried forward from the MFA will be increased by 16 per cent; for example, a quota which increased by 2 per cent per annum under MFA will now have to rise by 2.32 per cent a year. During the following four years, stage two of the new agreement, quotas will have to increase by 25 per cent with respect to those prevailing in stage one; in stage three, during the last three years of the transition period, they will have to be 27 per cent above stage two quota levels. So, say, a quota which was due to rise by 2 per cent a year prior to the Uruguay Round agreement, will now increase by 2.32 per cent in stage one, by 2.9 per cent in stage two and by 3.68 per cent in stage three.

Importing countries are free to choose which products should be liberalized and how. The requirement is that some products from each category (yarns, fabrics, textile products, clothing) should be liberalized, but the amount from each category is not fixed. This flexibility means that the most sensitive items will be excluded from the initial stages and will not be liberalized until the complete phasing out of MFA in 2004. Hence 49 per cent of trade covered by MFA quotas will not be freed from restrictions until the end of 2004.

Considerable uncertainty also surrounds the final outcome of the transition period: whether the final stage of the agreement will really be implemented and textiles and clothing brought fully under the GATT umbrella; or whether countries will succumb to the lobbying of domestic pressure groups and seek to extend the transitional period or revert to other forms of protectionism. Past history points at the fact that when one form of protectionism is banned and removed, a different, more subtle one replaces it. What exporting countries now fear is that protection will be shifted from quotas to safeguards and anti-dumping measures selectively allowed by the Uruguay agreement (Brenton, Scott and Sinclair 1997: 318).

The Uruguay Round agreement also included regulations of three areas not previously covered by GATT:

- trade in services now covered by the General Agreement on Trade in services (GATs);
- trade-related intellectual property rights (TRIPs);
- trade-related investment measures (TRIMs).

GATs provides a much needed initial framework for the liberalization of trade in services, given the increased importance of trade in services, which now accounts for approximately one-quarter of the value of world trade in goods.

The TRIPs agreement provides for copyright protection in a number of areas such as computer programs, pharmaceuticals and agricultural chemicals.

The TRIMs agreement represents a tentative first step towards liberalization of direct investment. It outlaws practices specifically intended to restrict foreign direct investment which are not consistent with treatment or conditions applied to domestic investment, such as local content requirements, trade balancing or foreign exchange balancing conditions. This agreement is also subject to revision in 1999.

CAUSES AND CONSEQUENCES OF NEW PROTECTIONISM

The difficulties and length of the Uruguay Round of negotiations are a clear testimony to the dire state of trade relations among the world's major industrial economies at the turn of this century. New and more subtle trade restrictions are used nowadays, as we have seen. New protectionism is the term often used to describe this process.

New protectionism represents the greatest threat to the liberal order envisaged after World War II. Protectionist pressures became particularly pronounced in the early 1980s, as tight monetary policies, designed to squeeze inflation out of the economic systems after the OPEC price rises of the 1970s, caused a major world recession. Countries plagued by unemployment and trapped in vicious circles of lower growth tried to shield domestic industries threatened by foreign competition, in order to minimize job losses. These policies had the effect of delaying the structural adjustments made necessary by the international specialization of production, without solving the problem at its root. It is easier to favour liberalism when economies are booming and unemployment is low, as in the 1950s and 1960s, than when economies are in the grip of severe contractions.

New protectionism and economic growth

The trend toward trade liberalization started to be reversed in 1975, when the world became engulfed in the deepest worldwide recession since the Great Depression of 1929. Recession in the 1970s triggered projectionist measures, as it did in the 1930s. This time, because of GATT restrictions on the imposition of tariffs, the measures had to be different, mostly non-tariff barriers (NTBs) and voluntary export restraints (VERs). Annual world trade growth fell to an all-time low of 3 per cent between 1980 and 1985, as opposed to the 8 per cent recorded on average in the previous two and a half decades.

The Uruguay Round was an attempt to reverse this trend by the establishment of firm rules for checking the proliferation of these new forms of protectionism. As we have just seen, the Uruguay Round was a qualified success in this respect.

New protectionism and economic theory

Further support of the use of protectionist measures has come from economic theory, as we have seen in Chapter 12. The benefits of free trade and liberalism are no longer clear-cut in a world where giant multinational corporations dominate the markets; where economies of scale give industries and economies substantial advantages; where technological innovation dictates the tempos and forms of international trade.

Japan is often offered as an example of a country which has used strategic and selective forms of protection to enhance domestic growth and world market penetration. Less aggressively and possibly less successfully, European economies have also attempted a strategic use of industrial protection.

International trade theory has been turned on its head: comparative advantage is no longer the basis for specialization and trade; rather, it is the result of it. Comparative advantage can be created by firms enjoying economies of scale through expansion to foreign markets or a cost advantage due to government industrial policies.

New protectionism and exchange rate volatility

The protectionist pressures which emerged in the 1970s and 1980s were also partly the result of large exchange rate fluctuations experienced by many currencies. Domestic goods competitiveness on foreign markets depends not only on the cost effectiveness and efficiency of home production, but also on the value of the currency. Exchange rates that remain overvalued for a prolonged period of time cause the decline of a country's export sector, just as undervalued exchange rates give a country an unfair advantage.

The overvaluation of the dollar by about 20 per cent between 1960 and 1973 made US goods uncompetitive on foreign markets and US markets an easy target for import penetration. The strong protectionist stance of the USA during that period and after was the logical consequence. The US introduction of quota restrictions on textiles, cars, steel and many other goods was an ill-conceived attempt to remedy a distortion with another distortion. What is worse, trade restrictions imposed during periods of exchange rate misalignment tend to have a ratchet effect. They cause an increase in the effective amount of protection, as often they are not removed when exchange rates return to equilibrium levels.

Protectionism and trade diversion: consolidation of trade blocs

As a result of increased protectionist pressures, international trade has become increasingly regionalized. Within preferential regional agreements, such as free trade areas, customs unions or common markets, countries enjoy the benefits of trade liberalization and larger domestic markets within the area of preferential trade, discriminating, via the use of tariffs and quota restrictions, against trade with the rest of the world.

The trend towards trade regionalization and the growth of intra-regional trade, as opposed to inter-regional trade, have grown in recent years. The original six-member European Economic Community, founded in 1957, expanded over the years to include 15 countries in 1998, with further enlargement planned by 2002 (Agenda 2000).

In 1988 the USA signed a comprehensive free trade agreement with Canada and created a North Atlantic Free Trade Area (NAFTA), subsequently extended to Mexico in 1993. Chile and Columbia are likely to join in the near future.

Regional trade blocs have emerged in many other areas of the world, while earlier ones have foundered. Economic unions in East Africa (Kenya, Uganda, Tanzania) and Central Africa (Malawi, Zambia and Zimbabwe, under their pre-independence names) collapsed in the 1960s. The Council for Mutual Economic Assistance (CMEA), which had presided over the rapidly expanding if strongly regulated trade between the former USSR and East Germany, Bulgaria, Czechoslovakia, Hungary, Poland and Romania, broke up with the collapse of the Communist regimes in 1990–91.

The South African customs union which links South Africa with Botswana, Lesotho, Namibia and Swaziland has survived. While Argentina, Brazil, Paraguay and Uruguay have formed a free trade area known as Mercosur. Other regional trading blocs exist among countries in Asia and the Pacific Rim.

VOLUME AND PATTERN OF INTERNATIONAL TRADE FLOWS

As stated before, a general feature of the global economy in the post-war period has been the unprecedented growth of international trade, which has exceeded the growth of world production. Figure 13.6 shows annual average aggregate growth rates for world GDP and world trade in real terms for various periods, from 1913 onwards.

✍ Activity 13.14

Look at Figure 13.6 and explain what it shows.

✓ Answer 13.14

The data show world production exceeding world trade for the period from 1913 to1950. This is in contrast with the situation after 1950, when average growth rates of world trade have exceeded those of world production. The pre-1950 situation reflects the effects of intense protectionism which characterized the inter-war period.

Since 1950 world growth rates of trade have exceeded those of world output. Growth rate trends of both world trade and world production declined in the 1980s, as a result of world recession and the increased protectionism. World trade regained strength in the 1990s, averaging 6 per cent, while world output growth on average was 2.5 per cent. This was accounted for by the fast expansion of growth and trade by the dynamic economies of Southeast Asia.

There are other characteristics of the global trade pattern, summarized in Figure 13.7 which are worth noticing at this point.

The characteristics of the global trade pattern include the following:

- The bulk of international trade takes place between industrialized countries.
- Trade takes place mostly between the main trade blocs: the EU, North America and Asia, trading with one another and the rest of the world.
- Trade has increased, both within and between regions, but overall it has become more regionalized, i.e. more trade tends to take place within trade blocs.
- Trade is increasingly intra-industry, particularly between industrialized countries. This means that countries both import and export the same category of goods, such as cars, refrigerators or computers. This again reflects increased specialization and other factors discussed earlier on in this chapter.
- Some countries have managed to improve their position on international markets, while for some the reverse is true.
- International trade is not equally important for all countries. Its importance is measured by the degree of openness of an economy (exports as a percentage of GNP). This tends to be greater, the smaller the economy. So, typically, international trade is less important for the USA than it is for countries like the UK or Netherlands.

Figure 13.6   Annual average aggregate growth rates for world GDP and world trade in real terms, 1913–98

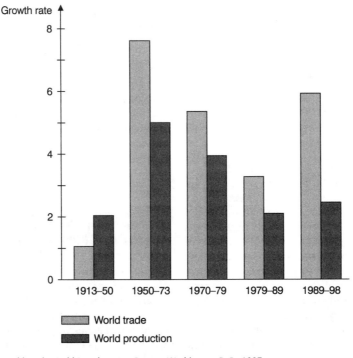

Source: Adapted from *The World Bank World Development Report*, Washington D.C., 1997

The rapid expansion of trade among industrial countries relative to trade with LDCs can be explained in the light of what has been said so far:

- built-in bias GATT trade liberalization efforts in favour of industrialized countries;
- high income elasticity of demand for intra-industry trade type products;
- intra-industry trade linked to multinational activities.

✍ Activity 13.15

Refer once more to Figure 13.7 on the regional structure of world trade and describe the main international trade flows in the 1990s, distinguishing between intra-regional and inter-regional trade.

✓ Answer 13.15

Regionalization of trade is particularly noticeable for the EU, where 60 per cent of all trade is intra-regional, i.e. between EU members, as opposed to inter-regional; only 9 per cent of EU trade is with North America and 6 per cent with Asia, while 25 per cent is with the rest of the world.

In North America, 40 per cent of trade is intra-regional, with Asia accounting for 23 per cent, the EU for 20 per cent, and the rest of the world for 17 per cent of North American exports.

Asian trade is relatively more outward looking, with intra-regional trade accounting for only 35 per cent of total trade. The main export outlet for Asian countries is increasingly North America, which accounts for 32 per cent of total exports, an increase of 8 per cent over a decade, followed by the rest of the world (17 per cent) and the EU (16 per cent).

TOWARDS A NEW GLOBAL AGE: A LONG-TERM SCENARIO

Over the next few decades the world economies face a variety of challenges and opportunities which will shape their growth and prosperity. New challenges and opportunities have been brought about by the following forces:

- rapid technological advances;
- gradual dismantling of barriers to trade, investment and capital movement;
- shift towards market economies of new, large sections of the world economy.

These forces have led to a steady opening up of the world economy and to unprecedented increases in worldwide trade in goods, services and financial assets. At the same time, however, the world economies face a range of problems:

- unfavourable demographic trends;
- increasing concentration of world production among few global players;
- deterioration of the global environment.

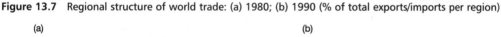

Figure 13.7   Regional structure of world trade: (a) 1980; (b) 1990 (% of total exports/imports per region)

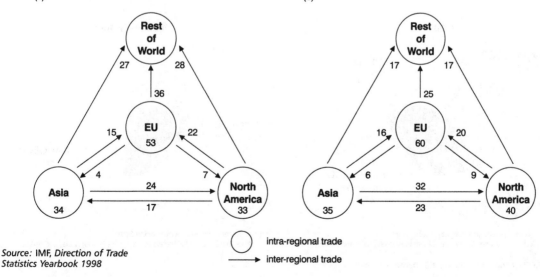

Source: IMF, Direction of Trade Statistics Yearbook 1998

○ intra-regional trade

→ inter-regional trade

To achieve higher growth in these circumstances will require special efforts. The explosion of world population implies in particular that:

■ the growth of investment and productivity will have to rise if global standards of living are to be maintained;

■ increased burden for public finances, which may have adverse effects on long-term interest rates if governments have to increase their borrowing – this in turn will have a negative impact on investment;

■ greater social spending on healthcare and pension systems.

Figure 13.8   Shares of world population and world GDP. In 1992 Purchasing Power Parities.

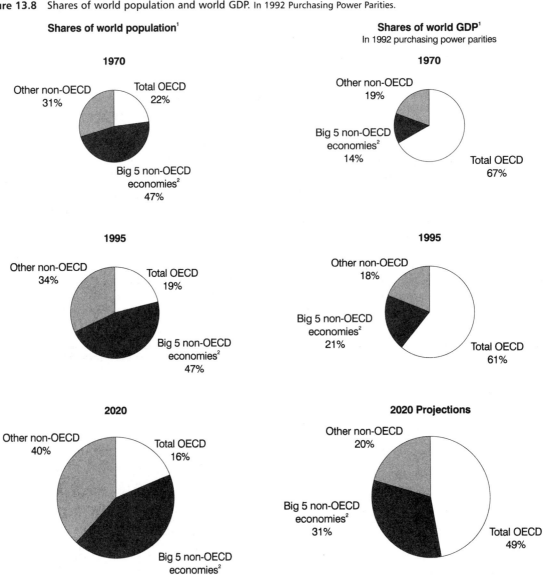

1. Pie-size reflects growth in world population
2. Brazil; China and Hong Kong, China; India; Indonesia; and Russia

1. Pie-size reflects growth in world GDP
2. Brazil; China and Hong Kong, China; India; Indonesia; and Russia

Source: OECD, Economic Outlook: 62, December 1997

Policies will need to provide a stable macroeconomic environment and to foster competition. Recent studies suggest that substantial gains in terms of growth could be achieved by DCs, thanks to the opportunities offered by the opening up of new large LDC markets which are eager to catch up with the more advanced economies. The greatest opportunities for world growth stem from the integration of the large economies of Brazil, China and Hong Kong, India, Indonesia and Russia (the big five non-OECD economies), as they increasingly pursue 'linkage-intensive' development strategies. These in turn will lead to greater trade, investment, co-operation and financial liberalization.

✍ Activity 13.16

Figure 13.8 shows the shares of world population and world's GDP to the year 2020. The pie size accurately reflects the projected growth in world population and world output. Describe what it shows.

✓ Answer 13.16

Figure 13.8 shows that the projected relative share of world output by the year 2020 will remain unevenly distributed, with the industrial economies retaining the greatest share. DC population will fall from 19 per cent to 16 per cent of total world population, while their projected share of world output will fall from 61 per cent in 1995 to 49 per cent in 2020. The relative share of world output of Brazil, China, India, Indonesia and Russia is projected to increase from 21 per cent to 31 per cent, the largest relative gain, thanks to a projected fall in population growth from 47 per cent of world population to 44 per cent. The share of world output by the rest of the world population, given its projected increase over the period, will remain roughly the same.

CASE STUDY: THREE CAPITALIST MODELS – USA, EUROPE AND JAPAN

After the collapse of the Communist regimes in central and eastern Europe, at a time when the whole world seems to have embraced the market philosophy of the capitalist system, it is good to be reminded by Hutton (1996) of the distinctive characteristics of the world's capitalisms (hence the plural). European, American and Japanese capitalism each have distinctive characteristics.

In this case study we start by discussing what they have in common, and move on to explain how and why they differ. A comparison of the outlooks of the US and Japanese economies in 1998 is also provided; statistics related to the EU economy have been discussed already on previous occasions throughout the book.

The common traits of capitalism

European, US and Japanese capitalism are all firmly based on a market system, whose pillar is provided by private property and the right to make profits by means of one's own enterprise. Production and distribution are organized through the market by individuals and companies pursuing the objective of profit maximisation. All three systems have stock markets to raise financial capital and a government which takes and gives, through a tax and a social security system. However, underneath the similarities are profound differences.

The US capitalist model

US capitalism is often regarded as the most extreme; one in which the frontiers of state intervention have been firmly rolled back (in fact never allowed to unroll, one could argue). Its main characteristics are:

■ Low personal and corporate taxation, matched by government's low spending on social welfare.
■ Flexible labour markets, which have proved able to generate jobs in recent years, but are characterized by job insecurity, very low wages (the bottom tenth of the workforce was earning 38 per cent of median earnings in 1995, compared with 67 per cent of median earnings earned by the bottom tenth in Europe), minimal employment regulation, high worker turnover, weak and fragmented trade unions. Unemployment benefits are paid for only six months and are equivalent to a meagre 36 per cent of average earnings.
■ A competitive business environment, safeguarded by tough anti-monopoly legislation, under constant threat of takeovers and hence geared towards short-term profits and maximization of dividends.
■ The extreme short-termism of private capital is mitigated by the existence of federal institutions, such as the Reconstruction Finance Corporation, and powerful state banks, dating back to Roosevelt's New Deal, which provide long-term finance to medium-sized companies and to housing construction and ownership.
■ Federal funding and support is available in the fields of education and research and development, which have greatly helped the high technology industry.
■ On the social front, there is a strong culture of participation and engagement and a tight network of intermediate public institutions, which mitigate the extremes of market capitalism.

To sum up, the US capitalist model combines the individualistic values of the market system and their celebration of profit and competition with vigorous public and private morality and a strong tradition of charity and solidarity.

US economic outlook into the year 2000

As Table 13.10 shows, the US economic outlook in the 1990s is quite good, as the economic performance in the second half of the 1990s has continued to improve.

Real GDP growth recorded in 1998 was among the highest of the industrialized economies, unemployment rate steady around the 5 per cent mark, budget deficit nearly eliminated and inflation coming down further.

continued overleaf

THREE CAPITALIST MODELS – USA, EUROPE AND JAPAN

Strong demand in 1999 is likely to cause inflation to pick up a little. The signs are that the economy might have reached the peak of its expansionary phase, showing a slow-down in inventory investment as stocks reach their desired level, and a less robust export growth associated with recent appreciation of the dollar and the ripple effects of the Asian financial crisis still being felt throughout the world economy.

The European capitalist model

The European model is an alternative form of capitalism, inspired by Germany's 'social market economy'. This brand of capitalism is less sanguine than the American, as political, economic and social institutions offer a solid framework and a constraint within which the forces of capitalism and the free market are allowed to develop.

Institutional structures favour co-operation, productivity and investment through a more direct link between financial institutions, business, government and trade unions. The main features of the European/German capitalist model are as follows:

■ A comprehensive welfare system, offering a high degree of social protection. Pensions and unemployment benefits are high with respect to average earnings. The education system gives young people in Germany a solid technical training, where the 'dual vocational system' offers them both an academic education and work experience.
■ The labour market is highly unionized – 75 per cent of German workers are covered by industry-wide wage settlements negotiated by powerful, large trade unions. The trade unions are highly integrated and present at decision level in the business structure of the economy. Turnover is low, wages are relatively high and a considerable degree of job security is enjoyed by workers in organizations, which try to minimize redundancies during recessions.
■ The business environment is collaborative rather than competitive and the focus is on medium to long-term returns, rather than on short-termism. Companies do not have to 'appear' highly profitable, but simply financially sound, as finance is mostly raised through the banking system rather than the stock market. Aggressive takeovers organized through the stock exchange are not common in Germany, unlike the USA or UK.
■ Social provisions and job protection offered by this system translate into a high tax burden and a rather inflexible system, unable to accommodate change rapidly, although change is accommodated eventually.
■ The social market philosophy permeates public institutions, regardless of political party divisions. This translates into strong independent regional governments and institutions.

These characteristics of the German capitalist model, which can be summed up in a rather large role for the state and in the importance of social cohesion, are generally shared by the other European economies and give this 'continental' brand of capitalism its own distinctive flavour. In contrast, British capitalism is more like the American than the continental: competitive and short-termist, as it is run by a financial system which demands quick, high returns, without the safeguard provided by strong, regulatory institutions. The labour market is characterized by high turnover, job insecurity and income inequality, but low functional and geographical mobility.

The Southeast Asian capitalist model

Finally, the third form of capitalism is the Japanese, Southeast Asian and just emerging Chinese model. Each country or group of countries presents its own variation within a theme, but they all share some common features.

The apparently contradictory principle that inspires this brand of capitalism is competition with co-operation, as competition is fierce but the spirit of co-operation which permeates society is equally strong. The main features of the east Asian capitalist model can be summarized as follows:

■ Rather than the government, it is the firm which provides the core social unit of which people are members. Unions are organized around the firm. Social provisions, such as security of employment, social protection and pensions, emanate from the firm and not from central government. Taxation is low by international standards and society is not divided by huge income inequalities.
■ Despite the fact that labour is recognized as the central element of the productive system and human relations in the workplace its focal point, the labour market is highly unstructured and not overtly mediated by the price mechanism. People do not work for wages, but to co-operate with management in the creation of the country's wealth. Of course they get paid, for their endeavours, and competitively, but they also get lifelong job security from the firms in return for their commitment.
■ The business environment within which firms operate is competitive and cooperative at the same time. The financial system is not market-based: the returns required from firms are low and the focus is once more on the personal relationship between the financial institution and its customers, the businesses. Long-termism, rather than short-termism, characterizes the financial system. Secure and long-term financial backing has allowed firms to be innovative both in terms of working practices and production technologies. This has produced the miracles of productivity which the world has admired.
■ Central government is small, as the boundaries between government, society and the economy are blurred. The result is an inclusive society, where the focus is on harmony and achievement, but where accountability and regulatory frameworks are weak as a result. This has often translated into fraud and corruption.

Southeast Asia economic outlook into the year 2000

Southeast Asian tiger economies provided world analysts with much needed new tales of economic miracles after Japan's extraordinary expansion was showing signs of slowing down in the second part of the 1990s. The fairytale of economic expansion came to a sudden end when the collapse of the Thai baht in July 1997 wobbled world financial markets. The string of devaluations, speculative attacks and stock market slumps which followed highlighted the fragility of the international monetary order and initiated a vicious circle of economic contraction of the whole area. The Japanese economy has also been caught by the recessionary spiral. A comparison of the basic statistics of the Southeast Asian economies for 1997 and 1998 is sufficient to illustrate the scale of the contraction (Table 13.11).

The origin of the economic instability in Southeast Asia

It could be argued with hindsight that the signs of trouble in Southeast Asia were visible well in advance.

✍ Activity 13.17

But what could be signs of trouble in a fast-expanding economy?

THREE CAPITALIST MODELS – USA, EUROPE AND JAPAN

Table 13.10   USA: basic indicators, 1995–9

Demand and output
Percentage changes from previous period, seasonally adjusted at annual rates, volume (1992 prices)

	1994 current prices billion $	1995	1996	1997	1998	1999
Private consumption	4717.0	2.4	2.6	3.3	3.1	2.4
Government consumption	1107.1	–0.1	0	1.2	1.0	0.2
Gross fixed investment	1152.5	4.4	7.5	7.1	8.1	3.8
Public	205.9	0.5	3.2	–0.3	1.5	0.5
Private residential	286.0	–3.8	5.9	2.4	3.4	0.2
Private non-residential	660.6	9.0	9.2	10.7	11.2	5.6
Final domestic demand	6976.6	2.4	3.0	3.6	3.7	2.4
*stockbuilding	61.2[a]	–0.5	0	0.5	–0.4	–0.3
Total domestic demand	7037.8	1.8	3.0	4.1	3.3	2.1
Exports of goods and services	721.2	11.1	8.3	12.6	7.6	6.4
Imports of goods and services	812.0	8.9	9.1	14.5	11.4	7.1
*net exports	–90.8[a]	0.1	–0.2	–0.5	–0.8	–0.3
GDP at market prices	6947.0	2.0	2.8	3.8	2.7	1.9
Industrial production	—	3.3	2.8	5.0	4.9	0.7

*Contributions to changes in real GDP (as a per cent of real GDP in the previous period)
[a]Actual amount

Employment, income and inflation
Percentage changes from previous period, seasonally adjusted at annual rates

	1995	1996	1997	1998	1999
Employment[a]	1.5	1.4	2.2	1.4	0.7
Unemployment rate[b]	5.6	5.4	5.0	4.7	5.0
Employment cost index	2.8	2.8	3.0	3.4	3.5
Compensation of employees	5.1	5.0	6.1	5.5	5.1
Unit labour cost	3.0	2.2	2.3	2.6	3.1
Household disposable income	5.8	4.3	4.9	5.4	5.1
GDP deflator	2.5	2.3	2.0	1.9	2.2
Private consumption deflator	2.6	2.4	2.1	2.0	2.3

[a]Household basis   [b]As a percentage of labour force

Financial indicators

	1995	1996	1997	1998	1999
Household saving ratio[a]	5.1	4.4	4.0	4.2	4.4
General government financial balance[b]	–1.9	–1.1	0.0	0.1	0.0
Current balance[b]	–1.8	–1.9	–2.1	–2.5	–2.6
Short-term interest rate[c]	4.4	5.0	5.1	5.6	5.6
Long-term interest rate[d]	6.6	6.4	6.4	6.4	6.5

[a]As a percentage of disposable income   [b]As a percentage of GDP   [c]3-month Treasury bills   [d]10-year government bonds

External indicators

			Seasonally adjusted at annual rates	
	1996	1997	1998	1999
	$ billion			
Merchandise exports	612.1	683	732	780
Merchandise imports	803.2	884	968	1,032
Trade balance	–191.2	–201	–236	–252
Invisibles, net	43.0	31	23	19
Current balance	–148.2	–171	–213	–233
	Percentage change			
Merchandise export volumes[a]	9.5	15.8	8.4	6.9
Merchandise import volumes[a]	9.9	15.3	12.0	7.3
Export performance[b]	3.3	6.2	0.1	–1.3
Terms of trade	–0.6	0.7	1.1	0.2

Source: OECD, 1997
[a]Derived from values and unit values on a national accounts basis.
[b]Ratio between the export volumes and export market of total goods.

continued overleaf

THREE CAPITALIST MODELS – USA, EUROPE AND JAPAN

Table 13.11   Southeast Asian economies: basic indicators, 1997–8

| | | 1998 | | | | Currency units | | Interest rates |
| | | % change | | $bn | | per $ | per £ | short-term % p.a. |
	GDP	Industrial production	Consumer prices	Trade balance	Current account	1998	1998	
China	+7.2	−4.4	−0.3	+44.9	+23.1	8.28	13.70	9.43
Hong Kong	−2.0	−0.2	+4.7	−18.4	−6.6	7.74	12.80	13.54
India	+5.6	−0.7	+8.3	−6.4	−4.8	42.20	69.90	7.33
Indonesia	−6.2	+10.7	+52.0	+15.4	−5.8	16745.00	27775.00	42.50
Malaysia	−1.8	−3.4	+5.4	+3.1	−4.8	3.93	6.52	11.10
Philippines	+1.7	+19.4	+9.2	−9.0	−4.3	40.90	67.80	14.43
Singapore	+5.6	+8.5	+0.6	−3.4	+13.6	1.67	2.77	8.00
South Korea	−3.8	−10.8	+8.2	+6.0	+14.4	1421.00	2356.00	17.00
Taiwan	+5.9	+6.3	+1.7	+44.0	+5.7	34.70	57.60	7.75
Thailand	+0.4	−21.1	+10.2	+1.1	−2.9	41.00	67.90	23.50

| | | 1997 | | | | Currency units | | Interest rates |
| | | % change | | $bn | | per $ | per £ | short-term % p.a. |
	GDP	Industrial production	Consumer prices	Trade balance	Current account	Sept	Sept	
China	+9.6	+10.9	+3.6	+31.0	+1.6	8.29	13.30	10.80
Hong Kong	+6.1	−3.1	+6.5	−20.4	−1.6	7.74	12.40	7.45
India	+7.0	+5.1	+5.6	−5.1	36.4	35.70	6.88	
Indonesia	+8.0	+7.1	+5.6	+9.0	−7.9	2970.00	4759.00	30.50
Malaysia	+8.4	+7.2	+2.4	−1.1	−4.4	3.00	4.81	7.58
Philippines	+5.7	−5.4	+4.5	−11.4	−2.0	33.50	53.70	12.88
Singapore	+7.8	+7.7	+2.1	−6.6	+15.5	1.51	2.43	4.16
South Korea	+6.3	+7.9	+4.0	−17.0	−22.8	909.00	1457.00	13.45
Taiwan	+6.3	+7.2	−0.6	+11.8	+9.7	28.60	45.80	8.15
Thailand	+6.7	+6.1	+6.6	−14.0	−10.0	35.90	57.50	24.50

Source: *The Economist*, June 1992; OECD, 1997

✓ Answer 13.17

You need to think in terms of what determines a sustainable and balanced growth. Is the growth of demand outstripping the economy's output capacity? Is demand mostly domestic or mostly foreign? Has it been sustained by borrowed funds? Is the inflow of capital likely to be volatile or long term? Is sectoral growth balanced or one sided?

If the Thai economy had been given this health check, the diagnosis would have been a worrying one well before July 1997:

■ Over-investment had fuelled a spurt in economic growth until 1995, eventually resulting in excessive domestic demand and spiralling current account deficits.

■ These current account deficits were financed by strong capital inflows from abroad, attracted to Thailand by its fast growth record, deregulation of its financial sector and relative stability of its exchange rate, pegged to the dollar like several other Southeast Asian currencies. The current account deficits were being compensated by capital account surpluses.

■ The inflow of capital had kept interest rates lower than domestic

economic conditions would have required; this in turn had fuelled an unsustainable surge in the property market.

■ Growth was also supported until 1995 by the weakness of the dollar, to which the bhat was pegged. As the dollar strengthened, so did the bhat, with the result that Thailand's competitiveness relative to Japan was eroded.

■ With China's vast manufacturing capacity coming onstream, doubts about Southeast Asia's long-term competitiveness in world markets were beginning to surface in the minds of international capital operators, making them less willing to invest capital in the country.

■ The weakening of US demand for electronic goods contributed to Thailand's export slowdown in 1996–7, just as the Thai banks were undermined by their excess supply of funds to the property market.

■ Many Thai companies had borrowed heavily from abroad, which made them particularly vulnerable to devaluation.

Some of the points mentioned above are specific to the Thai economy. Most, however, apply equally to other Southeast Asian economies and are the real causes of the whole area's long-term economic instability. The repercussions of this crisis are now being felt in Japan. (See Table 13.12.)

THREE CAPITALIST MODELS – USA, EUROPE AND JAPAN

Table 13.12 Japan: basic indicators, 1995–9

Demand and output

Percentage changes from previous period, seasonally adjusted at annual rates, volume (1990 prices)

	1994 current prices trillion ¥	1995	1996	1997	1998	1999
Private consumption	286.2	2.0	2.8	1.4	1.7	2.0
Government consumption	45.7	3.5	2.3	0.8	-0.2	-0.5
Gross fixed investment	137.3	1.1	8.7	-4.2	1.5	2.4
Public	41.3	0.7	9.9	-13.6	-0.8	-5.2
Private residential	25.7	-6.4	13.6	-12.6	-5.2	3.1
Private non-residential	70.2	3.9	6.6	3.9	4.5	5.6
Final domestic demand	469.2	1.9	4.6	-0.4	1.5	1.9
*stockbuilding	0.0[a]	0.3	-0.1	-0.1	0	0.1
Total domestic demand	469.2	2.2	4.5	-0.5	1.5	2.0
Exports of goods and services	44.4	5.4	2.3	10.4	8.2	7.6
Imports of goods and services	34.4	14.3	10.5	2.2	6.8	7.6
*net exports	-10.0[a]	-0.8	-0.9	1.0	0.3	0.1
GDP at market prices	479.3	1.4	3.5	0.5	1.7	2.1
Industrial production	–	3.5	2.7	4.4	0.1	1.7

*Contributions to changes in real GDP (as a per cent of real GDP in the previous period)
[a]Actual amount

Employment, income and inflation

Percentage changes from previous period, seasonally adjusted at annual rates

	1995	1996	1997	1998	1999
Employment	0.1	0.5	1.0	0.4	1.0
Unemployment rate[a]	3.1	3.4	3.4	3.4	3.3
Compensation of employees	2.1	2.1	2.7	2.0	2.6
Unit labour cost	0.7	-1.4	2.2	0.2	0.6
Household disposable income	1.3	1.7	2.3	2.5	3.1
GDP deflator	-0.6	0.0	1.1	0.8	0.5
Private consumption deflator	-0.5	0.2	1.7	1.0	0.6

[a]As a percentage of labour force

Financial indicators

	1995	1996	1997	1998	1999
Household saving ratio[a]	13.1	11.9	11.2	11.1	11.5
General government financial balance[b]	-3.7	-4.4	-2.8	-2.6	-2.4
Current balance[b]	2.1	1.4	2.2	2.4	2.5
Short-term interest rate[c]	1.2	0.6	0.6	0.6	1.1
Long-term interest rate[d]	3.4	3.1	2.4	2.1	2.6

[a]As a percentage of disposable income [b]As a percentage of GDP [c]3–6 month CD [d]Central government bonds

External indicators

Seasonally adjusted at annual rates

	1996	1997	1998	1999
	$ billion			
Merchandise exports	400.4	416	454	494
Merchandise imports	316.8	317	341	376
Trade balance	83.6	99	113	119
Invisibles, net	-17.8	-7	-8	-7
Current balance	65.8	92	105	112
	Percentage change			
Merchandise export volumes[a]	0.5	11.9	9.2	8.2
Merchandise import volumes[a]	3.4	4.8	7.6	8.7
Export performance[b]	-7.6	0.6	0.0	0.5
Terms of trade	-8.0	-2.7	0.0	-0.7

Source: OECD, 1998. Estimated values for 1999.
[a] Customs basis. [b] Ratio between the export volumes and export market of total goods.

continued overleaf

THREE CAPITALIST MODELS – USA, EUROPE AND JAPAN

Japans exports to the region are 2.5 times larger than the USA or Europe as a share of GDP. As a result, Japanese industrial production and GDP has fallen sharply for the first time in more than two decades. This contraction has to lead to bank and business failures, increased unemployment and fall in consumption, in other words to a depression.

Lessons for the world economy

After the collapse of the baht on the foreign exchange market and the subsequent sudden outflow of capital, a $16.7bn rescue package was put together by the IMF in August 1997 to stem the financial crisis. The measures did not prevent the economic malaise from spreading. The crisis could have been avoided if the following provisions had been made:

1 *Sounder financial systems*: the proposal under consideration by the world financial institutions is that the Basle Committee should draw up banking standards appropriate to the emerging markets. The IMF should police them and the World Bank should help countries to make improvements. Asia's crises are bound to give this agenda a push.

2 *Control of capital movements*: the Thai crisis has also contributed to the raising of some quite different concerns. The IMF, with its insistence on the liberalization of capital flows in its Articles of Agreement, might contribute to the difficulties being experienced by emerging economies. Capital flows can bring substantial benefits to an emerging economy by promoting growth and investment but they can be a double-edged sword, given their volatility.

3 *Balanced growth*: there are several steps that emerging economies need to take before liberalizing their capital movements, to ensure balanced growth and a reduction of speculation:

- government borrowing, inflation and current account deficits must be kept at safe levels;
- they must strengthen domestic financial markets;
- they must tackle any other structural economic distortions.

☆ **For revision of this chapter, see the Chapter Summaries at the end of the book, starting on page 411.**

Chapter summaries

CHAPTER 1

- Economics is divided into two main branches, microeconomics and macroeconomics, where the word 'macro', from Greek, means big and the word 'micro' means small.
- Microeconomics is concerned with individual, limited parts of the economy, like the demand and supply of a particular good or service, (cars, toothpaste or refrigerators).
- Macroeconomics is concerned with the study of the economy as a whole and with broad aggregates. It looks at:

  - aggregate demand for all the goods and services produced in an economy
  - total spending in the economy on the purchase of machinery by firms
  - spending by foreigners
  - government spending.

- Business is affected by macroeconomic variables such as interest rates, exchange rates, unemployment and inflation rates, the level and composition of government spending and taxation, business cycles and international monetary and trade policies.
- These macroeconomic variables affect business decisions but also affect each other. Their interdependence is the object of macroeconomic analysis.
- Macroeconomics tries to answer the following questions:

  - What determines national output and its growth over time?
  - What is inflation and what causes it?
  - What is unemployment? Why is it so high?
  - What causes Balance of Payment problems?
  - What can the government do to correct these problems?

- Macroeconomics makes use of models to reduce and make sense of the complexity of the economy as a whole.
- The most important and influential macroeconomic models, developed since the Second World War, have been the Keynesian and Monetarist models.

CHAPTER 2

- Macroeconomics is concerned with relationships between economic aggregates. Instead of discussing consumers, firms and individual markets, macroeconomics is concerned with the rate of growth of national income, unemployment, inflation, the money supply, the balance of payments, and so on. Macroeconomics is also concerned with government economic policies, such as fiscal policy and monetary policy.
- Different groups of economists have different interpretations of the workings of the macroeconomy, and these differences lead to alternative suggestions for policy.
- The most important division is that between Keynesians and Monetarists, though neither of these groups are as clearly defined as it is sometimes implied.
- It is important to have a measure of the economy's state of health. For this reason, national income figures are collected. National income figures are also commonly used to make comparisons of well-being across nations.
- A variety of different measures of national income are in use:

Gross domestic product (GDP)	=	value of all goods and services produced in the economy
Gross national product (GNP)	=	GDP plus net property income from abroad
Net domestic product (NDP)	=	GDP minus capital consumption
Net national product (NNP)	=	GNP minus capital consumption

- The various measures may be calculated at 'market prices' or at 'factor cost'. If at 'factor cost', then indirect taxes are subtracted from the figure at 'market prices' and subsidies are added on.
- As price levels change rapidly, national income figures are often quoted 'at 1990 prices', the current figure being deflated by a price index.
- The figures for national income may be arrived at in three equivalent ways. Firstly, the value of the output

of the economy can be added, industry by industry, using the value-added method. Value-added is the difference between the value of a firm's inputs and the value of its output. Secondly, all spending may be added up, avoiding double-counting by taking into account only final expenditures, to reach a total figure for spending on final goods and services. Thirdly, factor incomes (wages, rent, interest and profit) can be added up, reaching the same result, at least in principle. Although the three measures should arrive at the same answer in principle, in practice the shortcomings of the statistical system mean that they do not, and the official figures include a 'balancing-item'.

- National income figures are useful to assess the state of an economy. There are limits, however, to what they can show as measures of a country's well-being.

CHAPTER 3

- The circular flow model shows us that the economic system is in equilibrium when total income = total expenditure = total output.
- The circular flow is affected by withdrawals of money from its circulation, as well as by injections into it.
- Withdrawals are represented by savings, taxes and imports.
- Saving is that part of income which is not spent on goods and services. Savings are a leakage from the circular flow.
- Taxes reduce people's disposable income and their expenditure.
- Imports are goods produced abroad but purchased by people in the domestic economy. They represent a leakage of funds out of the circular flow.
- Injections into the circular flow are investment, government expenditure and export expenditure.
- Investment is the purchase of capital goods by firms, financed through borrowing or past savings.
- Government expenditure can take the form of direct expenditure on goods and services by the government or indirect expenditure such as subsidies to firms and transfer payments to households.
- Exports are domestically produced goods and services purchased by people in other countries.
- There is no automatic link between injections and withdrawals that ensures macroeconomic equilibrium.
- Planned injections may not equal planned withdrawals, hence expenditure ≠ output and income.

- If this is the case output will adjust to the level of aggregate expenditure.
- The level of employment in the economy depends, ceteris paribus, on the level of output firms decide to produce, which in turn depends on the level of aggregate expenditure.

CHAPTER 4

- According to Keynes, it is the level of aggregate demand or total desired expenditure that determines the level of output, income and employment in the economy.
- In order to reduce unemployment, we therefore need to stimulate aggregate demand or total desired expenditure.
- To be able to do that we need not only to know the components of aggregate demand but we also need to know what affects each component.
- The main components of aggregate demand or total expenditure are: consumption, investment, government spending and net exports. We need to explain what affects each one of them in order to be able to manipulate the level of aggregate demand.
- We have developed a theory of what affects consumption, which we have called the 'consumption function'. According to Keynes, it is the level of current disposable income that affects consumption decisions.
- This is a classic chicken and egg situation. The level of expenditure determines the level of output and income. But income determines the level of that expenditure we call consumption. So consumption cannot increase if income does not. But income does not increase if expenditure (consumption) does not. That is what we mean when we say that consumption is endogenously determined: it is an **endogenous** variable.
- The other important component of domestic expenditure is investment. Investment is not determined by current income; investment, is an **exogenous** variable.
- If investment demand or investment expenditure increases, so will the output, income and employment in the economy as they adjust to the higher level of investment spending. But as income increases because of the increased investment, so will consumption, as consumption increases when income increases. Output and income will then increase further, as they adjust to the higher consumption demand. This process of further successive increases in output and income on one hand and consumption on the other, triggered by an initial injection of exogenous expenditure (which

could be an increase in government spending or an increase in export demand and not just an increase in investment demand) eventually stops as further increases become smaller and smaller. This is due to the fact that only part of an increase in income is consumed. Part is saved. So the additional consumption demand gets smaller each time round and consequently 'triggers' a smaller increase in output and income. This process is known as the **multiplier effect**.

■ We have developed a theory of what affects investment, which we have summarised in an **investment function**. According to this theory, which only partly reflects Keynes' thinking on the subject but which is, nonetheless, currently used as the best approximation to it, it is the rate of interest that affects the level of investment.

■ Our next question then is: 'What determines the interest rate?'. As we see in Chapter 6, the interest rate is determined by monetary conditions. We have therefore found an important link between the **money sector** and the **real sector** of the economy in the Keynesian model.

■ Changes in the money supply affect the interest rate, which in turn determines investment demand, which ultimately affects the level of output, income and employment of the economy.

■ If however, investment is not very responsive to changes in interest rates, given that other factors like expectations of future sales also affect investment decisions, then direct government intervention – rather than monetary policy aimed at reducing the interest rate – might prove more effective to stimulate demand.

CHAPTER 5

■ Fiscal policies are government policies aimed at controlling the level of economic activity by varying government expenditure (G) and taxation (T).

■ If G exceeds T the government has a budget deficit. If G is smaller than T it has a budget surplus; if G is equal to T, the government has a balanced budget.

■ The budget deficit (surplus) refers to the debt (surplus) that the central government incurs in a year. The national debt is the stock of accumulated, outstanding government debt over the years.

■ The Public Sector Borrowing Requirement, the Public Sector Debt Repayment and the Public Sector Debt refer to the budget and debt position of the entire public sector, which includes central government, local government and public corporations.

■ Budgets deficits can be financed in three ways:
  – borrowing from the public by selling government bonds (Open Market Operations). This tends to push up interest rates and crowd out private investment.
  – borrowing from the Central Bank. This increases the money supply and can be inflationary.
  – borrowing from abroad. This is mostly used by developing countries and can create serious debt repayment and international liquidity problems.

■ Fiscal policy's main objective is to control aggregate demand and stabilize the economy by bringing **actual output** as close as possible to **potential output** and by reducing actual output's cyclical fluctuations by means of counter-cyclical policies.

■ Counter-cyclical policies are expansionary (G greater than T) when the economy shows signs of slowing down and contractionary (T greater than G) when the economy shows signs of overheating.

■ Fiscal policies can be distinguished as **automatic** or **discretionary**. A recession causes a budget deficit to develop automatically, just as economic expansion causes automatic budget surpluses (or reductions of deficits). Discretionary fiscal policies are deliberate changes by the government in its spending and taxation.

■ Government expenditure and taxation have a multiplier effect on the economy, just like any other form of injection or withdrawal of spending. We can distinguish four fiscal policy multipliers: direct government spending multiplier, tax multiplier, transfer payments multiplier and balanced budget multiplier.

■ Implementation of fiscal policy for stabilization purposes has proved difficult in practice for the following reasons: existence of time lags, use of 'estimated' variables, existence of shocks and unforeseen events, and displacements of other components of aggregate demand.

CHAPTER 6

■ This chapter explains how **interest rates** are determined, while the next one focuses on the effects of interest rates and changes in monetary policy on economic activity.

■ Interest rates are determined in **financial markets**, which are markets where financial assets are bought and sold.

- Financial markets are affected by government's **monetary policy**, which in turn affects the liquidity of the economic system by determining the quantity of money in the economy.
- **Money** is any medium of exchange that is widely accepted in payment for goods and services, and in settlement of debts. Money also serves as a standard of value for measuring the relative worth of different goods and services. The number of units of money required to buy a commodity represents the price of the commodity.
- The **official definitions** of money currently used in Britain are **M0** and **M4**. M0 comprises notes and coins in circulation outside the Bank of England *plus* bankers' operational deposits with the Bank. M4 comprises M0 *plus* UK private sector sterling deposits.
- The **money supply**, which is currency in circulation and bank deposits, is determined by the central bank and the banking sector.
- The amount of liquidity (money) people wish to have ready to hand, the **demand for money**, depends on their income. People will also want to have some liquidity handy to meet unforeseen expenses and not to incur the risks of capital losses associated with holding one's wealth in government bonds or other forms of financial assets. A capital loss occurs when the value of an asset falls.
- A **government bond** is a 'promise to pay' a fixed yield for a fixed period of time (five years, ten years) in exchange for a sum of money today (usually £100 for one government bond), after which time the Government undertakes to redeem the bond (return the money borrowed) at its face value (£100) and not its market value, which may be different.
- The **market value of bonds**, i.e. the price you can sell them at today, is inversely related to the interest rate. When interest rates fall, the price of bonds rises; when interest rates rise, the price of bonds falls.
- The amount of money supplied to the economy by the banking system, the money supply, and the amount of money (as opposed to bonds) people wish to hold determine the interest rate.

CHAPTER 7

- Keynes explains the determination of interest rates on the basis of **liquidity preference theory**. Money and financial assets, such as government bonds and treasury bills, are good substitutes for each other. Quite a small rise in the price of bonds will induce people to sell securities and hold money instead.

- An **increase in the money supply** will cause people to buy more bonds, rather than holding money. The increase in the demand for bonds, will push the price of bonds up, lowering the interest rate.
- A **lower interest rate** will stimulate investment spending and output, income and employment via the multiplier effect. Hence, according to the Keynesians, the interest rate and monetary policy affect the real sector of the economy, that is, output, income and employment. The interest rate affects investment expenditure decisions, which in turn affect the level of output and employment. This is the **transmission mechanism** that Keynes identifies between the money sector and the real sector of the economy, where decisions about how much to produce or how many people to employ are taken.
- According to Keynes, interest rates may not be very responsive to changes in the money supply and **investment decisions** are also affected by factors other than the exchange rate and are not very responsive to changes in the interest rate. For these reasons, Keynes favours the use of fiscal policies, rather than monetary policy, to control the economy.
- According to the **monetarists's portfolio balance approach**, changes in the money supply affect aggregate demand directly, consumption demand as well and not just investment demand (via the interest rate). But changes in aggregate demand, in their view, only affect the price level and not the level of output and employment.
- To affect the level of output and employment, according to the monetarists, the government must adopt 'supply side' policies aimed at increasing competition and price (wage) flexibility while maintaining price stability. Monetary and fiscal policy should only aim at reducing inflation.
- From a Keynesian viewpoint, an independent central bank reduces government ability to use fiscal and monetary tools for demand management.
- Monetarists oppose discretionary fiscal and monetary policies for stabilization purposes From their point of view, an independent central bank in charge of price stability is to be welcomed, as it is in line with their belief that inflation is always a monetary phenomenon and should be eliminated by gradual reduction of money supply.
- The creation of the European Union, of an independent European Central Bank and the introduction of a single currency represent major policy initiatives which go well beyond exchange rate stabilization and are likely to have profound effects on European governments' ability to conduct independent monetary and fiscal policies.

- There are potential gains from the introduction of a single currency, which include reduced transaction costs, reduced exchange rate uncertainty, increased intra-EU investment, increased inward direct investment, lower interest rates, increased price transparency and intra-EU competition, and economies of scale.
- There are also major potential costs associated with the introduction of a single currency, such as the loss of macroeconomic policy autonomy, loss of ability to react to country-specific shocks, risks of real misalignment within the union and the existence of asymmetric policy sensitivity among member countries.

CHAPTER 8

- The **effect of aggregate demand** on the economy largely depends on whether output and employment can increase or whether the economy has already reached its full-employment level of output.
- When the economy has reached its full-employment level, a further increase in aggregate demand only causes prices to rise and not output. This is a situation of demand-pull inflation.
- According to the monetarists, an increase in aggregate demand has no effect on output and employment; it simply leads to higher inflation. To increase output and stimulate employment, supply side policies are needed and not policies aimed at stimulating demand.
- **Inflation** is a generalised and persistent increase in prices. The rate of inflation is the percentage change in the overall price level, not the price level itself.
- There are two main **price indexes** that measure the price level and the rate of inflation: the retail price index and the GDP deflator.
- The **retail price index (RPI)** is the ratio of the value of a basket of goods at current year prices to the value of the same basket of goods at base-year prices, multiplied by 100. The goods included in the basket are those typically consumed by the average household in Britain.
- The **GDP deflator** index is obtained by dividing nominal GDP by real GDP (current year volume of goods valued at base-year prices), multiplied by 100.
- To discuss the **costs of inflation**, it is important to distinguish whether inflation is anticipated or unanticipated. **Unanticipated inflation** brings about unwanted and unplanned redistribution of income: from creditors to debtors, from employees to

employers. **Anticipated inflation** causes changes in relative prices, changes in relative interest rates and changes in output and employment.
- The **causes of inflation** are many. Inflation can be caused by demand-pull factors, cost-push factors, by a wage-price inflation spiral and by expectations. Inflation is always accompanied by, and may be caused by, an increase of the money supply.
- The **Phillips curve** showed the existence of a trade-off between unemployment and inflation in the late 50s and 60s. Data on inflation and unemployment in the 70s and 80s did not seem to support the existence of such a trade-off anymore. It is now argued that such a trade-off only exists in the short-run, as people are unprepared and do not correctly anticipate the rate of inflation, and when the economy does not suffer from other supply-side shocks.
- Policies to eliminate inflation include: deflationary fiscal policies and deflationary monetary policies.
- The **unemployment rate** is the percentage of the labour force which is out of work but willing to work.
- Unemployment can be distinguished as frictional, structural, cyclical, or voluntary.
- **Fricitional unemployment** is the amount of unemployment that is due to the normal working of the labour market. It represents people in between jobs and short-run problem of job/skills matching.
- **Structural unemployment** is the amount of unemployment caused by the changing pattern of demand and by technological innovations which cause certain industries to contract or disappear altogether. Structural unemployment is often also **regional**.
- **Demand-deficient or cyclical unemployment** is the amount of unemployment caused by lack of demand. This typically occurs during recessions and depressions, but is also associated to governments' deflationary policies. This form of unemployment is **involuntary**.
- **Classical unemployment** is supply-determined and measures the amount of unemployment due to people unwilling to take up the jobs available at the existing market wage. This form of unemployment is considered to be **voluntary**.
- The **natural rate of unemployment** is the amount of unemployment which persists when the labour market clears.
- To reduce unemployment Keynes prescribes demand-side policies of increasing government spending and reducing taxation; while Friedman advocates supply-side policies, such as cutting unemployment benefits or improving markets competitiveness.

CHAPTER 9

- The monetarist counter-revolution began to emerge in the early 1960s as an alternative explanation for the operation of the economy.
- Supply-side economics developed as an explicit repudiation of Keynes' demand-side principles.
- According to the monetarists, expansionary fiscal or monetary policies do not work as workers adjust their wage demand in line with inflation, preventing output and income from expanding. In this scenario, only supply-side policies can work to stimulate output growth.
- At the core of the monetarist model is the belief that:
  - if prices are flexible, markets will clear. This applies in particular to the market for labour, where workers do not suffer from money illusion.
  - markets are competitive and are better left to regulate themselves. This applies in particular to the money market, where interest rates are the equilibrating variable; to the open market, where exchange rate changes bring about equilibrium; and to the market for labour.
- Growth of potential ouput is determined by: the growth in the amount of productive resources, i.e. capital and labour; and the growth in the productivity of these resources.
- Supply-side policies, rather than macroeconomic policies, should be used to increase the productivity and competitiveness of the economy.
- Supply side policies are policies aimed at increasing the economy's efficiency and competitiveness through: increased wage flexibility, reformed welfare system, increased mobility of labour, tax rates cuts and regulations.
- Monetarism has inspired Government policies in the UK for a number of years.
- In June 1998 a statutory minimum wage was introduced in Britain, following the Low Pay Commission Report. Theory anticipates that there will be a substantial increase in inflation, before too long. The effect on the labour market will be very limited according to some; quite substantial, according to others.

CHAPTER 10

- The study of international economics focuses on the effects that international transactions have on the domestic economy.
- Countries export those goods for which they have the greatest comparative advantage and import those goods for which they have the greatest comparative disadvantage.
- To buy goods, services and assets from countries abroad, domestic residents need to acquire the relevant foreign currency first, and vice versa.
- The foreign exchange market is the market in which individuals, firms and banks buy and sell any tradable foreign currency.
- The demand for foreign currency arises because residents and domestic firms want to buy goods, services and assets from other countries.
- The supply of foreign currency to the foreign exchange market is provided by foreign people, firms and governments wanting to buy domestic goods and services or domestic financial assets.
- The exchange rate is the price of one unit of domestic currency expressed in terms of a foreign currency. Its value depends on demand and supply conditions on the foreign exchange market.
- The demand for imports is determined by the real exchange rate, i.e., relative prices multiplied by the nominal exchange rate, and by aggregate disposable income.
- The demand for exports is determined by real exchange rate and the level of income of foreign countries.
- Capital inflows/outflows are determined by relative, real rates of returns.
- An increased demand for imports causes a depreciation of the exchange rate and vice versa.
- An increased demand for exports causes an appreciation of the exchange rate and vice versa.
- There are two main exchange rate regimes: flexible exchange rates and fixed exchange rates.
- The Balance of Payments is a record of all the transactions between UK residents and the rest of the world involving the purchase or sale of domestic currency in a given period.
- It comprises two accounts: the current account and the capital account. The sum total of all the entries of the Balance of Payments is always equal to zero.
- Balance of Payments disequilibria can be corrected by the use of fiscal and monetary policies (aimed at reducing the demand for imports and increasing the inflow of portfolio capital), by the imposition of restrictions on convertibility of the currency and by tariffs and quotas on the import of goods.
- In an open economy, governments try to achieve **internal balance** (full employment and price stability) and **external balance** (current account balance).

CHAPTER 11

- The gold standard system assumed to ensure automatic achievement of external balance.
- The gold standard regime has conventionally been associated with three rules of the game:

  - In each participating country the price of the domestic currency must be fixed in terms of gold;
  - There must be a free import and export of gold;
  - The surplus country, which is gaining gold, should allow its volume of money to increase while the deficit country should allow its volume of money to fall.

- The gold standard system was abandoned at the outbreak of World War I.
- Attempts at reintroducing a watered down version of the gold standard, the gold-exchange standard, in 1918, were unsuccessful. The world economy moved into a deep recession after 1929 and economic integration weakened. In the very difficult years that followed, governments concentrated on domestic problems of recession and unemployment, partly shutting their economies off from the rest of the world. The result was intense protectionism and prolonged stagnation.
- After World War II the Bretton Woods system tried to restore an orderly international monetary system, based on fixed exchange rates and the dollar-gold convertibility. The aim of the system was to facilitate growth in a context of financial stability.
- Due to serious internal difficulties and the US macroeconomic policies of the 1960s, the system finally broke down in 1973.
- After the collapse of the Bretton Woods system, exchange rates were allowed to freely float in what became to be known as the 'non-system'.
- In 1979 the nine-member EC set up the European Monetary System (EMS) as part of its aim towards greater monetary integration.
- The EMS was based on the adoption of a system of relatively fixed exchange rates, known as the exchange rate mechanism (ERM), which set allowed bands of fluctuations for the participating currencies.
- The system almost broke down in 1992 due to lack of economic convergence, heightened capital mobility and differing political needs of member countries.
- Despite the difficulties of the ERM, EC members moved further down the path of monetary integration within the European economic and monetary union (EMU) with the adoption a single currency by eleven EU members.
- The present world system is one of managed flexibility of the exchange rates.
- The main reserve currencies are presently the dollar, followed by the Deutschmark, the yen and sterling.

CHAPTER 12

- Countries engage in trade to obtain the goods they cannot produce or they cannot produce as efficiently as other countries.
- Countries gain from specialization and trade.
- According to Ricardo, all participating countries can potentially benefit from trade if they specialize in the production of those goods for which they have a comparative advantage.
- According to Heckscher–Ohlin, countries should specialise in the production of those goods whose production is intensive in their abundant factor.
- There are however limits to the gains and scope for specialization.
- There are also other sources of comparative advantage, such as differences in demand, external and internal economies of scale, and scope for product differentiation.
- Contemporary trade theories include strategic trade theory, the Porter diamond and the exploitation of dynamic technological differences.
- Gains from trade are due to increased productivity, increased consumption possibilities, increased market efficiency and export led growth.
- There are arguments in favour of trade restrictions. They include: the infant industry argument, the senile industry argument, the anti-dumping argument, environmental arguments and non-economic arguments.
- Trade can be restricted through the use of tariffs, quotas, export subsidies, voluntary export restraints and technological barriers.
- Different forms of regional trade and economic association exist. They include: free-trade areas, customs unions, common markets and, economic and monetary unions.
- The European Union evolved from the original European community to create a more integrated common market.
- Agenda 2000 discusses the conditions for the enlargement of the EU to ten Central European countries.

CHAPTER 13

- The main country groupings currently used are: developed economies, European economies in transition, dynamic Asian economies and less developed countries.
- A liberal international economic order prevailed between 1870 and 1914. Before World War I, 43 per cent of world trade was in the hands of Britain, the US and Germany.
- The distribution of world trade changed significantly after World War I, as the US became the major world power. The Great Depression of 1929–31 which spread from the US to Europe, triggered a series of protectionist measures and caused a dramatic drop in the level of world trade.
- The international institutions created after World War II aimed to bring about a return to economic liberalism. The General Agreement on Tariff and Trade (**GATT**), signed in 1947, was the main institution which regulated international trade. In 1993 it was replaced by the World Trade Organization (WTO).
- GATT aimed to foster multilateralism in trade and a reduction of trade barriers, through a set of agreed rules for the conduct of international trade and a series of tariff cutting negotiations, called 'rounds'.

GATT succeeded in reducing tariff barriers. As a result of GATT's efforts, world trade grew faster than world output in the post-war period.
- Less developed countries remained outside GATT and pursued import-substitution policies aimed at self-sufficiency. These policies, however, proved detrimental to their development. In 1964, LDCs found in **UNCTAD** (United Nations Conference on Trade and Development) a forum where to voice their demands for a 'new economic order'.
- LDC requested the introduction of a **generalised system of preferences** (GSP) which would give their products unrestricted access to DCs markets, and the creation of a **commodity agreement** to stabilize the price of certain products. Both measures were endorsed by GATT in 1971 and 1976 respectively, but proved a victory only on paper.
- Allowing the newly created EC to become a member of GATT in 1957 represented an important exception to multilateralism.
- New forms of non-tariff barriers and new protectionist pressures spread in the 80s and 90s. Imports from LDCs and some NICs were limited by voluntary quotas (VERs).
- The global economy is characterised by trade between blocs and by an uneven distribution of world income. These features are likely to persist into the next century.

References

ALDCROFT, D. (1978) *The European Economy 1914–1970*, London: Croom Helm.

ANDREW, J. (1990) *How to understand the financial press*, London: Kogan Page.

ARGY, V. (1981) *The Postwar International Money Crisis*, London: George Allen & Unwin, pp 15–18.

ARROWSMITH, J. (1995) 'Economic and Monetary Union in a Multi-tier Europe', *The National Institute Economic Review*, 5: pp 32–37.

BARRO, R. and GRILLI, V. (1994) *European Macroeconomics*, London: Macmillan, pp 1–30, (on a cross-country comparison of the cyclical behaviour of output and output gaps).

BRANDER, J. and SPENCER, B. (1985) 'Export subsidies and international market share rivalry', *Journal of International Economics*, 18: pp 83–100.

BRENTON, P., SCOTT, H. and SINCLAIR, P. (1997) *International Trade*, Oxford: Oxford University Press.

BRIAULT, C., HALDANE, A. and KING, M. (1996) 'Central Bank Independence and Accountability: Theory and Evidence', *Bank of England Quarterly Bulletin*, 2: pp 12–18.

CURRIE, D. (1997) 'The Pros and Cons of EMU', London: The Economist Intelligence Unit.

CURRIE, D. (1998) 'Will the Euro work?', London: The Economist Intelligence Unit.

EUROPEAN COMMISSION (1990) 'One market, one money', *European Economy*, 44: pp 32–39.

EDYE, D. and LINTNER,V. (1996), *Contemporary Europe*, London: Prentice Hall.

FOLEY, P. (1996) 'EMU – the issues and arguments', *Lloyds Bank Economic Bulletin*, 7: pp 1–4.

FOLEY, P. (1997) 'The impending revolution in European saving', *Lloyds Bank Economic Bulletin*, 16: pp 1–6.

FOLEY, P. and WILLIAMS, T. (1997) 'The UK outlook: decision time approaches', *Lloyds Bank Economic Bulletin*, 17: pp 1–8.

FRIEDMAN, M. (1958) 'The Quantity Theory of Money: A Restatement', *Studies in the Quantity Theory of Money*, Chicago: University of Chicago Press.

FRIEDMAN, M. (1960) *A Program for Monetary Stability*, New York: Fordham University Press.

FRIEDMAN, M. (1969) *The Optimum Quantity of Money and Other Essays*, Chicago: Aldine.

FRIEDMAN, M. and SCHWARTZ, A. (1963) *A Monetary History of the United States 1867–1960*, Princeton: Princeton University Press.

GAYNOR, K. and KARAKITSOS, E. (1997) *Economic Convergence in a Multispeed Europe*, London: Macmillan Press.

GROS, D. and THYGESEN, N. (1998) *European Monetary Integration*, London : Longman.

GRIMWADE, N. (1989), *International Trade : New Patterns of Trade, Production and Investment*, London: Routledge.

HINE, R. C. (1985) *The Political Economy of European Trade*, Brighton: Wheatsheaf.

HUTTON, W. (1996) *The State We Are In*, New York: Vintage.

INGERSENT, K. A., RAYNER, A. and HINE, R. (1995) 'Ex-post Evaluation of the Uruguay Round of Agricultural Agreement', *The World Economy*, 18: pp 707–28.

INTERNATIONAL MONETARY FUND (1994), *International Financial Statistics*, Washington D.C.

INTERNATIONAL MONETARY FUND (1998), *International Trade Statistics Yearbook*, Washington D.C.

INTERNATIONAL MONETARY FUND (1998), *Economic Survey*, vol. 27, 15: pp 237–252.

JEPMA, C.J., JAGER, H. and KAMPHUIS, E. (1996) *Introduction to International Economics*, Longman.

JOVANOVIC, M. (1997), *European Economic Integration: Limits and Prospects*, London: Routledge Press.

KEYNES, J. M. (1977), *The General Theory of Employment, Interest and Money*, London: Macmillan. (First edition published in 1936).

KRUGMAN, P. and OBSTFELD, M. (1994) *International Economics*, New York: HarperCollins.

LINTNER,V. and MAZEY, S. (1991) *The European Community: Economic and Political Aspects*, London: McGraw-Hill.

LORANGE, P. and ROOS, J. (1992) *Strategic Alliances : Formation, Implementation and Evolution*, Oxford : Blackwell.

LUARD, E. (1983) *The Management of the World Economy*, London: Macmillan.

LUCAS, R. (1981) *Studies in Business Cycle Theory*, London: MIT Press.

MOON, P. (1996) 'Monetary Policy in Changing Times", *Lloyds Bank Economic Bulletin*, 8: pp 1–5.

NEWMAN, M. (1996) *Democracy, Sovereignty and the European Union*, London: Hurst and Company.

OECD (1993) *Trade Liberalisation: Global Economic Implications*, Paris: OECD.

O'SHEA, D. (1994) *Investing for Beginners*, London: Financial Times Business Information Ltd.

PELKMANS, J. (1997), *European Integration*, London: Longman

PHELPS, E. S. (1967) 'Money Wage Dynamics and Labour Market Equilibrium', *Journal of Political Economy*, 76.

PHELPS, E. S. et al. (1970), *Microeconomic Foundations of Employment and Inflation Theory*, London: Macmillan.

PHILLIPS, A. W. (1958) 'The Relation Between Unemployment and the Rate of Change of Money Wage Rates in the United Kingdom, 1861–1957, *Economica*, November.

POMFRET, R. (1977) *Development Economics*, New York: Prentice Hall.

POSNER, M.W. (1961) 'International Trade and Technical Change', *Oxford Economic Papers*, 13: pp 323–41.

RICARDO, D. (1977) *Principles of Political Economy and Taxation*, London: Aldine Press. (First edition published in 1817).

SACHS, J. and LARRAIN, F. (1993) *Macroeconomics and the Global Economy*, London: Prentice Hall.

SALVATORE, D. (1995) *International Economics*, New York: Prentice-Hall, pp 665, 704.

SAY, J. B. (1803) *A Treatise on Political Economy*, Paris.

SMITH, M. (1983) 'Trade relations between the European Community and the United States: common cause or divergent paths?', UACES Proceedings 3, London.

SOMERS, F. Ed. (1998) *European Union Economies*, London: Longman.

STEWART, M. (1983) *Keynes and After*, Harmondsworth: Penguin Books.

STEWART, M. (1983) *Controlling the Economic Future*, Brighton: Wheatsheaf.

TAYLOR, C. (1995) *EMU 2000?: Prospects for European Monetary Union*, London: Royal Institute of International Affairs.

THE INTERNATIONAL BANK FOR RECONSTRUCTION AND DEVELOPMENT (1997), *World Development Report*, Oxford: Oxford University Press.

THUROW, L. (1993) *Head to Head*, London: Nicolas Brealey Publishing.

TRIFFIN, R. (1960) *Gold and the Dollar Crisis*, New Haven: Yale University Press.

TSOUKALIS, L. (1997) *The New European Economy Revisited*, Oxford: Oxford University Press.

TURNER, P. (1998) 'Growth and the balance of payments', *Economic Review*,

UNITED NATIONS CENTRE ON TRANSNATIONAL CORPO-RATIONS (1992) *The Determinants of Foreign Direct Investment*, New York : United Nations.

UNITED NATIONS CONFERENCE ON TRADE AND DEVEL-OPMENT – Division on Transnational Corporations and Investment (1994) *World Investment Report*, New York: United Nations.

US DEPT OF LABOR (1995) Bureau of Labor Statistics, Washington DC: USGPO.

VERNON, R. (1966) 'International investment and interna-tional trade in the product cycle', *Quarterly Journal of Economics*, 80: pp 121–5.

VERNON, R. (1979) 'The product cycle hypothesis in a new international environment', *Oxford Bulletin of Economics and statistics*, 41: pp 255–67.

WELFORD, R. and PRESCOTT, K. (1994) *European Business*, London: Pitman Publishing.

WOOD, A. (1994) *North-South Trade, Employment and Inequality: Changing Fortunes in a Skills-Driven World*, Oxford: Clarendon Press.

Internet Sites

The European Commission : http: //europa.eu.int
The Financial Times : http: //www.ft.com
The International Monetary Fund : http: //www.imf.org

Index